NORTHWEST BEST PLACES

Restaurants, Lodgings, and Touring
in Oregon, Washington, and British Columbia

D0978409

David Brewster
Stephanie Irving

SASQUATCH BOOKS
Seattle, Washington

Assistant Editor: Emily Hall
Copy Editor: Alice Copp Smith
Proofreader: Edie Neeson
Contributors: Angela Allen, Carol Brown, Corbet Clark, Connie Cooper, Kimberlee Craig, Anne Depue, Les Dickason, Roger Downey, Susan English, Bob and Doris Evans, Larry and Stephanie Feeney, Richard Fencsak, Rob French, Paul Gregutt, Kitty Harmon, Joan Herman-Fencsak, Ron Holden, John Hughes, Jenn and Lou Jurcik, Lauren Kessler, Jessica Maxwell, Marnie McPhee, Theresa Morrow, Kristen Nelson, Rose Pike, John S. Robinson, Kathryn Robinson, Junius Rochester, David Sarasohn, William Skubi, Jane Steinberg, Fred and Marilyn Tausend, Brooks and Dorothy Tish, Cleve Twitchell, Laurie Underwood, Kathy Witowsky

Design: Jane Jeszeck and Karen Schober
Typeset by Typeworks, Vancouver, BC

This book is printed on recycled paper.

The *Best Places* guidebooks have been published continuously since 1975. Evaluations are based on numerous reports from locals and traveling inspectors. Final judgments are made by the editors. Our inspectors never identify themselves (except over the phone) and never take free meals or other favors. Readers are advised that places listed in previous editions may have closed or changed management or may no longer be recommended by this series. The editors welcome information conveyed by users of this book, as long as they have no financial connection with the establishment concerned. A report form is provided at the end of the book. Contact us at the address below for a catalog of our regional books.

Sasquatch Books
1931 Second Avenue
Seattle, Washington 98101
(206) 441-5555

CONTENTS

HOW TO USE THIS BOOK

Books in the *Best Places* series read like personal guidebooks, but our evaluations are based on numerous reports from local and traveling inspectors. Final judgments are made by the editors. Our inspectors never identify themselves (except over the phone) and never accept free meals or other favors.

Rating System. We rate establishments on value, performance measured against goals, uniqueness, enjoyability, loyalty of local clientele, cleanliness, and professionalism of service.

no stars Worth knowing about, if nearby
★ A good place
★★ Excellent; some outstanding qualities
★★★ Distinguished; many wonderful features
★★★★ The very best in the region
unrated New or undergoing major changes at press time.

Price Range. Prices are based on high-season rates. Prices throughout the British Columbia section are in Canadian dollars.

Expensive indicates a tab of more than $60 for dinner for two, including wine (but not tip), and more than $90 for one night's lodging for two.
Moderate falls between expensive and inexpensive.
Inexpensive indicates a tab of less than $30 for dinner for two, and less than $50 for lodging for two.

Checks and credit cards. Most establishments that accept checks also require a major credit card for identification. American Express is abbreviated as AE, Diner's Club as DC, MasterCard as MC, VISA as V.

Maps. About 50 town maps are included, though directions are included in every entry. Whenever possible, you should call ahead; many of the B&Bs are private homes and discourage drop-in visits. There is a map for each region in the book, normally found at the beginning of each geographic section, though some maps are combined to include several regions. All maps are oriented with north at the top of the page.

Reservations. Remember to call ahead whenever possible, as hours and days open sometimes change with the season. Prices also vary, reaching their peaks in high season. Corporate rates are sometimes available. It's also useful to know that some lodgings may accept checks to secure a reservation but may not accept them for payment in full.

Indexes. All restaurants, lodgings, and town names and some tourist attractions are listed alphabetically at the back of the book. The activities index that precedes it refers to activities specifically mentioned in the book, from beachcombing to bicycling to brew pubs.

Calendar. As an aid for your vacation planning, Northwest events from jazz festivals to tennis tournaments to slug races are listed by month.

Reader reports. At the end of the book is a report form. We receive hundreds of these reports from readers, suggesting new finds or agreeing or disagreeing with our assessments. They greatly help in our evaluations. We encourage readers to respond.

OREGON

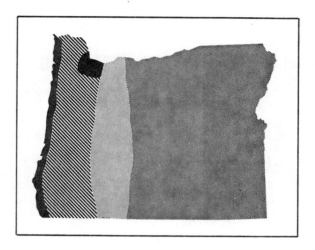

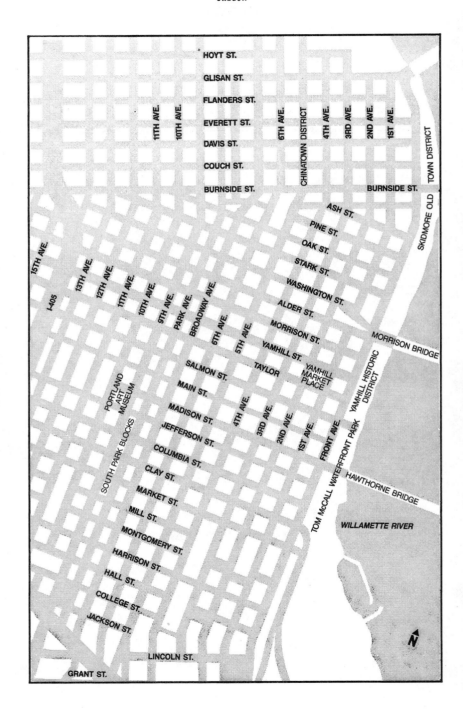

PORTLAND AND ENVIRONS

Including outlying areas: Beaverton, Hillsboro, and Tigard to the west, Lake Oswego to the south, and Gresham to the east.

Bit by bit, Portland is being dragged to major metropolitan status. During the last few years of the '80s and the first few of the '90s, the city that doesn't want to be a city has acquired a nationally noted light-rail service; a small jewel of a downtown performing-arts center (with a resident company from the Oregon Shakespeare Festival); a downtown shopping complex starring Saks Fifth Avenue; and a major convention center that may bring a new headquarters hotel in its wake. The downtown riverfront development was so popular people have since moved to match it on the other bank by attempting to relocate Interstate-5. And then there's the attraction that's most endearing to residents: a giant bronze statue of Portlandia, leaning off the new municipal building as though trying to play tag with the city buses.

The secret may be getting out, but Portlanders insist that a city is not for networking or catching planes to other places, but for living. What they prize about the place is not its per capita income but its rivers, its neighborhoods, its live jazz, its microbreweries, and its pro basketball Trailblazers. Below is a glimpse of Portland (followed by reviews of its top restaurants and lodgings): for a more comprehensive city guide, see our companion guide, *Portland Best Places*.

THE ARTS

Music. Nothing ever did so much for this city's aural offerings as the Arlene Schnitzer Concert Hall, Portlanders are packing the place 52 weeks a year. Besides the essential house "given"—the Oregon Symphony Orchestra, under conducter James DePreist—the "Schnitz" has expanded Portland's musical agenda significantly, (503) 248-4496. Chamber Music Northwest presents a five-week-long summer festival spanning four centuries of music, (503) 223-3202. From Johnny Mathis to Bad Company to Queen Ida, the importation of upscale entertainment is suddenly reality in a town that once struggled to maintain a local opera company.

Theater. Neighboring Schnitzer Hall is the Center for Performing Arts, which contains two performance spaces. Its full-time resident company is Portland Center Stage, a northern offshoot of the acclaimed Oregon Shakespeare Festival in Ashland. Portland Repertory continues to put on quality productions; Storefront is known as the operation that takes risks; Artists Repertory is the best small company; and musicals of any caliber land at the Portland Civic (home of the Portland Opera).

Visual Arts. The Portland art scene continues to grow. Gallery walks on the first Thursday of every month have encouraged the expansion of that community: The Portland Art Museum, Augen, Blue Sky, Blackfish, Elizabeth Leach,

Jamison/Thomas, Laura Russo, and Quartersaw are the hot showcases of both local and national work.

Dance. Two competent ballet companies have merged to become the Oregon Ballet Theatre, which now shares tenant status at the Civic Auditorium, (503) 227-6867. Nancy Matchek's Contemporary Dance Season at Portland State University brings in the hottest out-of-town dance action, (503) 725-3131; and probably the most creative productions are performed by Oslund and Company, (503) 236-3265.

Literature. Besides Powell's, the superpower of used (and new) bookstores, Portland has a flock of other strong hardcover contenders, including Cameron's, for back-issue magazines; the Catbird Seat, in the center of the city; Annie Bloom's Books, especially for Judaica; and Murder by the Book, which is to mysteries what Powell's is to everything else. Any of these, or a local church or college, might on any day be presenting readings by local or visiting writers. Portland Arts and Lectures produces a growing number of lectures by nationally known literary figures, (503) 241-0543.

Architecture. Portland's downtown skyline has become dramatically sophisticated in recent years. In March 1991, the American Institute of Architecture presented its most prestigious National Honor Award to Zimmer Gunsul Frasca's (ZGF) Convention Center, with its distinctive illuminated twin towers. Other outstanding buildings include Pietro Belluschi's glass-box Equitable Building, Michael Graves' controversial postmodern Portland Building, Will Martin's swank, complexly designed Pioneer Courthouse Square, A.E. Doyle's spectacularly ornate Old US Bank Building, ZGF's KOIN Center and its blue-reflective One Financial Center, and the city's most recent architectural entry, Broome, Oringdulth, O'Toole, Rudolf, Boles and Associates' 1000 Broadway, distinguished by its copper-colored glass and white illuminated dome.

OTHER THINGS TO DO

Nightlife. Portland's jazz community is picking up a national reputation: Remo's Brasserie Montmartre, The Hobbit, and DJs Village Jazz are the favored options. The Portland Art Museum is another hot spot; its After Hours gigs are each Wednesday evening. Rock fans get their best licks at Key Largo, Pine Street Theatre, and Starry Night. Music on or past the edge—and followers of the same—can be found at Satyricon in Old Town, north of Burnside between the river and 5th Street.

Sports. The town's only big-league action is the Portland Trailblazers basketball team. While they usually manage to make the finals, the Blazers have a penchant for fizzling in the playoffs; (503) 234-9291. Baseball fans like to follow the Portland Beavers, who play half of their 142-game schedule in the Portland Civic Stadium. Individual sports thrive in the region: runners have access to over 50 manicured miles of trail in the 5,000-acre Forest Park complex; rowers are guaranteed miles of flat water on the Willamette; and bicyclists use more than 100 miles of off-street paved bike path in the greater Portland area.

Parks and Gardens. Besides the sprawling and primitive Forest Park, there are nearly 150 other parks in the city . The Hoyt Arboretum, close to the Washington Park Zoo, has the most impressive collection of native and exotic flora, as well as the best-kept trails. More formalized grounds are the International Rose Test Garden, the Japanese Gardens, and the Rhododendron Gardens. A new World Forestry Center Building, also next to the Zoo, has ongoing displays worth checking. And the largest memorial of its kind in the nation, the Vietnam Veterans' Living Memorial, is an inspiring outdoor cathedral commemorating the

Oregon victims of that conflict; call Washington Park for more information, (503) 796-5274.

Shopping. Crafts and Renaissance-style goods can be found at Saturday Market under the Burnside Bridge; upscale specialty shops and eateries are found at New Market Theater, The Water Tower, Lloyd Center, Holiday Market, and Pioneer Place. Northwest Portland's 23rd Avenue and SE Hawthorne Boulevard between 35th and 45th feature great neighborhood merchants. Antiques are found in Sellwood, in the city's southeast corner.

Transportation. The city's public transportation system, Tri-Met, runs throughout the metropolitan area and is free in the downtown core area. The light-rail system, MAX, is a speedy conduit to the eastside, going as far as Gresham. Once a day, Amtrak heads north, south, and east. Plans are under way for a west-moving rail line, which should be completed in the next few years. The airport (PDX) is a $20 cab ride (or less than half that on shuttle buses from major hotels). Parking meters must be fed even on Saturdays in Portland.

RESTAURANTS

Genoa
NE 29th and Belmont,
(503) 238-1464
2832 SE Belmont St,
Portland
Expensive; wine only;
AE, DC, MC, V; checks
OK
Dinner Mon-Sat

Genoa marks its 20th anniversary by continuing to offer the most ambitious meal in town: Northern Italian dinners that span three hours and seven courses without ever running out of imagination. There's no view to act as drawing card: the windowless dining room is without much illumination, and it can be a couple of courses before you even know whom you're dining with. By then, however, you may hardly care; saffron-inflected fish soup, seafood ravioli, or spinach dumplings overshadow all other thoughts. Of the seven courses— appetizer, soup, pasta, fish, entrée, dessert, and fruit—not all will be spectacular, but a couple will certainly be, and the rest will be very good. The only choice of the evening comes with the entrée, when you're offered dishes such as pork tenderloin in a tomato and Marsala sauce or veal scallops in Madeira with morels. From the dessert tray, the showstopper boccone dolce (a baroque layering of meringue, chocolate, berries, and whipped cream) is pressed hard by simpler choices such as pear ice cream in caramel sauce. Theatergoers will be pleased with the abridged version of dinner (antipasto, pasta, entrée, dessert) served at 5:30pm and 6pm.

L'Auberge
26th and Vaughn,
(503) 223-3302
2601 NW Vaughn St,
Portland
Expensive; full bar; AE,
DC, MC, V; local checks
only

Those who think French restaurants are stuffy should wander into the bar here on Sunday nights. In a setting known for stylish informality, an innovative, eclectic menu, and—Sunday nights only—free screenings of classic movies, you'll discover terrific cheeseburgers and what might be the best barbecued ribs this side of the Mississippi. Welcome to L'Auberge's bar, a softly lit den of elegant rusticity and upscale hipness, with a well-stoked hearth in winter, a homey outdoor dining deck in summer and, in all seasons, a witty, personable staff. Changing every two weeks, the bar menu is

Dinner every day;
Sunday, bar menu
only

replete with great finds, such as grilled swordfish with cilantro pesto and a salad of wild edible greens cultivated on a farm in southern Oregon.

Downstairs takes a more serious approach. Execution is fairly understated—this is not a place to look for the shock of the new—and the dinners are among the most expensive in town. But L'Auberge, in business for over two decades, is distinguished by consistently high standards. Three- or six-course dinners are offered six nights a week in a country-inn atmosphere highlighted with contemporary touches. The kitchen emphasizes fresh local ingredients: entrees usually include game birds, veal, beef, or fresh fish. Options run from grilled quail with prune custard to rack of lamb marinated in pomegranate juice. Service is highly informed, the wine list astutely compiled.

Briggs and Crampton
Montgomery Park
between Thurman
and Vaughn,
(503) 223-8690
1902 NW 24th Ave,
Portland
Expensive; beer and wine;
MC, V; checks OK
Lunch Tues-Fri (by
appointment only)

If you're reading this anywhere near the time you expect to be hungry, forget it. There appears to be nothing like B&C's one-table one-lunch policy anywhere outside Portland, and people are flying in from afar to see what all the buzz is about. Reservations are taken once every three months (45 dates—aka tables—are available) and they book up in a matter of hours. It is, however, worth planning ahead. Nancy Briggs and Juanita Crampton's lunch table acts as a playground for their true passion—catering; in fact, they claim to have never prepared the same meal twice. Wintry fare may include a curried apple and potato soup and perhaps quail stuffed with wild rice sided with fresh pear chutney. Summers bring a lighter touch employing locally grown vegetables, edible flowers, fresh herbs, and often seafood. Choose a special person and take the afternoon off.

Cafe des Amis
Corner of 20th and NW
Kearney,
(503) 295-6487
1987 NW Kearney St,
Portland
Moderate; full bar; AE,
MC, V; checks OK
Dinner Mon-Sat

The now-upscale Cafe des Amis has shifted a bit from its beginnings as a down-home French cafe, but it still produces mostly satisfying meals that are surprisingly reasonable. The fragrant soups and hearty stews of provincial France and the Spanish Pyrenees are still around—although they're a smaller part of the menu. Look for mussels in a marvelous soup enriched with curry and cream. Add a salad with toasted walnuts, a basket of terrific oven-fresh French rolls, and one of the many bottles of good wine, and you have the makings of a light but satisfying meal. Moving upscale toward the entrée, you might find duck in wild blackberry sauce and a fillet of salmon, sautéed and then poached, in a sauce of crème fraîche and shallots. Chef Dennis Baker also makes the best steak in town, a buttery, two-inch-thick filet in a sauce that alchemizes port and garlic. The dessert tray always merits serious consideration, and you can rely on the serving staff to assess the day's offerings candidly.

The Heathman Restaurant and Bar

Salmon and SW Broadway,
(503) 241-4100
1009 SW Broadway,
Portland
Expensive;
full bar; AE, DC, MC, V; checks OK
Breakfast, lunch, dinner every day

★★★

Under the direction of executive chef Greg Higgins, the local leader in the Pacific Northwest cuisine movement has recently been broadening its horizons. Local seafood, game, and seasonal produce are still the themes, but they're more likely to be played to an accompaniment of Asian or Latin flavorings. Chinook salmon sharpened with Sichuan spices, prawns with black tea and wasabe or a Brazilian bean dish might flare up at lunch or dinner. With the return of wine expert John Poston from New York, the Heathman can match any of them with the appropriate vintage. Portland's official power breakfast is served in an elegant setting, with great attention to taste and detail. Eggs Benedict take on a Northwest flavor with smoked salmon replacing the ham; waffles come with a hint of malt and a mound of seasonal fruit; and cornmeal cakes with fresh blueberry compote take griddle food to new heights. The bar, a rich, glinting affair of marble and brass, features tapas and a fine selection of Portland's best microbrews.

Indigine

In Hawthorne neighborhood,
(503) 238-1470
3725 SE Division St,
Portland
Moderate; beer and wine; MC, V; checks OK
Dinner Tues-Sat

★★★

The regulars who fill this small, unpretentious eatery are a casually dressed group for whom eating out is serious business. They put great stock in the wizardry of owner-chef Millie Howe, whose maverick style and obsession with quality guarantee that nothing here will be routine or prepackaged. Saturdays are reserved for a blow-out East Indian feast. The four-course extravaganza starts with something unexpected, perhaps mango mousse and homemade goat cheese in phyllo. There's a choice of entrées, typically a searing rabbit vindaloo, lamb curry, seafood curry, or a collection of vegetarian options. At around $24, the quality and value here are outstanding. Some Indian dishes surface among the weeknight suppers, along with Latin American, European, or Pacific Northwest overtones: roast chicken stuffed beneath its skin with wildly garlicky pesto; a lovely salad basket overflowing with greens; and seafood enchiladas with hot chiles and cream. While there are numerous dessert offerings, Howe's pies are hard to beat.

La Mirabelle

Between Jefferson and Salmon, (503) 223-7113
1126 SW 18th Ave,
Portland

When Portland native Robert Kincaid moved back up from San Francisco in 1990, he expanded the range of French cuisine in his home town. In a small outpost with a dozen tables—most of them booked weeks ahead—he turns out impressive pre-Pritikin dishes: artichoke bottoms filled with chicken mousse dumplings and served with three sauces; saucissons en croute; roast duck with black currant sauce; lobster

Expensive; beer and wine; MC, V; checks OK Dinner Tues-Sat

ravioli; roast rack of lamb with mustard, herbs, and black pepper. But Kincaid can also flash in other directions, especially at dessert. While his tarte Tatin is classic French, his coffee milk shake in a chocolate box would be hard to find in Paris (and shortly after serving, the dish tends to disappear here as well). Matching the classic themes of the food, service is appropriately formal and ceremonial.

Regions
NW 1st and Couch in Old Town district, (503) 223-5033 53 NW 1st Ave, Portland Moderate; full bar; MC, V; local checks only Lunch Tues-Fri, dinner Wed-Sat

The only way to describe the food here is "cuisine de Mark Ross." The chef/owner's daily inspirations range from wild boar Tex-Mex style to Tuscan white beans with ahi tuna to an appetizer called Conversation Between Four Oregon Mushrooms in Puff Pastry. Ross may rely on worldwide inspiration, but he bases it strongly on the freshest local ingredients, and the mixture changes constantly (in fact, twice a day). Ross is keeping up one endearing pattern: most entrées approach or top $15, but there are always a couple running significantly less. This is likely to cause diners to spend the leftover on dessert, such as a chocolate biscotti cake best described as haunting. One change they do find: Ross celebrated his first anniversary by opening a separate room for after-dinner cigars and cognac. He insists it's co-ed.

Yen Ha
West Portland on SW Canyon Rd, (503) 292-0616 8640 SW Canyon Rd, Portland Moderate; full bar; MC, V; checks OK Lunch, dinner every day

Talented Vietnamese chef Bach Tuyet has moved her popular operation to the suburbs. Her new purple labyrinth digs are spacious enough to feed most of the large West Slope community. The food is still the same great fare that wowed *The New Yorker*'s food essayist Calvin Trillin on one Portland visit. While there's much to recommend, the classic is *bo noung vi*. For this amazing do-it-yourself dish, you plunge slivers of marinated beef into a pool of hot oil on a stove placed on your table. Once cooked to taste, the beef is wrapped with assorted fresh greens and mint in a pliable, edible rice skin. A frisky anchovy sauce is the finishing touch, bringing out all of the succulent package's exotic flavor. There is also a wonderful shrimp salad garnished with crushed peanuts, and a wide selection of chef's specials. Try the wonton soup, full of plump dumplings and Vietnamese herbs.

Zefiro's
Corner of NW 21st and Glisan, (503) 226-3394 500 NW 21st, Portland Moderate; AE, MC, V; local checks only

Zefiro may have landed on the Portland restaurant scene with the loudest bang of 1990, but the place was probably too busy to hear it. With a wide-ranging menu, bistro prices, and the LA feel of an Armani blazer, Zefiro became instantly popular as a place to be seen. And most were seen eating; the risotto of the day, which leads the menu, is reason enough to draw the hungry, but it's joined by imaginative dishes such as Gruyère-flavored butternut squash soup or grilled lamb

*Lunch Mon-Sat, dinner
every day*

Al-Amir
*Between 2nd and 3rd,
downtown,
(503) 274-0010
223 SW Stark St,
Portland*

*Between B and 2nd,
Country Square shopping
center, (503) 697-1900
455 SW 2nd, Lake Oswego
Moderate; full bar; AE,
MC, V; local checks only
Lunch Mon-Fri, dinner
Mon-Sat*

Alexis
*Between 2nd and 3rd
on Burnside,
(503) 224-8577
215 W Burnside,
Portland
Moderate; full bar;
AE, DC, MC, V; local
checks only
Lunch Mon-Fri, dinner
every day*

Atwater's
*Off Burnside on 5th,
(503) 275-3600
111 SW 5th Ave,
Portland
Expensive; full bar; AE,
DC, MC, V; no checks
Dinner every day, brunch
Sun*

chops with olive butter. The crush in the restaurant may lead you to spend some time waiting in the cozy bar, but diners don't seem to mind it; they just keep their profiles visible from the dining room.

The Bishop's House, complete with crosses and crenellations, seems an unlikely place to serve baba ghanouj. But Al-Amir, a solid Middle Eastern restaurant with both range and consistency, has finally conquered the original building. In addition to pungent kebabs, the menu includes *kharouf muammar*, a huge pile of moist, faintly sweet lamb chunks, and *dujaj musahab*, a charcoal-grilled chicken breast in lemon and olive oil. Holding everything together are pools of creamy hummus and baba ghanouj. Both the menu and the crowds here have increased recently, leading to a new branch expansion to Lake Oswego.

No place in Portland is quite like Alexis—a temple of good times that has evolved over the last nine years into something far beyond a little Greek eatery. Seven nights a week, members of the Alexis Bakouros family and their loyal staff patrol the premises with a professionalism all too rare on the West Coast. There's never a dearth of action, from lawyers' conventions to Old World folk dancing to Aurelia, the region's hottest Middle Eastern dancer. The food is authentic and of consistent quality. Some think you won't find better calamari this side of the Aegean, others find it across the street. Regardless, the bronzed oregano chicken is full of robust flavors. Complete dinners give you the most for your buck, but regulars also find the makings of a meal in the appetizers. Plan to dip into everything with Portland's finest house bread, which along with some of the appetizers is now available in Portland food stores.

The food at Atwater's may never match the drama of its setting, 30 floors up the US BanCorp Tower in a dressy design of peach and glass. But chef George Poston has elevated the food considerably, and if the experiments don't always work, nobody makes more imaginative use of Northwest seafood, game, wild mushrooms, and fruit. Here, a napoleon of wild Oregon mushrooms picks up an additional ingredient of elegance. The five-course formal dinner is $47, but the three-course version for $26 is a bargain. The all-you-can-eat Sunday buffet has been a particular hit, tables groaning with a vast assortment of traditional and contemporary items, chefs whipping up omelets, and only a few steam-table perennials. The star is the space itself, featuring an etched-glass wine cellar in the middle of the dining room and hundreds of miles of the Northwest stretching out beyond the windows.

B Moloch/The Heathman Bakery and Pub
At north end of South Park Blocks,
(503) 227-5700
901 SW Salmon St,
Portland
Moderate; beer and wine;
AE, DC, MC, V; local checks only
Breakfast, lunch, dinner every day

The huge wood-burning brick oven where some of the city's best pizzas and breads are born now shares attention with a bustling Widmer microbrewery bar with an ambitious Saturday night menu. That means on busy nights there are two lines to wait in—one to order (and pay for) your food and another to get a table. Oven products like beer bread and seafood calzone, stuffed with smoked mussels, shrimp, and plenty of ricotta, are wonderful, and the open oven resembles a particularly hypnotic illustration from Dante. Salmon, peppered ham, and sun-dried tomatoes are cured in a cold-smoker in back of the massive baking furnace. The breakfast menu offers creativity explosions such as hazelnut and stout beer waffles with marionberry syrup, but many still stick with the oatmeal.

Bangkok Kitchen
Corner of Belmont and 26th, (503) 236-7349
2534 SE Belmont St,
Portland
Inexpensive; beer and wine; no credit cards; local checks only
Lunch Tues-Fri, dinner Tues-Sat

Outstanding food makes up for the dearth of decor. The setting here is kitschy cafe, but authentic Thai offerings and the wacky good humor of owner-chef Srichan Miller and her family draws a loyal coterie of fans. They come for the heat treatment—the array of searing house soups, peanut sauces, and salads of fresh shrimp and lime. One of the popular specials is a whole fried fish covered in a feverish chile paste and deeply sautéed peppers, all decorated with basil leaves and other artful trimmings. Servers are in no hurry, and service can be a bit befuddled.

Berbati
1 block south of Burnside on 2nd,
(503) 226-2122
19 SW 2nd Ave,
Portland
Moderate; full bar;
AE, DC, MC, V; local checks only
Lunch Mon-Fri, dinner Mon-Sat

A few years after its opening in a neighborhood of high-octane Greek eateries, this unassuming establishment seems to have been here forever. Considerable numbers of its fans hope it's not going anywhere. A quiet storefront blossoms into a huge back room, nicely furnished with Hellenic simplicity. Service here is leisurely, if not laid back, so you have plenty of time to savor your retsina and sample some creamy, garlicky tzatziki on the warm, wholesome house bread. Entrées range from garlic-sautéed prawns with Berbati's signature lemon-basted roast potatoes to a finely blended pastitsio—lamb, pasta, cheese, tomatoes, and cream sauce combined in a Greek lasagne. Several dishes also provide nonsuffering options for vegetarians, and jazz now echoes on the weekends.

BJ's Brazilian Restaurant
½ block off Bybee on
Milwaukie,
(503) 236-9629
7019 SE Milwaukie Ave,
Portland
Inexpensive; beer and
wine; MC, V; checks OK
Lunch, dinner Mon-Sat

If there were nothing served here but Xingu "black beer of the Amazon," BJ's would still be making a contribution to Portland dining. Fortunately, there is considerably more, such as *feijoada* a black bean and pork stew, chicken in red palm oil, and small deep-fried meat pies called *pastels*. A specialty is *bobo de Camarao*: prawns with yucca, tomatoes, cashews, and coconut milk. Unexpected vegetables and spicy toppings, including one that mixes cilantro with red pepper, appear on all plates, and if you don't use all the spicing you're doing something wrong. You can alleviate the excess with more Xingu.

Brasserie Montmartre
Between Alder and
Morrison,
(503) 224-5552
626 SW Park Ave,
Portland
Moderate; full bar; AE,
DC, MC, V; checks OK
Lunch Mon-Fri, dinner
every day, brunch Sat-
Sun

This is a place where spiked heels compete with spiked hair. Brasserie Montmartre is not only one of Portland's few dining-and-dancing options, it's a place where you can do the dining part later than almost any place around. The extensive bistro menu runs until 2:30am weekdays, 3am weekends. Hot local jazz (no cover) is also a plus, and the bar is a scene of its own, inspired by huge mirrors and black-and-white checked floors. Tuesdays through Saturdays you might enjoy a live magic show. From the substantial lunch and dinner menus, a few of the pastas measure up to the operation's ambitions—linguine with pesto and scallops, for example—but the salmon with lingonberry sauce is the real triumph here. There are some good desserts: try the chocolate gâteau with almonds and currants, especially around 1am.

Bread and Ink Cafe
2 miles east of downtown,
(503) 239-4756
3610 SE Hawthorne
Blvd, Portland
Moderate; beer and wine;
MC, V; checks OK
Breakfast, lunch, dinner
Mon-Sat, brunch Sun

Considering the Hawthorne area's continuing boom, you might almost call Bread and Ink a neighborhood restaurant that created its neighborhood around it. The idiosyncratic menu boasts everything from the city's best homemade blintzes to a wild salad (with some 17 greens and flowers) to burgers in which the condiments—mayo, mustard, ketchup—are made right on the premises. Blackboard specials venture successfully into neo-American, Mediterranean, and Mexican specialties. Any place where lunch can consist of spring rolls, chicken enchiladas, and a sublime Italian cassata for dessert—before things get more ambitious at dinner—has both nerve and style. Not surprisingly, there's a loyal clientele who have learned to put up with the notoriously slow service. For breakfast there are delicious, billowing omelets, assorted homemade breads, and great coffee. On Sunday, bring *The New York Times* and settle in for a soul-satisfying four-course Jewish-style brunch.

Bush Garden
9th and Morrison near
Nordstrom,

Some of the city's best practitioners of sushi art pass through this kitchen. Chefs here have turned out versions of sushi and sashimi not found elsewhere: a bril-

(503) 226-7181
900 SW Morrison St,
Portland
Moderate; full bar; AE,
DC, MC, V; no checks
Lunch Mon-Fri, dinner
every day

liant flounder sushi dressed with chiles, sake, and soy sauce, for example; or spicy tuna roll. When they're available, try the hand-rolled maki containing small bouquets of radish sprouts and salmon-skin shavings. Regular Japanese fare is offered in tatami rooms; but among the standards, only teriyaki really shines. Things will be more interesting—and more successful—if you order the dishes that don't look familiar.

Campbell's Bar-B-Que

Powell Street exit off
I-205, corner 85th and
Powell, (503) 777-9795
8701 SE Powell,
Portland
Inexpensive; no alcohol;
MC, V; no checks
Lunch Tues-Fri, dinner
Tues-Sat

We'd go a heckuva lot farther than the east side of the county to rip into some of Portland's best barbecue. Four different barbecue sauces—mild, medium, hot, and smokey brown sugar—cascade over a range of different meats out of the barbecue oven, and do wonderful things for each. (Try the smokey brown sugar on turkey, or the hot on the homemade links. Or the other way around.) For a soothing respite, hit the dazzling home baked goods: pillowy white rolls, dense corn bread, or stunning peach cobbler. The decor isn't much, but the service—mostly by people named Campbell—is on a level with the food.

Casa-U-Betcha

Between Hoyt and Irving,
(503) 227-3887
612 NW 21st Ave,
Portland
Moderate; full bar; AE,
MC, V; no checks
Lunch Mon-Fri, dinner
every day

Welcome to Portland's first taco club. This wild and crazy eatery has become one of northwest Portland's most "happening" restaurants. One of the reasons is the interior, best described as hardware sci-fi. Galvanized stovepipe doubles for industrial-art cacti, sprouting from glitzy Formica banquettes and metal-topped tables, beneath an electric orange sunset of corrugated Fiberglas deck roofing. The bar is a psyche-delicized tile affair, generally full of people you might not see elsewhere. New chef Fernando Divina keeps up with the decor creating items like duck chimichangas, lamb chili, and grilled shrimp Mazatlan. The specials may be inconsistent, but the food is consistently imaginative.

Chen's Dynasty

Between Broadway and
SW 6th, (503) 248-9491
622 SW Washington St,
Portland
Moderate; full bar; AE,
DC, MC, V; no checks
Lunch, dinner every day

The 12-page menu must be one of the most complete anywhere this side of the People's Republic—you could explore culinary China here for years without repetition. Several dishes are rarities for these parts: sweet and pungent fish with honey-roasted pine nuts, squid cut to look like clusters of flowers and perfumed with Sichuan peppercorns, and pheasant, Hunan style. Standbys such as kung pao shrimp and General Tso's chicken are usually treated with respect, but the kitchen can also produce clunkers. The ambience belies the notion that Chinese restaurants must look like Fu Manchu sets. Among the nice touches is a rendering of the Great Wall and a doorway festooned with soft cotton serpent sculptures.

Eddie Lee's

2nd and Stark,
(503) 228-1874
409 SW 2nd Ave,
Portland
Inexpensive; full bar; AE,
DC, MC, V; checks OK
Lunch Mon-Fri, dinner
Mon-Sat

From a solid beginning with stunning sandwiches such as roast pork loin with fruit mustard and sweet onion relish on focaccia, and lighter entrées such as Portuguese mussels with chorizo, the restaurant has extended its hours and broadened its menu. Lunch now stretches from cioppino to a seafood Caesar salad to a marinated chicken and Italian sausage sandwich, and nighttime means grilled duck breast with smoked tea butter, pasta with black beans and prawns, or bouillabaisse. There have been reports of inconsistencies but the setting—two small dining rooms crowded with director's chairs across a lobby from one another—keeps a coterie of late-night regulars returning.

Elizabeth's

Corner of 32nd and
NE Broadway,
(503) 281-8337
3135 NE Broadway,
Portland
Moderate; beer and wine;
AE, MC, V; checks OK
Breakfast Sat-Sun, lunch
Mon-Fri, dinner Tues-
Sat

Grown out of a booming upscale deli operation, Elizabeth's is a successful, low-key restaurant with food and atmosphere that are always comfortable and sometimes inspired. On the first floor of an old northeast Portland house, the restaurant has won the dinnertime allegiance of Alameda and Laurelhurst locals. Soups, pâtés, and designer pizzas are lovely, and more ambitious entrées, although less consistent, are generally tasty and reasonably priced. Summertime expansion outward has only made the mood more appealing.

Esparza's Tex-Mex Cafe

Burnside and SE 28th,
(503) 234-7909
2735 SE Ankeny,
Portland
Inexpensive; full bar;
MC, V; no checks
Lunch, dinner Tues-Sat

In a Tex-Mex tortilla tornado, Esparza has flashed into Portland with a completely different kind of Mexican cooking. Joe and Martha Esparza's offerings range from eggs scrambled with cactus and hot sauce to fiery enchiladas to whatever they've got around—pork chops in salsa and, perhaps calf's brain tacos. All of it is served in an ambience of steer's-horn chairs and Tex-Mex hits on the jukebox. We're not talking formal, but we aré talking serious Mexican food.

Esplanade at RiverPlace (Alexis Hotel)

City Center exit off I-5;
Harbor Way off Front,
(503) 295-6166
1510 SW Harbor Way,
Portland
Expensive; full bar; AE,
DC, MC, V; checks OK
Breakfast, dinner every
day, lunch Mon-Fri,
brunch Sun

From high-price, low-success beginnings, Esplanade in the showcase RiverPlace Alexis Hotel continues to improve, although it still has a way to go. The strengths are still there: a lovely room, a wide-angle view of the Willamette, and a formality of service that convinces you something special is going on. Soups such as lobster bisque and apple-broccoli are outstanding, and salads—especially the endive and Stilton with apple slices and Calvados vinaigrette—are impressive and imaginative. Dishes such as chicken with pecan potato pancakes and smoked chile butter get attention—but the execution and the spicing are not always there. Still, with RiverPlace becoming a steadily more popular Portland hangout—and an extension of the park in the works—the restaurant is often full. Service is attentive without being intrusive. The fixed-price Sunday brunch, which includes an appetizer platter, breads and brioche, your choice of entrée, and a selection from the dessert tray, is far superior to all-you-can-eat offerings at the same price. There's a comfortable bar, staffed by a very knowledgeable wine steward.

Fong Chong
Everett and NW 4th,
(503) 220-0235
301 NW 4th Ave,
Portland
Inexpensive; full bar; no
credit cards; checks OK
Lunch, dinner every day

The setting—a cacophony of Chinese and Caucasian voices, clattering teacups, and clicking chopsticks—is far from sedate. From 11am to 3pm daily, young waiters scurry from table to table, hawking their hand-made morsels on miniature saucers. Welcome to Portland's finest dim sum parlor, where an array of steamed buns and savory dumplings is dispatched with gusto. Insist on the sticky rice wrapped in lotus leaves, and if the line gets too long, remember that the same people now own the House of Louie across the street (same menu). At night, Fong Chong is transformed into a quiet Cantonese eatery, with average preparations and a few surprises.

Fuji
(503) 233-0654
2878 SE Gladstone St,
Portland
Inexpensive; beer and
wine; MC, V; no checks
Lunch Tues-Fri, dinner
Tues-Sat

Fuji is, hands down, Portland's favorite sushi bar. There are those who eat here once a week just to challenge chef Fujio Handa's resourcefulness. Handa regularly departs from old school rules of sushi making to whip up creative concoctions (incorporating Western ingredients) that would make natives of Tokyo blush—and ask for more. Try "mountains in the snow," shavings of red snapper on ice dotted with fish eggs, or super California rolls resembling Abstract Impressionist sushi. The regular menu may be less exciting, but exceptions such as soft-shell crab or baked mussels could lure you from the sushi bar.

Jake's Famous Crawfish
Stark and SW 12th,
(503) 226-1419
401 SW 12th Ave,
Portland
Moderate; full bar; AE,
DC, MC, V; checks OK
Lunch Mon-Fri, dinner
every day

The length of its daily fresh list keeps this brass-and-mahogany Portland landmark on top of the Portland seafood restaurant list. No other local establishment of any kind can compete with it for style, atmosphere, and nonstop social scene. The faithful—and on some nights, one suspects, the unfaithful—pack the bar. In the dining room, the reservationless don't seem to mind the hour's wait for one of the coveted tables; they know their patience will be rewarded with some of the best seafood in the city and a grand old time. For sure satisfaction, order from the fresh sheet—local crawfish are available May through September, and increasingly the list is stocked from places such as Chile and New Zealand. Items on the regular menu, as well as some of the stabs at Cajun, can be inconsistent. But when the restaurant is hot (the bouillabaisse, packed with fish and fennel, is one example), it's hot. The ultrarich truffle cake leads the desserts, but the peach-and-pear crisp has loyal supporters.

Jarra's Ethiopian Restaurant
14th and Hawthorne,
(503) 230-8990
1435 SE Hawthorne Blvd, Portland
Inexpensive; full bar; MC, V; local checks only
Dinner Tues-Sat

Nothing, neither those four-alarm Texas chilis nor those palate-flogging peppers from Thailand, packs the wallop of this kitchen's wat stews. Made of chicken, lamb, or beef, they are deep red, oily, and packed with pepper after-kicks. Full dinners come with assorted stewed meats and vegetables, all permeated with vibrant spices and mounded on injera—the spongy Ethiopian bread that doubles as plate and fork. The variety is not extensive, but this is the area's unequaled heat champ. Be sure to take time to chat with the friendly owners, Petros Jarra and Ainalem Sultessa, who will explain the origins of the food, give you an Abyssinian history lesson, and debate Ethiopian politics. Take it all in with plenty of cold beer, the logical beverage with this cuisine. Downstairs, Petros and Ainalem recently opened Jarra's Cafe, a smaller establishment that doubles as espresso bar and pub.

Kashmir
17th and Couch,
(503) 238-3934
1705 NE Couch St, Portland
Moderate; no alcohol; AE, MC, V; checks OK
Dinner Tues-Sat

Teetotalism doesn't stand in the way of deep, purring contentment at the Pakistani-owned Kashmir restaurant: the melon smoothie will make you forget all the chateau-bottled delights you tried at the previous restaurant. When rents went up downtown, Kashmir moved into this turn-of-the-century house. The lights are low and the air is colored with tinkling, rambling-creek sounds of the East. A five-course dinner ($23) is generously portioned with crisp vegetable samosas with hot dip, a tangy cucumber and tomato salad alert with cilantro, a feather-light popadum, two chewy Frisbees of chapati, raita (yogurt with cucumbers, tomatoes, and spices), basmati rice, a choice of 17 entrées—try the Chana lamb or the prawn Jingha curry—and a dish of Indian almond ice cream. Close the meal with a milky tea spiced with cardamom.

London Grill (Benson)
SW Broadway at Oak St,
(503) 295-4110
309 SW Broadway, Portland
Expensive; full bar; AE, DC, MC, V; local checks only
Breakfast, lunch, dinner every day, brunch Sun

There was a time years ago when the London Grill was the place to go for a consistently fine meal in Portland. To some Portlanders it still is, for the Grill oozes tradition in its ambience, its service, its wine list (one of the best in town), and its menu. It is the dark, plush domain where anniversaries are celebrated and deals are made over a proven Caesar salad and steak Diane (both prepared at the table without a slip); especially at lunch, it's the rare table that's not on someone's expense account. Gradually, new flavors such as fresh grilled squab with butternut squash purée and sautéed eggplant with roasted peppers, goat cheese, and prosciutto are intruding into the restaurant's late-'50s world view. A change in the ownership of the hotel—now, once again, just the Benson (owned by WestCoast Hotels)—includes an overhaul of the London Grill.

McCormick & Schmick's Oak Street Restaurant
Oak and 1st,
(503) 224-7522
235 SW 1st Ave,
Portland
Moderate; full bar; AE, DC, MC, V; checks OK
Lunch Mon-Fri, dinner every day

We try but we seldom get past the appetizers—not because of the entrées but because the appetizers are so good. The house oyster arrangement combines half a dozen species from various waters, which says something about priorities here. There are at least two dozen seafood possibilities, as well as the fresh list—and that's just to start. Someday we'll return to sample the Pacific yellowfin tuna, the mahi mahi, and the Alaska prawns—although one can also get greatly distracted by the smokey smells that pour out onto the street and announce the presence of salmon and sturgeon. And for all of its attention to food that swims, M&S's also manages to dish up great cheeseburgers and golden fries.

Murata
Downtown between 2nd and 3rd, (503) 227-0080
200 SW Market,
Portland
Moderate; beer and wine; AE, MC, V; no checks
Lunch Mon-Fri, dinner every day

Murata not only produces sushi that others rarely cut—whole grilled sardines and the fatty toro cut of tuna—but it does dazzling things to seafood that require more than a knife. One night's special, a whole steamed crab, arrived with a totally unexpected vinegar dipping sauce that reoriented crab thinking. Grilled eel demonstrated why Japanese insist the creature is a delicacy, and grilled mackerel makes its own argument. But the strongest voice comes from huge, bubbling seafood stews called *nabes*, cooked on special tables in the tatami rooms. In a low-key environment—the restaurant is on the main floor of an office building—Murata reminds that Japan is an island surrounded by seafood.

Obi
Couch and 2nd, Old Town district,
(503) 226-3826
101 NW 2nd Ave,
Portland
Moderate; full bar; AE, DC, MC, V; no checks
Lunch Mon-Fri, dinner Mon-Sun

In this intoxicating temple of sushi run amok, the most striking innovations come in the maki section, where wild new combinations of gleamingly fresh seafood, vegetables, and Northwest mushrooms come wrapped in seaweed under names like Oregon Roll, Crazy Roll, and Rock 'n' Roll. Fish appears not just in the usual configurations but in items such as Tiger eyes—teardrop-shaped squid with a center of salmon and scallion. It's hard to choose a favorite, but let's just say that Rock 'n' Roll is here to stay.

Opus Too
Couch and 2nd, Old Town district,
(503) 222-6077
33 NW 2nd Ave,
Portland
Moderate; full bar; AE, DC, MC, V; no checks

The combination here is fish and fire; grilled seafood is so expertly done at this small operation that it has earned a devoted following even among the area's most diligent dieters. Great slabs of fresh seafood come away from the mesquite-fueled flames dripping with any of the restaurant's eight sauces, from béarnaise to beurre rouge. The decor is urban cool—tile floor, dark-wood booths, and a long swivel-chair bar overlooking

Lunch Mon-Sat, dinner every day

Panini
9th and Morrison, across from the Galleria, (503) 224-6001 620 SW 9th Ave, Portland Inexpensive; beer and wine; no credit cards; checks OK Breakfast, lunch, early dinner Mon-Sat

Papa Haydn
In Selwood district between Bybee and Holgate, (503) 232-9440 5829 SE Milwaukie Ave, Portland Moderate; beer and wine; AE, MC, V; local checks only Lunch, dinner Tues-Sat, brunch Sun

Irving and NW 23rd, (503) 228-7317 701 NW 23rd Ave, Portland Moderate; full bar; AE, MC, V; local checks only Lunch, dinner Tues-Sat, brunch Sun

The Ringside
2 blocks west of Civic Stadium, (503) 223-1513 2165 W Burnside, Portland Moderate; full bar; AE, MC, V; checks OK Dinner every day

the open kitchen and grills. The exuberant environment is complemented by a respectable wine list, some fine desserts, and piles of flavorful fettuccine. A terrific sourdough bread is part of the deal, and a recent change of ownership doesn't seem to have affected basic principles. Live jazz Tuesday and Wednesday nights starts at 9pm.

In size, it's just a hole-in-the-sidewalk; in spirit, however, it's chic and *molto italiano*—where the counter helpers don't just remember your name, they remember that you like your latte with a dash of cinnamon and just a little foam. Three-bite-sized panini (literally, "little sandwiches") are made of of anything from roast beef with homemade mayonnaise to pesto, fresh mozzarella, and tomato. Or drop by for a late afternoon tiramisu, or, on warm days, a soothing lemon mousse at a sidewalk table. The menu has recently been beefed up, not only at breakfast time but with muscular pastas at lunch and dinner. Some nights (at least during summer) the place stays open until 7pm.

This chocolate empire continues to expand: not only do the restaurants keep getting bigger, but the menu has grown to the point where you might eat there even if you *didn't* want dessert. Especially at the more ambitious Northwest 23rd outpost, entrées are increasingly imaginative (and increasingly expensive), with Thai and Mediterranean influences and less emphasis on sandwiches. But the core is still the display of dozens of towering, intense desserts, led by the Autumn Meringue—layers of chocolate mousse and baked meringue festooned with chocolate leaves—and the boccone dolce, a mountain of whipped cream, meringue, chocolate, and fresh berries. There are also subtler temptations, including a shocking purple blackberry ice and dense shortbread cookies. The northwest location has decent wine and beer lists and a full bar. The clientele there tends toward the upscale, while the southeast owes more to the cerebral Reed college crowd. Both have lines running out the door.

The mythically juicy steaks here might not bowl over those beef connoisseurs in Kansas, but in this territory they're hard to beat; for texture, color, flavor, and character, they're everything you could want from a hunk of steer. The degree of cooking is as ordered, and deviations are few. Still, it's the plump but light, slightly salty onion rings, made with Walla Walla sweets, that single-handedly made the Ringside famous—an order is essential. The menu has recently expanded into ocean fare; other house specialties include crackling fried chicken and nicely charred burgers. Appetizers and salads are limited, although the marinated herring deserves attention; the desserts do not. The dignified, black-jacketed staff is always professional.

Ristorante Medici

1 block south of 30th,
bordering Laurelhurst
district, (503) 232-9022
2924 E Burnside,
Portland
Moderate; full bar; AE,
MC, V; checks OK
Dinner Tues-Sun

After some inconsistency in its early years, this break-through Northern Italian restaurant seems to be getting its pots in a row. The menu now leaps to more experimentation, with inspiring homemade pasta dishes such as sweet potato ravioli with caramelized onions. Scallops in aioli exemplify the vigor of the entrées, and polenta blooms pungently in surprising corners of the menu—including dessert. The room itself is crowded but homey, with an alluring view of East Burnside and outside dining in summer. The service is gentle and helpful. The wine list goes on and on, with especially impressive numbers of Oregon pinots noirs and Italian reds; most impressive of all is a steward who can explain them all.

Ron Paul Catering and Charcuterie

Everett St Market,
(503) 223-2121
2310 NW Everett St,
Portland
Moderate; beer and wine;
MC, V; checks OK
Breakfast, lunch, dinner
every day

The vegetable stand next door has departed for even greener pastures, but Ron Paul, restaurant flagship of a growing catering operation, isn't going anywhere. Paul himself is a serious chef, recently invited to cook the James Beard Memorial Dinner in Manhattan, and his restaurant takes all its food seriously, from its home-cured lox to its pot pie of the day. (Hope for the Mexican chicken.) Also on the menu are individualized pizzas, barbecued chicken, spicy Sichuan noodles, and some of the best specialty breads in town (try the rich, dark walnut wheat). Desserts rank high. If you're looking for a morning spot, you won't find better coffee or rum-glazed bran muffins anywhere. Bring a sweater—the concrete floors and glass walls keep the place cool.

Salty's on the Columbia

Marine Drive exit from
I-5, (503) 288-4444
3839 NE Marine Dr,
Portland
Moderate; full bar; AE,
DC, MC, V; checks OK
Lunch Mon-Sat, dinner
every day, brunch Sun

Salty's on the Columbia washed in on a wave of doubt created by the mediocre performance of Salty's on the Willamette. But this operation is not only on a more exciting river, it has a considerably more exciting menu, served up with consistency and style. Stick to the daily fresh list of about 20 items, spurring inspirations that only appear at this particular Salty's, such as an explosive Columbia River sturgeon saltimbocca. And there are just about always briny local oysters. The restaurant is usually jammed, both the dining room downstairs and the upper deck lounge—the latter for the view as well as the food.

Sumida's

NE Sandy and 67th,
(503) 287-9162
6744 NE Sandy Blvd,
Portland
Moderate; beer and wine;
MC, V; no checks
Dinner Wed-Sun

Etsuo Sumida is nothing less than the patron saint of Portland's sushi scene, and his restaurant is where you come to indulge your raw-fish fetish. Just watching this master's virtuoso knifework is an experience: he's the Toshiro Mifune of seafood carving. Everything in this cozy neighborhood eatery is impeccably fresh. Sumida is also an expert at sushi rice preparation: proper vinegared rice must be sticky enough to hold fish, avocado, and such inside, yet easy to handle on the outside. This difficult balance is something of a litmus test for true sushi chefs, rare in the Northwest. Most of the grilled seafood is reliable here, if your taste for the raw is limited, and familiar items like tempura and teriyaki chicken are well executed.

Thanh Thao

Off 39th in Hawthorne
district, (503) 238-6232
4005 SE Hawthorne
Blvd, Portland
Inexpensive; beer and
wine; MC, V; checks OK
Lunch, dinner Wed-Mon

Thanh Thao II

On Powell off 82nd,
(503) 775-0306
8355 SE Powell Blvd,
Portland
Inexpensive; beer and
wine; AE, MC, V;
checks OK
Lunch, dinner every day

From low-key beginnings, this Vietnamese eatery and its branch are overshadowing the originally dominant Vietnamese establishments in Portland's northeast. The friendly Nguyen family can tell you everything you need to know about Vietnamese or Thai food. A bowl of vegetable curry (crisp broccoli, snow peas, and sprouts in a creamy curry broth with fresh pineapple and cilantro) warms the body. You'll find some ordinary dishes here (like cashew chicken), but there's also barbecued goat, and pigeon salad. Try the *muc xao thap camp* (squid sautéed with pineapple, tomato, mushroom, and celery), or the *dau hu chua ngot* (sweet-and-sour tofu) for a delicately steamed and sauced dinner. Thanh Thao's popularity led to the 1988 opening of the second place, on Powell.

Vat & Tonsure

1 block south of Broadway
between Yamhill and
Taylor, (503) 227-1845
822 SW Park Ave,
Portland
Inexpensive; beer and
wine; no credit cards;
checks OK
Lunch, dinner Mon-Sat

You'll find a considerably warmer reception at the Vat if you're one of the numerous regulars, but even outsiders will find solid American food, an extensive wine list and, frequently, the mayor having a beer. The high-backed wooden booths on the upper and lower decks of this split-level eatery are filled with cerebral and arty types (and, not surprisingly, plenty of smoke) who wax philosophical to a background of classical music. Owner Mike Quinn runs the bar and offers one of the town's most complete wine cellars. His wife, Rose-Marie Barbeau, handles the kitchen, turning out some fine stuffed Cornish hens, sautéed prawns, and lamb chops. Each year, the restaurant closes for a month while the proprietors go to Europe.

Winterborne
NE 42nd and Fremont in
Beaumont district,
(503) 249-8486
3520 NE 42nd Ave,
Portland
Moderate; beer and wine;
AE, MC, V; checks OK
Dinner Fri-Sat

A sense of '60s solemnity still seems to pervade Portland's first nonsmoking restaurant. For years it has been quietly turning out some of the most respectable fish dishes in town. No pretensions to elegance here—there's not a pastry wagon or a maitre d' in sight. Instead, plain dishware, dim lights, classical music, and a few lithographs set the tone. Chef/owner Dwight Bacon's menu is small, and entrées are complemented by fresh whole-wheat bread, a simple salad, and fragrant fish soup. None of the half-dozen main courses are overwhelmed by their simple sauces, although flounder stuffed with roasted almonds and lavender is pretty flashy. Pan-fried oysters with homemade tartar sauce make an excellent starter. For dessert, try some Death by Chocolate—so popular, it's beginning to show up in other local establishments.

Zell's: An American Cafe
13 blocks up from
Morrison Bridge,
(503) 239-0196
1300 SE Morrison St,
Portland
Inexpensive;
beer and wine; AE, MC,
V; checks OK
Breakfast, lunch
every day

Now *this* is breakfast: smoked sturgeon omelet, spring Chinook salmon and scrambled eggs, huckleberry pancakes, home-baked scones and two jams. The powerful coffee and fresh-squeezed orange juice are the kinds of touches that make getting up in the morning worthwhile. This establishment boasts one of the few soda fountains around that is not a campy imitation of the originals: Zell's is a converted '50s drugstore whose owners wisely spared the fountain counter from the remodeler's saw. Finally, if you can't resist recklessly sweet things in the morning, try the German pancakes with apples. Zell's is stunningly accommodating to kids, but the typical wait for a table may complicate things.

Zen
9th and Salmon,
downtown,
(503) 222-3056
910 SW Salmon St,
Portland
Expensive; full bar; AE,
DC, MC; local checks
only
Lunch Mon-Fri, dinner
Mon-Sat

The oldest Japanese restaurant around, Zen still sets the standard for the basic Japanese repertoire. Beef and seafood dishes are strongest, and a dish of spicy grilled beef (*yakiniku*) is a highlight. The sushi bar is more of an afterthought. Zen is the only restaurant around offering *kaiseki*, the formal, multicourse Japanese banquet (arrange in advance). The chef manages to fulfill both the artistic and culinary challenges it provides, but come sometime when you've got nothing planned for later on.

Cajun Cafe and Bistro
Corner of 21st and NW
Lovejoy, (503) 227-0227
2074 NW Lovejoy St,
Portland
Moderate; full bar; AE,
DC, MC, V; no checks

During a stretch when the Cajun Cafe turned first to the southwest and then toward mediocrity, some of the Cajun specialties continued to carry the flame. The blackening always kept its color, and the baking was solid. Recent changes may provide renewed energy. New chef Robin Milam brings in a background in French provincial cuisine, plus a short course with

*Lunch Mon-Fri, dinner
every day*

Bruce Livingston, the Cajun Cafe's founding chef. Milam could send the cafe down a whole new path—but for now the front dining room is a fast-food Mediterranean place called "Garbanzos." We just hope the Cajun martinis and Dixie beer will endure.

Couch Street Fish House
*Between Couch and
Davis, (503) 223-6173
105 NW 3rd Ave,
Portland
Expensive; full bar; AE,
MC, V; checks OK
Dinner Mon-Sat*

Couch Street works hard, from a board at the entrance welcoming the names on the reservation list to waiters converging on the table to whisk the covers off the entrées to a dessert of strawberries dipped in chocolate, injected with Grand Marnier, and served on a plate with the restaurant's name written in chocolate. Waiters in formal dress bring warm hand towels before the meal and, much later, whipped cream and brown sugar with your coffee. Food is not adventurous (Horst Mager keeps a tight rein on his chefs), but ingredients are strong, and some of the preparations are splendid, especially appetizers such as warm smoked trout. This is going to cost considerably anyway, so start things off with the delectable alder-smoked salmon.

Doris' Cafe
*North end of town, near
Kirby exit off I-5
northbound,
(503) 287-9249
3240 N Williams St,
Portland
Inexpensive; no alcohol;
AE, MC, V; local checks
only
Lunch, dinner Mon-Sat*

A hickory-burning brick pit and two hinged oil drums outside produce serious beef and pork ribs, with a sauce that is more sweet than angry. If you've sworn off barbecue, fried chicken is lovely, fresh, and gently complex. Desserts vary, but the buttery pound cake and the mousselike sweet potato pie should not be missed. Most take their food to go, but stay or go: nothing's going to come too quickly.

Hunan
*Between Washington and
Alder on SW Broadway,
(503) 224-8063
515 SW Broadway,
Portland
Moderate; full bar; MC,
V; local checks only
Lunch, dinner Mon-Sat*

To get acquainted with some of the more fervid aspects of Chinese cooking, there's Hunan; it's one of the most consistently on-target Chinese eateries in town. Among the standouts: Hunan beef, Lake T'ung T'ing shrimp, and minced Sichuan chicken wrapped in pancakes. The restaurant's versions of the spicy standards—General Tso's chicken, twice-cooked pork, chicken in tangy sauce—are pungent and massively popular. Service is fast and impersonal.

Koji Osakaya Japanese Fish House
*John's Landing area,
Texas and Macadam,
(503) 293-1066*

High on atmosphere, low on frills, and with enough noise to drown out a fraternity party, this is the Japanese answer to the neighborhood tavern. Koji's is also

*7007 SW Macadam Ave,
Portland
Moderate; full bar; AE,
DC, MC, V; no checks
Lunch Mon-Fri, dinner
every day*

where you come to catch up on the latest in sumo wrestling—Nippon's most popular sport is broadcast on a television perched above the sushi bar. Sushi fans pack the 23-seat raw-fish counter to watch dueling behemoths ritualize the physics of overfed flesh. Most of the standard sushi preparations can be had here, as well as a few rarities such as the pungent plum-mint rolls. It's a busy place, and service can be leisurely.

Marrakesh

*NW 23rd and
W Burnside,
(503) 248-9442
121 NW 23rd Ave,
Portland
Moderate; beer and wine;
AE, MC, V; checks OK
Dinner Tues-Sun*

In Portland's first Moroccan restaurant, your meal will begin with the customary finger-washing ceremony and end with the sprinkling of rose water over your hands. In between, you will experience—without the benefit of utensils—five courses of considerable interest but uneven success. Ben H. Alaoui's formula worked in Seattle, and seems to be working here. You sit on cushions along a tapestried wall and begin with *harira Marrakshia*, the cumin-and-coriander lentil soup of North Africa and the Middle East. The meal continues through a Moroccan eggplant salad and a Bastela Royale (a dry chicken-and-nut mixture covered with phyllo dusted with powdered sugar). Some of the entrées are too sweet and others are uninspired. Try instead the lamb with eggplant or the braised hare in a rich cumin and paprika sauce. Or visit with a large group and order the *mechoui*, Morocco's famous roast lamb (three days' notice required)—but don't expect any special treatment. For $14.50 you get a lot of food, but pay attention when ordering and reordering wine; the total bill can rise quickly.

The Original Pancake House

*Barbur Blvd exit of I-5
south; SW 24th and
Barbur, (503) 246-9007
8600 SW Barbur Blvd,
Portland
Inexpensive; no alcohol;
no credit cards;
checks OK
Breakfast, lunch Wed-
Sun*

This restaurant has clearly attained Portland landmark status, along with several of its namesake dishes. Nearly 20 species of pancake are here produced from scratch, from wine-spiked cherry to wheat-germ to a behemoth apple variety with sticky cinnamon glaze—a coffee cake masquerading as a pancake. A good bet is the ultrathin, egg-rich Dutch baby, dusted with powdered sugar and served with fresh lemon (essential to its overall flavor). And if you need a little something less sweet, this is one of the few places that can do decent scrambled eggs. Drawbacks are a painfully long wait for seating (bring a copy of *War and Peace* if you're thinking of weekend breakfast), a 90-decibel interior, and the town's weakest coffee. Once you're seated, the service is rushed and aloof.

Plainfield's Mayur

*1 block west of Civic
Stadium, (503) 223-2995
852 SW 21st Ave,
Portland*

This is the only spot in Portland with an authentic tandoor oven. The style is basically Mogul, with an emphasis on subtle flavors and aromatic spices. The setting is sparse and somewhat formal: bone china, crystal, candles, and linen-covered tables, although outdoor tables during the summer loosen the mood up some-

*Moderate; full bar; AE,
DC, MC, V; checks OK
Dinner every day*

what. Portions are small and tariffs a bit steeper than one usually expects for this cuisine. For starters, bypass the traditional offerings for something unusual, such as tomato coconut soup. The tandoori dishes—roasted prawns in tandoori jhinga, for one—are outstanding, and a recent addition to the menu, lobster in a spicy brown sauce, is so good you probably won't even wonder whether India actually has lobsters.

Vietnam's Pearl

*10th and Morrison,
(503) 241-4740
1037 SW Morrison St,
Portland
Inexpensive; beer and
wine; MC, V; no checks
Lunch, dinner Mon-Sat*

Portland's first Vietnamese restaurant remains the city's most accessible, both in downtown location and in food. After a period of uneven quality, its original owner reacquired it, and the Pearl is now a popular and consistent downtown fixture. Try the sour soups, the peanutty charcoal-grilled pork appetizer, and chicken with ginger or lemon grass. The menu goes on at some length, and while some choices might be uneven, chances for a satisfying, inexpensive meal are high.

Yen Ha (East)

*Off NE 67th and Sandy
Blvd, (503) 287-3698
6820 NE Sandy Blvd,
Portland
Inexpensive; beer and
wine; MC, V; checks OK
Lunch Tues-Fri, dinner
Tues-Sun*

Last year, Duck Van Tran inherited the original Yen Ha from his celebrated culinary cousin, Bach Tuyet (now stationed on Canyon Road), and he's made it his own: Yen Ha East is a bustling Vietnamese cafe with an innovative kitchen. Try the superb soups, the succulent salt-fried Dungeness crab in tangy sauce, or the hot pot with seafood, vegetables, and Asian exotica. This is a menu worth exploring, and service is better than in most Vietnamese operations.

LODGINGS

The Heathman Hotel

*SW Broadway at Salmon,
(503) 241-4100 or toll
free (800) 551-0011
1009 SW Broadway,
Portland, OR 97205
Expensive; AE, DC, MC,
V; checks OK*

This is the place to stay in town: afternoon tea each day, exquisite bar, elegant rooms, one of Portland's finest restaurants. The Heathman is also a historic landmark, restored about a decade ago by the Stevenson family. The most notable feature of the interior is the generous use of Burmese teak paneling—the owner, Mark Stevenson, is a timber magnate. Small guest rooms are furnished with leather-and-rattan chairs, marble-topped bathroom pieces with brass fittings, chintz window shades, celadon lamps, and original prints and paintings. Colors are soft green, rose, and cream. Among the amenities are a choice of approximately 300 complimentary movies, European soaps, bathrobes, and a nightly turn-down service. One of the Heathman's nicest qualities is the service—its employees are low-key (a highly valued quality in Oregon) but meticulously attentive. Guests feel well taken care of but not fussed over. Rooms facing away from Broadway are best; the hotel is on downtown

Portland's busiest street. Rooms start at $140 (double).

**RiverPlace
Alexis Hotel**
*Harbor Way off Front
Ave, (503) 228-3233 or
toll-free (800) 227-1333
1510 SW Harbor Way,
Portland, OR 97201
Expensive; AE, DC, MC,
V; checks OK*

The Portland counterpart to Seattle's elegant Alexis Hotel is situated in Portland's showcase riverfront district. It features 10 chic condominiums, 74 rooms, specialty shops, two restaurants (one, the Patio, is open summers only), scenic jogging paths, and an upscale bar. Inside are plush furnishings, postmodern colors, televisions concealed in armoires, complimentary sherry in the bar, smashing views of the river, and a lively night scene. The best rooms face the Willamette River or look north across park lawns to the downtown cityscape (though there's no guarantee of a river-view room). A jogging path, extending along the riverfront from the hotel's front door to downtown, is so popular with guests that hotel management has added to its complimentaries list the loan of jogging suits and athletic shoes. Use of the adjacent RiverPlace Athletic Club facilities is an extra $8. The hotel restaurant, Esplanade, is strong in New American cuisine, and the bar is staffed by one of the most knowledgeable wine stewards around.

Heron Haus B&B
*NW 25th and Johnson,
(503) 274-1846
2545 NW Westover Rd,
Portland, OR 97210
Expensive; MC, V;
checks OK*

It's located in the exclusive Northwest Hills overlooking Portland, and you won't find more luxurious lodging. Built in 1904 for a local cranberry baron, Heron Haus maintains many original touches, including parquet flooring on the main level. Updated amenities, however, are no less pleasant: one of the five rooms has an elevated spa offering a view of the city below. Each room has its own bath, and one even features a turn-of-the-century seven-nozzle shower. This is a spacious operation for a B&B, 7,500 square feet. There's a living room with modern furniture, a handsome, well-stocked library, a TV room, an enclosed sun room, and an outside pool. A very comfortable spot, especially for the business traveler; there are phones in every room, and downstairs you'll find a fax machine and a work area. If you're visiting in late summer, you'll get in on the harvest from a miniature orchard of pear, apple, and cherry trees. It's also two blocks from the city's most popular shopping district.

The Benson
*Corner of SW Broadway
and Oak, (503) 228-9611
309 SW Broadway,
Portland, OR 97205
Expensive; AE, DC, MC,
V; checks OK*

Simon Benson was a philanthropic lumber tycoon who in 1912-13 built the Benson Hotel, giving orders to spare no expense. The creation was a noble 13-story affair of brick and marble (the latter has by now acquired a pale-green patina), with a palatial lobby featuring a stamped-tin ceiling, mammoth chandeliers, stately columns, a generous fireplace, and surrounding panels of carved Circassian walnut imported from Russia. For decades this was the only classy lodging in town. Competition brought an end to the Benson's exclusive status; however, under the new ownership of WestCoast Hotels, a major renovation taking place at press time may just bring it back up to its original stature. The lobby and lounge is being restored to its marbled elegance. Upon completion (expected by late 1991) there will be fewer rooms in the older north wing, where the rooms were generally small, with utilitarian baths; now they're bigger (bath and all). The newer portion of the building—the south wing, with more forgiving accommodations—will be open until the plumbing, wiring, and looks of the north wing are brought out of the 1890s. There are two pricey restaurants in the hotel, the London Grill (with a stunning wine cellar) and Trader Vic's.

Hotel Vintage Plaza

Broadway at Washington,
(503) 228-1212
422 SW Broadway,
Portland, OR 97205
Expensive; full bar; AE,
DC, MC, V; no checks
Breakfast, lunch, dinner
every day

One of Portland's oldest hotels is now the city's newest. Bill Kimpton of San Francisco's Kimco Hotels saved this 1894 hotel (originally the Imperial) from being converted into office space. The 107 rooms are individually decorated with cherry wood furnishings and rich colors. Request a starlight room with greenhouse style windows perfect for stargazing. A complimentary winetasting is held every evening in the atrium lobby on the main floor (there's a wine cellar here too). Each suite in the hotel is named after an Oregon vineyard. Service is personable and all rooms come with complimentary shoe shine, nightly turn-down service, morning coffee in the lobby, and the *Oregonian* delivered to your door. Pazzo Ristorante on the main floor serves Northern Italian cuisine. An extra $8 a day gets you into the Princeton Athletic Club nearby.

Mumford Manor

Follow Burnside west to
King, (503) 243-2443
1130 SW King Ave,
Portland, OR 97205
Expensive; AE, MC, V;
checks OK

The Mumford is a fully restored Queen Anne from the turn of the century. The blue-shuttered, three-story beige structure is ideally located in the heart of the commercial triangle—walking distance from the business hub of downtown, the indulgence shops of the northwest district, and the sequestered beauty of Washington Park. The master suite is Victorian (if you don't count the electric towel warmer), done in reds and chintz, and has a fireplace. The three other rooms are equally stylish, from their designer wallpaper and goose-down pillows and comforters to the antique pedestal sinks in the bathrooms. There's a grand piano and fireplace for all in the living room, and a game room downstairs, where there's often a jigsaw puzzle in the works. A wholesome breakfast is served on fine china and crystal.

Portland Guest House

NE Broadway and 15th,
(503) 282-1402

What PGH lacks in grandeur, it makes up for in simplicity and class. Since owner Susan Gisvold doesn't live here, she runs it like a small hotel; she's usually

1720 NE 15th Ave,
Portland, OR 97212
Moderate; AE, DC, MC,
V; checks OK

around just long enough to advise you on Portland doings and bake a batch of cookies. The rest of the time, guests have full run of the parlor, dining room, and—dare she?—the fully stocked fridge. In the morning, Susan drops in to cook a fine breakfast of fresh fruit, scones, maybe even a basil omelet. With five rooms (three with baths), privacy is seldom a problem. Each room has its own phone and clock, items that, we're finding, are not standard in many B&Bs. The newest suite is a good choice for families (one queen and two single beds). When the weather's warm, the garden's the spot. You'll probably sample Susan's fresh corn, tomatoes, pumpkins, and herbs.

Portland's White House

Coliseum exit from I-5,
head east to NE 22nd,
(503) 287-7131
1914 NE 22nd Ave,
Portland, OR 97212
Expensive; MC, V; checks
OK

Another local timber baron, Robert F. Lytle, built to last what is now a popular B&B—it's constructed of solid Honduras mahogany. From the outside it's an imposing white mansion with all the trappings of Brahmin taste: fountain, carriage house, and a grand circular driveway. Inside are six roomy units, exquisite Oriental rugs, and other elegant appointments. The Canopy Room has a private bath, its own balcony, and a large canopied bed. Another room, equally romantic, has a vintage brass bed and delicate lace curtains. Teatime is quiet time... unless your visit coincides with a wedding (for which they're consistently booked three times a month).

Sheraton Airport Hotel

On Airport Way just
before the terminal,
(503) 281-2500, toll-free
(800) 325-3535
8235 NE Airport Way,
Portland, OR 97220
Expensive; AE, DC, MC,
V; checks OK

For the traveling businessperson the airport's Sheraton tops the list. For one thing, it's located—literally—on the airport grounds (Fed Ex planes load up next door, and arrival and departure times are broadcast at the main entrance). Inside, amenities abound: everything from meeting rooms and a complete, complimentary business center (IBM computer, printer, fax machine, and secretarial services), to an indoor swimming pool, sauna, and workout room. Details down to hair dryers in the women's room (we didn't check the men's) are covered here. The executive suites consider the personal needs of the businessperson with extra touches such as two phones, sitting areas, and pullout makeup mirrors in the bathrooms. We only wish they would give the hotel a quarter turn: Mount Hood stands tall to the east, but you'd never know it from the airport-facing rooms.

General Hooker's B&B

¾ mile south of the
Marriott Hotel, between
SW 1st and 2nd,
(503) 222-4435 or toll
free (800) 745-4135
125 SW Hooker St,

Happy Hooker, an Abyssinian cat, greets you at the door of this gracious Victorian B&B in a quiet southwest neighborhood. The General's house offers four rooms with handmade batik quilts and other homey touches, including a large wood stove, an eclectic library, hanging metal artwork by owner Lori Hall's mother, and a sun deck. There's a VCR in each room,

Portland, OR 97201
Moderate; AE, MC, V;
checks OK

and the building has central air conditioning. The best unit is the Rose Room, with a king-size bed, private entrance, and skylit bath. Kids can stay in the bunk room downstairs. Wine is served to guests nightly on the roof decks, and there is half-price use of the nearby Metro YMCA. Duniway Park running track, Terwilliger Boulevard bike path, and the Lair Hill public tennis court are also within walking distance. Downtown is five minutes by car and is also accessible by bus.

Hartman's Hearth B&B

Stanton and 20th in
Irvington district,
(503) 281-2182
2937 NE 20th Ave,
Portland, OR 97212
Moderate; AE, DC, MC,
V; checks OK

Katie and Chris Hartman opened their B&B a few years ahead of schedule. But now (though both fully employed elsewhere) they have settled marvelously into juggling the responsibilities of B&B owners. Of the three upstairs rooms, choose the spacious Art Deco one (the entire third floor), which is only $20 more than its two shared-bath partners. There's a cedar sauna in the basement and a gazebo-covered Jacuzzi in the back yard. Robes and, of course, breakfast provided.

MacMaster House

Below Washington Park,
near corner of Burnside
and Vista,
(503) 223-7362
1041 SW Vista Ave,
Portland, OR 97205
Expensive; AE, MC, V;
checks OK

This colonial is 2 blocks from the largest municipal park in the country—the Washington Park–Forest Park complex, which incorporates Portland's renowned Rose Gardens and Hoyt Arboretum. From the outside, MacMaster is a restored B&B, with a massive portico set off by Doric columns, a spacious manse with seven fireplaces and leaded glass windows. Inside, things get a bit bizarre: a wall painted with palm trees in one room, Greek columns in the next, erotic art in another. Still, if you can stand the odd decor, five spacious rooms have queen beds and cable TV and share two baths. Four have colonial fireplaces. Not everyone will feel comfortable in the safarilike sixth room (the three-room suite): bamboo-canopied bed, zebra-skin rugs, and cowhide chair. Breakfast is served communally in the stately dining room.

Mallory Motor Hotel

Corner of SW 15th and
Yamhill, (503) 223-6311,
or toll-free
(800) 228-8657
729 SW 15th Ave,
Portland, OR 97205
Inexpensive; AE, DC,
MC, V; checks OK

This place is an older establishment in every sense—from the massive hunks of ornate wooden lobby furniture to the clientele to the senior staff. It's also one of the best bargains in town, starting at $45 for a double, with vast suites for $75. While rooms are spacious, they bear no resemblance to the hotel's more elaborate entrance. On the other hand, this is one of the few areas bordering downtown Portland that is genuinely quiet. Parking is easy to find (Mallory has two lots across the street), and several of the rooms have good views of the city or the west hills. The bar, a kind of bizarre hybrid of '50s dark-plushy and '60s eccentric-cutesy, is not the major attraction here. The irritating Muzak in every corner of the ground floor is a drawback. The flaws fade, however, next to simple, charming touches such as the small, lace-trimmed pillow with needle, thread, and buttons left in your room and the almost motherly service.

Marriott Residence Inn/Lloyd Center
2 blocks east of Lloyd Center on Multnomah,
(503) 288-1400
176 NE Multnomah,
Portland, OR 97232
Expensive; AE, DC, MC, V; checks OK

This new hotel near the Lloyd Center Cinema has 168 rooms. It's geared toward longer stays (4-7 days): each room has a full kitchen and most have wood-burning fireplaces. Extras include a continental breakfast (bagels, muffins, cereal and fruits) served in the lobby. There isn't much of a view and no restaurant, but the rooms are bigger than other standard hotels. There are a couple of Jacuzzis for guest use and a heated outdoor pool. An extra $4 gains you access to the Lloyd Center Athletic Club seven blocks away.

Marriott Hotel
Between SW Clay and Columbia streets facing the Willamette,
(503) 226-7600
1401 SW Front Ave,
Portland, OR 97201
Expensive; AE, DC, MC, V; checks OK

This big, urban place looks like standard convention lodging in every big city in the country. Redeeming that is its location overlooking the Willamette River. There are 503 rooms in the 14-story structure, and facilities include a 24-hour health club, an indoor pool, two restaurants, and two bars. This is the kind of operation where callers can expect a chirpy-voiced clerk to put them on hold for five minutes, then field rate queries in terms of "current, tomorrow, and weekend." Don't settle for the first price quoted—if you probe them you might just find you qualify for more moderate prices (ask about weekend, senior citizen, AAA, and other special rates).

Red Lion at Lloyd Center
Lloyd Center/Weidler exit from I-5, (503) 281-6111
toll-free (800) 547-8010
1000 NE Multnomah St,
Portland, OR 97232
Expensive; AE, DC, MC, V; checks OK

Its daunting size (a map in the lobby directs you to the three restaurants) and proximity to Lloyd Center, Memorial Coliseum, and the new Convention Center make this corporate hotel a good choice for eastside conventions or seminars. With 476 guest rooms, it's Oregon's second-largest hotel (the Marriott is slightly bigger), with a number of well-organized meeting rooms, an outdoor pool, a workout room, and a courtesy airport van. Reserve a west-facing room above the fifth floor for a view of Mount Hood.

TIGARD

LODGINGS

Embassy Suites Hotel
Off Hwy 217, follow signs to Washington Square,
(503) 644-4000
9000 SW Washington Square Rd, Tigard,
OR 97223

This is the westside equivalent of the Marriott. The Embassy is urban-moderno, right down to its location, adjacent to the sprawling Washington Square shopping complex in Tigard, about 15 minutes' driving time from Portland. The only feature that really recommends this monolithic structure is its quick access to Oregon's "Silicon Valley" business district in the flat plains be-

Expensive; AE, DC, MC, V; checks OK

tween Beaverton and Tigard. At press time, a major new wing that will add 110 more rooms, an elaborate ballroom, and a swanky conference center was imminent. Complimentaries include full breakfast, athletic club use (five minutes away by complimentary limo), and shopping-mall limo service. Restaurant and lounge are the usual Denny's-gone-velvet found in all hotels of this genre. Double occupancy begins at $127.

LAKE OSWEGO
RESTAURANTS

Thai Villa
Downtown Lake Oswego, (503) 635-6164
340 N 1st St, Lake Oswego
Inexpensive; beer and wine; MC, V; checks OK
Lunch Mon-Fri, dinner every day

Hidden away in a corner of a municipal parking lot next to the Lake Oswego fire station is a Thai restaurant with few matches but a lot of fire. Thai Villa specializes in pungent soups served swirling in a moat around a pillar of flame, and a wide range of seafood dishes. The spicing is up to you, but the highest level of heat is called "volcano," and they're not kidding. The chef is also handy with basil, garlic, and subtle hints of sweetness, and the prices are reasonable, especially on a cost-per-tingle basis. Hit the King's Favorite Chile— the king knows his stuff—or the accurately named "Seafood World."

LODGINGS

Howard Johnson Plaza Hotel
Intersection of I-5 and Hwy 217, (503) 624-8400 or toll-free (800) 654-2000
14811 SW Kruse Oaks Blvd, Lake Oswego, OR 97035
Moderate; AE, DC, MC, V; checks OK

Howard Johnson's come a long way from its signature burnt orange of the '60s. This blue-and-tinted-glass six-story tower seems to fit in well with the new corporate parks sprouting in the 'burbs, but contrasts with the few remaining Lake Oswego farms near the intersection of I-5 and Highway 217. The rooms are standard, but we suggest you request one on the outside of the "V" lest you wake up staring at your neighbor across the way. There's an indoor/outdoor pool, exercise facilities, a sauna, and a Jacuzzi.

GRESHAM
RESTAURANTS

Roland's
Right off Powell (Hwy 26); 2 blocks from downtown Gresham,

The road through Germany, Sweden, Australia, Brazil, and San Francisco doesn't usually end in Gresham, but Roland Blasi's did, and all of east Multnomah County is

(503) 665-7215
155 SE Vista,
Gresham
Moderate; beer and wine;
MC, V; local checks OK
Dinner Tues-Sat

grateful. A mile from the MAX line, Blasi has produced a splendid continental restaurant—continental not in the sense of the 38th version of veal Oskar, but in surefooted and imaginative menu choices drawn from all over Western Europe. Try the Pasta Angelo with an unusually subtle Italian sausage, and hope that the specials include the poached salmon with two sauces. Torta di formaggio is actually cheesecake, but this version can call itself anything it wants to.

MILWAUKIE
RESTAURANTS

Buster's Smokehouse Texas-Style Bar-Be-Que
2 miles north of I-205,
take Oregon City exit,
(503) 652-1076
17883 SE McLoughlin
Blvd, Milwaukie
Inexpensive; beer and
wine; MC, V; local
checks only
Lunch, dinner every day

From I-84 East, take
Wood Village exit; in
Hood Center shopping
mall, (503) 667-4811
1355 E Burnside,
Gresham

One deep whiff as you come in tells you all you need to know about Buster's, where huge wood-smoke ovens leave their mark on both the meat and the atmosphere. Brisket, chicken, beef and pork ribs, and links all pass through the cooker and come out estimably pink and juicy. The pungent barbecue sauce helps considerably, and beer is the beverage of choice. Accompaniments are simple: fries, slaw, barbecue beans, and, for the daredevil, stuffed jalapeño peppers. Pecan pie is a solid finish. Equal emphasis on barbecue essentials at both the original Milwaukie location and the newer Gresham branch.

HILLSBORO
RESTAURANTS

Helvetia Tavern
2½ miles north of Sunset
Hwy, (503) 647-5286
Helvetia Rd,
Hillsboro
Inexpensive; beer and
wine; no credit cards;
no checks
Lunch, dinner every day

Sports cars and motorcycles share space in the parking lot of this regular joint, where locals and highway travelers pack the premises and there's much backslapping between staff and patrons. Hamburgers and fries are the establishment's raison d'être—beyond these options, proceed at your own risk. Burgers are topped with mildly sautéed onion rings, crisp lettuce, and tomatoes, and finished with a light mayonnaise sauce—a decent old-fashioned burger. The fries are terrific, long and lean with brown skins intact, and heaped into a mound that covers half the plate like a golden haystack.

BEAVERTON

RESTAURANTS

Chen's China Clipper
Near Scholl's Ferry Rd,
(503) 292-4898
6750 SW Beaverton
Hillsdale Hwy,
Beaverton
Moderate; full bar; AE,
DC, MC, V; no checks
Lunch, dinner every day

In the middle of 1988 chef Chi-Siung Chen jumped his Portland ship. Leaving downtown for the suburbs, he opened a restaurant specializing intensely in seafood (note the giant papier-maché fish hanging from the ceiling), including 28 different shrimp dishes. The results are sometimes uneven but often brilliant, and usually well worth getting your feet wet. Shanghai Harbor Crab, a whole Dungeness in a hoisin sauce flecked with ginger and scallions, is a good example of the place at its best. *Chiang siu* (whole crispy fish) and scallops in a nest, Hunan style, demonstrate how effectively Northwestern seafood and Far Eastern inspiration can blend. Be warned: you're going to pay more than you might expect for Chinese food, and when Chen himself is not in the kitchen, standards dip toward the waterline.

Hall Street Bar & Grill
Canyon Road to Cedar
Hills Blvd, right on Hall,
(503) 641-6161
3775 SW Hall St,
Beaverton
Moderate; full bar; AE,
MC, V; checks OK
Lunch Mon-Sat, dinner
every day

With high vaulted ceilings and oak floors, Hall Street looks and acts like a typical fern bar. The difference is in the food, featuring rock salt–roasted prime rib and mesquite-grilled steaks from Nebraska. An inventive daily menu includes another half dozen entrée selections, mostly nouvelle fish prepared with ingredients like lime, ginger, basil, hazelnuts, and/or avocado salsa. A recent wine list (usually a dozen Northwest and California wines) offered three different nouveaux Beaujolais, and the beer list goes on for quite a distance. A superb burnt crème with a hard sugar crust leads the list of strong desserts.

LODGINGS

Greenwood Inn
Hwy 217 and Allen Blvd,
(503) 643-7444
10700 SW Allen Blvd,
Beaverton, OR 97005
Moderate; AE, DC, MC,
V; checks OK

The best thing about this modern 253-room motel and convention complex is its location just off Highway 217, the freeway connecting the Sunset Highway in the northwest with the teeming southwest suburbs of Beaverton and Tigard. The rooms are nothing special, although a few of the suites have Jacuzzis and kitchens, and some rooms are set aside for guests with pets. The courtyard and trapezoidal pool are quite pretty. One unusual feature for a motel is room service, including complimentary coffee and a choice of newspapers in the morning; place an order the night before with the wake-up operator. From 5pm to 6pm there are complimentary cocktails. Inside the Pavillion Bar and Grill, lights are soft, and service treads the delicate line between chummy and concerned. The food's absolutely OK without being remarkable.

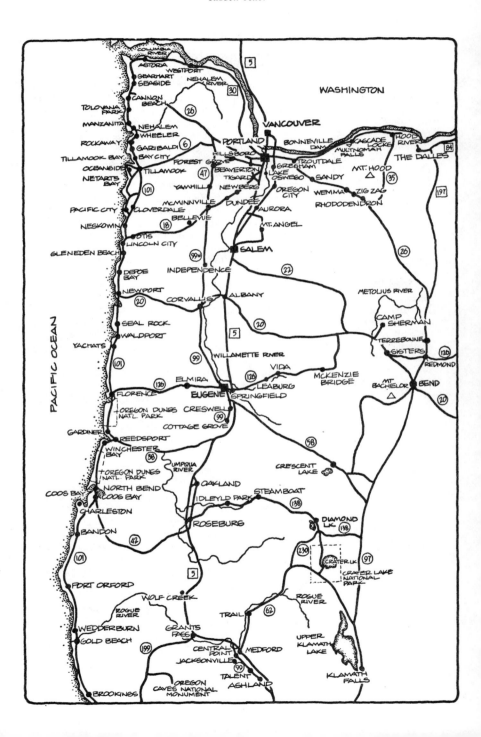

OREGON COAST

From Westport (on the Columbia River, some 30 miles inland), a southward route down the coast.

WESTPORT

LODGINGS

King Salmon Lodge
Just off Hwy 30 at the ferry dock,
(503) 455-2400
Mail: PO Box 5111, Westport, OR 97016
Moderate; no alcohol, no credit cards; checks OK
Lunch, dinner Mon-Sat, brunch Sun, by reservation only,

Westport is the tiny Columbia River town connected to Puget Island by ferry, then by bridge to Cathlamet, Washington, and the Washington mainland. The King Salmon Lodge, formerly a barracks for Chinese salmon-cannery workers, is now a bed and breakfast with a restaurant. The setting, on a gurgling creek lined with alders and maples, is idyllic. Lunch and dinner are open to non-guests, though you must call ahead to guarantee a spot. A $10 all-you-can-eat buffet lunch might include some decent lasagne and pretty good clam chowder. Dinners are more elaborate ($12.50 and up) and might feature prime rib, calamari, or Willapa Bay oysters, with soup, salad, and dessert included. A Sunday-only brunch is an all-you-can-eat opportunity.

If time permits, take the 20-minute ferry ride to Puget Island, a land of farms, forests, and abundant wildlife and a bicyclist's paradise. You might spot deer, elk, or even a bald eagle on the wide-open rural roads.

ASTORIA

This fishing and cannery town founded in 1811 lays claim as the first permanent American settlement west of the Rockies. Recently, the city has begun touting its historical attractions, and visitors from Portland and Puget Sound are discovering that the North Coast has more to offer than sandy beaches.

Boston's Robert Gray first sailed into the Columbia in May of 1792 (Oregon and Washington are planning a 200th anniversary celebration for 1992) and named the river for his ship. In 1805-1806, explorers Lewis and Clark spent a miserably rainy winter at the now-restored Fort Clatsop, six miles southwest of town. Noting that only 12 of 106 days were without rain, these two intrepid explorers gave the Northwest coast its permanent reputation for dampness. Five years later, New Yorker John Jacob Astor, one of America's wealthiest individuals, sent out the fur-trading company that founded Fort Astoria (now partially restored at 15th and Exchange streets).

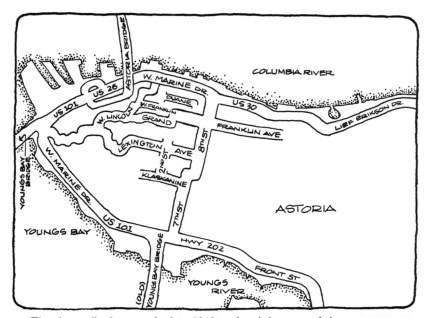

The city really dates to the late 1840s, when it began to thrive as a customs-house town and shipping center. The well-maintained Victorian homes lining the harbor hillside at Franklin and Grand avenues provide glimpses of that era. Now, Astoria is a museum without walls, an unstirred mix of the old and new that finds common ground along the busy waterfront—once the locale for canneries and river steamers, now an active port for oceangoing vessels and Russian fish-processing ships. Salmon- and bottom-fishing trips leave from here.

The Columbia River Maritime Museum is the best maritime museum in the Northwest. Located at 17th Street along Marine Drive, (503) 325-2323, the museum boasts a Great Hall with restored small craft and seven thematic galleries, each depicting a different aspect of the Northwest's maritime heritage: sailing vessels, river commerce, marine safety, etc. The *Lightship Columbia,* the last of its kind on the Pacific coast, is moored outside the museum and is included in the admission price.

Fort Clatsop National Memorial, 6 miles southwest of Astoria off Highway 101, reconstructs Lewis and Clark's 1805-1806 winter encampment. A visitor center features audiovisual displays about the Lewis and Clark expedition, limited exhibits, and a small collection of books and souvenirs; a new, larger, and more modern visitor center is scheduled to open in late 1991.

Captain George Flavel House/Heritage Museum. Operated by the Clatsop County Historical Society, these two museums feature local historical displays. The Flavel House, named after a prominent 19th-century businessman and Columbia River bar pilot, is the city's best example of ornate Queen Anne architecture; 8th and Duane streets, (503) 325-2563. The recently restored Heritage Museum, (503) 325-2203, is 8 blocks away at 1618 Exchange Street.

The Astoria Column, atop the city's highest point, Coxcomb Hill, offers an endless view of the Columbia River estuary out to the Pacific and beyond. Well worth the 160-plus-step climb. Spiral murals of the region's history wrap around the column, which is being restored by the city. To get there, drive up to the top of 16th Street and follow the signs.

Sixth Street River Park has an always-open, covered observation tower providing the best vantage point to view river commerce, observe bar and river pilots boarding tankers and freighters, and watch seals and sea lions looking for a free lunch.

Josephson's Smokehouse, 106 Marine Drive, (503) 325-2190, prepares alder-smoked salmon that's as good as you'll find anywhere. Other smoked fish includes tuna and sturgeon. Third-generation owners Linda and Mike Josephson are good sources for local information.

Fort Stevens State Park, 20 minutes southwest of Astoria off Highway 101, is a 3,500-acre outdoor wonderland of uncrowded beaches--including the permanent resting spot of the hulk of the *Peter Iredale*, wrecked in 1906. With 605 camping sites, Fort Stevens is Oregon's largest publicly owned campground.

The South Jetty lookout tower, located at Oregon's northwesternmost point, is a supreme storm-watching spot. It also marks the start of the Oregon Coast Trail, the 62-mile trail along the beach and coastal hills to Tillamook Bay.

Ricciardi Gallery, the newest kid on the 10th Street block (108 10th Street, (503) 325-5450), offers a nice selection of regional art displayed in an airy, attractive setting. Espresso, juices, and desserts are offered up front.

Stop in **Peri's Sandwich Express** (915 Commercial St, 325-5560) for the best sandwiches in town. Since there aren't any tables, the Sixth Street River Park is a nice spot for picnicking.

RESTAURANTS

Columbian Cafe

Corner of 11th St and Marine Dr,
(503) 325-2233
1114 Marine Dr,
Astoria
Inexpensive; beer and wine; no credit cards; checks OK
Breakfast, lunch Mon-Sat, dinner Wed-Sat

This vegetarian, nonsmoking, smallish cafe just happens to be Astoria's best bet for good grub. Locals know it and recommend it, so every noontime is crowded. You could rub shoulders with the city manager on the next counter stool or share a booth with the drummer from the coast's hottest garage band. As long as you enter prepared for cramped quarters, uneven service, an eccentric chef, and erratic hours, you'll leave happy. Chef Uriah Hulsey may engage you in stimulating conversation, offer up-to-the-minute tidbits on Astoria happenings, or totally ignore you. But the delicately crafted crêpes, sumptuous soups, excellent omelets, and black bean burritos make it all worthwhile. If you're feeling adventuresome, order the "chef's mercy," an eclectic concoction of the day's best (and freshest) ingredients; duplicates are a rarity. Dinners, which change nightly, center around fish and fresh pasta topped with garden veggies and handmade cilantro and garlic sauces.

Kim's Kitchen

Corner of 14th and Marine Dr,
(503) 325-1047
225 14th, Astoria
Inexpensive; no alcohol; no credit cards; local

Tucked in between a bike shop and an art gallery, Kim's Kitchen brings a bit of Korean ethnicity to this side of the Pacific Rim. Proprietor Kim Fuhrmann's tiny (eight tables) restaurant isn't fancy, but the food is good, the portions ample, and the hostess eager to please. A daily specials board features a handful of Korean dishes, such as bolgoki —spicy slices of top

checks only
Lunch Mon-Sat, dinner
Fri-Sat

sirloin—or a simple meal of rice and tiny prawns. Ask for kimchi, a spicy cabbage that will clear your sinuses. In a gesture to her adopted country, Kim offers a decent banana cream pie.

Pacific Rim
Next to Doughboy
Monument on Marine
Drive beneath Interstate
Bridge, (503) 325-4481
229 W Marine Dr,
Astoria
Inexpensive; full bar;
MC, V; checks OK
Lunch, dinner every day

In a city aching to tap into the East Asian trade scene, it's appropriate that a restaurant with a view of oceangoing vessels be named the Pacific Rim. But don't expect any Oriental cuisine; here, the rim of choice is chewy, doughy pizza. You can choose between a traditional New York–style pie or a thicker, more filling Sicilian square. Toppings include San Francisco Italian sausage and pepperoni, along with the usual array of veggies and such. Other things Italian include the lasagne lunch, a thick wedge of layered pasta oozing cheeses, meat, and sauce. It's tough to take the service seriously, especially on summer weekends, when the smallish Rim gets crowded, smoky, and disorganized. But the diverse dining clientele seem to appreciate the absence of canned mushrooms and prefab dough found in most coastal pizzerias.

The Ship Inn
On the west end of town,
at the foot of 2nd St on the
waterfront,
(503) 325-0033
1 2nd St, Astoria
Moderate; full bar; MC,
V; local checks only
Lunch, dinner every day

An Astoria waterfront institution, the Ship Inn is owned and operated by English expatriates Jill and Fenton Stokeld. Your best bet is fish 'n' chips, and for this your best choice is halibut. All fish is double-dipped in a delicately seasoned batter and cooked moist in fresh oil, while the chips are made from large potato slices. Neither is greasy. Wash your meal down with a pint of Watney's ale or Labatt's beer, both on tap. The place gets crowded almost every weekend, and since no reservations are accepted, you'll wait awhile for your table. Grab a chair in the congenial (but smoky) bar up front—a wonderful place to enjoy a brew, take in some local chit-chat, or listen to occasional live acoustic music. When it's time to eat, ask for a window table, where you can watch bar and river pilots get on and off oceangoing freighters and tankers in the river channel just a hundred yards away.

LODGINGS

Franklin House
Franklin Ave and 17th,
(503) 325-5044
1681 Franklin Ave,
Astoria, OR 97103
Moderate; MC, V;
checks OK

Matronly innkeeper Karen Nelson scurries around this remodeled Victorian B&B with the brightly painted exterior, looking after her guests like an indulgent grandmother. Giant sequoias and other evergreens dominate the grounds, and the quiet residential location just down the street from some of Astoria's finest Victorians ensures serenity. Inside, the furnishings—including a rich wrought-iron fireplace with paneled mirrors—were chosen with meticulous care. Mrs. Nelson named each of the home's five spacious guest rooms after a Northwest lighthouse; each has a private bath, including the beautiful burgundy-tiled washroom in the Cape Flattery Room (which doubles as the bridal suite). The home's only basement room, Grays Harbor, is the largest and least attractive, but the best choice for families with children.

Franklin Street Station
Between 11th and 12th on Franklin,
(503) 325-4314
1140 Franklin Ave,
Astoria, OR 97103
Moderate; MC, V;
checks OK

The location of Jim and Renee Caldwell's B&B, three blocks from downtown on a rather ordinary street, could be better, but most everything else is done with style and elegance. The building was constructed in the 1900s by a local shipbuilder for his son; rich woodwork attests to dad's fondness for local forest products. Local art decorates the hallways, sleeping rooms, and parlor. The five guest rooms (one is a two-bedroom suite) all have private baths, large closets, and two have decks with river views. All rooms are exquisitely appointed with Victorian furnishings and trimmed with ruffles and lace. Renee and her mother, Karen Nelson (who operates her own B&B six blocks away), sewed every frilly drapery, cherry-patterned quilt, and pillowcase in the house. The Astor Suite has a claw-footed tub, a wet bar, and a deck.

KC's Mansion-by-the-Sea
Duane St and 37th,
(503) 325-6172
3652 Duane St, Astoria,
OR 97103
Expensive; MC, V;
checks OK

Something of a misnomer—the sea being 8 miles distant—this B&B is nonetheless a spectacular, restored Victorian structure, decked out in a frilly golden color. Spacious landscaped grounds, wide-open views and sounds of the Columbia River (ships' booming foghorns at night sound like they're right outside your bedroom window, and almost are), and unrestrained service add to the total experience. There are four guest rooms, all with private baths. Owner/operator Cher Jenkins will attend to your every need, so kick back and enjoy the luxury. The ample breakfast, prepared and served by Cher and fellow innkeeper Gus Karas, keeps pace with the other amenities.

Crest Motel
2 miles east of downtown,
on Hwy 30,
(503) 325-3141
5366 Leif Erikson Dr,
Astoria, OR 97103
Moderate; AE, DC, MC,
V; no checks

This tidy, well-maintained motel perches on a bluff overlooking the Columbia River. In the large back yard, guests may recline in lawn chairs and enjoy a bird's-eye view of the international shipping traffic, or unwind in a gazebo-enclosed whirlpool. The motel's 40 rooms come equipped with coffeepots, and some enjoy spectacular views. Pets are welcome, and one section is designated nonsmoking.

GEARHART

Gearhart should win the prize for having the most examples of "Oregon Coast" architecture, with large weathered-wood homes in shades of gray and white.

Fashionable Portlanders first put their summer cottages here—some of which are substantial dwellings—when the coast was "discovered." Unlike other coastal towns, Gearhart is mostly residential. Razor-clam digging is popular here, and many gas stations rent shovels. The wide beach is backed by lovely dunes.

Gearhart Golf Course, opened in 1892, is the second-oldest course in the West—a 6,089-yard layout with sandy soil that dries quickly; open to the public, (503) 738-5248.

RESTAURANTS

Pacific Way Bakery and Cafe
Downtown Gearhart, corner of Cottage and Pacific Way,
(503) 738-0245
601 Pacific Way, Gearhart
Moderate; beer and wine; MC, V; checks OK
Breakfast, lunch Wed-Sun (every day in summer)

This four-year-old establishment is airy and impeccably clean, with hardwood floors, lots of windows, white wooden walls, minimalist (but hip) service, cool sounds, and hot espresso. And it continues to thrive on an odd mix of suspender-and-clam-shovel locals and out-of-area "gearheads," the BMW and summer-beachfront-home crowd. They come to hang out, hob-nob, and sample the best cinnamon rolls, French apple turnovers, pecan buns, cheesecake, and breads the North Coast has to offer. Sandwiches are also a good bet, including the Greek sandwich, a lusty affair with gobs of salami, olives, mozzarella, and feta on French bread. A new outdoor dining area with gazebo is a recent addition, and at press time they were considering dinners on Friday and Saturdays in summer.

SEASIDE

One hundred years ago, affluent Portland beachgoers rode Columbia River steamers to Astoria, then hopped a stagecoach to Seaside, the Oregon Coast's first resort town. Seemingly, the place has become more crowded every year since. Destination resort hotels, shops, and tourist amenities of all sorts are springing up at a rapid pace. The crowds mill along Broadway, eyeing the entertainment parlors, the taffy concession, and the bumper cars, then emerge at the Prom, the two-mile-long cement "boardwalk" that's ideal for strolling.

Fishing. Surf fishing is popular here. Your best bet lies at the south end of town in the cove area (also frequented by surfers). Steelhead and salmon only may be taken from the Necanicum River, which flows through town. Seaside has good razor-clam beaches.

Hiking. The trailhead for the 6-mile hike over Tillamook Head is at the end of Sunset Boulevard at the town's south end. The spectacular and rugged trail ends at Indian Beach in Ecola State Park near Cannon Beach.

Recreation. The Sunset Empire Park and Recreation District, headquartered at Sunset Pool (1140 Broadway, (503) 738-3311) promotes various activities from biathlons to lap swims to seasonal outdoor music events open to the public.

Art. The Weary Fox Gallery in Sand Dollar Square on Broadway features Northwest arts and crafts, (503) 738-3363.

RESTAURANTS

Christiano's
North side of Broadway,

The ambience is warm and homey, with Spanish background music and south-of-the-border decor—like a

*across from Dooger's
Restaurant,
(503) 738-5058
412 Broadway,
Seaside
Moderate; full bar; AE,
MC, V; checks OK
Lunch, dinner every day
(winter hours vary)*

small cantina somewhere below Ensenada. Your hosts, the Gutierrez family, want you to be comfortable; stick with the Cal-Mex basics and you will be. The fajitas are particularly tasty. The fish specials deserve a look, especially the halibut or snapper (in reality, Pacific rockfish). Service is usually attentive; chips and salsa arrive at your table pronto. In the summer when the place is packed, though, you might think your meal came all the way from Mexico. There's a larger second Christiano's in Astoria, but Seaside's is substantially better.

Dooger's
*Broadway and Franklin,
(503) 738-3773
505 Broadway,
Seaside
Moderate; beer and wine;
MC, V; local checks only
Lunch, dinner, every day*

If you're determined to satisfy your longing for good clam chowder while in Seaside, this is the place. Most summer evenings you'll have to wait in line, since Dooger's is also Seaside's best bet for decent sandwiches and moderately priced seafood dinners. Stick with the simpler offerings and avoid anything that didn't come from Northwest waters. Order a microbrew to round out your meal. Dooger's is nonsmoking and a good place to take the kids. Also try the second outlet in Cannon Beach (1371 S Hemlock, (503) 436-2225).

LODGINGS

The Boarding House
*N Holladay and 3rd,
(503) 738-9055
208 N Holladay Dr,
Seaside, OR 97138
Moderate; MC, V; checks
OK*

This well-restored, circa-1898 Victorian retains many of the features of a traditional boardinghouse: fir tongue-and-groove walls, beamed ceilings, and paneling. The location fronts Seaside's busy Holladay Drive, but the back yard slopes gently down to the banks of the Necanicum River. In any case, you're just 3 blocks from the beach. All five rooms have private baths, TV, and a beachy feeling. Full breakfast included. There's also a miniature Victorian cottage with one bedroom, living quarters, fully equipped kitchen, and a loft with a bird's-eye view. At $95, it's a good deal for families.

Gaston's Beachside Bed and Breakfast
*Avenue I and the Prom,
(503) 738-8320
921 S Prom, Seaside,
OR 97138
Inexpensive; no credit
cards; checks OK*

This place falls into the "great deal" category. There are only two rooms, but the location on Seaside's Prom affords panoramic ocean views and direct access to one of Seaside's less crowded stretches of beach. Proprietor Helen Gaston, a fountain of local information, sets a mean breakfast table that might include interesting egg dishes or waffles, fresh fruits, and various home-baked goodies. Although guests share a bath, rates are only $40 to $50, and children are welcome. If you've a family or just want more privacy and a private bath, rent both rooms ($65 for two people, $80 for four).

Gilbert Inn Bed and Breakfast
*Beach Dr and Ave A,
(503) 738-9770
341 Beach Dr,*

Seaside's only Queen Anne–style Victorian now sports 10 guest rooms. The original building dates to 1880 and, unfortunately, the five-room addition sticks out like a sore thumb. Nonetheless, the full breakfast is good, and the turn-of-the-century architecture is a joy

Seaside, OR 97138
Moderate; MC, V;
checks OK

to behold. Ask for the light, cheery turret room, located on the second floor; all rooms come with private baths. The Gilbert Inn is on the edge of downtown, and the beach is just a block away.

Shilo Inn
N Prom and Broadway at
Seaside's turnaround,
(503) 738-9571 or toll
free (800) 222-2244
30 N Prom,
Seaside, OR 97138
Expensive; AE, DC, MC,
V; checks OK

We're wary of glitzy establishments that hog the shore, but this one has a good and well-deserved reputation. The setting is superb—on the beach at Broadway in downtown Seaside. The lobby and restaurant are upbeat and stylish, and all the usual amenities expected in a full-service resort hotel are here: indoor swimming pool, steam room, sauna, workout room, and therapy pool. The choicest rooms are facing the ocean, with fireplaces, full kitchens, and private patios. Prices are stratospheric. The Shilo frequently hosts conventions, and it's not the place to get away from the hubbub of urban life. The on-premises restaurant is improving and is your best bet in town for a full-course dinner in a spectacular setting. Ask for a window seat.

Riverside Inn Bed and Breakfast
1½ blocks south of
Broadway at S Holladay,
(503) 738-8254
430 S Holladay Dr,
Seaside, OR 97138
Moderate; MC, V;
checks OK

Lodgelike, the Riverside Inn is comfortable and spacious. The inn and adjacent cottages total 11 guest accommodations. The setting on Seaside's Necanicum River is three blocks or so from the beach, but the backside of the inn feels quietly removed from the main-street comotion. Each unit includes TV and private bath although there have been reports of uncomfortable mattresses. Rates are reasonable (and include full breakfast), ranging from $40 to $70, except for a larger cottage with full amenities (including washer, dryer, and barbecue) that accommodates five and rents by the week.

CANNON BEACH

Cannon Beach is the Carmel of the Northwest, an arts community with a hip ambience and strict building codes that prohibit neon and ensure that only aesthetically pleasing structures of weathered cedar and wood products are built here.

Still, the town is tourist-oriented, and during the summer it explodes with visitors who come to browse through its galleries and crafts shops or rub shoulders with coastal intelligentsia on crowded Hemlock Street. Its main draw is the spectacular beach--wide, inviting, and among the prettiest anywhere.

Haystack Rock, one of the world's largest coastal monoliths, dominates the long, sandy stretch. It's impressive enough just to gaze at, but check it out at low tide and observe the rich marine life in the tidal pools.

Ecola State Park (on the town's north side) has fine overlooks, picnic tables, and good hiking trails. If you hike to Tillamook Head, you can see the Tillamook Rock Light Station, a lighthouse built offshore under severe conditions more than 100 years ago and abandoned in 1957. Today it is a columbarium (a facility where cremated remains are stored) called "Eternity at Sea." No camping along the trail, except for summer campsites atop the Head.

Haystack Program in the Arts, (503) 725-4081, offered through Portland State University, conducts arts workshops (coordinated with family vacation plans).

Coaster Theater hosts good summer plays as well as local and out-of-town shows year-round; 108 N Hemlock, (503) 436-1242.

Galleries abound in the area, all on Hemlock Street, the main drag. Three especially good ones are the White Bird, which has a variety of arts and crafts, (503) 436-2681; the Haystack Gallery (503) 436-2547, with a wide range of prints and photography; and Jeffery Hull Watercolors in Sandpiper Square, a collection of delicately brushed seascapes, (503) 436-2523.

Other shops of interest, also on Hemlock, include Once Upon a Breeze, a kite store at the north end of town, (503) 436-1112; Osburn's Ice Creamery & Deli, with excellent picnic and takeout supplies and ice cream, (503) 436-2234; Cannon Beach Bakery, with one of the few remaining brick oil-fired hearth ovens on the West Coast, supplying a good assortment of breads, cookies and pastries, (503) 436-2592; Cannon Beach Book Company, with a surprisingly extensive selection and an owner who lets customers browse indefinitely, (503) 436-1301; and El Mundo Ltd. Clothing for Women and El Mundo for Men, with natural-fiber clothing in youthful styles, (503) 436-1572 (women's), (503) 436-1002 (men's).

RESTAURANTS

Cafe de la Mer
Hemlock and Dawes,
(503) 436-1179
1287 S Hemlock St,
Cannon Beach
Expensive; beer and wine;
AE, MC, V; local checks
only
Dinner Wed-Sun (days
vary in winter)

★★★

One of the original high-end eateries on the North Coast, the upscale Cafe de la Mer has won a considerable following among Willamette Valley visitors and the moneyed old guard with vacation homes in Tolovana Park and Gearhart. Husband and wife owners Ron Schiffman and Pat Noonan have transformed a post-'60s coffeehouse into a fine dining establishment. An open kitchen divides 15 or so tables into two areas—a newly renovated glassed-in patio and a homey, wood-paneled room. Patrons receive pampered but purposeful service (though lately we've heard reports of it verging on arrogant). The food is glorious. A country mushroom soup smells like an Oregon coast autumn forest and tastes as earthy as fresh-picked chanterelles. Tender slices of veal (a rare find on the coast) are served with a marvelous melted blue cheese. Bouillabaisse contains a lusty mix of Dungeness crab, salmon, and white fish chunks in an exquisite bread-dipping broth. For the above epicurean delights, you pay dearly, even by Cannon Beach standards. The wine list is well rounded but expensive.

The Bistro
Opposite Spruce in
downtown Cannon
Beach, (503) 436-2661
263 N Hemlock St,
Cannon Beach
Moderate; full bar; MC,

Owned and operated by Cannon Beach native Matt Dueber and his wife Anita, the Bistro feels like an inn on the Brittany coast. Of course, the patrons here speak Cannon Beach chic instead of French, and the cuisine is Northwest-oriented. The intimate interior has a dozen or so closely spaced tables with an adjacent cozy bar. Soft chamber music, flower boxes, and an

*V; local checks only
Dinner every day (closed
for a few weeks in
January)*

herb garden out back contribute to the country-inn ambience. In step with the times, the Bistro is a nonsmoking establishment, except for the bar. Dinners are imaginatively prepared and should satisfy an assortment of culinary tastes. On one recent visit, a fresh spring Columbia River salmon steak—the choicest of the choice salmon, becoming ever more rare—was foil-baked with leeks, asparagus, and dill sauce. Luckily, Matt knows where to procure the finest local ingredients, including halibut so fresh it needed only baking in its own juices. Occasional glitches surface in dishes other than seafood but service is pleasant and responsive. Matt frequently makes the rounds himself to ensure that all is well with your meal.

Lazy Susan Cafe
*Hemlock and 1st,
(503) 436-2816
126 N Hemlock,
Cannon Beach
Moderate; beer and wine;
no credit cards; local
checks only
Breakfast Thurs-Mon,
lunch, dinner Thurs-Sat
(winter days vary)*

★

Very Oregon. Definitely Cannon Beach. Everyone in town seems to gather at this airy, sunny, double-decker restaurant in a courtyard opposite the Coaster Theater. The nonsmoking interior is bright with natural wood, plants hanging from the balcony, and local art on the walls. Breakfast is the best time here, when you can order omelets, oatmeal, waffles topped with fresh fruit and yogurt, and excellent coffee to prolong your stay. Eggs—sided with fresh home-fries—are correctly cooked. Lunch includes quiche and some interesting sandwiches, such as the turkey exotica, made with curried mayonnaise and a chutney garnish. Expect long waits on sunny weekends.

Midtown Cafe
*6 blocks south
of downtown,
(503) 436-1016
1235 S Hemlock,
Cannon Beach
Inexpensive; beer and
wine; no credit cards;
local checks only
Breakfast, lunch Wed-
Sun, coffee and dessert
Fri-Sat*

Sit at the cherrywood bar stools (salvaged from Portland's former Meier and Frank) and spy into the kitchen of this small restaurant with a Mediterranean appeal (bright white with Grecian-blue trim). It's a casual place, run in the spirit of Bainbridge Island's Streamliner Diner (where owner Mimi Kaufman used to work) and Seattle's Surrogate Hostess. Breakfasts (fresh bagels, frittatas, eggs and nitrate-free bacon, or tofeta—a scramble of tofu, feta, onions, and spices) have been getting good reports. The homemade marmalades and house-ground flour give breakfast scones a fresh twist. Lunches range from a raging Jamaican seafood stew (shrimp, snapper, and bell peppers with coconut milk, lime juice, curry, and a cilantro sauce) to simple toasted cheese sandwiches. Smoothies are usually made with seasonal fruit, but the chocolate, banana, espresso version is year 'round.

LODGINGS

The Argonauta Inn
*Corner of 2nd and Larch,
(503) 436-2601*

This is not really an inn, but rather an unusual lodging arrangement consisting of five nicely situated cottages, all within a stone's throw of the beach and a couple of

Mail: PO Box 3,
Cannon Beach,
OR 97110
Moderate; MC, V;
checks OK

blocks from the heart of town. They come equipped with fireplaces and color TVs, and all but one have complete kitchens. All feature comfy beds and are nicely appointed with artwork and a smattering of turn-of-the-century furnishings. The two-person Lower Lighthouse is a deal at $59. The Beach House, like a miniature lodge, can accommodate up to 11 guests.

The Waves Motel

Between Hemlock and
Larch off 2nd St,
(503) 436-2205
Mail: PO Box 3,
Cannon Beach,
OR 97110
Moderate; MC, V;
checks OK

Managed by the folks at the Argonauta, The Waves is an intriguing collection of accommodations situated in a spacious but built-up area that fronts the Elk Creek estuary and the beach, yet is only a block or so away from the downtown core. You can choose a two- or three-person ocean-front apartment with fireplace, kitchen, and deck, or select a one- to three-bedroom ocean-view cottage. Most have kitchens and many feature fireplaces. A few units are nonsmoking and some are passively solar-heated ($65-$125). Also within the Waves complex is the White Heron Lodge, consisting of one duplex and a "Victorian-style" fourplex.

TOLOVANA PARK

Nestled on Cannon Beach's south side, Tolovana Park is laid back and less crowded, and possesses a residential character. Leave your vehicle at the **Tolovana Park Wayside** (with parking and restrooms) and stroll an uncluttered beach, especially in the off season. At low tide you can walk all the way to Arch Cape, some 5 miles south. (Be careful, the incoming tide might block your return.) **Hane's Bakerie**, 3116 S Hemlock, sells myriad varieties of muffins, cheesecakes, French bread, and croissants; (503) 436-1719.

LODGINGS

Sea Sprite Motel

Nebesna and Ocean front,
(503) 436-2266
Mail: PO Box 66,
Tolovana Park, OR
97145
Moderate; MC, V;
checks OK

This cute ocean-front motel has six small units on the beach, each with a color TV and kitchen and most with woodstoves. There's a washer and dryer on the premises, and firewood, beach towels, and blankets are provided. Recently, the linen seems a bit worn and some windows don't open to let in the ocean breeze (not acceptable at $125). If the Sea Sprite is full, ask about the Hearthstone Inn, located in Cannon Beach and under the same ownership.

MANZANITA

Resting mostly on a sandy peninsula with undulating dunes covered in beach grass, shore pine, and Scotch broom, Manzanita is a lazy but growing community gaining popularity as a beach getaway for in-the-know Portlanders. Adjacent Nehalem Bay has become a windsurfing hot spot, and **Nehalem Bay State Park**, just south of town, offers hiking and bike trails, as well as miles of little-used beaches. Overlooking it all sits nearby Neahkahnie Mountain with a steep, switchbacked trail leading to the 1,600-foot summit, the best viewpoint on Oregon's North Coast. Hundreds of miles of Coast Range logging roads offer unlimited mountain-biking thrills.

Just north of town, **Oswald West State Park** has one of the finest camping grounds on any coast in the world. You walk a half mile from the parking lot (where wheelbarrows are available to carry your gear) to tent sites among old-growth trees; the ocean, with a massive cove and tidepools, is just beyond. Surfing, kayaking, and sun-bathing are favorite summer activities. No reservations, as the walk deters the crowds that would otherwise come. Call (503) 238-7488 for advance word on availability.

RESTAURANTS

Blue Sky Cafe
Laneda and 2nd,
(503) 368-5712
154 Laneda Ave,
Manzanita
Moderate; beer and wine;
MC, V; local checks only
Dinner every day,
brunch Sun

There's an exciting dining development along Oregon's northern coastline—intimate, cafe-style restaurants serving creatively prepared meals, particularly seafood. For diners accustomed to second-rate surf 'n' turf roadhouses on the coast, this trend promises long-awaited culinary relief. The four-year-old Blue Sky fulfills the promise. This non-glitzy establishment has a decidedly untraditional feel—one wall is plastered with paper-menu artwork done by patrons, and each table features salt-and-pepper shakers with a different plant or animal motif. Overall, the mood is casual and unpretentious (though an additional dining area will add about fifty percent more space). The menu is ambitious and far-flung, particularly for a smallish cafe. It features Northwest shellfish and seafood prepared in styles that range from Southwest (a chicken Santa Fe with sweet red peppers and mushrooms) to Southeast (a superb sweet potato cheesecake for dessert) to Chinese (spicy Sichuan chicken). A flavorful Brie with hazelnuts and chutney is particularly yummy with the house brown bread. A main course of correctly cooked snapper suffers from a way-too-sweet orange, lime, and cilantro glaze. Pesto prawns, large, succulent and lightly dusted with basil and garlic, are superb.

Jarboe's
Laneda and Carmel,
(503) 368-5113
137 Laneda Ave,
Manzanita
Moderate; beer and wine;
MC, V; checks OK
Dinner Thurs-Tues (days
vary in winter)

Housed in a remodeled cottage in Manzanita, Jarboe's ties with the Blue Sky for the best eats in town. A snug, eight-table interior is simply decorated with plants, artwork featuring fish and flora, and inverted-flowerpot lampshades. It's a tad more formal than the Blue Sky, and some like it better. The daily menu is short, offering four or five entrées along with an equal number of appetizers and desserts. The kitchen is in the capable hands of Danish-born owner and chef Klaus Monberg, whose imagination and feel for food are evident from the start of your meal (a superb green salad with radishes, endive, filberts, and sun-dried tomatoes or an enchanting duck bouillon with herbs and vegetables) Although most reports have been favorable, there have been a few disappointments: running out of salmon by 8 pm, an uninspired salmon and oyster tartare, and a miscooked New York steak. But, the accompanying vegetables, such as eggplant and scalloped potatoes, are exemplary. The wine list, although well chosen, is too heavily weighted toward California wines, with not enough Northwest selections.

Cassandra's
Laneda and 4th,
(503) 368-5593
411 Laneda Ave,
Manzanita
Inexpensive; beer and
wine; no credit cards;
local checks only
Lunch, dinner Fri-Tues

Travelers take note: the newly opened, beachy but sophisticated Cassandra's purveys the best pizza on the north Oregon coast. Owner Fawn de Turk (who formerly operated Manzanita's Creative Catering and Deli) serves pizzazzy pies with interesting names and (for some diners) unusual ingredients (at least for this territory), such as artichoke hearts and feta cheese. But she realizes that the heart and soul of any good pizza begins with correctly prepared dough, gobs of cheese, and a zesty sauce. There's something for everyone here, from one-meat or one-veggie pies to the primavera, a savory affair built on a base of olive oil, garlic, and herbs, with mushrooms, green pepper, red onion, and tomatoes, heaped wih provolone, Romano, and mozzarella. Fawn's salads are good too.

LODGINGS

The Inn at Manzanita
1 block from the beach at
67 Laneda,
(503) 368-6754
Mail: PO Box 243,
Manzanita, OR 97130
Expensive; MC, V;
checks OK

One block off the beach, occupying a multilevel setting similar to a Japanese garden, the Inn at Manzanita is a quiet, tranquil retreat. Inside, each of the eight spacious units is finished in pine or cedar, with panels of stained glass here and there. All units enjoy a fireplace, a good-sized spa, a wet bar with refrigerator, a view deck, and a TV with VCR. And the luxury doesn't stop there. Friendly but unobtrusive innkeepers Larry and Linda Martin also have attended to the little things: bathrobes hanging in your room, a pile of wood for your fire, and a daily paper at your door. Continental breakfast served in your room is available for an additional $20. This is a subdued, romantic getaway, not a place for the kids. Smoking and pets are not allowed.

WHEELER

Two miles south of Nehalem at Wheeler, the Nehalem River widens into an estuary. Although you'd never know it today, Wheeler once was touted as a potential San Francisco of the Northwest. Instead, it became a retirement community and a stopover for recreational fishermen and crabbers.

RESTAURANTS

River Sea Inn
Just off Hwy 101 at

There's a surprising variety of dishes offered at this Nehalem Bay–front restaurant just off Highway 101.

Marine Dr,
(503) 368-5789
380 Marine Dr,
Wheeler
Moderate; full bar (beer
and wine only Oct-
March); MC, V; local
checks only
Breakfast, lunch, dinner
every day, brunch Sun
(days vary in winter)

Chicken, veal, prime rib, a Mexican combination plate, and Italian fare are just some of the ambitious menu's many choices. The Sunday brunch is a good deal at $5.25; it includes a glass of champagne, a choice of eggs prepared several ways (with chopped sirloin or oysters, for example), and homemade muffins. There's even a Chateaubriand for two at $34.95, served with a day's advance notice.

ROCKAWAY BEACH

This is a strip-development town with little to offer except touristy schlock. The beach, however, is lovely and usually uncrowded. The **Twin Rocks** area at the south end of town has the nicest stretches of beach.

RESTAURANTS

Karla's Krabs 'n' Quiche
Delight
At the north end of
Rockaway Beach on Hwy
101, (503) 355-2362
2010 Hwy 101 N,
Rockaway Beach
Moderate; no alcohol;
MC, V; local checks only
Lunch, dinner Tues-Sat
(closed Nov through mid-
March)

★

At 50mph Karla's appears as just another shell-shop/greasy-spoon combo on the northern reaches of the Rockaway strip. Not so. Folks in the know, including former Oregon governor Neil Goldschmidt, hit the brakes here. Karla doles out good old-fashioned home cooking in as friendly an atmosphere as you're likely to find. No fast-food mediocrity; just casual quick service. A large five-piece order of halibut (rather than cod, which most places use) fish 'n' chips nesting on a pile of hand-hewn fries with salad and garlic bread is not only a treat, it's a super deal at $8.95. Ample sandwiches, such as smoked salmon with cream cheese on rye, are served with salad and an excellent clam chowder, perhaps the best on the North Coast. Prawns, salmon, and oysters are smoked on the premises. For dessert, try the hot sweet-potato pie—more than enough for two, and only $3. Catering is available, and you can buy smoked fish to go. Karla opened another location in Portland, which her original partner, Amelia, is managing (2138 SE Division, Portland, (503) 232-7546).

GARIBALDI/BAY CITY

The Tillamook bay front is one of the seasonal homes for the summer salmon fleet. If you don't mind wading through an RV park, greasy-spoon restaurants, and tacky surroundings, there are several Garibaldi establishments that sell the area's freshest seafood, including salmon, shrimp, sole, bottom fish, and crab. **Miller Seafood** on Highway 101 is the easiest to find. Fresh salmon, lingcod, and bottom fish are featured; (503) 322-0355. **Smith's Pacific Shrimp Co.** sells fine shrimp and has viewing rooms at 608 Commercial Drive; (503) 322-3316. **Hayes Oysters** is the best place to buy oysters (check whether the rare and wondrous Kumamotos are available); on Highway 101 in Bay City, (503) 377-2210.

RESTAURANTS

Downie's Cafe
5th & C streets,
(503) 377-2220
9230 5th St,
Bay City
Inexpensive; no alcohol;
no credit cards; local
checks only
Breakfast, lunch, dinner
every day

Downie's is right off the set of the '60s television show *Mayberry R.F.D.*, so don't be surprised if Andy Griffith strolls in during your meal and sits in the booth behind you. Clean, tidy, unpretentious, and small (one lit cigarette would fill the room), Downie's offers down-home service and food, specializing in fresh fish from nearby Tillamook Bay and ocean waters. Formica tabletops with plastic booths and a tiny counter offer seating for 25 or so. Clam chowder is a can't-miss: a rich, creamy potion of potatoes, celery, and thick chunks—not bits—of clam. Although the toasted bread and hand-hewn chips are greasy, the fish (lingcod), fried in light batter, is not. Avoid the bland coleslaw.

TILLAMOOK

A broad, flat expanse of bottomland created by the confluence of three rivers (Tillamook, Trask, and Wilson), Tillamook is best known as dairy country. On the north end of town along Highway 101 sits the home of Tillamook cheese, the remodeled and expanded Tillamook County Creamery Association at 4175 Highway 101 N. The parking lot is always full, the tour self-guided, the samples minuscule, and the cheese overpriced for tourists; (503) 842-4481. Instead, opt for the **Blue Heron French Cheese Company**, about 1 mile south on 101. Less kitschy and better stocked than the Tillamook Creamery, Blue Heron offers a variety of cheeses and other made-in-Oregon munchies. There's also a wine-tasting room for Oregon-made wines; 2001 Blue Heron Dr, (503) 842-8281.

The **Pioneer Museum** occupies three floors of the 1905 county courthouse. Shipwreck buffs will be interested in the artifacts (including huge chunks of beeswax with Spanish markings) from the unnamed 18th-century Spanish galleon that wrecked near the base of Neahkahnie Mountain, a few miles north; Second and Pacific, (503) 842-4553.

Clamming is good at Netarts Bay, 7 miles west of Tillamook. Supplies can be had in the tiny town of Netarts.

OCEANSIDE

Oceanside, a tiny seaside resort that defines "quaint," lies 8 miles west of Tillamook. The road to town is part of the 22-mile **Three Capes Scenic Drive**, one of Oregon's most beautiful stretches of coastline. The narrow, winding road skirts the outline of Tillamook Bay, climbs over Cape Meares, then traverses the shores of Netarts Bay. **Cape Lookout State Park**, another jewel in Oregon's park system, offers 250 campsites, along with headland-hugging trails and a huge stretch of virtually unused beach; call (503) 842-3182. Continuing south, the scenic drive scales **Cape Lookout**, the westernmost headland on the North

Oregon coast. The trail from the parking lot at the cape's summit (also part of the state park) meanders through primeval forests of stately cedar and Sitka spruce. Spectacular ocean vistas fill the lower side of the drive. Back at sea level lies a desertlike landscape of thousands of acres of sandy dunes, a favorite area for off-road recreational vehicles (which are required to stay in designated areas). The road to Pacific City and the route's third cape, **Kiwanda**, runs through lush, green dairy country.

RESTAURANTS

Roseanna's Oceanside Cafe
On the west side of Hwy 101, (503) 842-7351
1490 Pacific, Oceanside
Moderate; beer and wine; MC, V; no checks
Breakfast, lunch, dinner every day (closed Mon in winter)

The only restaurant in pint-sized, picturesque Oceanside (well, except for the tavern across the street), Roseanna's feels like a funky fern bar—lots of plants, a piano, an overdone pink-and-mauve motif with a ubiquitous signature parrot, all packed into an old converted grocery store with wooden floors. After a day spent windsurfing in Netarts Bay or hang gliding off Maxwell Mountain, there's nothing better than a bowl of tasty clam chowder, a wedge of crab or shrimp quiche, or a plate of grilled oysters. Desserts score high points, especially an oven-warmed Toll House pie topped with Tillamook ice cream. Service is laid back but efficient; the location scenic, on a small bluff above the ocean, Maxwell Mountain, and Three Arch Rocks.

LODGINGS

House on the Hill
Maxwell Mountain Rd on Maxwell Point, (503) 842-6030
Mail: PO Box 187, Oceanside, OR 97134
Moderate; MC, V; no checks (except for advance reservations)

Three two-story buildings, housing a total of fifteen units and a honeymoon suite, make up this clean, beachy, out-of-the-way motel. The setting, on a bluff halfway up a dead-end road, is unbeatable. And the views are gorgeous, with Three Arch Rocks (a bird, seal, and sea lion sanctuary) and the blue Pacific just below. The trapezoidal architecture is unusual at best. Recent renovations include a brand-new main building with a conference room, and a "rock room," where telescopes look out over the water, perfect for scanning the horizon for whales. Inside, there are too many Motel 6–type furnishings. Outside, wooden walls block too much of the lovely view. Choose a unit with a kitchen and stock up with groceries from Tillamook, since local pickings are pretty slim. Kids are okay here, and pets are allowed in two of the units.

Whiskey Creek
On Three Capes Scenic Drive, between Netarts and Cape Lookout State Park, (503) 842-2408
7500 Whiskey Creek Rd, Tillamook, OR 97141
Moderate; MC, V; checks OK

On the outskirts of the Netarts/Oceanside environs, on a little cove in Netarts Bay in the lee of Cape Lookout, sits Whiskey Creek B&B. Seabirds will likely be your only bay-front visitors as you enjoy the view of one of the nation's most pristine estuaries. There are only two rooms: the larger downstairs room goes for $80 and includes a kitchen and living quarters; the upstairs accommodations ($60) are pretty basic, kind of like summer camp. A full breakfast is served.

PACIFIC CITY

The dory fleet comes home to Pacific City, where salmon-fishing boats are launched from trailers in the south lee of Cape Kiwanda. This town is lately known for another kind of fleet: hang gliders, which swoop off the slopes of the cape and land on the sandy expanses below. The region's second Haystack Rock (Cannon Beach has the other) sits a half mile offshore. Even if you have never visited before, this area may look familiar; nationally acclaimed Oregon photographer Ray Atkeson has made Cape Kiwanda a most-photographed spot on the Oregon coast. **Robert Straub State Park**, worth visiting, sits at the south end of town and occupies most of the Nestucca beach sandspit.

RESTAURANTS

Riverhouse Restaurant
¼ mile north of the stoplight on Brouten Rd,
(503) 965-6722
34450 Brouten Rd,
Pacific City
Moderate; full bar; MC, V; checks OK
Lunch, dinner every day (Wed-Sun in winter)

You might see a great blue heron perched on a log on the Nestucca River, which flows idly to the sea right outside the window. The Riverhouse is a cozy, calming stop, 3 miles off 101 in the little town of Pacific City, and many people go far out of their way to come here. It's small—10 or so tables—with hanging plants and a piano in the corner for the local folk musicians who perform here on weekends. Everything's homemade: soup might be a chunky fresh vegetable or French onion. The deluxe hamburgers are consistently good. This is an apple-pie sort of place, and their's is especially good.

CLOVERDALE

LODGINGS

Hudson House Bed & Breakfast
2½ miles south of Cloverdale, closer to Pacific City,
(503) 392-3533
37700 Hwy 101 S,
Cloverdale, OR 97112
Moderate; MC, V; checks OK

Perched on a bluff in the middle of nowhere, the historic Hudson House, built in 1906 and on the Historic Register, evokes memories of a country weekend at Grandma's house. The entire residence has been dedicated to the guests. Your hosts, the amicable Kulju family, reside next door. There are six sleeping rooms, all nicely decorated in an early-century country style. The four upstairs rooms (with shared baths) overlook forested hillsides surrounding the pastoral Nestucca River valley, home for contented Holsteins, Herefords, and Jerseys. The two larger downstairs rooms have private baths. Anne Kulju whips up full breakfasts of six courses or more from her country kitchen, including unusual treats such as the English sausages known as bangers and light, buttery croissants filled with eggs and topped with white Cheddar cheese.

NESKOWIN

A diminutive, mostly residential community lying in the lee of Cascade Head, a steeply sloped, forested promontory, Neskowin affords the final port of refuge before the touristy "20 miracle miles" (as the stretch from Lincoln City to Newport used to be called). Although the beach here is narrower here than in other locales, it nevertheless provides opportunities for lonely strolls or, in winter months, excellent beachcombing. **Cascade Head** has miles of little-used hiking trails that traverse rain forests and meadows, then skirt rocky cliffs. They begin at a marked trailhead about 2 miles south. The old Neskowin road, a narrow route that winds through horse farms and old-growth forests, is an enchanting side trip.

The **Sitka Center for Art and Ecology** operates on the south side of Cascade Head and offers summer classes on many subjects, plus numerous talks and exhibits; (503) 994-5485.

LODGINGS

The Chelan
Off Salem Blvd at 48750
Breakers Blvd,
(503) 392-3270
Mail: PO Box 732,
Neskowin, OR 97149
Moderate; MC, V; no
checks

★

This attractive, cream-colored adobe structure encompasses nine condominium units, all with lovely ocean views. Most units have two bedrooms, a well-equipped kitchen, and a large living room with a picture window and brick fireplace. Ground-floor units have a double doorway leading to a small back yard; upstairs accommodations have private balconies. The front lawn and gardens are inviting. In fact, the whole place has a cared-for, welcoming look.

Pacific Sands
Breakers Blvd and
Amity, (503) 392-3101
Mail: PO Box 356,
Neskowin, OR 97149
Moderate; MC, V; no
checks

This well-maintained resort motel with an average, bland, exterior enjoys a spectacular setting, literally a stone's throw from breaking waves. The spacious rooms have so-so furnishings; some have fireplaces and full kitchens. Opt for a beachfront unit—an ideal getaway spot with miles of untrampled sand just outside your door and primitive Cascade Head a short distance to the south.

OTIS

RESTAURANTS

Otis Cafe
Otis Junction,
(503) 994-2813
Hwy 18, Otis
Inexpensive; beer and
wine; no credit cards;
checks OK
Breakfast, lunch every
day, dinner Thurs-Sun

The Otis Cafe does all the things small-town cafes all over America used to do—only better. Even the prices are a bit old-fashioned. Proprietors Gale and Jim Powers cook up beefy burgers, soups, and complete breakfasts. Dinner specials are also available. Try the huge malts and milk shakes, wonderful throwbacks to soda-fountain days and a deal for $2.50. As a concession to our times, a small selection of wines is available, including a featured white each week. Baked items are surprisingly good and available to go. The black bread is simply delicious, as are the pies. Service can be slow.

LINCOLN CITY

September-'til-spring used to be the ideal time to visit the coast and escape the summer hordes. Now, some areas of coastline, such as the super-congested stretch between Lincoln City and Newport, have no off season. Every weekend is crowded. Weather is no longer a factor, since visitors come almost hoping for winter storms or to observe the whale migrations (best on an overcast day).

Barnacle Bill's seafood store is famous for fresh and smoked fish: salmon, sturgeon, albacore tuna, and black cod. Open daily; 2174 NE Highway 101, (503) 994-3022. Mossy Creek Pottery in Kernville, just south of Lincoln City, sells some of the area's best locally made high-fired stoneware and porcelain. Open daily; ½ mile up Immonen Road, (503) 996-2415.

Catch the Wind Kite Shop (266 SE Highway 101, (503) 994-9500) is the headquarters for a successful kite manufacturing and sales company, with eight outlets along the coast from Seaside to Florence. The operators often fly some of their more spectacular designs at the D River beach wayside, across the highway from the shop, and at Beverly Beach, north of Newport along Highway 101.

RESTAURANTS

The Bay House
On Hwy 101 within the city limits,
(503) 996-3222
5911 SW Hwy 101,
Lincoln City
Moderate; full bar; MC, V; checks OK
Dinner every day (closed Mon-Tues in winter)

★★★

Shoreside restaurants with spectacular views can often get away with serving overpriced, mediocre food. This is not the case at the Bay House, located on the banks of Siletz Bay, just out of reach of the glitzy Lincoln City tourist trade. Inside, the mood is traditional, with dark gray walls, white tablecloths and napkins, soft track lighting, and black-tied waiters. Most tables possess a splendid view of the bay's driftwood-covered shores. The Bay House's menu matches the mood—understated, with mostly conventional preparations rather than innovative dishes. The creamy onion soup with tiny Pacific shrimp, a house specialty, compliments the garlicky crisp bread (or you can sop it up with sourdough, also offered). Chef William Purdy creates the evening's specials list out of whatever's fresh; recent entrée selections included petrale sole, mild and flaky, with Dungeness crab served in a dill cream sauce. The sole is heavenly, the sauce thin and subtly seasoned. The roast duckling with wild rice and berries and the Oregon lamb are also good bets. For dessert, try the lemon-almond cheesecake, the best we've encountered on the coast. Time your reservations with sunset and experience Siletz Bay's daily light show at dusk—like the food, a treat worth savoring.

Road's End Dory Cove
Next to state park,
(503) 994-5180
5819 Logan Rd,
Lincoln City
Inexpensive; beer and wine; MC, V; checks OK
Lunch, dinner every day

A crowded parking lot and long lines (a covered walkway is proof that appreciative throngs wait rain or shine) attest to this place's popularity. They come for hamburgers (including a half-pound monster), clam chowder, fish 'n' chips, and homemade pies. The food is hearty Americana, Oregon Coast style. Road's End Wayside, a small state park, is right next door and offers good beach access and decent clamming.

GLENEDEN BEACH

RESTAURANTS

Chez Jeannette
*¼ mile south of Salishan
Lodge, (503) 764-3434
7150 Old Hwy 101,
Gleneden Beach
Expensive; beer and wine;
AE, MC, V; checks OK
Dinner every day (closed
Sun-Mon in winter)*

Flower boxes by the windows and whitewashed brick walls in an intimate, woodsy setting just off the beaten path, with trees pressed right up to the building, give this establishment the appearance of a French country inn. The clientele is upscale, but the atmosphere is noticeably less formal than at Salishan, just a half mile away. Two fireplaces, usually blazing away in the winter, add to the ambience. Owner and part-time chef Joan Westerberg makes certain no detail is overlooked, in or out of the kitchen. Skillful preparations of squab, quail, or even venison might be offered as specials on the same night; deep-sea selections such as salmon and halibut are also here. Carnivores should opt for the carpetbagger steak, stuffed with Yaquina Bay oysters, wrapped in bacon, and served with a sauce of crème fraîche, bacon, spinach, and scallions. Every course (even the soups and salads) challenges the imagination without going over the edge. A cream of potato is smooth and sumptuous; vegetable curry is pungent and spicy. Well-chosen salad greens are combined with artichoke hearts, olives, radishes, even pear slices. Vegetables might include enticing combinations such as carrots and mangoes, or cabbage with walnuts and onions. Desserts are equally inspired.

LODGINGS

Salishan Lodge
*Hwy 101 in Gleneden
Beach, (503) 764-3600 or
toll-free (800) 452-2300
Mail: PO Box 118,
Gleneden Beach,
OR 97388
Expensive; AE, DC, MC,
V; checks OK
Breakfast, lunch, dinner
every day*

Drive into the Salishan resort complex and your first impression might be one of exclusivity. The place *is* special. You'll be pampered throughout the visit with service that may be unmatched on the Oregon coast. Sprawled out over thousands of acres, the resort includes 205 guest rooms, arranged in eightplex units nicely dispersed over the lush, green landscape. There's an 18-hole (par 72) golf course, plus driving range, pro shop, and resident PGA pro. A tennis facility features outdoor and indoor courts, complete with pro shop and teaching professional. You can swim in an indoor pool, work out in the sizable fitness center, sweat in a sauna, or jog on the trails through the 750-acre forest. Kids even have their own gameroom and play area. The resort's focal point is a huge lodge with restaurants, a nightclub, a library, meeting rooms, and a gift shop. The guest units are spacious and tastefully furnished but not extravagant, with brick fireplaces, view balconies, splashes of regional art, and individual covered carports. Distances within the resort are considerable, so specify your locale depending on what you want to be near (for example: Spruce, Fairway,

Chieftain House South, and Sunset Suite overlook the links; Tennis House is near the courts; and the Blue Heron and Tide units have the best views of Siletz Bay and the ocean). The beach is a good half mile away.

While you're purposely pampered elsewhere in the resort, you may be disappointed by what the main dining room has to offer. While the food is good (Salishan regularly touts its "award-winning" kitchen), it doesn't match the resort's overall excellence, and the dining room staff seems to compensate with sometimes-overindulgent service. Diners who aren't staying at the resort are likely to describe the place as pretentious and expensive. Entrées can be exciting and unusual, but they can also be downright uninspired (the paella was dry and tasteless). The voluminous wine list is superlative, representing a cellar stocked with almost 20,000 bottles and some real bargains. Be sure to ask wine steward Phil deVito for his advice.

DEPOE BAY

Once a charming coastal community, Depoe Bay today is mostly an extension of Lincoln City's strip development. Driving down Highway 101, it's hard to tell where one community ends and the other begins. Fortunately, some of the original Depoe Bay, including its tiny harbor, remains intact. During the gray whale migratory season (January through April), the leviathans cruise within hailing distance of headlands, at times purposefully scraping off troublesome barnacles against offshore rocks. Deep Sea Trollers is one of several operations offering whale-watching cruises; the one-hour trip costs $7 per person (with a minimum of five), or you can charter a boat for up to 20 passengers for $100; (503) 765-2248.

LODGINGS

Inn at Otter Crest
*Otter Crest Loop, 2 miles south of Depoe Bay, (503) 765-2111, toll-free (800) 452-2101 in Oregon, (800) 547-2181 outside Oregon
Mail: PO Box 50, Otter Rock, OR 97369
Expensive; AE, DC, MC, V; no checks*

The 100-acre parklike setting of this attractive and secluded destination resort on Cape Foulweather is exquisitely and lushly landscaped with rhododendrons, evergreens, and coastal shrubs—a seeming oasis of serenity with an isolated beach and a breathtaking view. Regrettably, all is not as it seems. For starters, Cape Foulweather is aptly named, as fog often enshrouds the cape, even though sunny skies may beam just north and south. As for the resort, there's a history of less-than-top-notch service—an occasional misplaced reservation, an unfriendly clerk—that detracts from the positive attributes. The Inn is so large (over 280 rooms and suites) that the personal touch can sometimes be lacking. The many conventions held here can be intrusive. The tennis facilities—two indoor and two outdoor courts—are inadequate for the resort's size. The nearest golf course is about five miles south, and the inn's restaurant is ordinary. Still, most of the rooms enjoy marvelous ocean views from private decks (request one of these) and are part of four- and eightplex units that blend in well with their surroundings. You leave your car a short distance away and hop a shuttle van to your room. Many have fireplaces and fully equipped kitchens. All in all, a nice but expensive ($77 to $145) alternative to beachfront motel life.

Channel House
35 Ellingson St at the end of the street,
(503) 765-2140 or toll-free (800) 447-2140
Mail: PO Box 56, Depoe Bay, OR 97341
Expensive; MC, V; checks OK

This is a large B&B, more like an inn really, with a spectacular setting: perched on a cliff's edge overlooking the ocean and the Depoe Bay channel. The place has grown to nine rooms, with rates ranging from $52 for the smallish "Crow's Nest" to $150 for an ocean-front suite with gas fireplace, kitchenette, and a deck with hot tub. Full breakfasts are served to all visitors. Be sure to bring your binoculars, especially during whale-watching season.

NEWPORT

The most popular tourist destination on the Oregon Coast, Newport demonstrates the pitfalls of development. The place has grown—in some instances, not attractively—as the older downtown core gives way to shopping-center sprawl on the north end of town. Veer off Highway 101's commercial chaos and seek out the real Newport.

The **bay front** is a working waterfront going full tilt, where fishing boats of all types—trollers, trawlers, shrimpers, and crabbers—berth year-round. Nearby, take a drive out on the **South Jetty Road** for sea-level views of harbor traffic. The friendly **Nye Beach** area houses a potpourri of neo-professionals, tourists, writers, artists, and fishermen.

Art galleries. Oceanic Arts Center, 444 SW Bay Blvd, (503) 265-5963, and the Wood Gallery, 818 SW Bay Blvd, (503) 265-6843, both on the bay front, offer fine selections—the former primarily jewelry, paintings, pottery, and sculpture, the latter functional sculpture, woodwork, pottery, and weaving.

Fishing charters. Most provide bait and tackle, clean and fillet your catch, and even smoke or can it for you. Many charter operators have initiated whale-watching excursions, as well as half- and full-day fishing trips. Sea Gull Charters, 343 SW Bay Blvd, (503) 265-7441, and Newport Sport Fishing, 1000 SE Bay Blvd, (503) 265-7558, are two popular operators.

Oregon State University's **Hatfield Marine Science Center** offers displays, a facsimile tidepool, educational programs, and a full range of free nature walks, field trips, and films, especially during the summer Seatauqua program. 2030 S Marine Science Drive in South Beach; (503) 867-0100.

Newport Performing Arts Center is an attractive new structure that hosts shows and events, some of national caliber; 777 W Olive, (503) 265-ARTS.

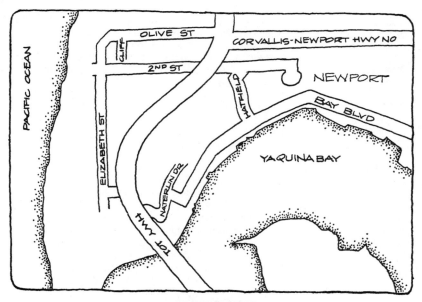

RESTAURANTS

Canyon Way Restaurant and Bookstore

*At the bottom of Herbert
off Hwy 101,
(503) 265-8319
1216 SW Canyon Way,
Newport
Moderate; full bar; AE,
MC, V; local checks only
Lunch Mon-Sat, dinner
every day (dinner Tues-
Sat in winter)*

The entrance is a bit odd, since it's now a restaurant, bookstore, gift shop, and deli. While you're waiting for a table, you can browse the books or sip an espresso. Or buy a book and read during lunch in the newly expanded deli. There are sandwiches, pastries, and other munchies to go, so you can stroll down the hill to the bay front well fortified. The restaurant features knowledgeable, efficient, and friendly service. Pasta and seafood fill the lunch menu, as well as unusual sandwiches—Cajun turkey, barbecued beef with angel hair onion rings, a grilled filet of lingcod—bouillabaisse, ginger-garlic chicken, a variety of salads, and tasty omelets served with pan-fried red potatoes. Desserts are made daily. There have been reports of inconsistency lately, but keep with the simple seafood preparations and you'll be well fed. On sunny days, request an outdoor table overlooking the bay.

The Whale's Tale

*SW Bay and Fall,
(503) 265-8660
452 SW Bay Blvd,
Newport
Moderate; beer and wine;
AE, DC, MC, V;
checks OK*

In tourist-infested Newport, where mediocre restaurants come and go, Whale's Tale owner Dick Schwartz has been purveying the best food in town inside the bay front's hippest setting for over 15 years. And he loves (almost) every minute of it. Witness his table-tapping jigs to live music on boisterous summer weekends, or his manner in which he mingles with locals and tourists alike. Breakfasts are outstanding, with fresh jalapeño omelets, memorable poppyseed pancakes, and home-fried potatoes with onions and green chili smothered in

Breakfast, lunch, dinner every day (may vary in winter)

cheese. There's fresh, strong coffee and espressos. Lunches are full of good-sized sandwiches (even a garden burger for veggie fans) and sumptuous, well-seasoned soups. Dinners are equally inspired, mostly seafood affairs such as grilled Yaquina oysters and mussels marinara. There's also lasagne and a German sausage, potato salad, and sauerkraut plate served with black bread. Save room for the signature mousse-in-a-bag dessert.

LODGINGS

Sylvia Beach Hotel

West on NW 3rd off Hwy 101, 6 blocks to NW Cliff, (503) 265-5428
267 NW Cliff, Newport, OR 97365
Moderate; AE, MC, V; no checks

Owners Goody Cable (of Portland's Rimsky-Korsakoffee House) and Sally Ford have dedicated their blufftop hotel to bookworms and their literary heroes and heroines. They gave several like-minded friends the task of decorating each of the 20 rooms, and the results are rich in whimsy and fresh, distinct personality. Most luxurious are the three "classics" (Mark Twain, Agatha Christie, and Colette). The Agatha Christie suite, for instance, is decorated in lush green English chintz, with a tiled fireplace, a large deck facing out over the seacliff below, and—best of all—clues from the writer's many murders: men's shoes peeking out from beneath a curtain, notes on the walnut secretary, bottles labeled "poison" in the medicine cabinet. The "best sellers" (views) and the "novels" (non-views) are quite small, not as impressive (some even look a bit tattered) but they are equally imaginative. A mechanized pendulum swings over the Edgar Allan Poe bed (consider the possibilities), the Cat in the Hat smirks on the wall of the Dr. Seuss room. There aren't any reading chairs in the best sellers or novel rooms but upstairs books and comfortable chairs abound in the library. Hot wine is served nightly at 10pm. Breakfast (open to non-guests by reservation) is included in the price of a room. Prepare for a stay sans phones, TVs, and stress.

Dinners in the hotel's Tables of Content restaurant, located downstairs and just above the beach, are prix-fixe affairs, open to the public on a reservation-only basis. The main attraction here is the company; the food gets secondary billing. Meals, eight or so "chapters" long, cost about $17. Courses are brought to your table family style, making dinner more like a picnic than a gourmet meal; still, portions at dinner and breakfast are plentiful. But the stories told here are what you'll remember.

Ocean House

Just off Hwy 101 N in Agate Beach,
(503) 265-6158
4920 NW Woody Way,

Hosts Bob and Bette Garrard have created a homey, congenial ambience at Ocean House, the first B&B in these parts. The setting overlooking the surf at Agate Beach is striking. A short trail leads from a well-kept garden to one of Newport's less crowded beaches in

Newport, OR 97365
Moderate; MC, V;
checks OK

the lee of Yaquina Head, with Yaquina Lighthouse towering nearby. The four rooms are neither elegant nor luxurious, but are comfortable and well appointed, and Michelle's Room has a private deck. There's a small library with cushy chairs, a good place to curl up with a good book. Outside, you can relax and sunbathe protected from the summer northwest wind (but not from the neighbors) in the sheltered back yard. The Garrards are gracious and helpful but never obtrusive. Luscious full breakfasts complement their hospitality.

The Vikings

Between 6th and 8th on
NW Coast,
(503) 265-2477
729 NW Coast St,
Newport, OR 97365
Moderate; DC, MC, V;
checks OK

No missing this place: there's a reproduction Viking longboat complete with dragon figurehead perched on the lawn in front of the office. But the natives are very friendly, and the Nye Beach cliffside setting is superb. The best bet here is a 13-unit collection of beach cabins built in 1925. They fit right in to the eclectic blend of Nye Beach architecture—rustic cottages among massive, modern motels. All units have color TVs, some have fireplaces, and 11 have full kitchens. A steep but sturdy staircase leads from cabin level to the beach below. A cozy second-story "crow's nest" in one of the cottages enjoys an unbeatable Pacific panorama; this wood-paneled one-room unit with a double bed and teeny kitchen comes complete with a table preset with napkins, silverware, and wine glasses. Very romantic, and a bargain at $60. The adjoining Pacific Crest Condos, although enjoying an equally stunning view, are not nearly as much fun.

Embarcadero

West off Hwy 101 on Bay
Blvd, (503) 265-8521
1000 SE Bay Blvd,
Newport, OR 97365
Expensive; AE, DC, MC,
V; checks OK

This huge complex, situated right on the bay, is quite attractive. The facility offers all the amenities one might expect of a destination resort, including indoor heated pool, sauna, whirlpool, children's play area, outdoor crab cooker, and even a private crabbing and fishing dock (a nearby marina is available for moorage). But the best feature of all is the sweeping view of the harbor, the Newport Bay bridge, and the blue Pacific beyond. Each roomy unit has tasteful furnishings, a deck, and a view. Kitchen units have fireplaces as well. The grounds are well landscaped, the architecture well conceived. The restaurant has a pleasant bar view and offers a Sunday champagne brunch.

SEAL ROCK

RESTAURANTS

Yu Zen

7 Miles South of Newport,
(503) 563-4766

One of Oregon's best Japanese restaurants is in this coastal town of 200 that is nothing more than the proverbial "wide spot in the road," in a Bavarian-styled

Hwy 101, Seal Rock,
OR 98376

building (a holdover from its former life) with a female choir singing "What a friend we have in Jesus" in Japanese. The sushi bar is extraordinary. The sukiyaki, as good as we have encountered in the Northwest, was served with the traditional raw egg on the side for dipping sauce. Miso soup and salad accompany most entrees. The Don Zen dishes are excellent choices as are the Bento dinner specials.

WALDPORT

This small, unpretentious, quiet town at the Alsea River's mouth was named in the 1870s by German settlers who floated downriver to what was formerly an Alsi Indian burial ground. At one time, the area had several sawmills and salmon canneries. There's still good clamming and crabbing in the bay, and equipment can be rented at the dock in the Old Town section, on the water just east of Highway 101.

Fudge. On Highway 101 in Seal Rock is a tiny storefront selling varieties of scrumptious light and dark fudge. Good ice cream is also available; (503) 563-2766.

LODGINGS

Cliff House
Bed and Breakfast
1 block west of Hwy 101
on Adahi Rd,
(503) 563-2506
Mail: PO Box 436,
Waldport, OR 97394
Expensive; MC, V; no
checks

★★★

Precious few places can capture your attention and keep it long after you've departed. This place is one of them. The Cliff House is a whimsical retreat, thanks to the efforts of owners Gabriella Duvall and D.J. Novgrad. The house is exactly where it claims to be—perched on a cliff on what must surely be one of the Oregon Coast's most prized parcels. The ocean vistas are endless. Alsea River–mouth seals, salmon-hungry sea lions, and migrating whales occupy the watery panorama below. Every room in the house enjoys an ocean or bay view. Each of the five bedrooms has a balcony, a full bath, and a chandelier. The loft, appropriately named the Redwood Room, is akin to sleeping in a comfy, padded cedar chest. The bridal suite is luxurious—with a skylight, a Jacuzzi, and a fully mirrored bathroom. There's a deck with hot tub out back, and a spa is planned with sauna, steam room, and shower. Breakfasts are first-rate: a smorgasbord of fresh fruits, homemade yogurt, granola, just-squeezed juices, and perhaps a huge fluffy soufflé. Gabriella and D.J. will give you as little or as much attention as you want. . . and they always seem to know how much.

Cape Cod Cottages
2½ miles south of
Waldport,

These cozy spic-and-span duplexes a couple of miles south of Waldport are usually packed. There are four two-bedroom duplexes and five one-bedroom units,

(503) 563-2106
4150 SW Pacific Coast,
Waldport, OR 97394
Moderate; AE, MC, V;
checks OK

each with kitchen, some with garage. Decks on the ocean side have fireplaces in which to burn the real logs provided by the owners.

Edgewater Cottages
2½ miles south of
Waldport on Hwy 101,
(503) 563-2240
3978 SW Pacific Coast
Hwy, Waldport,
OR 97394
Inexpensive; no credit
cards; checks OK

Each unit has good beach access and views, deck, windbreaks from the summer winds, TV, fireplace, and kitchen. They range from a duplex and a fourplex to separate cottages that sleep two to eight, and the crow's nest. Usually booked from the beginning of the tourist season; lots of honeymooners.

YACHATS

Yachats (pronounced Ya-Hots) is a tiny settlement straddling the mellow Yachats River on the bare basaltic marine terrace tucked between mountains and sea. In fact, the name Yachats means "at the foot of the mountain." Nearby, the most untrammeled and dramatic rocky beaches in Oregon yield rich tidepools, wildife breeding grounds, whooshing geysers, and near-shore whale watching. It's little wonder that Yachats has dubbed itself "The Gem of the Oregon Coast."

Cape Perpetua. The newly remodeled visitors' center offers films and dioramas to orient you to the surrounding natural formations. Under Highway 101 at Cook's Chasm, the ocean churns in a deep cleft. From the visitors' center you can drive or hike to the highest point on the Oregon Coast. The 19-mile auto tour begins 3 miles south of Yachats on Highway 101; (503) 547-3289.

RESTAURANTS

La Serre
Downtown Yachats,
(503) 547-3420
2nd and Beach,
Yachats
Moderate; full bar; AE,
MC, V; checks OK
Dinner every day, brunch
Sun; closed January
(dinner Wed-Mon,
brunch Sun in winter)

The skylight-domed, arched ceiling, whitewashed walls, and lace-curtained windows create an airy, open frame in this country French eatery. Antiques and healthy plants add warmth. It's consistently good; add a bit of panache and it could be great. Shrimp omelets, poppyseed pancakes, and good espresso are morning favorites. For lunch, stick with the entrée salads and seafood specials. There's even a Distraction Plate of fruit chunks for children. Candlelight softens the room at night. Try the clam puff appetizers, steamed Umpqua Pacific oysters, most any fresh fish special, and the zesty cioppino. The spinach salad is a meal in itself. And top it off with summer's freshest fruit pie or a cordial in the cozy fireplace bar where there's live folk music on weekends.

New Morning Coffeehouse
Across from the bank,

Blythe Collins and Don Niskanen adopted this previously vacant building in May 1988. They let in the sun

Hwy 101 and 4th St,
(503) 547-3848
373 Hwy 101 N,
Yachats
Inexpensive; no alcohol;
no credit cards;
checks OK
Breakfast, lunch Wed-
Sun

through sparkling panes of beveled glass, softened the space with plants and handmade quilts, and allowed the cathedral ceiling to show off its handsome blond beams. But it's not only the company or the solitude that draws locals and travelers here. Boy, can Blythe bake! Our carrot cake was unforgettable, the marionberry pie superb. The light menu features very good soups (lots of vegetarian choices), salads, and sandwiches on homemade bread. They're in the process of adding a deck out back for outdoor dining.

LODGINGS

The Adobe Resort

In downtown Yachats at
1555 Hwy 101,
(503) 547-3141
Mail: PO Box 219,
Yachats, OR 97498
Moderate; AE, DC, MC,
V; local checks only
Breakfast, lunch Mon-
Sat, dinner every day,
brunch Sun

This resort—both the original section and the newer complex—was built with respect for the landscape. The Adobe fans out around the edge of a basalt-bumpy shore. Waves crash onto the rocks; their thunder echoes into the rooms. The original rooms were made out of the resort's namesake: local adobe bricks. Those rooms—knotty pine, beamed ceilings, fireplaces, and ocean views—are still popular. The two newer wings have refrigerators and coffee makers; some have fireplaces. There's a six-person Jacuzzi and a sauna for all. Children are welcome, and with advance notice so is your dog. The restaurant emphasizes fresh fish and produce, with a slight French influence. Breakfasts facing the ocean are decadent; dinners at sunset are delightful. Service is slow, but with so much window gazing you barely notice. The bar has a full ocean view, but the loft is the perfect perch for a drink or a snack.

Ziggurat

6½ miles south of Yachats
on Hwy 101,
(503) 547-3925
95330 Hwy 101, Yachats,
OR 97498
Moderate; no credit cards;
checks OK

This stunning glass-and-wood four-story pyramid was named after an ancient Sumerian pyramid found near Babylon. Its radical triangular design works well—as a beach house and as a well-placed sculpture. Owners Mary Lou Cavendish and Irv Tebold will gladly discuss its architectural fine points, such as the spectacular views from all 40 windows. Guests share the 2,000-square-foot first-floor living and reading rooms complete with refrigerator, books, and games; two guest rooms share a bath and can be used as a suite. One more guest bedroom upstairs has a private bath-cum-sauna. A tiled, glassed-in atrium wraps around the second floor, providing a wind-free spot for everyone to read or weather-watch and a baby grand piano (guest concerts encouraged). The hosts will serve you a full breakfast wherever you please. No inside smoking.

Gull Haven Lodge

7 miles south of Yachats
on Hwy 101,
(503) 547-3583
94770 Hwy 101,

Mary Fike picks up her mail in Florence, but her popular haven for beachcombers is technically in Yachats. The main lodge sits on a bluff overlooking the ocean—and so do most of the rooms (with private baths and kitchen privileges). The rooms are reasonably

Florence, OR 97439
Inexpensive; MC, V;
checks OK

priced, though for $40 you might consider the Shag's Nest, a separate cabin with 180-degree ocean views, a fireplace, and a kitchen. The only problem: it has no bath (and it's a 30-yard dash to the lodge). But reserve it early anyway, as it's usually booked well in advance. There's a separate unit with a commercial kitchen—ideal for meetings.

Shamrock Lodgettes
On Hwy 101 S, just south
of Yachats,
(503) 547-3312 or toll-
free (800) 845-5028
Mail: PO Box 346,
Yachats, OR 97498
Moderate; AE, DC, MC,
V; local checks only

Rustic cabins and newer motel units are nicely spaced on immaculate grounds adjacent to the mouth of the Yachats River. Kids race on the grass and dig in the sand on the protected beach. Bring friends and stay in one of the well-maintained but older log cabins with cedar paneling, fireplaces, and two-burner kitchenettes. Less private but nicely appointed are the newer motel rooms with fireplaces and ocean or bay views. The deluxe units have kitchenettes and Jacuzzi bathtubs. Owners Bob and Mary Oxley added a separate spa building with sauna, Jacuzzi, and exercise room (no equipment, though). As Bob makes his morning rounds he deposits a copy of *The Oregonian* at your front door. The reservation policy can be quite severe; be aware that if you don't arrive on time, you may lose your room (and get charged for it too).

FLORENCE

Florence is surrounded by the beauty of the Oregon Dunes National Recreation Area, the Siuslaw River, several large freshwater lakes, and in May, bright pink native rhododendron flowers. Old Town is the heart of Florence: a continually upgraded few blocks of shops, restaurants, and some of the town's oldest structures on Bay Street east of Highway 101 along the banks of the Siuslaw. Though it does draw tourists, the traffic won't crush you. You can rent crab rings and catch your dinner right off the city dock in Old Town. The **Old Town Coffee Company** is the daytime hangout. **Catch the Wind Kite Shop** displays airborne creations. And Ken Kesey modeled his mythical bar, "The Snag" in *Sometimes a Great Notion*, after the Fisherman's Wharf.

    The Oregon Dunes National Recreation Area. Orient yourself to this intriguing ecosystem at the Oregon Dunes Overlook, 12 miles south of town. Hike or ride a dune buggy into a land of 600-foot-high dunes, dark lakes, and tree islands. Dune buggies are available at **Sand Dunes Frontier,** 83960 Highway 101 S, (503) 997-3544, or at **Sandland Adventures Inc.,** Highway 101 at 10th Street, (503) 997-8087.

    Heceta Head Lighthouse and the light-keeper's home, 12 miles north, offer *the* postcard shot on the coast. The supposedly haunted but truly lovely light-keeper's home can be reserved for college classes or unusual weddings; (503) 747-4501, extension 2558.

    Sea Lion Caves, (503) 547-3111, 10 miles north, is the only known mainland breeding colony of the Steller's sea lion.

    Darlingtonia Botanical Wayside is a bog 5 miles north of town with insect-eating plants called cobra lilies. Look for their unusual burgundy flowers in May.

The **Toy Factory**, 5 miles north, has fine toys which are made locally and sold internationally.

Indian Forest, (503) 997-3677, 4 miles north, has buffalo and deer grazing near authentic models of Native American structures. Open from early May to mid-October.

RESTAURANTS

Windward Inn

*1½ miles north of
Florence on Hwy 101,*
(503) 997-8243
3757 Hwy 101 N,
Florence
Moderate; full bar; AE,
DC, MC, V; local
checks only
Breakfast, lunch, dinner
every day

The pride of Florence, this large, handsome, though somewhat pretentious restaurant is the town's best, containing a coffee shop (where there are sweatshirts and other knick knacks for sale), a comfortable room with a few books, a formal hall with a grand piano and, most recently, a spacious courtyard lounge decorated with Palladian windows and barrel-vault ceilings, where live entertainment happens on Friday and Saturday nights. Owner David Haskell has added a dozen or so seafood items, but dinner favorites remain the veal in Madeira cream and the superb boudin blanc made with chicken. The inn is exceptionally proud of its breads and pastries, baked on the premises, and its sumptuous dark chocolate truffles.

Old English Tea Company

*In Old Town across from
Johnson House Bed &
Breakfast,*
(503) 997-8890
239 Maple St,
Florence
*Inexpensive; beer and
wine; MC, V; no checks*
*Breakfast, lunch, and tea
every day, dinner Mon-
Sat*

In this transplanted English cottage, everything that can be is made from scratch . The locals have made this one of Florence's most popular places to have lunch. The fare is hardy English, but the vegetables are not overcooked and the steak and kidney pie (when offered on special) is on the mild side. The shepherd's pie is the best you'll find in a restaurant, and the chicken and mushroom pie and the sweet potato soup are almost as good. There's a superb afternoon tea with good cream cheese and cucumber sandwiches. The house tea is industrial-strength PG Tips; however, the most popular is English breakfast. Scones and other goodies (try the peach cobbler) are all made on the premises. A back garden with two decks, open in warm weather, is the only area where smoking is permitted.

LODGINGS

Johnson House
Bed & Breakfast

*1 block north of the river
at 216 Maple St,*
(503) 997-8000
Mail: PO Box 1892,
Florence, OR 97439
Moderate; MC, V;
checks OK

Jayne and Ron Fraese bring wit, curiosity, and high aesthetic standards to this perennially popular Victorian B&B in Old Town. Reflecting the Fraeses' interests (he's a political science prof, she's an English teacher), the library is strong on local history, natural history, politics, and collections of essays, letters, cartoons, and poetry. Each of the six bedrooms (three with private baths) is pillowed in down. Jayne uses asparagus, blueberries, rhubarb, cherries, and herbs from the garden in her full breakfasts. The lovely ground floor room near the kitchen is not recommended if you plan to sleep past 7am. The Fraeses will loan you crabbing gear for the day or sell their own conserves for guests to take home. The well-kept secrets, however, are the two independent cottages run by the Fraeses: Moonset, a two-person octagonal cabin facing Lily Lake (9 miles up the road) and the Coast House, 10 miles north at the water's edge. The latter is a remodeled artist's shack (five levels high) clinging to a cliff, with two skylit sleeping lofts, an ocean-viewing claw-footed tub, an exceptional library and tape collection, and a living room with wood stove. Moonset has a two-day minimum; Coast House requires three. We worry, however, about the recent grumblings of overbooking and then moving people to lesser quarters. Breakfasts are outstanding.

Driftwood Shores Surfside Resort Inn
3 miles north of Florence,
(503) 997-8263,
(800) 422-5091 or
(800) 824-8774
outside Oregon
88416 1st Ave,
Florence, OR 97439
Moderate; AE, DC, MC,
V; local checks only
Breakfast, lunch, dinner
every day

This is one of the few places on the south central coast where you can stay right on the beach—actually, 10 miles of uninterrupted beach. The four-story resort contains 121 plain but tasteful rooms. All have views and balconies; most have kitchens. Groups can get large units with fireplaces, kitchens, and up to three bedrooms for about $135 for two people, $10 per additional person. Amenities include an indoor pool, sauna, and Jacuzzi.

The Surfside Restaurant and Lounge serves acceptable food in extraordinary surroundings. Some dinner favorites: scampi flambé, rack of lamb, Chateaubriand, and the Captain's Plate. Breakfasts are standard, but portions are quite substantial.

REEDSPORT

This port town on the Umpqua River has gained a new attraction: the **Dean Creek Elk Reserve**, about 4 miles east of town on Route 38, where you can observe a wild herd grazing on protected land.

The staff at the **Oregon Dunes National Recreation Area** at the intersection of Highway 101 and Route 38 offer educational programs on this country's highest coastal dunes (summers only); call (503) 271-3611.

NORTH BEND

RESTAURANTS

The Brass Rail
Right on Hwy 101 S,
(503) 756-2121
2072 Sherman Ave,

Forget the highway and breeze into the quiet garden courtyard of North Bend's best eatery. Deli sandwiches, seafood, fresh soups, special salads (try the orange-almond), and daily specials such as stuffed cab-

North Bend
Inexpensive; beer and
wine; AE, MC, V;
checks OK
Lunch every day,
breakfast Sat-Sun

bage rolls and enchiladas keep the regulars coming. Not to mention the desserts, about 50 of them— notably the lemon meringue, coconut-apricot, and French silk pies.

LODGINGS

Highlands Bed & Breakfast
5 miles east of Hwy 101
on Ridge Rd (call for
directions),
(503) 756-0300
608 Ridge Rd, North
Bend, OR 97459
Moderate; MC, V;
checks OK

It's the view of the Coast Range (and Coos Bay), the deer (and an occasional elk), and the steelhead (but not the skunks) that lure people to these six acres of highlands. Not to mention the comfortable 2,000-square-foot lower level of Marilyn and Jim Dow's contemporary cedar home. There's a huge living room with a soapstone stove and wraparound windows, and a private solarium deck with a spa. Both bedrooms have private baths and use of the kitchen. Breakfast is best on the wraparound deck, with Marilyn's marvelous baked French toast with fresh fruit. If you want to try your hand at crabbing, the Dows will loan you their crab ring and cook whatever good creatures you net. No children under ten, please, unless both rooms are taken together as a suite.

Sherman House
Hwy 101 S, 3 blocks above
the old town center,
(503) 756-3496
2380 Sherman Ave,
North Bend, OR 97459
Moderate; AE; checks OK

The house is Pennsylvania Dutch and the hostess is from Arkansas, but you're very much in Oregon, 3 blocks above North Bend's old town district. There are three bedrooms (two with city or harbor views), all decorated with Jennifer and Phillip Williams' antiques. Guests have free run of the top two floors of this three-story home; upstairs there's a sitting room; downstairs there's a full kitchen, dining room with fireplace, and living room. Business meetings, however, can be held in complete privacy. Jennifer Williams dishes up biscuits and gravy (true to her Southern roots), omelets, or lighter fare for breakfast, depending on your appetite. Smoking allowed in certain areas.

CHARLESTON

Charleston's docks moor the bay's commercial fishing fleet. Fresh fish is inexpensive, the pace is slow, and there's lots to do.

Oregon Institute of Marine Biology is the University of Oregon's respected research station, (503) 888-2581. You can also visit the **South Slough National Estuarine Reserve**, (503) 888-5558, the first of 21 such reserves in the U.S., and **Qualman Oyster Farms**, 4898 Crown Point Road, (503) 888-3145.

To the west, a trio of state parks. **Sunset Bay** features a large cove with fossil-filled sandstone walls, a sandy beach, and ample camping space. **Shore Acres**

Botanical Gardens' spectacular geology, crazy surf, and quiet pocket beach convinced timber baron Louis J. Simpson to build his estate here. The mansions are gone, but the views and the gardens (Japanese, formal, and rose) remain. Farther south, listen for and observe Steller's and California sea lions and harbor seals on tiny islands offshore from **Cape Arago State Park.**

RESTAURANTS

Portside
*Follow Cape Arago
Highway, right at
drawbridge, right again at
Captain John's,*
(503) 888-5544
*8001 Kingfisher Rd,
Charleston*
*Moderate; full bar; AE,
DC, MC, V; local checks
only*
Lunch, dinner every day

From your table, watch tidal fluctuations and the boat traffic in the mouth of the Charleston Boat Basin. Fish, direct from the boat and simply prepared, is the specialty. Try the Dungeness crab steamed with melted butter; the calamari sautéed in garlic, wine, and butter; the grilled Empire clams; or the refreshing combination of shrimp, crab, and smoked salmon in cucumber dressing, served in a hollowed-out cucumber. Owner Joe Tang expresses his Chinese heritage in the sumptuous Friday seafood buffet. For $13.95 you can sample hot-and-spicy octopus, shrimp egg rolls, and chilled steamed shrimp, plus steamer clams, pickled herring, oysters on the half shell, and cold cracked crab. Of course, you'll see a few meat entrées (including barbecued ribs) in the lineup, but why bother?

COOS BAY

As the largest natural harbor between San Francisco and Seattle, surrounded by some of the richest forests in the world, Coos Bay has long been a busy port. Ships carrying logs, lumber, and wood chips to Asian markets have kept local tugboat companies and longshoremen busy. Ship crews have infused cultural diversity into this Scandinavian/German town.

But the forests have been felled and the big mills have closed, so Coos Bay's base may be shifting from trees to tourists. As a result, the town is undergoing a facelift. The downtown mall is being remodeled, and a San Francisco architect is helping redesign the waterfront. Riverboat, harbor, and charter cruises are available in the area; contact the Chamber of Commerce, (503) 269-0215.

Coos Bay hosts the **Oregon Coast Music Festival** in July, the **Blackberry Arts Festival** in August, and the **Bay Area Fun Festival** (including a 10k run) in September. The **Coos Bay Art Museum,** 235 Anderson Avenue, (503) 267-3901, brings in high-quality displays. The **Marshfield Sun Printing Museum** has been restored (Highway 101 and Front Street). And the **Playwrights' American Conservatory Theatre** has improved local theater (On Broadway Theater, 226 S. Broadway, (503) 269-2501).

RESTAURANTS

Blue Heron Bistro
*Hwy 101 and
Commercial,*
(503) 267-3933
*100 Commercial St,
Coos Bay*

Wim de Vriend's consistency, from-scratch recipes, and European flair keep his cafe bustling. Dinners are more eclectic than when this place was the Hurry Back!; try the Indonesian grilled chicken with a spicy peanut sauce or the bay scallops, shrimp, and snow peas on homemade spinach linguine. De Vriend handles

Moderate; beer and wine;
MC, V; checks OK
Breakfast, lunch, dinner
every day

fish so that the herbs, wine, and sauces enhance rather than overpower the subtleties. His homemade pastas are al dente, with vibrant sauces. Salads are as fresh and innovative as local supply allows. His soups are superb, especially a recent beer-cheese potage and the just-spicy chicken soup with green chiles. Breakfasts will satisfy any appetite, with freshly made croissants, cinnamon rolls, and Danishes or more filling entrées. The Lollobrigida omelet (salami, cream cheese, pesto, mushrooms, and onions) is a standout. There are lots of desserts, but apple pie is the best bet.

Kum-Yon's
On the main drag,
(503) 269-2662
835 S. Broadway,
Coos Bay
Inexpensive; beer and
wine; MC, V; checks OK
Lunch, dinner every day

Kum-Yon transformed a former fast-food eatery into a showcase of her native South Korean plus Japanese and Sichuan specialties. Food is still fast but very fresh. Sushi, dim sum, hot and sour soup, and Sichuan entrées stand out in a menu that also includes Mongolian beef, shrimp tempura, and beef teriyaki. Japanese visitors (among the many other knowledgeable diners) order off the menu. Kum-Yon's American mother-in-law bakes the desserts. Kum-Yon has opened a new eatery in Newport (1006 South Coast Highway, Newport).

1887 Union
California and Union,
(503) 756-7378
1887 Union,
North Bend
Expensive; MC, V;
checks OK
Lunch Tues-Fri, dinner
Tues-Sat

unrated

Michael Petchekovitch, who gained quite a following for his creations at Port Orford's Whale Cove, opened his own restaurant in an 1890 Victorian just about the same day we went to press. We're unable to review it, but we couldn't resist mentioning this 30-seat dining room. Petchekovitch, himself equal parts Russian, Irish, and painter, wanders freely among many cuisines and plays with the color and taste of local top-grade ingredients which, claims Petchekovitch, will be a whole lot easier to get here than in Port Orford.

LODGINGS

Captain's Quarters
Bed & Breakfast
West side of the bay,
(503) 888-6895
265 S Empire Blvd, Coos
Bay, OR 97420
Moderate; no credit cards;
checks OK

Captain John McGenn, known fondly as the "Poet of the Pacific," built this home in 1892. Over the past few years, owners Jean and John Griswold have tracked McGenn's relatives and have assembled his history, including some of his poetry. The two guest bedrooms overlook the bay; they cost about $45 per night. Johnny's seven-grain waffles are a hit in the dining room or on the sunny porch next to the rose garden. No smoking inside, please.

This Olde House
Corner of 2nd St,

Edward and Jean Mosieur decorated their 1893 Victorian with love (including the lampshades they made

downtown,
(503) 267-5224
202 Alder Ave, Coos Bay,
OR 97420
Moderate; no credit cards;
checks OK

themselves) and humor; the Mosieurs' "instant family" consists of secondhand portraits they've hung inside antique frames Jean's collected for about 60 years. The trees surrounding this B&B (just four blocks from the heart of downtown) keep it quiet. They have four bedrooms, one with a private bath. French toast for breakfast, along with Edward's superb bran muffins. There's room for kids, but no pets.

BANDON

Some locals believe Bandon sits on a "ley line," an underground crystalline structure that is reputed to be the focus of powerful cosmic energies. Certainly there's magic here: this little community at the mouth of the Coquille River bustles. North of town is the **Coquille River Lighthouse**, accessible through **Bullards Beach State Park.**

In town, sample the famous cheddar cheeses (especially the squeaky cheese curds) at **Bandon Cheese** at 680 East Second, (503) 347-2456. For another treat, try the *New York Times*–touted handmade candies (fudge, creams, and taffy) at **Cranberry Sweets**, (503) 347-9475, First and Chicago. Bandon's cranberry bogs make it the nation's fifth-largest producer. Call (503) 347-3230 for a tour (May through November).

Old Town features **Harbor Hall,** which books ballet to blues and is the home of the Encore Presenters acting troupe, (503) 347-4404. There are also **Second Street Gallery** and other fine crafts shops and at least 11 food purveyors. The stern-wheeler *Rose* takes slow-paced trips up the Coquille River, including dinner cruises in summer, (503) 347-3942.

The south jetty has the best beach access: **Coquille Point** at the end of 11th Street or the **Face Rock Viewpoint** on Beach Loop Road. Six miles south of Bandon is the **West Coast Game Park Safari,** a special "petting" park where you can pet lions, tigers, and elk, among others. (503) 347-3106.

RESTAURANTS

Andrea's
1 block east of ocean,
(503) 347-3022
160 Baltimore,
Bandon
Moderate; beer and wine;
no credit cards;
checks OK
Breakfast, lunch Mon-
Sat, dinner every day,
brunch Sun

Andrea Gatov-Beck's eclectic south coast restaurant continues to be very popular, in part because it doubles as the unofficial information hub of Bandon. Breakfasts are filling. Substantial sandwiches on homemade whole-grain breads, soups, and pizza by the slice round out the lunch menu. For dinner, Andrea draws on many traditions (sometimes too many?), from Cajun to Russian. She's strong on seafood cooked any of six different ways, from blackened to fat-free. Her lamb is home-grown. And on Friday nights, locals descend on the place for pizza.

Books in the Best Places *series read like personal guidebooks, but our evaluations are based on numerous reports from local experts. Final judgments are made by the editors. Our inspectors never identify themselves (except over the phone) and never accept free meals or other favors. You can help too, by sending us a report.*

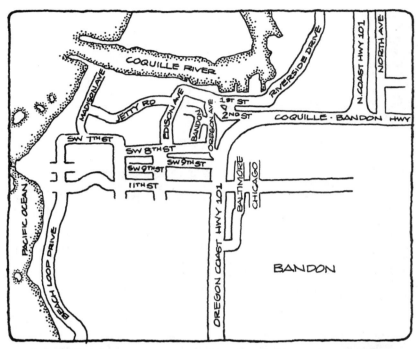

Bandon Boatworks

Follow River Rd out to the jetty, (503) 347-2111
S Jetty Rd, Bandon
Moderate; beer and wine; AE, MC, V; checks OK
Lunch, dinner Tues-Sun, brunch Sun (closed January)

Always a local favorite, the Boatworks takes advantage of its location near the south jetty on the Coquille River to provide fine dining with an equally fine view. The restaurant has expanded, with seating downstairs overlooking the river. If the restaurant is packed, wait anyway for a table upstairs; it's a shame to miss the sunset on the river and ocean. Dinner selections include baked butterflied shrimp served in a light and tangy mustard sauce; fresh oysters roasted in anisette; and an excellent rack of lamb. The decent salad bar includes warm loaves of sweet, if crumbly, cranberry bread (cranberries are an important local crop). For lunch, the sauteed calamari is especially good. On Sundays the Boatworks features brunch and an above-average Mexican menu. Service is excellent.

Lord Bennett's

From Hwy 101, turn right on 11th St, then left on Beach Loop Rd,
(503) 347-3663
1695 Beach Loop Rd, Bandon
Moderate; full bar; AE,

The town's newest dinner house offers a spacious dining room, tall windows, a grand ocean view, and decent food. Try the sole stuffed with mushrooms, artichokes, cream cheese, and bay shrimp, topped with Mornay sauce. Our plate came with fresh asparagus, squash, and baby carrots, with a hint of cheese, garnished with citrus and strawberry slices. On the minus side, the soup may be lukewarm, and don't be surprised if they're out of the wine you ordered.

MC, V; checks OK
Lunch, dinner every day

The adjacent Sunset Motel (not under the same ownership) offers everything from $29 economy rooms (sans view) to $85 ocean front suites with kitchen, fireplace, and an equally spectacular view.

LODGINGS

Cliff Harbor Guest House
Beach Loop Rd at 9th St,
(503) 347-3956
Mail: PO Box 769,
Bandon, OR 97411
Expensive; no credit
cards; checks OK

This modern ocean- and bay-fronting home, with only two guest units, sits on a bluff overlooking the Pacific and the Coquille River harbor. The Harbor Suite features a bedroom, sitting room, window seat, bath, sun deck, and private entrance with wheelchair access. Upstairs, the Cliffside Studio has two double beds, kitchen, bath, fireplace, window seat, and private entrance. Owner Douglas Haines, a master craftsman who built the lovely contemporary home, will create a substantial morning spread, using organically grown meats and produce. It's one of the best breakfasts a five-spot could buy. The place is grand, but hard to find at night. No smoking, no pets.

**Lighthouse
Bed and Breakfast**
First St at 650 Jetty Rd,
(503) 347-9316
Mail: PO Box 24,
Bandon, OR 97411
Moderate; MC, V;
checks OK

Spacious and appealing, this contemporary has windows opening toward the Coquille River, its lighthouse, and the ocean. Nonsmoking guests can watch fishing boats, seals, and seabirds nearby or stroll into Old Town. Hosts Linda and Bruce Sisson serve local organically grown strawberries for the morning's meal of French toast. The Sissons offer four rooms year-round, all with private baths: two view the ocean, the others look at the river and the town. Three rooms with queen beds run about $80 depending on the season; the fourth, the Green House Room—with king bed, fireplace, whirlpool tub, and TV—runs about $90 in the high season.

Inn at Face Rock
2 miles south of Bandon,
right turn at Seabird
Lane, (503) 347-9441
3225 Beach Loop Rd,
Bandon, OR 97411
Moderate, AE, MC, V;
local checks only
Breakfast, lunch, dinner
every day (hours vary in winter)

This elegant resort is just across the road from the beach. Choose from one-bedrooms to two-bedroom two-bath suites with kitchens, queen hideabeds, fireplace, and balconies. Many rooms have views (except for the 24 newer units in back). Prices vary as dramatically as the weather ($40-$105). The rooms are large, comfortable, and very attractive. There are two nonsmoking king units. The Jacuzzi is exclusive to guests; the nine-hole golf course, restaurant, and bar are not. The resort's golf pros can give you a lesson in coping with the often-irritating winds. The ocean-view dining room is inviting, but the quality of the meals flip-flops. The bar is relaxing, especially on a stormy night.

**Sea Star Hostel
and Guest House**
Take 2nd St off Hwy 101
into Old Town,

We'd like this place even if it weren't under $12 a night. Okay, so it's a hostel; but it's a hostel in the loosest sense of the word—and a popular one. The place offers small men's and women's dorms, private rooms for

(503) 347-9632
375 2nd St, Bandon,
OR 97411
Inexpensive to moderate;
MC, V; local checks only

couples and families, a common room, kitchen, secluded courtyard, and sun decks. The Guest House (connected to the hostel by a courtyard), with natural wood interior, skylights, and harbor-view deck, offers a comparatively lavish alternative to its less formal neighbor. Apartments have an open floorplan with an extra queen hideabed, kitchen, living room, and deck. These fancier units run from $50 to $85. Proprietors Dave and Monica Jennings also operate the Bistro restaurant next door.

Windermere Motel
1½ miles south of
Bandon, west on Seabird
Lane, (503) 347-3710
3250 Beach Loop Rd,
Bandon, OR 97411
Moderate; MC, V;
no checks

Many guests wouldn't change a thing about this quintessential family motel. Where else can you find wonderfully battered oceanside cottages with kitchenettes and room for kids to run, all at moderate rates? For years it was nothing fancy, even a little run-down, but recently the place has been extensively remodeled. The rooms are clustered in units of three or four. The best are those with sleeping lofts, but all rooms have truly magnificent ocean views and access to an uncrowded beach. No deposit is required for reservations which sometimes results in overbooking.

PORT ORFORD

It's got history (the oldest townsite on the Oregon coast), location (prime views and beaches with summer wind protection), mild climate, natural resources, and talented residents. Sheep ranching, fishing, sea-urchin harvesting, and cranberries dominate. Several surprises await. **Cape Blanco State Park**, 6 miles north of town, is the westernmost point in the contiguous U.S., with empty beaches, a scenic lighthouse, and the nearby historic **Hughes House**, built in 1898; the **Elk** and **Sixes** rivers are prime fishing streams. Check out the once-thriving **Lakeport**, now a ghost town, on Floras Lake Road a little farther north, near Langlois. South of town, halfway to Gold Beach, the **Prehistoric Gardens** offer a somewhat educational, if touristy, display of dinosaur replicas, (503) 332-4463. It costs $4.50 to get in.

One warning: from here south, poison oak grows close to the ocean. Watch out for it on Battle Rock.

RESTAURANTS

**Truculent Oyster Restaurant
and Peg Leg Saloon**
At the south end of town,
(503) 332-9461
236 6th St,
Port Orford
Moderate; full bar; AE,
DC, MC, V;
local checks only
Lunch, dinner every day

Enter the dark nautical interior of the Truculent Oyster through the Peg Leg Saloon. The fresh oyster shooters, homemade soups (clam chowder, split pea with ham), weekend prime rib, and mild Mexican entrées are the strong points of the eclectic menu. The slow-broiled Chinook salmon (seasonal) can be outstanding. Portions are sizable, service prompt, and coffee miserable.

The Whale Cove

Across from Battle Rock Park, (503) 332-7575
190 6th St (Hwy 101 S), Port Orford
Moderate; full bar; MC, V; checks OK
Lunch, dinner Thurs-Mon, brunch Sun

unrated

It's a treasure, though you'd hardly suspect it from the unassuming gray exterior. First there's a casually elegant ambience: a wide-open Pacific view, live baroque music on Monday nights; and fresh flowers. The place reopened at press time after an extended closure in 1991; however, the notable chef, Michael Petchekovitch, departed to open his own restaurant in Coos Bay. We were unable to review this under the new chef/owner, Christolphe Baudry, formerly of the Crystal Room in Ashland's Mark Antony Hotel, but early reports were promising. In the past we've enjoyed the cranberry and strawberry vinaigrettes made from local ingredients, cream of cilantro soup with peppers and rose petals, rich seafood bisques, herb-flavored vegetarian pastas. Under Petchekovitch there wasn't a bland bite—granted, a tough act to follow.

LODGINGS

Castaway by the Sea

Between Ocean and Harbor Drives on W 5th, (503) 332-4502
Mail: PO Box 844, Port Orford, OR 97465
Moderate; AE, MC, V; checks OK

This bluff-top 14-unit, two-story motel sits on history; ancient Indian artifacts, plus the former sites of both Fort Orford, the oldest military installation on the Oregon coast, and the Castaway Lodge, once frequented by Jack London. The two three-bedroom units have kitchenettes and glassed-in sundecks with harbor and ocean views ($45-$85). Avoid the dank older section under the office, except in a pinch. It's an easy stroll to the beach, harbor, or shops. Look for off-season specials.

Gwendolyn's Bed & Breakfast

Just off Hwy 101 at 735 Oregon St, (503) 332-4373
Mail: PO Box 913, Port Orford, OR 97465
Inexpensive; MC, V; no checks

Like roadside guest homes of the past, Gwendolyn's provides home-style comfort, in a gingerbread-cute 1921 home next to Highway 101 in downtown Port Orford. All four bedrooms have brass beds. Hostess Gwendolyn Guerin enjoys serving her salmon and crab pie and fresh-baked breads.

GOLD BEACH

This is famous as the town at the ocean end of the Rogue River, a favorite with Zane Grey and one of the dozen "wild and scenic" rivers in the US. It's also a supply town for hikers heading into the remote Kalmiopsis Wilderness Area.

Fishing. The river is famous for steelhead and salmon. You might want to visit some of the lodges favored by fisherfolk to pick up tips, or rent clam shovels and fishing gear at the **Rogue Outdoor Store,** 560 N Ellensburg, (503) 247-7142.

Jet boat trips. Guides will discuss the area's natural history and stop to observe wildlife on these thrilling trips from 64 to 104 miles up the Rogue River. You'll even get a hearty lunch or dinner, with local sweet corn and tomatoes, at one of the inns along the way (extra charge). One caution: prepare for sun exposure, as most of these boats are open. Call **Court's White Water Trips** at Jot's Resort, 94360 Wedderburn Loop, Box J, Gold Beach, OR 97444, toll-free (800) 451-3645; **Jerry's Rogue Jets,** Port of Gold Beach, PO Box 1011, Gold Beach, OR 97444, (503) 247-7601 for information or toll-free (800) 451-3645 for reservations; **Mail Boat Hydro-Jets,** PO Box 1165-G, Gold Beach, OR 97444, (503) 247-7033 for information or toll-free (800) 458-3511 for reservations. Better yet, a call to **Rogue River Reservations,** (503) 247-6504 or (800) 525-2161 can gain information on or arrange bookings on just about any Rogue River outing, jet boat trip or overnight stay in the wilderness.

Whitewater trips. Traffic on the all-too-popular wild and scenic part of the Rogue is controlled. People interested in unsupervised trips must sign up for a lottery—the first six weeks in the new year—with the Galice Ranger District; (503) 479-3735.

Hiking. Trails cut deep into the Kalmiopsis Wilderness or the Siskiyou National Forest, or follow the Rogue River. A jet boat can drop you off to explore part or all of the 40-mile-long Rogue River Trail along the river's north bank. Spring is the best time for a trek, before 90-degree heat makes the rockface trail intolerable. Stay at any or all of seven remote lodges, where—for prices ranging from $40 to $155 per night—you end your day with a shower and dinner, and begin with breakfast and sack lunch for the next day. (Reservations are a must.)

In the Agness area the lodges are **Cougar Lane Lodge,** 04219 Agness Road, Agness, OR 97406, (503) 247-7233; **Lucas Pioneer Ranch,** 03904 Cougar Lane (PO Box 37), Agness, OR 97406, (503) 247-7443, and **Singing Springs Ranch,** 34501 Agness-Illahee Road (PO Box 68), Agness, OR 97406, (503) 247-6162.

In the Rogue River Wilderness contact **Clay Hill Lodge** and **Wild River Lodge,** PO Box 18, Agness, OR 97406, (503) 247-6215; **Half Moon Bar Lodge,** 719 NW 3rd Street, Grants Pass, OR 97526, (503) 476-4002, or the crown jewel, the **Paradise Bar Lodge,** PO Box 456, Gold Beach, OR 97444, (503) 247-6022. For information about trails contact the Gold Beach Ranger District, 1225 S Ellensburg, Gold Beach, OR 97444, (503) 247-6651. The Rogue-Pacific Interpretive Center (920 S Ellensburg Avenue, (503) 247-6113), can prepare you for your trip with an overview of the area. It also offers a whale-watching seminar from January through April.

RESTAURANTS

The Captain's Table
Hwy 101, south end of town, (503) 247-6308
1295 S. Ellensburg Ave,
Gold Beach
Moderate; full bar; MC, V; checks OK
Dinner every day

This is Gold Beach's old favorite, though recent reports of poorly prepared seafood have been registered. The corn-fed beef from Kansas City is meat you can't often get this far west. One nice touch: the salad is served family style and you can help yourself to as much as you want. The dining area is moderately small, furnished with antiques, and can get smoky from the popular bar. Both dining room and bar have nice ocean views. The staff is courteous, enthusiastic (if a bit hovering), and speedy.

Chowderhead
Hwy 101, middle of town,
(503) 247-7174
910 S Ellensburg Ave,
Gold Beach
Moderate; full bar; AE,
MC, V; checks OK
Lunch, dinner every day

The view isn't as grand here which is probably why it's popular with locals. Who needs a view when Rob and Kelley Biewend serve the best broiled cod in town? At lunchtime, it comes with Mornay sauce, vegetables, and cheese. At night look for cod amandine. The halibut and salmon can also be fine here. Service is attentive.

Nor'Wester
On the waterfront,
(503) 247-2333
Port of Gold Beach,
Gold Beach
Moderate; full bar; MC,
V; checks OK
Dinner every day

From the windows of the Nor'Wester you may watch fishermen delivering your meal: local sole, snapper, halibut, lingcod, and salmon. Most seafood is served simply: broiled or sautéed, perhaps sprinkled with some almonds. The sole amandine is respectable. Dinners feature both soup and salad, served simultaneously. Try a spinach salad, either the classic with bacon and chopped egg or the house recipe, with mandarin oranges, shrimp, and avocado in a tangy dressing.

LODGINGS

Tu Tu Tun Lodge
Follow the Rogue River
from the bridge up the
north bank for 7 miles,
(503) 247-6664
96550 North Bank
Rogue, Gold Beach,
OR 97444
Expensive; full bar; MC,
V; checks OK

The lodge is one of the loveliest on the coast, though you are 7 miles inland from the ocean. Tall, mist-cloudy trees line the north shore of the Rogue River. The building is handsomely designed, with such niceties as private porches overlooking the river, racks to hold fishing gear, and stylish, rustic decor throughout. There are 16 units in the two-story main building and two larger, noisier kitchen suites in the lodge. In the apple orchard is a lovely garden house (sleeps six) with all the amenities including two baths, kitchen, deck, and old stone fireplace. You can swim in the heated lap pool, use the four-hole pitch-and-putt course, play horseshoes, relax around the mammoth rock fireplace, or hike. Most people come to fish for the Chinook salmon and steelhead, of course.

Three meals a day are served in the lodge or on the patio, family style, from lazy Susans. The prix-fixe dinner begins with hors d'oeuvres in the bar. Your own fish might be the entrée, or perhaps chicken breasts with a champagne sauce, or prime rib, along with freshly made soup, salad, bread, and dessert. Only two river suites and garden house are available in winter. Fido's welcome spring and fall: $3 charge.

Gold Beach Resort
Hwy 101, near south end
of town, (503) 247-7066

If you want a fairly fancy motel room with a good ocean view, this is probably your best bet in Gold Beach. During the summer season the 39 units range from $69

*1330 S Ellensburg Ave,
Gold Beach, OR 97444
Moderate; AE, DC, MC,
V; checks OK*

for a standard room to $95 for a condo with fireplace and kitchen. Most are quite spacious. It's an easy walk to the beach. There's an indoor swimming pool and Jacuzzi, and hosts Pravin and Mridula Patel serve a complimentary continental breakfast in the lobby for early risers, May through September.

Jot's Resort
*At the Rogue River Bridge
at 94630 Waterfront
Loop, (503) 247-6676 or
toll-free
(800) FOR-JOTS
Mail: PO Box J, Gold
Beach, OR 97444
Moderate; AE, DC, MC,
V; checks OK*

The manicured grounds of this lovely resort spread out on the north bank of the Rogue River near the historic Rogue River Bridge; the lights (and the traffic) of Gold Beach are just across the river. The 140 rooms are spacious, tastefully decorated, and well furnished. Summer rates range from about $65 for a standard room to $165 for a two-bedroom condo accommodating six. There's an outdoor pool and an indoor spa and weight room. Rent a bike (or a boat!) to explore the riverfront. Rogue River jet boats and guided fishing trips leave right from the resort's docks. An unexpected fishing trip? The lodge rents necessary gear.

**Ireland's
Rustic Lodges, Inc.**
*On Hwy 101 at 1120 S
Ellensburg Ave,
(503) 247-7718
Mail: PO Box 774,
Gold Beach, OR 97444
Inexpensive; no credit
cards; checks OK*

The original eight cabins live up to the name they got when the Irelands owned the place: rustic log structures with driftwood handrails and nice stonework set amid lovely, well-maintained gardens. Some are a bit run-down. Others have been remodeled. All have one or two bedrooms and fireplaces, but unfortunately no kitchens. Under the present owners there are new cabins and about 24 motel rooms; most have queen beds, fireplaces, and decks overlooking the Pacific. Two complete three- and four-bedroom houses are available, as are some nonsmoking rooms. Rooms have no telephones.

BROOKINGS

Brookings sits in Oregon's "banana belt," just 6 miles north of the California line: it enjoys the state's mildest winter temperatures. In addition, the town is bookended by breathtaking beauty. To the northwest are the **Samuel H. Boardman** and **Harris Beach state parks**. To the east are the verdant Siskiyou Mountains, deeply cut by the Chetco and Winchuck rivers. Brookings also boasts the safest harbor on the Oregon Coast—and therefore a busy port.

Chetco Valley Historical Museum. The standard pioneer items are here, plus a haunting iron casting of a face, which may have been left by Sir Francis Drake in 1579. Near the museum is the nation's largest cypress tree. Highway 101 south of town, (503) 469-6651.

Azalea State Park just east of 101. Fragrant Western azaleas bloom in May, alongside wild strawberries, fruit trees, and violets; you can picnic amid all this splendor on hand-hewn myrtlewood tables. Myrtlewood, which grows here and in Palestine, can be seen in groves in Loeb Park, 8 miles east of town on North Bank Chetco River Road, or carved up into far too many souvenir knickknacks.

Outdoor activities. Fishing is usually good here: a small fleet operates at the south end of town. And there's access from Brookings to trails into the Kalmiopsis Wilderness Area and the Siskiyou National Forest. The Redwood Nature Trail winds through one of the few remaining groves of coastal redwoods in Oregon.

RESTAURANTS

Chetco River House Seafood Restaurant

West of Hwy 101 on north bank of Chetco River,
(503) 469-7539
241 Chetco River Rd,
Brookings
Moderate; beer and wine;
MC, V; local checks only
Dinner Mon-Sat in
summer (sometimes Sun)

Larry O'Neill is originally from Dublin. He and his wife and daughters ran restaurants in New Jersey and San Diego before buying the former Christmas Tree and renaming it in the mid-1980s. The fresh seafood here often includes snapper stuffed O'Neill style (bread crumbs, shrimp, celery, and spices). Fresh halibut and salmon are often available. Or there are Prawns O'Neill, with the shrimp sautéed with tomatoes, green onions, and mushrooms and served over linguine. Soups are special here, notably the purée of onion as well as the chowder. O'Neill's wine list strays from the norm too—16 of the 17 entries cost the same ($13).

Plum Pudding

At the north end of town,
(503) 469-6961
1011 Chetco Ave,
Brookings
Inexpensive; no alcohol;
MC, V; checks OK
Breakfast, lunch Tues-Sat

Unfortunately, Plumm Smith sold her popular restaurant a few years ago; fortunately, her 11-year employee, Karen Thom, bought it. Plumm's touch is still evident, right down to her favorite calligraphed motto: "Eat dessert first, life is uncertain." The desserts and gourmet breads are grand, but you'll also be hard pressed to finish many of the rich breakfast and luncheon entrées. Try the chicken enchirito—a large flour tortilla filled with chicken, potato chunks, onions, and olives in a mild Mexican sauce, covered with cheddar cheese, baked, and served with sour cream and salsa. Breakfasts run from light to overwhelming. Cream cheese is a Thom staple. Everything comes off wonderfully here, and Thom's commitment to freshness is always evident. Too bad they don't serve dinner. No smoking.

River Manor

On North Bank Chetco River Rd, ¼ mile east of Hwy 101, (503) 469-3332
97666 North Bank Chetco River Rd,
Brookings
Moderate; full bar; MC, V; checks OK
Dinner Tues-Sun

He's from Italy, she England, so Al and Eloise Rosichelli merged their heritages with this restaurant on the Chetco River. They serve Italian/European fare amid medieval British decor. After an antipasto appetizer or escargots aux champignons, diners choose a pasta course with one of five sauces. Try the puttanesca, with bacon, mushrooms, and peas. For the main course, there's orange roughy in pastry shell and daily specials such as beef Wellington. They also serve more standard fare like lasagne and scampi, accompanied by polenta fritta. The wine list is adequate.

Rubio's

At the north end of town,
(503) 469-4919
1136 Chetco Ave,
Brookings
Moderate; beer and wine;
AE, MC, V; local checks
Lunch, dinner Tues-Sat

The salsa is outstanding; you can buy bottles of it here and elsewhere in Brookings. But the restaurant itself is the only place you can get Rubio's incredible chiles rellenos and chile verde. And—wow—the seafood à la Rubio combines fresh lingcod, scallops, and prawns in a butter, garlic, wine, and jalapeño sauce. There are 13 tables inside and 5 on the patio; reservations are suggested. There's also a drive-thru for take-out orders.

LODGINGS

Chetco River Inn

Follow North Bank Rd
16 miles, left after South
Fork Bridge, take second
guest driveway on left,
(503) 469-2114, ext.
4628 (radio phone); toll-
free (800) 327-2688
Pelican Bay Travel)
21202 High Prairie Rd,
Brookings, OR 97415
Moderate; MC, V;
checks OK

Expect a culture shock: the fishing retreat sits on 35-acres of a peninsula wrapped by the turquoise Chetco River, 17 miles east of Brookings (pavement ends after 14 miles) and 6 miles from a phone. There's a radio-phone operator, but forget private conversations. The lovely deep-green marble floors are a purposefully practical choice for muddy fishermen's boots. All three rooms have private baths and view river or forest, but the place is not so remote that you can't read by safety propane lights and watch TV via satellite (there's even a VCR). The large, open main floor offers views of the river, myrtlewood groves, and wildlife. Porch overhangs and clerestory windows keep the building cool in summer; solid construction and a wood stove provide winter warmth. A fisherman-sized breakfast comes with a night's stay. Packages include early-riser breakfast service, a deluxe sack lunch, and an exemplary five-course dinner. All told, this is getting away from it all in fishing style.

Chetco Inn

In town behind the Shell
station at 417 Fern St,
(503) 469-5347
Mail: PO Box 1386,
Brookings, OR 97415
Inexpensive; MC, V;
checks OK

For years nobody but vagrants would touch this once-elegant 1915 hotel. In 1985 the Roberts and Schroder families bought the big blue building in the middle of town, rolled up their sleeves, and threw everything out. It's taken years to restore it to some semblance of the grandeur that once attracted Clark Gable and Carole Lombard to downtown Brookings. And it may take a few more years to finish the job. For now, it's an improvement; how much of one depends on your point of view. Period antiques and handcrafted items decorate the 44 rooms; ten have ocean views, most have private baths, and a half dozen come with kitchenettes. Manager Bernita Lockwood offers guests a complimentary fruit basket upon arrival. Other amenities are lacking (portable electric heaters for warmth), and the place can be noisy.

For a more detailed guide to the Rose City, consult Portland Best Places, *which includes more restaurants and lodgings as well as tips on local nightlife, shopping, excursions, and events.*

Nendels

On Lower Harbor Road,
south of the Port of
Brookings,
(503) 469-7779
Mail: PO Box 2729,
Brookings, OR 97415
Moderate; MC, V;
checks OK

Sure, it's only another in the Nendels chain, but if you want an ocean-front motel room in Brookings, this is the closest you can get. The three-story structure opened in 1990 with 39 rooms. Nothing special, but the view and beach access are pluses.

WILLAMETTE VALLEY AND SOUTHERN OREGON

North to south along the I-5 corridor from Yamhill and Washington counties in the north to the Rogue River Valley in Southern Oregon.

AURORA

In 1856 Dr. William Keil brought a group of Pennsylvania Germans here to establish a communal settlement of Harmonites. The commune faded away after Keil's death, but the town remains a well preserved turn-of-the-century village that's been put on the National Register of Historic Places. Two dozen or so clapboard and Victorian houses line the highway; many contain antique shops. The **Old Aurora Colony Museum** recounts the history of the town, (503) 678-5754.

RESTAURANTS

Chez Moustache
Corner of Hwy 99E and Main St, (503) 678-1866
21527 Hwy 99E, Aurora
Moderate; full bar; MC, V; checks OK
Dinner Tues-Sat

Until the town gets a new sewer system, no new restaurant will be allowed to open. So Chez Moustache has the market to itself. Chez Moustache began life as a tavern, taking its name from a Frenchman who migrated up from California. Joel and Barbara Miller run the place, seating the guests at oilcloth-covered tables in a series of small rooms and verandahs. They spend nothing on advertising, preferring to put money into fresh ingredients. Three-course dinners (about $13) begin with a soup, followed by a salad with a marvelous (and secret) vinaigrette. The main course— depending on the season and on what's fresh and available— might be a fillet florentine David, served on a bed of spinach with fresh bay shrimp and béarnaise sauce. The best desserts consist of fresh fruit.

WILLAMETTE VALLEY WINERIES

The Oregon wine country now stretches from Portland all the way south to the California border, with the greatest concentration of vineyards in **Yamhill County,** where among rolling oak-covered hills increasing numbers of wineries keep touring wine lovers more than busy.

It is not Napa; nevertheless, weekends are quite busy. Still, seek out the small family operations well off the beaten track and you'll receive a hearty welcome. It's best to call ahead; some wineries have limited hours and some are not open to

See page 38 for a map that includes the Willamette Valley and Southern Oregon.

the public at all. Arm yourself with a map and a good guidebook—the Oregon Winegrowers Association publishes a good pamphlet, and many member wineries carry it as well: (503) 228-8403, 1200 NW Front Avenue, Suite 400, Portland, OR 97209. In fine weather take along a picnic lunch; many vineyards have tables, some sell chilled wine and picnic supplies.

As you drive south on Highway 99W (the state's official wine road), the first stops are **Veritas Vineyards**, Newberg, (503) 538-1470, makers of excellent chardonnay, and **Rex Hill Vineyards**, Newberg, (503) 538-0666, a decidedly upscale winery with a splendid tasting room and outstanding (if pricey) pinot noir. In the hills west of Newberg is **Autumn Wind Vineyard** (503) 538-6931, a small new place with a promising pinot noir. In Dundee, the **Elk Cove tasting room** (503) 538-0911 offers not only its own fine rieslings and pinots noirs but also the wines of **Adelsheim Vineyard**, the industry's pioneer in Oregon—and a decent light lunch as well. Behind the town are **Cameron Winery** (503) 538-0336, with its lovely view, and the new **Lange Winery** (503) 538-6476, where an interesting pinot gris is emerging as the new find in Oregon whites. Nearby are two much larger wineries: **Knudsen Erath**, Dundee, (503) 538-3318, one of the oldest and largest in the state (near Crabtree Park and a nice midday stop), with a full lineup of wines in a variety of prices, including one of the best values in pinot noir, and **Sokol Blosser Winery**, Dundee, (503) 864-2282 whose handsome tasting room and broad range of wines also offer a worthwhile stop. Just south, outside Lafayette (which boasts one of the few Trappist monasteries in the country), **Chateau Benoit**, (503) 864-3666, sits right on the crest of a ridge, with spacious visitor facilities. Try their Müller-Thurgau (a great picnic wine), sauvignon blanc, and sparkling wines.

Near the railway tracks in the heart of McMinnville are another couple of vintners worth a visit: both **Arterberry Winery** (503) 472-1587 and **Panther Creek Winery** (503) 472-8080 make fine pinots noirs. South of McMinnville on Highway 18, the lovely **Yamhill Valley Vineyards** (503) 843-3100 are set among old oaks—a good shade for sipping their long-aging pinot noir on a hot day. Just a bit further along is the **Oregon Wine Tasting Room**, 17 miles south of McMinnville on Hwy 18, (503) 843-3787, which sells a huge variety of wines and always has an interesting assortment to taste, including some from top-notch producer **Eyrie Vineyards**, McMinnville, (503) 472-6315, which is not open to the public on a regular basis.

Highway 99W out of McMinnville meanders through the Eola Hills, home to another half dozen wineries, including **Amity Vineyards**, Amity, (503) 835-2362, a small, rustic winery that consistently produces excellent pinot noir, gewurztraminer, and dry riesling. **Bethel Heights Vineyard**, 7 miles northwest of Salem, (503) 581-2262, is one of the oldest vineyard sites in the area, and **Eola Hills Winery**, Rickreall, (503) 623-2405, makes good chenin blanc and cabernet sauvignon—rarities in the Willamette Valley.

Still further south are two neighboring wineries, both very small and definitely off the beaten track. **Airlie Winery**, Monmouth, (503) 838-6013, makes excellent Müller-Thurgau and has well-priced wines; take some extra time and visit the birds at their pond. **Serendipity Cellars**, near Monmouth, (503) 838-4284, produces some unusual wines, including Marechal Foch, a very rare (and very good) red. **Tyee Wine Cellars**, (503) 753-8754, south of Corvallis, makes excellent whites—especially pinot gris and gewurztraminer. **Broadley Vineyards**, Monroe, (503) 847-5934, is a modest storefront winery that offers a powerful pinot. To the west is picturesque **Alpine Vineyards**, Alpine, (503) 424-5851, one of the only wineries in the Willamette Valley to make a consistently good cabernet, and a fine producer of riesling as well.

The Tualatin Valley lies west of Portland. An excellent close-in destination (ten minutes outside Beaverton) is **Ponzi Vineyards,** Beaverton, (503) 628-1227. This modern pioneer winery produces an outstanding lineup, including a powerful pinot noir, an elegant chardonnay, and fine pinot gris and dry riesling. **Cooper Mountain Vineyards,** outside Beaverton near Hillsboro, (503) 649-0027, makes a good pinot noir at its beautiful hilltop site; in an old dairy barn south of town, **Oak Knoll Winery,** Hillsboro, (503)[th]648-8198, maintains an Oregon tradition of very good fruit wines and also produces a variety of other wines at good prices. Several wineries out near Forest Grove include the huge new **Montinore Vineyards,** (503) 359-5012, which has a fancy tasting room, plenty of room to wander, and wines that are improving with each vintage. **Laurel Ridge Winery,** (503) 359-5436, on the site of a historic Oregon winery, specializes in sparkling wines and sauvignon blanc. **Shafer Vineyards,** (503) 357-6604 has produced some agreeable chardonnays, and **Tualatin Vineyards,** (503) 357-5005, in their best vintages produces exquisite chardonnay and a tasty Müller-Thurgau. **Elk Cove Vineyards,** Gaston, (503) 985-7760, has a spectacular tasting room perched on a forest ridge.

NEWBERG

A mill town at the gateway to the wine country, Newberg is rapidly being suburbanized. Away from the 99W strip, however, there are some lovely neighborhoods and old houses; **Minthorn House,** where Herbert Hoover spent his youth, has been restored and is open to visitors (follow signs from Highway 99W).

RESTAURANTS

Valenti's
Just north of Newberg on Hwy 99W,
(503) 538-6637
2320 Highway 99W,
Newberg
Moderate; full bar; AE, MC, V; checks OK
Lunch Sat-Sun, dinner Tues-Sun, (dinner only in winter)

★

When Roland Gotti moved up from Sonoma to be in the heart of the Northwest wine country, he bought and gutted this old house and created a place where the goal is serious Italian cuisine. And, indeed, one the attention to detail might make this a very good restaurant rather than simply an okay one. The low ceilings and minimal lighting make the room cramped rather than intimate, and the food seemed to suffer from excessive zeal in some places and inattention in others. A big, beautiful, crisp salad was doused in too much vinaigrette, while a perfectly cooked piece of chicken lacked flavor. There are nice touches, including a loaf of fresh bread and a plate of olive oil for dipping. The house specialty is bistecca al pepe di pinot—tenderloin with fresh peppercorns and Oregon pinot noir demiglacé. The subtle approach to dessert pays off in a delicate Italian rum cake. Wine by the glass off a decent—if pricey—list is the best bet.

LODGINGS

Hess Canyon Estate
South from Hwy 99W on River St, then east on 4th to Wynooski,

This B&B has the convenience of being just a few blocks from Newberg's main street, but you'd never know it once you're there. Peter and Susan Mitchell run a cheerful, relaxed establishment (full of dark wood

(503) 538-1139
712 Wynooski, Newberg,
OR 97132
Moderate; MC, V;
checks OK

and overstuffed furniture) that overlooks a creek and a horse pasture. There are three small rooms, each with its own bathroom (including one with a Jacuzzi); an additional room with twin beds is perfect for kids. Guests have the run of downstairs and are welcome to visit the horse barn. Breakfast might feature fresh blueberry pancakes, quiche lorraine, or potato pancakes. There's a stack of board games and a closet of toys for children; in late summer, you can pick fresh blueberries.

Spring Creek Llama Ranch
From 99W going south,
go right on Benjamin Rd
[f]4/10 mile past Rex Hill
Winery, (503) 538-5717
14700 NE Spring Creek
Lane, Newberg,
OR 97132
Moderate; MC, V;
checks OK

Dave and Melinda Van Bossuyt discovered that llamas make great pack animals when they began taking their new baby on backpacking trips. The Van Bossuyts have been aficionados ever since. Their llamas are gentle and eager for visitors (especially at mealtime) and provide fine diversion for children three years and up. This large, airy, modern home is tastefully and simply furnished, and has three guest rooms (one with twin beds). Privacy seekers may feel the openness of the ranch is not to their taste, but its proximity to the trails in the woods, Newberg, and Highway 99W (though the house is secluded from the highway's noise) is a plus.

DUNDEE
RESTAURANTS

Red Hills Cafe
On Hwy 99W,
(503) 538-8224
976 Hwy 99W, Dundee
Inexpensive; beer and
wine; no credit cards;
checks OK
Breakfast Mon-Sat,
lunch Mon-Fri, dinner
Fri-Sat

This tiny roadside place has just a half dozen good-sized wooden tables, most likely occupied by overall-clad regulars on a first-name basis with owner Alice Halstead (formerly of Alice's Restaurant at the same location). She's broadened her menu—this one includes a homemade sandwiches, soups, and desserts—and it's all just "really good." Sure enough, the beef barley soup is full of fresh vegetables; the tender meat loaf sandwich drew raves all around. Add a huge piece of homemade pie and you'll walk out happy, full, and little the poorer.

YAMHILL
LODGINGS

Flying M Ranch
10 miles west of Yamhill;
follow the little red Ms

The lodge (completely rebuilt after in burned down years ago) contains a Western-style lounge (the bar is made from six-ton logs) and a restaurant that serves

with flying wings,
(503) 662-3222
23029 NW Flying M Rd,
Yamhill, OR 97148
Moderate; AE, DC, MC,
V; checks OK

decent breakfasts and straightforward steaks. The food is a far third behind the clean, restful setting and the modest accommodations: several simple cabins under the alder and maple trees are the obvious favorites. Other choices include a primitive dude-ranch bunkhouse (with motel-style rooms) or shaded campsites at the confluence of Hanna Creek and the North Yamhill River. Some just come up for the day, to enjoy the plentiful picnic grounds for families and enormous picnic shelters for large groups and to swim in the pond. There is an airstrip (for those who bring their own plane) and stables (for those who bring their own horse). For a fee, local cowboys can take you trail riding on one of Flying M's horses and maybe even grill steak on the way. Breakfast rides, too.

McMINNVILLE

McMinnville *is* small-town Oregon, where teenagers still cruise bumper-to-bumper down the main drag on Friday night. The growing wine industry has enlivened things a bit; the town's central location and a surprising number of tourist facilities make it good headquarters for wine touring. Serious enophiles attend the three-day **International Pinot Noir Celebration** in late July on the gracious old campus of Linfield College: (503) 472-8964.

RESTAURANTS

Lavender's Blue,
A Tea Room
1 block east of Hwy 99W
on Cowles,
(503) 472-4594
535 N Cowles,
McMinnville
Inexpensive; no alcohol;
no credit cards;
checks OK
Afternoon tea Wed-Sun

★★★

McMinnville—a farming town—may seem an unlikely location for a tradition English-style tea, but Montanan Terese Blanding has created an oasis of quiet elegance in a pleasant family neighborhood. The sprawling old house is surrounded by a tidy garden with attention paid to detail: soothing blues and pretty floral patterns, books for reading piled on each table, soft music in the background, and linen, china, and silver at each place. Even small children seem subdued in this restful atmosphere. The wonderful house specialty tea includes lavender and lemon peel; black or herb teas are served along with excellent scones, shortbread; a small savory dish such as marinated asparagus or hot, creamy artichoke puffs, and a sweet dessert, and can make a satisfying supper at $8. An ideal place to recover from a day's wine-tasting, but also worth its own trip from Portland. Reservations are recommended.

Nick's Italian Cafe
Off Hwy 99W, across
from the movie theater,
(503) 434-4471
521 E 3rd St,
McMinnville

Located in a small burg outside of Portland, Nick's would be extraordinary wherever it was—Seattle, San Francisco, even New York—for it combines two qualities rarely found in one restaurant: outstanding food and total lack of pretension. Nick Peirano is an inventive but mercifully untrendy Northern Italian cook who

Moderate; beer and wine; no credit cards; checks OK Dinner Tues-Sun

has created a friendly, relaxed atmosphere in which to eat marvelous meals. Nick's matter-of-fact approach to service and atmosphere (the cafe was once a luncheonette) puts the food in sharp focus, where it belongs. The five-course meal always includes a second-course tureen of Nick's grandmother's rich, garlicky minestrone, followed by a fresh, simply dressed green salad and chewy, dense French bread. The fourth course is always pasta, always homemade, and always delicious (possibly a hazelnut-filled ravioli in a Gorgonzola sauce). Entrée choices might be fresh halibut grilled in butter and olive oil with a light pesto sauce or sirloin steak with capers. Homemade pastries make up the dessert list, including Italian specialties created by Nick's mother. Appropriately, the wine list includes impressive local bottlings at very reasonable prices, and the knowledgeable staff won't steer you wrong.

Kame

At Evans and 3rd, (503) 434-4326 228 N Evans, McMinnville Inexpensive; beer and wine; MC, V; local checks only Lunch Mon-Fri, dinner Tues-Sat

McMinnvilleites aren't used to getting their change counted out in Japanese, but for food this good and this inexpensive, they don't seem to mind one bit. A tiny storefront place with white walls, plain wood tables and chairs, a few artfully placed decorations, and simple Japanese food served graciously. Owner Mieko Nordin learned to cook family style from her mother. A basic (and satisfying) meal might include tasty miso soup, a small salad of pickled cabbage, and chicken or pork with vegetables on a bed of steaming rice. Tempura and teriyaki, too.

La Maison Surrette

On 3rd near Ford St, (503) 472-3787 729 E 3rd St, McMinnville Moderate; beer and wine; AE, MC, V; no checks Dinner Fri-Sat

This immaculately restored Victorian house, complete with antique furnishings, is the setting for chef John Surrett's restaurant (he added the final "e" to make the restaurant sound more French). The prix-fixe meal begins with a simple appetizer, followed by soup, perhaps seafood bisque (more of a chowder really, studded with bay scallops and potatoes). Main courses might range from fresh halibut with sauce béarnaise to filet mignon with hunter sauce or medallions of pork with a white wine-butter-Dijon sauce. Desserts are prepared by Surrett's wife, Carol, who doubles as the waitstaff. Choices could be a rich bittersweet chocolate cheesecake or fresh apple pie. This leisurely, moderately priced meal is available only on weekends; your hosts have full-time careers in Portland.

Roger's

Corner of 27th St and Hwy 99W, (503) 472-0917 2121 E 27th St, McMinnville

Roger's grew out of an adjoining seafood market, which still provides both the basis for the restaurant's menu and the rationale for the dining room's nautical motif. The decor is enhanced by bentwood chairs and fresh carnations and, above all, by the calm setting: a quiet stream running through natural greenery just outside.

Moderate; full bar; AE,
DC, MC, V; checks OK
Lunch Mon-Fri, dinner
every day

In good weather you can eat out on the patio; at night the trees twinkle with hundreds of tiny lights. The execution of Roger's deep-fried items—especially the fish and chips—can be ideal, but it's not a sure thing, according to local reports. Baked and sautéed items show a steadier hand. A dish of snapper arrived hot from the oven, topped with a tarragon glaze, accompanied by perfectly done fries (crunchy outside, moist inside). The highlight, surprisingly, was a delightful pine-nut torte, moist without being gooey or cloying. The desserts are homemade and seasonal.

LODGINGS

Youngberg Hill Farm
Old Sheridan Hwy to
Peavine Rd and
Youngberg Hill Rd,
(503) 472-2727
10660 Youngberg Hill
Rd, McMinnville,
OR 97128
Moderate; AE, MC, V;
checks OK

A more spectacular setting would be hard to devise. At the crest of a 650-foot hill the view stretches 180 degrees from an exquisite small pastoral valley to the hills of the wine country and across to Mount Hood and the Cascades. It's so pleasant that even in the dead of winter guests take their coffee out to the wraparound porch. Eve and Norman Barnett (who also run a sheep ranch and vineyard on this 700 acres) take an obvious delight in their surroundings and clearly enjoy pampering their guests. The house is brand-new, but has the design and feel of an old country house. The five spacious bedrooms are furnished in dark colors and heavy wood furniture and each has its own view and bathroom (two have fireplaces). The cozy sitting room has a wood stove. There's a conference room that accommodates 20. A daily menu in the foyer announces the breakfast selections, which might include puffed pancakes, smoked ham, and fresh fruit. Austrian dinners with a variety of wines are served on occasion. The Barnetts are knowledgable wine lovers, and will soon add a formal tasting room to their extensive wine cellar. An easy place to stay, a difficult one to leave.

Mattey House
¼ mile south of Lafayette
on Hwy 99W,
(503) 434-5058
10221 NE Mattey Lane,
McMinnville, OR 97128
Moderate; MC, V;
checks OK

Standing behind its own little vineyard—an acre of Müller-Thurgau—like a remote French manor house, it's actually an 1890s Victorian mansion, beautifully restored by Gene and Susan Irvin. Each of the four guest rooms is named for a wine variety (pinot noir, chardonnay), and is decorated with antiques; all but one share baths. Extra touches include fresh flowers, plush bathrobes, bedtime chocolates, and an afternoon glass of wine in the parlor. The Irvins are perfect hosts and knowledgeable, enthusiastic guides to the local wine scene. There have been reports of waning upkeep, but on our last visit all seemed in good order.

Steiger House
From 99W, turn east on

Decks wrap around the chalet-style house at a couple of levels, offering plenty of opportunities to sip coffee

Cowls at the hospital,
(503) 472-0821
360 Wilson St,
McMinnville, OR 97128
Moderate; no credit cards;
checks OK

outside and enjoy the large woodsy back yard. Three rooms (each with private bath) are downstairs. The two upstairs rooms (with *real* feather beds) share a bath but are usually rented en suite. Owner Doris Steiger is a weaver who sells woolen goods in a small guest shop. You breakfast on Doris's homemade granola. Children over 10 are welcome.

Safari Motor Inn
19th St and Hwy 99W,
(503) 472-5187
345 N Hwy 99W,
McMinnville, OR 97128
Inexpensive; AE, DC,
MC, V; no checks

Just off Highway 99 as it enters McMinnville, this unassuming motor lodge doesn't offer anything fancy, but it's ideally located for visitors who shy away from the B&B scene. The Safari offers relatively new, perfectly quiet rooms with wonderfully comfortable beds. A small exercise facility with Jacuzzi is available, and the coffee shop is fine for breakfasts. No pets, please.

BELLEVUE/SHERIDAN

Bellevue (a little bump on the road) is the site of three fine establishments, all under one roof. The **Oregon Wine Tasting Room**, (503) 843-3787, offers tastes of the best bottlings from two dozen Oregon wineries. **The Lawrence Gallery**, (503) 843-3633, is an excellent showcase of fine regional talent in all media. Upstairs is **Augustine's**, one of the region's better restaurants.

RESTAURANTS

Augustine's
Hwy 18, 7 miles west of
McMinnville,
(503) 843-3225
19706 Hwy 18,
Bellevue
Moderate; full bar; MC,
V; checks OK
Lunch, dinner Wed-Mon,
brunch Sun (closed Mon
in winter)

With assured, knowledgeable service and fine fresh ingredients carefully and imaginatively prepared, Augustine's has become a real star in the Willamette Valley dining scene. The clean, open space has scenic views out both sides: farmland on one side and down into the Lawrence Gallery on the other. You could start your meal with a smoked seafood platter (salmon, mussels, halibut, and cream cheese) or some of the excellent creamy clam chowder. Soup or a pleasant green salad is included with the entrée. For the main course, there are pasta dishes, filet mignon, and lamb chops, but seafood is a real focus at Augustine's (owner/chef Jeff Quatraro worked at the Couch Street Fish House in Portland). Poached salmon was a huge fillet served with a simple herb butter. Fresh sturgeon fillet piccata—a special one night—was tender and delicious. Desserts are deservedly popular. The legendary hazelnut cheesecake is rich, light, and not too sweet; citrus tart (orange, lemon, and grapefruit curd) is tangy and refreshing. The all-Oregon wine list is reasonably priced and changes four times a year. Many fine vintages are offered by the glass.

LODGINGS

Sheridan Country Inn
*1 mile west of Bridge St
on Hwy 18 (business
loop), (503) 843-3151
1330 W Main, Sheridan,
OR 97378
Moderate; DC, MC, V;
checks OK*

This old house is now an inn, located in sleepy Sheridan. There are ten rooms, six in the funky but spacious mansion and four in the outside duplexes. The rooms ($45-$55) are large and comfortable, with views of the acre of grounds surrounding the house. All have private bath, phone, TV, and a small refrigerator to chill your latest wine discoveries. Room 7 ($95) is a huge suite with a private Jacuzzi. The location isn't particularly convenient to the wineries, but the rates are reasonable, and kids are welcome, making the inn a nice alternative to a motel. During summer, you can relax in the outdoor Jacuzzi. A serve-yourself continental breakfast is included.

MOUNT ANGEL

The town stages a Bavarian folk festival in mid-September that's enthusiastically supported by neighboring residents. **Mount Angel Abbey**, a Benedictine seminary for the last hundred years, is a fully accredited college atop a butte the Indians considered sacred. The campus is worth a visit, not only for the view but for the architecture (the library is a gem by the internationally celebrated Finnish architect Alvar Aalto). For hours, call (503) 845-3030.

SALEM

For a city of its size (pop. 100,000), Salem is remarkably low-key. Despite the state Capitol building and the office buildings, Salem retains the appearance of a small town, and looks to stay that way—downtown, redevelopment lacks focus and some of the interesting ideas, such as the Reed Opera House, have not panned out very well. The newish (1938) **Capitol building** is worth a visit. Attractive parks flank the Art Deco-cum-classical building; just behind it stretches the campus of **Willamette University**, the oldest in the West, where a happy blend of old and new brick buildings are merged with pretty landscaping. Gardeners should visit the small but well-cared-for **botanical gardens** on the east side of the campus.

Across the road from the University is **Mission Mill Village**, 1313 Mill Street SE, (503) 585-7012, an impressive 4½-acre cluster of restored buildings from the 1800s: a woolen mill, a parsonage, a Presbyterian church, and several homes. The mill itself drew its power from Mill Creek, which runs through the Willamette University campus and now houses a museum that literally makes the sounds of the factory come alive. The Jason Lee House, dating from 1841, is the oldest remaining frame house in the Northwest; regular tours of the premises run from 10 to 4:30pm Tuesday-Saturday. Picnic along the stream and feed the ducks, if you like. The Salem Visitor Information Center is part of the complex, as are several shops selling handcrafted clothing, gifts, and antiques.

Bush House, 600 Mission Street SE, (503) 363-4714, is a genuine Victorian home built in 1877 by pioneer newspaper publisher Asahel Bush. It sits in an large

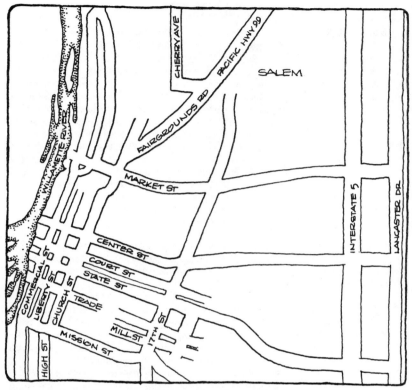

park, complete with conservatory, rose gardens, hiking paths, and a barn-turned-art-gallery. Tours available.

Gilbert House Children's Museum, (503) 371-3631, on the downtown river-front between the bridges, has hands-on learning activities for young children.

Salem is off the beaten winery track, but it's not to be passed by. The **Willamette Valley Vineyards** (503) 588-9463, a big new investor-owned winery, is just off I-5 south of town. **Evesham Wood Vineyard**, (503) 371-8478, in west Salem—a tiny winery making some top-notch wines—receives visitors by appointment; **St. Innocent Winery** is not far from downtown at 2701 22nd Ave, Salem, (503) 378-1526.

Old-fashioned ferries, operated by cable, still cross the Willamette River in a few places and are a good alternative to bridges if you've got some extra time. Two run in the Salem area: the Wheatland ferry, just north of town in Keizer (follow Highway 219 north from downtown to Wheatland Road), and the Buena Vista (from I-5 take exit 243, west on Talbot Road). The ferries run every day (except during storms or high water) and cost very little.

If you're in the area around Labor Day, don't miss the **Oregon State Fair** (see calendar). This 10-day event is one of the biggest in the Northwest and there's room enough for everyone.

For excursions further south, keep an eye out for Northern California Best Places, *due in 1992, from a team of California reviewers.*

RESTAURANTS

Alessandro's Park Plaza
Trade and High streets,
(503) 370-9951
325 High St, Salem
Moderate; full bar; AE,
MC, V; checks OK
Lunch Mon-Fri, dinner
Mon-Sat

Alessandro Fasani (who also owns Alessandro's in Portland) runs this lovely urban oasis overlooking Mill Creek Park. You will feel out of place here if you don't dress up. The interior is handsome: layers of red, white, and green napery give the two-story interior an elegant Italian look (Fasani calls it Roman); wildflowers add a nice touch to the tables, contrasting with the just-short-of-pretentious service and the supercilious menu (it is permissible to point). The hearty bouillabaisse is laced with saffron and studded with shellfish and chunks of tomato. In addition to the regular menu, a multi-course dinner is offered daily: the staff asks only if there's a particular dish you don't like, and they surprise you with the rest. For a $25 tariff you enjoy three appetizers (maybe smoked salmon over linguine), an entrée such as veal Marsala, and an elaborate dessert.

Inn at Orchard Heights
West side of Salem, off
Wallace Rd,
(503) 378-1780
695 Orchard Heights Rd
NW, Salem
Moderate; full bar; AE,
DC, MC, V; checks OK
Lunch Mon-Fri, dinner
Mon-Sat

It took a sense of humor to turn the inside of this 1937-vintage home overlooking Salem into a thoroughly slick restaurant full of glass, chrome, and mirrors, then adorn the outside with enough twinkling lights to illuminate the Capitol building. You sit in the bar, sipping a glass of fragrant Yamhill Valley Vineyards elderblossom wine, and see a gray deer in the bushes: it's a fake, made from twigs and vineyard clippings. It's not surprising that recent reports claim the kitchen has been relying more on pretension than on quality—not going the extra step we know they're capable of. When they're on, the preparations can be first-rate, beginning with homemade appetizers such as freshly marinated herring in sour cream. Follow that up with an unusual soup (cream of dill pickle?). Then proceed to the entrées—many stuffed seafood and pasta dishes as well as sautés and curries of veal and pork. Owner-chef Hans d'Alessio's continental sauces go well with the local wines; try a Sokol Blosser chardonnay with appetizers or fish.

Lazio
In the Evergreen
Shopping Center,
(503) 585-3948
3826 Center St, Salem
Moderate; beer and wine;
AE, MC, V; checks OK
Lunch Mon-Fri, dinner
Mon-Sat

Lazio is less than a year old, but it's already been discovered. Even on weeknights, locals flock to John Andrich's mall storefront spot, which confirms the good cooking going on inside. Muted earth tones, stark lighting, big tables, and comfortable chairs set the tone for some serious Italian food, covering a broad range of interesting pastas, seafood, veal, and other meats. Flavorings are zesty, with capers and artichoke hearts ladled out generously—occasionally a little *too* zealously. Highlights include a mild-flavored smoked chicken, a perfectly balanced chicken saltimbocca, and tortellini stuffed with veal, excellently sauced with lovely mushrooms. Servings are plentiful, and there are lots of extras. Desserts on a recent visit were a battalion of cheesecakes. The staff works hard at professional style despite a few minor gaffes. The fair-priced wine list combines a small assortment of Italian vintages with wines by the glass from nearby Oregon wineries. No smoking here. At press time, expansion into a neighboring space was underway.

Morton's Bistro Northwest
Across the Marion St bridge from downtown Salem, (503) 585-1113
1128 Edgewater, West Salem
Moderate; beer and wine; MC, V; checks OK
Dinner Tues-Sat

Clever design puts the diner *below* roadway level, looking out on an attractive courtyard backed by an ivy-covered wall. The interior is intimate, with dark wood beams and soft lighting. The menu (predominantly Northwest cuisine with hints of French and Oriental influences) features fresh seafood, veal, and a short list of pasta dishes, but the prevailing theme is cream sauce and calories. Veal with calvados was drenched with a rich sauce of apples, onions, and mushrooms, and the veal was a tad overdone. The tortellini stuffed with pumpkin is a great combination—but again, heavy. Add hearty soup like cream of asparagus (lots of asparagus, lots of cream) and a dessert like chocolate mousse, and you may be hard pressed to make it back up the stairs. Still, there's a serious intent here: the service is expert and pleasant, and the wine list features a very good selection of Northwest wines at responsible prices. No smoking; wheelchair-accessible.

Off Center Cafe
17th and Center,
(503) 363-9245
1741 Center NE, Salem
Inexpensive; no alcohol; no credit cards; checks OK
Breakfast Tues-Sun, lunch Tues-Fri, dinner Thurs-Sat

A throwback to the '60s, the Off Center Cafe features a genuine soda fountain, demure classical music or rock & roll (depending on the chef's mood), a clientele ranging from aging hippies to professors grading papers to bankers in three-piece suits, and intriguing food: scrambled tofu for breakfast, black Cuban beans and rice at lunch, fresh halibut with lime at dinner, and fruit pies all day long. It's not a fancy place, but one that offers "real food" and prides itself on serving its customers well. Many have their own special concoctions listed on the menu: try Ed's Cooler, a mixture of ice cream, mocha, and Pepsi. Mmmmm.

LODGINGS

Chumaree
Market St exit off I-5,
(503) 370-7888, or
(800)248-6273
3301 Market St NE,
Salem, OR 97303
Moderate; AE, DC, MC, V; checks OK

Of all the motels near the Capitol buildings, this one has the most to offer. The rooms are what you'd expect—except the luxury suites with Jacuzzis. Still, it's the courtesy car to the airport, direct-dial phones, and the indoor garden—all free to all guests—that place this convention-oriented motel one step above the others.

**State House
Bed and Breakfast**
21st and State,
(503) 588-1340
2146 State St, Salem,
OR 97301
Moderate; MC, V;
checks OK

Behind Mike Winsett and Judy Uselman's B&B you'll discover a handsomely landscaped garden: a wide spot along Mill Creek with its own gazebo, hot tub, ducks, and geese. You can barely hear the traffic as you sit in the shade of the red maples (some landscaping was being done on a recent visit). But all's not quiet: the TV is often on in the family-style living room (with Nintendo if there are kids around). The four-bedroom B&B boasts queen beds, brass fixtures, chandeliers, and terrycloth bathrobes and phones in all the rooms. The three cottages include small kitchens and are good for families. Breakfast is included for those staying in the main house but an extra $5 for cottage guests.

INDEPENDENCE

As long as anyone can remember, **Taylor's Fountain & Gift**, on the corner of Main and Monmouth, has been serving up old-fashioned sodas, burgers, and breakfasts. Marge Taylor, her daughter, and two granddaughters run the place and haven't changed it much in its 44 years.

RESTAURANTS

Amador's
Hoffman Rd and Main
St, (503) 838-0170
870 N Main St,
Independence
Inexpensive; beer and
wine; MC, V; checks OK
Lunch, dinner Mon-Sat

Here's a little gem: just north of the restored main part of town, tucked into a fading strip mall, which produces some of the most honest Mexican fare around. Brothers Manuel and Antonio Amador do the cooking while their families (down to the youngest children) wait on the customers. Nothing elaborate in the way of decor: a whitewashed space, a few Mexican fans, paper flowers, a painted parrot on the floor. But you know it's going to be good as soon as the first basket of chips arrives (thick, crunchy, homemade), along with a fresh salsa; you can taste the corn and tomatoes. Everything from tacos to enchiladas is exquisitely fresh, piping hot, and lavishly garnished with sour cream, avocado, fresh tomatoes, and green onions.

ALBANY

Sure, there's a pulp mill next to the freeway, but Albany is really quite a pleasant stop, recalling the small-town Oregon of an earlier era with its broad, quiet streets, neat houses, and slow pace. Once an important transportation hub in the Willamette Valley, Albany has watched progress pass it by; the highlights here are the **historic homes** and buildings in a wide variety of styles, many of them lovingly restored. A self-guided tour displays 13 distinct architectural styles in the 50-block, 368-building Monteith Historic District alone. Then there are the Hackleman District (28 blocks, 210 buildings) and downtown (9½ blocks, 80 buildings). Many of the buildings are open for inspection on annual tours—the last Saturday in July and the Sunday evening before Christmas Eve. A handy guide is available free of charge from the Albany Convention and Visitors Commission, 435 West 1st Avenue, (503) 926-1517, and tours through Experience Albany, 2697 NW Quince, (503) 926-5652 or (503) 926-1517. The tree-lined path alongside the Willamette to Monteith and Bryant parks makes for a pleasant stroll.

Covered bridges. In 1930, more than 300 covered bridges spanned streams and rivers in western Oregon. Today only 50-some remain, most of them in the Willamette Valley counties of Lane, Lincoln, and Linn, but that's more than in any state west of the Mississippi. Many have aged gracefully, while others—sagging precariously—are candidates for restoration by the Covered Bridge Society of Oregon. Best starting points for easy-to-follow circuits of the bridges are Albany, Eugene, and Cottage Grove; in addition, many handsome bridges dot the woods of the Oregon Coast Range. Eight of these bridges lie within an 8-mile radius of Scio, northeast of Albany. For details and maps of wooden bridges, send SASE with 52 cents postage to the Covered Bridge Society of Oregon, PO Box 1804, Newport, OR 97365, or call (503) 265-2934.

RESTAURANTS

Novak's Hungarian Paprikas
Take exit 233B toward town, (503) 967-9488
2835 Santiam Hwy SE, Albany
Inexpensive; no alcohol; MC, V; checks OK
Lunch Sun-Fri, dinner every day

Refugees from Pecs in south central Hungary, Joe and Matilda Novak run this roadside restaurant with help from their family: daughter Karen bakes the desserts, son Ed helps with the sausages, big Joe dispenses the bear hugs. And another brother may soon be on the plane from Hungary, importing another Novak talent, no doubt. Dinners begin with a tasty chicken-and-vegetable soup and a salad of chopped lettuce covered with a house dressing, which falls somewhere between French and Italian. Then come the Hungarian specialties, well executed though on the bland side: beef *szelet* and *pariszi* (pork) *szelet* are tender cutlets, battered and fried to crisp perfection; *kolbászok* are mild homemade sausages served with deliciously tangy sweet-and-sour shredded cabbage. Everything tastes fine, if a bit underseasoned; you long for a bold, assertive hand in the kitchen, or at least for a glass of wine to spice up the meal. For dessert, choose the Dobos torte over "Mama's Favorite."

LODGINGS

Lilla's
Ellsworth and 7th,
(503) 928-9437
206 7th Ave SW, Albany,
OR 97321
Moderate; MC, V;
checks OK
Lunch, dinner Tues-Sat,
brunch Sun

Located amid the grand old homes of Albany's Monteith Historic District, Lilla's is one of the best preserved Victorian mansions in town. There's a respectable restaurant downstairs and four guest rooms upstairs. You might think you're visiting friends at a vintage beach house with hooked rugs on the plank floors, comfortable bedding, and a claw-footed tub with a ring shower; yet the place is lacking in some of the amenities you'd expect at home—no bedside tables or lamps, for instance. Breakfasts are filling: fresh orange juice; homemade nut and raisin bread; an omelet with mushrooms, Italian sausage, red and green peppers, basil, and two cheeses. The Gilliams don't live in the house, so be sure to ask for a key if you (or your children) plan to stay out late.

CORVALLIS

Corvallis is dominated by Oregon State University, which gives it a more cosmopolitan flavor than most towns of its size. The campus is typical of other Northwest megaversities, with a gracious core of old buildings, magnificent giant trees, and lots of open space surrounded by a maze of modern, boxlike classroom and residential buildings of little character. Sports are big here, especially "Beaver" basketball and gymnastics, but culture flourishes as well. The **Horner Museum**, housed in the basement of Gill Coliseum, has a wonderfully eclectic, rather dilapidated collection that traces the history of Oregon's development from Native Americans to Oregon Trail to more recent economic growth. A grand place for kids, (503) 754-2951. **Corvallis Art Center**, located in a renovated 1889 Episcopal church off Central Park, displays local crafts and hosts weekly lunchtime concerts, (503) 754-1551.

Corvallis is ideal for biking and running; most streets include a wide bike lane, and routes follow both the Willamette and Mary's rivers. Avery Park, 15th Street and US 20, offers a maze of wooded trails as well as prime picnic sites and a rose garden. Arborists will also enjoy the hiking trails and picnic facilities of OSU's 40-acre **Peavy Arboretum**, 8 miles north of town on Highway 99W.

RESTAURANTS

The Gables
Follow Harrison to 9th,
(503) 752-3364
1121 NW 9th St,
Corvallis
Moderate; full bar; AE,
DC, MC, V; checks OK
Dinner every day

For years, this was *the* only place to go for dinner in Corvallis. It's not the only place any more, but it's still the best. The atmosphere is homey, with dark wood furnishings, low beams, and a fireplace, and the staff is courteous. The menu features tried-and-true American fare: prime rib, lamb chops, teriyaki chicken and, more recently, seafood. Dinners are huge (especially given the price) and come with all the trimmings: sourdough bread, relish tray, salad or chicken bisque, veggies, and rice or potato. Fresh herbs from The Gables' own garden enhance the meals. The prime rib has a reputation as the best in town, and the seafood sauté we tried was a generous crock full of prawns, scallops, salmon, and halibut in a delicate lemon-butter-and-wine sauce. A heaping bowlful of homemade garlic croutons comes to your table for soup and salad. The wine cellar is often used for special occasions.

Nearly Normal's
Near the corner of Monroe
and 15th, (503) 753-0791
109 NW 15th St,
Corvallis
Inexpensive; beer and
wine; no credit cards;
checks OK

Normal's is not normal. It's funk: a gigantic mural of orchids out front, a fine collection of pink plastic flamingos on the back porch, and sometimes-barefoot waiters in shorts. Inside, Normal's is a noisy den of mismatched tables and chairs crowded with OSU folk enjoying generous helpings of the restaurant's "gonzo cuisine"— vegetarian fare prepared with gusto. Variations of the oversized burritos are the specialty, but Normal's also

Breakfast, lunch, dinner
Mon-Sat

dabbles in pastas, Middle Eastern dishes, and stir-fries. The falafel is a hearty mix of spicy garbanzo patties packed into pita with fresh veggies and a cool yogurt sauce, and the sunburger (made with sunflower seeds, eggs, and veggies on a whole-wheat bun) satisfies even the most skeptical carnivore. There's live music Wednesday, Thursday, and Saturday nights, but there's never any smoking, and there's a suggested two-drink maximum.

La Estrellita
In the Timberhill
shopping center at Walnut
and Kings Blvds,
(503) 754-0514
2309 NW Kings Blvd,
Corvallis
Moderate; full bar; AE,
MC, V; checks OK
Lunch, dinner every day

A little star in the middle of Corvallis where the choices off the large Mexican menu are cooked in the style of the Jalisco region. It may seem mild to those who like their Mexican hot and spicy, but the chips are fresh and crisp, the salsa tangy, and the servings enormous. The friendly and lightning-fast service softens somewhat the uncomfortable hard bench backs in the booths, and the list of Mexican brews is as long as you're likely to find in these parts. A cut above chain restaurants, though this one is quickly becoming a chain itself with two others in Salem (1111 NW Edgewater, 362-0522, and 3295 Silverton Road NE, 362-7032), and a third is planned in Kaiser. Children welcomed here, and there are lots of them.

LODGINGS

Hanson Country Inn
Five minutes west of town
off West Hills,
(503) 752-2919795 SW
Hanson St, Corvallis,
OR 97333
Moderate; AE, DC, MC,
V; checks OK

You follow a country road to a grand wood-and-brick 1928 farmhouse on a knoll overlooking the Willamette Valley. Formerly a prosperous poultry-breeding ranch, it's now, thanks to an extensive renovation by San Franciscan Patricia Covey, a registered historic home. A hand-carved staircase of imported New Zealand gumwood leads up to the four guest rooms with original hardwood floors and built-in cabinetry. The living room (with piano and fireplace), sun room, and library are often used for weddings. Upstairs, a queen-size four-poster bed, a private bath, and a study compose the best suite. After a gourmet breakfast, explore the grounds and the original egg house. Bring the kids, but not the dog; the chickens, sheep, and rabbits are company enough.

Madison Inn
Corner of 7th and
Madison, near the
University,
(503) 757-1274
660 Madison Ave,
Corvallis, OR 97333
Moderate; MC, V;
checks OK

A stately five-story Tudor opposite Central Park, downtown. Owner Paige Down grew up in the house (which her mother, Kathryn Brandis, began as a bed and breakfast over a decade ago), and the seven guest bedrooms are named after Paige and her siblings. Furnished with antique beds and woolen patchwork quilts, the wood-floored rooms have a rustic, cozy feel. Request the Kathryn Room on the top floor for a cathedral ceiling and the best view of the park, or the Matt and Mike Room for a private entry (and private bath). A new cottage has been added (Rachael's) that includes all the amenities of a one-bedroom apartment. Paige and husband Richard prepare a full breakfast for guests that includes such daily specialties as quiche, scones, or Dutch babies. The inn has secured a solid reputation in the area, and advance reservations are advised.

ELMIRA

LODGINGS

McGillivray's Log Home Bed and Breakfast
14 miles west of Eugene off Hwy 126,
(503) 935-3564
88680 Evers Rd, Elmira, OR 97437
Moderate; MC, V; checks OK

This peaceful, spacious log home has two huge guest rooms, both with private baths. Skylights let the sun in to the upstairs room (with a king-size bed and two twins—great for families). A pancake and egg-and-bacon breakfast is prepared on the wood cookstove with an antique griddle. But contemporary comforts are not forgotten—the log building is both air-conditioned and wheelchair-accessible.

EUGENE

Oregon's second-largest city is more overgrown town than throbbing metropolis, which to the visitor means less hustle but also less hassle. Traversing the city by foot, public transportation, or car will not age you appreciably, and finding a parking spot is not only possible but likely.

A study in contrasts, Eugene is an odd mix of cultured urbanites, back-country loggers, and persevering hippies—possibly one of the few places on earth where a 10-block skyline includes both a grain elevator and a world-class performing arts center. Home to the state's flagship institution of higher learning, the University of Oregon, the area also includes one of Weyerhaeuser's largest mills and a thriving alternative community. Eugene has its own symphony, plus theater, ballet, and opera companies.

Although downtown has been ailing for a decade, there's renewed energy just 3 blocks north in Eugene's Fifth Street district. It begins at the **Oregon Electric Station**, a historical landmark that features the city's loveliest bar; continues west past the newly constructed Station Square, two floors of upscale retail anchored by Eugene's newest brew pub, **Steelhead**; and ends at the Fifth Pearl Building, home to Eugene's best restaurant, **Chanterelle**, and the now-venerable Fifth Street Public Market.

Hult Center for the Performing Arts is a top concert facility with two architecturally striking, acoustically perfect halls. The 24-hour concert telephone number is (503) 342-5746.

University of Oregon features an art museum with a permanent collection of noteworthy Oriental pieces and a variety of speakers and events.

Wistech, a small but nicely conceived hands-on science and technology museum (with accompanying planetarium) is the place to take kids on rainy weekends; open Saturday and Sunday, 10am-5pm, 2300 Centennial Blvd, (503) 484-9027.

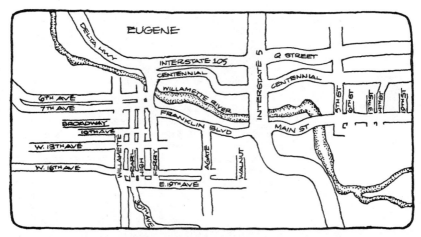

Lane County Museum offers a large homesteading collection and excellent historical photography; open Tuesday-Sunday, 740 W 13th, (503) 687-4239.

Saturday Market, a thriving open-air crafts and food fair, is the ultimate Eugene experience. For people-watching, unique gift buying, and continental noshing, this is the place; open April-December on High Street at Broadway.

Fifth Street Public Market has three levels of shops surrounding a lovely brick courtyard and fountain. Relax at an outdoor table while reading the out-of-town papers (from Marketplace Books) and treating yourself to a snack or a full meal from any of the Market's many food vendors (Italian, Greek, Middle Eastern, or nouvelle cuisine). One of Eugene's best breakfast spots, Terry's Diner, is here, as is the city's best bakery, The Metropole. Musicians perform most weekends.

Outdoors. Two rivers run through town, the Willamette and the McKenzie, and thanks to the farsighted environmentalism of the late governor Tom McCall, they run clear and clean. Rafting and canoeing are favorite summertime activities, from easy flat-water runs (great for families) between Eugene and Harrisburg on the Willamette to more challenging whitewater experiences on the McKenzie. Hikers will find miles of forest trails just outside the city limits. Runners—Eugene is known as the nation's track capital—will love the well-groomed, packed running paths that travel through parks and follow the river.

Parks. Run along the banks of the Willamette through Alton Baker Park on the 6.3-kilometer groomed Prefontaine Trail. Women will feel safer on the sloughside 1.6-kilometer track that borders Amazon Park, the site of spirited outdoor concerts in summer months. Hendricks Park, the city's oldest, features an outstanding 10-acre rhododendron garden (best blooms in May and early June). Skinner's Butte Park, which skirts the Willamette, includes a lovely rose garden, several playgrounds, picnic areas, and a 12-mile bike path. Spencer's Butte, at the south end of town, offers sweeping urban and pastoral views. Two relatively easy trails wend their way to the top.

RESTAURANTS

Cafe Central
W 13th and Lawrence,
(503) 343-9510
384 W 13th, Eugene

Intimate but not claustrophobic, this pretty restaurant offers quiet dining in a lovely clerestory-lit back room, with more public seating at a handful of storefront tables. Cafe Central is exactly what a Northwest res-

Moderate; full bar; MC,
V; checks OK
Lunch Mon-Fri, dinner
Mon-Sat

taurant should be: a solid connection to local suppliers, light preparations infused with intense flavors, and an eclectic menu with a real base in European cuisine. The menu changes seasonally, and the fresh seafood list changes almost daily. For the most part, Cafe Central offers sublime meals, beautifully presented. A multi-dimensional salmon entrée came criss-crossed with crème fraiche and a raspberry coulis atop a deep green bed of mustard greens and fennel. The marinated chicken breast with sautéed apples, rosemary and garlic was sweet and succulent, but the ahi had barely touched the grill (on another visit it was cooked perfectly). Northwest and international wine selection is commendable; service and presentation are always lovely. Most important, the poached cheesecake (chocolate or lemon) has got to be Eugene's best dessert—quite an accomplishment, considering that the town is as competitive in desserts as it is in track.

Chanterelle

Corner of 5th and Pearl
(503) 484-4065
207 E 5th, Eugene
Moderate; full bar; AE,
MC, V; Checks OK
Dinner Tues-Sat

Chanterelle, a small and lovely place, is one you can truly count on. Chef Ralf Schmidt, working alone in a kitchen the size of a walk-in closet, never has had a day off. The printed menu is always enhanced by a wide selection of chef's seasonal specials from sturgeon to antelope. In the spring, there are dishes showcasing local lamb and Chinook salmon. In the winter, there is Ralf's wonderfully hearty onion soup. In between, try the venison from New Zealand, ahi from Hawaii, and snails from France. The desserts, the bailiwick of Mrs. Schmidt, are superb. Chef Schmidt achieves a balance of innovation and consistency, a quiet sophistication in the menu and its presentation, an understated implication that you are a valued patron.

The Excelsior Cafe

Across from Sacred Heart
Hospital, (503) 342-6963
754 E 13th Ave, Eugene
Moderate; full bar; AE,
MC, V; checks OK
Lunch, dinner every day

Although other restaurants in town now offer the inventive nouvelle and Northwest concoctions and masterful desserts that made Excelsior famous, few do it with such consistency and charm as this grande dame of Eugene's sophisticated dining scene. The elegant but informal restaurant and its small, bustling bar are favorites with the university crowd. The menu changes daily to reflect both seasonal finds—locally grown lamb, spring asparagus, for example—and the whims of the talented chefs. The seafood, from grilled marlin to deep-fried Yaquina Bay oysters to baked Chinook salmon, is invariably noteworthy. The soups are outstanding (particularly the delicate carrot bisque). Excelsior's salads are also a delight, especially the butter-leaf lettuce, toasted hazelnuts, apples, and crumbled blue cheese combination. Desserts (Frangelico cheesecake, whiskey-apricot torte—need we say more?) are terrific. From 5pm to 6:30pm you can select from the regular dinner menu at a "bistro" price.

Zenon Cafe

*Corner of Broadway and
Pearl, (503) 343-3005
898 Pearl St, Eugene
Moderate; beer and wine;
MC, V; checks OK
Breakfast, lunch, dinner
every day*

This is where upscale locals go for the most urban—and urbane—eating experience Eugene has to offer. Zenon is a noisy, active, exciting place with a formidable, always interesting, always changing international menu. The cuisine roams the world, from the Northwest to North Africa, Appalachia to the Mediterranean, Indonesia to India. Possibly too much to pull off, but not here. Zenon's large kitchen staff does an always credible, sometimes inspired job: a mixed grill of venison sausage, pork chops, boar ribs served with champagne sauerkraut, a wonderful spicy swordfish, and a fiery Cajun red snapper. Regional wines, many by the glass, are well represented. Desserts are a must. Zenon, now open on Sundays, offers wonderful breakfasts (especially the huevos rancheros and frittatas) and pleasant outdoor seating in the summer.

Ambrosia

*Corner of Broadway and
Pearl, (503) 342-4141
174 E Broadway, Eugene
Inexpensive; full bar;
MC, V; checks OK
Lunch Mon-Sat, dinner
every day*

Despite a sign that looks as though it belongs on a teenage disco and mediocre antiques inherited from the previous occupant, this place has a lot going for it—including a massive oak bar presided over by Eugene's friendliest barkeep. Pizza is the acknowledged speciality here. The huge wood-burning ovens turn out wonderfully crisp pies topped with rich plum-tomato sauce and your choice of trendy ingredients (sun-dried tomatoes, artichoke hearts, roasted eggplant). The entrées, from the superbly creamy lasagne florentine to the credible saltimbocca, are the reason to come here. A gelato provides the finishing touch. Ambrosia is much more than a designer pizzeria.

Baja Cafe

*Pearl between Broadway
and 8th, (503) 683-8606
860 Pearl, Eugene
Inexpensive; beer and
wine; MC, V; checks OK
Lunch Mon-Fri, dinner
Mon-Sat*

With a zany decor—watermelon piñatas, a 7-foot mounted swordfish, and lots of turquoise—and an eclectic menu, this informal eatery is a welcome addition to downtown Eugene. Ethnic-food purists, be forewarned: the Mexican food you'll find here has never been seen south of the border. The chips come with blue-cheese dip; the beans are black, not pinto; the cheese is a sprinkling of Parmesan; and the cooks use no lard. Our favorites are the fish tacos and the chicken fajitas. It's an informal spot with fast counter service and menu flexibility, which makes it a fine place to take the kids. Mexican beers await the adults.

Hilda's Latin American Restaurant

*Take W 6th to Blair,
(503) 343-4322
400 Blair Blvd, Eugene
Inexpensive; wine and
beer; MC, V; checks OK
Dinner Tues-Sat*

Tucked away in a downwardly mobile westside neighborhood and housed in a middling 1930s bungalow, Hilda's, with its exotic menu of Latin-American dishes, comes as a lovely surprise. Here you'll find the cuisines of Brazil, Peru, Argentina, Chile, Guatemala, and Venezuela represented with a pleasing diversity of meat, seafood, and vegetarian offerings. Some come for the half dozen tapas; others favor the full meals such as the *aji de gallina*, a rich, spicy casserole of chicken, Parmesan cheese, almonds, and onions. This place lacks all pretension (wear jeans), but expect to pay what in Eugene passes for "uptown prices."

Lou & Ev's
Gilbert Shopping Center,
(503) 688-5553
1295 Pacific Hwy 99 N,
Eugene
Inexpensive; full bar;
MC, V; checks OK
Dinner every day

Lou & Ev's should be next door to Ralph's Pretty Good Grocery and down the street from the Chatterbox Cafe; but it's in north Eugene and has been for 45 years. There are other items on the menu, but the world-class fried chicken is what brings 'em in. The chicken is served with a wonderful twice-baked potato, a decent salad, and, oddly enough, a stack of toast.

Mekala's
In the Public Market
Building on 5th,
(503) 342-4872
296 E 5th Ave, Eugene
Inexpensive; beer and
wine; MC, V; checks OK
Lunch, dinner every day

Chef Payung Van Slyke runs an ambitious operation. This pretty restaurant with its light-filled dining area overlooking the Public Market courtyard features a six-page menu with more than a dozen fiery curries and two dozen vegetarian dishes. Payung and her kitchen staff are sensitive to a wide range of palates and will spice up or cool down most any dish. Whatever you choose for an entrée—from the vegetables with hot-sweet mint leaves and chile to the rich *homoke* soufflé (shrimp, scallops, and fish in a curry and coconut sauce with fresh lime leaves, green pepper, and cabbage)—begin your meal with the terrific Angel Wings (deboned chicken wings stuffed with ground pork, glass noodles, and bean sprouts) and end it with a dish of homemade coconut ice cream.

North Bank
West of the Ferry St
Bridge, (503) 343-5622
22 Club Road, Eugene
Moderate; full bar; AE,
DC, MC, V; checks OK
Dinner every day

Notable for its beautiful view of the Willamette River, relaxed ambience, lively bar, and reasonable prices, this is the place to go if you want a pleasant meal with little fuss. The serve-yourself homemade-soup-and-salad bar is varied and fresh—no pallid greens or bland offerings here. The seafood (varies seasonally) is cooked nicely, but the beef and chicken dishes are rather standard. Drinks on the deck overlooking the river are a must on summer evenings.

Taj Mahal
Under the Overpark at
10th and Oak,
(503) 342-1976
1050 Oak, Eugene
Inexpensive; no alcohol;
AE, MC, V; checks OK
Lunch Mon-Sat, dinner
every day

It's as if Eugene had been waiting for Indian cuisine. Harbhajan Singh Dhuna, owner of the Taj Mahal in Portland, just opened this eatery, and the response has been overwhelming—a little too overwhelming for the untrained service staff. But you forgive the spotty service and the orange-and-yellow plastic decor (courtesy of the previous tenant) because the food is so wonderful. The East Indian menu features a number of authentic lamb and chicken dishes as well as half a dozen vegetarian entrées. Begin with samosas, pastry shells stuffed with spiced potatoes and peas, a kind of Indian knish. Then try the light and delicately spiced *jhinga*

105

WILLAMETTE VALLEY AND SOUTHERN OREGON

malai, prawns sautéed with onions and garlic and simmered in a sauce of almonds, saffron, and coconut milk. The chicken tikka, boneless chicken marinated in garlic, ginger, mint, and coriander leaves, is a perfect blend of tang and sweetness. Soon Taj Mahal will install a tandoor oven, which will enable Dhuna to add a number of special charcoal-grilled dishes, and (none too soon) will unveil a new decor.

Jamie's
18th and Chambers,
(503) 343-0485
1810 Chambers St,
Eugene
Inexpensive; no alcohol;
AE, MC, V; checks OK
Lunch, dinner every day

Take the kids to Jamie's, where they (and you) can get terrific burgers (11 varieties), inspired onion rings, and real—yes, real—milk shakes. There's also a great chargrilled chicken sandwich and a just-like-Mom's grilled cheese sandwich. Avoid the ordinary fries. Kids can play on the red Vespa and sidecar displayed in the center of the restaurant while you listen to tunes from the '50s jukebox and wait for your order. There's a second location in Eugene at 2445 Hilyard Street, (503) 342-2206, a third in Corvallis, and a fourth in Portland.

Napoli
Across from Sacred Heart
Hospital, (503) 485-4552
686 E 13th, Eugene
Inexpensive; beer and
wine; MC, V; checks OK
Breakfast, lunch, dinner
Mon-Sat

As the name promises, Napoli's strong suit is Southern Italian food—you know, those wonderful cheesy, tomato-y lasagnes and calzones that have all but been replaced by the more delicate Northern Italian cuisine that overtook America in the 1970s. Pasta of all sorts is good here, from gnocchi to manicotti to ziti. The pizzas are disappointing. Locals prefer the *focaccia,* Italian bread baked with olive oil, garlic, and Parmesan cheese. Desserts (including a lovely ricotta cheesecake) are temptingly displayed as you enter. This is a good lunch place.

LODGINGS

Campus Cottage
1 block south of the
university on E 19th,
(503) 342-5346
1136 E 19th Eugene,
OR 97403
Moderate; no credit cards;
checks OK

Eugene's original bed and breakfast is classy, cozy, comfortable, and convenient. The three guest rooms, all with private baths, are beautifully furnished with antiques. One of the rooms is very private (with its own entrance) and features a vaulted ceiling and bay windows overlooking a pretty garden and deck. Innkeeper Ursula Bates, the godmother of the Eugene B&B scene, runs a flawless operation, including an elegantly served full breakfast. This friendly place is a favorite with visiting professionals and faculty.

Maryellen's Guest House
East side of Hendricks
Park (503) 342-7375
1583 Fircrest, Eugene,
OR 97403

This airy Northwest contemporary tucked into a wooded hillside is just three minutes from the University of Oregon campus. There are only two rooms, but they rank among Eugene's best. The country French suite, tastefully decorated with brass bed and antiques, has a bathroom with a double shower and a Roman soaking tub. The contemporary suite also with its own

Moderate; AE, MC, V;
checks OK

bath, is understated Deco. Both rooms have private decks, although the house's main deck features a lovely pool and an all-season hot tub. Innkeeper Maryellen Larson is everything you could want in a hostess: gracious, friendly, flexible, and respectful of privacy. She accommodates all tastes for breakfast—from pork chops with biscuits and gravy to vegetarian omelets—but baked German pancakes are her specialty. Bikes available. No smoking in the house.

Valley River Inn
Exit 194B off I-5 to West
105, then exit 3,
(503) 687-0123
1000 Valley River Way,
Eugene, OR 97401
Expensive; AE, DC, MC,
V; checks OK

Although next to a regional shopping mall, this sprawling complex effectively creates a world of its own, with pretty inner courtyards, lovely plantings, and an inviting pool area. The best rooms face the Willamette River. All rooms are large and tastefully decorated. The food's nothing special, but the public spaces offer river views, and the lobby provides a good selection of West Coast newspapers. The newly opened outdoor dining area along the river is a wonderful place to relax in the summer months.

Duckworth's
Bed and Breakfast
1 block south of the
university on E 19th,
(503) 686-2451
987 E 19th, Eugene,
OR 97403
Moderate; no credit cards;
checks OK

This fully restored English Tudor home just blocks from the university features three rooms (two share a bath, one has a private bath). All have pretty antiques, lace curtains, window seats, fresh flowers—and their own VCRs. There's a 600-movie video library downstairs, and a comfortable overstuffed sofa in front of the living-room fireplace. In the summer, there's apricot iced tea in the English garden, and bikes for the asking. Innkeeper Peggy Ward is proud of her three-course breakfasts.

Eugene Hilton
Exit 194B off I-5, then
exit 1 to City Center,
(503) 342-2000
66 E 6th Ave, Eugene,
OR 97401
Expensive; AE, DC, MC,
V; checks OK

An excellent downtown location and terrific city views save this from being just another stamped-from-the-same-mold Hilton. The Hult Center for the Performing Arts is across a brick courtyard; the city's convention center is attached; the downtown mall is a block away. The 271 rooms are spacious and comfortable, but predictable. Amenities include an indoor pool, sauna, Jacuzzi, and game room. Breakfast can be included in the price, but don't plan to eat other meals at either of the hotel's two lackluster restaurants.

New Oregon Motel
Across from the U,
(503) 683-3669
1655 Franklin Blvd,
Eugene, OR 97403
Inexpensive; AE, DC,
MC, V; checks OK

The free sports center and this Best Western's location just across from the University of Oregon put this place in a slightly different class from other strip motels. The 128 rooms are a cut above motel standards. The sports facility includes an indoor pool, a Jacuzzi, two saunas, and two racquetball courts.

SPRINGFIELD

RESTAURANTS

Spring Garden
Downtown Springfield,
(503) 747-0338
215 Main St, Springfield
Inexpensive; full bar;AE,
MC, V; local checks only
Lunch, dinner every day

This steadfastly uncharming place, with its panoramic view of a Goodwill Industries outlet, offers some of the best Chinese food south of Portland: a truly inspired sizzling rice soup, egg rolls that are both crunchy and eggy, and a variety of fresh, flavorful entrées. Seafood lovers should make a beeline for the stuffed garlic prawns or the pan-fried shrimp, two of the best items on the menu. Avoid the combination dinners.

Kuraya's
Market and Mohawk,
(503) 746-2951
1410 Mohawk Blvd,
Springfield
Inexpensive; beer and
wine; MC, V; checks OK
Lunch Mon-Sat, dinner
every day

Although the location is somewhat off the beaten path, the area's first Thai restaurant is a popular spot with its energetic atmosphere and inventive menu, recently infused with new variety. Bangkok prawns, charcoal-broiled and served with a crabmeat-and-peanut dipping sauce, are very popular. Or try the seafood basket, shrimp and scallops in a bracingly hot, coconutty sauce. Service has greatly improved in this friendly, well-run restaurant.

LEABURG

LODGINGS

MarJon Bed & Breakfast
See review for directions,
(503) 896-3145
44975 Leaburg Dam Rd,
Leaburg, OR 97489
Expensive; MC, V;
checks OK

Three miles east of Leaburg on McKenzie Highway, turn at the Leaburg Dam Road (milepost 24). Don't worry about the "dead end" signs—you're on the right track. Nestled at the edge of the blue-green McKenzie River is Marjorie Haas's contemporary home. The house itself is an immaculate blend of Oriental and French Provincial. The junior room, at $80 a night, is a nice-sized bedroom with his-and-hers bathrobes so that you can cross the hall to the bathroom (complete with fishbowl shower). The master suite ($100 a night) has a 7-by-12-foot bed, an adjoining bath with sunken tub, and a Japanese garden view. Marjorie calls her house the oyster and the grounds the pearl—she's right; it's a lovely, landscaped property.

Wondering about our standards? We rate establishments on value, performance measured against the place's goals, uniqueness, enjoyability, loyalty of clientele, cleanliness, excellence and ambition of the cooking, and professionalism of the service. For an explanation of the star system, see "How to Use This Book."

CRESWELL

RESTAURANTS

Emerald Valley Dining Room
10 miles south of Eugene,
(503) 485-6796
83293 N Dale Kuni Rd,
Creswell
Moderate; full bar; AE,
DC, MC, V; checks OK
Dinner Wed-Sun, brunch
Sun

★

Creswell's Emerald Valley is undergoing some major changes over the next few years. It's soon to be a major resort community, complete with homes, a hotel, and a shopping center. So far, however, there's no place to stay—just an athletic club and this elegant steak-and-seafood centerpiece, restaurant. The dining room with its panoramic view of the adjoining 18-hole championship golf course and the Cascade foothills, is popular for business dinners. The food served at large meetings is excellent for the genre. The Sunday brunch is bountiful, the prime rib widely praised, and the Northwest wines on the card extensive. A lounge hums with live music Friday and Saturday nights. In short, a very nice spot, particularly if you've had a successful round of golf.

COTTAGE GROVE

Mining country. There once was gold fever in these parts, and although the old steam engine The Goose is no longer running, you can still tour the old mines and mining towns by car or bus; you head east toward Bohemia, on roads that can be quite treacherous; call the Forest Service, (503) 942-5591, for road conditions and directions.

Old houses. Tour along the River Road, south from Main Street. **Cottage Grove Historical Museum** has more memorabilia, particularly from the mining era; Birch Avenue at H Street, (503) 942-3963, for irregular hours.

LODGINGS

Best Western
Village Green Resort
I-5 at Cottage Grove exit,
(503) 942-2491, or
(800) 343-ROOM
725 Row River Rd,
Cottage Grove, OR 97424
Moderate; AE, DC, MC,
V; local checks only

★

It's a self-contained little resort, nicely laid out, small (96 rooms), yet with lots of facilities: tennis, a playground, a heart-shaped pool, lawn games. Rates are reasonable and rooms diverse: try a poolside suite with a family room and fireplace. Unfortunately, there are no rooms with kitchens.

Books in the Best Places *series read like personal guidebooks, but our evaluations are based on numerous reports from local experts. Final judgments are made by the editors. Our inspectors never identify themselves (except over the phone) and never accept free meals or other favors. You can help too, by sending us a report.*

OAKLAND

RESTAURANTS

Tolly's
Exit 138 off I-5 to middle of Oakland,
(503) 459-3796
115 Locust St, Oakland
Moderate; full bar; MC, V; checks OK
Lunch, dinner every day

Oakland is one of Oregon's older towns, dating back to the 1850s. Tolly's is a special-occasion place for locals; still, it's a bit of an oddity. Downstairs there's an old-fashioned ice cream parlor, candy counter, and antique gift shop. Upstairs the Tollefsons get a bit more serious. One elegant room, with high wingback chairs and candlelight, is reserved for couples only. The menu leans toward standard steak (prime rib on weekends) and seafood entrées. Some, like the salmon with pesto sauce, can verge on the ordinary, but chef Maureen Schlers also prepares such relatively interesting dishes as chicken in spicy peanut sauce over fettuccine.

STEAMBOAT

LODGINGS

Steamboat Inn
38 miles east of Roseburg on Hwy 138,
(503) 498-2411
Mail: Steamboat Inn, Steamboat, OR 97447
Expensive; MC, V; checks OK
Breakfast, lunch and dinner every day;

On the banks of a fly-only fishing stream is the plain-seeming lodge run for many years by Jim and Sharon Van Loan. Linked by a long verandah paralleling the North Umpqua River are eight small guest cabins; rooms have knotty-pine walls, a bath, and just enough space. In the woods are five secluded cottages with living rooms and kitchens. Latest additions are two riverside suites. Prices begin at $85 for a stream-view double and end at $175 for a suite. Remarkably good family-style dinners are served in the main building each night a half hour after dark, by reservation only ($25 per person, including wine). That's just enough time to prepare your fishing stories. The meals are elegant multicourse feasts, and (with advance notice) chef Sharon can design one around your special tastes or diet. A recent meal included spinach balls with mustard sauce, chilled avocado, garden salad, barbecued beef tenderloin, and dessert.

ROSEBURG

The Roseburg area now has five wineries, open for tours and tastings: **Callahan Ridge**, 340 Busenbark Lane, (503) 673-7901; **Davidson Winery**, 2637 Retton Road, (503) 679-6950; **Girardet Wine Cellars**, 895 Reston Road, (503) 679-7252; **Henry Winery**, Highway 9, Umpqua, (503) 459-5120; and **HillCrest Vineyards**, 240 Vineyard Lane, (503) 673-3709.

Wildlife Safari allows you to drive through rolling country to see a quasi-natural wildlife preserve, with predators discreetly fenced from their prey, and to watch baby animals close up. Daily 9am-8pm, shorter hours in winter; Route 99, four miles west of I-5, exit 119, (503) 679-6761.

Douglas County Museum imaginatively displays logging, fur-trapping, and pioneer items in one of the handsomest contemporary structures you'll find. It's free and open Tuesday-Sunday; off I-5 at the fairgrounds, exit 123, (503) 440-4507.

K&R's Drive Inn dishes out huge scoops of Umpqua ice cream. One scoop is really two; two scoops is actually four. Located 20 miles north of Roseburg, at the Rice Hill exit off I-5; the parking lot is full from before noon to after dark, year-round.

RESTAURANTS

Cafe Espresso
Corner of Douglas and Jackson, (503) 672-1859
368 SE Jackson St,
Roseburg
Inexpensive; no alcohol;
MC, V; local checks OK
Breakfast, lunch
Mon-Fri

It's a smart, sunny cafe with black-and-white tiled floor, red-and-white-checked tablecloths, and Roseburg's only espresso bar. They have good coffee and croissants at breakfast and Italian sodas, soups, and salads for lunch. Daily specials range from beef stroganoff to quiche to lasagne. Low prices and weekday-only hours confirm our hunch that the locals want to keep this place all to themselves.

AZALEA

RESTAURANTS

Heaven on Earth
Exit 86 off I-5,
(503) 837-3596
703 Quines Creek Rd,
Azalea
Moderate; no alcohol; no
credit cards;
local checks OK
Breakfast, lunch, dinner
every day

Heaven this is not, but it's at least partway there. Six-inch-diameter cinnamon rolls weigh in at a pound or more. It's all very quaint; they serve water in canning jars. Food is basic (roast beef, chicken-fried steak) and the soups superior, notably the split pea. Owner Christine Jackson likes to chat with guests, who are usually frequent travelers of I-5.

WOLF CREEK

LODGINGS

Wolf Creek Tavern
Exit 76 off I-5 at 100
Railroad Ave,
(503) 866-2474
Mail: PO Box 97,
Wolf Creek, OR 97497
Inexpensive; MC, V;

An old 1850s stagecoach stop, this inn was purchased by the state and restored in 1979. There are eight guest rooms, seven that rent for about $45 and one larger one for $55. All have private baths. Downstairs there's an attractive parlor and a dining room open to the public for all meals including Sunday brunch. The fare is standard but hearty and inexpensive. It's open

checks OK

year-round (except sometimes in early January). Children are okay; pets are okay with payment of a deposit.

GRANTS PASS

The Rogue is one of Oregon's most beautiful rivers, chiseled into the coastal mountains from here to Gold Beach, protected by the million-acre Siskiyou National Forest, flecked with abandoned gold-mining sites, and inhabited by splendid steelhead and roaming Californians. Two companies offer jet boat tours. **Hellgate Excursions**, (503) 479-7204, departs from the Riverside Inn in Grants Pass. **Jet Boat River Excursions**, (503) 582-0800, leaves from the city of Rogue River, 8 miles upstream. One guide service that conducts wild and daring whitewater trips is **Orange Torpedo Trips**, (503) 479-5061. Or you can hike the Rogue, a very hot trip in the summer; see Gold Beach listing.

RESTAURANTS

Pongsri's
*Take the North Grants
Pass exit off I-5, continue
1 mile, (503) 479-1345
1571 NE 6th St,
Grants Pass
Inexpensive; beer and
wine; MC, V; checks OK
Lunch, dinner Tues-Sun*

You don't need to dress up or bring much money to Don and Pongsri Von Essen's Thai restaurant. Still, you can choose from more than 75 selections. Hot and spicy dishes such as massamam (beef curry with peanuts and potatoes, onions, and coconut milk) are marked on the menu with an asterisk. Order a two-asterisk dish like pla kung—spicy shrimp salad—and be prepared for an adventure.

The Brewery
*North Grants Pass exit off
I-5, 1½ miles to G St,
(503) 479-9850
509 SW G St,
Grants Pass
Moderate; full bar; AE,
MC, V; local checks OK
Lunch Tues-Fri, dinner
Tues-Sun, brunch Sun*

The newest brewery in Grants Pass is in the oldest brewery in town. And, truthfully, we like it best for its comfortable atmosphere and well-brewed beer. The menu, main-line American, only occasionally rises above steak and lobster. Soup and pasta are passable, but the shrimp—sautéed unbreaded in garlic and lemon butter and topped with Parmesan—is superior.

LODGINGS

Paradise Ranch Inn
*Hugo St exit off I-5,
(503) 479-4333
7000-D Monument Dr,
Grants Pass, OR 97526
Expensive; MC, V;
checks OK
Breakfast, dinner Wed-*

Paradise, once a working dude ranch, is now a full-service resort, right in the heart of the verdant Rogue River Valley. Activities abound: fishing for trout or bass, swimming in a heated pool, boating on a 3-acre lake, playing tennis on two lighted courts, riding bicycles or hiking along miles of trails, relaxing in a hot tub. Three holes of an eventual 18-hole golf course have opened. With all this planned action, you might

Sun (every day in summer)

expect a sprawling modern resort, but Paradise Ranch Inn defies that image: there are only 17 large Early American–style guest rooms. Best are those that overlook one of the three ponds. The emphasis is on peace and quiet: no TVs or phones in rooms. The four-bedroom Sunset House on the back 40 is a good choice for a couple of families or small groups. Dinner explores smoked duck, fresh pasta, fresh fish, and rack of lamb; the restaurant is open to non-guests. The menu changes from time to time, and so do the chefs; but all in all, this is a divine getaway.

Riverbanks Inn
8 miles south of town on Hwy 99, then right on Riverbanks Rd for another 8,
(503) 479-1118
8401 Riverbanks Rd,
Grants Pass, OR 97527
Expensive; MC, V;
checks OK

It's on the Rogue, so you'd expect a fine river ambience. You might not expect parklike surroundings with an Oriental garden, a teahouse for meditation, and a therapeutic massage room (Myrtle Franklin, who opened this gorgeous B&B in 1988, is a licensed therapist). The rooms are quite exotic: Caribbean Dream Suite with plantation canopy queen bed draped with Mombasa netting; Rain Forest room wetted with a bar, Jacuzzi, and two private patios; Casablanca furnished with Peruvian carved furniture and tribal carpets. All units have private baths; most have VCRs with a movie selection that corresponds to the room's motif. The emphasis here is on fun and imagination. For breakfast, Franklin often prepares Christmas hash—sausage, red potatoes, and vegetables—or sheepherder's-bread French toast. Smoking is permitted outside only. No pets.

Lawnridge House
Savage and Lawnridge,
(503) 476-8518
1304 NW Lawnridge,
Grants Pass, OR 97526
Moderate; no credit cards;
checks OK

This restored historic (1909) home turned B&B permits easy access to Ashland (45 minutes) or Jacksonville (25 minutes). The place has two suites, each with private bath. One is designed for families; the other has a king-size curtained canopy bed. Breakfasts are Northwest hearty: baked salmon, crab cakes, croissants, and quiche. Innkeeper/chef Barbara Head makes an effort to accommodate special dietary requests, so speak up. Reservations required in winter.

The Washington Inn
North Grants Pass exit,
503) 476-1131
1002 NW Washington
Blvd, Grants Pass,
OR 97526
Moderate; AE, MC, V;
checks OK

In an 1864 National Historic Place, this B&B offers nostalgia as its theme. The three guest rooms are named for the children of owners Maryan and Bill Thompson: Linda's Love Nest, Pattie's Parlor, and Sally's Sunny View. The first two have fireplaces; the last has a canopy bed and, yes—on nice days—a sunny view. Two have private baths; the third shares. For breakfast Maryan makes things like banana splits (minus the ice cream), Belgian waffles and omelets.

JACKSONVILLE

The town started with a boom when gold was discovered in Rich Gulch in 1851. Then the railroad bypassed it, and the tidy little city struggled to avoid becoming a ghost town. Much of the 19th-century city has been restored; Jacksonville now boasts 85 historic homes and buildings open to the public. The strip of authentic Gold Rush-era shops, hotels, and saloons along California Street has become a popular stage set for films, including *The Great Northfield, Minnesota Raid* and the TV movie *Inherit the Wind*. Jacksonville is renowned for antique shops.

Britt Festival, an outdoor music and arts series, runs from late June through September on the hillside field where Peter Britt, a famous local photographer and horticulturist, used to have his home. Listeners gather on benches or flop onto blankets on the grass to enjoy open-stage performances of jazz, bluegrass, folk, country, classical music, musical theatre, and dance. Quality of performances varies, but the series includes big-name artists from the various categories, and listening to the music under a twinkling night sky makes for a memorable evening. Begun in 1963, the festival now draws some 50,000 viewers through the summer. For tickets and information call the Britt Festival office, (503) 773-6077.

Jacksonville Museum, housed in the stately 1883 courthouse, follows the history of the Central Oregon Railroad in the Rogue Valley with plenty of photos and artifacts. Another section displays works of Peter Britt. The adjacent children's museum lets kids walk through various miniaturized pioneer settings (jail, tepee, schoolhouse) and features a collection of the cartoons and memorabilia of Pinto Colvig, the Jacksonville kid who became Bozo the Clown and the voice of Disney's Pluto, Goofy, and three of the Seven Dwarfs; (503) 773-6536.

Valley View Winery, the area's oldest, is at Ruch, five miles west of here; (503) 899-8469.

RESTAURANTS

Jacksonville Inn

On California St, the town's main thoroughfare,
(503) 899-1900
175 E California St, Jacksonville
Moderate; full bar; AE, DC, MC, V; checks OK
Lunch Mon-Sat, dinner every day, brunch Sun

Ask a native to name the area's best, and the answer will often be the Jacksonville Inn. The staff is considerate, and the antique-furnished dining room, housed in the original 1863 building, is elegant and intimate. Executive chef Diane Menzie expertly creates the full realm of continental cuisine: steak, seafood, pasta, plus health-minded low-cholesterol fare and an expanded variety of vegetarian entrées. Dinners can be ordered as a leisurely seven-course feast or à la carte (or save money by ordering from the bistro menu in the lounge); the latter is substantial enough. The petrale sole is a favorite, as are the veal piccata and the beef Richelieu with Madeira sauce. Desserts are lovely European creations. The place is full of locals during weekday lunch. The twice-monthly Opera Pops dinner takes place in the upstairs dining room. Jerry Evans exhibits one of the best-stocked wine cellars in Oregon, with more than 600 domestic and imported labels on hand.

Upstairs, eight refurbished rooms are decorated with 19th-century details: antique four-poster beds, patchwork quilts, and original brickwork on the walls. Modern amenities include private bathrooms and air conditioning (a boon in the 100-degree summer swelter). The rooms, especially the sought-after corner room, are a bit noisy—street sounds easily penetrate the walls. Guests enjoy a full breakfast. Reserve rooms in advance, especially during the Britt Festival.

Bella Union

On California St,
(503) 899-1770
170 W California St,
Jacksonville
Moderate; full bar; AE,
MC, V; checks OK
Lunch, dinner every day

This restaurant, in the original century-old Bella Union Saloon (half of which was constructed when *The Great Northfield, Minnesota Raid* (1969) was filmed in Jacksonville), has grown into a first-rate dinner house with everything from pizza and pasta to elegant dinners to picnic baskets for the summertime Britt Music Festival. The place has a good fresh sheet with choices like Cajun-style swordfish with black bean sauce and salsa, petrale sole with pesto, lingcod, flounder, and steamed mussels. The garden out back is pleasant in warm weather. Proprietor Jerry Hayes is a wine fancier and pours 35 labels by the glass as well as by the bottle.

LODGINGS

Old Stage Inn

Take Oregon St just
beyond Livingston Rd to
883 Old Stage Rd,
(503) 899-1776, or
(800) US-STAGE
Mail: PO Box 579,
Jacksonville, OR 97530
Moderate to expensive;
MC, V; checks OK

This is Jacksonville's classiest B&B: a century-old farmhouse renovated by Hugh and Carla Jones and opened in 1990. There's an extensive library, a parlor, and a formal sitting room with a rare 1865 Hallett & Comston square parlor grand piano. Early guests of the Old Stage Inn have included the governor of Oregon and a German minister of finance. The two rooms with king-size beds (one of them wheelchair-accessible), have their own baths, while two rooms with queen-size beds share a magnificent bath. In her kitchen, the size of a living room in most normal homes, Carla creates breakfasts of homemade breads, poached pears with raspberry purée, and entrées such as croissants stuffed with mushrooms, cheese, and fresh herbs.

McCully House Inn

Follow the signs from I-5
to 5th and E California,
(503) 899-1942
240 E California St,
Jacksonville, OR 97503
Moderate; full bar; MC,
V; checks OK

One of the first six homes in the city, McCully House was built in 1861 for Jacksonville's first doctor, and later housed the first girls' school. It's elegant inside, with hardwood floors, fresh paint, lace curtains, and lovely antiques. The three guest rooms have private baths, and the McCully Room flaunts a fireplace, a claw-footed pedestal tub, and the original black-walnut furnishings that traveled 'round the Horn with JW McCully. Downstairs, the inn's cafe is open to the public, serving creative variations on comfort foods (lamb burgers and chili with cilantro cream at lunch, salmon with cabernet butter sauce and roast rabbit with linguine for dinner).

CENTRAL POINT

RESTAURANTS

Mon Desir
Exit 32 off I-5, east ½
mile to Hamrick, turn
left, down ¼ mile,
(503) 664-6661
4615 Hamrick Rd,
Central Point
Moderate; full bar; AE,
DC, MC, V; checks OK
Dinner every day,
brunch Sun

The mansion was built in 1910 by a Chicago millionaire who had married an actress; no expense was spared. Since it became a restaurant it has at times traded more on its decor and rose gardens than on its food. Current owner Russ Walters and three generations of his family changed that; the ambience is a little less formal and the food a little more appealing. The focus is mainly on steak and seafood, but there are some vegetarian offerings, such as quiche, broccoli crêpes, and cheese lasagne. The cream of zucchini soup has acquired a following. The atmosphere is still grand: chandeliers, ornate bars, Victorian furniture, and three acres of manicured lawn and rose gardens.

SHADY COVE/TRAIL

The Upper Rogue area, between Medford and Crater Lake, offers some of the region's most invigorating scenery—rugged mountains, timbered hillsides, and whitewater rapids.

RESTAURANTS

Bel Di's
North side of Shady
Cove's bridge, first drive
after BP station,
(503) 878-2010
21900 Hwy 62,
Shady Cove
Moderate; full bar; MC,
V; checks OK
Dinner Tues-Sun

Ray and Joan Novosad took over this riverside country dinner house a couple of years ago and have maintained the quality that makes it a special place. The dining room has a grand view of the Rogue River. The full dinner is served with elegance, but you're out in the boonies and don't need to dress up. The overall ambience, the attentive service, and the fine soups and salad dressing are more special than many of the entrées, but try the scampi or the Louisiana stuffed prawns. If your visit comes in summertime, ask about the float trip package: an escorted 2½-hour ride down the Rogue River, followed by dinner. It's great fun.

Rogue River Lodge
25 miles from Medford on
Hwy 62, (503) 878-2555
24904 Hwy 62, Trail
Moderate; full bar; AE,
MC, V; checks OK
Dinner every day

The oldest dinner house in Jackson County has been owned by ex–Navy man Ken Meirstin for nearly two decades now. The walls are decorated with his collection of ship paintings. Dory, his wife, supervises the cooking here and maintains a high standard of consistent quality with a somewhat predictable menu: steaks, scampi, teriyaki chicken, and prime rib (on weekends). The view of the Rogue isn't as good as at Bel Di's down the road, but the locals like the place.

MEDFORD

Southern Oregon's largest city may not win any contests with nearby towns for prettiness, but it is the center of things in this part of the world. The city is well known across the nation due to the marketing efforts of Harry and David, the mail-order giant known for its pears, other fruit, and condiments.

Harry and David's Original Country Store, Highway 99 south of town, offers "seconds" from gift packs and numerous other items, as well as tours of the complex, which is also the home of **Jackson & Perkins,** the world's largest rose growers. The firm ships from Medford, although most of the flowers are grown in California, (503) 776-2277.

The Grub Street Grill, the Rogue Valley's best pub, serves up Irish stout as well as Northwest microbrews, (503) 779-2635.

River rafting on a nearby stretch of the Rogue, between Gold Hill and the city of Rogue River, is safe for beginners. You can rent a raft at River Trips in Gold Hill, (503) 855-7238, or try one of the shop's Rogue Drifters, a large sack filled with styrofoam balls.

The Oregon Vortex at the House of Mystery, between Medford and Grants Pass, is a "whirlpool of force" that causes some people to experience strange phenomena such as an inability to stand erect and apparent changes in the laws of perspective; 18 miles northwest of Medford on Sardine Creek Road, Gold Hill, (503) 855-1543. Closed in winter.

RESTAURANTS

Hungry Woodsman
Just down from the Rogue Valley Mall,
(503) 772-2050
2001 N Pacific Hwy,
Medford
Moderate; full bar; AE, DC, MC, V; no checks
Lunch Mon-Fri, dinner every day

Bob LaFontaine, owner of a Medford hardware store, tired of the rowdy nightclub next door, bought it 17 years ago, tore it down, and erected the Hungry Woodsman. The building is a testimonial to the forest products industry. Old saws, photos, and other logging memorabilia adorn the walls. The menu is pretty basic: steak, prime rib, shrimp, crab, lobster. You're probably best off with a steak or an English cut of prime rib; crab tends to be too pricey here. Locals like the Woodsman, as they call it. Few patrons dress up; the waiters wear jeans.

The Sandpiper
Take the Barnett Rd exit east off I-5,
(503) 779-0100
1841 Barnett Rd,
Medford
Moderate; full bar; AE, DC, MC, V; no checks
Dinner every day

Although part of a chain (four of the five other Sandpipers are in Idaho), the Medford branch offers the sincere service and quality food that one associates with smaller operations. The fresh sheet here is the city's best. Salmon and lingcod are mainstays. On the regular menu, try the brandied pork or Steak Sandpiper, a classic bacon-wrapped filet served with both béarnaise and burgundy sauces. The pretty, split-level dining room has lots of flowers and soft lighting. The lounge is very popular with young singles during weekends and late in the evening, so you may want to plan accordingly.

LODGINGS

Under the Greenwood Tree

Exit 27 off I-5, Barnett
#27 to Stewart, left on
Hull, right on Bellinger,
(503) 776-0000
3045 Bellinger Lane,
Medford, OR 97501
Expensive; MC, V;
checks OK

Its name refers to a popular Elizabethan song that appears in *As You Like It.* And it certainly is: green lawns, 300-year-old trees, and a 10-acre farm with an orchard, riding ring, beautiful rose gardens and gazebo, and antique farm buildings. The 1862 home has four guest rooms, each with private bath. Innkeeper Renate Ellam, a Cordon Bleu chef, goes all out. Guests who arrive by 4:30pm receive British-style afternoon tea, and her elaborate three-course breakfasts may include dishes like vanilla-poached pears with Chantilly cream or strawberry blintzes with eggs-and-yogurt filling and strawberry preserves.

Red Lion Inn

Right off I-5; look for the
signs, (503) 779-5811
200 N Riverside Ave,
Medford, OR 97501
Moderate; AE, DC, MC,
V; checks OK

It's only a Red Lion, smack in the middle of Motel Row and smack in the middle of the price range. But it's the best of its kind. Some units overlook a small creek, which in turn overlooks I-5. A better strategy is to get a room facing the small inner courtyard with garden and pool. The restaurant isn't bad, the only place in town with tableside flambé, if you're into that sort of thing. Nothing keeps locals from their favorite brunch.

TALENT

RESTAURANTS

Chata

Talent exit off I-5; watch
for signs, (503) 535-2575
1212 S Pacific Hwy,
Talent
Moderate; full bar; MC,
V; checks OK
Dinner every day

The name (pronounced HAH-tah) means "cottage" in Polish, but the restaurant is neither small nor strictly Polish. The eastern and central European menu features dishes like *bigos*, Polish hunter's stew, and *mamaliga de aur* ("bread of gold")—Romanian cornmeal cakes sprinkled with cheese and served in a sauce of mushrooms, cream, and wine. Owners Jozef and Eileen Slowikowski have had the smooth service and splendid consistency in the food down to a practiced art—which they are now gradually turning over to their children. On our last visit we chose the Yugoslav *juvec*, with layers of pork roast and vegetables swimming in tomato sauce. Our seafood selection—curried lingcod with vegetables—was equally fine. The wine list presents Oregon labels side by side with white riesling from Yugoslavia, among others from that region. And, of course, there's Polish vodka and Serbian plum brandy.

New Sammy's Cowboy Bistro

Halfway between Talent
and Ashland on Hwy 99
(Pacific Hwy),

Proprietors Vernon and Charleen Rollins do no advertising, rely entirely on word of mouth (they didn't even want us to include them here). There's no sign other than a flashing light at night. And the outside looks barely a cut above a shack. Inside, though, is as

(503) 535-2779
2210 S Pacific Hwy,
Talent
*Moderate; wine only; no
credit cards; checks OK
Dinner Wed-Sun*

charming a dinner house as you're likely to find in southern Oregon. There are just six tables; reservations are a must. The French-inspired menu usually lists just a handful of entrées—salmon, veal stew, a beef dish (the New York steak was perfectly cooked). The wine list is extensive: 40 choices from Oregon, California, and French wineries.

Arbor House

*Talent Ave to the RR
tracks, west on Wagner,*
(503) 535-6817
*103 W Wagner St, Talent
Moderate; beer and wine;
no credit cards;
checks OK
Dinner Wed-Sun*

The exterior, recently enhanced by a Japanese garden, is still modest enough to fool you. Aging granola types consider this place a find, as it remains surprisingly congenial—one of the most comfortable restaurants in the Rogue Valley. The menu ranges the world—vegetarian plates, curries, sauerbraten, jambalaya, enchiladas, eggplant parmigiana, and good old American steak. Not open on Wednesdays in winter.

ASHLAND

The remarkable success of the Oregon Shakespeare Festival, now over 50 years old, has transformed this sleepy town into one with, per capita, the best tourist amenities in the region. The Festival now draws a total audience of nearly 350,000 through the eight-month season, filling its theaters to an extraordinary 94 percent capacity. Visitors pour into this town of 17,000, spawning fine shops, restaurants, and bed-and-breakfast places as they do. Amazingly, the town still has its soul: for the most part, it seems a happy little college town, set amid lovely ranch country, that just happens to house the fifth-largest theater company in the land.

The Festival mounts plays in three theaters. In the outdoor Elizabethan Theatre, which seats 1,200, appear the famous and authentic nighttime productions of Shakespeare (three different plays) each summer. Stretching from February to October, the season for the two indoor theaters includes comedies, contemporary fare, and some experimental works; in these the large repertory company is more likely to excel, for Shakespeare outdoors takes a toll on voices and subtlety. Visit the Exhibit Center, where you can clown around in costumes from plays past. There are also lectures and concerts at noon, excellent backstage tours each morning, Renaissance music and dance nightly in the courtyard—plus all the nearby daytime attractions of river rafting, picnicking, and historical touring. The best way to get information and tickets (last-minute tickets in the summer are rare) is through a comprehensive agency: Southern Oregon Reservation Center, (503) 488-1011, (800) 547-8052; PO Box 477, Ashland, OR 97520. Festival box office is (503) 482-4331.

Actor's Theatre of Ashland, Ashland's growing experimental theater productions (often called **Off Shakespeare** or **Off Bardway**), are worth checking into. Festival actors often join in these small companies, giving audiences a chance to see Shakespearean actors having a bit of fun and going out on a theatrical limb. A

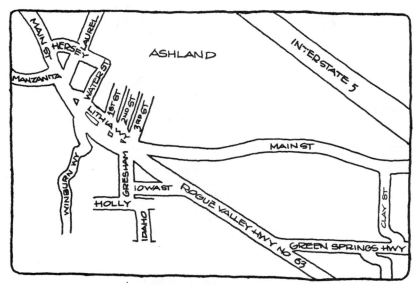

full listing of productions is available at the Chamber of Commerce, 110 E Main, (503) 482-3486.

Oregon Cabaret Theatre presents musicals and comedies through much of the year. Caterer Tracy Darling supervises a menu of dinners, hors d'oeuvres, and desserts for theater patrons, as well as European country fare, in her new Primavera Restaurant, First and Hargadine Streets, (503) 488-2902.

Touring. The Rogue River Recreation Area has fine swimming for the sizzling summer days, as does the lovely Applegate River. Twenty-two scenic miles up Dead Indian Road is Howard Prairie Lake Resort, where you can camp, park your trailer, shower, rent a boat, and fish all day; (503) 482-1979.

Mount Ashland Ski Area, (503) 482-2897, 18 miles south of town, offers 22 runs for all classes of skiers, Thanksgiving to April.

Lithia Park. Designed by the creator of San Francisco's Golden Gate Park, Ashland's central park runs for 100 acres behind the outdoor theater, providing a lovely mix of duck ponds, Japanese gardens, grassy lawns, playgrounds, groomed or dirt trails for hikes and jogging, and the pungent mineral water that gave the park its name. Great for picnicking, especially after stocking up at nearby Greenleaf Deli (49 N Main, (503) 482-2808).

Manna From Heaven Bakery is a distinguished Old World bakery famous for elaborate breads and pastries, plus good coffee. Definitely worth a visit for breakfast. 358 E Main Street, (503) 482-5831.

Mark Antony Hotel. This downtown landmark is of some historic interest. The hotel fell on hard economic times in the 1970s and '80s, with several changes of ownership. But ownership has stabilized and food service has improved notably in recent months; 212 E Main Street, (503) 482-1721.

Weisinger Ashland Winery, Ashland Vineyards and **Rogue Brewery & Public House** offer opportunities to sample Ashland products. The Weisinger winery is snuggled in a Bavarian-style building; the gift shop offers jams, jellies, sauces and, of course, their wines for sale (Highway 99 just outside Ashland, (503) 488-5989). Ashland Vineyards is near the Highway 66 exit from I-5. Turn north onto

East Main Street and follow signs; (503) 488-0088. Wash down a sandwich or a pizza with a Golden Ale at the Brewery, located at 31-B Water Street—a good place to unwind after a day of theater; (503) 488-5061.

RESTAURANTS

Chateaulin

Down the walkway from Angus Bowmer Theatre, (503) 482-2264 50 E Main, Ashland Moderate; full bar; AE, DC, MC, V; checks OK Dinner every day

Less than a block from the theaters you'll find a romantic cafe reminiscent of New York's upper West Side; the dark wood-and-brick dining rooms (one is nonsmoking) are accented with copper kettles hung from the ceiling and displays of vintage wine bottles. During the Shakespeare season, the place bustles with before- and after-theater crowds gathered for the fine French cuisine or for drinks at the bar. House specialties are pâtés and veal dishes, but seafood is also impressive; the delicate butterflied shrimp in a subtle sauce of sherry, cream, tomato, and brandy, were delicious. Chef David Taub and co-owner Michael Donovan change the menu seasonally, and several daily specials feature seasonal entrées prepared with classical French flair. The "cafe menu" is a favorite of the after-show crowd: baked goat cheese marinated in olive oil on featherweight squares of toast, an outrageous onion soup. Service is polished and smooth even during the rush of theater crowds. The owners have recently opened a small shop inside, "Chateaulin Selections," which features rare and gourmet foods and fine wines.

China Korea

Across from Chamber of Commerce, (503) 488-0235 139 E Main, Ashland Moderate; full bar; MC, V; local checks only Dinner Tues-Sat

Busy Ashland restaurateur Beasy McMillan has a place for almost every taste, Macaroni's for Italian, Beasy's for steaks, Thai Pepper for Thai and Señor Gator's for Mexican—all sharing facilities with the seasonal (outdoor) Backporch Barbecue. His newest is this Chinese and Korean outpost. It's a busy place where with a beautiful view of the Ashland hills. People pack the place primarily for the Korean specialties (faintly smoked ginger chicken served on top chinese vegetables). The bulgoki is excellent as are the Chinese greens. You'll do best to start with the salmon and cream cheese wrapping in a crispy dough and to end with cheese cake.

Primavera

Below Oregon Cabaret Theatre, (503) 488-1994 241-A Hargadine, Ashland Moderate; beer and wine; MC, V; checks OK Dinner Wed-Sun (days vary in summer)

Even if you find the bold red, blue, and orange decor a bit much, wait for the appetizers—they're among the best in Southern Oregon. Spring rolls filled with duck, served with a raspberry catsup, will forever alter your feelings about both duck and catsup. The warm roasted garlic soup with pesto and lavender was perfectly balanced. Chévre is served grilled on toast or in grape leaves. Or try the grilled zucchini served with pesto and roasted-red-bell-pepper mayonnaise. Entrées usually include beef, duck, chicken, and a vegetarian choice or two. None reach the inspiration or execution of the appetizers, but they are still very good and like the halibut with mustard and fennel with a tomato coulis, capture intense, clean, flavors. Desserts, like everything else, are made on the premises. A thoughtfully selected wine list complements the food. No smoking. The garden is a gorgeous place for a midsummer's night dinner.

The Winchester Country Inn
Half a block from Main St, (503) 488-1113
35 S 2nd St, Ashland
Moderate; full bar; MC, V; checks OK
Dinner every day, brunch Sun (closed Mon in winter)

Pay a visit to the Winchester when you feel like being pampered. You sit amid crisp country furnishings on the slightly sunken ground floor of this century-old Queen Anne–style home and look out on tiers of neatly snipped garden outside. The staff attends to your every need. Chef Mark Warriner creates from an ambitious range of entrées, from roast duck with mango bigarade sauce to Vietnamese marinated broiled *teng dah* beef to lamb du jour to Oregon rabbit. The baked apple in a pretty puff pastry deserves an encore. Smoking was recently banned from the dining room.

In addition to being one of Ashland's finer restaurants, the Winchester provides seven antique-furnished guest rooms upstairs. Guests are treated to full breakfasts.

Green Springs Inn
17½ miles east Ashland, (503) 482-0614
11470 Hwy 66, Ashland
Moderate; beer and wine; AE, MC, V; no checks
Breakfast, lunch, dinner every day

Here's an escape from the tourist crowds of Ashland—a cozy, rustic spot dishing up Italian specialties in the midst of the splendid hills. Ernie and Diane Croteau are the new owners, and their restaurant doubles as a neighborhood convenience store. The 35-minute drive through the red-soil hills, jutting cliffs, and thick evergreens is worth the trip in itself, especially if you want to hike or cross-country ski along the Pacific Crest Trail that runs ¼ mile from the restaurant. The hearty soups, sandwiches, and 12 different pasta dishes make this a welcome stopping point. Our black bean soup was a generous dish, rich and lightly garlicked—perfect when lapped up with sweet, just-baked brown bread.

Il Giardino
1½ blocks from Shakespeare Festival, (503) 488-0816
#5 Granite St, Ashland
Moderate; beer and wine; MC, V; local checks only
Lunch Thurs-Fri, dinner Tues-Sun

Order the risotto when you place your reservation—it's as close to Italy as you'll get without a plane ticket. It's not on the menu and it's time-consuming to make, but Franco Minniti and Maurizio Contartese love to cook and are anxious to please. Both are recent immigrants from Italy and know just enough English to be dangerously charming. If Minniti and Contartese don't win your heart their capellini con pomidoro and basilico (angel-hair pasta with tomato and basil) will. The carpaccio is a flawless antipasto, and the black ravioli with salmon, tarragon, and cream sauce is one of Il Giardino's most popular entrées. Still, there's an obvious lack of confidence here, a simple dish like the chicken Marsala was way overcooked and the nervous service, on one visit, destroyed the mood the owners try so hard to set.

Thai Pepper

Main St near Water St,
(503) 482-8058
84 N Main St, Ashland
Moderate; beer and wine;
MC, V; local checks only
Lunch Tues-Sat, dinner
every day

Another Beasy MacMillan restaurant and, yes, he has done it again. His Thai restaurant has become another Ashland favorite. Even though true Thai connoisseurs might cringe while perusing the menu, locals don't seem to mind that not a word of Thai appears on the menu or that the dishes listed would be rarities in Bangkok. Even if they're not entirely authentic, items like tiger rolls (cream cheese, crab, and shrimp) and garlic pork with coriander and fresh chile are popular.

LODGINGS

Chanticleer
Bed & Breakfast Inn

2 blocks from the library
off Main St,
(503) 482-1919
120 Gresham St,
Ashland, OR 97520
Expensive; MC, V;
checks OK

Despite growing competition, Chanticleer has maintained its roost as the preferred B&B through nearly a decade of Shakespeare seasons now—mostly due to hosts Jim and Nancy Beaver's extraordinarily high standards. The home has an uncluttered country charm, with an open-hearth fireplace in the spacious sitting room and carefully chosen antiques throughout, plus the plush extras of fresh-cut flowers, imported soaps and lotions in the rooms, and scripts of all the plays running at the Shakespeare Festival. In the morning, a lavish breakfast is served in the dining room or (on request) brought to your room for breakfast in bed. It's a setting that promises to rejuvenate your soul. . . and your romance. There are seven rooms: Aerie and Fleur overlook Bear Creek Valley and the foothills of the Cascade range, and the Chanticleer Suite provides guests with two bedrooms, full kitchen, parlor stove, private bath, and private garden outside. Chanticleer is 4 blocks from the theaters, but surprisingly quiet. Make reservations early. No smoking.

Mount Ashland Inn

Follow signs to Mt.
Ashland Ski Area,
(503) 482-8707
550 Mt Ashland Rd,
Ashland, OR 97520
Expensive; MC, V;
Checks OK

Wind your way up Mt. Ashland Road and you discover a huge, custom-made two-story log cabin. This is the dream home of Jerry and Elaine Shanafelt, who designed and built the lodge in 1987, using some 275 cedar trees cut from their 160-acre property in the Siskiyous. The magnificent inn is more posh inside than you'd expect from a log house; golden aromatic-cedar logs, high beamed ceilings, large windows, and a huge stone fireplace. Examples of Jerry's handiwork are seen throughout the house: stained-glass windows, a spiral cedar staircase with madrona railing. Guests sleep in handcrafted beds covered with elaborate patchwork quilts, and each of the five units has a private bath. Try for the new Sky Lakes suite with a two-person whirlpool bathtub, king-size bed, wet bar, private entrance and a sitting room, plus a view of Mt. McLoughlin. A new meeting room makes this an ideal inn for an 8- to 10-person retreat. Be prepared for snow (November to April). No smoking.

Romeo Inn
Idaho and Holly,
(503) 488-0884
295 Idaho St, Ashland,
OR 97520
Expensive; MC, V;
checks OK

This imposing Cape Cod home has four plush guest rooms and two suites decorated in contemporary and antique furnishings. The spacious rooms, all have king-size beds—covered with hand-stitched Amish quilts—phones, and private baths; the Stratford suite is a separate structure with its own bedroom, bath, and kitchen; it features a vaulted ceiling with skylight, a marble-tiled fireplace, and a raised whirlpool bathtub-for-two. Owners Bruce and Margaret Halverson recently gave up their own quarters to create the second suite, the Cambridge, with fireplace, patio, and private entrance. There's a baby grand piano in the living room, and the heated pool and hot tub on the large back deck are open year-round. No smoking, please.

The generous breakfast of baked fruit, specialty main course (chosen from 40 possibilities), and fresh baked goods reportedly satisfies through dinnertime. The Halversons keep a computerized record of what they served you last time, so regular clientele never get the same meal twice. Clever.

Country Willows
4 blocks south on Clay St
from Siskiyou Blvd,
(503) 488-1590
1313 Clay St, Ashland,
OR 97520
Moderate to expensive;
MC, V; checks OK

Set on five acres of farmland six minutes from downtown Ashland, this rebuilt 1896 country home offers peace and quiet and a lovely view of the hills. Bill and Barbara Huntley offer five rooms and two suites, with air conditioning and private baths, plus a swimming pool and a newly built hot tub on the large back deck. The best room is, well, in the barn: it has a two-person soaking tub, fireplace, and private deck. Breakfast is presented on a pretty sun porch. The grounds outside offer running and hiking trails; and the owners keep a small flock of ducks, a gaggle of geese, and a herd of horses on the property. No smoking, please.

Fox House Inn
2nd and B off Main,
(503) 488-1055
269 B St, Ashland,
OR 97520
Expensive; no credit
cards; checks OK

★★

Jim and Jacqueline Sims remodeled an early Victorian home to create this two-bedroom inn that offers guests the utmost privacy, perfect for families or two couples traveling together. The rooms (no smoking) are furnished with brass beds with half-canopies and private baths with claw-footed tubs. The Garden Room downstairs, highlighted with stained and etched glasswork, opens into an enclosed flower garden. Annabel's Suite upstairs is well suited for a romantic getaway: guests have the entire second story, with private sitting room and dressing room, and a lavish satin-and-lace bedroom. Breakfast, of course.

Arden Forest Inn
On Hersey at Laurel,

Walking distance from Shakespeare, this remodeled folk (but not folksy) farmhouse is a refreshing change of

(503) 488-1496
261 Hersey, Ashland,
OR 97520
Moderate; AE, MC, V;
checks OK

pace from the antique motif that abounds in bed and breakfasts. The light and airy living room and each of the four guest rooms are decorated with lovely examples of host/artist Audrey Sochor's vividly hued paintings. Host/Shakespeare teacher Art Sochor's extensive theater library is available for guests' perusal, and the longtime theater buff welcomes chats with his show-bound guests. The hosts have made the common room and three of the bedrooms wheelchair-accessible. The two carriage-house rooms offer optimum privacy, and all rooms have private baths and air conditioning. Children are welcome, smoking is not.

Cowslip's Belle

3 blocks north of the
theaters on Main,
(503) 488-2901
159 N Main St, Ashland,
OR 97520
Moderate; MC, V;
checks OK

Unintentionally named after a song in *A Midsummer-Night's Dream*, the home has a cheery charm with its swing chair on the front porch, vintage furniture and fresh flowers inside. There are two lovely bedrooms in the main house, two more in a romantic carriage house in the back, with extra privacy. A main attraction here is proximity to the theaters, downtown, and Lithia Park, three to four blocks away.

Morical House

Exit 19 from I-5, turn left
onto Hwy 99,
(503) 482-2254
668 N Main St, Ashland,
OR 97520
Expensive; MC, V;
checks OK

This large farmhouse dates back to the 1880s. Its proximity to busy Main Street somewhat takes away from its ambience, but owners Patricia and Peter Dahl have worked hard to soundproof the five bedrooms and provide back-yard views into the fields and mountains beyond. The rooms are furnished with antiques, handmade quilts, and family heirlooms. The attractive grounds include a putting green and a place to play croquet. Breakfasts are substantial. As with most B&Bs, smoking is permitted outside only. Children over 12 are welcome; pets are not.

Windmill's Ashland Hills Inn

Hwy 66 exit from I-5,
(503) 482-8310
2525 Ashland St,
Ashland, OR 97520
Moderate; AE, DC, MC,
V; checks OK

For those who prefer motels to B&Bs, this is the best Ashland has to offer, with 159 rooms, several elegant suites, a pool, and tennis courts. The food is not bad; locals like the Sunday brunch. The banquet area, Ashland's largest, plays host to everything from wine-tastings to formal balls.

CAVE JUNCTION

Though the tight quarters can get awfully packed with tourists, the **Oregon Caves National Monument** is a group of intriguing formations of marble and limestone. Tours leave periodically each day year-round. They are a bit strenuous, and the caves are a chilly 41 degrees. Children under 6 are allowed if they meet the height requirement. However, babysitting service is available. Arrive early during summertime, or you may have a long wait; (503) 592-3400.

LODGINGS

Oregon Caves Chateau
Route 46, 20 miles east of Cave Junction, follow signs, (503) 592-3400
Mail: PO Box 128, Cave Junction, OR 97523
Moderate; MC, V; checks OK
Open June through September

This fine old wooden lodge is set amid tall trees and a deep canyon. Doors don't always close properly, but the place is restful. The sound of falling water from numerous nearby mountain streams will help lull you to sleep. Views are splendid, the public rooms have the requisite massive fireplaces, and the down-home cooking in the dining room is quite good. The wine list features lots of local bottlings. There are 22 rooms in the lodge—nothing fancy, but clean.

OREGON CASCADES

The Columbia River Gorge—Troutdale to The Dalles—followed by two easterly Cascade crossings: Sandy to Mount Hood in the north, McKenzie Bridge to Bend mid-state. Finally, a southward progression through the heart of the mountains to Klamath Falls.

COLUMBIA RIVER GORGE

The wild Columbia has been dammed into near lakehood, but its fjord like majesty is part magnificent waterfalls, part dramatic cliffs and rock formations cut by the country's second-largest river, and part wind tunnel. Watch for the colorful fleet of sailboarders who have made this stretch of the river world-renowned.

Most of the traffic is out on I-84, which leaves the old **Columbia Gorge Scenic Highway (Route 30)** for take-your-time wanderers. This 22-mile detour traverses the waterfall-riddled stretch from Troutdale to Ainsworth Park. Popular viewpoints and attractions are as follows: **Crown Point**, 725 feet above the river, features an English Tudor–style vista house. Below, at Rooster Rock State Park, one of the attractions is a nude bathing beach. **Larch Mountain**, 14 miles upriver from Crown Point, is even more spectacular than the more famous overlooks. **Multnomah Falls** ranks second highest in the country at 620 feet (in two steps). **Multnomah Falls Lodge**, (503) 695-2376, at the foot of the falls, was designed in 1925 by Albert E. Doyle, of Benson Hotel fame, in a rustic stone style. Now a National Historic Landmark, the lodge houses a naturalists' and a popular visitors' center. It also has a large restaurant that is a good stop for breakfast, but dinners are unremarkable (better just to go for dessert). **Oneonta Gorge** is a narrow, dramatic cleft through which a slippery half-mile trail winds to secluded Oneonta Falls. **Bonneville Dam**, the first Federal dam on the Columbia, offers tours of the dam, the fish ladders (seen through underwater viewing windows), and the navigational locks; (503) 374-8820. You can tour the Bonneville Fish Hatchery (next to the dam) year-round; however, the best time is in September and November when the Chinook are spawning; (503) 374-8393.

The old highway disappears briefly at Hood River; it picks up again between Mosier and The Dalles, where the forests give way to grasslands, and the clouds vanish. Wildflowers abound from February to May.

TROUTDALE

RESTAURANTS

Tad's Chicken 'n' Dumplings
Exit 18 off I-84,
(503) 666-5337
943 SE Crown Point
Troutdale
Moderate; full bar; AE,

A down-home country restaurant, 20 miles east of Portland as you head up the Columbia Gorge, this decades-old Oregon institution is popular with kids, bargain-hungry families, tourists—and fanciers of chicken. You can make quite an evening of it: a drink on the back deck, dinner at a window table where you can

MC, V; checks OK
Dinner every day

watch the sunset, a family-style meal (you should know what to order), topped off with ice cream or homemade pie. The place is usually packed, so call ahead to get on the waiting list, particularly for Sunday dinner.

CASCADE LOCKS

Before the dams, the riverboats often foundered on nasty rapids here. Locks smoothed things out; their remains are the centerpiece of the town's Marina Park. A fine little museum at the **Bridge of the Gods** explains the legend of the rapids. There are also the Port of Cascade Locks Visitor Center, a sailboard launch and oodles of picnic spots. The **Sternwheeler Columbia Gorge** revives the Columbia's riverboat past; there are three trips daily and extra lunch, brunch, and dinner cruises, mid-June through the end of September, with stops at Bonneville Dam and Stevenson Landing; (503) 374-8427.

RESTAURANTS

CharBurger Restaurant
Cascade Locks off I-84,
(503) 374-8477
714 SW Wa-Na-Pa St,
Cascade Locks
Moderate; full bar; MC,
V; checks OK
Breakfast, lunch, dinner
every day, brunch Sun

Service is cafeteria style in this barny place high on a bluff; get a window table for the view through the trees to the river below. Amid hokey, Old West decor, you choose from a truck-stop standard menu. Enjoy portions of all-American roadhouse food at a reasonable price. Best is the bakery, in which you can buy warm, homemade cinnamon and pecan rolls for just a buck apiece, and marvelous cookies. Downstairs there's a mediocre attempt at "fine dining."

LODGINGS

Scandian Motor Lodge
Wa-Na-Pa St in town,
(503) 374-8417
Mail: PO Box 217,
Cascade Locks,
OR 97014
Inexpensive; AE, DC,
MC, V; no checks

Norway wandered west and landed here. The large rooms are woodsy, with bright Scandinavian colors and tiled baths (one with a sauna). Try for an upstairs room near the office for the best river views. Even in these, the rates are quite reasonable. Very clean and not too much *Uff da!* There are several nonsmoking rooms. Reserve early for summer months.

HOOD RIVER

Fruit orchards are everywhere. Hood River is ideally located on the climatic cusp between the wetter west side and the drier east side of the Cascades, alongside the mighty Columbia, so it gets the sun *and* enough moisture (about 31 inches annually) to keep the creeks flowing and the orchards bearing. Thirty miles to the south, 11,245-foot Mount Hood supervises; however, from the town itself, the views are of Washington's Mount Adams, the Columbia, and its ubiquitous

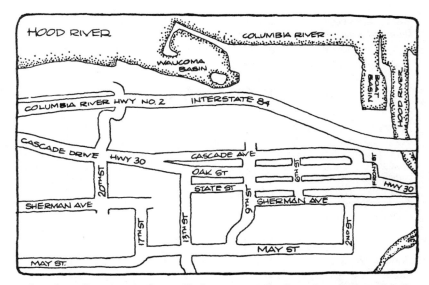

saiboarders. In town, you're as likely to see orchard workers as boardheads, two-inch steaks as espresso. New restaurants, inns, and shops are constantly opening (and closing) in flux with the high and low seasons.

Visitors come to hike, fish, climb, and ski on Mount Hood and Mount Adams. In between is the Columbia river. And on it are the boardheads who can't get enough of the famous winds that blow in at that ideal opposite-to-the-current direction. At least 27 local businesses cater to the sailboard crowd; several offer lessons and rentals, and all will tell you where the winds are on any given day. The **West Jetty** and **Columbia Gorge Sailpark/Marina** are favorites. The latter also features a fitness course, a marina, and a cafe.

As locals strongly attest, there was life in Hood River before sailboarders descended. Native American artifacts are on exhibit in the **Hood River County Museum**; (503) 386-6772, open 10am-4pm Wednesday through Saturday, 10am-5pm Sunday, April through October, or when flags are flying. The town's Visitor Information Center adjoins, though it's inexplicably closed on winter weekends; (503) 386-2000.

Orchards and vineyards are the valley's other economic mainstays. The wonderful small-town **Blossom Festival** (mid-April) celebrates the flower-to-fruit cycle. From Highway 35 you can catch the vista of the orchards fanning out from the north slopes of **Mount Hood Scenic Railroad**. The Fruit Blossom Special departs the quaint Hood River depot April through December. You can buy the fruit bounty at **The Fruit Tree** near the Columbia Gorge Hotel, or at **River Bend Country Store** (2363 Tucker Road; (503) 386-8766 or toll-free (800) 755-7568); the latter specializes in organically grown produce. Or visit the tasting rooms of the **Three Rivers Winery**, 275 Country Club Road, (503) 386-5453; the **Hood River Vineyards**, 4693 Westwood Drive, (503) 386-3772, known for its pear and raspberry dessert wines; or **Elk Cove Vineyards Tasting Room** at The Marketplace at Hood River Village, (503) 386-9466. Beer aficionados will head for the **WhiteCap BrewPub**, 506 Columbia Street, (503) 386-2247, for handcrafted Full Sail ales and light meals. The outdoor deck (live music on weekends) provides a fitting place for tired sailboarders to unwind while keeping the river in sight.

For a breath-taker, head half a mile south of town on Highway 35 to **Panorama Point.** Or go east on I-84, exit at Mosier, and climb to the **Rowena Crest Viewpoint** on old Highway 30; the grandstand Columbia River view is complemented by a wildflower show in the Tom McCall Preserve, maintained by the Nature Conservancy. **The Coffee Spot** (Oak Street and 1st, (503) 386-1772) is a good spot to pick up sandwiches for a picnic.

RESTAURANTS

Peter B's
13th and B streets,
(503) 386-2111
1302 13th St,
Hood River
Moderate; full bar; MC,
V; checks OK
Dinner every day

Peter B's is the happy metamorphosis of the former Reflections of the Past, located in one of the few charming houses left that's not a bed and breakfast. Peter Bollinger's place is gracious and very good. Chef Nan Bains ventures broadly, but fish is her thing. There's an ahi with black beans and saffron rice, a really garlicky fettuccine alfredo, and a spicy prawn and scallop curry with homemade pear chutney. Specials are a little more adventurous and equally successful: two recent ones were a sautéed morel appetizer and Oriental prawns with a mango/ginger/vinegar sauce. On one visit it took two convicted chocoholics to finish the Belgian chocolate cake with raspberry sauce.

Stonehedge Inn
Exit 62 off I-84,
(503) 386-3940
3405 Cascade Dr,
Hood River
Moderate; full bar; AE,
DC, MC, V; checks OK
Dinner Wed-Sun

Beyond the funky markers and up a mildly rutted gravel drive to this turn-of-the-century summer estate, owner Jean Harmon makes you instantly at home. She'll get the kids looking through her stereopticon viewer and tell the history behind each decoration as she leads you to a table in the fire-warmed and dark-paneled main room, the garden-viewing porch room, the homey library, or the intimate bar. Chef Patrick Edwards' pâté is delectable, as were the appetizers (spicy pepper-rubbed smoked salmon and Willapa Bay oysters on the half shell), and the cabbage-caraway soup is delicious. Meats are Edwards' forte. The rack of lamb, deglazed in rosemary, wine, and other herbs, was perfectly pink. Skip the accompanying mint sauce (bottled). There were, however, a few disappointments: no more of the warm rosemary bread we used to love; the famous twice-baked potato tasted as though it was also twice-salted; and the salad appeared thoughtlessly prepared. Nevertheless, the sincere service and general high quality keep this on our favorites list.

Chianti's Ristorante
6th and Cascade,
(503) 386-5737
509 Cascade St,
Hood River
Moderate; full bar; AE,
MC, V; checks OK

The casual congeniality of a drop-in Italian restaurant fits snugly into Hood River. Chianti's is a bustling spot with a menu of about eight pastas, a half dozen meat or seafood specials, and a few salads. It's all no-nonsense food: a robust, creamy Caesar; pollo fettuccine, fragrant with rosemary; rosemary-flecked bread sticks; and big bowls of hearty spaghetti-for-two. Hang around

Lunch Mon-Fri, dinner every day

awhile with your coffee: the day's best sailboarding stories are sure to be overheard from the next table.

The Mesquitery
12th and B streets,
(503) 386-2002
1219 12th St, Hood River
Inexpensive; beer and wine; MC, V; checks OK
Lunch Mon-Fri, dinner Mon-Sat

The mesquite grill takes center stage here. It's housed in a glass-enclosed frame surrounded by booths and small tables. So it's barbecue—not super-hot, but A-OK. There are baby back ribs, a chicken combo, pollo vaquero (grilled chicken to roll in tortillas with pico de gallo), and fish, including a recent special: tender, moist halibut in a ginger/lime/honey sauce. Fill up with soup or salad, a roll, and two of eight side dishes, from coleslaw to barbecued baked beans to fettuccine pesto. The apple crisp à la mode is dandy; so are the service and the bill. A good, nonsmoking place to bring the kids, too.

River Wind Cafe
Exit 62 off I-84 to Cascade St,
(503) 386-7789
1810 W Cascade St, Hood River
Moderate; beer and wine; MC, V; checks OK
Breakfast, lunch, dinner Wed-Mon (summer)
(hours vary in winter)

It's a sign of Hood River's times that the virtual landmark, Jose's Mexican Restaurant, became an uptown eatery. But if it had to be, this is a winner. It's light, even in a drizzle. And the food is fine, from the huevos rancheros (though we would have preferred a homemade salsa) and seven-grain cereal to the two daily soups, tasty veggie lasagne, Thai peanut chicken, and a rummy Jamaican snapper. Desserts try a little too hard: pears baked with walnuts and brown sugar, served on a bed of blackberry-flavored chocolate?

Bette's Place
Oak St and 4th,
(503) 386-1880
416 Oak St, Hood River
Inexpensive; no alcohol; no credit cards; checks OK
Breakfast, lunch daily

Where the boardheads go. Bette's is the last of the old-time coffee shops in town, with platters of hash browns, thick omelets, and homemade blueberry muffins (or legendary cinnamon rolls if it's Wednesday) and, what the heck, a piece of pie to finish. Come at lunch and order a Barge Burger; no complaints when your tummy is this full.

LODGINGS

Columbia Gorge Hotel
Exit 62 off I-84,
(503) 386-5566, toll-free
(800) 345-1921
4000 Westcliff Dr, Hood River, OR 97031
Expensive; AE, DC, MC, V; no checks

From the beginning, this has been a luxury hotel. Lumber baron Simon Benson built the showcase in 1921, brought in his famous chef Henry Thiele, and thereby capped his successful completion of the Columbia Gorge Scenic Highway. Instantly it became a favorite of honeymooners and tourists. After several non-hotel incarnations, it was restored and reopened in 1979 and then remodeled again in 1989. It's posh, pricey, and pretentious. We hope it gets this luxury bit down because it has all the pluses: a stunning structure, with a private window on Wah-Gwin-Gwin Falls of the Columbia River, and a colorful past, which included visits by Rudolph Valentino.

The public rooms are large and elegant. Each guest room has its own color scheme. Aim for a gorge-side room; they're quieter and have the best views. The complimentary basket of scented soaps and bath oils is a nice touch, but that doesn't make up for the small rooms (starting at $175) and the almost insultingly large breakfast with its notorious Honey from the Sky ($22.95 for non-guests). Dinners are slightly better but overpriced for what they are. A spring meal of Chinook salmon in a light chardonnay sauce was fresh but uninspired; the rack of Eastern Oregon lamb with a tamarind-mint sauce was flawless. Service is fawning. What the place needs to strive for is true panache.

Hood River Hotel
Oak and 1st,
(503) 386-1900
102 Oak St, Hood River,
OR 97031
Moderate; full bar; AE,
DC, MC, V; checks OK

Last year's restoration revived this hostelry's past as a turn-of-the-century country hotel. Thirty-two rooms, including eight kitchen suites, come with four-poster canopy beds, pedestal sinks, and plenty of cheerful floral chintz. Since it's in the center of town, there's some noise from the street, the railroad, and I-84. A small downstairs dining room serves reasonably priced breakfasts, lunches, and dinners that are strong on Italian specialties and local fruit and fish. Enjoy your espresso or after-dinner drink in front of the lobby fireplace or at an outside table. A casual place, with live jazz and Celtic music on weekends.

Lakecliff Estate
Exit 62 off I-84, ½ mile
west of Hood River at
3820 Westcliff Dr,
(503) 386-7000
Mail: PO Box 1220,
Hood River, OR 97031
Moderate; no credit cards,
checks OK

Everyone's favorite Hood River bed and breakfast, Lakecliff Estate delivers fine hospitality in outstanding surroundings. The forest-green home, just a short jog off I-84, is sheltered by woods to create quiet seclusion with an astonishing view of the Columbia River. Built in 1908 by architect Albert E. Doyle (who also designed Multnomah Falls Lodge and the Benson Hotel in Portland) as a summer estate for a Portland businessman, Lakecliff now is listed on the National Register of Historic Places. It features five fireplaces of locally quarried stone, a large and inviting living room, a cheerful sun porch, and an elegant dining room where breakfast is served. Some rooms have fireplaces, others have views. Owners Bruce and Judy Thesanga are friendly and fun. Guests often linger over their oatmeal with sautéed nectarines or Dutch babies with fruit sauce while watching windsurfers below.

State Street Inn
Near the corner of State
and 10th, (503) 386-1899
1005 State St,

Mac and Amy Lee fled aerospace careers to live in Hood River. Now Amy's a technical writer and Mac runs the B&B. He does it right. The place, an impeccable and well-crafted 1932 English Tudor, is ideally

Hood River, OR 97031
Moderate; MC, V;
checks OK

located on a quiet street that's still close to everything. The queen beds are comfy. Four nonsmoking rooms share two baths; the decor of each reflects the character of the states where the Lees used to live. The Chesapeake-inspired Maryland Room and the bright and colorful California Room are the largest, with views of Mount Adams. Most everyone gathers around the fire or in the game room at night and meets again for breakfast (whole-wheat waffles or lemony cream cheese–filled crepes with fresh fruit) in a dining room in which they sit eye-to-eye with Mount Adams.

Duckwall House
State and Oak,
(503) 386-6635
811 Oak St, Hood River,
OR 97031
Moderate; AE, MC, V;
checks OK

Jack and Doris Kent and their guests occupy this tidy home close to the center of things on Oak Street. Four rooms (sharing two baths) are done up in peaches and pinks and pretty antiques, and are priced at a reasonable $65 a night for a double room. Unfortunately, the room with the nicest view of the river also has the most traffic noise. The best part of the stay, however, is Doris and Jack's gracious, but not obsequious hospitality. Breakfast is a big treat: baked eggs, fresh fruit, potatoes, cinnamon buns, orange juice, and coffee.

Vagabond Lodge
Exit 62 off I-84,
(503) 386-2992
4070 Westcliff Dr,
Hood River, OR 97031
Inexpensive; MC, V;
checks OK

So close to the Columbia Gorge Hotel it could almost be another wing. It's got the identical view as (some say better than) CGH; the rooms are twice the size and a fraction of the price. The front building is nothing but a nondescript highway-facing unit. The surprise is in back. Ask for a room in the riverfront building. If there are four of you, get a suite with a fireplace and separate bedroom ($82).

THE DALLES

The Dalles is *the* historical stop along this stretch. For centuries, this area was the meeting place for Native Americans. In the 1840s, it was the official end of the Oregon Trail. Later it served as the only military fort in the Northwest and the county seat of Wasco County, then a 130,000-square-mile vastness that spread from the Cascades to the Rockies. Gold miners loaded up here. Thomas Condon, Oregon's father of geology, got his start amid local basalts.

Signs of all this remain—the Native American petroglyphs, the 1850 surgeon's house from the old Fort Dalles (now a museum at 15th and Garrison streets), the east side's "houses of entertainment," and nicely maintained examples of Colonial, Gothic Revival, Italianate, and American Renaissance architecture. Take a tour by car or on foot; maps are available at The Dalles Convention and Visitor Bureau, 901 E 2nd St, (800) 255-3385 or (503) 296-6616.

Uphill from downtown are irrigated cherry orchards; Wasco County is the largest producer in the U.S. and celebrates its **Cherry Festival** in mid-April. Spreading far to the east are the grainfields and grasslands of drier Eastern Oregon. Annual precipitation is no more than 15 inches; trees thin out quickly, and rocks protrude more visibly. Most of the year the ground is golden, except for the wild-flowers in spring.

RESTAURANTS

Ole's Supper Club
Exit 84 off I-84, go west 1 mile, (503) 296-6708 2620 W 2nd St, The Dalles
Moderate; full bar; MC, V; checks OK
Dinner Tues-Sat

Ole's isn't glamorous. In fact, it's in the industrial west end of The Dalles. But locals like it this way. The consistent quality of the food and the commitment to good wine make it notable—in spite of the fact that it looks like a double-wide mobile home. The house special turns out to be one of the best cuts of prime rib we've tasted anywhere. Everything is included: delicious homemade soup, a standard salad, an individual loaf of hot homemade bread, and a potato, rice, or a vegetable. Although the restaurant has established its reputation on beef, it also features chicken, seafood, and lamb. When fresh razor clams are available, it treats them well. The wine list is notable because the bar is one of the few in Oregon that doubles as a wine shop; it's known regionally for a wide selection, and wine prices in the restaurant are just over retail.

LODGINGS

Williams House Inn
Corner of Trevett and 6th, (503) 296-2889 608 W 6th St, The Dalles, OR 97058
Moderate; AE, MC, V; checks OK

A manicured three-acre arboretum surrounds this classic 1899 Queen Anne house. It has been in the Williams family for more than 60 years and is now on the National Register of Historic Places and run as a bed and breakfast by Don and Barbara Williams. Nicaraguan mahogany decorates the walls, and Oriental rugs cover the floor of the large living room that contains a piano, Don's bass fiddle, and a fireplace. Two of the three rooms have their own balcony. We especially like the downstairs Elizabeth Suite with its separate bedroom, writing desk, hideabed, and private bath with marble-topped washbasin and a six-foot-long claw-footed tub. The Williamses serve a fine breakfast of fresh or canned local fruits, including cherries from their own orchard, home-roasted granola, muffins, fresh-ground coffees, and eggs. Don Williams happily shares his love and encyclopedic knowledge of the area's rich history, which includes his own.

MOUNT HOOD

At 11,245 feet, Hood may not be the highest in the chain of volcanoes in the Cascades, but it is one of the best developed. The Timberline Day Lodge at the 6,000-foot level has plenty of facilities to equip the mountaineer, hiker, or skier (see review). Chair lifts take you to the Palmer Snowfield, up in the glaciers, where you can ski in the middle of summer. The lower parts are ablaze with rhododendrons (peaking in June) and wildflowers (peaking in July); all are easily reachable from trails that spread out from Timberline Lodge. One of the best trails leads 4½ miles west from Timberline Lodge to flower-studded Paradise Park. Like Rainier, the mountain is girt by a long trail (called Timberline Trail), a 40-mile circuit of the entire peak that traverses snowfields and ancient forests.

Mid-May to mid-July is the prime time for climbing Mount Hood, a peak that looks easier than it is, since the last 1,500 feet involve very steep snow climbing. Timberline Mountain Guides, in the Timberline Day Lodge, equip and conduct climbers to the summit; (503) 548-0749.

LODGINGS

Timberline Lodge
60 miles due east of Portland off Hwy 26, (503) 272-3311, toll-free (800) 547-1406 outside Oregon
Mail: Timberline Ski Area, OR 97028
Moderate; AE, MC, V; checks OK
Breakfast, lunch, dinner every day

Built in 1937 as a WPA project, Timberline Lodge is a wonderland of American crafts—carved stone, worked metal, massive beams with adze marks plain to see, rugged fireplaces everywhere, and a huge, octagonal lobby that is an inspiring centerpiece for the steep-roofed hotel. In 1975 an organization called Friends of Timberline was formed to supervise and finance the restoration of the magnificent craftsmanship. Since then, many of the upholsteries, draperies, rugs, and bedspreads in the public and guest rooms have been re-created in their original patterns—in some cases with the help of the original craftspeople. When the lodge was declared a National Historic Landmark in 1978, a full-time curator was employed to ensure proper maintenance and care for the furnishings. With the opening of the Wy'East Day Lodge in 1981, much of the ski traffic was diverted from the historic lodge. The personality of the place is best expressed by Heidi, the latest in a long string of faithful St. Bernard greeters.

Visits here are quite special. There are bunk rooms for $52, but it's worth it to book a room with a fireplace for $135. The resort is known for its year-round downhill skiing, but come also for cross-country skiing and other wintertime activities. During the summer, Timberline offers great hiking, picnicking, chair-lift rides, and guided nature tours (the staff is a great source for suggestions). There's also a sauna and heated pool. The lobby's best for lounging (as the rooms are quite small); desk nooks upstairs are *the* postcard-writing spots.

The restaurant menu is getting better all the time under the direction of chef Leif Eric Benson. Fish is his strong point. The food in the Ram's Head Lounge is not quite as good but do take time for a drink while looking into the heart of the mountain. Fast food is available in the Wy'East Lodge.

Inn at Cooper Spur
23 miles south of Hood River on Hwy 35, (503) 352-6692 or (503) 352-6037

This resort is located between Hood River and the summit of Mount Hood. You can stay in a sleeping room in the main lodge, but get a log cabin instead: each has two bedrooms (with queen-size beds), sleeping lofts with three single beds, a fully equipped

*10755 Cooper Spur Rd,
Mount Hood, OR 97041
Moderate; full bar; MC,
V (AE at Inn only); local
checks OK
Breakfast, lunch Sat-
Sun, dinner every day*

kitchen, 1½ baths, and all the wood you could want for the huge fireplace. Tennis, basketball, and croquet await warm-weather guests. Ski packages and cross-country equipment rental are available in winter. In any season, you have the use of your own hot tub. Recent reports tell us that the service is not always on a par with the tranquillity of the setting. The food at the adjacent restaurant is good but not fancy. Hours vary in the off season.

ZIG ZAG

RESTAURANTS

Salazar's

*Hwy 26, 1 mile east of Zig
Zag, (503) 622-3775
71545 E. Hwy 26,
Rhododendron
Moderate; full bar; AE,
DC, MC, V; checks OK
Dinner every day*

All three dining rooms have been filled with the fruits of owner-chef Al Salazar's 30-odd years of collecting: antique lamps, tapestries, stained glass, ornate carving knives, a huge collection of doorknobs, and so on. The effect is as disconcerting as it is fascinating. The cuisine is equally eclectic and somewhat uneven: blackened cod, Oriental duck, lamb shanks, Swiss steak. The wine list is adequate. Our advice is to order a tender steak, dine in the upstairs loft for the view (particularly if there's a snowscape), and be sure to enjoy the doorknob collection.

Barlow Trail Inn

*Hwy 26 in Zig Zag,
(503) 622-3877
69580 E Hwy 26, Zig Zag
Moderate; full bar; AE,
MC, V; no checks
Breakfast, lunch, dinner
every day*

Warm and friendly, this log lodge caters to the locals, serving up big breakfasts, juicy burgers, thick steaks, and nothing unexpected. Have fried chicken or a burger, and sit outside. The place is so popular for breakfast that you might consider making reservations.

LODGINGS

Mountain Shadows Bed and Breakfast

*3 miles north of Zig Zag
off east Lolo Pass Rd,
(503) 622-4746
Mail: PO Box 147,
Welches
Moderate; no credit cards;
checks OK*

It's definitely off the beaten path—on a rutted gravel road that passes through a clear-cut under power lines. But its forested surroundings and spectacular view of Mount Hood are worth the drive. There are three large guest rooms—one with a private bath—in this handcrafted log house. New owners Cathy and Paul Townsend genuinely like preparing your full breakfast; in summer they'll serve it on the deck with Mount Hood almost in your lap. And maybe you'll also see elk, river otters, and deer. Extensive hiking trails abound. Kids are welcome; but no smoking in the rooms.

SANDY

A pleasant town on the way to Mount Hood, Sandy (named for the nearby river) offers a white-steepled church, quaint shops, a weekend country market, ski rentals, and big fruit stands purveying the local fruits, vegetables, wines, juices, and filberts. In short—a nice stop en route to the mountains.

The **Oregon Candy Farm** features Bavarian truffles (85 cents each) along with hand-dipped chocolates, caramels, barks, chocolate-covered prunes, apricot-walnut jellies and on and on. Kids can watch the candymakers in action. It's 5½ miles east of Sandy on Highway 26; (503) 668-5066.

Oral Hull Park is designed for the blind, with splashing water and plants to smell or touch; it is a moving experience even for the sighted; (503) 668-6195.

RESTAURANTS

Calamity Jane's
Hwy 26, 1 mile east of Sandy, (503) 668-7817 42015 Hwy 26, Sandy Inexpensive; beer and wine; MC, V; checks OK Lunch, dinner every day

After a short hiatus, the original owners are back and have beefed up their list of hamburgers from 15 to 30, plus 15 pizzaburgers. They've gotten a bit silly—adding burgers with peanut butter, hot fudge with marshmallow sauce, or pineapple sauce and sour cream. The word is that somebody really does eat them. The decor is rustic Old Wild West; the exterior looks a little too rustic. The old-fashioned shakes, served in the big stainless-steel shakers, are very good; ditto the ice cream sundaes. Kids' meals are really a deal.

WEMME (aka WELCHES)

This pretty little town is known as Wemme on maps, but Welches at the post office because so many Welches settled here. The meadows nearby were destinations for pioneers and later for early Portlanders needing a mountain break.

RESTAURANTS

Chalet Swiss
Hwy 26 and E Welches Rd, (503) 622-3600 24371 E Welches Rd, Welches Moderate, full bar; AE, DC, MC, V; checks OK Dinner Wed-Sun

Open the door and walk into Oregon's version of Switzerland—a world of peasant dresses, cowbells, and hand-carved wooden furniture. And consistently excellent food. Owner-chef Kurt Mezger prepares classics with élan: *Bündnerfleisch* (paper-thin slices of beef salt-cured in alpine air), traditional fondues, raclette (cheese broiled on potatoes and served with pickles and onions), a superb salmon bisque, greens dressed with lemon, garlic, and herbs, and fresh vegetables cooked just right. Try the *Zurcher Geschnitzeltes* (veal in cream sauce with mushrooms) or the trout amandine. You may be tempted to take an order of the homemade spaetzle (noodles) with you. It's all filling and delightful fare, and we actually managed to save room for tiramisu and fresh strawberries. Chalet Swiss seats only 75, so make reservations a day before.

LODGINGS

The Resort at the Mountain

½ mile south of Hwy 26 on E Welches Rd,
(800) 669-ROOM or
(503) 622-3101
68010 E Fairway Ave,
Welches
Expensive; AE, DC, MC, V; checks OK
Breakfast, lunch, dinner every day, brunch Sun

Finally, this resort has found an ownership that works. Newly remodeled and renamed, it is, at last, very good. The 160 rooms are large and quiet; each has a deck or patio and a view of the pool, forest or, yes, freeways. Most have a sports-gear closet (a necessity here) and many have fireplaces. And, as if the mountain and nearby rivers didn't offer enough recreational options, the resort lists a 27-hole golf course, six tennis courts, an outdoor heated pool and Jacuzzi, a fitness center, mountain-bike rentals, hikes, horseshoes, golf lessons, volleyball, badminton, croquet, and basketball. Of course, it's also a very popular conference center. Rates run anywhere from $99 for a regular resort room to $185 for a two-bedroom suite.

The food is above par. The Tartans Grill and Tartans Pub are golf-course-and-mountain-viewing casual; the Highlands restaurant and Highlands Quiet Bar are subdued/elegant, with views of the pool and mountains. Executive chef Dale Rasmussen does well with Italian, Northwest, and Scottish specialties. Given the upscale nature of the place, the prices aren't unreasonable.

Old Welches Inn

1 mile south of Hwy 26 on E Welches Rd,
(503) 622-3754
26401 E Welches Rd,
Welches
Inexpensive; AE, MC, V; checks OK

Judi and Ted Mondun have reopened what was the first summer inn on Mount Hood (1890). A hundred years later it's still perfectly placed: French windows overlook The Resort at the Mountain's 27-hole golf course, mountains ring the valley, and a yard filled with wildflowers stretches down to the Salmon River. The three upstairs rooms are small and share two full baths, but all are attractive and have views. Relax by the fire, read in the sun room, and pat good old Rocky the dog (your own dog is welcome with Rocky's approval). Larger groups may prefer to rent the adjacent and comfy no-frills two-bedroom cabin, with fireplace, kitchen, and views. Kids over 12 welcome.

McKENZIE RIVER

The highway through this river valley is the most beautiful of all the Cascade crossings. Following Highway 126 from Eugene, you pass through farm country alongside the green water of the McKenzie River. Soon you see lovely campgrounds and come to waterfalls and amazingly transparent lakes. At Foley Springs you catch Highway 242 for the pass (opens about July 1 each year). This is volcanic country, with vast lava beds that cooled off only 2,000 years ago.

McKenzie River runs. Long celebrated for trout fishing, the McKenzie has become known for river-runs in rafts or the famous McKenzie River boats, rakish dories with upturned bows and sterns. **Dave Helfrich River Outfitter** in Vida, conducts springtime day trips on the river and also arranges for fly-fishing expeditions in drift boats; (503) 896-3786.

McKENZIE BRIDGE

Tokatee Golf Course, 3 miles west of McKenzie Bridge, is commonly rated one of the five finest in the Northwest: lots of trees, rolling terrain, and concentration-distracting views of the scenery; (503) 822-3220.

RESTAURANTS

Log Cabin Inn
50 miles east of I-5 on Hwy 126, (503) 822-3432
56483 McKenzie Hwy, McKenzie Bridge
Moderate; full bar; MC, V; local checks only
Breakfast Sat-Sun, lunch, dinner every day; (winter hours vary)
Lodging closed Jan-Feb

The fundamentals of home cooking and clean, comfortable lodging are enshrined here in eight cabins on the water. You can opt for a continental breakfast delivered to your door ($4 extra) or you can order from the menu at the going rate. Dinners are popular and offer a range as broad as cod, wild boar, buffalo, venison, and quail, as well as more traditional prime rib. Folks come from miles around to top it all off with marionberry cobbler for dessert.

LODGINGS

Holiday Farm
McKenzie River Dr, 3 miles west of McKenzie Bridge, (503) 822-3715
54455 McKenzie River Dr, Blue River, OR 97413
Expensive; full bar; no credit cards; checks OK
Breakfast, lunch, dinner every day

First-time visitors to Holiday Farm wouldn't know at a glance that the resort encloses 90 acres and a hidden lake or three. They would find a freshly painted main house (an old stagecoach stop), pleasant dining in the restaurant, and some amiable riverside cottages with knockout views of the McKenzie. Open April through November, all of the cabins feature decks and bright windows. Some are older green and white (with a rebuilt porch here and there); others are cedar-sided and more contemporary. Low foot-lamps light the path that connects them. Big and Little Rainbow is a large and modern unit that can be joined for a larger group (two families) or split for individual parties.

The restaurant, open to tourists passing through, makes a very pleasant dining stop on a porch overhanging the river. Burgers are typical fare for lunch; steaks, seafood, and game for dinner.

CAMP SHERMAN

LODGINGS

House on the Metolius
Forest Service Rd 1420, 2½ miles north of Camp Sherman, (503) 595-6620
Mail: PO Box 601, Camp Sherman, OR 97730

This private fly-fishing resort is open all year now (and it's still hard to get into and impossible to drop by), set in 200 acres of gorgeous scenery, with the Metolius River nearby. The cabins are lovely, fully equipped with fireplace, kitchenette, and king, double, or twin

Expensive; MC, V;
checks OK

beds. Reservations needed at least a week in advance. Well-behaved pets are okay. Don't forget your fly rod.

Lake Creek Lodge
4 miles north of Hwy 20 at
Camp Sherman turnoff,
(503) 595-6331
Mail: Star Route, Sisters,
OR 97759
Expensive ; no credit
cards; checks OK
Breakfast, dinner every
day (restaurant summers
only)

The resort has been here for over 60 years, popular with families who want a knotty-pine cabin from which to enjoy the fishing, the tiny pond, and the hearty food at the lodge. Best choice is a lodge house, a cheerful, open-ceilinged home with two or three bedrooms, one or two baths, possibly a fireplace, a complete kitchen, living room, and screened porch; less expensive are the two-bedroom cottages, which have no kitchens. The cabins are spread around grassy grounds dotted with pines, overlooking the small lake made from a dammed stream. Facilities are extensive: tennis (two courts), fishing, hiking and biking, and children's activities. The lodge serves excellent breakfasts and dinners, and if it's not too busy with guests, it is also open for outsiders by reservation. You bring your own wine.

SISTERS

Named after the three mountain peaks that dominate the horizon (Faith, Hope, and Charity), this little community is becoming a bit of a mecca for tired urban types looking for a taste of cowboy escapism. On a clear day (and there are about 250 of them a year), Sisters is exquisitely beautiful. Surrounded by mountains, trout streams, and pine and cedar forests, this little town is beginning to capitalize on the influx of winter skiers and summer camping and fishing enthusiasts.

There's mixed sentiment about the pseudo-Western storefronts that are thematically organizing the town's commerce, but then again, Sisters does host 50,000 visitors for its annual June rodeo. If cowboy isn't your style, there are a very good art gallery at the corner of Elm and Main, a mini-mall called Barclay Square (with a nice tile boutique), a knowledgeable mountain supply store, and even a store for freshly roasted coffee beans.

Although the population of the town itself is only about 820, more than 3,000 folks get mail at the Sisters PO. Many of them run boarding and ranch facilities. The most famous ranch is **The Patterson Ranch**, breeders of Polish Arabian horses, South American llamas, and elk. Call (503) 549-3831 for information.

RESTAURANTS

Hotel Sisters and
Bronco Billy's Saloon
Cascade and Fir streets,
(503) 549-RIBS
101 Cascade St, Sisters
Moderate; full bar; MC,
V; local checks only
Lunch, dinner every day

The social centerpiece of Western-theme Sisters, this bar and eatery serves up Western-style ranch cooking, with good burgers and some Mexican fare as well. It's string ties all around on the friendly and diligent waitstaff. Seafood is fresh (deliveries thrice weekly from Salem), but we recommend you stay with the chicken and ribs and avoid the odd taco-shell preparations dredged in Parmesan and paprika. Owners John

(in winter, lunch Sat-Sun only, dinner every day)

Keenan, Bill Reed, and John Tehan have succeeded in turning old friendships into a going business consortium, re-creating the look of a first-class hotel, circa 1900. The old upstairs hotel rooms are now private meeting rooms, and historical photos enhance the pleasant dining decor downstairs. Drop-ins often eat in the saloon, or on good days take a drink on the deck.

Papandrea's Pizza

East end of town,
(503) 549-6081
Cascade Hwy, Sisters
Inexpensive; beer and
wine; MC, V;
local checks only
Lunch, dinner every day

Oregonians love this place. The original link in a small chain of pizzerias, Papandrea's has built a quality reputation on fresh dough, homemade sauce, real cheese, and fresh vegetables. Because of all this freshness, the place does seem to abide by its disclaimer sign—"We will not sacrifice quality for speed, so expect to wait a little longer." Actually, you wait quite a bit longer for the original thick-crust pies, but there's a You-Bake line for take-out.

The Gallery

Corner of Cascade and
Hood streets,
(503) 549-2631
230 W Cascade St,
Sisters
Inexpensive; full bar;
MC, V; checks OK
Breakfast, lunch, dinner
every day

The breakfast omelets draw the morning crowd, and the lunch burgers pull the afternoon business at this no-nonsense spot. There are always weekly specials (meat loaf, German sausage, sirloin tips), and the prices (up to $11.95) are still modest for the value (even though they're almost double what they used to be). Owners Jim and Carrie Cheatham are proud of their Ray Eyerling paintings and also display the largest Northwest collection of Winchester rifles. Drop in for some peanut-butter pie and coffee just to check it out.

LODGINGS

Black Butte Ranch

Hwy 20, 8 miles west of
Sisters, (503) 595-6211
Mail: PO Box 8000,
Black Butte Ranch,
OR 97759
Expensive; AE, MC, V;
checks OK
Breakfast, lunch, dinner
every day (closed Mon-
Tues from January
through April)

With 1,800 acres, this vacation and recreation wonderland remains the darling of Northwest resorts. Rimmed by the Three Sisters mountains, scented by a plain of ponderosa pines, and expertly developed by the Brooks Scanlon Company, these rental condos and private homes draw families year-round to swim, ski, fish, golf, bike, boat, ride horses (summer only), and play tennis. The best way to make a reservation is to state the size of your party and whether or not you want a home (most are quite large and contemporary) or simply a good-sized bed and bath (in the latter case, the lodge condominiums will suffice, although they are dark and dated, with too much orange Formica and brown furniture). The main lodge is a handsome but not overwhelming building that serves as dining headquarters. Tables at The Lodge Restaurant are tiered so that everyone can appreciate the meadow panorama beyond. Food is straightforward and hearty, and servings are generous.

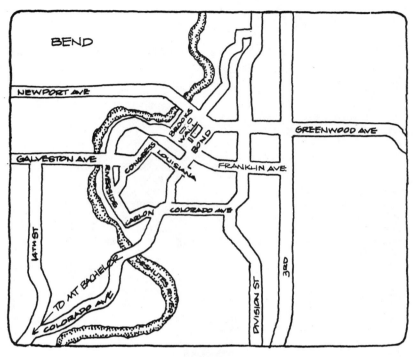

BEND

Bend was a quiet, undiscovered high-desert paradise until a push in the 1960s to develop recreation and tourism potential tamed Bachelor Butte into an alpine playground. Then came the golf courses, the airstrip, the bike trails, the river-rafting companies, the hikers, the tennis players, the rockhounds, and the skiers. Bend's popularity and population (currently 19,510) have been on a steady increase ever since, propelling it in the last three years to serious destination status. The main thoroughfare (3rd Street) bypasses the town center, which thrives just to the west between two one-way streets, Wall and Bond. Part of the charm of the town comes from the blinding blue sky and the sage-scented air. The other part of its appeal is due to its proximity to the following attractions.

Mount Bachelor Ski Area (22 miles southwest). With a fourth express quad (skyliner) opened a few years ago, Mount Bachelor now has 9 lifts feeding skiers onto 3,100 vertical feet of dry and groomed skiing. **The Skier's Palate**, serves excellent lunches of grilled pistachio oysters or a hot sandwich of Dungeness crab and bay shrimp (and the best margarita around). The 9,065-foot elevation at the summit makes for all-season skiing. High-season amenities include ski school, racing, day care, rentals, an entire Nordic program and trails, and better-than-average ski food at six different lodges. Call (800) 547-6858; inside Oregon, (503) 382-8334 or the ski report at (503) 382-7888.

The High Desert Museum (59800 S Hwy 97, Bend, OR 97702) is an outstanding nonprofit center for natural and cultural history, located 6 miles south of Bend on Highway 97, that includes among other things a live animal educational presentation. Inside, the new expanded center is a walk through 100 years of history, featuring excellent dioramas from Native Americans times through the 1890s. Twenty acres of natural trails and outdoor exhibits offer replicas of covered wagons, a sheepherder's camp, a settlers' cabin, and an Indian wickiup, and supports a couple of resident river otters and porcupines. Open every day from 9am to 5pm; call (503) 382-4754.

Pilot Butte (just east of town). This cinder cone with a road to the top is a good first stop, offering a knockout panorama of the city and the mountains beyond.

Lava River Caves (12 miles south of Bend on Highway 97). Tours of the lava caves include a mile-long lava tube. As you descend into the dark and surprisingly eerie depths, you'll need a warm sweater. **Lava Lands Visitor Center**, atop a high butte formed by a volcanic fissure, is a lookout point with accompanying geology lessons about the "moonscape" panorama caused by Central Oregon's volcanic history. Call (503) 593-2421; open mid-March to the end of October.

Pine Mountain Observatory (30 miles southeast of Bend on Highway 20, (503) 382-8331) is the University of Oregon's astronomy research facility. One of its three telescopes is the largest in the Northwest.

Deschutes Historical Center (corner of NW Idaho and Wall). The museum features regional history and interesting pioneer paraphernalia but keeps limited hours. Call (503)389-1813 (open Wed-Sun, 1pm to 4:30pm).

Cascade Lakes Highway/Century Drive. This 100-mile tour needs several hours and a picnic lunch for full appreciation; there are a number of lakes along the way. Begin in Bend along the Deschutes, using the National Forest Service's booklet "Cascade Lakes Discovery Tour."

Smith Rock State Park. Twenty-two miles north of Bend in Terrebonne, some of the finest rock climbers gather to test their skills on the red rock cliffs.

RESTAURANTS

Pine Tavern Restaurant
*Foot of Oregon Ave
downtown at Mirror
Pond, (503) 382-5581
967 NW Brooks, Bend
Moderate; full bar; AE,
DC, MC, V; checks OK
Lunch Mon-Sat, dinner
every day, brunch Sun*

Buttonhole three out of four Bend citizens on the street and tell them you're ready for a fancy night out, with good food, service, atmosphere, and a decent value for your dollar. The recommendation time and time again will be the Pine Tavern. Under the ownership of Bert Bender, Joe Cenarrussa, and Brad and Theresa Hollenbeck, this establishment—and 50 years of history make it truly established—is regaining its reputation for quality. Consider window-shopping at the Brooks Street Mercantile across the street while you wait for a table (yes, even with reservations). Request a table by the window in the main dining room and marvel at the tree growing through the floor. The menu runs about $10 to $16 for various beef entrées, but a lighter dinner menu offers smaller cuts of steak and petite portions of veal. The prime rib petite cut is ample even for a hungry diner, but prime rib is the forte of the restaurant and few can resist the larger cut.

Le Bistro
*1 block off Greenwood on
Hwy 97, (503) 389-7274
1203 NE 3rd St,
Bend*

Owner Axel Hoch remains at the helm in the kitchen, and his wife, Salli, handles the front at this French specialty restaurant. Don't be put off by the austere old church facade; inside, the sidewalk-cafe decor warms things up, as does the superlative waitstaff. Yes, it's

Moderate; full bar; DC, MC, V; no checks
Dinner Tues-Sat

expensive and pretentious, but it's tough to fault the food. The duck breast with plum sauce begins the meal with a gentle flair. Though Hoch's sauces (nantua, béarnaise, pepper-cream) are ever-present on the seafood entrées, we prefer the simple preparations of lamb and Chateaubriand. The rice, a Dixie cup–size tower that topples onto the tablecloth when you try to eat it, is silly. Don't miss the very attractive lounge downstairs; it's a good place to sample from an appetizer menu or to take your after-dinner coffee.

Pescatore

Minnesota at Gasoline Alley, (503) 389-6276
119 NW Minnesota, Bend
Moderate; full bar; AE, MC, V; checks OK
Lunch Mon-Fri, dinner every day, Sunday brunch

Terry Vibbert and Brad Haun's new restaurant in the former Cyrano's space is nowhere close to the water, but Pescatore (it means "fisherman") is proud of its Italian renditions of seafood. Pasta Pescatore is a mixture of clams, mussels, calamari, ahi and salmon in a spicy marinara served atop capellini. They also do a "risotto" version, but it's really just on riso. However, we prefer the appetizers— recently, grilled thin slices of ahi and eggplant with an excellent tomato-basil vinaigrette. Every entrée comes with a salad or soup (often minestrone). At press time, chef Vibbert was concocting what he believed would become their signature dessert, a quadruple-chocolate flourless cake. Unfortunately, the test samples were still in the oven, so we'll be back.

Westside Bakery and Cafe

Right on Franklin from Division; opposite Drake Park, (503) 382-3426
1005½ NW Galveston, Bend
Inexpensive; no alcohol; no credit cards; local checks only
Breakfast, lunch every day

Once just a bakery in the corner of the building, the ever-popular Westside has recently taken over the entire building (at last count there were four rooms). You can still get good coffee and wholesome baked goods to go, but most choose to stay for the huevos rancheros, blueberry, pancakes or homemade granola for breakfast. Lunches consist of turkey, ham, or pastrami piled high on thick slabs of homemade bread. The staff and prices are some of the friendliest in town.

Deschutes Brewery & Public House

Near the corner of Bond and Greenwood, (503) 382-9242
1044 NW Bond St, Bend
Inexpensive; beer and wine; MC, V; local checks OK
Lunch, dinner every day

A very social spot, whether you're a local or not. The place was designed by Portland city folk, with urbanites in mind: exposed rafters and dark wood wainscoting. The beer is dark, too: a rich Black Butte Porter, a hoppy Cascade Golden Ale, a robust Bachelor Bitter and, for nondrinkers, a tasty, not-too-sweet *rootbier*. The kitchen has created light gourmet bar food for lunch (spicy lamb-vegetable soup, black bean chili, and bratwurst with sauerkraut) that has been attracting lunching professionals, and a full dinner menu. Many locals are proud to see Bend on a beer-bottle label; but they can also bring in a sealable bottle and get brew to go.

Yoko's Japanese Restaurant
Bond at Oregon St,
(503) 382-2999
1028 NW Bond St, Bend
Moderate; beer and wine;
AE, MC, V; checks OK
Lunch Tues-Fri, dinner
Tues-Sat

Steve Detatie, who appreciates Japanese cooking and recognized a lack of it in central Oregon, opened this restaurant two years ago and has been busy ever since. He leaves the cooking up to chef Yoychiro Mori, who does a commendable job. Try the boat, a wooden replica of a Japanese fishing boat that sails over to you brimming with chicken and beef teriyaki, tempura, and an assortment of sushi.

LODGINGS

Sunriver Lodge
Off Hwy 97, 15 miles
south of Bend,
(503) 593-1221 or
(800) 547-3922
Mail: PO Box 3609,
Sunriver, OR 97707
Expensive; full bar; AE,
MC, V; checks OK
Breakfast, lunch, dinner
every day

More than a resort, Sunriver is an organized community with its own post office, realty offices, grocery store, and 1,000 or so full-time residents. The unincorporated town now sprawls over 3,300 acres, and its own paved runway for private air commuting does a brisk business. Nevertheless, its specialty is big-time escapist vacationing, and this resort has all the facilities to keep families, couples, or groups of friends busy all week long, year-round. Summer months offer golf (two 18-hole courses), tennis (22 courts), rafting, canoeing, fishing, swimming (two pools, seven hot tubs), biking (25 miles of paved trails), and riding. In winter the resort is home base for skiing, both Nordic and alpine, ice skating, snowmobiling, and indoor racquetball. You can stay in a condo or one of the privately owned homes (reserved through the resort). For the best bargain, request one of the large and contemporary homes (these often have luxuries like Jacuzzis, barbecues, and decks) and split expenses with another family. If you want access to the pool and hot-tub facility, be sure to request a house that has a pass. Rates run from $79 to $155. Even the minimal bedroom units have a small deck and fireplace. When you rent through the resort (rather than individual owners) all condos come with four daily passes to the racquet-and-pool facility and golf course.

Dining at Sunriver offers decent spicy fare at Cheng's Chinese Restaurant and the popular Mexican menu at spacious Casa de Ricardo. We like to catch the inexpensive breakfast down at the Provision Company or at the Trout House, while The Meadows is the much-acclaimed showplace for fine dining. The locals rave over the Sunday brunch.

Inn of the
Seventh Mountain
18575 S Century Dr,
5 miles west of Bend,
(503) 382-8711, or toll-
free in Oregon
(800) 542-6810
Mail: PO Box 1207,

The Inn offers the closest accommodation to Mount Bachelor and is especially popular with families, no doubt due to the vast menu of activities built into the multi-condominium facility. In the winter it has the biggest (though not full-size) ice rink around, one sauna large and hot enough to accommodate a group of about 15 guests, three cloverleaf-shaped, bubbling hot tubs, and two moderately heated swimming pools. In the

Bend, OR 97709
Expensive; full bar; AE,
DC, MC, V; checks OK

summer the pools are the centerpiece of activity—there's a whole layout complete with water slide and wading pool. By 1992, guests can play a new 18-hole golf course. The Inn does a terrific job of social planning and offers fabulous off-season rates. An activities roster for the week gives the rundown on tennis, riding, biking, skating, snowmobiling, skiing, aerobics, frisbee, golf... you name it. The rooms are beginning to show their age in decor and wear. Avoid buildings 18 and 19; they are the least scenic and the most removed from the center.

There is plenty of good eating at the resort. The Poppy Seed puts on a plentiful and tasty breakfast. Barron's, a deli/hamburger joint, is perfect for those who prefer less formal surroundings. El Crab Catcher, though it's going through chef and management changes, remains a local favorite for stepping out. We like the après-ski Warren Miller films in the lounge.

Mount Bachelor Village
Toward Mount Bachelor
on Century Dr,
(503) 389-5900, toll-free
(800) 452-9846 in
Oregon, (800) 547-5204
outside Oregon
19717 Mount Bachelor
Dr, Bend, OR 97702
Expensive; AE, MC, V;
checks OK

You don't want a social chairman, you can live without an adjacent dining room, and you rarely need a hot-tub soak after 11pm? Then Mount Bachelor Village may be your style. What this development has over some of its more famous neighbor resorts is spacious rooms (there are no studios—all accommodations have one-bedroom, one-bedroom/loft, or two-bedroom floor plans). Every unit has a completely furnished kitchen, wood-burning fireplace, and private deck. We like the newer units, where the color scheme is modern and light and where the soundproofing helps mute the thud of ski boots in the morning. The views aren't particularly breathtaking (some units look out to the busy mountain road). There are around 75 units to choose from, with prices starting at $75 a night. Outdoor Jacuzzi, seasonal outdoor pool, six tennis courts, and a 2.2-mile nature trail round out the amenities.

The Riverhouse
On Hwy 97 in Bend,
(503) 389-3111, toll-free
(800) 547-3928
3075 N Hwy 97, Bend
OR 97701
Moderate; AE, DC, MC,
V; checks OK
Breakfast, lunch, dinner
every day

The Riverhouse has become an institution in Bend for comfortable stays at more reasonable rates than the out-of-town recreation resorts offer. Amenities are still abundant: a good-sized pool (heated year-round), saunas, whirlpool, exercise room, and indoor Jacuzzi; rooms with river views, walkable shopping, and adjacent restaurants. The Deschutes creates welcome white noise as it rushes over rocks and under the connector bridge. Rooms range from merely utilitarian to fancy suites with spas ($40 to $130).

This is where you'll find Tito's, serving authentic Mexican cuisine, and the Riverhouse Dining Room, respected for its continental cuisine (with some tableside preparations). The poolside cafe serves appetizers, soups, and sandwiches. The après-ski lounge rocks with contemporary bands six nights a week, so avoid nearby rooms unless you plan to dance all night.

Rock Springs Guest Ranch

On Hwy 20, 7 miles from Bend and 20 miles from Sisters, (503) 382-1957 64201 Tyler Rd, Bend, OR 97701 Moderate; AE, DC, MC, V; checks OK

★★

The emphasis here is very much on family vacations. Counselors take care of the kids in special programs all day while adults hit the trail, laze in the pool, play tennis, or gobble down hearty meals in the ranch dining room (open only for those staying at the resort). The cabins are quite nice—comfy knotty-pine duplexes with fireplaces. There are only about 25 units, so it's easy to get to know everyone staying at the ranch, particularly since everyone eats together in the lodge. The setting, amid ponderosa pines and junipers alongside a small lake, is secluded and lovely.

The main activity here is riding, with nine wranglers and a stable of 68 horses. Summer season is booked by the week only, starting at $1,100 per person, which includes virtually everything with your room (meals, snacks, riding, spa, and special events). Tennis courts are lit, and there's fishing in the ranch pond. Note the special financial arrangements (like reduced-price meals and accommodations) for babysitters brought for young children. You'll have to leave your pets at home.

Rock Springs is a guest ranch only from the end of June through Labor Day; the rest of the year it functions as a top-notch conference center (only one group at a time). Facilities include a 4,500-square-foot conference room with pine paneling and a rock fireplace.

Entrada Lodge

7 miles from Bend on Century Dr, (503) 382-4080 19221 Century Dr, Bend, OR 97702 Moderate; AE, DC, MC, V; no checks

★

Whether you're a weary traveler or just an avid skier looking for a firm mattress, a dependable shower, a clean room, and decent TV reception, you'll get that and more here. The "more" is a covered outdoor hot tub that cooks all season long, closer proximity to the mountain than town lodgings provide, and a straightforward breakfast menu (your choice of three offerings). Friendly owner Brett Evert works hard to personalize this 79-room ranch-style Best Western motel. There're hot chocolate and snacks après-ski by the office fireplace and a spa room, and pets are allowable, with some restrictions. The price is thrifty, and the proximity to the mountain is a plus. Brett also owns another Best Western in town, The Woodstone Inn (721 NE 3rd St, Bend, OR 97701, (503) 382-1515).

House at the Water's Edge

On Mirror Pond directly across from Pine Tavern, (503) 382-1266 36 NW Pinecrest Ct, Bend, OR 97701 Moderate; no credit cards;

Behind the cul-de-sac entrance is a very dramatic contemporary home on the Deschutes River's Mirror Pond. This stunning bed-and-breakfast is both tranquil and centrally located. High-beamed cathedral ceilings, open kitchen/living area, and plenty of windows create a relaxing ambience. A wood stove with a glass front is lit when there's even the slightest chill in the air. In the warmer weather, the deck is about as inviting a place

OREGON CASCADES

checks OK

Lara House
Bed and Breakfast
Louisiana and Congress,
(503) 388-4064
640 NW Congress, Bend,
OR 97701
Moderate; MC, V;
checks OK

as you'd want. Inside, the two bed-and--breakfast rooms have their own baths. If you don't get along with teddy bears get the north room. Hors d'oeuvres in the afternoon and a full breakfast come morning.

One of Bend's largest and oldest (1910) homes, Lara House has been renovated from a run-down boarding-house to a bright and homey bed and breakfast. At press time it was changing ownership, but *everything* else was to remain the same—phone number, furnishings and all. The main room is perfect for small-group socializing—large stone fireplace, upright piano, and sunny adjacent solarium that looks out over the large yard onto the river parkway. The lighting is warm, and there's a wonderful community oak table that guests gather around in the morning for a breakfast that would keep any skier or biker pumped all day long. Each of the four guest rooms upstairs has a queen-size bed, cheery wallpaper, and its own shower and vanity sink. There's a sauna and hot tub in the basement.

ELK LAKE
LODGINGS

Elk Lake Resort
Century Dr, Elk Lake,
radio phone YP7 3954
Mail: PO Box 789, Bend,
OR 97709
Moderate; MC, V; no
checks

Elk Lake is a small mountain lake about 30 miles west of Bend on the edge of the Three Sisters Wilderness Area. This remote lodge—reached by snow-cat or 10 miles of cross-country skiing in the winter—consists of a dozen self-contained cabins, most with fireplace, kitchen, bathroom, and sleeping quarters for two to eight people. It's nothing grand, but the place is much favored by Bend dwellers (a good recommendation) and the scenery is wonderful. There is a dining room with standard American grub; reservations required.

Getting a reservation can be almost as tough as getting here, since there's only a radio phone (you'll probably have to inquire by mail) and the place is often booked up to a year in advance.

CULTUS LAKE
LODGINGS

Cultus Lake Resort
Century Drive at Cultus
Lake, winter phone
(503) 389-3230, summer
radio phone YP7-3903
Mail: PO Box 262, Bend,

You're well into the mountains, in the Deschutes National Forest 50 miles southwest of Bend, alongside a large lake popular with anglers and boaters. The resort has 23 acceptable cabins (19 with kitchens), all paneled in wood and some with big windows looking over the lakefront, at good prices ($42-$78). A serviceable res-

OR 97709
Moderate; AE, MC, V;
checks OK

taurant and a small grocery store are in the handsome main lodge, and boat rentals are easily managed. Cabins 7, 8, 9, and 10 are the most desirable. Open May to October.

MOUNT BAILEY

Mount Bailey Alpine Ski Tours offers a true backcountry skiing experience, with snow-cats instead of helicopters to take you to the top of this 8,363-foot ancient volcano and experienced guides who stress safety. Diamond Lake Resort, (503) 793-3333, headquarters the guide service, offering multiple-day packages including lodging and meals; otherwise, the cost is $110 a day (lunch included). When the snow melts, the operation turns to mountain-bike tours.

CRATER LAKE

Some 6,500 years ago, 15,000-foot Mount Mazama became the Mount St. Helens of its day, blew up, and left behind a deep crater that is now filled with Crater Lake. The area is extraordinary: the impossibly blue lake, the eerie volcanic formations, the vast geological wonderland. The visitor center, at the park headquarters, (503) 594-2211, has been reopened, with a theater, an information desk, and a good interpretive exhibit. Visitors to Crater Lake should plan to camp, since the lodge is being remodeled (scheduled to open in 1995); Mazama campground is a good place. Be sure to take the two-hour boat ride from Cleetwood Cove out to Wizard Island and around the lake. There are dozens of trails and climbs to magnificent lookouts. In the winter, when the crowds finally thin out, only the south and west entrance roads are kept open.

KLAMATH FALLS

This city of 19,000 people, the largest for 100 miles, is so isolated that it once led a movement to secede from Oregon and become the state of Jefferson. Now the residents happily welcome tourists, bird watchers, and sportspersons from both Oregon and California (just 25 miles south).

Favell Museum of Western Art is a true Western museum, with arrowheads, Indian artifacts, and the works of more than 200 Western artists; 125 West Main Street, (503) 882-9996.

The **Klamath County Museum** exhibits the volcanic geology of the region, Indian artifacts from all over Oregon, and relics from the Modoc wars; 1451 Main Street, (503) 883-4208.

Baldwin Hotel Museum, in an old (1907) hotel, retains many fixtures of the era; 31 Main Street, June through September, (503) 882-2501.

Ross Ragland Theater, a onetime Art Deco movie theater, now presents stage plays, concerts, and the like, an impressive 130 nights a year, (503) 884-0651.

Upper Klamath Lake, 143 square miles, is the largest lake in Oregon; it's fine for fishing and serves as the nesting grounds for many birds, including white pelicans. The Williamson River, which flows into the lake, yields plenty of trout.

RESTAURANTS

Alice's Saddle Rock Cafe
Main and 10th streets,
(503) 884-1444
1012 Main St,
Klamath Falls
Moderate; full bar; MC,
V; checks OK
Breakfast, lunch Sun-
Fri, dinner available with
reservations.

The Saddle Rock, from the outside, appears a consistent part of the timeworn Klamath Falls: a battered facade that says "old main street" cafe all over it. Inside, though, it's up to the minute: brick walls adorned with abstract black-and-white artwork. The fare is equally progressive: three excellent fresh pastas with distinctive sauces, Oregon beef, poultry, and magnificent burgers. Unfortunately, service can be ragged at times. Full-service catering available.

Fiorella's
S 6th St to Simmers,
(503) 882-1878
6139 Simmers Ave,
Klamath Falls
Moderate; full bar; MC,
V; local checks only
Dinner Tues-Sat

Residents of Klamath Falls appreciate the Northern Italian fare at Fiorella and Renato Durighello's restaurant. On a recent visit we had fine scaloppine Marsala and the house special, pasticio, both of which came with soup, salad and garlic bread. The pasta is homemade and delicious. Reservations welcome.

LODGINGS

Thompson's Bed and Breakfast by the Lake
Call for directions,
(503) 882-7938
1420 Wild Plum Court,
Klamath Falls,
OR 97601
Moderate; no credit cards;
checks OK

The Thompsons offer three full bedrooms with king-size beds and private entrances and baths. Sunsets over the Cascade Range provide a backdrop to the spectacular view of Upper Klamath Lake. Deer are frequent visitors to the back yard; bring your binoculars for bird watching. Owner Mary Thompson will cook almost anything you'd like for breakfast.

LAKEVIEW

At an elevation of nearly 4,300 feet, Lakeview also calls itself "Oregon's Tallest Town." It's better known for its geyser, Old Perpetual—which doesn't exactly rival Yellowstone's Old Faithful, but it's Oregon's only geyser. It's located in a pond at **Hunter's Hot Springs**, a 47-acre property dotted by hot-springs pools, on the west side of Highway 395 about 2 miles north of town. The geyser goes off once every 30 seconds or so, shooting 75 feet into the air for 3 to 5 seconds. It's been erupting regularly for some 60 years, apparently unleashed by someone trying to drill a well. **Hunter's Hot Springs resort**, built in the 1920s, now includes a pizza restaurant and a motel, (503) 947-2127.

Abert Lake, 20 miles north of Lakeview, is a stark, shallow body of water over which looms **Abert Rim**, a massive fault scarp. One of the highest exposed geologic faults in North America, the rim towers 2,000 feet above the lake.

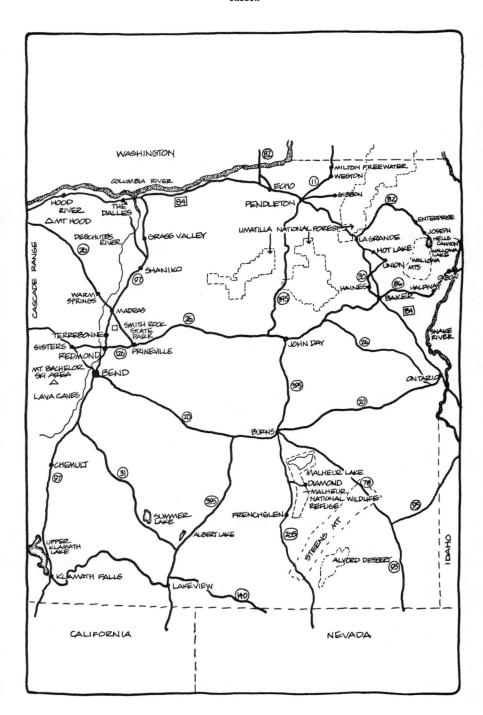

EASTERN OREGON

Two major routes: eastward mid-state from Warm Springs to John Day, and southeastward along I-84 from Pendleton to Ontario (with a diversion into the Wallowas), turning in-state again to Burns and Frenchglen.

GRASS VALLEY
RESTAURANTS

Carol's Kitchen
Easy, (503) 333-2255
Highway 97,
Grass Valley
Inexpensive; no alcohol;
no credit cards;
checks OK
Breakfast, lunch, every
day; dinner Mon-Sat

Wheat and barley farmers, ranchers, and Bend-bound truckers and travelers have one thing in common: an affection for Carol Grout's homemade cinnamon rolls, breads, and pies. Carol and Virgil Grout and their two daughters began this roadside diner nearly 10 years ago—and it's been a favorite Highway 97 stop ever since, with great malted milk shakes, meaty cheese-burgers, and fresh-cut fries. All road trips deserve a stop like this.

SHANIKO
LODGINGS

Shaniko Historic Hotel
Downtown Shaniko,
(503) 489-3441
Mail: PO Box 86,
Shaniko, OR 97057
Inexpensive; MC, V;
checks OK

Shaniko once boasted the Columbia Southern Railway (1900-1911), terrific vitality in shipping wool and gold, 13 saloons, the lot—and then died when the railhead moved. History buffs Jean and Dorothy Farrall bought this wreck of a hotel in the near-abandoned town in 1985, and they now rent out 18 grandmotherly, spot-less rooms. Each room has its own bath (previously, one bathroom served the whole place). Downstairs, you're never lonely: ranchers amble in to sit and yarn. After dinner stroll the false-fronted town, with its 11 occupied homes, so like the set of a John Wayne movie.

WARM SPRINGS
LODGINGS

Kah-Nee-Ta Resort
11 miles north of Warm
Springs on Hwy 3,
(503) 553-1112 or toll-
free (800) 831-0100
Mail: PO Box K, Warm

The Confederated Tribes of Warm Springs Reserva-tion some years ago built this posh resort, complete with a large arrowhead-shaped motel, a vast mineral-springs pool, tepees and cottages for rent, and such amenities as golf, tennis, riding, river rafting, and fancy restaurants. The Indian fry-bread and the bird-in-clay

Springs, OR 97761
Expensive; AE, DC, MC,
V; checks OK

dish are the crowd-pleasers, but the flavors are uninspired. Even so, Kah-Nee-Ta is a unusual experience with excellent service. You might stay in a roomy tepee (the lodge rooms are usually small), for instance, gathering the family around the fire pit in the evening. During the day, you can ride into the desert countryside, splash in the pool, or watch Indian dances.

REDMOND

LODGINGS

Inn at Eagle's Crest
5 miles west of Redmond
on Hwy 126, turn south
on Cline Falls Rd,
(503) 923-2453 or toll-
free (800) MUCH-SUN
Mail: PO Box 1215,
Redmond, OR 97756
Moderate; full bar; AE,
MC, V; checks OK
Breakfast, lunch, dinner
every day

Sisters has Black Butte, Bend has Sunriver, and now the high desert of Redmond has a full resort all its own. Eagle's Crest's large new private homes rim the 18-hole golf course and visitors choose one of the 75 rooms in the resort's hotel (the best ones have a golf course-facing deck) or a condominium. The condos are the better deal, especially if you come with four to eight people. They've got kitchens and access to the recreation center (not available to those who stay in the main building) with its indoor tennis, squash, and racquetball courts, workout room, masseuse, tanning salon, heated outdoor pool and Jacuzzi. Even if you don't get access to the rec room, there's plenty to do here: another outdoor pool and tennis courts, miles of biking and jogging trails, an equestrian center and playfields. The food at the resort's formal Canyon Club is predictable for such a clubby atmosphere with rancher-size portions. Service can be slow. The three-tiered deck outside provides a good view.

JOHN DAY

You are in the midst of dry cattle country in an area loaded with history: John Day is just off the old Oregon Trail, and the whole region was full of gold (during the height of the Gold Rush in 1862, $26 million in gold was mined in the neighboring town of Canyon City).

Kam Wah Chung Museum, next to the city park, was the stone-walled home of two Chinese herbal doctors at the turn of the century. A tour makes for an interesting glimpse of the Chinese settlement in the West: opium-stained walls, Chinese shrines, and herbal medicines are on display, as well as a small general store. Open May-October.

John Day Fossil Beds Monument lies 40 to 120 miles west, in three distinct groupings: the banded Painted Hills, extremely ancient fossils, and fascinating geological layers; 420 W Main Street, (503) 575-0721, for maps and brochures.

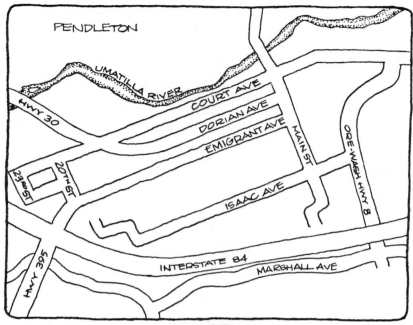

PENDLETON

In these parts, the name of this town is synonymous with the Wild West. Each September the Pendleton Round-Up rolls around—a big event since 1910 that features a dandy rodeo; call toll-free (800) 524-2984 for tickets and information. **Hamley's Saddlery** has been selling Western clothing, boots, hats, tack items, and custom-made saddles since 1883. It's a kind of shrine, the L.L. Bean of the West; 30 SE Court Street, (503) 276-2321.

Pendleton Woolen Mills gives tours Monday through Friday, and sells woolen yardage and imperfect blankets at reduced prices; 1307 SE Court Place, (503) 276-6911.

RESTAURANTS

Raphael's Restaurant and Lounge

Court and Dorion,
(503) 276-8500
233 SE 4th, Pendleton
Moderate; full bar; AE,
MC, V; checks OK
Lunch Tues-Fri, dinner
Tues-Sat

The successful Skyroom has flown its former coop at the Pendleton airport and landed in the historic Roy Raley House in downtown Pendleton. In this new space the Hoffmans continue to run their popular combination of authentic Native American fine art gallery (Raphael Hoffman is a member of the Nez Perce tribe) and reputable restaurant. Her husband Robert Hoffman, the chef, is not Indian—so don't expect any Native American dishes. The dinner menu runs heavily to well-prepared and well-presented seafood. Steamer clams are generally available—a treat in the deserts of eastern Oregon. An unusual entrée is the applewood-smoked prime rib; many of the patrons are crazy about it, but others resist such liberties with a standard favorite. There is a good-sized wine list, featuring moderately priced selections.

LODGINGS

Indian Hills Motor Inn
Exit 210 off I-84 at
304 SE Nye Ave,
(503) 276-6111
Mail: PO Box 1556,
Pendleton, OR 97801
Moderate; AE, DC, MC,
V; checks OK

A little to the south of Pendleton is the Red Lion's Indian Hills Motor Inn, the most lavish motel in town. Amenities include heated pool, lounge, dining room, and coffee shop. There are outsized, gaudy Western bas-reliefs in the reception areas. The view from your balcony over the low mountains and tilled fields of eastern Oregon can be inspiring—more so than the food, which ranges from indifferent to passable. Well-behaved pets okay.

ECHO

RESTAURANTS

The Echo Hotel
Restaurant and Lounge
20 miles west of Pendleton
on US 84 in Echo,
(503) 376-8354
110 Main St, Echo
Inexpensive; full bar;
MC, V; local checks only
Breakfast, lunch, dinner
every day

★

The simple exterior blends in with Old West symbols of Main Street—antique shops, a sturdy bank building, a wandering dog. The Echo's cedar-shake interior is filled with a curved bar, a split-level dining area, and three blackjack tables. Co-proprietor Susan Sperr greets every guest. This former rabbit cannery and historic hotel (there are hopes of reopening the upstairs as a bed and breakfast) serves up generous portions of 16-ounce prime rib and ranch-wagon specials. The house doesn't bother with vegetables or garnishes, just salad. The Echo prefers to emphasize real drinks (rather than local wines), hearty fare, and Oregon conviviality. This experience is especially popular on weekends with Pendleton residents.

WESTON

RESTAURANTS

Tollgate Mountain Chalet
16 miles E of Weston,
(503) 566-2123
Tollgate Mtn Hwy,
Weston
Moderate; full bar; MC,
V; local checks only
Breakfast Sat-Sun;
lunch, dinner every day

Walla Walla folks often drive 50 miles south through the lovely, waving wheatfields to this rustic eating place in the Blue Mountain forest. Locals order the chili, a hamburger, a Reuben sandwich, or a reasonable steak; the pies are homemade and different every day. It makes a particularly good spot for breakfast before a day of hiking or touring.

MILTON-FREEWATER

RESTAURANTS

The Oasis
Old Milton-Freewater
Hwy and State Line Rd,
(503) 938-4776
Milton-Freewater
Inexpensive; full bar;
MC, V; local checks only
Breakfast, lunch, dinner
Tues-Sun

This isn't a copy of a 1920s Western roadhouse, it's the real thing—and it hasn't ever changed: linoleum floors, lots of chrome. Eat in the bar and eavesdrop on the cowboys swapping stories. New owners Jack and Pat Koch are sticking with the roadhouse atmosphere. Although not every dish on the menu is a culinary triumph, the steaks are uniformly reliable and gigantic. Prime rib is good. On Sundays, chicken and dumplings are served family style, all you can eat, for about $7 per person—and a fine meal it is. For breakfast, a platter of biscuits and gravy goes for just over two bucks. Students from Walla Walla are fascinated with this place.

LODGINGS

Bar-M Guest Ranch
8 miles east of Gibbon on
river rd, (503) 566-3381
Mail: Rt 1, Box 263,
Adams, OR 97810
Moderate; no credit cards;
checks OK

The Bar-M is a 2,500-acre working dude ranch operated by the Baker family in the lovely Blue Mountains. The main ranch house (eight guest rooms and three baths) dates back to 1864, when it was built as a stage stop; its hand-hewn logs are still in good shape, and the interior is decorated with period pieces. There are also cabins near a brook, waterfall and a small lake. The ranch takes families (no pets and they prefer no children under 6) for a one-week-minimum stay (except during off-season). Included are excellent meals (local trout and home-grown vegetables) plus use of the mountain-savvy horses. Youngsters are encouraged to help with chores—mending fences, slopping pigs, or picking vegetables—if they want to. The riding, bird watching, and trout fishing are superb; there's a large warm-water pool; and evenings offer camp-outs, volleyball, and square dancing. Open April through September; many come just for raspberry season in July.

LA GRANDE

RESTAURANTS

Mamacita's
On Depot near Adams,
(503) 963-6223
110 Depot St, La Grande
Inexpensive; beer and
wine; no credit cards;
checks OK
Lunch Tues-Fri, dinner

Not only is this the liveliest place in town—this pueblo hops even on Sunday nights—but the Mexican food is fresh and tasty. We gave it high marks right from the start for its spicy and fresh salsa. House specials are usually the best things coming out of the kitchen, and at bargain prices. Add to the good food pleasant, helpful service, wine margaritas, and an adobe-colored wall

Tues-Sun

adorned with bright splotches of Mexicana, and you have our vote for best meal in La Grande.

Golden Crown Restaurant
Corner of Adams and Elm, (503) 963-5907
1116 Adams Ave,
La Grande
Inexpensive; beer and wine; MC, V; local checks only
Lunch, dinner every day

It's not hard to find. The bright vermilion-and-gold sign is so garish that you might not give this Chinese-American eatery a second glance. Even after you're inside, the vinyl booths give no hint of the menu's treasures. The wonton soup is heaped with freshly wrapped wontons, shrimp, pork, pea pods, mushrooms, and bok choy. The dish called Three Ingredients is a full platter of medium-sized shrimp, shreds of chicken, tender slices of barbecued pork, and an assortment of at least six kinds of vegetables.

LODGINGS

Stange Manor
Bed and Breakfast
Corner of Spring and Walnut, (503) 963-2400
1612 Walnut St,
La Grande, OR 97850
Moderate; AE, MC, V; checks OK

This restored timber baron's house on the hill behind town returns an elegance to this once-booming town. A sweeping staircase leads up to the five bedrooms; three have private baths, while the other two (usually rented as a suite) share a bath adjoining a sitting room with stone fireplace. The master suite is, of course, the best—and biggest—accommodation, but even if you opt for the maid's quarters, you won't have to lift a finger. The four hosts graciously welcome even unexpected guests (winter blizzards frequently close I-84) with tea in the living room. Breakfasts vary but favorites include German pancakes and French toast.

JOSEPH

This is the fabled land of the Wallowas, ancestral home of Chief Joseph, from which he fled with a band of Nez Perce warriors to his last stand near the Canadian border. Although Chief Joseph's remains are interred far from his beloved "land of the winding water," he saw to it that his father, Old Chief Joseph, would be buried here, in an Indian burial ground on the north shore of Wallowa Lake.

Wallowa Lake State Park on the edge of the **Wallowa Whitman National Forest** and **Eagle Cap Wilderness**, is perhaps the only state park in the country where locals still lament the fact that there are "never enough people." An Alpenfest with music, dancing, and Bavarian feasts happens every September, but the peak season is still midsummer, when the pristine lake and its shores are abuzz with go-carts, sailboats, and windsurfers. In winter the attraction is miles and miles of unpeopled cross-country trails throughout the lovely Wallowa highlands.

Wallowa Lake Tramway takes you by a steep ascent in a four-passenger gondola to the top of 8,200-foot Mount Howard, with spectacular overlooks and two miles of hiking trails. Summer only; PO Box 1261, La Grande, OR 97850, (503) 432-5331.

Hells Canyon, 35 miles east of Joseph, is the continent's deepest gorge, an awesome trench cut by the Snake River through sheer lava walls. The best view is from Hat Point near Imnaha, though McGraw Lookout is more accessible if you don't have four-wheel drive. Maps of the region's roads and trails, and information on conditions, are available at the Wallowa Valley Ranger District in Joseph, (503) 426-4978.

Hurricane Creek Llamas. You explore the lake-laden Eagle Cap Wilderness with a naturalist, while smiling llamas lug your gear. Hikes vary in length; hearty country meals are included (May-September). Call in advance, (503) 432-4455.

Wallowa Alpine Huts. Experienced backcountry ski guides offer 3-to-5-day powder-bound tours for skiers seeking the best of the Wallowa winterland. You stay in spartan tents and dine in a yurt (208) 882-1955.

RESTAURANTS

Vali's Alpine Deli and Restaurant
Wallow Lake State Park, (503) 432-5691
Joseph
Inexpensive; beer and wine; no credit cards; checks OK
Breakfast, dinner Tues-Sun (Winters Sat-Sun)

Don't let its "deli" status mislead; a dinner at Vali's usually requires reservations. The food here is Hungarian-German (and so is the decor) interspersed with a few authentic renditions from other cuisines: on a recent visit a savory shish kabob replaced Sunday's usually exceptional wiener schnitzel. At breakfast, Maggie Vali's homemade doughnuts are local legend, but don't show up hungry—the morning meal ends there. In the summer, sausage and cheese are available to take out for picnics.

LODGINGS

Chandlers—Bed, Bread, and Trail Inn
700 S Main St,
(503) 432-9765
Mail: PO Box 639,
Joseph, OR 97846
Inexpensive; MC, V; checks OK

Cedar shingles, multiangled roof lines, and cushiony wall-to-wall carpets make this bed and breakfast resemble an alpine ski lodge—in the middle of Joseph. A log staircase climbs from the comfortable living room to a loft where five simple bedrooms share three baths, a sitting room, and a workable kitchenette. The substantial breakfast and knowledgeable hosts make this a wonderful stopover for area explorers. No pets, children under 12, or smoking.

Wallowa Lake Lodge
Wallowa Lake State Park, (503) 432-9821
Mail: Route 1, Box 320,
Joseph, OR 97846
Moderate; beer and wine; MC, V; checks OK
Breakfast and dinner every day (dinner Fri-Sat winter)

After a few years of renovation, this historic lodge is still not perfect, but it's a big step up from its past. At check-in you must promise not to smoke in the rooms and they ask you not to eat or to drink alcohol there. The rooms are very small (especially the $40 ones). You'll do best if you reserve one of the originally restored rooms with a lake view. If you plan to stay longer, the rustic pine cabins on the lake with a living room, fireplace, and a kitchen allow for a bit more flexibility. Even if the rooms *were* spacious, we'd spend most of the evening in front of the magnificent stone fireplace in the knotty-pine lobby, and the days on the lake or in the mountains. A new deck is a splendid addition. Winters are painfully slow, especially in the dining room.

HAINES

RESTAURANTS

Haines Steak House

A short detour from I-84, exit 285 (eastbound) or exit 306 (westbound); (503) 856-3639 Old Hwy 30, Haines Moderate; full bar; AE, MC, V; checks OK Dinner Wed-Mon

There's no mistaking that you're in cattle country, pilgrim. Most of the vehicles surrounding this ever-busy spot are of four-wheel-drive breed and many of the men wear their cowboy hats while eating. Cowbells add to the ranchlike bedlam about every five minutes to announce a birthday or anniversary. This landmark burned to the ground on May 1, 1989. A year later, it returned to life as a now two-story eatery. Designer Phyllis Brownlee, known for her interior design work for several major hotels in Hawaii and the South Pacific, worked in collaboration with owners Steve and Gail Hart and sculptor Mick Brownlee to develop the "new-old" Haines Steak House. We particularly like the log-cabin type booths and the singletree "curtains." Although chicken and fish dishes are offered, stay with the beef; it's well selected, cut, and cooked. Next to beef, the hashbrowns are the best thing on the menu.

UNION

RESTAURANTS

Golden Harvest Chinese and American Restaurant

Main St at the railroad tracks, (503) 562-5105 101 S Main St, Union Inexpensive; beer and wine; MC, V; checks OK Lunch, dinner every day

Albert So and his wife, Monita, were born in China and Hong Kong respectively. In 1989, they laid claim to the former Knotty Pine Cafe. The counter with stools and the booths in this bright little restaurant are right out of the 1930s. Egg rolls, made from scratch, are some of the best we have found anywhere. (Try the vegetarian version.) The Sichuan dishes are our favorites. It adds only seven miles to swing through the Grande Ronde Valley between Baker and La Grande, and for such a small distance you will be treated to the best Asian food between Portland and Boise. Trust us.

LODGINGS

Queen Ann Inn Bed and Breakfast

On 5th, (503) 562-5566 782 N 5th St, Union, Oregon 97883 Moderate; MC, V; checks OK

If the immaculately kept grounds at the edge of town and the picture-perfect 1894 Victorian don't draw you in, then the smells from the kitchen and the warmth of your hostess, Blanche Kohler, surely will. It has four oak and ceramic tiled fireplaces, fancy moldings and gingerbread trim to spare. Three guest rooms are on the second floor and a fourth takes up the third floor. At press time, only one bath on the second floor served all rooms, although a bath on the third floor is planned. No smoking. No young children.

BAKER

Baker's restful city park, old-time main street, and mature shade trees may give it a Midwest flavor, but the backdrop is decidedly Northwest. Located in the valley between the Wallowas and the Elkhorns, Baker makes a good base camp for forays into the nearby mountain gold-rush towns.

The Elkhorn Mountains, west of Baker, contain most of the old mining towns, which you can tour on a 100-mile loop from Baker (some on unpaved roads).

Ghost towns. There's a restored narrow-gauge steam train at Sumpter, and the deserted towns of Granite, Bourne, Bonanza, and Whitney are well worth visiting.

Anthony Lakes Ski Area, 20 miles west of North Powder, has good powder snow, a chair lift, and cross-country trails; (503) 856-3277.

RESTAURANTS

The Anthony
1st St and Washington,
(503) 523-4475
1926 1st St, Baker
Moderate; beer and wine;
no credit cards;
checks OK
Dinner every day

Restaurateur Anthony Silvers single-handedly runs Baker's most unusual restaurant. Busts of General Grant and other classic fellows blend with strange paintings and leaping plaster lions to create an atmosphere that is weirdly eclectic, yet candlelit and intimate. A fine wine list is The Anthony's greatest coup, with far and away the most extensive selection in Baker. For dinner we found the poached whitefish tender and succulent; the sauces over some of the dishes are a bit too rich and assertive.

LODGINGS

Best Western Sunridge Inn
Off City Center exit,
(503) 523-6444
1 Sunridge Lane, Baker,
OR 97814
Inexpensive; AE, DC,
MC, V; checks OK

A sprawling Best Western, it's still the best of the lodgings in town, with 124 comfortable, spacious, air-conditioned rooms and an attractive pine finish. In the hot summer, you'll appreciate the grassy courtyard/pool area (summers only). Come winter, move indoors to the 18-foot whirlpool.

HALFWAY

Once just a midway stop between two bustling mining towns, Halfway is now the quiet centerpiece of Pine Valley—stashed between the fruitful southern slopes of the Wallowa mountains and the steep cliffs of Hells Canyon. The old church in the middle of town is now the headquarters of **Wildflowers of Oregon,** which dries locally picked flowers and sells the arrangements internationally, (503) 742-6474.

Hells Canyon, the continent's deepest gorge begins at Oxbow Dam, 16 miles east of Halfway. For spectacular views of the Snake River, drive from Oxbow to Joseph (take Highway 86 to Forest Road #39; summers only). Maps of the region's roads and trails are available from the Forest Service, just outside Halfway, (503) 742-7511.

The folks at **Wallowa Llamas** lead 3-to-8-day trips along the edge of Hells Canyon or into the pristine Eagle Cap Wilderness high in the Wallowas, while their friendly sure-footed beasts lug your gear and plenty of food; for a brochure or information call (503) 742-4930.

For those who would rather experience the raging river up close, **Hells Canyon Adventures** in Oxbow arranges jet boat tours or float-and-horseback combination excursions leaving from Hells Canyon Dam; call (503) 785-3352 or **Cornucopia Wilderness Pack Station** at (503) 893-6400.

LODGINGS

Clear Creek Farm
Call ahead for directions,
(503) 742-2238
Mail: Rt 1, Box 138,
Halfway, OR 97834
Moderate; MC, V; checks
OK

Once you find this somewhat quirky paradise, you'll know why Mary Ann Carr, her mother, and 373 other residents of Halfway have carefully chosen this fertile valley as home. There are four homey bedrooms in the farmhouse, but during summer families and small groups bunk up in either of the two board-and-batten cabins. It's delightfully campish, with bathrooms in a separate building. There are several small ponds for swimming, a field of lavender, fragrant herb garden, and 500 peach trees. When the snow falls, getting up the driveway can be treacherous, but the cross-country skiing is unbeatable. Billowing Dutch babies, luscious peaches (seasonal), and fresh-squeezed grapefruit juice await you in the morning. Bring your friends; group rates are cheaper, *and* Mary Ann might just throw in a wonderful Mexican dinner. Cha cha cha.

ONTARIO

RESTAURANTS

Casa Jaramillo
2 blocks south of Idaho
Ave, (503) 889-9258
157 SE 2nd St, Ontario
Inexpensive; full bar;AE,
MC, V; checks OK
Lunch, dinner Tues-Sun

★

This Mexican cantina gives cool respite from the hot eastern Oregon desert. Recently expanded and remodeled, its tropical atmosphere is perfect for families. For the past 24 years, John Jaramillo and his family have been turning out authentic Mexican fare. Try the enchiladas rancheros, with fresh crunchy onions and a chile verde sauce that delivers. Great guacamole.

LODGINGS

Tapadera Motor Inn
Off I-84 in Ontario,
(503) 889-8621,
1249 Tapadera Ave,

The Tapadera is no longer a Best Western and has removed its sauna; nevertheless, it continues to be Ontario's finest. Its 97 rooms have all been recarpeted and about half are now designated non-smoking. Some

Ontario, OR 97914
Moderate, AE, DC, MC,
V; checks OK

suites have king-size waterbeds. No charge for children 11 and under.

BURNS

The town of Burns, once the center of impressive cattle kingdoms ruled by legendary figures Pete French and William Hanley, is a welcome oasis in this desolate high-desert country. The look of the land, formed by 10 million years of volcanic activity, was branded on the American consciousness in a few decades by the thousands of Western movies filmed in the area.

Malheur National Wildlife Refuge, 37 miles south on Route 205, is one of the country's major bird refuges—184,000 acres of verdant marshland and lakes. It is an important stop for migrating waterfowl in spring and fall, and the summer breeding grounds for magnificent sandhill cranes (with wingspans approaching 100 inches), trumpeter swans, and many other birds; (503) 493-2612.

RESTAURANTS

Pine Room Cafe
On Monroe and Egan,
(503) 573-6631
543 W Monroe St, Burns
Moderate; full bar; MC,
V; checks OK
Dinner Tues-Sat

For more than 30 years the Kinder family has operated this pleasant cafe, and they've built up a faithful clientele. Careful preparations and interesting recipes are the reason: the chicken livers in brandy and wine sauce are different and popular, and the Kinders still refuse to give out the secret ingredients of their German potato-dumpling soup, a local favorite. They also make their own bread and cut their own steaks in the kitchen.

The Powerhouse
East side of town,
(503) 573-9060
305 E Monroe, Burns
Moderate; full bar; MC,
V; local checks only
Lunch, dinner every day

This is where the locals go. A restaurant in a stone-built former power station (1924), it's lined inside with barn wood and ranch artifacts. Monday nights they pack 'em in with fresh roasted prime rib, done just the way you like it. The menu's pretty standard with burgers and the works, but the extras like homemade bread and daily-baked pies really light up the meal.

LODGINGS

Best Western Ponderosa
Hwy 20, (503) 573-2047
577 W Monroe, Burns,
OR 97720
Inexpensive; AE, DC,
MC, V; no checks

With 52 rooms, this is the preferred place to stay in Burns. It's blessed with a swimming pool to cool you off after a hot day's drive. What more? Pets are okay.

DIAMOND

LODGINGS

Diamond Hotel
12 miles east of Hwy 205,
(503) 493-1898
Mail: Box 10, Diamond,
OR 97722
Inexpensive; beer and
wine; MC, V; checks OK
Breakfast, dinner every
day for hotel guests only.

Except for the new paint on the Diamond Hotel (and a couple of trucks parked out front) you might mistake Diamond for a ghost town. Its six residents keep the looming ghosts at bay. In 1991, Judy and Jerry Santillie, formerly of the Frenchglen Hotel, remodeled this building and opened it to those exploring Malheur territory. It now quintuples as hotel, general store, deli, post office and—late in the afternoon—local watering hole. The five small bedrooms upstairs share two baths and a sitting area on both floors. The Santillies have lived in the area for seven years and are filled with high-desert stories. Judy used to be a ranch cook (there's always meat, potatoes, vegetables, salad, bread). A platter of tenderloin comes with slabs for every taste from well-done to "so rare that a good vet could get it back up on its feet." Desserts (perhaps a marionberry cobbler with ice cream or Judy's Guadalupe River Bottom Cake) are double, no triple, the size you need them to be—and that's okay with us.

FRENCHGLEN

The flooding around Harney Lake kept tourists away from this beautiful little town (population 15) a few years back, but now, happily, the highway is above water and tourists are once again stopping in while touring Malheur (see Burns introduction) or to spy **Steens Mountain**, Frenchglen's biggest tourist attraction. It rises gently from the west to an elevation of 9,670 feet, then drops sharply to the Alvord Desert in the east. A dirt road goes all the way to the ridgetop (summers only), and another skirts around this massive escarpment (an adventurous day trip by the vast borax wastelands of the once Alvord Lake, numerous hot springs, and fishing lakes near the northeastern end of the route). Neither route is recommended if there's been much precipitation. Geologically, Steens forms the world's largest block fault, created by volcanic lava flows and glacial action.

LODGINGS

Frenchglen Hotel
60 miles south of Burns
(503) 493-2825
Mail: General Delivery,
Frenchglen, OR 97736
Inexpensive; beer and
wine; MC, V; checks OK
Breakfast, lunch, dinner
every day (closed mid-Nov
through mid-Feb)

★

A small, white frame building that dates back to 1916 has eight small, plain bedrooms upstairs with shared baths, renting for about $40 a night; Room 2 is the largest, nicest, and the only one with a view of Steens. Nothing's very square or level here, and that's part of the charm. Downstairs are a large screened-in verandah and the dining room. The current managers, John Ross and Karla Litzenberger, cook up good simple meals for guests and drop-by visitors. Ranch-style dinner is one seating only (6:30pm sharp) and reservations are a must. But if you miss dinner, John and Karla won't let you go hungry (this is ranch country).

WASHINGTON

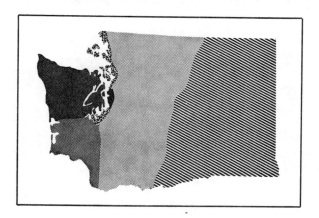

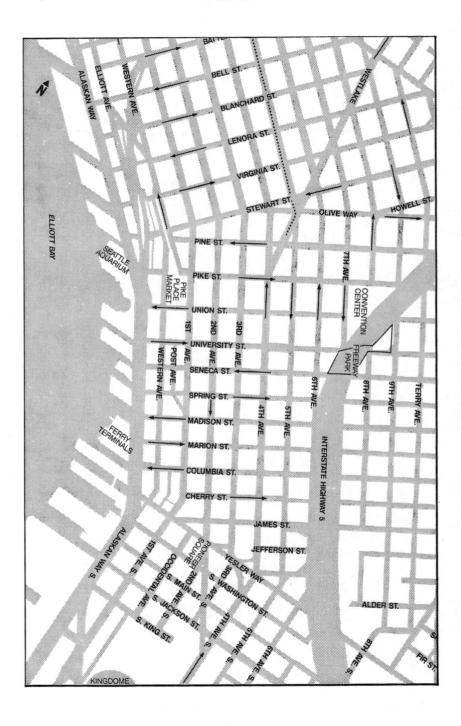

SEATTLE AND ENVIRONS

▲

Including the suburbs: Edmonds and Bothell to the north, Woodinville, Redmond, Kirkland, Bellevue, Mercer Island, and Issaquah to the east; Bainbridge Island to the west; Tukwila, Burien, Des Moines, and Kent to the south.

In the past few years, it seemed the entire nation, in one way or another, had turned its eyes on this far corner of the United States. National polls voted it the best city for virtually everything, housing prices were still competitive, TV hit series (*Twin Peaks, Northern Exposure*) were filmed in nearby towns, and it was one of the few places in the country unscathed by the recession. With all this attention, the Emerald City chances losing a little of its sparkle. The traffic (barely alleviated by the opening of the new bus tunnel) is getting more and more congested, and the skyline is cluttered with major new buildings. The Convention Center was built literally *over* I-5 in the middle of downtown.

Despite all this, the city remains a gem, with its striking views of Puget Sound and the Olympic Mountains to the west, the Cascades to the east, and Mount Rainier just to the south. The up side of this rapid growth and international sophistication is outstanding restaurants, thriving cultural organizations, fine sports, and fabulous citywide festivals. The Seattle area supports such abundance because it has a highly educated population dedicated to making it work, a surplus of singles (who like to go out), lots of young families (determined to make it a kids' place), and a climate as temperate in weather as it is tolerant in politics. Add to this one of the largest universities in the West, and you can see why the populace has a striving, bettering cast of mind.

What follows are a few highlights of Seattle's entertainment; for a detailed city guide, we refer you to our companion book, *Seattle Best Places.*

THE ARTS

Music. Seattle Opera has entered the big leagues with productions of often stunning brilliance. The Seattle Symphony, under conductor Gerard Schwarz, maintains a high level of consistency and artistic acclaim. Chamber music has become a local passion, with the Santa Fe Chamber Music Festival (at University of Washington's Meany Hall) and the Seattle Chamber Music Festival (at bucolic Lakeside School) during the summer; Seattle Camerata, the Early Music Guild, the Northwest Chamber Orchestra, the Ladies Musical Club, and the International Chamber Music Series at Meany Hall fill out the winter and spring seasons.

Theater. This is this city's strongest cultural card, with a dozen professional theaters (the third-largest number per capita in the U.S.) and twice as many small groups producing a great deal of quality work. The Seattle Repertory Theatre mounts classics and contemporary fare with the highest production values. A Contemporary Theatre excels at modern drama in an intimate space (summer season); The Empty Space, in Pioneer Square, has a national reputation for new works, crazy comedies, and classics (winter season); Intiman is the place for classics and some more adventurous works (summer); The Seattle Group Theatre, in the Ethnic Cultural Theatre, is the city's only theater company with a strong ethnic approach.

Dance. Pacific Northwest Ballet has evolved into a company of national stature; its regular season mixes Balanchine masterworks with new pieces, and the Christmas highlight is a breathtaking realization of *Nutcracker* with sets by Maurice Sendak. Meany's World Dance Series and On The Boards present touring companies.

Visual Arts. At press time, the opening of the new Robert Venturi–designed Seattle Art Museum was imminent. The museum's permanent collections will be moved to the new location on University Street between 1st and 2nd avenues, at which time the Volunteer Park branch will close for remodeling. The Henry Art Gallery at the UW mounts thoughtful and challenging shows. The main galleries— it's a very good scene—are found predominantly in Pioneer Square; gallery openings are the first Thursday of every month; (206) 448-4938.

There are more than 1,000 works of art on public display in the city (due in part to a city ordinance calling for 1 percent of capital improvement funds to be spent on public art); for a free map to these places, call the Seattle Arts Commission, (206) 684-7171.

Architecture. Seattle's skyline is forever changing with the most recent striking additions being NBBJ's Two Union Square (6th and Union); the AT&T Gateway Tower, designed by Bassetti/Norton/Metler/Rekebics; the Callison Partnership's elegant Pacific First Centre (5th Avenue and Pike Street); and most recently Zimmer Gunsul Frasca's boxy Second and Seneca Building, with its distinctive dome on top. Pioneer Square, rebuilt after the fire of 1889, has a coherence that is rare in American "old towns" and makes for a lovely stroll. Pike Place Market is a shrine for architects, in part because no architect had much to do with its jumbled, exuberant vitality.

OTHER THINGS TO DO

Nightlife. There are clubs all over town, but Seattle's music scene is centered around two neighborhoods: Pioneer Square offers every kind of music from jazz to sophisticated rock, and Ballard brings in the blues, as well as traditional and new folk music. The jazz scene is often very good. There are good coffeehouses on Capitol Hill and in the University District; the new music scene is found in the Denny Regrade.

Exhibits. The Woodland Park Zoo is a world leader in naturalistic displays, particularly the uncannily "open" African savannah and the exotic Asian elephant forest. The Museum of Flight, to the south of the city, is notable for its sophisticated design and impressive collection. Pacific Science Center, with a planetarium and revolving displays on all sorts of subjects, graces Seattle Center, that legacy of the 1962 World's Fair; there is a decent aquarium on the central waterfront; and at the Hiram M. Chittenden Locks in Ballard, where the ships are lifted to Lake Washington, salmon climb the ladders on their way to spawn.

Parks. Seattle's horticultural climate is among the finest in the world—damp and mild all year—so the parks are spectacular and numerous. The Washington Park Arboretum, with 5,500 species of plants and gentle pathways amid azaleas, is the loveliest; Discovery Park, with grassy meadows and steep sea cliffs, is the wildest; Green Lake, with its 2.8-mile running-walking-rollerblading track, is by far the most active. Freeway Park, built over I-5 downtown, is the most urban.

Sports. The town is football-mad, which means there are hardly any tickets (test your concierge's powers). The UW Huskies, usually contenders, play in one of the land's most beautiful stadiums, with arrival by boat a local custom; the

Seahawks lift the roof off the drab Kingdome. The SuperSonics are playing good basketball again in the bandbox Coliseum until their new facility is built near the Kingdome; the UW women's basketball team is one of the top 20 in the country; Seattle's baseball team, the Mariners are on an upswing in the ill-suited Dome.

Shopping. The downtown area has many of the designer-name stores, plus some excellent, full-line department stores, and Westlake Center, a glossy new mall smack in the middle of the downtown congestion, across from Nordstrom's headquarters store. Of the specialty shopping areas, we favor the Pike Place Market (for foodstuffs), Capitol Hill (for funky clothes and furnishings), the U District (for books), and Pioneer Square (for fine arts and crafts).

Transportation. The Metro bus is free in downtown's commercial core; otherwise, the fare is 75 cents within the city ($1 during peak hours), and $1 if you cross the city line ($1.50 peak hours). Another common commute is on the Washington State Ferries, which cross Puget Sound frequently. Riding the ferries also happens to be one of the most enjoyable ways to view the city's skyline. Ferries to both the Navy town of Bremerton (1 hour one way) and rural Bainbridge Island (½ hour one way) leave from Colman Dock.

RESTAURANTS

Georgian Room (Four Seasons Olympic Hotel)
Between 4th and 5th on University,
(206) 621-7889
411 University St, Seattle
Expensive; full bar; AE, DC, MC, V; checks OK
Breakfast every day, lunch Mon-Fri, dinner Mon-Sat, brunch Sun

The Georgian Room at the Four Seasons Olympic Hotel is a grand, elegant space with high ceilings, huge chandeliers, and all the accoutrements of formal dining, right down to the silver-domed covers on the plates of food and the linen napkins placed in your lap. Live piano music tinkles unobtrusively from the center of the room. Chef Kerry Sear, originally from England by way of Chartwell's of the Four Seasons in Canada, is the Georgian Room's new hotshot executive chef. He's turning what was once not much more than a formidable hotel dining experience into an evening elegant, innovative, and very unexpected: tempura basil sprigs garnish a salad of bitter greens, a pear consommé is the broth for a wild-mushroom ravioli soup. The lamb rib eye with foie gras and whipped potatoes was unconventionally stacked in the middle of your plate. The silky smooth and brilliant blood orange–colored red pepper and smoked salmon bisque was a fine example of why this restaurant is so good. Moist venison was served on a bed of wild mushroom risotto. From the main menu came lobster and imaginative blackened tomato lasagne with smoked tomatillo butter. The best way to sample Sear's talents is to order the four-course chef's menu ($40). For $20 more, the courses are complemented by carefully selected wines by the glass (1981 Sauternes, 1985 Bordeaux)—an excellent value. Dessert might be tarte Tatin with a butter caramel sauce, or a layered sorbet cake with mango sauce.

Labuznik
On 1st between Stewart and Virginia,
(206) 441-8899

Artistic temperament has always been part of the charm of Labuznik and its perfectionist owner, Peter Cipra. Customers who've known Labuznik since its inception 14 years ago claim that service is as exact and

1924 1st Ave,
Seattle
Expensive; full bar; AE,
MC, V; no checks
Dinner Tues-Sat

★★★★

professional as ever. While other chefs have followed fads and experimented with showy Mediterranean, Japanese, and nouvelle influences, Cipra has stuck steadfastly by the stolid traditions of his native Czechoslovakia. His restaurant is the apotheosis of meat and potatoes, with sublime dumplings and sauerkraut on the side. You have to admire the confidence of a chef who dares ignore color in presentation; still, the uniformly monochromatic meals are elegant and comforting. Concentrating as he does on a narrow, near-changeless menu, it's no surprise that Cipra has found the very best meats, and simple preparations that clear the stage to show off their virtues: a richly sauced seasonal special of pork medallions with fresh chanterelles, the excellent Tournedos Black and White and veal Orloff. Labuznik's wine list is a wise and succinct selection from moderate to very high price levels. The cafe in the front of the restaurant is a bargain, relatively speaking. Desserts are the one disappointment.

Adriatica

Corner of Aloha
and Dexter,
(206) 285-5000
1107 Dexter Ave N,
Seattle
Expensive; full bar; AE,
DC, MC, V; checks OK
Dinner every day

★★★

The quiet crowd is urban and sophisticated, the site a glossy refurbished house perched on a hillside (up a long flight of stairs) overlooking the broad expanse of Lake Union. This is Mediterranean food brought to the city, polished to perfection but with an earthy lustiness. All is overseen in cordial style by owner/host Jim Malevitsis, who leaves the kitchen in the estimable hands of chef Nancy Flume. Her skill there is evidenced by a remarkable record of consistency. Most diners start with fried calamari and garlic dip, probably the best-known appetizers in the city, but as successful are the taramasalata spread on bread or the delicate, paper-thin carpaccio. The menu runs to savory grilled meats, expertly done pastas, and some of the finest fish in the city, cooked to perfection and presented under inspired sauces. A baklava-like dessert—dates, walnuts, and brandy baked in phyllo with Cognac and almond whipped cream—is rich and delicious. There aren't tables for two near the window. An extensive cellar includes over 20 champagnes and 300 wines.

Al Boccalino

At Yesler and Alaskan
Way, (206) 622-7688
1 Yesler Way,
Seattle
Expensive; beer andwine;
AE, MC, V; checks OK
Lunch Mon-Fri, dinner
Mon-Sat

★★★

It's tucked inconspicuously almost under the Alaskan Way viaduct, but Al Boccalino has drawn quite a bit of attention to its stunning Italian fare. Co-owner Luigi de Nunzio has gathered recipes from his native Apulia, the heel of the Italian boot, and with chef Tim Roth produces renditions of these to make your palate sing. Some dishes, like an herbed saddle of lamb, reflect the Arabic and Greek influence on southern Italian cuisine, but de Nunzio isn't so strict about regional food that a couple of resplendent risottos didn't find their way onto the menu. Intriguing salads and antipasti make use of the best ingredients, elevating sometimes-simple dishes to sublime heights of taste and texture. Luigi seems to be everywhere at once, joking with diners, yelling good-naturedly in Italian at his waiters, and attending to too many favored customers; there have been complaints of slow service, and dinners are pricy for such comfort food. Chic mottled-mustard and raw-brick walls are accented with dark wood and stained glass; a skewed shape to the rooms creates the desired atmosphere of intimacy and intrigue.

Botticelli Cafe
Corner of 1st and Stewart, (206) 441-9235
101 Stewart St, Seattle
Inexpensive; no alcohol; no credit cards; checks OK
Breakfast, lunch Mon-Sat

This very polished, very Italian four-table aperitif bar is a place to linger over one of Seattle's finest espressos or irresistible panini (toasted Italian sandwiches). If you so much as peek in the door you might be coaxed in by Angelo Belgrano and expected to stay awhile. Even if he's not there, the excellent sandwiches are enough of a draw—Sicilian focaccia bread toasted warm with fresh mozzarella, artichoke hearts, Roma tomatoes, and sweet red peppers and drizzled with thyme, oregano, and extra-virgin olive oil. Expect exceptional quality and freshness. Espresso, Italian mineral waters, and fresh fruit ices are for sipping. At press time, Belgrano was planning to add some gelati to his summer menu and keep his small cafe open until early evening.

Cafe Sport
1 block north of Pike
Place Market, on
Western, (206) 443-6000
2020 Western Ave, Seattle
Moderate; full bar; AE, DC, MC, V; checks OK
Breakfast, lunch, dinner every day

Cafe Sport/Bellevue
Bellevue Way and NE 8th, (206) 453-1111
Winter Garden in Bellevue Place, Bellevue
Moderate; full bar; AE, DC, MC, V; checks OK
Lunch Mon-Fri, dinner Mon-Sat

A few years ago, Cafe Sport became one of Seattle's most distinctive restaurants, the standard-bearer for a consistently fresh blend of New American and Pacific Rim cuisines. Even after a turmoil of chef changes, the classic Sport dishes (Dungeness crab cakes, grilled chicken breast on spicy noodles, and the fabulously messy shoestring potatoes) still receive many accolades. We've become accustomed to the excellent soups (like the famous black bean with crème fraîche and tomato salsa), the spicy pan-fried oysters, the usually outstanding seafood dishes (grilled swordfish with fresh tomato vinaigrette), and the perky and intelligent service. However, lately we've noticed some slips: service has been less attentive, meats have been improperly cooked, one pasta arrived cold and congealed, and a puttanesca sauce was a planet away from the original recipe—no red peppers, no capers, no anchovies. For now, enjoy the casual cafe half of the original Sport and choose the always superb preparations of yellowfin tuna, or nibble on the antipasto plate, loaded with marinated vegetables, a whole roasted head of garlic, and goat cheese. Each entrée is paired with a recommended wine—a very helpful feature. Among our favorite desserts are a dark chocolate terrine with white chocolate sauce. We know what this restaurant's capable of, but recently it seems as if someone has let this sport slip out of first place. The Bellevue restaurant is attempting a more Mediterranean/Middle Eastern inclination (though Sport fans will recognize more than a few of the dishes).

Cafe Lago
On 24th Ave E, 6 blocks south of Hwy 520, (206) 329-8005 2305 24th Ave E, Seattle Moderate; beer and wine; no credit cards; checks OK Dinner Tues-Sun

Little Cafe Lago in Montlake has garnered a lot of admiration. Carla Leonardi and Jordi Viladas hail from Tuscany and Calabria (by way of Connecticut) respectively, and here they've combined the flavors of both cuisines. This exuberant and friendly little restaurant comes closer in atmosphere than almost any place in town to the essence of a genuine Italian trattoria, from the rough red wine to the basket of Ciro Pasciuto's chewy, rustic bread that arrives on the paper-covered table as soon as you sit down. The simple menu, which changes twice a week or so, includes real Italian antipasti (braseola and coppa instead of salami, plus fontina, fresh mozzarella, and roasted red peppers). One-person pizzas bake in the wood-fired oven in the back and emerge with a crisp crust and an outstanding herbed tomato sauce and fresh mozzarella. The fresh ravioli is sometimes filled with sweet butternut squash or the four-cheese lasagna with a hint of nutmeg. There's a lot of good cheer here. And the exemplary service has been known to go beyond the call of duty.

Dahlia Lounge
4th Ave between Stewart and Virginia, (206)682-4142 1904 4th Ave, Seattle Moderate; full bar; AE, DC, MC, V; checks OK Lunch Mon-Fri, dinner every day

Tom Douglas' Dahlia Lounge has blossomed into one of Seattle's finest restaurants. The space is vermilion with floral-upholstered booths and artful papier-mâché fish lamps, and the menu brilliantly captures the pioneer spirit of Northwest cuisine. If it has to be defined, it's somewhere between the comfort food of the '50s and Northwest cuisine of the '90s. Who else would dare feature roast pork with sweet-potato hashbrowns, delicate Dungeness crab cakes with Wild West Salsa, and charred rare tuna puttanesca with egg noodles on the same menu? Douglas not only gets away with it, he does a superb job at delighting foodies with tastes they never expected to like: the hoisin barbecued salmon with fried rice was simultaneously light and spicy; the roast duck with green peppercorn sauce came with a soothing butternut squash risotto. Lunches run a similarly unexpected multiethnic course, from tomato-and-sweet-red-pepper soup with sorrel cream to a pita sandwich filled with grilled chicken, hummus and tzatziki. The desserts are light on chocolate and heavy on invention—the pear tart is ethereal. Douglas's relaxed, casual, and professional tone (he likes to chat with the diners) has rubbed off on his outstanding staff.

Fullers
(Seattle Sheraton Hotel)
Between Pike and Union on 6th, (206) 447-5544 1400 6th Ave, Seattle

In the late '80s, repeated doses of national publicity boosted the reputation of the Seattle Sheraton's top-of-the-line restaurant to unsustainable levels. The room, with its original artworks by Northwest masters, is dignified and agreeable, the service assiduous, and the

Expensive; full bar; AE, MC, V; checks OK
Lunch Mon-Fri, dinner Mon-Sat

kitchen staff, under youthful chef Caprial Pence, first-rate. But Fuller's is a hotel restaurant which owes a lot of its turnover (if not reputation) to catered affairs, banquets, and once-in-a-generation graduation or anniversary celebrations: its output can't consistently live up to the level of smaller restaurants devoted exclusively to demanding individual gourmet diners. That said, Fuller's has maintained a respectable if not outstanding record among top-end Seattle dining rooms, and with co-chef John Pence joining his wife in the kitchen, morale and dedication to results seem to be on the rise. Appetizers tend to be outstanding, and fresh seafood is always a reliable choice (sea scallops with hummus and roast-onion-tomato confit, kasuzuke cod with black-bean vinaigrette and spicy rice cakes, salmon in a rhubarb-orange compote). There's a new emphasis on game among the meat items: roast duck in a five-peppercorn plum glaze, guinea hen with north African seasonings on a bed of red lentils. Desserts have never been Fullers' strong point, though under John Pence that may improve. The wine list is moderately extensive, moderately imaginative, and expensive.

The Hunt Club (Sorrento Hotel)

Madison and Terry,
(206) 622-6400
900 Madison St, Seattle
Expensive; full bar; AE, DC, MC, V; checks OK
Breakfast, lunch, tea, dinner every day, brunch weekends

Dark with burnished mahogany paneling and deep red bricks, this is one of the most pleasant restaurants in the city, especially in the winter. When the days are longer, we prefer to eat outdoors in the courtyard. Barbara Figueroa offers the kinds of dishes that make the traveling executive feel well fed, as well as the kind of outrageous combinations that make nouvelle cuisine the object of so many ambivalent feelings. The kitchen has a tendency toward overcomplication: entrées occasionally come with so many little surprises you find yourself wondering what it all is and why it's sharing the same plate. But as you work your way around the plate from a tender bite of Ellensburg lamb to a Brussels sprout to eggplant stuffed with lamb sausage and Oregon blue cheese, it can also be a pleasant journey, with no need to surmise why. Overall, it would be difficult to imagine getting an unsatisfying meal at the Hunt Club. After dinner, savvy patrons retire to the lobby bar for dessert and coffee . Afternoon tea with pastries and finger sandwiches is served here every day.

Le Gourmand

Corner of 6th NW and Market, (206) 784-3463
425 NW Market St, Seattle
Expensive; beer andwine; AE, MC, V; checks OK
Dinner Wed-Sat

Inside an unlikely Ballard storefront on an unlikely street for a French restaurant lives the spirit of Parisian dining. Owners Robin Sanders and Bruce Naftaly have created a calm, intimate dining space, simply appointed with fresh linens and candles, and filmy curtains to obscure the traffic on busy NW Market Street. Seasonal mushrooms, blossoms, and bottom fish arrive daily from Naftaly's carefully chosen list of local suppliers, all to be generously embellished with Naftaly's forte, sauces. Each meal might start with Whidbey Island steamed mussels in tomato/garlic/basil broth, or zucchini and mint soup. Entrées may include an unbelievably tender venison with a dark elderberry and pinot noir stock, simultaneously tart and sweet; roast rack of lamb coated with mustard seed crumbs; or beef tenderloin infused with shallot butter and homemade mustard. The accompaniment one winter was a platter of Russian kale, red and green chard, New Zealand spinach, and amaranth. Finish with a wild-greens salad feathered with calendulas, nasturtiums, and rose petals. A divine crème brulée garnished with chopped hazelnuts and brandied raspberries nearly gilds the lily.

Nikko
Fifth and Stewart
(Westin), (206)322-4905
1900 Fifth Ave, Seattle
Moderate; full bar; AE,
DC, MC, V; no checks
Dinner Mon-Sat

Shiro Kashiba, a master showman who claims position as Seattle's first sushi chef, is still among the best. But by the end of 1991, he's moving his venerable restaurant from the International District to a large new space in the Westin. For now, go to King and 13th where Shiro's art packs the house with diners who queue up at the sushi bar to watch the expert craft bite-size Japanese delicacies—squid gut, fish liver, fish skin—with remarkable alacrity. Trouble is, newcomers to Japanese cuisine (or those who don't favor ordering in the traditional Japanese way, by asking the chef to prepare whatever's freshest) receive the same first-rate fish, but with second-rate presentation and service. Menu items have also been inconsistent lately: we've encountered tempura that was light and lacy one night, almost gummy the next. If you can't wait for a seat at Nikko's bar, you have a choice of the dining tables or tatami rooms (one of which can hold a private party of 40). Either place, ask for the Japanese menu for more esoteric (and more carefully prepared) items, including snack-size portions of wonderful things like steamed clams with sake and cold spinach with soy and sesame.

Ray's Boathouse
60th NW and Seaview,
(206) 789-3770
6049 Seaview Ave NW,
Seattle
Moderate; full bar; AE,
DC, MC, V; checks OK
Lunch Mon-Fri (Sat-Sun
cafe only), dinner
every day

The self-confident Ray's has bounced back from a fire a few years ago, and it feels unchanged—same attention to very fresh seafood (it doesn't come any fresher), same casual cafe/bar up a flight, same three-week wait for a Saturday night two-top, same peerless (and unabashedly romantic) vista of the Sound, the Olympics, the sunset. In composing your meal, concentrate on the simple fresh items that Ray's has proven it can do: grilled rockfish splashed with white wine, capers, and lemon juice; smoked black cod, meltingly broiled; scallop sauté (and little danger of overcooking here). Ray's appetizers prove tempting and substantially sized. The superb wine list (beautifully organized by country and varietal, with a page devoted to splits) and the extremely professional service help nudge the whole experience into the realm your final tab reflects. If the reservation wait for the dining room proves weeks long, try the upstairs cafe. Walk-ins are often successful, and the prices are more moderate.

Rover's
1½ blocks from the Arboretum at 28th and Madison, (206) 325-7442
2808 E Madison St, Seattle
Expensive; beer and wine; AE, DC, MC, V; checks OK
Dinner Tues-Sat

Chef Thierry Rautureau has created a neighborhood restaurant that reaches beyond the boundaries of any neighborhood. The semiformal setting offers quiet intimacy, but the simultaneously unobtrusive and attentive service puts you at ease. Great for a three-hour meal—never rushed. Dinners are marvelously sauced, classically French-inspired treatments of Northwest fare. Rautureau's forte is seafood, and he's adept at finding the best quality ingredients. All in all, the food is a tad fussy and expensive, but meals are portioned with a generous hand. The outstanding Columbia River sturgeon with Maine lobster, served on a bed of ocean salad (seaweed, agar, Japanese mushrooms, sesame, rice vinegar, and white sesame seed) and complemented by a rich, fresh black truffle sauce. The steamed halibut was served with caviar, braised leeks, and lobster sauce. Rautureau's silky crème brulée is gently flavored with ginger and a hint of lavender. Wines are carefully chosen from the Northwest and France, with many half-bottles available. Or try a five-course feast: the *menu dégustation*, Rautureau's masterpiece, for a fixed price ($39.50; vegetarian version also available). Wonderful on a summer night when you can eat in the enclosed garden.

Saleh al Lago
On the east side of Green Lake, (206) 522-7943 or (206) 524-4044
6804 E Green Lake Way, Seattle
Expensive; full bar; AE, DC, MC, V; local checks only
Lunch Mon-Fri, dinner Mon-Sat

Saleh Joudeh puts out some of the some of the best Italian food in Seattle. It's style slightly heavier and spicier than Northern Italian, in an understatedly austere space. The ravioli al burro nero is a preparation of pasta stuffed with ricotta and spinach that takes on a deeper hue with the addition of a rich brown garlic sauce. Favorites which almost always have a berth on the menu are the calamari antipasto and the simple yet exquisite risotto verde (arborio rice with spinach, cream, and Parmesan). The *assaggini* plate is a wonderful array of tidbits that takes full advantage of Northwest ingredients, such as chanterelles, perfectly marinated. Seafood is usually prepared simply and with care though the emphasis here is decidedly meat-oriented. Try the veal medallions; we like the quattro formaggi, with its dense, delicate cream sauce of fontina, Bel Paese, Romano, and Gorgonzola. The cafe is ideal for a drink, snack, or late-night dessert and espresso; it opens in summer onto a sunny patio.

Union Bay Cafe
Between University Village and Children's

Part local hangout, part serious restaurant, this comfortable Laurelhurst storefront offers seasonal fare in a low-key setting. Chef/owner Mark Manley is likely to

Hospital, off Sand Point Way, (206) 527-8364 3505 NE 45th St, Seattle Moderate; beer and wine; AE, DC, MC, V; checks OK Dinner Tues-Sun

leave his open kitchen to wander among the linen-topped tables, discussing his carefully chosen dishes. The menu, which changes daily, is small and emphasizes fresh seafood. Appetizers might include tender squid with lime and roasted garlic aioli or chanterelles sautéed with leeks, garlic, and port. Seasonal entrées have included white sturgeon grilled with sun-dried tomato, garlic, olives, and mustard greens. Two small lamb chops with eggplant and sun-dried tomato were perfectly cooked. Seasonal produce shows up again in desserts (nectarine and huckleberry crisp and fresh fig tart with blackberry sauce, for instance), but the smooth and creamy chocolate mousse is a standout. The small wine list offers some interesting choices by the glass.

Wild Ginger

1 block east of the waterfront on the corner of Western and Union, (206) 623-4450 1400 Western Ave, Seattle Moderate; full bar; AE, DC, MC, V; checks OK Lunch Mon-Sat, dinner every day

A glimpse at this self-proclaimed Asian menu—Chinese broccoli, Japanese eggplant, squid Singapore, Mongolian steak—made us wonder whether they weren't reaching in too many directions, especially in a city infused with myriad Cambodian, Thai, Chinese, and Vietnamese restaurants. But taste the food, and hesitations vanish. Rick Yoder, who spent two years in the South Pacific and Southeast Asia, came up the first (and at the moment the only) satay bar in the country. Sit at the Honduran mahogany satay bar and try some grilled marinated prawns with soy black vinegar sauce or the chicken satay with a mild peanut sauce. At lunch, a plate of asparagus with black bean sauce was good enough to stand on its own as an entrée; the seven elements soup (crunchy with egg noodles, smooth and hot with coconut curry chicken, and tangy with lime juice) was a wonderful combination of textures and tastes. For dinner try the panang beef curry—hot with ginger and red chile—or the fragrant crisp duck with anise. Many are fond of this eclectically Southeast Asian restaurant that happens to be run by a Westerner.

Arrowhead Cafe

On Westlake across from Franco's Hidden Harbor, (206) 283-8768 1515 Westlake Ave N, Seattle Moderate; full bar; MC, V; local checks only Breakfast, lunch every day, dinner Mon-Sat, brunch Sat-Sun

Owner Greg Beckley gave a rakish new look to the interior of the narrow, arrowhead-shaped building that once housed Liz's Tavern: butter-colored walls, Deco sconces, stylish black-and-white checkerboard floor tiles. The air is rich with swing and bluesy jazz, and the waitstaff dashes around taking good and friendly care of guests. The name and the ingredients (Navajo fry-bread, hominy, melons) say Southwest, but the food, when it's heaped in front of you, is imaginative and unprescribed. The Anasazi mud pie is nachos by way of New Mexico, and the grilled papaya, melon, and onion that sided a dinner of grilled fresh scallops with a hint of blue cheese were a refreshing twist. Fruit is used here in all sorts of unusual ways, from a breakfast side of a mild apple sausage to a surprisingly good watermelon salad drizzled with raspberry purée and walnut oil, sprinkled with black pepper and sweet red onions.

Asuka

2nd and Madison,
(206) 682-8050
1000 2nd Ave, Seattle
Expensive; full bar; AE,
MC, V; no checks
Lunch Mon-Fri, dinner
Mon-Sat

In Jun Miwa's downtown location, there's no longer a tempura bar; however, you'll find superior sushi, private tatami rooms, and a skyline view of the city. Classic Japanese dishes are augmented by more unusual lobster arrangements. Provided you have ordered a day in advance you can be served *omakase*, a multicourse "chef's choice" dinner. The food is very subtle and quite good, though the prices are particularly high. The decor is especially beautiful, with the private, rice paper–paneled dining rooms prefabricated in Japan. It makes an elegant place for consummating business deals, in the Japanese manner. Service is better midweek. In summer, sit outside in the pretty courtyard.

Ayutthaya

1 block west of Broadway
at Harvard and Pike,
(206) 324-8833
727 E Pike St, Seattle
Inexpensive; beer and
wine; AE, MC, V;
no checks
Lunch Mon-Fri, dinner
Mon-Sat

★★

One of the best Thai restaurants in town attracts a mixed clientele: couples in their finery, young families, and savvy businesspeople. Soft pastel colors and clean, smooth lines create a calming antidote to the fiery food, which is prepared carefully and authentically by the Fuangaromya family (members of which also own Thai Restaurant on Lower Queen Anne). It's good to make reservations as there's little waiting room. The showy seafood is excellent—perhaps a sizzling platter of shrimp spiked with basil, chile, and garlic that's a show in itself. With the exception of the fried noodles (too sweet), everything is good: Naked Bathing Rama; a Thai meat-and-potato dish called massaman beef in a toned-down curry sauce; exceptionally delicate grilled chicken in coconut milk. Local businesspeople are catching on to the best lunch deal in town, so arrive early. Service is patient and sweet.

Beeliner Diner

Across from the Guild
45th movie theater,
(206) 547-6313
2114 N 45th St, Seattle
Inexpensive; beer and
wine; no credit cards;
checks OK
Breakfast, lunch, dinner
every day

The 5-Spot and Counterbalance Room

Queen Anne and Galer,
(206) 285-SPOT
1502 Queen Anne Ave N,
Seattle
Inexpensive, full bar;
MC, V; local checks only

Peter Levy and Jeremy Hardy's Beeliner was the city's first example of what is now a trend—genuine fake diners dishing out genuine real (and improved) American food. This is where meat loaf and macaroni and cheese have gone, along with flaky-crusted chicken pot pie, charcoal-grilled pork chops, Parker House rolls, roast chicken with mashed potatoes, and the Blue Plate Special. Grab a booth or a counter stool, order some cheap white wine, sink into a creamy slice of coconut cake to finish. It isn't perfect (watch out for tepid soup, dry chops, and intentionally obnoxious service), but it's got personality to burn.

The Beeliner's sister restaurant is the 5-Spot, located at the top of Queen Anne's counterbalance (the steep hill the streetcar climbed in the old days, aided by a heavy weight going in the opposite direction). It is a suitably noisy place to bring the tots, Granny, or the canasta girls for a quick supper of just about anything

Brunch every day, lunch Mon-Fri, dinner every day

you want (anything, that is, that's Made in the U.S.A.). Or just drop by for a nip in the Counterbalance Room.

Cactus

In Madison Park near lake, (206) 324-4140 4220 E Madison St, Seattle Moderate; beer and wine; MC, V; checks OK Breakfast Sat-Sun, lunch, dinner Mon-Sat

Cactus has quickly gained a very loyal following. Chef Marco Casabeaux—Italian-born, Argentina-raised, and Spanish-trained—consolidates his talents in this colorful new Madison Park bistro. The terra-cotta floors and center table piled with peppers, Serrano ham, and garlic create a Mexican utopia. The menu travels farther afield, to the food of Spanish people all over (Argentina, Peru, Spain, New Mexico). The antojitos, called tapas here as in Spain, include Moorish-style dishes such as roasted eggplant with cumin and cilantro pesto. The Navajo fry-bread, posole, and enchiladas are pure New Mexico. The Yucatán-style grilled fish comes directly from the Mexican Gulf Coast. The pork steak adobo, a hefty pork loin marinated in achiote seed, peppers, orange juice, garlic, and herbs and then grilled, is authentic in all but one respect—there's not enough of it. Skip the worshipful tableside preparation of guacamole ($5.50 to watch your waiter mash an avocado). Instead, poke into the excellent and unusual de-prickled prickly pear cactus salad. A festive atmosphere with sidewalk tables in summer, and one of the best flans in town.

Cafe Alexis
(The Alexis Hotel)

1st and Madison, (206) 624-3646 1007 1st Ave, Seattle Expensive; full bar; AE, DC, MC, V; checks OK Lunch Mon-Sat, dinner every day

For the past five or so years Cafe Alexis has managed the unlikely: culinary consistency in the face of chef inconsistency. The latest in the kitchen parade is Charles Ramseyer, a Four Seasons Hotels recruit whose creations are exemplified by a superb fall menu of grilled New York steak with cabernet/onion marmalade, lamb sausage with fennel in warm huckleberry coulis, peppered ahi with saffron risotto cakes. Aside from a minor flaw in a special (a slightly overcooked venison) we found the food on the whole delicious and exactingly executed. No longer does service in this cozy brocade drawing room of a restaurant match the dinners we tested; servers have been youthful and awkward on recent visits. And making a reservation doesn't alway guarantee you'll be able to be seated. If you can overlook these problems, you'll have a meal to remember, all the way through to the fruity homemade ice cream for desser; until they are solved, we're compelled to withhold a third star Ramseyer's food definitely merits.

Campagne

Below 1st Ave, between Pine and Stewart, at the Inn at the Market,

No longer focused solely on the foods of Provence, Campagne is still a good bet for hearty fare at bourgeois prices. Owner Peter Lewis's province is the front—a light, quietly elegant space in the Inn at the

(206) 728-2800
86 Pine St, Seattle
Expensive; full bar; AE,
MC, V; no checks
Lunch Mon-Sat, dinner
every day

Market courtyard, with wood floors, Oriental rugs, and a view of the bay—and the highly individualistic wine list (from which you can actually order a good Côtes du Rhone by the glass). New chef Tamara Murphy (formerly of Dominique's Place) premiers her own menu after press time, but a recent meal showed that she's good with sauces, local ingredients, and hearty meats. An order of ravioli filled with wild mushrooms, sun dried tomatoes, and goat cheese was superb. Puréed asparagus soup was velvety in texture but disappointingly bland (more cream than asparagus). Entrées are priced high and lack any accompaniments (if you want vegetables, request them). A special duck preparation slated for the new menu promises great entrées ahead. The whole duck is roasted, then deboned and marinated with herbs, then quickly grilled just before serving. Desserts are equally pricey as is the fashionable café filtre served à la table. If the weather is warm, lunches in the courtyard are especially pleasant.

Chau's Chinese Restaurant
4th and Jackson,
(206) 621-0006
310 4th Ave S, Seattle
Inexpensive; beer and
wine; MC, V; no checks
Lunch Mon-Fri, dinner
every day

Chau's gets a big zero for atmosphere and even less for cleanliness, and yet some insist that Jimmy Yick serves up the best Cantonese seafood this side of the Far East, taking advantage of the Northwest's abundant selection of undersea edibles. Customers in the know head straight for the steamed oysters with garlic sauce or the heady and flavorful wok-baked Dungeness crab with ginger and green onions. Reports are dismal on the rest of the fare, so stick with the seafood. Try Chau's with a large group: a 10-course seafood banquet can cost as little as $15 per person (in a room that accommodates up to 80 people). Open late.

Chez Shea
Pike Place Market,
(206) 467-9990
Corner Market Bldg,
Seattle
Expensive; beer and wine;
AE, DC, MC, V;
checks OK
Dinner Tues-Sun

In many ways, Chez Shea is the quintessential Market restaurant: the freshest ingredients, a real love for the bounty of the region, and a cozy, elegant setting with half-moon windows overlooking the Market rooftops to the Sound and the Olympics. Candles and subdued lighting provide just enough illumination to keep conversations low and the experience romantic. The four-course meals are prix-fixe ($33); you choose one of four entrées. Recent meals have not been up to the same high standards of imagination we remember from executive chef Sandy Shea's previous years. The courses that surrounded the entrée seemed perfunctory: a light tomato and red pepper terrine pepped up with a vinaigrette, followed by a stark-naked white risotto garnished with only a sprig of parsley, and a salad built of only red lettuce and two precious slices of tomato. For entrées, the pan-roasted beef tenderloin in wine, basil, and garlic sauce was butter-knife tender, topped with Gorgonzola and walnuts and perfectly rare (as requested); however, the yellowfin ahi (though competently cooked) was oversauced with mediocre béarnaise. The wine list, while not long, has an excellent mix of top West Coast and European vintages, carefully chosen by manager Lotta Hashizume.

El Puerco Lloron

On the Pike Place Market Hillclimb,
(206) 624-0541
1501 Western Ave, Seattle
Inexpensive; beer and wine; AE, MC, V; no checks
Lunch, dinner every day

For authenticity of decor and cooking (at cheaper-than-authentic prices), few Mexican places in Seattle beat "The Crying Pig," on the Pike Market Hillclimb. The metal card tables and folding chairs, complete with scars and Cerveza Superior logos, were imported from a cafe in Tijuana. The vivid hues of ordinary Mexico—pink, aqua, yellow—were splashed on the ceiling and walls. Everything here is handmade with fresh ingredients. The masa for the tortillas—from American corn, and therefore yellower—is ground daily. The menu is small and so are the prices. Two popular items are tacos de carne asada (soft-shelled tacos the way the Mexicans make them, filled with freshly grilled strips of steak) and taquitos, a plate of three small corn tortillas stuffed with your choice of meat. Dinner ends at 9pm, 7pm on Sundays.

Hien Vuong

On King at 5th,
(206) 624-2611
502 S King St, Seattle
Inexpensive; no alcohol; no credit cards; no checks
Lunch, dinner Wed-Mon

Simple food has never been so exquisite. The atmosphere is nothing much, just a cubbyhole across from Uwajimaya. It's the food that draws, for its freshness and vibrancy of flavors. The beef noodles come in a light but miraculously resonant broth. Papaya with beef jerky combines grated, still-green papaya with delicate shreds of spiced, dried beef in a tangy dressing. The shrimp rolls are some of the best in town: very fresh shrimp with romaine, mint, and cilantro wrapped in rice paper, with scallion ends peeking out like little green tails. They come with a rich, brown peanut sauce for dipping. All the hot dishes come to your table straight off the stove. Crisp, clean, and delightful. Two can eat dinner for under $10.

Il Bistro

Just below Read All About It in Pike Place Market,
(206) 682-3049
93-A Pike St, Seattle
Expensive; full bar; DC, MC, V; no checks
Lunch Mon-Fri, dinner every day

This Pike Place Market walk-down makes fine use of its low ceilings and warrenlike space. Rounded arches, white plaster, low amber lights, much rich, dark oak, and a few Oriental rugs on the walls combine for a mood that's part Moorish, part Continental, and irresistibly cozy. Small wonder the bar is a cherished refuge on damp winter nights; soft recorded jazz and fine brandy and malt whiskey selections abet lingering. Seafoods—shellfish in particular—play a distinguished role in many of the entrées. Trouble is, there have been numerous reports of inconsistencies in preparation, suspicious lack of fresh fish (when market-fresh seafood is just steps away), and lackadaisical (even rude on one visit) service. Hopefully, owner Frank Daquila will either hire a second waitress for those busy nights or ask the maitre d' to step in and help out. Until then, stick with the standbys (a tangy cioppino, a marinated lamb) and expect a wait. Desserts are good, and one as simple as marionberry-blackcurrant sorbet can be lovely.

Il Terrazzo Carmine

Between Jackson and King, in the courtyard,
(206) 467-7797
411 1st Ave S, Seattle
Expensive; full bar; AE, DC, MC, V; checks OK
Lunch Mon-Fri, dinner Mon-Sat

At Il Terrazzo, floor-to-ceiling floral drapes dominate the comfortable room, an opera is often playing, and in the summer you can eat on the outdoor patio, where a fountain is supposed to drown out the noise of the viaduct (unfortunately, it doesn't—if it's rush hour and you want to talk, go inside). There are more gold chains around necks here than in any other Seattle restaurant, but the elegance is subdued and the clientele somewhat older and upscale—all enjoying the great presentation, consistently flavored dishes, excellent wine, and sometimes odd service. Be sure to take notice of the antipasti on the way in; they're all laid out for perusal, and the taste matches the presentation. We've had stunning veal piccata (lightly sauced and zipped with capers), superb pillows of ravioli filled with venison, and rich tender medallions of venison sautéed with wild mushrooms and Marsala. The half chicken roasted with oregano sauce is *meraviglioso*. Service, however, can be a bit confused (and tends to favor regulars and celebrities). If you choose carefully and take advantage of the extensive Italian wine list, the food is certainly worth the considerable expense (a dinner for four can run $160), and the ambience is *molto invitante*.

Carmine's Grill (83 S King St, (206) 622-6743) offers grilled anything, from half chickens to duck to fish. Not primarily Italian, it's slightly less expensive than its big brother up the street.

Islabelle Caribbean Food

45th and Woodlawn,
(206) 632-8011
1501 N 45th St, Seattle
Inexpensive; no alcohol; no credit cards; checks OK
Lunch, dinner Tues-Sun

Islabelle is a tropical oasis on busy 45th Street. Amid sun-splashed colors on industrial-metal walls and the exotic aromas of tamarinds and cumin, plantains and garlic, there are only a few tiny tables, so in the summer most take their dinner to nearby Green Lake. From Lorenzo Lorenzo's repertoire of spicy Caribbean classics come tender, marinated halibut, broiled and served with cumin-fragrant black beans and two domes of rice; a mighty and marinated pork sandwich; and the towering Caribbean Burger, topped with homemade salsa, sautéed onion, bright slices of tomato, and fresh, leafy watercress. There has been talk on and off for months of returning breakfast items to the menu; at press time we began to hear these rumors again—we hope they're true. What we remember was very good.

Italia

Between Madison and Spring on Western,
(206) 623-1917

The energy at this upscale, unpretentious urban cafe continues to make Italia well worth aiming for especially in the evenings for the creations of former Chez Shea chef Scott Craig. It's a cavernous space run simul-

1010 Western Ave,
Seattle
Moderate; beer and wine;
AE, DC, MC, V;
checks OK
Breakfast, lunch, dinner
Mon-Sat (open Sun for
dinner in summer)

taneously as art gallery, gourmet food store, concert hall, lunch cafeteria, and restaurant. By day the food can be hit or miss—there's an excellent pizza with a crackerlike crust that lets the tomato sauce and cheese (sometimes with smoked chicken, pancetta, leek, or chèvre) take over, but other lunch items can seem indifferent. Evenings, the menu assumes a greater degree of sophistication, and marvelous meals can be had, like a recent plate of firm pappardelle pasta with subtly seasoned homemade lamb sausage. Pastas tend to be trusty under Craig's sure hand; the only recent problem was an over-lemoned sauce for tortellini. Proprietor David Holt brings his renaissance interests to his restaurant; hence the interested diner will find art lectures the second Thursday of each month, and a solid wine list including a fine selection by the glass. Now, if Holt could just smooth out the oft-scattered service.

Kaspar's by the Bay
1st and Cedar,
(206) 441-4805
2701 1st Avenue, Seattle
Moderate; full bar; AE,
MC, V; no checks
Lunch Mon-Fri, dinner
Mon-Sat

Kaspar Donier came to Seattle a few years ago from Vancouver's Four Seasons. His menu shows an imaginative pairing of international ingredients that doesn't quite jibe with the large fifth-floor office-tower dining room. The expansive views west to Elliott Bay or north to the Queen Anne skyline almost divert your attention from the bland decor. The best thing to do is concentrate on the menu, where Donier has proven that good food can overcome lack of ambience and gaffes in service. A meal might start with crab and salmon hash-cake with silky mushroom sauce, a revelation for crab-cake fans, or ratatouille-filled won ton ravioli with jumbo garlic prawns. The menu offers a large selection of interesting salads and soups (cream of spinach soup with blue cheese ravioli). Entrées may include a lightly grilled wild salmon caught off Neah Bay with complementary chanterelle rosemary sauce on the side. The moist pork tenderloin with crisp bacon and port wine–soaked prunes was simultaneously fruity, tangy, and smokey. Desserts show the deft hand of an expert: an individual pear tart in puff pastry shaped like a pear was artfully drizzled with chocolate and sprinkled with lacy powdered sugar. For lunch, try one of the outrageous pizzas that change daily (venison, chile, fried onions, and Monterey jack cheese on one visit).

Kokeb
12th and Spring,
(206) 322-0485
926 12th Ave, Seattle
Inexpensive; full bar;AE,
DC, MC, V; no checks
Lunch Mon-Fri, dinner
every day

There are now at least two other Ethiopian places in town—proving that Seattle has truly arrived as a culinary crossroads—but the first remains the best. It's plain and inexpensive, with a steady clientele of Seattle University students and faculty. The food is distinctive and exotic, and because it's eaten with the fingers, it appeals to children. Be forewarned, though: nearly all of the entrées are spicy. The base of a meal, literally, is injera, a flat, spongy bread. A round of this on a platter holds an entire party's entrée choices, soaks up their sauces, and is eaten to climax the meal. Service can be blasé, but this food is worth the wait.

La Rive Gauche
On 2nd between
Blanchard and Bell,
(206) 441-8121
2214 2nd Ave, Seattle
Moderate; full bar; AE,
DC, MC, V; checks OK
Dinner Mon-Sat

An effervescent collage of lively jazz piano, echoing lights and voices, and the inimitable charm of a casual Left Bank bistro. Jean-Paul and Nina Kissel have created an atmosphere comfortable enough for dropping in for a bowl of French onion soup or a full four-course meal. The short menu stars simple neighborhood food of France, from an excellent bouillabaisse to Paris's ubiquitous steak and *pommes frites*. The linger-awhile mood prevails with Kissel at the helm, neighborhood regulars at the bar, and live jazz on weekends. The prix-fixe dinner ($24) may include a pâté plate with a mild terrine or a rich chicken liver mousse, a wild green salad studded with goat cheese and walnuts, succulent halibut poached in a rich tarragon butter sauce and sided with sautéed garlic potatoes, and a much-raved-about hard-crusted French bread. In the past, the kitchen's been uneven, but recently reports have only been favorable. The Kissels know chocolate; confirm that by ending the evening with a layered slice of bittersweet chocolate hazelnut torte.

Le Tastevin
Corner of 1st W and
Harrison,
(206) 283-0991
19 W Harrison St, Seattle
Expensive; full bar; AE,
DC, MC, V;
local checks only
Lunch Tues-Fri, dinner
Mon-Sat

Le Tastevin has boasted ardent regulars since 1976—and the airy, trellised space hidden on Lower Queen Anne is large enough to hold many of them at once. The menu emphasizes slightly lightened versions of traditional French fare; however, it isn't quite as showy as it used to be, and some of the dishes, such as the coquilles St. Jacques, were too uninspired to justify such prices. But we still enjoy the ever-so-satisfying bouillabaisse, the meltingly tender sweetbreads, and the stellar prawns Villemarie in a creamy, Pernod-spiked sauce (thankfully, still a fixture). We recommend that you dine in the bar, from a lighter, lower-priced appetizer menu for the urban crowd. The extraordinary wine cellar, presided over by Emile Ninaud, boasts everything from moderate Northwest selections to rare French vintages. There are interesting iced, flavored vodkas to start, and at the end of the meal, check out the exquisite Cognacs and dessert wines (such as a 50-year-old raisin sherry), many of which are quite reasonably priced. The desserts are very good.

Maple Leaf Grill
89th and Roosevelt NE,
(206) 523-8449
8909 Roosevelt Way NE,
Seattle
Moderate; beer and wine;
MC, V; checks OK

Laid back, and discriminating in taste but never in welcome, the Maple Leaf is fast becoming the grill of dreams. Formerly a sports bar (occasionally an event—sans sound—will be on TV), this tavern is kid-free without being too terribly adult. The vigor of the menu lies on the specials board. Chef Stuart Ripley, known simply as "Rip," seems to know what our collective ap-

*Lunch Mon-Fri, dinner
Mon-Sat*

petite hankers for: fresh, timeless eats tweaked with (occasionally too much) chic. He's fond of chiles and scrupulous about freshness, producing such mouth-watering meals as swordfish with mango salsa or grilled rabbit glazed with apple cider, ginger, and cranberries, and such first-class appetizers as pork and rabbit pâté or salmon mousse to savor at the glossy bar or in one of the booths. Not everything works well, but slight inconsistencies in taste and texture serve mostly to make the Maple Leaf seem that much more like the dining room of a fond friend.

McCormick and Schmick's
1st and Spring,
(206) 623-5500
1103 1st Ave, Seattle
Moderate; full bar; AE,
DC, MC, V;
local checks only
*Lunch Mon-Fri, dinner
every day*

This seafood restaurant is an encyclopedia of San Francisco clichés: dark wood paneling, booths, glitter bar, and waiters with black bow ties. You'd think they'd been grilling lamb chops and salmon steaks since the turn of the century. Don't smirk—they do it well, if not with perfect consistency. Just remember to keep it simple: order seafood, and stay away from the pasta. Start with roasted garlic and some fresh oysters; then get the fresh fish of the day, usually done in a tasty, uncomplicated sauce. The straightforward work at the grill also includes meat, game, and poultry. At lunch it's too busy for its own good—service adopts a hurry-up attitude, and they make you sit in the hall until your whole party assembles—but dinners are more relaxed, with the bar suppers a nice feature for solo diners. A private room holds up to 15 guests.

**McCormick's
Fish House and Bar**
4th and Columbia,
(206) 682-3900
722 4th Ave, Seattle
Moderate; full bar; AE,
DC, MC, V;
local checks only
*Lunch Mon-Fri, dinner
every day*

This may be the best of the downtown fish houses and it certainly is the most popular. Lunch is noisy and frenetic, the bar jams up with City Hall types after 5pm, and even dinners feel crowded, particularly during the tourist season. Somehow, the waiters remain cheerful amid the bustle. The formula here is simple: the heavy-on-seafood menu, printed daily, offers several types of fish prepared in simple ways (grilled with a flavored butter) sautéed with another butter, baked more elaborately. Preparation can be uneven—we've had both tough tuna and near-perfect halibut—but you can usually rely on decent cooking (especially when you order your fish broiled) and generous portions. Oysters are fine, salads pedestrian, the wine list carefully chosen and overpriced, the beautifully fresh sourdough bread always a treat.

Mikado
Jackson and 5th,
(206) 622-5206
514 S Jackson St,
Seattle
Moderate; full bar; AE,

You can still eat well (or mostly well) at Mikado, but its food is merely good, no longer surpassing. It is still a very cozy place for one so large, broken up into a warren of distinct, intimate dining settings and styles. You can sit at Formica tables and order from any of the menu genres; far better to sit at the sushi bar or the robata-yaki (grill), where the Japanese diners con-

MC, V; local checks only
Dinner Mon-Sat

gregate. (At the former, the presentation makes for a good show, but on our last visit the sashimi was less than exceptional.) If you must settle for the main dining room, grab a stuffed-vinyl corner booth. If you're in a large party, reserve a straw-matted, low-seated tatami room; the food perks up in this traditional setting, and a big steaming pot of *toban-yaki*—meat, fish, shrimp, and vegetables cooked at your table—is a marvelously sociable antidote to winter blahs. Service is quick, maybe a bit *too* quick with the check. Veteran waitresses delight in decoding Japanese cuisine for novices.

Omar Al-Khayam
77th and Aurora (and branches),
(206) 782-5295
7617 Aurora Ave N,
Seattle
Inexpensive; beer and wine; AE, DC, MC, V; no checks
Dinner every day

Try to overlook the plastic flowers on the tables and the New England calendar scenes on the wall—Omar Al-Khayam is one of the least expensive, most authentic purveyors of Middle Eastern food in town. The menu includes generous shish kabobs (try the very lemony, very garlicky chicken kabob), a sublimely smokey baba ghanouj, and *fatoush*, a bread salad. Now there are three neighborhood branches: the Greenwood original, Renton, and Hadi's in Georgetown (the last two serve lunch). Banquet facilities in Greenwood hold parties of up to 30.

Panda's
NE 75th and 35th Ave,
(206) 526-5115
7347 35th Ave NE,
Seattle
Inexpensive; beer and wine; AE, MC, V; local checks only
Lunch Mon-Sat, dinner every day

Panda's is the North End's favorite Chinese restaurant. Occupying a small storefront in a new strip mall, Panda's has a contemporary look, with an open kitchen and high-backed stools at the counter. As three cooks work the wok line, a hostess covers delivery orders on the phone, someone else bags them up, and two drivers run in and out in a constant flurry of motion. Smoked tea duck is smokey and moist, served with hoisin sauce and soft steamed buns. The mu-shu pork is nicely done here: the vegetables are crisp and distinct, the pork strips are tender, and the accompanying pancakes are homemade. Beef and asparagus in black-bean garlic sauce shows how skilled the cooks are—neither the asparagus nor the beef is cooked a moment too long. All noodles, dumplings, buns, and sauces are made on the premises. The waitstaff is friendly and helpful and can be trusted to make good suggestions, especially for the adventurous.

Phoenecia Restaurant
1st and Mercer,
(206) 285-6739
100 Mercer St, Seattle
Moderate; beer and wine;
MC, V; checks OK
Dinner Tues-Sat

Owner/chef Hussein Khazaal has built his reputation on excellent service, highest-quality Mediterranean delicacies, and a warmth and generosity practically unknown in other Seattle restaurants. He greets his diners warmly, fusses over them, and makes sure they're being taken care of. The restaurant, in the Hansen Baking complex, is an elegant spot done up in cerulean and purple and divided into separate rooms to accommodate private parties. The menu essentials are smokey baba ghanouj, creamy hummus, and delicate lamb kababs. Too bad he has to limit his printed menu to what will work for the hurry-up pre-curtain crowd. The best plan for fully appreciating Phoenecia is to bring a crowd of friends in and order one of Khazaal's famous *mezas* (feasts), for $18 to $25 per person. For the next couple of hours you will be served an embarrassment of incredible food, probably enough for twice the size of your group, with dishes you will not find elsewhere. When (and if) the Hansen Baking complex is remodeled into condominiums, Khazaal will have to move Phoenecia to a new location. In the meantime, he is making moves toward an inexpensive version of his Queen Anne establishment in Pike Place Market—word is, he'll even be offering box lunches.

The Pink Door
*Post Alley between
Stewart and Virginia,
Pike Place Market,
(206) 443-3241
1919 Post Alley, Seattle
Moderate; full bar; MC,
V; local checks only
Lunch, dinner Tues-Sat*

We like this Post Alley spot despite its flaws. The idea is exemplary: an inexpensive trattoria with cheap wine, reasonably good pasta, and a sort of built-in cachet (you enter through the pink door on Post Alley; there's no sign). At lunch, the large room grows noisy around a burbling fountain, and the service becomes forgetful. To be safe, stick with the pasta selections—especially anything with the puttanesca sauce, or the spinach fettuccine with salmon and cream. In warm weather, Jackie Roberts opens a splendid outdoor cafe on the roof with a pleasant view of the Sound. At night when the pace slows down, the tables are lit by candlelight, the service becomes more attentive, and you can dine—prix-fixe—on four courses (no choices). Later, you can order appetizers in the bar and watch the occasional entertainment. The quality of cooking is still uneven, but certain dishes—a full-bodied cioppino, wonderful bubbling lasagne, a Gorgonzola soup we'll never forget—can shine. The place overflows with Italian kitsch, but it's cheerful.

Place Pigalle
*Pike Place Market,
(206) 624-1756
5 Pike Place Market,
Seattle
Expensive; full bar; MC,
V; no checks
Lunch, dinner Mon-Sat*

This spiffy bistro boasts breathtaking views over Elliott Bay, windows that open to the breeze, and a thoughtful, inventive menu. Seafood is as fresh as it should be with Pike Place Fish just an alley away. It shows up in the form of daily specials (salmon in brandy–Bing cherry sauce) and seasonal dishes (spot prawns grilled with shiitake mushrooms, radicchio, and scallions and served with a salad of arugula). A parade of talented chefs has passed through the Place's tiny kitchen en route to fame and glory; now it's Colin Hill's turn, and he's retained perennial favorites such as the rich French onion soup and the lightly gingered calamari in a mustard cream. Other dishes toss tradition right out the window: pan-roasted duck breast with demiglaze and fresh plum and jalapeño chutney. Dishes have been always artful, always entertaining, always fresh, and usually disarmingly successful. Service ranges from attentive to aloof. You can eat outdoors at one of the few tables in the skyway in summer, or perch at the tiny bar with a local ale and lounge the afternoon away.

Ponti Seafood Grill
Under the Fremont Bridge, (206)284-3000 3014 3rd N, Seattle Moderate; full bar; AE, DC, MC, V; checks OK Lunch Mon-Sat, dinner every day, brunch Sun

On the ship canal, in the shadow of the Fremont Bridge, Jim and Connie Malevitsis (Adriatica) opened their second restaurant with Richard and Sharon Malia (remember Malia's Northwest?). It's a large, new space split into comfortably sized rooms, with a view from nearly every seat. As for the food, chef Alvin Binuya helped to create a menu featuring seafood tweaked with influences of Italian, Middle Eastern, Asian, and French. There are excellent salads (a warm spinach and smoked prawn with a light vinaigrette and a mixed green salad spiked with Oregon blue cheese, caramelized walnuts, and pomegranate seeds). Tender scallops seared with a tomato-basil vinegar appear alongside a snappy Asian cabbage slaw. The service can sometimes be a bit disorganized, but that's nothing a little time can't fix. Desserts are outstanding, try the chocolate croissant pudding with a crème anglaise.

Queen City Grill
Corner of Blanchard and 1st, (206) 443-0975 2201 1st Ave, Seattle Moderate; full bar; AE, MC, V; checks OK Lunch Mon-Fri, dinner every day

You sink into a glossy, high-backed booth and disappear from the world to schmooze with friends. In a très chic little drop-in space with mottled ochre walls, and Art Deco wall sconces, Peter Lamb and Steven Good have peeled off the veneer of formality to allow a more casual style of eating out, perfect for its Belltown location. Chef Paul Michael has a way with the grill, from the swordfish to the New York steak, and he occasionally brings his Texas know-how and barbecue sauce to an andouille sausage lunch. We've come to expect good, fresh fish, though they'd do well to be a bit more generous with the portions, and on one occasion we encountered aloof and unprofessional service that detracted from what would otherwise have been an enjoyable evening. At lunch, more spicy dishes (a Sichuan prawn plate, a Creole-style sea bass with Jamaican lime butter) appear on the menu. Good wine, prompt service at lunch, and lotsa garlic.

Reiner's
Between Seneca and Spring, (206) 624-2222 1106 8th Ave, Seattle Moderate; full bar; MC, V, DC; no checks Lunch Tues-Fri, Dinner Tues-Sat, Brunch Sun

A European oasis from back before nouvelle. German-born owner and chef Reiner Greubel recently opened his own place after years as a prize-winning chef with major hotels. Just down the hill from Virginia Mason Hospital, Reiner's is a small, elegant space reminiscent of a classic European tearoom. Starters are good: a delicate terrine of tuna and sturgeon mousse in a sauce verte of watercress and cream, with sautéed fennel on the side; a superb cream of asparagus soup; a luscious soup of tortellini, chicken, and pesto. Main courses are in the Grand Hotel tradition. Three very tender veal medallions were served with sautéed mushrooms and a pinot noir sauce that lacked richness. Fresh tuna au poivre was cooked properly but had a one-dimensional flavor of peppercorns. Desserts disappoint, except for a wonderful orange bittersweet chocolate mousse with raspberry sauce. Reiner's is just across Freeway Park from several downtown hotels and caters to a clientele put off by more trendy restaurants.

Ristorante Buongusto
Queen Anne Ave and McGraw, (206) 284-9040
2232 Queen Anne Ave N, Seattle
Moderate; full bar; MC, V; checks OK
Lunch Tues-Fri, dinner Tues-Sun

Mamma Melina's
Roosevelt at NE 50th, (206) 632-2271
4759 Roosevelt Way NE, Seattle
Moderate; beer and wine; MC, V; local checks only
Dinner Mon-Sat

Melina Auriemma has three sons, Salvio, Roberto, and Leo Varchetta. A year ago, Salvio and Roberto created a restaurant worth climbing the counterbalance for. Buongusto has become more of a special-occasion restaurant than a drop-in trattoria; reservations, unless you come quite late in the evening, are a must. Patrons come for appetizers like garlicky pan-fried calamari or a plate of assorted marinated vegetables, sopped up with Ciro Pasciuto's now-famous bread. Dinner portions are huge. A steaming plate of *creste di gallo* (cockscomb-shaped pasta topped by a perfectly spiced tomato sauce and heaped with Isernio sausage and eggplant) can be split between two for a first course. In addition to the usual dessert offerings, a unexpectedly wonderful Sambuca gelato is a refreshing finale.

In early 1991, the third son, Leo (and his mamma) opened Mamma Melina's on Roosevelt. The results are equally endearing. The menu is brief, utterly simple, and moderately priced. Try the luscious *lasagne casareccia* (homemade pasta with tomato sauce, fresh mozzarella, and tiny, tiny homemade meatballs) or the fisherman's soup. The Varchettas have brought a true taste of Italian home cooking home to Seattle.

Romio's Pizza
20th W and W Dravus, (and branches)
(206) 284-5420
2001 W Dravus St, Seattle
Inexpensive; beer and wine; MC, V; checks OK
Lunch, dinner every day

Gasp! This fine Interbay institution is as busy a neighborhood eatery as we've ever seen; the last thing it needs is press. Even more, it delivers—literally and figuratively—a magnificent product. The pies, with a thick, crisp (yet chewy inside) crust, feature ingredients that are almost abnormally flavorful. In the Zorba, each part—onion, tomato, feta, Greek olives, gyro beef, and homemade tzatziki—contributes nobly to the whole. Romio's signature pizza, with garlic, artichoke hearts, sun-dried tomatoes, and pesto, achieves an integration of flavors and textures that seems somehow inevitable. Order it on a garlic crust (which they tend to run out of early) and you've got yourself a bona fide GASP! Other branches are downtown (917 Howell, 622-6878), in Pioneer Square (616 1st Avenue, 621-8500), on Eastlake (3242 Eastlake Ave E, 322-4453), and a new one in Greenwood, slated to open summer of 1991.

Salvatore Ristorante Italiano

1 block north of Ravenna Blvd on Roosevelt, (206) 527-9301
6100 Roosevelt Way NE, Seattle
Moderate; beer and wine; MC, V; checks OK
Lunch Mon-Fri, dinner Mon-Sat

You'll be struck by the Italian heartiness of this northeast neighborhood place. A whole wall is painted with a bright mural of a village street scene, peopled with artfully pasted-in photos of crew and friends. Much of the warmth, however, stems from Salvatore Anania himself, who brings his *amore* for the Southern Italian food of Basilicata—one of the country's lesser-known regions—to his North End landing. The penne puttanesca was a fine example of the region's fondness for red pepper, while the linguine alle cozze, with an unusual meld of herbs and rich sweet mussels, was spiced with restraint. All in all, you will not be disappointed, especially if you're here on an evening when the dessert menu perks up with a tiramisu.

Sea Garden

Jackson and 7th, (206) 623-2100
509 7th Ave S, Seattle
Inexpensive; full bar;AE, MC, V; no checks
Lunch, dinner every day

The Sea Garden has emerged as one of Seattle's finest Chinese eateries. Over the years it has draped linen over its Formica-topped tables and prettied itself up a bit with a coat of pastel; but, elegance or not, we've always been enamored with its ability to keep such consistently excellent seafood so reasonably priced. It's subtle, elegant Cantonese fare, the tamely spiced food we all enjoyed before we developed our culinary crush on fiery Sichuan or Hunan food. The seafood is scrupulously fresh, from the steamed crab in black bean sauce (taken from the holding tank minutes before arriving at your table) to the thinly sliced geoduck with a soy-based dipping sauce, and an excellent braised black cod. Such standards as wonton soup and chow mein are infused with new subtleties; all are served with fresh vegetables and, if requested, prepared without MSG. The place is usually filled with Asians (although that's been changing lately) and, after midnight, the all-night mah-jongg crowd from the District. The upstairs room sits private parties of up to 50.

Septieme

2nd between Battery and Bell, (206) 448-1506
2331 2nd Ave, Seattle
Inexpensive; beer and wine; no credit cards; checks OK
Breakfast, lunch, dinner every day

In the Paris of the *septième arrondissement*, a vigorous intellectual culture exists in tiny cafes, where the propriétaires let the literati linger, and conversation is fueled with coffee and rich pastries. Septieme is Kurt Timmermeister's tribute to the student life he remembers there. He features the same lush pastries, the same easy atmosphere, the same compact quarters and small brick courtyard. Septieme pays attention to what's important: rich and delicious lattes served in china teacups (or bowls for the real addicts), on white linen–covered tables. You choose from a spread of beautiful pastries at the counter, and they're delivered to you on pretty, gold-rimmed white china plates with heavy silver forks. Timmermeister has added about four sandwiches (a recent version bulged with eggplant, roasted red peppers, tapenade, and truly fresh mozzarella layered between slices of chewy Italian bread) and an excellent Caesar salad ($5). Septieme opens early and closes late.

Settebello
Denny and Olive,
(206) 323-7772
1525 E Olive Way,
Seattle
Moderate; full bar; AE,
DC, MC, V; checks OK
Lunch Mon-Fri, dinner
every day

Few restaurants in Seattle have had such a rocky history as the "beautiful seven," perched at the triangle where Denny crosses Olive Way. What used to be an often-intimidating lineup of achingly innovative chefs and a veritable Who's Who in Seattle might now regain its footing with the rest of us. New owner Amir Hefhmatpour, in his first months of ownership, seems, at press time to be trying to bring back the kind of patrons that the old place scared away. His first move was to restructure the prices and streamline the menu, making Settebello a more accessible restaurant for those who enjoy a good meal out but aren't necessarily dedicated foodies. There's a nice degree of authenticity to the Northern Italian food (antipasti like bruschetta topped with tomatoes, Roman style, and a spicy linguine tuttomare heaped with shellfish), and the service is attentive. Not exactly a neighborhood trattoria yet, but the former glitz has been toned down a little. A jazz duo has been added on Sunday nights.

Siam on Broadway
Broadway E and E Roy,
(206) 324-0892
616 Broadway E, Seattle
Inexpensive; beer and
wine; AE, MC, V;
checks OK
Lunch Mon-Fri, dinner
every day

Among Seattle's burgeoning collection of Thai restaurants, Chai Asavadejkajorn and John Sariwatanarong's tiny Siam on Broadway is one of the most aesthetically pleasing and smoothly run Thai restaurants in town. The menu doesn't stray far from the Bangkok standards, but the food is distinctive. The open kitchen makes a fun diversion—it's probably the only place in town where you can enjoy Thai cooking from a front-row seat (and undoubtedly will if you don't make reservations at least 24 hours in advance for a table in back). Regulars agree that this restaurant takes its hot chiles seriously, especially in the soups. However, a three-star chicken curry was no hotter than the two-star soup during a recent visit. Try the crisp yum wuun sen, a salad of bean threads with pork, squid, and onions piquant with fresh lime and cilantro.

Szmania's
33rd Ave W and
McGraw, (206) 284-7305
3321 W McGraw St,
Seattle
Moderate; full bar; DC,
MC, V; checks OK
Lunch Mon-Fri, dinner
Mon-Sat, brunch Sat

Joining the esteemed culinary tradition established by chefs who bravely ply their trade in the residential hinterlands, Ludger and Julie Szmania have opened a fine neighborhood restaurant in Magnolia. This restaurant's sleek contemporary style feels altogether out of sync with the dry cleaners and pizza parlors of folksy Magnolia Village—surely one reason it's caught on so solidly. The food also has something to do with it. Ludger (late of the Four Seasons Olympic) cooks wonderfully and with suggestions of his native Germany, from an appetizer of toothsome chanterelle risotto to entrées such as cinnamon-smoked chicken breast with herb sauce and smoked pork loin with homemade sauerkraut. One special, salmon in mushroom sauce, was rich and meltingly textured. Szmania might combine pasta with pesto cream and serve with blackened scallops or toss it with lightly grilled prawns in a fragrant smoked tomato sauce. There are problems—an overdressed Caesar, occasionally unprofessional service—but in the main, this young restaurant is gaining more fans than detractors.

Toyoda Sushi
125th and Lake City Way,
(206) 367-7972
12543 Lake City Way
NE, Seattle
Moderate; beer and wine;
MC, V; checks OK
Dinner Wed-Mon

Stacks of wooden sake cups with people's names burned onto them is evidence that there are a lot of regulars at this North End Japanese restaurant—and with reason. The owner, Natsuyoshi Toyoda (formerly of Aoki), is extremely conscious of freshness, and the fish is exquisitely so, even on Sunday. The kasuzuke black cod (marinated in sake lees), the *saba shioyaki* (mackerel grilled with salt), and the *kakifry* (deep-fried oysters) are all absolutely superb. Some things on this menu are not found elsewhere—for instance, *yamakake* (raw tuna with grated mountain potato) and *hamachi no kamayaki* (yellowtail with sweet potato). Five dollars gets you six big, browned, gingery dumplings. Try the *unagi maki* (six slices of *uramaki* with eel and cucumber, brushed with teriyaki sauce). Tea is served in black plastic with a gold design (imitation lacquer), but it is freshly made for each pot. Service is lightning-fast, even when the place is busy, which is often.

Trolleyman Pub
2 blocks west of the
Fremont Bridge on 34th
(206) 548-8000
3400 Phinney Ave N,
Seattle
Inexpensive; beer only;
MC, V; checks OK
Lunch, dinner Mon-Sat
(open Sun, but no food)

Seattle's first brew pub pouring utterly fresh Red Hook beers has added a few light meals for beer drinkers who love to linger over an Extra Special Bitter or a Ballard Bitter. The menu's nothing fancy, and if you arrive late there may be even fewer choices. The food, like the beer, is seasonal; a different soup graces the menu each day. Try the assertively spicy black bean chili served with pools of cool sour cream or the hearty sausage lasagne. You can sit at the long, curved wooden bar, nestle in front of the fireplace on an overstuffed couch, or join your friends at one of the long community tables. It's the social casualness of this pub which entices locals night after night.

The Two Bells Tavern
4th and Bell,
(206) 441-3050
2313 4th Ave, Seattle
Inexpensive; beer and
wine; no credit cards;
no checks
Lunch, dinner every day

Everybody likes this new-wave, slightly seedy, urban tav-cum-eatery for its engaging blend of artsy atmo and cheap, delicious food. There's always a daily homemade soup or sandwich, a good Caesar, a couple of cold plates, a hot beer sausage sandwich (two split wieners facedown in sweet-hot mustard with Swiss cheese melting over the top), and, of course, the famed burger, a thick hunk of beef and plenty of onions on crusty French bread, with good chunky potato salad. There are 25 kinds of beer. We wonder what would happen to the arts scene in town if there weren't a Two Bells to nourish the artists so cheaply.

Viet My

Just off 4th near Washington,
(206) 382-9923
129 Prefontaine Pl S, Seattle
Inexpensive; no alcohol; no credit cards; local checks only
Lunch, dinner Mon-Fri

When Chau Tran arrived in Seattle, she began cooking out of her home for appreciative friends. When her living room was no longer large enough, she opened this little storefront on Prefontaine, where she serves authentic, delicious Vietnamese dishes: chicken curry with rice, rice-paper rolls with shrimp and pork, and an incredible seafood soup. Tran imports many of her ingredients from her homeland, and aficionados can taste the difference. Consult the list of specials taped to the wall and plan on a wait—Chau is a one-woman show, so lunch may take a while. Very inexpensive.

Copacabana

Pike Place Market,
(206) 622-6359
1520½ Pike Place, Seattle
Inexpensive; beer and wine; AE, DC, MC, V; no checks
Lunch, dinner Mon-Sat (summer); lunch Mon-Sat, dinner Sat (winter)

Seattle's only Bolivian restaurant doesn't quite recall the authenticity of Ramon Paleaz's original Pike Place Market dive—the one with the counter that tilted so much that servers had to jam forks beneath the plates to keep them upright—but the splendid sun deck (great for viewing Elliott Bay and Pike Place) comes close. The family recipes are still used: the spicy shrimp soup; *salteñas*, juicy meat-and-raisin-stuffed pastries; *huminta*, a piquant corn pie topped with cheeses; poached halibut with sautéed onion and tomato in a mild saffron sauce. Like the Spanish, Bolivians seem to cook everything to death, and everything here is a tad pricier than you'd expect.

House of Hong

8th S and Jackson,
(206) 622-7997
409 8th Ave S, Seattle
Inexpensive; full bar;AE, DC, MC, V; no checks
Lunch, dinner every day

Faye Hong, whose family previously made the Atlas Cafe a local favorite, operates a more elegant model of what most folks still mean by "Chinese restaurant"— uncorrupted Cantonese cuisine, not especially exciting, but usually reliably and speedily prepared. The setting is a match: handsome dusty pink in a courtyardlike indoor layout, yet still a place you feel comfortable taking the kids. Which is just what the regulars do on weekends, for one of the district's better dim sums (come before the 11am opening). At 75 items, Hong's is also one of the most diverse. Even simple classics like ginger beef dumplings and *ha gow* are refined in flavor and texture and are wheeled in piping hot. We found the dough in the baked *hum bow* cloyingly sweet, somewhat balanced by an overly salty filling, and the steamed dumplings are more dependable than the fried. Seafood carries the banner at dinner: prawns in lobster sauce are ambrosial, steamed black cod in ginger oil a special delight. Others praise the earthy quality of the home-cooked fare (salted fish and fried rice), the order-ahead banquets (in a private room), and the parking lot—no small plus in this crowded district. Food until midnight on weekends.

India Taj

Cherry and 1st,
(206) 233-0160
625 1st Ave, Seattle
Inexpensive; beer and
wine; AE, DC, MC, V;
checks OK
Lunch Mon-Sat, dinner
every day

When Makhan Gill is cooking, almost everything that comes out of the 800-degree tandoori oven approaches perfection: chicken that's improbably moist, vibrantly coral-colored, and smoldering with smoke; tender, irresistibly puffy breads infused with the same smokiness. Vegetables here are never treated as afterthoughts; vegetarians and committed carnivores alike spoon up forkfuls of *aloo-gobi* (a sauté of potato and cauliflower chunks) or *malai kofka* (homemade cheese and vegetable nuggets in tomato-butter sauce) with mounds of sunny basmati rice. When Gill's not in the kitchen, however, India Taj can be off its stride. Servers are very courteous while helping you wade through the unfamiliar territory of tandoori cooking.

Lao Chearn

Off Washington, between
3rd and 4th,
(206) 223-9456
121 Prefontaine Pl S,
Seattle
Inexpensive; beer only; no
credit cards; checks OK
Lunch, dinner Mon-Sat

This unprepossessing little restaurant on Prefontaine Place is already too crowded (especially at lunch), but word continues to spread about its delightful Laotian and Thai food. Order the Lao spring rolls, filled with a peppery mixture of ground pork, cabbage, carrots, and cellophane noodles, tightly wrapped and deep-fried to a deep, nutty brown. The hot-and-sour shrimp soup, a tingling lime and lemongrass broth, arrives in a hot pot belching fire through its chimney. Enjoy the *gai yarng*, chargrilled chicken marinated in coconut milk and spices; the preparation takes a while, but it's the best dish on the menu. A small private room for 15 to 20 people can be reserved—great for lunch meetings.

Leschi Lakecafe

Alder and Lakeside S,
(206) 328-2233
102 Lakeside Ave S,
Seattle
Inexpensive; full bar;AE,
DC, MC, V; checks OK
Lunch, dinner every day

This place simply tries too hard. You are besieged with information about the historic site, the sources of seafood, exactly how the tea is brewed, and on and on. Despite the overload, the staff is less than helpful when you ask a question they're not programmed to answer, and service can be shaky even with all the drilling. The result is a place that ends up making you nervous and a little embarrassed for all its effort to produce passable dining. The seafood is good, if they get the orders right, and the beer selection in the bar is extensive. Best to come for fish 'n' chips, sit outside (it's very pretty). In summer, crowds arrive by boat and BMW.

Marrakesh

Just north of Group
Health, 15th Ave E at
Mercer, (206) 328-4577
605 15th Ave E,
Seattle
Moderate; full bar; MC,
V; no checks
Dinner Tues-Sun

Your traditional Moroccan meal begins with the customary finger-washing ceremony and ends with the sprinkling of rosewater over your hands (which are your utensils). At the Marrakesh, $14.50 buys a substantial five-course meal (but wine, which seems to flow here, increases the bill substantially). Everyone begins with the ubiquitous lentil soup of North Africa and the Middle East. The meal continues through a Moroccan eggplant salad (served too cold on our visit) and a dry and rather uninteresting *bastela royale* (poultry pie). Entrées include the lackadaisical cous-

cous with honey-prune chicken, or the tender braised Vashon Island rabbit in a rich, warm paprika sauce. Or visit with a large group and order the *mechoui*—Morocco's famous roast lamb. Hosting a group may, in fact, be Marrakesh's best function. Don't plan on whispering sweet nothings, however; the din can really escalate in here, especially when the bedizened belly dancer starts to sway. Ben Alaoui has opened a similar version of this restaurant in northwest Portland.

Maximilien-in-the-Market
Pike Place Market,
(206) 682-7270
81-A Pike Place Market,
Seattle
Moderate; full bar; AE,
DC, MC, V; no checks
Breakfast, lunch, dinner
Mon-Sat, brunch Sunday

François and Julia Kissel's French market cafe in the Main Arcade is such a splendid *place*—full of noble dark wood antiques and blessed with a view of Elliott Bay. François is one of the town's best chefs, but unfortunately, he's usually not involved in the kitchen. Meals are inconsistent. In addition to croissants and espresso, breakfasts include a soufflé and homemade sage sausage. At lunch, stick with steamed mussels with wine and cream or the excellent fish 'n' chips. Dinners include grilled sweetbreads in mustard-caper sauce, a halibut and red snapper soup, and chicken with apples and veal sausage. The specials are often the most successful preparations here. Finish with bread pudding, topped with François's incomparable caramel sauce—desserts are a consistent strong point at Maximilien's. The pretty upstairs bar area is available for rent by parties of up to 30.

Metropolitan Grill
2nd and Marion,
(206) 624-3287
818 2nd Ave,
Seattle
Expensive; full bar; AE,
DC, MC, V; checks OK
Lunch Mon-Fri, dinner
every day

This handsome haunt in the heart of the financial district does a booming business among stockbrokers and Asian tourists. The soul of the restaurant is its steaks, and you'd do well to stick to them, since they really do live up to the hoopla. Pastas and appetizers are less well executed, but a growing list of large, appealing salads (and a terrific clam chowder) present good alternatives to beef for the lunch crowd. There's a lot of table-hopping going on here, which puts the waiters in even nastier spirits. Financiers like to use the Met's 30-person private room as a dependable dinner venue.

LODGINGS

Four Seasons
Olympic Hotel
5th and University,
(206) 621-1700
411 University St, Seattle,
WA 98101
Expensive; AE, DC, MC,
V; checks OK

The Olympic has been a Seattle landmark since the 1920s. It has been refurbished in a style befitting its earlier grandeur; the rooms (450 on 11 floors) are now quite spacious, softly lit, and tastefully furnished in period reproductions. Welcome touches include valet parking, 24-hour full room service, a stocked bar, chocolates on your pillow, complimentary shoeshines, and a terrycloth robe for each guest. A team of well-informed concierges, on call 24 hours, offers uncommonly good service; indeed, the staff exudes just the right blend of unobtrusiveness and thorough care.

The public rooms are grand verging on gaudy: armchairs, potted plants, marble galore, tapestries, wood paneling. You can lounge amid the swaying palms in the skylit Garden Court, taking high tea if you wish. The showcase dining room, the Georgian Room, is a handsome space (see review); downstairs is the livelier Shuckers, an oyster bar with excellent mixed drinks. There are several elegant meeting rooms (the ornate Spanish Ballroom for large affairs), and retail spaces off the lobby make for the best boutique shopping in town. The Olympic now features special amenities for Japanese guests including an elaborate, authentic breakfast. A classy health club rounds out the amenities with a pool, Jacuzzi, and licensed masseuse. Prices are steep, especially considering there are few views, but this is Seattle's one venerable, world-class contender, and the service (and location) cannot be bested.

Alexis Hotel
1st and Madison,
(206) 624-4844
1007 1st Ave, Seattle,
WA 98104
Expensive; AE, DC, MC,
V; checks OK

The Alexis is a gem carved out of a lovely turn-of-the-century building in a stylish section of downtown near the waterfront. It's small (54 rooms), full of tasteful touches (televisions concealed in armoires, complimentary sherry upon arrival), and decorated with the suave modernity of Michael Graves's postmodernist colors. You'll be pampered here, with Jacuzzis and real-wood fireplaces in some of the suites, a steam room that can be reserved just for you, nicely insulated walls between rooms to ensure privacy, and a concierge at the ready. Other amenities include valet parking, complimentary continental breakfasts, a morning newspaper of your choice, shoeshines, a guest membership in the nearby Seattle Club ($15) or Northwest Nautilus ($5), and a range of dining options, from elegant Northwest cuisine to a steak house. No convention facilities: the Alexis favors well-heeled travelers who prefer quiet poshness. Pets are accepted.

However, the Alexis is still not a hotel of world-class performance. The staff is very young and lacks the air (and polished skill) of seasoned help. Lately, we've gotten reports of understocked rooms and loud air-conditioner noise. And there are no views. We suggest booking a room that faces the inner courtyard—rooms facing First Avenue can be noisy. Or book one of the 39 condos five doors down in the jointly managed Arlington Suites, spaces geared for longer stays with views, kitchens, and (for a little bit extra) full Alexis maid and room service.

Inn at the Market
1st and Pine,
(206) 443-3600

It's become one of the finest places to stay in the city, largely because of the location. You are right in the famous Pike Place Market, looking out over its

86 Pine St, Seattle,
WA 98101
Expensive; AE, DC, MC,
V; checks OK

rooftops to the lovely bay beyond. The hotel is small—65 rooms—so service can approximate that of a country inn; and you won't feel oppressed by conventioneers (there are limited conference facilities, in the form of one meeting room and one outdoor deck). The architecture is quite good (by the local firm of Ibsen Nelsen Associates/Peter Greaves), with oversized rooms, bay windows that let even some of the side rooms enjoy big views, a Laura Ashley lobby, and a configuration that is built around a central courtyard. Opening off the courtyard are smart shops, a sumptuous spa, and the elegant Campagne restaurant (see Restaurants section of this chapter). There is no complimentary breakfast (order breakfast room service from the Gravity Bar). Dinner room service is offered by Campagne. A hotel in America's finest public market is a marvel.

Sorrento Hotel
9th and Madison,
(206) 622-6400
900 Madison St, Seattle,
WA 98104
Expensive; AE, DC, MC,
V; checks OK

When the Sorrento opened in 1909—in time for the Alaska-Yukon-Pacific Exposition—it commanded a bluff overlooking the young city and Puget Sound. For years thereafter, it was the most elegant hotel in the city, with Renaissance architecture modeled after a castle in Sorrento, Honduras mahogany in the lobby, and a famous dining room on the top floor. The place faded badly, though, and the view was partly lost as the city grew up around the hotel. A decade ago it was fixed up and reopened. They couldn't bring back the view, but they brought back its beauty. Downstairs there's a clubby restaurant. The mahogany lobby is now an superb lounge. The rooms, 76 of them, are decorated in muted, tasteful coziness with a slight Oriental accent. We recommend the 08 series of suites, in the corners. Suites on the top floor make elegant quarters for special meetings or parties—the showstopper being the $700 penthouse, with its grand piano, patio, Jacuzzi, view of the bay, and luxurious multiple rooms. The location, uphill five blocks from the heart of downtown, may be inconvenient, but it's quieter. The Hunt Club is a clubby restaurant with excellent food (see restaurants section of this chapter).

Westin Hotel
Between Stewart and
Virginia on 5th,
(206) 728-1000
1900 5th Ave,
Seattle, WA 98101
Expensive; AE, DC, MC,
V; checks OK

Westin, a major international chain, is headquartered in Seattle, so this flagship hotel has quite a few extras. The twin cylindrical towers may be called corncobs by the natives, but they afford spacious rooms with superb views, particularly above the 20th floor. Convention facilities, spread over several floors of meeting rooms, are quite complete. There is a pool, along with an exercise room supervised by conditioning experts. On the top floors are some ritzy, glitzy suites. The location, near shopping and the Monorail station, is excellent. The longtime Trader Vic's is closed with plans to reopen as a Japanese restaurant. The posh Palm Court is still here. For more casual dining try the good (though overpriced) Market Cafe.

Chambered Nautilus
East on NE 50th St to 21st Ave and circle around the block,
(206) 522-2536
5005 22nd Ave NE, Seattle, WA 98105
Moderate; AE, DC, MC, V; checks OK

This blue 1915 Georgian colonial (with a fresh coat of paint and a bright red door) on a hillside street in the U District offers six airy guest rooms beautifully furnished with antiques. Several rooms open onto porches with tree-webbed views of the Cascades, and four private baths are newly added. You are just across the street from shared student housing units, and a few blocks from Fraternity Row, so it can get noisy here during rush (other times, though, it's surprisingly quiet). Bunny and Bill Hagemeyer serve a full breakfast and complimentary afternoon tea. A spacious public room, meeting facilities, and an enclosed porch/reading room with soothing chamber music round out this tasteful hostelry.

Gaslight Inn
15th and Howell,
(206) 325-3654
1727 15th Ave, Seattle, WA 98122
Inexpensive; AE, MC, V; checks OK

Praised by repeat guests and bed-and-breakfast owners alike, the Gaslight is one of the loveliest, most reasonably priced, and friendliest bed and breakfasts in town. Trevor Logan and Steve Bennett have polished this turn-of-the-century mansion into a ten-guestroom jewel, six with private baths, two with fireplaces, each decorated in a distinct style—some contemporary, some antique, some Art Deco. Outside are three decks and a large heated swimming pool. No pets or kids. Smoking is okay.

Holiday Inn Crowne Plaza
6th and Seneca,
(206) 464-1980
6th Ave and Seneca St, Seattle, WA 98101
Expensive; AE, DC, MC, V; checks OK

This hotel bends over backward for the repeat and corporate visitor. The upper-floor rooms, which are corporate, comfortable, and very clean, have been refurbished in striking maroons, mauves, and dark wood and receive a lot of individual attention (at a slightly higher price): free newspapers, a lounge, and their own concierge desk. Lower-floor guests stay in spacious but rather bland rooms, and though concierge services are available to all, there's no lower-floor desk. The lobby is elegant and comfortable, the staff attentive and accommodating. In addition to the pleasant Parkside Cafe, the pricier Parkside Restaurant has recently opened and features continental fare. Conference rooms and parking (for a fee) are available. The location is ideal—right downtown, near the freeway, and two blocks from the Convention Center.

Lake Union B&B
3 blocks north of Gas Works Park,
(206) 547-9965
2217 N 36th St, Seattle, WA 98103

Shoes off. If you don't have any socks, they're provided. Then sink into the white cloud of carpet and couches of this modern three-story house not far from Gas Works Park—a refreshing break from the Victoriana that plagues most B&Bs. There are two rooms upstairs, both stunning, though one—with its solarium,

Moderate; MC, V;
checks OK

Mayflower Park Hotel
4th and Olive,
(206)623-8700
405 Olive Way, Seattle,
WA 98101
Expensive; AE, DC, MC,
V; checks OK

Meany Tower Hotel
45th and Brooklyn, in the
University District,
(206) 634-2000
4507 Brooklyn Ave NE,
Seattle, WA 98105
Moderate; AE, DC, MC,
V; checks OK

Roberta's
16th E near Prospect,
(206) 329-3326
1147 16th Ave E, Seattle,
WA 98112
Moderate; AE, DC, MC,
V; checks OK

fireplace, and a view of Lake Union and the Seattle skyline from the Jacuzzi or peeked at through the resident telescope—is probably Seattle's finest affordable bedroom. There's a sauna in the downstairs bath.

Renovations have paid off at this handsome 1927 hotel right in the heart of the downtown shopping district. A coolly elegant lobby opens onto Oliver's (bar and lounge) on one side, and Clipper's, one of the prettiest breakfast places in town, on the other. Rooms are small, bearing charming reminders of the hotel's past: lovely Oriental brass and antique appointments; large, deep tubs; thick walls that trap noise. Modern intrusions are for both better and worse: double-glazed windows in all rooms to keep out traffic noise, and the addition of undistinguished furnishings in many of the rooms. The deluxe rooms are slightly bigger and have corner views; aim for one on a higher floor or you may find yourself facing a brick wall. Prices, $100 to $275 for doubles, are average for this part of town, and $20 more gets you a guest membership in a fancy athletic club (Seattle Club) four blocks away.

The distinguished 1930s design of the former University Tower Hotel remains, but inside there are double-glazed windows and air conditioning. The whole place— lobby and rooms—is quite cloyingly turned out in shades of peach. Each room has a bay window with a good view, and those on the south side are sunny. An exercise room is the latest addition. You're one block from shopping on the Ave, two blocks from the University of Washington campus. The hotel's restaurant, The Meany Grill, is prettified with brass and deep green, but the food isn't much. The bar boasts a big-screen TV in the lounge for sports fans.

Roberta is the gracious, somewhat loquacious lady of this Capitol Hill house a few blocks from Volunteer Park, the Seattle Art Museum, and the funky Broadway district. Inside it's lovely: gleaming refinished floors throughout, a comfortable blue couch and an old upright piano, books everywhere, and a large oval dining table and country-style chairs. Of the five rooms, the cheery Hideaway Suite (the entire third floor) with window seats, a sitting area with a futon couch and a small desk, and a full bath with a tub, is our favorite. Others prefer the one in peach tones with an antique desk, bay window, love seat, and queen-size oak bed. Early risers will enjoy the Madrona Room, with its morning sun and full bath. All five rooms have their own private tubs and pretty ceramic sinks, but one room's toilet is across the hall. In the morning, Roberta brings you a wake-up cup of coffee, then later puts out a smashing full breakfast (no meat, though), maybe homemade cinnamon rolls or grainy raisin bread with blackberry jam. No children. No smoking except on the porch.

Salisbury House
Corner of Aloha and 16th, (206) 328-8682
750 16th Ave E, Seattle, WA 98112
Moderate; AE, MC, V; checks OK

A welcoming porch wraps around this big, bright Capitol Hill home, an exquisite hostelry neighboring Volunteer Park. Glossy maple floors and lofty beamed ceilings lend a sophisticated air to the guest library (with a chess table and a fireplace) and living room. Up the wide staircase and past the second-level sun porch are four guest rooms (one with a canopy bed) that share two large baths. Our favorite is the Rose Room, with its bay window and walk-in closet; if you can stand lots of purple, the Lavender Room comes in second. Breakfast is taken in the dining room or on the sunny terrace. Classy, dignified, and devoid of children (under 12) and pets.

Seattle Sheraton Hotel and Towers
6th and Pike,
(206) 621-9000
1400 6th Ave, Seattle, WA 98101
Expensive; AE, DC, MC, V; checks OK

Seattle's Sheraton is an 841-room tower rising as a sleek triangle, the Convention Center in its shadow. It, too, aims at the convention business, so the rooms are smallish and standard, and the emphasis is on the meeting rooms, VIP floors upstairs, and the restaurants. Banner's restaurant offers mainstream continental fare, plus a 27-foot-long dessert spread; Gooey's is the night club; and the outstanding Fullers is adorned with fine Northwest paintings (see Restaurants section of this chapter). Service is quite efficient. Convention facilities are complete, and the kitchen staff can handle the most complex assignments. Snootier business travelers will want to head for the upper four "VIP" floors, where a hotel-within-a-hotel offers its own lobby, concierge, and considerably more amenities in the (same size as economy) rooms. The top floors feature a health club, pool, and a private lounge with a knockout city panorama. You pay for parking.

Stouffer Madison Hotel
6th and Madison,
(206) 583-0300
515 Madison St, Seattle, WA 98104
Expensive; AE, DC, MC, V; checks OK

This large hotel at the southeast edge of downtown successfully conveys a sense of warmth and intimacy inside. The lobby, dressed in signature greens and peach with Dale Chihuly glass sculpture, is tasteful and uncluttered, upstairs hallways are softly lit, and the rooms sport elegant marble countertops, coffered ceilings, and wood cabinetry. Extras include feather pillows, oversized towels, coffee, morning papers, and a concierge on duty. The pricey "Club Floors" (25 and 26) offer exclusive check-in privileges, their own concierge services, hors d'oeuvres and continental breakfast at "Club Lounge," a library, and the best views (although views from most rooms are quite good). Complimentary green tea service (24 hours), robe and slippers, the city's first traditional Japanese breakfast, and city information printed in Japanese are offered to the Japanese traveler. Comfortable conference facilities, parking (for a fee), and free in-town transportation, round out the offerings. Prego, on the 28th floor, offers a surprisingly fine selection of seafood.

The College Inn Guest House
40th and University Way,
(206) 633-4441
4000 University Way NE,
Seattle, WA 98105
Inexpensive; AE, DC,
MC, V; checks OK

Burgundy carpets, window seats, antiques, and pastel comforters create a cozy if somewhat spartan atmosphere in this hospitable inn designed along the lines of a European pension. Housed in a renovated 1909 Tudor building that is on the National Register of Historic Places, it's in the heart of the lively U District, with a cafe and rathskeller pub below. (Late-night noise travels quite handily into west-side rooms.) Each of the 25 guest rooms has a sink but no toilet, TV, radio, or phone. For the musically inclined, there's an upright piano in room 305. Bathrooms are at the end of each hall, and a guest living room is tucked away on the fourth floor. A generous continental breakfast is included—a good deal at these budget prices.

Edgewater Inn
Pier 67 at Wall St and
Alaskan Way,
(206) 728-7000
Pier 67, 2411 Alaskan
Way, Seattle, WA 98121
Moderate; AE, DC, MC,
V; checks OK

Alas, you can't fish from the famous west windows of this waterfront institution anymore. The place has been spiffed up quite a bit (so no more fish-cleaning in the rooms), giving the lobby and rooms a rustic tone, with bleached oak and overstuffed chairs. It's like an urban motel (parking is free), but with a serviceable restaurant and a decent bar with a piano. Waterside rooms are quietest, with the best views and $125-to-$175 price tags. The Edgewater is just a block from the Victoria Clipper terminal.

MV Challenger
Henry Pier at Chandler's
Cove on Lake Union
(behind Benjamin's),
(206) 340-1201
809 Fairview Pl N,
Seattle, WA 98109
Moderate; AE, MC, V;
checks OK

This friendly little retired tugboat docked at the south end of Lake Union is the city's only bunk and breakfast. When you come aboard, owner Jerry Brown may offer you a refreshment from the hardwood bar and a seat in the conversation pit—a sunken living space with two couches and a fireplace. His engine room is a gleaming nautical beauty; up top there's a deck, ideal for lolling in the sun. As for sleeping, you have two boat choices (three in winter). We prefer the classic tug, where you might stay in the unbelievably small main-floor berths (two bunk rooms, one double, which share a head). Better is the suite state-room, with its own bath, VCR, and stereo, and the newly renovated wood-paneled "upstairs" rooms. However, the nearby yacht is more spacious—and more contemporary—with two rooms (each with big double berths). Wintertime guests overflow (Jerry's tug is often full) onto the *Alaska Adventurer*, which summers as a charter fishing boat. Jerry makes breakfast in the *Challenger*'s galley, using a diesel-powered stove and a microwave oven. In the evening, it's a pleasant stroll to Lake Union's growing number of restaurants. A very Seattle experience.

Villa Heidelberg
Corner of 45th SW and Erskine Way,
(206) 938-3658
4845 45th Ave SW,
Seattle 98116
Moderate; AE; checks OK

Leaded glass windows, beamed ceilings, Puget Sound views, and a wraparound covered porch distinguish this 1909 minimansion in West Seattle, built and named by a German immigrant. The three guest rooms ($55 to $75) share one bathroom. One has an Olympics-facing sundeck, another has a fireplace and a phone. Owners John and Barb Thompson serve a breakfast of popovers and fruit, waffles, or French toast. Look for extras like a bouquet of roses on the table.

WestCoast Camlin Hotel
9th and Olive,
(206) 682-0100
1619 9th Ave, Seattle,
WA 98101
Moderate; AE, DC, MC, V; checks OK

Like many older hotels in Seattle, this 1926 grande dame has been remodeled and made soundproof with double-glazed windows. (The elevator and the ventilation system, however, both hark back to an earlier era.) Though there are no conference facilities, the Camlin appeals to the business traveler (the large rooms have small sitting/work areas), and it's a good buy for the money. Rooms have been redecorated with sophistication, featuring spacious closets and spotless bathrooms; those whose numbers end in 10 have windows on three sides. Avoid the cabanas (they're small and dreary and for smokers) and the room service, which is quite slow. There's rooftop dining in the newly restored Cloud Room. The downtown location is close to the retail district and the Convention Center.

WestCoast Roosevelt Hotel
7th and Pine,
(206) 621-1200
1531 7th Ave, Seattle,
WA 98101
Moderate; AE, DC, MC, V; checks OK

Gone is the grand skylit lobby that so distinguished the Roosevelt when it first opened its doors in 1930; new owners who reopened it in 1987 deemed that space better suited to Von's Restaurant (a McRory's-type outpost). The new lobby is low-ceilinged and cramped, but elsewhere the WestCoast installation has somewhat preserved the Roosevelt's Art Deco sensibilities. The hotel's 20 stories have been redivided for the contemporary traveler, but standards are still almost comically small. The deluxes (only $20 more than a standard) are a better choice, with adjoining sitting areas; the 11 superior-class rooms each boast a Jacuzzi, a separate sitting area, and a perspective northwest toward Puget Sound. Five floors are nonsmoking, and you can request nonsmoking, but it's never guaranteed. Considering its proximity to the Convention Center and the shopping district, the Roosevelt's prices—$89 to $119—are decent, but the service needs some polish.

The Williams House
Galer and 4th N,
(206) 285-0810
1505 4th Ave N, Seattle,
WA 98109

In its 89-year history, this residence on the south slope of Queen Anne Hill has also done stints as a gentlemen's boardinghouse and an emergency medical clinic for the 1962 Seattle World's Fair. Doug and Sue Williams still own the establishment; however, they've

Moderate; AE, DC, MC, V; checks OK

Lake Union's first full-scale hotel, too new to review at presstime, is not exactly on the lake but across busy

moved out and have turned the management over to the reliable Ruth McGill, who offers plenty of Southern hospitality. There are five guest rooms, four with views and two with private baths. The enclosed south sun porch is a nice meeting spot. Brass beds, original fixtures, fireplaces, ornate Italian tiles, and oak floors hark back to the home's Edwardian past. You will get a full breakfast that may include Ruth's special South of the Border quiche.

Marriott Residence Inn Lake Union
On Lake Union at Fairview, (206) 624-6000
800 Fairview Ave N,
Seattle, WA 98109
Expensive; AE, DC, MC, V; checks OK

unrated

Lake Union's first full-scale hotel, too new to review at presstime, is not exactly on the lake but across busy Fairview Avenue. Still, the 234 rooms, most of which boast lake views, are decorated in tasteful '90s colors, with touches of peach, mauve, and teal; the one-bedroom suites are spacious, but the studios feel cozier. All rooms have fully outfitted kitchenettes, and continental breakfast may be enjoyed in the lobby—a light, plant-lined courtyard with an atrium and waterfall—or taken back to your room. There isn't a hotel restaurant, but there are plenty of lakeside eateries across the street at which guests can charge meals to their room. Amenities include five quiet meeting rooms, a lap pool, exercise room, sauna, and spa.

GREATER SEATTLE: EDMONDS

The area thought of as Edmonds is really just a small village in a much larger area. Funky stores, wide sidewalks, and waterfront views encourage evening strolls through town. The ferry departs to Kingston; for information call (206) 464-6400. Edmonds bills itself as the City of Celebrations. Most popular are the **Edmonds Art Festival** (second weekend in June) and **A Taste of Edmonds** (third weekend in August).

Brackett's Landing Beach Park, just north of the ferry terminal, has a jetty and an offshore underwater marine-life park that draws lots of scuba divers. **Edmonds Historic Walk** was prepared by the Centennial Committee and offers a look at old Edmonds. Stop by the Chamber of Commerce (120 5th Street N) for a free map of the walk.

RESTAURANTS

brusseau's
Corner of 5th and Dayton, (206) 774-4166
117 5th Ave S, Edmonds
Inexpensive; beer and wine; MC, V; local checks only
Breakfast, lunch, early dinner every day; brunch Sun

Seattleites used to make weekend pilgrimages to Jerilyn Brusseau's restaurant for one of her excellent cinnamon rolls. As the years passed, and Edmonds' favorite boulangerie/charcuterie/patisserie grew, Brusseau spoiled us with her fabulous French toast (more like a gigantic slice of bread pudding) and her thick, hearty soups. Maybe we got too used to the high standards, for recently we've encountered a few blunders (a bland soup, perfunctory salads). With executive chef William Keegan helping out in the kitchen (especially when Brusseau's off on the TV talk show circuit), the restaurant seems to be pulling itself back together. Overall, the food is good and the baked goods better.

Chanterelle Specialty Foods
Up from ferry terminal on Main, (206) 774-0650
316 Main St, Edmonds
Inexpensive; beer and wine; MC, V;
local checks only
Breakfast, lunch Tues-Sun, dinner Tues-Sat

Stunning, inventive creations come out of Jochen Bettag's Edmonds kitchen, the most exciting of which is his seafood sausage. The place is stocked with gourmet foodstuffs, salads, and such, which can be packaged to go. You order and pay up front, but because of the freshness and vibrancy of the food, that doesn't detract from the experience. Pesto-cheese eggs for breakfast are light and flavorful; spanakopita is dripping with spinach, pine nuts, and feta cheese. Every night Bettag offers a half-dozen entrées, a couple of soups, and several salads. Prices are great.

Ciao Italia
Downtown Edmonds, (206) 771-7950
512 5th Ave S, Edmonds
Moderate; beer and wine; MC, V; local checks only
Dinner Tues-Sun

Gino and Tama Borriello have taken over the old Bel Piemonte site and imbued it with an openness and ambience Piemonte lacked. It is now a pleasure to be here (families too). Diners coo over the calamari, quickly poached and served with a pesto marinade. The pizza margherita was sensational—a light crust and a well-herbed sauce (Gino was well trained at Salute! and Saleh al Lago). We recommend the creamy pollo pesto, the tender veal spiked with artichokes and mushrooms, and the penne with ricotta, mozzarella, Parmesan, and eggplant in marinara sauce. The salads and soups are a little disappointing; nevertheless, it's a very comfortable spot where children are always *benvenuti*.

Provinces
Asian Restaurant and Bar
In upper level of Old Mill Town Mall at 5th and Maple, (206) 744-0288
201 5th Ave S, Edmonds
Inexpensive; full bar;AE, DC, MC, V;
local checks only
Lunch Mon-Sat, dinner every day

Years ago, Asian fare was either Chinese, Japanese, Cambodian, or Vietnamese. The thought of a pan-Asian restaurant was an aberration most foodies would have snubbed. Today, such culinary journeys actually work. Pan-Asian food in a clean-lined restaurant has caught on, first in Seattle (Wild Ginger) and now in Edmonds at Cambodian-Chinese Ken Lee's restaurant. Favorites include Hong Kong–style pan-fried noodles topped with vegetables, beef, chicken, and prawns served on a medium-pizza-sized platter, and the Triple Mushrooms (black, straw, and oyster). Portions vary, however: the serving of prawns in black bean sauce with pea pods was meager. Desserts make no attempt to stay within the Asian continent, originating instead at Seattle's own Pacific Desserts—and that's fine with us.

LODGINGS

Pinkham's Pillow
Corner of Dayton and 3rd, (206) 774-3406
202 3rd Ave S, Edmonds, WA 98020

This clean, ageless home is right in the heart of downtown Edmonds, two blocks from the waterfront, with views of Puget Sound. Don't worry about the name: Pinkham's Pillow does lean toward lace and ruffles, heart-shaped rugs and antique-style furnishings,

Moderate; MC, V; checks OK

★★

but still remains comfortable and uncluttered, with an overriding sense of organization and welcome. Each of the five guest rooms—Melissa, Shannon, Lacey, Joy, and Adria, named after the owners' daughters–has a private bath; Lacey has handicapped access. Prices are $56 to $86 and include breakfast.

Edmonds Harbor Inn
*Dayton and Edmonds Way, (206) 771-5021
130 W Dayton St, Edmonds, WA 98020
Moderate; AE, DC, MC, V; checks OK*

★

Strategically located near the Edmonds ferry and train terminals (20 minutes north of Seattle) is an attractive choice for a night in Edmonds: 61 large rooms, oak furnishings, continental breakfast, and access to a nearby athletic club. Get directions—the place is near the harborfront, but a little difficult to find in the gray sea of new office and shopping developments. No views.

GREATER SEATTLE: BOTHELL

The town stands at the north end of Lake Washington, on the way into more open country. **Bothell Landing** is a pleasant park, and from here you can take a 9.5-mile hike, bike ride, or roller-skating tour along the Sammamish River, stopping part of the way at the Ste. Michelle winery for a picnic; food and wine can be purchased at the winery (see Woodinville).

RESTAURANTS

Gerard's Relais de Lyon
*Just inside Bothell city limits, north of Seattle, (206) 485-7600
17121 Bothell Way NE, Bothell
Expensive; full bar; DC, MC, V; checks OK
Dinner every day*

★★★

Tucked away beneath the tall pines off Bothell Way, Gerard Parrat's Lyonnaise restaurant has not only survived but has grown modestly in its almost 15 years. The only thing you need to do to forget where you are is walk through the door, for to eat here is to send the senses to France, in a country inn appointed with crisp linen, Wedgwood china, leaded glass, fresh flowers, and a fireplace. Presentation is important, but Parrat never overreaches. But for all its sophistication of assembly and presentation, Parrat's cuisine remains firmly within his Lyonnaise heritage with lighter tastes: rabbit fricassee with chanterelles, cabbage-stuffed partridge in puff pastry; potato and corn blinis topped with his own smoked salmon and caviar. To appreciate the full extent of Parrat's talents, try the six-course *menu découverte* or a 10-course *menu dégustation*—a good deal at $55 (though the wine list is rather pricey). The only quibbles are that the tables are too close together and the restaurant can get quite noisy, although a new patio with a fountain (and a fragrant herb garden) is a pleasant addition for warm-weather dining. Plan on spending at least three hours over dinner—this is a meal worth savoring, and there's no reason for the staff to rush you.

GREATER SEATTLE: WOODINVILLE

The suburbs have caught up with this formerly rural outback, but some of the country ambience remains, especially to the east where Woodinville fades into dairy farms of the Snoqualmie Valley. Woodinville's claim to fame is the **Chateau Ste. Michelle**, the state's largest winery. The grapes come from Eastern Washington, but experimental vineyards are on site, and tours of the operation, complete with tastings, run daily between 10am and 4:30pm; 14111 NE 145th, (206) 488-1133. Just across the street from Ste. Michelle is **Columbia Winery**, the state's oldest premium-wine company. Columbia now offers tours on weekends, and the tasting room is open daily from 10am to 5pm; 14030 NE 145th, (206) 488-2776.

Gardeners from around the region flock to **Molbaks**, the massive nursery and greenhouse at 13625 NE 175th, (206) 483-5000.

Woodinville also carries a leg of the **Sammamish River Trail**, a paved bike path that runs from Lake Sammamish in Redmond to Lake Union in Seattle.

RESTAURANTS

Maltby Cafe
From Hwy 405, go 4½ miles east on Monroe Hwy 522, turn left at the light,
206 483-3123
8809 212th St SE (Maltby Rd), Maltby
Inexpensive; beer and wine; MC, V;
local checks only
Breakfast, lunch every day

Four women have taught the old Maltby schoolhouse cafeteria a new lesson: how to cook. It's now a tough-to-find country cafe, contemporary in design but not overly trendy. Unhurried breakfasts feature delicious, rich omelets (the sauces and sausages in the Italian omelet were not too tangy or spicy), good new potatoes, and old-fashioned oatmeal with nuts, raisins, and cream. The giant cinnamon rolls are so legendary that the cafe often runs out (go early). If you do miss breakfast (which is served *all day* on weekends), lunch is even better. You can take a seat at one of the nine counter stools for a thick Reuben sandwich (they cook their own corned beef), grilled tuna on a huge slab of bread, big toothsome hamburgers, a bowl of home-made soup, and local beer. Leave your cigarettes at home. Long lines are the norm now, so you may want to call ahead.

Pacifica
1 block east of Chateau Ste. Michelle,
(206) 487-1530
14450 Woodinville-Redmond Rd, Woodinville
Moderate; full bar; AE, DC, MC, V;
local checks only
Lunch Tues-Sat, dinner

What Pacifica does well, it does very well—the staff is educated in cooking and wines (good thing, as this has become a popular stopping point during tours of the nearby wineries). A recent chowder was excellent (though heavy-handed on the pepper). In contrast, seafood entrées were faultless: the Atlantic sea scallops with chanterelles and the fresh halibut with a mild lime sauce were sublime. It seems that people come here not only to consume good food and good wine but also to talk about it. Order a full bottle of wine: this res-

Tues-Sun, brunch Sun

taurant seems to favor those who at least appear to be aficionados. Superb cheesecake.

Armadillo Barbecue
*Take Woodinville exit
from 522E, on the main
drag, (206) 481-1417
13109 NE 175th St,
Woodinville
Inexpensive; beer and
wine; AE, MC, V;
checks OK
Lunch, dinner every day*

A West Texas barbecue joint plopped down in West Woodinville might not measure up to the standards of an oil-state expatriate, but never mind. People come here for camaraderie, an icy beer (from the six draft selections), and a refill of the smokey sauce with its rich hot tang. The pork is lean and tender and the chicken's extra moist, *and* they both come with a side of molasses-y beans and cake-y corn bread. The salads are merely passable. Brothers Bob and Bruce Gill have done up this place with a freewheeling, slightly perverse sense of humor. Specials of the day (Cement Soup, for example) are scrawled on the front windows and the menu includes some inspired descriptions.

GREATER SEATTLE: REDMOND

It may be best known for its corporate top gun, **Microsoft**, but this city perched above Lake Sammamish also claims to be the cycling capital of the country. Every summer at the **Marymoor Velodrome**, the nation's best bicyclists gather for the U.S. Track Cycling Championships in **Marymoor Park**. Covering the north shore of Lake Sammamish, the park is a huge expanse of ball fields and semi-wild grassland that makes for great bird watching. On weekends, hundreds of dog owners bring their pets to the vast and legally leashless dog run in the fields along the Sammamish River.

Less ambitious peddlers enjoy the **Sammamish River Trail**, which runs north from the lake along the Sammamish River. In Woodinville, the trail connects with the Burke Gilman trail, which stretches around Lake Washington all the way to Lake Union in Seattle.

Redmond's downtown is a traditional suburban amalgamation of strip malls and shopping centers, but Anglophiles should stop for afternoon tea at the **British Pantry**; 8125 161st Ave NE, (206) 883-7511.

RESTAURANTS

Kikuya
*Off the Redmond-
Kirkland Hwy on 161st
NE, (206) 881-8771
8105 161st NE,
Redmond
Moderate; beer and wine;
MC, V; no checks
Lunch Tues-Fri, dinner
Tues-Sat*

Stuck in the back of an undistinguished shopping center in Redmond is this small, family-run, informal Japanese restaurant where the food is wonderful. No kimonos or tatami rooms here—the draw is the excellent sushi bar. As for the rest, it's the kind of place where you order good, honest, simple things—spicy yakisoba (which you can see the chef cooking), gyoza, donburi, and a tempura you can always count on. The fresh, full-flavored meats and fish aren't overseasoned; they're allowed to command the entrée. Everything comes with pickled cucumbers, miso soup, a simple salad, and green tea. Kikuya, a favorite with local Japanese, doesn't take reservations. There's frequently a line at the door, and once seated you may find the service disconcertingly rushed.

Big Time Pizza
Leary Way and W Lake Sammamish,
(206) 885-6425
7281 W Lake Sammamish Pkwy NE,
Redmond, 98052
Inexpensive; beer and wine; no credit cards; checks OK
Lunch, dinner every day

Big Time Pizza may be named like a chain, it may look like a chain (in a 7-Eleven strip mall at the end of Highway 520), it may at times even *act* like a chain—but it isn't. Here, the pies are all about flavor and nuance, enlightenment and restraint—like our favorite, the Pesto Plus, a harmonious blend of pesto, mushrooms, artichoke hearts, and sun-dried tomatoes. Crusts are aromatic and chewy, toppings are applied with an even hand and an epicurean's light touch. Owner Bill Tamiesie also makes focaccia bread, breadsticks, calzones, and terrific (try the Greek) salads. At press time he was gearing up for a move to a bigger space a few doors down with enough room that you'll even be able to sit down and eat. There's also a playground next door, where there will be a few tables come summer.

GREATER SEATTLE: KIRKLAND

This city's comfortable downtown on Lake Washington's Moss Bay is a popular summer destination. Art galleries, restaurants, bookstores and boutiques line the two-story main street. Several restaurants look out over boats docked at the marina. Have breakfast at Cousin's, on Central Way, or grab a muffin and coffee at Archie's, a storefront coffee shop near the corner of Central and Lake Street, and walk a block to the waterfront park, where ducks beg scraps and dodge children on the small sandy beach.

On Yarrow Bay at the south end of town lies **Carillon Point**, a new hotel and shopping complex which lines a round, red-brick courtyard that overlooks the lake, with the Olympic Mountains in the background.

To the north, at **Saint Edward State Park**, spectacular rolling trails amble through old stands of Douglas fir and Western red cedar, eventually winding up on the lakefront.

RESTAURANTS

Cafe Juanita
116th exit off 405, west to 97th, take a right, 1½ blocks to 120th Pl,
(206) 823-1505
9702 NE 120th Pl,
Kirkland
Moderate; limited bar; MC, V; checks OK
Dinner every day

For a dozen years, owner Peter Dow has threaded happily among tables of pasta eaters in this charming white house restaurant. He's often seen presenting a bottle of his own Cavatappi sauvignon blanc, cabernet sauvignon, or Maddalena (he makes them all on the premises) and fresh-baked bread flaked with green olives and rosemary, or perhaps describing with gusto the home-bottled vinegar that makes the cafe's salads so wonderful. Pasta is Dow's forte and consistency his recipe. A primo piatto, the cheese ravioli redolent with garlic, was delightful. The menu consists of a half dozen specials rotating around three excellent and unchanging main dishes: chicken in a near-luminous pistachio cream sauce, lamb chops grilled in garlic, rosemary, and olive oil, and sturdy lasagne. Of the specials, try the *spiedini misti* (two skewers of lamb and Italian sausage, chicken marinated in herbs and olive oil, and chicken livers), perfectly roasted, or a succulent veal chop sauced with a stirring blend of veal stock, brandy, and sage. The wine list carries one of the best selections of inexpensive Italian wines we've seen locally. For dessert, be sure to include Dow's crème de monforte, a wonderful, dense variation of crème caramel. A private room with its fireplace and sofa is particularly good for a party of up to 25. Reservations suggested.

Stresa

Kirkland exit off 520, north on Lake Washington Blvd NE to Carillon Point,
(206) 889-9006
2220 Carillon Point, Kirkland
Moderate; full bar; AE, DC, MC, V; checks OK
Lunch, dinner every day

★★★

Named for an elegant resort on the Lago Maggiore in northern Italy, Stresa displays the guiding spirit of Luciano Bardinelli, the original owner of Settebello in Seattle. It's a cool, spare, informal jewel on the eastern shore of Lake Washington, with dark wood chairs, starched white napery, white china. Tables look out past the expansive waterfront lawns of Yarrow Point, across the lake to Seattle's residential hills and the Olympics. Begin with an appetizer of tuna tartare (garnished with strips of red and yellow peppers, suffused with basil and fresh tomatoes) or a true special like baseball-sized porcini mushrooms, oven-roasted and drizzled with extra-virgin olive oil. Veal is excellent here: a hearty osso buco with wild mushrooms and herbs, a sublime veal chop with rosemary and roast potatoes. The pasta dishes are imaginative and well-executed. At lunch, opt for the plate-size pizzas, with crisp crusts and delicate toppings. For dessert, we recommend Luciano's tiramisu or the "salami" of chocolate, berries and nuts. The wine list is admirable and the service usually impeccable except when you're seated outside.

Izumi

Totem Lake West shopping center at 116th and 124th,
(206) 821-1959
12539 116th Ave NE, Kirkland,
Moderate; beer and wine; AE, MC, V; checks OK
Lunch Tues-Fri, dinner Tues-Sun

★★

Chef Hiroyuki Matsushima'Izumi gets consistent raves from Japanese eaters in the area, many of whom consider it the best moderately priced Japanese eatery in greater Seattle. Located at Totem Lake West shopping center, Izumi rubs shoulders with hamburger joints and ersatz Mexican chain restaurants. Chef Matsushima wields the sushi knife with conspicuous flair and exacting standards. His waitstaff is friendly and efficient, making Izumi the kind of place where families feel right at home. Lunches are tasty and reasonably priced—try the Izumi *makunouchi*, served in a lidded lacquer box with six sections. The sections are fastidiously packed with sushi topped with shrimp, fish, vegetables, and tempura prawns.

Le Provençal

Downtown Kirkland,
(206) 821-3300

Owner Philippe Gayte, a native of Avignon, has made Le Provençal an institution with the genuine hospitality and the solid fare of a French cafe. At dinner, he's out

212 Central Way,
Kirkland
Moderate; full bar; AE,
DC, MC, V;
local checks only
Dinner every day

front, greeting guests who choose from a bistro-style menu. The three course version includes a hearty soup or spicy pâté; a main course (maybe breast of chicken with sundried tomatoes); and a simple dessert of crème caramel or fruit and cheese. The *menu gastronomique* (about $30) offers five courses, beginning with oysters or smoked salmon, a goat cheese salad, a sorbet, then perhaps duck with a port sauce or monkfish bathed in lobster, followed by desserts. From the à la carte menu, the garlicky rack of lamb and tender pepper steak make good choices. The admirably priced wine list concentrates on France, with bottles of the house wine, from vineyards owned by Gaite's cousin in Provence. A private room seats up to 20.

Third Floor Fish Cafe

In downtown Kirkland,
above the marina,
(206) 822-3553
205 Lake St S,
Kirkland
Moderate; full bar; AE,
DC, MC, V;
local checks only
Lunch Mon-Fri, dinner
Mon-Sat

Formerly a steak house with a men's club atmosphere, this waterfront restaurant is now a popular fish house, jazzed up with a flotilla of fanciful styrofoam fish swimming through waves of vermilion, orange, aqua and yellow. Credit goes to Kathy Casey, Seattle's celebrity restaurant consultant, who revitalized the menu as well. Appetizers are meant to be shared, especially crab cakes with confetti relish, roasted garlic with an eggplant caponata, mussels in lemon-thyme cream. Regular main courses feature cutting edge flavors, especially the smoked chicken ginger ravioli and the Northwest shellfish stew with garlic mayonnaise. Desserts include a lovely cobbler with fresh berries. The bar offers a dozen zany concoctions, such as Electric Fish Bowl and Moss Bay Slimer. The view, across the lake to the Olympics, remains the same.

Shamiana

In the Houghton Village
at 108th and 68th,
(206) 827-4902
10724 NE 68th St,
Kirkland
Moderate; beer and wine;
AE, MC, V; checks OK
Lunch Mon-Fri, dinner
every day

Shamiana is named after the canopy made of brilliant, primary-colored cotton banners used for celebrations and weddings. It's run by an American brother/sister team who grew up in Bangladesh and Pakistan. Open just a few months at press time, the service is eager and quite capable, and the Indian and Paksitani food is prepared with contemporary American sensibility for each ingredient and its contribution to a dish. Eggplant bharta is a good example—it's a sweet, rich Indian ratatouille, but rather than the mush that's often served elsewhere, you can still see each soft chunk of eggplant and pieces of tomato; it's presented with a generous scattering of pistachios and sliced scallions on top. We tried fish *tikka*, billed as Pakistani barbecue—a hunk of perfectly cooked cod, faintly pink and slightly smokey, was served atop a pile of *pulao*, brilliant yellow, slightly overcooked rice. Kabuli chicken curry is a superbly balanced stew, rich but light (reminiscent of many Thai curries); coriander and cream play against the pepper.

Yarrow Bay Grill and Beach Cafe

Off Lake Washington
Blvd, (206) 889-0303 or
(206) 889-9052
1270 Carillon Point,
Kirkland
Moderate; full bar; AE,
DC, MC, V;
local checks only
Breakfast Sat-Sun,
lunch, dinner every day
(in the Cafe);
dinner every day
(in the Grill)

This cousin to the classic Ray's Boathouse at Shilshole has been suggesting lately that magical chemistry cannot be duplicated. Like Ray's, it's on the water—the lovely Kirkland shore of Lake Washington—and, like Ray's, it's two restaurants in one: the hushed and fancy Grill upstairs, and the livelier, come-as-you-are Beach Cafe below. The former, with its teak booths and Edward S. Curtis photographs, too often manages to turn exquisite wild-caught seafood into perfunctory, inept dinners. At press time, Vicky McCaffree was introducing a new, non-traditional menu with items such as steamed salmon with sake and ginger and topped with shiitake pickled-ginger butter. Until then, our advice: stay with simple entrées instead of busier preparations; be prepared to let the lax servers know you are a demanding diner. The wine list (on both levels) is well conceived. Your best bet, however, is to eat downstairs in the Beach Cafe for its just-off-the-boat spirit and less expensive food. You choose things like ravioli stuffed with three cheeses, hazelnuts, and roasted garlic in a mustard and salmon cream sauce or Whidbey Island mussels Dijonnaise. Portions are large—recently, the half portion of spinach salad doused with a tangy Dijon-shallot vinaigrette and a plate of mesquite-grilled chicken glazed with herb butter were more than enough for two hungry eaters.

LODGINGS

Woodmark Hotel

Kirkland exit off SR 520,
north on Lake
Washington Blvd NE to
Carillon Point,
(206) 822-3700
1200 Carillon Point,
Kirkland, WA 98033
Expensive; AE, DC, MC,
V; checks OK

On the eastern shore of Lake Washington, this hotel resembles any new office building. Nearby there's still a lot of construction at Carillon Point, and parking access is a bit of a maze, but inside one encounters the soft touches of a fine hotel: 100 plush rooms (the best have lake views) with fully stocked minibars, VCRs (with complimentary movies available at the front desk), baths equipped with a second TV, terrycloth robes, and oversized towels, with service (from laundry to valet) to match. They serve a full breakfast—with a newspaper—and if you get late-night cravings, the refrigerator is yours to raid. Downstairs on the lake level there's a comfortable living room with a grand piano and a well-tended fire. The hotel has its own clubby restaurant, the Carillon Room, but you'll be happier at one of the better restaurants next door.

Shumway Mansion

Near NE 116th on 99th
Pl NE, (206) 823-2303
11410 99th Pl NE,
Kirkland, WA 98033

When Richard and Salli Harris heard that developers wanted to demolish this historic 1909 mansion to make room for condos, they hauled the four-story house to a safe location near Kirkland's Juanita Bay. Now it's a gracious bed and breakfast with an equal emphasis on seminars and receptions. Their daughter Julie Blakemore is the resident manager. Seven guest rooms are

Moderate; AE, MC, V;
checks OK

furnished with antiques (each has a private bath), and antique-filled public rooms overlook the bay (just a short walk away) and the lower parking lots. The ballroom downstairs is often used for weddings or special meetings. In summer, it opens onto a flowering patio. A full breakfast is served on linen in the dining room. The Columbia Athletic Club (available free for guest use) is a block away; downtown Seattle is 20 minutes away. Children over 12 are okay. No pets or smoking.

GREATER SEATTLE: BELLEVUE

This former quiet suburban hamlet is developing into a sister-city of Seattle, boasting a downtown skyline of hotels and office towers. Bellevue is the heart of the Eastside, the region between Lake Washington and the Cascade Mountains that is rapidly becoming the Silicon Valley of the Northwest. As many commuters now leave Seattle in the morning for work on the Eastside as do make the traditional suburb-to-Seattle trek.

The city's most recent commercial gem is **Bellevue Place**, a hotel, restaurant, and shopping complex in the center of downtown. Daniel's Broiler on the 21st floor of the Seafirst Office Building offers stunning views of Seattle, the San Juan Islands and the Olympics.

Across the street, **Bellevue Square** hosts Nordstrom and hundreds of other stores, but it's also one of the first malls in the country to house a museum—**The Bellevue Art Museum**, specializing in Northwest crafts, (206) 454-6021.

Much of what makes Bellevue such a livable city is the quiet neighborhoods that ring the downtown. The neighborhood surrounding **Bridle Trails State Park** on the Kirkland border looks like a condensed version of Virginia equestrian country, with backyards of horses and stables. The park features miles of riding and hiking trails through vast stands of Douglas Fir. Day-hikers can also explore **Cougar Mountain**, the forested, western-most hill of an ancient mountain range that stretches from Lake Washington to the younger Cascades.

RESTAURANTS

Azalea's Fountain Court
Just off Main in old
Bellevue, (206) 451-0426
22 103rd Ave NE,
Bellevue
Expensive; full bar; AE,
DC, MC, V; checks OK
Lunch Mon-Fri, dinner
Tues-Sat

Lovely, mannered, garbed in crisp florals, and possessed of quiet good taste, Azalea's Fountain Court (formerly the Fountain Court off Main) is the dowager empress of restaurants. New owners Shelley Kuni and Kathy Birkner have whipped this elegant old Bellevue home back into shape, with service that's an unaffected blend of hospitality and efficiency, and food that's for the most part as intelligent as it is pretty. Chef Tracie Putnam has compiled an intriguing list of Northwest inventive foods—plenty of salads at lunch, and a nice mix of poultry, fish, meat, and pasta at dinner—and doesn't shy away from strong flavors. One warm seafood salad, for instance, amounted to a lush pile of fresh greens, aswoon from their bath in warm port dressing, heaped with flawlessly steamed mussels, salmon, ahi, and prawns, and strewn with a relish of herbs and

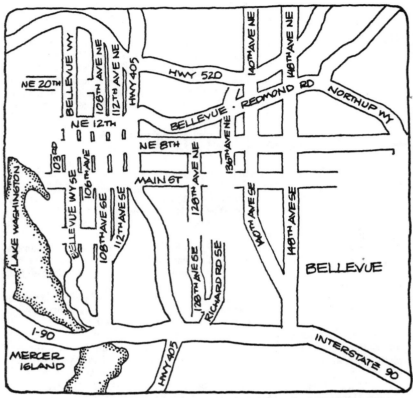

marinated mushrooms. Some thought the sauce was overwhelming, and there have been reports of chewy over-buttered crab-filled raviolis. With its lady-like decor, this place is not for everyone but for the most of us, the results are pleasing. Have dessert (a sumptuous crème caramel, a cloudlike raspberry Grand Marnier mousse cake) and linger amid restaurant surroundings so classic they impart a sense of rootedness in shiny Bellevue.

Eques
(Hyatt Regency Hotel)
Across from Bellevue
Square, (206) 451-3012
NE 8th and Bellevue
Way, Bellevue
Moderate; full bar; AE,
DC, MC, V; no checks

Formal but nonetheless warm and pleasing in pastel tones and natural wood, Eques dispels the presumption that hotel dining is bound to disappoint. The menu is divided: the right side lists the daily specials, which let chef Peter Kelly exhibit his culinary creativity; the left side presents tried-and-true Eques classics, which have earned that status by virtue of diners' repeated requests and raves. We can only hope that the duck and spinach salad with mustard dressing moves over to the left side and becomes available every night. Another favorite is veal medallions with artichoke hearts

*Breakfast Mon-Sat,
dinner every day,
brunch Sun*

in red wine and Gorgonzola, a meltingly tender combination. Their rendition of chowder—infused with puréed salmon—is an excellent choice, as is the spinach fettuccine served with blackened tuna and lemon-thyme cream. Prices in this glitzy Bellevue Place spot are quite reasonable and the service properly subdued. Children's portions are available at half price, although the atmosphere—with a roaring fire in the fireplace and a classical guitarist in the background—is only for the best behaved.

Ristorante Allegria
*Inside Quadrant Plaza at
the corner of NE 8th and
112th, (206) 453-1981
11100 NE 8th St,
Bellevue
Expensive; full bar; AE,
MC, V; checks OK
Lunch Mon-Fri, dinner
Mon-Sat*

Allegria means "happiness," and there's plenty of it in this classic Italian restaurant. It's not of the jam-packed, red-checked-tablecloth variety; Allegria is elegantly stark, with white table linens, stucco walls, and tables spaced comfortably apart. The knowledgeable and well-trained waitstaff and the location (just off I-405 on NE 8th Street in Bellevue) predict an uptown experience, and that's what is delivered. Best of all, the food lives up to any and all unspoken promises made by the surroundings. The seafood is excellent—start with the *sauté di pesce misto* (clams, mussels, calamari, prawns, and scallops in olive oil, garlic, and white wine sauce) or the *gamberi al limone* (prawns in lemon sauce with red pepper and garlic). The pasta is cooked to perfection (including the special round ravioli stuffed with smoked salmon in a light tomato, basil, and cream sauce), and the sauces are so good that even the most proper of Allegria's diners can be caught discreetly dipping bits of bread to get the last drop. Don't waste time looking for street parking on NE 8th—use the underground lot and have the ticket validated.

André's Gourmet Cuisine
*Between 148th NE and
140th NE on NE 20th,
(206) 747-6551
14125 NE 20th St,
Bellevue
Moderate; beer and wine;
MC, V; no checks
Lunch Mon-Fri, dinner
Mon-Sat*

André Nguyen, a young Vietnamese-born chef who earned his stripes at Fullers, Daniel's Broiler, and the Lakeside, has brought inexpensive, innovative Eurasian cuisine to Bellevue. From a menu about equally divided between Vietnamese and European selections, you choose carefully prepared food that's served with a color-conscious nouvelle flair. Some puzzling lapses, though. We had scallops served in a scallop-shaped ceramic bowl and bathed in a buttery, beautifully balanced mushroom and cream sauce with fresh dill; they were meltingly excellent. Oddly, they came with a side of Chef Boy-ar-dee–style spaghetti. Lamb au garlic featured four tender pink slices of lamb seasoned with a whisper of rosemary and topped with broiled garlic cloves, but sitting in a bland, eggy sauce. Some of the Vietnamese combinations explode with vibrant, complex spicings; others are merely routine. We'll come back, though, because what André does well, he does wonderfully.

Pogacha

*In Bellevue Plaza near
106th NE and NE 8th,*
(206) 455-5670
119 106th Ave NE,
Bellevue
*Inexpensive; beer and
wine; AE, MC, V;
no checks*
*Lunch Mon-Fri, dinner
Tues-Sat*

★

Pogacha, a sauceless Croatian relative of Italian pizza, is the specialty of the house in this odd, sterile Bellevue strip-mall space. The light, crisp—but chewy on the inside—disks are baked in the brick oven centerpiece and topped with any of a half dozen combinations, which include mushrooms, pesto, salami, red onions, basil, tomatoes, and various cheeses. There are also some generously sauced pastas, hearty peasant soups, and good salads, and buttery pastries by the score. The terrific wine-by-the-glass is an unexpected delight.

Seoul Olympic Restaurant

NE 8th and 112th NE,
(206) 455-9305
1200 112th Avenue NE,
Bellevue
*Inexpensive; full bar;
MC, V; checks OK*
*Lunch Mon-Fri, dinner
every day*

★

Some of the best Korean food in the Seattle area is to be found in a nondescript office complex in Bellevue. There's a whole page of untranslated Korean-only entrées, and if you ask what they are, the waitress will just shake her head and say "too hot" or "not cooked" or "too strange." Well, you don't need to *read* Korean to order the Korean barbecued beef (grilled beef that's been marinated in soy sauce, sugar, and wine). Traditionally, you grill your own, which you can do here in the small barbecue room in back. Adventuresome eaters who do end up randomly ordering off the Korean-only page may find themselves faced with a hearty soup of beef, tripe, and tubular animal innards.

Landau's

*Between 4th and 8th in
Koll Center,*
(206) 646-6644
500 108th Ave NE,
Bellevue
*Moderate; full bar; AE,
DC, MC, V; checks OK*
*Lunch Mon-Fri, dinner
Mon-Sat*

unrated

This restaurant seems to be constantly undergoing major changes every time we go to press. You'll still find the polished granite, enormous flower arrangements, plush carpeting, and satiny upholstery in this Koll Center restaurant, but the former wide open space is now two. Recently Mary Jane Landau has worked hard to create an atmosphere that's more inviting to the drop-in-after-work crowd (hence the more appealing bar) and has rewritten the menu to include more pastas and a detailed daily fresh sheet (so the pricing is less exclusive). A noble attempt to become less intimidating, though the details of a fine restaurant are still evident: for instance, complimentary bite-size hors d'oeuvres begin the meal and artfully arranged petits fours end it. The menu has broad appeal, with classic continental dishes (lamb chops, scallops of veal, roast duck breast) and a few more trendy items (smoked salmon linguine, black bean soup, tequila chicken). We've come to expect a delicacy of flavor here and true finesse. In the bar, where a few nostalgic photographs have been hung on the walls, there's a smaller menu (at deli prices). For later in the day, the bar has 21 different vodkas and complimentary hors d'oeuvres.

LODGINGS

Hyatt Regency at Bellevue Place

NE 8th St and Bellevue Way, (206) 462-1234, toll-free (800)233-1234
900 Bellevue Way, Bellevue, WA 98104
Expensive; AE, DC, MC, V; checks OK

Hyatt Regency is just one part of Kemper Freeman's splashy, sprawling retail-office-restaurant-hotel-health-club complex called Bellevue Place. It's a 382-room hotel with 24 stories (the highest in Bellevue), which offers all the extras: two pricier "Regency Club" floors, two big ballrooms and several satellite conference rooms, an adjoining health club (for a $10 fee), and an excellent restaurant, Eques (see Restaurants section). The best rooms (doubles start at $165) are those on the south side above the seventh floor. Plenty of people come to Bellevue just to shop—and now they have a place to stay.

The Bellevue Hilton

Main and 112th NE, (206) 455-3330, toll-free (800)BEL-HILT
100 112th Ave NE, Bellevue, WA 98004
Expensive; AE, DC, MC, V; checks OK

With every amenity in the book, the Bellevue Hilton is one of the best bets on the Eastside's Hotel Row. Rooms are tastefully done in soft, warm colors; extras include use of a nearby health and racquet club, free transportation around Bellevue, 24-hour security and room service, cable TV (or movies) in every room, and three restaurants. Meeting rooms recently have been renovated. Doubles run from $97 to $105; parlor suites, at $225, have sitting rooms, partial kitchens, and dining tables.

Bellevue Holiday Inn

112th and Main, (206) 455-5240
11211 Main St, Bellevue, WA 98004
Moderate; AE, DC, MC, V; checks OK

This understated two-story motel neither stimulates nor overloads the senses; many regular visitors to Bellevue won't stay anywhere else. The units are arranged campus style around a well-manicured lawn and heated pool. The suites are nothing special; the fancy dining room, Jonah's, is better than most.

GREATER SEATTLE: MERCER ISLAND
RESTAURANTS

Subito

Take Island Crest exit off I-90, (206) 232-9009
2448 76th Ave SE, Mercer Island
Moderate; beer and wine; MC, V; checks OK
Lunch Mon-Fri, dinner every day

Eric and Vicki Napoleone have succeeded in avoiding Mercerfication—the tendency to cater to otherwise bland tastes as so many other Island restaurants do. The tangy antipasti are excellent, and the marinara, bolognese, and cream sauces do well with the pasta, chicken, and veal dishes. Chef Napoleone has found the establishment's niche and narrowed his menu to mostly traditional Italian (OK, so there are a few burgers for the kids, on request). The insalata di mare catches five types of seafood with a lemon-jalapeño vinaigrette in a net of lettuce, red bell peppers, and fresh vegetables. The fettuccine Mario (herbed artichokes and chicken in cream sauce) is satisfying. The cool, contemporary dining space beams with big, colorful paintings, and there are moderately priced wines and numerous microbrewed beers. Subito means "in a hurry" and even if you are, the service is not. Two semiprivate rooms in back work nicely for larger parties.

GREATER SEATTLE: ISSAQUAH

Fast food franchises now line the Interstate, but the center of this old coal mining town still resembles small-town America, complete with butcher shop and a working dairy. On good days, Mount Rainier appears between the hills that form the town's southern and eastern borders.

Gilman Village on Gilman Boulevard is a shopping complex with a twist: the developers refurnished old farmhouses, a barn and feed store, then filled them with craft and clothing shops, restaurants, and a woodworking gallery. **Boehm's Candies** on the edge of town still dips its chocolates by hand, and offers tours most weekdays, but reservations are needed, (206) 392-6652.

The **Issaquah Farmer's Market** is open Saturdays throughout the summer, across from the **Issaquah State Salmon Hatchery**, on Sunset Way, which is open to visitors daily from 8am to 7:30pm.

Lake Sammamish State Park lies between town and Lake Sammamish, and offers swimming and boat access. **Tiger Mountain**, the sprawling 13,000-acre state forest that looms to the east, is a favorite weekend destination for hikers. Trails wind through alder and evergreen forests and past old coal mine shafts.

RESTAURANTS

Mandarin Garden
Exit 17 off I-90 to Sunset,
(206) 392-9476
40 E Sunset Way,
Issaquah
Inexpensive; beer and
wine; MC, V;
local checks only
Lunch Tues-Sat, dinner
Tues-Sun

This Issaquah restaurant has the distinction of producing spiciness where promised—a rarity among Chinese restaurants in the area, and all the more admirable since chef and owner Andy Wang is a native of Shanghai. The minimal decor and the down-at-heels ambience mask Wang's understanding of Sichuan, Hunan, and Mandarin cooking and warm, efficient service. Praiseworthy dishes include melt-in-your-mouth kung pao chicken, mixed seafood Sichuan, and variations on bean curd. Two private rooms (one holding up to 50 guests) are available for banquets. Peking duck should be ordered a day in advance.

LODGINGS

The Wildflower
Exit 17 from I-90, head
left 2 blocks, then right
onto Issaquah–Fall City
Rd for 1 mile, turn right
at light, (206) 392-1196
25237 SE Issaquah–Fall
City Rd, Issaquah,
WA 98027

Laureita Caldwell has decorated the four guest rooms of her log-house bed and breakfast in floral themes, based on plants native to Issaquah: the Strawberry Room, the Fern Room, the Daisy Room, the Rose Room. The last boasts the classiest decor (although it shares a bath with Daisy); all rooms have raw pine walls, charming window seats (great for reading), and handmade quilts. Downstairs there's a cozy common room where guests can relax by the wood stove. All

Inexpensive; no credit cards; checks OK

this and breakfast too for $50. The massive cabin sits quite impressively in the lonesome woods just north of Issaquah—a terrific base camp for travelers torn between the mountains and the metropolis.

GREATER SEATTLE: BAINBRIDGE ISLAND

Once a major logging port, Bainbridge Island is now a semirural haven for city professionals (who don't mind the half-hour commute via ferry from downtown Seattle), writers, artists, and people seeking simpler lives. It makes a pleasant tour, by car or bike, during which you can see some small pastoral farms, enviable waterfront homes, and spectacular cityscapes (especially from **Fay Bainbridge State Park** on the northeast corner of the island). The wooded and waterfront trails in **Fort Ward State Park**, on the south end of the island, make for a nice afternoon stroll (good picnic spots, too).

Bloedel Reserve is 150 acres of lush tranquil gardens, woods, meadows, and ponds. Plants from all over the world make the grounds interesting at any time of the year. Reservations are required and limited, taken for Wednesdays through Sundays only, (206) 842-7631.

A simpler trip is to ride over on the ferry, sans car, and walk a few strides up the road to the **Bainbridge Island Winery**, a small family winery which makes a number of good wines including a superb strawberry. Then walk a few blocks into downtown Winslow, take in the shops, have coffee and pastry at **Pegasus Espresso House** at the foot of Madison Avenue S, and float back to Seattle.

RESTAURANTS

Pleasant Beach Grill
Follow signs toward Fort Ward State Park,
(206) 842-4347
4738 Lynwood Center NE
Bainbridge Island
Moderate; full bar; AE, MC, V; local checks only
Dinner every day

★★

Bainbridge Island's only white-linen restaurant remains quietly tucked away in a large Tudor house on the south end of the island. Islanders have always favored the pine-paneled bar, warmed by a fireplace and with two couches, as the place to sink into a drink and dessert (a luscious slice of rich shortcake crowned with crimson berries, or an excellent chocolate mousse). In the past the food has been uneven, but recent meals, under the direction of chef Hussein Ramadan, have proved delightful, from the sauté of prawns, scallops, and white fish (in a sauce of curry, cool lemongrass, and coconut milk and adorned with mushrooms and a tri-colored mosaic of peppers) to an excellent 10-ounce slab of New York pepper steak with a green peppercorn, mustard, and brandy sauce. There are oysters on the half shell; however, most oysters here are baked with garlic butter, Parmesan, and brandy. Stick with simple grills and seafoods; enjoy the ample portions and skilled service. The dining room's pleasant, but in the summer, ask for the terrace. In winter, reserve a table in the comfortable bar.

Four Swallows
Follow signs toward Fort

With its high booths, comfortable couch, and fresh flowers, the Four Swallows on the south end of Bain-

Ward State Park,
(206) 842-3397
4569 Lynwood Center Rd
Bainbridge Island
Inexpensive; beer and
wine; MC, V;
local checks only
Dinner Tues-Sat

bridge Island is appreciated by locals for its friendliness and, lately, its very good food. The menu changes daily and is written on a large paper tablet in the entryway. Somehow, it's always exactly right: a savory heap of fall-off-the-bone pork with black beans, sour cream, salsa, and tortillas; a platter of perfectly ripe pears, slices of kiwi fruit, goat cheese rolled in pine nuts, crackers, and a large head of roasted garlic; or a plate-sized pizza margherita (tomato sauce, fresh basil, and three cheeses). Salads are an excellent toss of wild greens. The service is excellent, and if you've been there more than once, they'll probably even remember your favorite wine.

Streamliner Diner

Winslow Way and
Bejune, (206) 842-8595
397 Winslow Way,
Bainbridge Island
Inexpensive; beer and
wine; no credit cards;
local checks only
Breakfast every day,
lunch Mon-Sat (light
lunch Sun)

You don't need a better excuse than breakfast to hop the ferry to Bainbridge Island. The Streamliner Diner (an easy walk from the Winslow ferry) has been an Island breakfast institution for nearly a decade. As we went to press, new owners had stepped in, but the rest—the staff, the menu, and the prices—appears to remain the same. With its kitchen-table decor and sweet saxophone swing coming through the sound system, this no-smoking restaurant oozes small-town personality. Breakfasts include inventive omelets, incomparable buttermilk waffles with real maple syrup, nutritious homemade granola, and Potatoes Deluxe—the famed spiced potatoes stir-fried with vegetables and topped with Cheddar cheese. Lunches are natural homemade soups, salads, quiches, and sandwiches. A delightful spot on any morn, except on weekends, when the lines are quite long.

LODGINGS

The Bombay House

4 miles south of the ferry,
just off W Blakely Ave,
(206) 842-3926
8490 Beck Rd NE,
Bainbridge Island,
WA 98110
Moderate; AE, MC, V;
checks OK

A sweet stroll from Fort Ward State Park on the south end of the island, the Bombay House has a hearty dose of the country-hideaway mood that's so much of the bed-and-breakfast mystique. It's a sprawling turn-of-the-century house with a wrap around porch, set in a lavish flower garden with a rough-cedar gazebo overlooking scenic Rich Passage. The large living room has a huge fireplace, and all five bedrooms are done up in country antiques (three have private baths). The vast second-floor Captain's Suite has a wood parlor stove and a claw-footed tub. Innkeepers Roger Kanchuk, Bunny Cameron and their charming daughter are friendly hosts; their breakfast includes homemade muffins and breads and fresh fruits. Children over 6 years are accepted. Smoking is restricted.

Beach Cottage B&B

4 miles from the ferry off
Eagle Harbor Dr,

Right across Eagle Harbor from the ferry-stop town of Winslow is this charming, flower-bedecked four-cottage setup. Each cottage has a queen-size bed, a

(206) 842-6081
5831 Ward NE,
Bainbridge Island,
WA 98110
Moderate; no credit cards;
checks OK

kitchen (stocked with breakfast fixings), logs for the fireplace, and stereo. Two are right on the beach, and all four boast a view of Eagle Harbor and its marina (the brand-new two-bedroom on the hill even views Seattle and Mount Rainier on clear days). Each goes for $75 for two people ($95 for four). Smoking is allowed (pets and children aren't), and there's a rowboat for loan.

GREATER SEATTLE: SEA-TAC/AIRPORT

LODGINGS

Seattle Airport Hilton Hotel
188th St exit off I-5, north
1½ miles,
(206) 244-4800, toll-free
(800) HILTONS
17620 Pacific Hwy S,
Sea-Tac, WA, 98188
Expensive; AE, DC, MC,
V; checks OK

This streamlined building miraculously manages to create a resort atmosphere along an airport strip. Plush rooms (at posh prices) circle a large, landscaped courtyard with pool and indoor/outdoor Jacuzzi. The architecture is by the distinguished national firm of SOM. Exercise room and meeting and party rooms available. A versatile menu offers continental cuisine.

Seattle Marriott at Sea-Tac
Off Pacific Hwy S on
176th, (206) 241-2000,
toll-free (800)228-9290
3201 S 176th St,
Sea-Tac, WA 98188
Expensive; AE, DC, MC,
V; checks OK

Another megamotel, but on a human scale. The Alaska motif is warm, although it makes the lobby somewhat cluttered. Rooms are standard but suites are spacious. A pool and a courtyard area are part of an enormous covered atrium; there are also two Jacuzzis, a sauna, and a well-equipped exercise room. Lobby bar open until 2am.

GREATER SEATTLE: TUKWILA

LODGINGS

Doubletree Inn and Plaza
Take Southcenter exit off
I-5, (206) 246-8220,
toll-free (800) 528-0444
16500 Southcenter Pkwy,
Tukwila, WA 98188
Moderate; AE, DC, MC,
V; checks OK

The Doubletree, fixed between I-5 and the Southcenter shopping mall, is two hotels. The Plaza has handsome luxury suites ($99 to $156) with refrigerators, TVs (you pay per cable movie), and small wet bars. Southeast-facing rooms have views of Mount Rainier. There's a Jacuzzi and a sauna at the Plaza; the pool is across the street in a secluded courtyard at the Doubletree Inn, the more plebeian sibling. The woody Northwest lobby is nice, but rooms here ($69 to $104) are average; avoid the north-facing ones, which hum with the sounds of I-5 and offer views of the Frederick & Nelson department store. Service is quite friendly.

GREATER SEATTLE: BURIEN

RESTAURANTS

Filiberto's
Off Highway 518,
(206) 248-1944
14401 Des Moines-
Memorial Dr S, Burien
Moderate; full bar; AE,
MC, V; checks OK
Lunch Tues-Sat, dinner
Tues-Sun

Filiberto's is the most authentic and, on a good day, among the best of the south Seattle Italian restaurants. The look is cheery and trattoria-perfect, with even the dishwashing section in back finished in imported tile. Service can be erratic, but the food seems to have gotten more consistent, with good attention to the basics. The long menu emphasizes Roman and other midregion preparations of pasta, veal, poultry, and rabbit, right down to the real stracciatella alla Romana egg-drop soup (not too salty, as it often is in Rome). Three special treats: the huge, very well-priced selection of Italian wines in a take-your-pick glass case (here's where you'll find that unforgettable label with the forgotten name), Filiberto's pizza oven, and a bocce court out back (if you're lucky you'll get asked to play).

Satsuma
Off 148th on Ambaum,
(206) 242-1747
14301 Ambaum Blvd SW
Burien
Inexpensive; beer and
wine; AE, MC, V;
no checks
Lunch Tues-Wed, Fri,
dinner Tues-Sun

Plain as a box on the outside, this tranquil Burien hideaway has captured the interest of the local Japanese, who come to enjoy the cooking of Tak Suetsugu, formerly of the Mikado. The tempura is light as air, the sushi merely creditable. For a twist, try the Washington roll, with smoked salmon, *tamagoyaki* (similar to an omelet), cucumber, and strips of Washington apple. The black cod kasuzuke, marinated in sake lees and broiled, is a velvety ambrosia. Tatami rooms are available, including one that holds 20—great for a private function. Service is gracious.

GREATER SEATTLE: KENT

RESTAURANTS

Cave Man Kitchens
W Valley Hwy at the
James intersection,
(206) 854-1210
807 W Valley Hwy, Kent
Inexpensive; no alcohol;
MC, V; checks OK
Lunch, dinner every day

The late Dick Donley spent years experimenting with methods of smoking ribs, chicken, turkey, sausage, and salmon over alder and (when available) apple wood. What he finally achieved was outstanding—expecially the moist smoked turkey. Donley's six children carry on after him, and nothing has changed. There is no inside seating, but in warm weather you can eat outside on picnic tables. Most people take out, loading up on the smoked goods and accompaniments such as beans, potato salad, coleslaw, and a terrific bread pudding with butterscotch whiskey sauce.

GREATER SEATTLE: DES MOINES

RESTAURANTS

Le Bonaparte
S 216th St and Marine View Dr, (206) 878-4412
21630 Marine View Drive, Des Moines
Expensive; full bar; AE, DC, MC, V; no checks
Lunch Mon-Fri, dinner every day, brunch Sun

By mining the territory between traditional French and nouvelle cuisines, this restaurant-in-a-house has been known to draw diners from the entire region to the shoreline of Des Moines. But as things begin to slip, fewer are inspired to make an evening of it. Owner/chef Jacques Mason normally offers up to four game birds (squab, duck, quail, pheasant) prepared in different sauces. Not all of them are successful. A recent lamb dish was overpowered by Pernod. There are, however, some surprising touches, the veal dishes are often exemplary, and the chocolate Marie Antoinette gâteau made without flour continues to wow even reluctant chocoholics. The service has been known to attempt to cover up incompetence with snobbery. Le Bonaparte is especially lovely in summer, when you can eat on the verandah in the shade of venerable fruit trees. On Sundays, a five-course brunch features everything from omelets and fruit to seafood and escargots. Chef Mason puts together imaginative menus for private groups of up to 70.

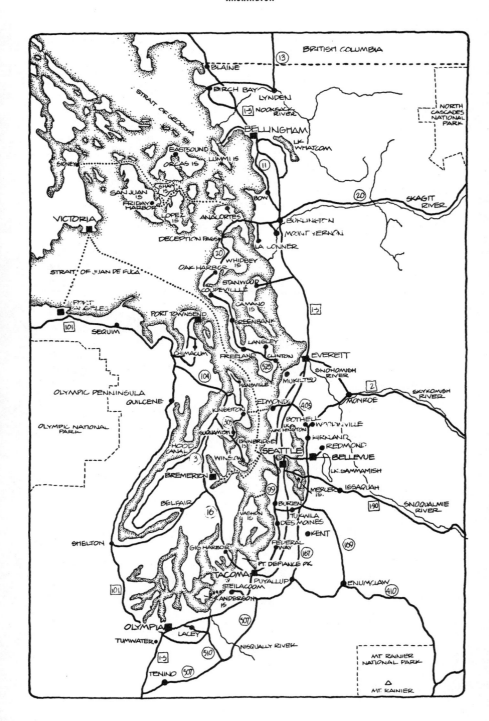

PUGET SOUND

North to south along the I-5 corridor, including side trips to the islands.

BLAINE

Blaine is, well, plain. Not exactly the kind of spot you're likely to make a travel destination unless you have some other reason for visiting this little community snugged up against the border. The flower-bright gardens and the lawns at the border-crossing park around the International Peace Arch are quite lovely, so if you want to picnic en route to or from British Columbia, this a good, if sometimes crowded, place.

LODGINGS

Inn at Semiahmoo
Take exit 270 off I-5, travel west, watch for signs at 9565 Semiahmoo Pkwy (206) 371-2000
Mail: PO Box 790, Blaine, WA 98230-0790
Expensive; AE, DC, MC, V; checks OK
Breakfast, lunch, dinner every day

Semiahmoo Spit is a stunning site for a resort, with beachward views of the sea and the San Juans from many of the buildings. It sports lots of amenities: a 300-slip marina convenient to the inn; a house cruise vessel on which you can book excursions through the San Juans or scenic fishing trips; a thoroughly outfitted athletic club (swimming pool, racquetball, squash, tennis, aerobics, weight lifting, tanning, massage, sauna, and Jacuzzi); an endless stretch of beach. Three restaurants (Stars, the Northwest gourmet dining room, plus two more casual spots) provide the necessary range of culinary alternatives. The golf course, designed by Arnold Palmer, may be the best in the state: long, unencumbered fairways surrounded by dense woods, excellent use of water (some very clever water shots here), and lovely, sculptural sand traps.

So why isn't it the best resort in the West? Lots of little things, which leave us feeling vaguely as though Semiahmoo is more glorified motel than luxury resort. The adjacent convention center, where revamped cannery buildings make top-notch meeting arenas, is really Semiahmoo's greatest strength: it's a nice place to do business. But vacationers might well be disappointed by the mindless clichés of decor. Systems noises have been far too audible through the walls. Views, splendid from the bayside rooms, are nonexistent in others.

BIRCH BAY

It's just the place for 1950s teenage nostalgia. The crescent-shaped beach draws throngs of kids—cruising the strip, go-carting, hanging out in the arcade (open Memorial Day through Labor Day). Frankie and Annette are all that's missing.

There's a state park for camping and lots of sandy beach to wiggle between your toes. Off season can be very off.

LODGINGS

Jacobs Landing Rentals
Take exit 270 off I-5, head
west for 5 miles, follow
signs, (206) 371-7633
7824 Birch Bay Dr,
Birch Bay, WA 98230
Moderate; AE, MC, V;
checks OK

This is the best of the condo developments, right in the "middle of town," across the main street from the beach. Units are set at angles among the beautifully maintained grounds—affording some of them better water views than others. Suites (one-, two-, and three-bedroom units) are modern and deluxe, with fireplaces, kitchens, and washers and dryers. There are outdoor tennis courts, an indoor heated pool, a Jacuzzi, and racquetball courts to keep everyone busy.

LYNDEN

This picture-perfect, neat and tidy community sports immaculate yards and colorful gardens lining the shady avenue into downtown, which has adopted a Dutch theme (slightly overdone) in tribute to a community of early inhabitants. Be sure to visit the charming and informative **Pioneer Museum** full of local memorabilia and antique buggies and motorcars; (206) 354-3675.

RESTAURANTS

Hollandia
In the Dutch Village at
Guide Meridian and
Front St, (206) 354-4133
655 Front St, Lynden
Inexpensive; beer and
wine; MC, V; local
checks only
Lunch Mon-Sat, dinner
Tues-Sat

Riding on the tail of bigger Dutchified establishments is a slightly more tasteful and quiet bistro that offers a selection of authentic fare imported from The Netherlands. It's located just off the base of the windmill in the center of town. Chef Dini Mollink works competently on what is, to the American palate, rather heavy cuisine. A safe choice is, believe it or not, the *Toeristenmenu: Groentesoep* (Dutch meatball soup—firm, tasty meatballs in a luscious homemade broth with bits of vegetable), schnitzel Hollandia (chicken breast in a just-crunchy light breading), and dessert (we adored the little almond tarts). A less filling selection would be the *Koninginnesoep met crackers* (the Queen's cream soup, a rich chicken soup served with fresh raisin bread and thin slices of Gouda cheese). A small spice cookie accompanies your after-dinner coffee—a nice touch.

LODGINGS

Dutch Village Inn
Front St and Guide
Meridian,
(206) 354-4440
655 Front St,
Lynden, WA 98264
Moderate; MC, V;
checks OK

One might question an inn located in a windmill in a Dutch-theme village. This particular inn, however, provides six authentically designed, tastefully furnished, and luxuriously appointed rooms to please all but the most jaded of travelers. Not surprisingly, the rooms are named for the Dutch provinces; Friesland Kamer, the room named for the northernmost province, occupies the top of the windmill. Views are lovely, but interrupted rhythmically as the giant blades of the wind-mill pass by (turning, fully lit, until 10pm). There are special touches in all the rooms—two have extra beds fitted into curtained alcoves in true Dutch fashion, and several have two-person tubs. Breakfast is served from the full menu of the cafe, just off the lobby and along the village "canal."

FERNDALE

Hovander Homestead Park. At this county-run working farm, kids can pat the animals or prowl the barn, and families can picnic along the Nooksack River. The centerpiece is the gabled farmhouse and its gardens, built in 1903 by a retired Swedish architect, Holand Hovander. 5299 Nielsen Road, south of Ferndale off Hovander Road, (206) 384-3444. Call ahead for hours.

Adjacent to Hovander Park, the **Tenant Lake Interpretive Center and Fragrance Garden** offers boardwalk access to an abundance of birdlife in a wetland setting. The garden was developed with the visually impaired and handicapped in mind, so many of the raised-bed plantings are identified with Braille labels and the garden is very wheelchair accessible.

RESTAURANTS

Douglas House
½ mile west of Ferndale city center,
(206) 384-5262
2254 Douglas Dr,
Ferndale
Moderate; beer and wine;
MC, V; checks OK
Dinner Wed-Sun

Few restaurants north of Bellingham have aspired to the level of cuisine that Douglas House attempts, and it is much to the kitchen's credit that it can turn out carefully prepared and diverse dishes on a night when the whole world has decided to show up. Many things are fine here: moist, deboned charbroiled trout fillets in a subtle beurre rouge, a robust rack of lamb that came as ordered and was served with mint crème fraîche. There are some lapses in service, although we chalk these up to inexperience (the limited wine list lacks depth, the rolls are brown-n-serve); owners Rod and Susan Zoske take these things in stride and correct them willingly. The place is located on Ferndale's main thoroughfare in an older remodeled house, with a fetching view of the elusive Mount Baker. Plans to enlarge last year's herb garden—to which the Zoskes and chef David Wallace are obviously devoted—are underway, as is a deck for outdoor dining.

SUMAS

LODGINGS

Sumas Mountain Lodge
Downtown Sumas,
(206) 988-4483
819 Cherry St, Sumas,

Although Sumas, a small border-crossing town east of Lynden, is not a destination community, it's a good jumping-off point for a trip into Canada. This place deserves a more rustic setting than Sumas's main drag,

WA 98295
Moderate; MC, V;
checks OK

steps away from the Canadian border. This handsome log lodge is a small-scale replica of the classic Mount Baker Lodge, which was destroyed by fire in 1931. The nine rustic rooms recapture the aura of the old lodge, with peeled-log beds, wooden floors with braided rugs, and framed black-and-white reproduction photos of Mount Baker Lodge. Six rooms have Jacuzzis; two have river-stone fireplaces. Room 6, Twin Sisters, where the queen-size bed is supplemented with a dandy bunk bed and red tartan curtains, is perfect for families. Guest receive a $5-per-person credit toward breakfast in the lodge's attractive restaurant. In deference to the fiery finale of its predecessor, this is a nonsmoking establishment.

BELLINGHAM

The mishmash grid of Bellingham's streets is a reminder of its former days as four smaller towns. Only recently has the downtown architecture of this city, situated on three rivers flowing into one bay, been rediscovered: the town is full of fine old houses, award-winning architecture at Western Washington University, stately streets, and lovely parks. An economic boom is bringing change and expansion to Whatcom County, most notably at the handsome port facility that now houses the southern terminus (built at great expense in 1989) of the **Alaska Marine Highway System**. For information on weekly sailings for passengers and vehicles along the Inside Passage, call (800) 642-0066 or 206 676-8445.

Whatcom Museum of History and Art, a massive Romanesque building dating from 1892, was used as a city hall until 1940. It has been beautifully restored, and the exhibits—Eskimo and Northwest Coast Indian artifacts, pioneer photographs, logging lore—are imaginatively mounted; 121 Prospect Street, (206) 676-6981. One block from the museum is **R.R. Henderson**, one of the best used bookstores in the state; 112 Grand Ave (206) 734-6855.

Old homes. Wonderful turn-of-the-century mansions abound in Bellingham: check out Utter Street, between Madison and Monroe; West Holly Street, from Broadway to C Street; Eldridge Avenue; and North Garden Street, from Myrtle to Champion. Also worth a visit, in the south end of town, are the homes on Knox Avenue from 12th to 17th and on Mill Street near 15th; the 1890 Roland G. Gamwell House at 16th and Douglas; and the Craftsman-style Roeder Home on Sunset Drive, open to the public.

Big Rock Garden Nursery and Gardens of Art. A vast array of azaleas, rhododendrons, and Japanese maples share this wonderful woodland site with a unique outdoor gallery of garden art. Plans are in the works for free music in the garden on Sunday afternoons from May to August. 2900 Sylvan, near Lake Whatcom; (206) 734-4167.

The **Old Town** around West Holly and Commercial Streets hosts antique and junk shops and some decent eateries. **Fairhaven**, the product of a short-lived railroad boom from 1889 to 1893, is good for exploring—there has been a resurgence of life in the red brick buildings. **The Marketplace**, the grand dame and central figure among the attractive old buildings, was restored in 1988 and houses a number of interesting shops and dining options. The district is rich with

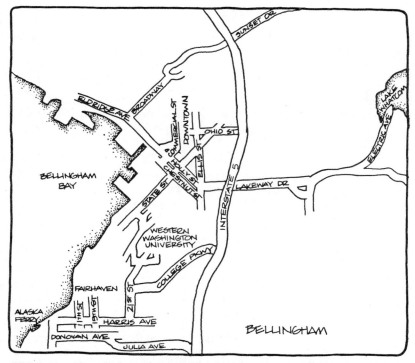

diversion: crafts galleries, coffeehouses, bookstores, a charming garden/nursery emporium, and a lively evening scene unique for Bellingham.

Western Washington University, on Sehome Hill south of downtown, is a fine expression of the spirit of Northwest architecture: warm materials, formal echoes of European styles, respect for context and the natural backdrop. The Ridgeway Dormitory complex by Bassetti and Morse demonstrates an extraordinary sensitivity to terrain; also notable are the Social Sciences Building, with its elaborate concrete structural patterns; Mathes and Nash halls, with a curvilinear echo of Aalto; and the Central Quadrangle, with its feelings of a Danish town square.

Lake Whatcom Railway—located not on Lake Whatcom but on Highway 9 at Wickersham—makes scenic summer runs using an old Northern Pacific engine; (206) 595-2218.

Mount Baker Vineyards. This attractive, cedar-sided, skylit facility specializes in some of the lesser-known varietals, such as Müller-Thurgau and Madeleine Angevine, and various less exotic blushes and blends. The tasting room is located 11 miles east of Bellingham on Mount Baker Highway; (206) 592-2300.

The Ski to Sea Race attracts teams from all over the world to participate in this annual event over Memorial Day weekend (see Calendar).

The **Island Shuttle Express** provides passenger-only ferry service from Bellingham to the San Juan Islands, May through September. Call for reservations: (206) 671-1137.

RESTAURANTS

il fiasco

*Across from the Parkade
at Commercial and Holly,
(206) 676-9136
1309 Commercial St,
Bellingham
Moderate; full bar; MC,
V; local checks only
Lunch Mon-Fri, dinner
every day*

il fiasco (Italian for "the flask") has built a dedicated clientele who come often because the welcome is warm and sincere, the staff friendly and knowledgeable, the decor sophisticated and comfortable, and the food interesting and ambitious. Head chef Christopher Stift, owner Terry Treat, and the staff have masterfully orchestrated a menu featuring Northern Italian classics, often with a contemporary twist—for example, a traditional carpaccio (beef tenderloin sliced paper-thin) accompanied by fresh-grated Reggiana Parmesan and a caper/mustard sauce. Dinners are accompanied by a choice of the day's soup (often rather eclectic combinations, consistently sensational) or mixed greens (always nicely done, making this a tough choice), vegetable, and an angel hair soufflè. Many selections can be ordered as either appetizer- or entrée-sized portions—a relief when you're stymied by indecision. There's a fine selection of Italian wines (some available by the glass) spanning the entire price range.

Pacific Cafe

*Off Holly on Commercial,
(206) 647-0800
100 N Commercial,
Bellingham
Moderate; beer and wine;
AE, MC, V; checks OK
Lunch Tues-Fri, dinner
Tues-Sat, brunch Sun*

The Pacific Cafe, tucked into the historic Mount Baker Theater building, has always been a leader on Bellingham's gastronomic front. But recently here seems to have been something of a renaissance going on in Robert Fong's kitchen, and the results are even more exciting than usual. The menu—and the tasteful decor—reflect a bit of Fong's Asian influence (he comes to Washington via Hawaii, supplemented with years of travel in Europe, India, China, and Malaysia). The satay sauces are complex, light and fragrant. Specials may include a buttery truffle and cognac pâté and perfectly fried Brie with fresh fruit. Entrées are prepared with care; the roast duck with ginger-shiitake mushroom sauce is rich and moist; lamb grilled with rosemary and garlic rock salt comes adorned with a sweet and tangy chutney. Fong is a serious wine collector, and the quality of the vintages presented reflects a fine-tuned palate. No smoking, please.

The Bagelry

*Railroad near Champion,
(206) 676-5288
1319 Railroad Ave,
Bellingham
Inexpensive; no alcohol;
no credit cards; local
checks only
Breakfast, lunch
every day*

Expatriate East Coasters will delight in the dense crusty New York–style bagels, six or seven kinds of which are offered hot from the ovens throughout the day. The pumpernickel is especially good, with onion running a close second. The tasty bialys, which look like large flat bagels without a hole, make an addictive base for a sandwich—tender smoked Virginia ham, for example. Other bagel sandwiches come open-faced and piled with freshly made spreads and salads (we like the rich chopped chicken liver and creamy scallion spread). Dharma juices, a local product, are fresh and flavorful. No smoking.

Bluewater Bistro

Holly and Cornwall,
(206) 733-6762
1215½ Cornwall Ave,
Bellingham
Inexpensive; beer and
wine; MC, V;
checks OK
Breakfast, lunch Mon-
Sat, dinner Tues-Sat,
brunch Sun

The Bluewater has filled a long-empty niche in downtown Bellingham, providing a cheerful atmosphere, energetic staff, an adventurous attitude in the kitchen, and even a live jazz brunch on Sundays (Thursday night jazz in summer). It's supposed to be fun—and for the most part it is. The delicious garlic burger is served on the Bistro's own brioche bun, with provolone and a tasty marinara dip. The Mexican quiche is a lesson in taco-as-quiche in a so-so crust. At brunch you might try the hearty Italian eggs (eggs on polenta with the house marinara) or the mild and creamy basil, chèvre, and tomato omelet. In keeping with its bistro heritage, wines here tend toward the less patrician (and less expensive) covering the territory from Australia to California to the Northwest, and the brews can take you from Kalama, Washington to Czechoslovakia.

Cafe Toulouse

Downtown near Railroad
Ave, (206) 733-8996
133 E Holly St,
Bellingham
Inexpensive; beer and
wine; no credit cards;
local checks only
Breakfast Mon-Sat,
lunch Mon-Fri

This unselfconscious lunch counter–style cafe has already developed a diverse and fiercely loyal following. Students, businesspeople, and weary shoppers make up a clientele as eclectic as the menu. Stop in for a whole- or half-sandwich—perhaps smoked turkey served on generous slices of homemade breads with a cranberry/apple/cream cheese spread, or roast pork loin with mixed pepper and fresh mint jelly. The flavorful Toulouse country terrine is marvelous as a sandwich (served with caper/herb cream cheese and Dijon on French bread) or by itself. Potato pancakes are a specialty at breakfast. Try to avoid the obvious breakfast and lunch hours in this popular—and tiny—cafe.

La Patisserie

North end of town in
Northwest shopping
center, (206) 671-3671
3090 Northwest Ave,
Bellingham
Inexpensive; beer and
wine; MC, V;
checks OK
Breakfast, lunch, dinner
every day

As the name suggests, La Patisserie is a bakery, the sort that makes its own croissants and a terrific pastrami sandwich. The real draw here, however, is soul-satisfying Vietnamese food—homemade soups, egg rolls, and an infinite variety of noodle dishes (such as barbecued duck with rice noodle soup, or the *bun bo*—a fiery beef-and-noodle affair that is definitely not for the timid. Dinners focus exclusively on Vietnamese cuisine: translucent steamed dumplings, generously stuffed with shrimp, daikon, and onion—or a refreshing salad of beef, anchovy, and onion marinated with lemon juice. There are three kinds of entrées: hot pots, trays, and noodle dishes, most of which involve some element of do-it-yourself cooking.

Thai House

Across from Bellis
Fair Mall,
(206) 734-5111
3930 Meridian Village,
Bellingham
Inexpensive; beer and
wine; MC, V;

Peggy Sripoom has fashioned a most comfortable spot located (as many of the great Thai restaurants seem to be) in a strip mall. Bellingham's best Thai house caters to the most discerning Thai food lovers. It's a nice environment in which to savor one's fish cakes or linger over the flavorful hot-and-sour soup chock full of tender seafood and redolent of fresh lemon grass. Tried-and-true favorites include a whole flatfish, deep-fried and

checks OK
Lunch, dinner every day

then smothered in a spicy red sauce) or any one of the curries. The Thai House offers a more restricted but reasonably priced menu for lunch, which includes steamed rice and a rather forgettable cup of soup. Thai House can also cater your next party.

Colophon Cafe
11th near Harris (in
Village Books),
Fairhaven,
(206) 647-0092
1210 11th St, Bellingham
Inexpensive; no alcohol;
MC, V; checks OK
Breakfast, lunch, dinner
every day

Located in the best bookstore in town, Colophon Cafe offers table service on its lower level, counter service above. The food here can be playful—a peanut-butter jambon (on a French roll, of course), or a Reese's sandwich (PB&J with chocolate chips)—or serious and hearty, like the incredible African peanut soup (in vegetarian and nonvegetarian versions), which is chunky with fresh tomatoes, grainy with peanuts, and pungent with gingerroot. The Colophon encourages patrons to tarry over their espresso with a book or with friends for a lively discussion. The gallery space around the walls is dedicated to local artists.

LODGINGS

Schnauzer Crossing
Take exit 253 off I-5, go
3.2 miles on Lakeway Dr
and turn left,
(206) 733-0055 or
(206) 734-2808
4421 Lakeway Dr,
Bellingham, WA 98226
Expensive; MC, V;
checks OK

This sophisticated and unique B&B overlooking Lake Whatcom attracts a surprising range of visitors, from newlyweds to businesspeople to discerning foreign travelers—and graciously accommodates them all. Donna and Monte McAllister open their lovely contemporary home, gardens, and grounds to their guests, many of whom return time and again. A charming new cottage will vie in popularity with the spacious and elegant suite, which also has a king-size bed, fireplace, Jacuzzi, TV/VCR, and a tranquil garden view. The McAllisters are sensitive to guests' needs for privacy and have a finely tuned sense of hospitality that's obvious in the details such as extra-thick towels and gorgeous flowers year-round. A superior gourmet breakfast might include jazzy French toast with fresh fruit and espresso. A private tennis court, hot tub in a Japanese garden setting, canoe, decks, and use of the living room are all available to guests. There really are schnauzers here.

Best Western Heritage Inn
Take I-5 exit 256,
(800) 528-1234 or
(206) 647-1912
151 E McLeod Rd,
Bellingham, WA 98226
Moderate; AE, DC, MC,
V; checks OK

Three tasteful, Wedgwood-blue, shuttered and dormered structures nestling amid a small grove of trees and a stream seem incongruous adjacent to I-5 and a conglomeration of malls; however, this Best Western is one of the most elegantly furnished, professionally run hotels in the area. Exquisite cherrywood four-poster beds (stair-step up included), high- and low-boys, wingback chairs in rich fabrics, and stylish desks with a comfortable chair. Other thoughtful touches include in-room coffee and tea, hair dryers, guest laundry facility, an attractive outdoor pool (in season) and indoor hot tub. A free continental breakfast is served in front of the fire in the lobby or can be taken back to your room. Rates are extremely reasonable. Request a room away from the freeway.

Anderson Creek Lodge
East of Bellingham, off
Mt. Baker Hwy,
(206) 966-2126
5602 Mission Rd,
Bellingham, WA 98226
Moderate; AE, MC, V;
checks OK

Once a private school, the main house is now an intimate bed and breakfast with six individually designed rooms, three of which have their own fireplaces (for the others, the massive stone hearth in the common area is quite inviting). The remainder of the facility has been developed as a conference center, though it is quite conceivable to nestle into the Lodge without the slightest hint that 70 physicists are conferring just down the lane. Most guests will be lured out to the hot tub or to walk the parklike trail through the woods; nearby rural back roads promise great biking. An inviting pool and sauna are scheduled so as not to conflict with conference-attendee use. While exploring, be sure to seek out resident sculptor James Lapp's studio; his work is exhibited in the Lodge. A hearty, homey, full breakfast is thoughtfully prepared each morning.

DeCann House
West on Holly, which
turns into Eldridge,
(206) 734-9172
2610 Eldridge Ave,
Bellingham, WA 98225
Moderate; no credit cards;
checks OK

Within this neighborhood of historic homes overlooking Squalicum Harbor Marina, Bellingham Bay, and the San Juan Islands, this unpretentious Victorian bed and breakfast welcomes visitors to a quiet and comfortable haven. Test your skills at the ornate pool table in the front parlor or the interesting collection of wooden mazes in the sitting room. Barbara and Van Hudson maintain an extensive current library of travel-related material and provide a log in which you can pass along your impressions to other travelers—a nice touch. A complete breakfast, beautifully served, assures a cheery start to the day.

North Garden Inn
Maple and N Garden,
(206) 671-7828
1014 N Garden St,
Bellingham, WA 98225
Moderate; MC, V;
checks OK

This Victorian house (on the National Register of Historic Places) boasts over two dozen rooms plus seven baths, the result of additions early in the century. Only ten are rented as guest rooms (seven in winter); some have lovely views over Bellingham Bay and the islands. Five full baths are shared. All the rooms are attractive, clean, and with a bit more character than usual—due partly to the antique house, partly to the influence of the energetic and talented hosts. Barbara and Frank DeFreytas are both musical—two grand pianos in performance condition are available to guests, and musical or dramatic evenings take place here just as they probably did at the turn of the century. In the morning, Barbara serves a full breakfast and freshly ground coffee.

Sunrise Bay
On the north shore of
Lake Whatcom,

Hosts Karen and Jim Moren have crafted a most attractive and welcoming retreat on the north shore of Lake Whatcom at Sunrise Cove. The Morens offer a cheerful

(206) 647-0376
2141 N Shore Rd,
Bellingham, WA 98226
Moderate; MC, V;
checks OK

pair of rooms in a detached cottage, where huge windows overlook their expansive lawn to the lake (at times at the expense of guests' privacy). Thoughtful touches reveal extensive travel experience and knowledge of what makes guests comfortable: TVs with VCRs, private phones, private baths (with skylights), and reading lights on both sides of the beds. A creative breakfast is served in the Morens' contemporary home. Families are welcome and Katie, the youngest host, provides her special welcome. A heated swimming pool (seasonal), hot tub, beach, canoes, and dock are also available.

LUMMI ISLAND

This pastoral island just off Gooseberry Point northwest of Bellingham is perhaps one of the most overlooked islands of the ferry-accessible San Juans. It's serviced not by the Washington State Ferries but by the tiny **Whatcom County Ferry**, which leaves Gooseberry Point almost every hour from 6:20am to midnight. It's easy to find (just follow the signs to Lummi Island from I-5, north of Bellingham) and cheap ($4 round trip for a car and two passengers). It's a ten-minute crossing; call ahead for schedule, (206) 676-6730 or (206) 398-1310.

Just a few yards from the ferry landing is **The Islander**, the island's only mercantile, (206) 758-2190. A couple of low-tech bikes are available for rent ($5 half-day; $10 all day) at **Island Rental** next door. **The Beach Store**, a new restaurant in the old store near the island's ferry terminal, is a good place to drop by for breakfast and lunch.

LODGINGS

The Willows
From ferry, north on
Nugent for 3½ miles,
(206) 758-2620
2579 W Shore Dr,
Lummi Island,
WA 98262
Moderate; beer and wine;
MC, V; checks OK
Dinner Fri-Sat (Sat only
in winter)

Run as a resort since the late 1920s, the old Taft family house stands on a bluff, 100 feet above the accessible beach, offering a sweeping view of the San Juan and Gulf Islands, active with ship and boat traffic of all sorts. There are four rooms in the main building (two view rooms upstairs share a bath, two downstairs in the back have their own baths), a small cottage for two, and a newly remodeled two-bedroom apartment that looks out over the rose garden to the ocean (with a little of the kitchen roof in between). For couples traveling together, the last is our favorite. Each bedroom has a bathroom en suite (one with a Jacuzzi and the other with a shower for two). There are a convincingly toasty gas-log fireplace and a thoughtfully equipped kitchen. Hostess Victoria Taft Flynn quietly delivers a beautiful tray with coffee and a loaf of hot Irish soda bread first thing in the morning—to get you going and tide you over until you emerge for her superb breakfast. For the rest of the meals you're on your own, unless you're staying over a Saturday.

On Saturday evenings at 6:30pm, up to 24 dinner

guests gather in the sitting room for sherry and appetizers, soaking in the expansive view to the strains of a harpist and a classical guitarist. The five-course meal always incorporates the freshest ingredients, with many herbs from the Flynns' garden, and each course is accompanied by an appropriate wine. After dinner, guests repair in civilized fashion to the sitting room for port. This superb feast has become quite popular among locals (who often come from Bellingham just for dinner) and requires reservations often months in advance. Friday night dinners (summers only) are casual.

Loganita
From ferry, right on Nugent for 3 miles,
(206) 758-2651
2825 W Shore Dr,
Lummi Island,
WA 98262
Expensive; MC, V;
checks OK

A stunning location. This nearly 100-year-old retreat has for a number of years been used exclusively for executive think-tank conferences. Last year, owners Ann and Glen Gossage decided to also share their second home with the bed-and-breakfast public (gently scheduled around the corporate meetings). The house sprawls (as do the decks). There's an unobstructed view of Georgia Strait from almost any spot on the well-manicured grounds. Two huge stone fireplaces bookend the two spacious living rooms. Ten guest rooms (all with baths) range from the fully equipped three-bedroom apartment in the carriage house (good for families) to the pretty blue room in the main house to the honeymoon suite with its own sitting room, deck, fireplace and west-facing window seat. There's a hot tub on the back porch and a long sandy beach just across the street. Seals frequently sunbathe on the tiny rock island just off the coast. When you've had enough of the beach (a rarity) how about ping-pong or pool?

West Shore Farm
From ferry, north on Nugent for 3 miles,
(206) 758-2600
2781 W Shore Dr,
Lummi Island,
WA 98262
Inexpensive; MC, V;
checks OK

Carl and Polly Hanson's handbuilt octagonal house tucks into a slope overlooking the north tip of the island and the Georgia Strait. Accommodations on the lower level have sweeping views and ground-floor entrances. Readers will appreciate the plethora of interesting books and magazines, comfortable seating, and individual reading lights above the beds. The two guest rooms each have (not en suite but handy) a cedar-paneled and thoughtfully appointed bath. A substantial breakfast is served at the big round table in the inviting quarters; lunch and dinner are available on request. Little to do but sleep late, walk the secluded beach, or laze on the deck. Don't bother to bring your car; the Hansons will pick you up at the ferry if you like.

CHUCKANUT DRIVE

This famous stretch of road between Bellingham and Bow used to be part of the Pacific Highway; now it is one of the prettiest drives in the state, curving along the mountainlike hills and looking out over the water and the San Juans. Unfortunately, if you're in the driver's seat you'll have to keep your eyes on the road and wait for turnoffs for the view; the road is narrow and winding. Take the Chuckanut Drive exit off I-5 north, or follow 12th Street south in Bellingham.

Teddy Bear Cove is a nudist beach, and a pretty one at that, on a secluded shore along Chuckanut Drive just south of the Bellingham city limit. No signs; watch for the crowd of cars.

Interurban Trail, once the electric rail route from Bellingham to Mount Vernon, is now a five-mile running, walking, riding, and mountain-biking trail connecting three parks at the north end of Chuckanut Drive: Fairhaven Park to Arroyo Park to Larrabee State Park.

Larrabee State Park, seven miles south of Bellingham, was Washington's first state park. Beautiful sandstone sculpture along the beaches and cliffs provides a backdrop for exploration of the abundant sea life. Good picnic areas and camping.

The Blau Oyster Company sells not only excellent Samish Bay oysters and clams but an array of other seafoods as well. Call 24 hours ahead (Monday-Thursday) and get a discount on all orders. Seven miles west of Edison via the Bayview-Edison Road and the Samish Island Road, and follow the signs to the shucking sheds; 919 Blue Heron Road, Bow, (206) 766-6171.

BOW

RESTAURANTS

The Oyster Bar
Exit 250 off I-5,
(206) 766-6185
240 Chuckanut Dr, Bow
Expensive; beer and wine;
AE, MC, V; checks OK
Dinner every day

This tiny 12-table restaurant, perched high above quiet Samish Bay, often draws diners who have come just for the evening from as far away as Seattle or Vancouver. There are elements here of a world-class restaurant: breathtaking sunsets and spectacular views in all seasons, an award-winning wine list, and an incredible oyster bar stocked with bivalves from the adjoining Rock Point Oyster Farm. However, many who might be drawn here (and who conceivably will drop $90 per person for meal and wine) will find that the food, while sometimes quite good, is far from world-class. The menu selection is small—which is not to say that these offerings can't be delectable (they usually are)—but it amplifies the occasional lapses. The namesake oysters are fresh in all their incarnations: dusted with curry flour, sautéed and served with caviar and a wine-garlic-shallot butter sauce, delicately smoked or simply raw. A generous salmon terrine was rather muted, the luscious mousseline its best feature; an unusual tomato soup, chunky and herby, was garnished with crumbled chèvre. The kitchen did an admirable job of marrying the always difficult grilled ahi (a lean, lean fish) with a fan of moist avocado and a lime beurre blanc.

Oyster Creek Inn
*About a half hour's drive
south of Bellingham on
Chuckanut Dr,*
(206) 766-6179
190 Chuckanut Dr, Bow
*Moderate; beer and wine;
MC, V; checks OK*
Lunch, dinner every day

Tucked into the woods alongside a boisterous creek, this peaceful place is cool in summer, cozy in winter. Located directly adjacent to teeming oyster beds, the Inn has a long history of dedication to seafood (with a good selection of lamb, chicken, and such as well). Dishes have been imaginative and generally well prepared, with interesting twists to classic favorites: light, crisp fried calamari rings with apple and garlic mayonnaise; mussels in a fragrant basil cream sauce. With a recent change in the long-standing menu, however, has come occasional disappointment: the selection is less enticing and the quality inconsistent. However, with the new menu also came a widely expanded and very exciting wine list. Still exclusively Northwest, this list has matured with the industry and now contains some fine—and hard-to-come-by—wines.

The Rhododendron Cafe
*At the Bow-Edison
junction,*
(206) 766-6667
553 Chuckanut Dr, Bow
*Moderate; beer and wine;
MC, V; local checks only*
*Lunch Fri-Sat, dinner
Wed-Sun, brunch Sun*

The Rhododenron Cafe continues to be a pleasant destination for travelers on Chuckanut Drive, even if it does not possess the view of some restaurants or the elegance of others. The cafe's sunny patio, carefully screened from any breeze coming up the Skagit Valley, is a perfect spot to savor the delights of good wines, carefully selected, and good food, adventurously prepared. Be sure to ask about the specials. On a recent visits, our options included luncheon crêpes, stuffed with chicken, green peppers, and sausage, and hot coppa, topped with cheese sauce. The African peanut soup—dotted with fresh tomato bits—was flavorful yet light. The Italian meat loaf, here served with an herby, tangy marinara sauce, bears only a faint resemblance to the substance you came to know in college. In fact, it's just the thing to accompany one of the lusty Italian reds from the wine list.

LODGINGS

Alice Bay B&B
*Just right of the map
billboard at the base of
Samish Island, at the end
of Scott Road,*
(206) 766-6396
*982 Scott Road,
Bow, WA 98232*
*Moderate; no credit cards;
checks OK*

Overlooking the eelgrass beds and clamming flats of Samish Bay, on the southeast side of Samish Island, rests this small, quiet B&B. There's only one guest room, but it has a private entrance and its own bath. Guests have access to a private beach, wonderful for solitary rambling, and the hot tub is a pleasure at night. A heron rookery adjoins the property, and you might see several hundred of these glorious creatures fishing in the small bay. Nonsmokers only. If the tides are right, your hosts, the Rousseaus, will harvest the excellent local clams and oysters from the beach, serving them steamed or on the half shell; obviously, nothing could be fresher.

BURLINGTON

RESTAURANTS

El Gitano
Across from Memorial Park at E Fairhaven,
(206) 755-9010
624 E Fairhaven, Burlington
Inexpensive; beer and wine; AE, MC, V; checks OK
Lunch, dinner every day

El Gitano started out as a Mexican/Hungarian restaurant, logically enough: founders John and Angie Bosver are of, respectively, Hungarian and Mexican origin. However, due to a thriving Latino community and not much interest in Hungarian food, the Bosvers decided to serve exclusively Mexican food. Now nephew Adrian Ivarra is carrying on that tradition, using locally procured vegetables and meats to make hot homemade salsas and some of the most sumptuous nachos around. Highly variable—but when it's good, it's marvelous.

ANACORTES

RESTAURANTS

La Petite
34th and Commercial,
(206) 293-4644
3401 Commercial Ave, Anacortes
Moderate; full bar; AE, DC, MC, V; checks OK
Breakfast every day, dinner Tues-Sun

La Petite, hidden in the modest Islands Inn, is the brightest spot in Anacortes' generally humdrum eating offerings. The food is predominantly French-inspired with a few Dutch touches, reflecting the heritage of the Hulscher family, the longtime owners. The limited menu changes regularly and seasonally; the perfectionist kitchen will prepare only three different entrées per table (some favorites are pork in mustard sauce and the lamb loin marinated in wine and fresh herbs and roasted with garlic). There are always a couple of good appetizers, but you probably won't need them. With each meal comes a soup (maybe the Madeira-laced tomato and beet), salad (simple and topped with Parmesan), and delicious, crackling-crusted dinner-size bread loaves popped in the oven the minute you walk in the door (each loaf takes eight minutes to bake). Desserts are heavy on chocolate; for something different, try the *Griesmeel Pap*, a soothing pudding of ground almonds and farina with raspberry sauce. The fixed-price Dutch breakfast is intended primarily for (but not exclusive to) motel guests.

LODGINGS

Channel House
At Oakes and Dakota,
(206) 293-9382
2902 Oakes Ave,
Anacortes, WA 98221
Moderate; MC, V;
checks OK

Just a mile and a half from the ferry dock, Dennis and Pat McIntyre's Channel House is a 1902 Victorian home designed by an Italian count. There are four antique-filled rooms in the main house, two with private baths, all with grand views of Puget Sound. A cottage contains two suite-style units, complete with fireplaces and private whirlpool baths; the Victorian Rose room has its own deck and is especially nice. There is a large hot tub out back and the McIntyres serve cozy breakfasts (before a roaring fire on chilly days). Freshly baked cookies and Irish cream coffee await guests returning from dinner.

The Majestic Hotel
Between 4th and 5th on Commercial,
(206) 293-3355 or
(800) 950-3323
419 Commercial Ave,
Anacortes, WA 98221
Expensive; AE, MC, V;
checks OK

Truly majestic, this 1889 hotel has been through a number of incarnations (apartments, mercantile, offices), but this is surely the grandest. New owners Virginia and Jeff Wetmore reopened the hotel at the north end of town in 1991. The two-story lobby is adorned with lots of marble and deep, rich colors and lightened by tall windows. Every one of the 23 rooms (on three floors) is unique, with individualized English antiques; some have oversized tubs with skylights above, some have decks, others have VCRs, and a few have everything. Our favorites are dubbed "majestic" rooms, especially the corner ones. On the second floor (the only smoking level) there's a small library with a chess table. And up top, a cupola with a 360-degree view of Anacortes, Mount Baker, the Olympics, and the San Juans. There's no better perch in sight for a glass of wine at sunset.

SAN JUAN ISLANDS

There are 743 at low tide and 428 at high tide; 172 have names; 60 are populated; and only 4 have major ferry service. The San Juan Islands are varied, remote, and breathtakingly beautiful. They are also located in the rain shadow of the Olympics, and most receive half the rainfall of Seattle. Great! But, as expected, the sparsely populated islands are rather overrun in the summer months, and getting a ferry out of Anacortes can be a long, dull 3-hour-and-up wait. Bring a good book—or park the car and board with a bike. The lineup for accommodations can be even more troublesome: reserve early.

The four main islands—Lopez, Shaw, Orcas, and San Juan— have lodgings and eateries and some beautiful parks. Lopez, Orcas, and San Juan are discussed below; Shaw has little on it other than the world's only ferry landing run by nuns (they also have a certified dairy—three cows—and a campground with eight sites).

SAN JUAN ISLANDS: LOPEZ

Lopez Island, flat and shaped like a jigsaw-puzzle piece, is a sleepy, rural place, famous for its friendly locals (they always wave) and its cozy coves and full pastures. It has the easiest bicycling in the islands: a 30-mile circuit suitable for the whole family to ride in a day. You can camp at **Odlin County Park** (80 acres) or **Spencer Spit State Park** (130 acres), both on the north side. Odlin has many nooks and crannies, and grassy sites set among Douglas firs, shrubs, and clover. Spencer Spit has around 30 conventional campsites, and more primitive sites on the hillside. Both parks have water, toilets, and fire pits. **Agate County Park**, at the southwest tip of the island, has a pleasant, rocky beach for the tired cyclist. A great place for a sunset.

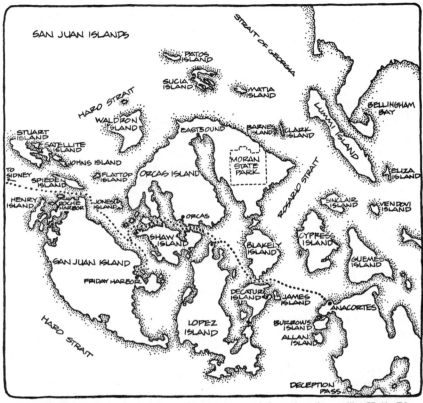

Lopez Village is basic, but has a few spots worth knowing about, like **Holly B's Bakery** in the Lopez Plaza, with celebrated fresh bread and pastries and coffee to wash them down (open June through September).

RESTAURANTS

Bay Cafe

Across from the post office in Lopez, (206) 468-3700
Lopez Town, Lopez Island
Moderate; beer and wine;
MC, V; local checks only
Dinner every day in summer; winter days vary

Without sacrificing any of its cheerful, personal appeal, owner/chef Bob Wood has expanded the Bay Cafe to occupy the whole of this former storefront space in "downtown Lopez." Entertaining a full house of both tourists and Lopezians most nights, the restaurant seems only to be increasing in popularity. Specializing in ethnic dishes, Bob changes the menu often to include innovative preparations which span many cuisines from Dungeness crab enchiladas to pork tenderloin with Indonesian-style peanut sauce, with at least one continental entrée (such as London broil), and one vegetarian dish (perhaps red and black bean quesadillas, or a curry of the day). For dessert we sampled a refreshing raspberry sorbet and passed on a lusciouslooking chocolate fudge cake. Prices are reasonable: if we were lucky enough to live nearby we'd be regulars as well.

Gail's
Lopez Town,
(206) 468-2150
Lopez Island
Moderate; beer and wine;
MC, V; checks OK
Breakfast, lunch every
day, dinner Thurs-Mon

Now that Gail's husband Bob has opened a neighboring deli, the lunchtime roar has subsided a bit, much to our relief. It's still crammed with loyal customers, but now that the retail crowd is next door, more attention can be paid to the daily lunch offerings of quiches, vegetable pastries, and soups. Deli sandwiches and burgers are basic but satisfying, and soups, entrées, and decadent desserts are all homemade. A complete wine and beer list is available. Dinners are quieter, more formal affairs (reservations suggested) featuring locally grown foods in faintly ethnic preparations (black bean sauce gracing fresh roasted halibut, a pork loin roast infused with Cajun seasoning).

LODGINGS

Inn at Swift's Bay
Head 1 mile south of ferry
to Port Stanley Rd, left 1
more mile,
(206) 468-3636
Mail: Rt 2, Box 3402,
Lopez Island, WA 98261
Expensive; MC, V;
checks OK

With their remarkable knack for knowing how to care for guests without ever appearing intrusive, Robert Herrmann and Christopher Brandmeir have turned this former summer home into the most appealing accommodation on Lopez Island. Choose from two large and comfortable bedrooms with shared bath, or two luxurious suites—one with a magnificent view of the fir-lined yard, the other a highly successful renovation of the attic, featuring an antique sleigh bed and several rectangular skylights ($115). There's also a secluded outdoor hot tub that can be scheduled for private sittings (towels, robes, and slippers provided). There's a first-class selection of recorded music and movies on tape for evening entertainment (only available, though, from November to April; in temperate months you really ought to be outside). Expect to be pampered. Christopher is an excellent breakfast chef and serves the morning meal in the bright and cozy dining room.

MacKaye Harbor Inn
12 miles south of the ferry
landing on MacKaye
Harbor Rd,
(206) 468-2253
Mail: Rt 1, Box 1940,
Lopez Island, WA 98261
Moderate; MC, V;
checks OK

Bicyclists call it paradise after their sweaty trek from the ferry to this little harbor. The tall house sits above a sandy, shell-strewn beach, perfect for sunset strolls or pushing off to explore the scenic waterways—which makes the crowd at the inn sometimes seem like a kayaking mini-convention. In addition, Mike and Robin Bergstrom offer guided kayak tours from March through October. For nature lovers not of the paddling persuasion, there's plenty of bird and other wildlife to enjoy on land as well. Inside, the five rooms have been done up a bit sparsely but tastefully, with a second-story deck for lounging and sunset-ogling. The Bergstroms have stopped serving their successful dinners; the former dining room is now a cozy library with a fireplace and comfortable couches for reading. Breakfasts—with entrées from a different European country every morning—are full and filling.

Blue Fjord Cabins
Elliott Rd at Jasper Cove,
(206) 468-2749
Mail: Rt 1, Box 1450,
Lopez Island, WA 98261
Moderate; no credit cards;
checks OK

Lopez is the most secluded and tranquil of the three islands with tourist offerings, and the Blue Fjord Cabins are the most secluded and tranquil getaway on Lopez. The three log cabins are tucked away up an unmarked dirt road, each concealed from the others by thick woods. They're of modern chalet design, clean and airy, with full kitchens. Rates are a deal; $58-$68 a night with a two-night minimum (three nights in July and August). Doing nothing never had such a congenial setting.

SAN JUAN ISLANDS: ORCAS

It was named by a Spanish explorer for Don Juan Vicente de Guemes Pacheco y Padilla Orcasitas y Aguayo Conde de Revilla Gigedo, but let's just call it Orcas for short. Orcas is the hilliest of the four big San Juans, boasting Mount Constitution, from whose old stone lookout tower you can see Vancouver, Mount Rainier, and everything in between. You can drive to the top, but the trail through 4,800-acre **Moran State Park** is prettier. Moran has one lake for freshwater swimming, three more for fishing and boating, and nice campsites, but you must write at least two weeks ahead for reservations: Moran, Star Route Box 22, Eastsound, WA 98245.

RESTAURANTS

Bilbo's Festivo
Northbeach Rd and A St,
(206) 376-4728
Eastsound
Inexpensive; full bar;AE,
MC, V; local checks only
Dinner every day, closed
Mon in winter;
seasonal lunch

Orcas Islanders, and off-island fans who keep coming back, speak of this cozy little place with reverence. Its decor and setting—mud walls, Mexican tiles, arched windows, big fireplace, handmade wooden benches, spinning fans, in a small house with a flowered courtyard—are charming, and the Navajo and Chimayo weavings on the walls are indeed from New Mexico. The fare is a combination of Mexican, Spanish, and New Mexican influences with original improvisation on the themes of enchiladas, burritos, and chiles rellenos, distinctively seasoned but only moderately fiery. Nightly specials grilled over mesquite might be carne asada (lime-marinated sirloin strips) served with Spanish rice, refried beans, and flour tortillas, or pollo en naranjas (chicken marinated in orange sauce) served with new potatoes, fresh asparagus, and salad. Lunch includes ceviche salad (raw fish or seafood marinated for 24 hours in lime juice) and a wide array of soups, salads, and grilled white fish. In winter, no lunches, and variable dinners; in summer, the courtyard is a pleasant place to dine. Get a margarita.

Christina's

North Beach Rd and
Horseshoe Hwy,
(206) 376-4904
Eastsound
Moderate; full bar; DC,
MC, V; checks OK
Dinner every day
(summer), Thurs-Mon
(winter) (closed Jan–
mid-Feb)

Christina's varies from superb to merely good—a result not of sloppiness but rather of continual experimentation within the neo-Northwest genres. This means that Christina's doesn't grow boring with repeated visits. The decor is a nice balance of elegance and natural-wood simplicity; try for one of the small tables on the enclosed porch, where the view of the sunset over East Sound makes lingering even easier, or if weather permits, a seat on the rooftop terrace. Christina's works hard to land the best seafood and other fresh local ingredients: *fresh* oysters from Crescent Beach Farm, a lamb chop with juniper aioli. The sumptuously creamy six-lilies soup (garlic, leek, scallion, etc.) is not to be missed, and a recent diner raved about the unbelievably fresh halibut in plum chutney. The changing dessert selections—espresso profiteroles with with caramel and chocolate, various cheesecakes, delicate ice cream puffs in loganberry sauce—tend toward the irresistible.

Downstairs, Christina's Cafe, which opened June 1991, offers coffee and retail foods, with a couple of tables for enjoying waffles, baked goods, salads, or whatever treat the kitchen is putting out. Christina plans to open ten French-styled hotel guest rooms in the next few years.

Deer Harbor Lodge and Inn

Follow signs to Deer
Harbor, Orcas Island,
(206) 376-4110
Mail: PO Box 142, Deer
Harbor, WA 98243
Moderate; beer and wine;
AE, MC, V; checks OK
Dinner every day
(weekends only in winter)

This expansive, rustic dining room with a large view deck is a cozy, soothing place despite its size, done up nicely in dark blue prints and natural wood. Pam and Craig Carpenter have rescued the inn from its long career as a purveyor of battered chicken and made it home to the island's best seafood, with generous portions and a strong emphasis on fresh, local ingredients. About a dozen entrées, including beef, chicken, and a staple vegetarian fettuccine, are outlined on the blackboard at the door and varied according to what's in season. Soups and salads arrive in large serving bowls, allowing each diner to partake according to capacity with a minimum of fuss. Fresh homemade bread comes with them. Not only the wine list but the beer list is thoughtfully conceived, with novelties like German wheat beer. Dessert may be homemade ice cream.

For lodging, there's a two-story log-cabin with eight rooms, and two decks; breakfast arrives in a picnic basket outside your door.

Cafe Olga

Near Moran State Park
at Olga Junction,
(206) 376-5098, Olga
Inexpensive; beer and
wine; MC, V; local

Olga is the name of the hamlet, not the owner. Marcy Lund runs a cozy, inexpensive country kitchen in one corner of the Orcas Island Artworks, a sprawling cooperative crafts gallery in a picturesque renovated strawberry-packing barn. The cooking, usually good, may suffer on Lund's days off. The food is wholesome, international home-style: Greek salad, cheese-spinach

checks only
Lunch every day

manicotti, blackberry pie ("the best in the world," according to islanders) and other fruit cobblers according to season, fresh-baked cinnamon rolls (beloved by the locals) and pastries, and daily specials. Espresso or chilled applemint cooler wash it all down nicely and make Cafe Olga a favorite local rest station on chilly and sweaty days alike, from brunch to early supper.

La Famiglia
A St and North Beach Rd, Orcas Island, (206) 376-2335 Eastsound Inexpensive; full bar;AE, MC, V; local checks only Lunch Mon-Sat, dinner every day (Mon-Sat in winter)

Here's a mainstream Italian lunch and dinner spot that seems to have achieved the consistency to match its pleasant, sunny decor, friendly service, and reasonable prices, as witnessed by the many discriminating locals who've become regulars. The emphasis is on fresh pasta, calzone, and other hearty family fare befitting the name; try the chunks of veal sautéed in butter, wine, and lemon, nestled nicely alongside pasta and vegetables.

LODGINGS

Beach Haven Resort
9 miles from the ferry at President Channel, (206) 376-2288 Mail: Rt 1, Box 12, Eastsound, WA 98245 Moderate; no credit cards; checks OK

The sign as you exit on the dirt road reads "Leaving Beach Haven. Entering the world." Cute, but appropriate, especially after the seven-day minimum summer stay. The cabins, shielded by tall trees, are of the genuine log variety, with wood stoves. Accommodations range through various grades of rustic to modern apartments and one "Spectacular Beachcomber" four-bedroom house. Everything faces on the long pebble beach, canoes and rowboats are ready if you feel energetic, and the air of tranquillity is palpable enough to chew. A great place to bring the kids.

Turtleback Farm Inn
10 minutes from the ferry on Crow Valley Rd, Orcas Island, (206) 376-4914, Mail: Rt 1, Box 650, Eastsound, WA 98245 Expensive; MC, V; checks OK

The Turtleback is inland, but still scenically located amidst tall trees, rolling pastures, and private ponds. In 1984 it was just another dilapidated farmhouse, used to store hay. Bill and Susan Fletcher have redone it entirely and added a wing, but kept the country flavor with natural wood, wide floor planks, private claw-footed tubs for six of the seven rooms, and excellent antiques. They live in a separate house past the pond, so you won't suffer the B&B horror of feeling you're imposing on Aunt Irma and Uncle Ralph. A glass of sherry tops the evening. Their breakfasts, which may be taken in the well-appointed dining room or on the sunny deck, are the most praised on the island. Besides the usual bacon and eggs, they may include fresh yogurt, crêpes with lingonberry sauce, and an example of the ultimate B&B staple that reportedly won the San Juan granola contest.

Kangaroo House

North Beach Rd,
(206) 376-2175
Mail: PO Box 334,
Eastsound, WA 98245
Moderate; MC, V;
checks OK

The location of this bed and breakfast, just past the Orcas airport, isn't scenic, but it's convenient to Eastsound and North Beach. And it's a pleasant, attractive old bungalow, done up in period fashion with good antiques and classic wallpaper. Three of the five rooms are a tad on the small side but well appointed; a downstairs suite and large bedroom upstairs have private baths. And the big front porch and rear deck suit lounging in the sun any time of day. Owners Jan and Mike Russillo have added a bit of their personality to the furnishings and have been busy upgrading the turn-of-the-century Craftsman-style place (new mattresses, wallpaper, gardens) since they took over in 1988. The namesake kangaroo that "Cap" Ferris brought here in 1953 is no longer resident.

North Beach Inn

1½ miles west of the airport at North Beach,
(206) 376-2660
Mail: PO Box 80,
Eastsound, WA 98245
Moderate; no credit cards;
checks OK

The Gibson family home, once but no longer the main dining lodge, is a movie-set dream of a turn-of-the-century summer camp. It's high-gabled and surrounded by tall trees; the beach-fronting porch, lined with massive log pillars, will inspire you to put up your feet and start into a very long novel. The 11 little cottages up the rocky beach are nearly buried in blackberries and are worn down to the funky side of rustic. (The spiffier Columbia, Shamrock, and Fraser are available for a price.) But the splendid view and ambience may distract you entirely from the vintage linoleum. The sense of history here is no illusion, as the Gibson family has presided over the North Beach Inn since 1932. The privacy of their visitors is well guarded; the grounds are closed to all but registered guests. Pets okay.

Orcas Hotel

Orcas ferry landing,
(206) 376-4300
Mail: PO Box 155,
Orcas, WA 98280
Expensive; AE, MC, V;
checks OK
Breakfast, lunch, dinner
every day

Renovated and reopened just a few years ago, this Victorian hostelry is an indispensable addition to the local scene. Sited scenically and conveniently, it perches grandly above the Orcas dock; its deck is the perfect place to wait out a tardy ferry. In 1990, Orcas Hotel Inc. bought this bed and breakfast, but wisely hasn't altered the level of gracious solicitude at this larger 12-room inn or the equally cheerful, accommodating staff. The rooms are clean, simple, and full of the appropriate period furnishings. Ten rooms, three of which have half-baths, share showers down the hall, and two new, larger rooms have private balconies and whirlpool tubs. The kitchen has a new chef who has expanded the menu of fresh seafood and Northwest continental dishes. Good, inexpensive soup and sandwiches are served for lunch in the dining room and bar, the latter a convivial local meeting ground.

Rosario Resort

Horseshoe Hwy, east side
of Orcas Island,

Rosario, claiming to be the region's premier large resort, has had its share of financial and operational problems. The centerpiece of the complex is a spec-

(206) 376-2222
Mail: 1 Rosario Way,
Eastsound, WA 98245
Expensive; AE, DC, MC,
V; checks OK

tacular one, worth a sightseeing stop: the lavish old mansion of shipbuilding tycoon Robert Moran, decked out with memorabilia and an awesome pipe organ still frequently played. Unfortunately you can't stay in the Moran Mansion and you can't eat the view. The "villas" and "haciendas" (hotel units) up the hill are rather less exciting, with some reports of spotty maintenance. And the food, in the gracious Orcas Room, is nothing to write home about. The common facilities—bayside pool, tennis, marina, and a full spa in the basement of the mansion (whose architecture lends an elegant, antique touch to aerobics or hot-tubbing)—are excellent. They also tend to be underused, which should leave you plenty of room while everyone else tours the island. The stunning grounds provide a good location for special events; however, the disorganized staff makes for a nervous bride.

Sand Dollar Inn

½ mile from the center of
Olga, (206) 376-5696
Star Rt Box 10,
Olga, WA 98279
Expensive; AE, MC, V;
checks OK

While not on the water proper, this quiet, peaceful spot, run by a couple of California emigrants, has three lovely rooms, each with a view of Buck Bay (a less expensive room downstairs is sans view). The best is the library with its own deck (and walls of books); and you can see the bay while lying in bed (though you trek across the hall to the bathroom). For a place with such a high per-night charge, owners Ann and Ric Sanchez, workday refugees themselves, are surprisingly and refreshingly anti-anything else touristy on the island. They serve a big, mean breakfast, usually including fresh salmon baked in a cream sauce served on an English muffin with scrambled egg or an intensely flavored raspberry crumble followed by sizable stacks of blueberry pancakes, with plenty of sparkling cider to wash them down.

Doe Bay Village Resort

4 miles east of Olga,
(206) 376-2291
Mail: Star Rt Box 86,
Olga, WA 98279
Inexpensive; AE, MC, V;
checks OK
Breakfast, dinner Wed-
Sun (summer); breakfast
weekends (winter)

Doe Bay offers not only the cheapest but some of the most peaceful and scenic lodgings on Orcas. The old boat landing on a pretty bay at the island's west end sprouted a ramshackle cluster of cabins that became a resort, then an artist's colony, then the still-much-talked-about Polarity Institute. Lately returned to resort use, the "village" retains some countercultural ambience, but also draws plenty of families driven by noise or overfilling from Moran State Park. Bathing suits are optional at the bathhouse, where the giant wood-fired sauna and three outdoor tubs (two hot, one cold) overlooking an inlet are a joyous discovery, especially in winter (the resort's open year-round), and massage is available for further relaxation. Accommodations range from campsites to hostel berths to inexpensive cabins with worn or minimal furnishings to better-appointed cottages at moderate prices. There are communal kitchen facilities, a cafe serving scrumptious, wholesome breakfasts and healthful dinners, kayak trips to a nearby wildlife refuge, and a general store (they'll open it up for you in winter) full of whole-wheat pasta, tofu, and natural body-care products. Retreat facilities are now available, and, for folks just passing through, the hot tubs are open to non-guests at a $5 charge.

Outlook Inn
Eastsound, Orcas Island,
(206) 376-2581
Mail: PO Box 210,
Eastsound, WA 98245
Moderate; AE, MC, V;
local checks only

Built as a cabin in 1938, this dwelling has had a long history, expanding slowly into a 27-room white clapboard inn (including the ten-room motel-ish annex) and restaurant. The current tenants have labored with nostalgic zeal to restore it to its original homey ambience. They've antiqued the rooms to hearken back to Grandpa Walton's salad days; the atmosphere is cheery and the motifs relentlessly floral. The restaurant has a family feel—it's a good place to bring kids.

SAN JUAN ISLANDS: SAN JUAN

San Juan Island is the biggest in the archipelago, and it sports the biggest town, Friday Harbor. Attractions include the **University of Washington Oceanographic Laboratory**, which gives tours in July and August, and the sites of the **American and English Camps** during the famous Pig War of 1859-72, so called because the sole casualty was a pig. The English had the nicer camp; American Camp looks like a desert and is occupied only by rabbits. If you want to do some camping yourself, there's **San Juan County Park**, a dozen often-crowded acres on Smallpox Bay (reservations suggested especially July-August), and **Lakedale Campground** (reservations suggested but not required), 4½ miles from Friday Harbor on Roche Harbor Road, (206) 378-2350 a favorite campground for bicyclists with 82-acres and three private lakes for swimming and fishing. The best **diving** in the whole archipelago can be had here at **Henry Island**, across from **Snug Harbor Marina Resort**; (206) 378-4762. **Anacortes Diving and Supply,** 2502 Commercial Avenue in Anacortes, is the nearest outfitter; (206) 293-2070.

One interesting stop is the nation's first official **whale-watching park**. Pods of orca and minke whales swim regularly by the western shore of San Juan; here you can spot them (best in late spring, summer, and fall) and the interpreter can answer your questions. West Side Road, six miles from Friday Harbor. There's also **The Whale Museum** downtown, 62 1st Street North, (206) 378-4710.

Jazz Festival. Throngs of people infest the streets of Friday Harbor for three days of Dixieland jazz, mid- to late-July; for information, call (206) 378-5509.

RESTAURANTS

Cafe Bissett
1st and West,
(206) 378-3109
Friday Harbor
Moderate; beer and wine;
MC, V; checks OK
Dinner Thurs-Mon (every

Any local will tell you their favorite restaurant on San Juan Island is this bistro-sized side street cafe. For six years now, Cafe Bissett has been serving dinners of precision and remarkable flavor: crisp duck in a green peppercorn and brandy sauce, smoked chicken with black-eyed peas, fragrant fish stews, rack of lamb. The atmosphere departs from the usual island style (or

day from mid-June through Aug)

Duck Soup Inn
4½ miles north of Friday Harbor on Roche Harbor Rd, (206) 378-4878
3090 Roche Harbor Rd, Friday Harbor
Moderate; beer and wine; no credit cards; checks OK
Dinner Wed-Sun (closed in winter)

Springtree Eating Establishment and Farm
Under the elm at 310 Spring, (206) 378-4848
Friday Harbor
Moderate; beer and wine; MC, V; checks OK
Breakfast, lunch, dinner every day

Duffy House
Take Argyle Road south from town to Pear Point Rd, (206) 378-5604
760 Pear Point Rd, Friday Harbor, WA 98250
Moderate; MC, V; checks OK

stylelessness)—the furnishings are elegant and harmonious, and the linen white. Service is usually meticulous and polished, but not intimidating. Trouble is, when the owners are not around we've encountered spotty service and lapses in execution. This place is too pricey for such inconsistencies.

Changes of ownership of this pretty, barnlike restaurant seem to be a biennial occurrence. New owner Gretchen Allison seems committed to continuing the ambitious reach of the kitchen. For the most part, she's maintained the emphasis on fresh, local seafoods and seasonal ingredients, adding game dishes and pastas to round out the selection. It's a charming restaurant, that's tough to get to, but the playful entrées can be hit or miss. On any given day the menu might hint of Thai, Cajun, and German influences, as well as offering home-smoked salmon or oysters. The wine list has been expanded and internationalized by Gretchen's husband Richard, the maître d' and wine steward.

Using produce, herbs, and flowers grown organically at their own farm, Springtree serves up a varied menu ranging from arugula-stuffed chicken breasts to Island cod florinada (fresh citrus and garden mint sauce over freshly caught cod) to New York steak with sweet pepper salsa. The price of the generous entrées includes a crisp green salad, soup or seafood chowder, seasonal vegetables, and basmati rice or potatoes. Meal-sized salads, pasta, and burgers are also available, and the desserts are heavenly.

The homey decor verges on Victorian. Even the waitresses dress in floral prints, enhancing the visual effect. The management is clearly dedicated to service, and over the pleasant din of conversation and laughter, we heard more than one party effusively thanking their waitperson for making their evening such an enjoyable one. Patio dining is available.

LODGINGS

Duffy House bed and breakfast displays an architectural style (Tudor) that's rare in the islands, in a splendid, isolated site overlooking Griffin Bay and the Olympics. A secluded beach and nearby gardens, woods, and orchard offer plenty of room for contemplation. The large farmhouse, with leaded glass and much mahogany, is attractive enough to merit its setting, and plenty roomy for five guest parties. Get ready for a tasty breakfast of quiche, fresh fruit, coffee cake, and muffins. A small beachside cabin that sleeps four with its own hot tub (currently undergoing a facelift).

Lonesome Cove Resort

*Take Roche Harbor Rd 9
miles north to Lonesome
Cove Rd, (206) 378-4477
5810 Lonesome Cove Rd,
Friday Harbor,
WA 98250
Moderate; MC, V;
checks OK*

Back in 1945, Roy and Neva Durhack sailed their 35-foot yacht here from the Hawaiian Islands. They were getting ready to sail it around the world, but once they saw Lonesome Cove their wanderlust subsided. Now, under newer management, the resort remains a pretty spot. The six immaculate little cabins (recently renovated with hand-laid red cedar walls) set among trees at the water's edge, the manicured lawns, and the domesticated deer that wander the 75-acre woods make the place a favorite for honeymooners—fully 30 percent of Lonesome Cove's guests are newlyweds. The sunsets are spectacular, and there's a fine view of nearby Speiden Island. Cabins start at $75 a day and have a 5-night minimum in the summer months. No pets—too many baby ducks around.

Olympic Lights

*Take Argyle Ave out of
Friday Harbor to Cattle
Point Rd,
(206) 378-3186
4531-A Cattle Point Rd,
Friday Harbor,
WA 98250
Moderate; no credit cards;
checks OK*

As you approach this isolated bed and breakfast, you may recall the movie *Days of Heaven*: the tall Victorian farmhouse sits lonely as a lighthouse in a sea of open meadow. The renovated interior is more modern, and quite elegant: four upstairs rooms, all with queen beds, done up in bright whites and soft pastels, and furnished with antiques. The downstairs room, however, is the only one with a private bath. You must remove your shoes to tread the off-white pile carpet. All the rooms are lavishly bathed in sunlight. The panorama of Olympic Mountains and Strait of Juan de Fuca from the south rooms adds to the effect. The proprietors, Christian and Lea Andrade, are San Francisco refugees who came to San Juan's empty south tip seeking a more calming, contemplative milieu. Breakfast includes fresh eggs from the resident hen; they also have four cats who roam downstairs. No smoking.

Roche Harbor Resort

*Roche Harbor,
(206) 378-2155
Mail: PO Box 4001,
Roche Harbor, WA 98250
Expensive; MC, V;
checks OK*

Remember that old Patrick McGoohan TV show *The Prisoner*? When you walk out of the stately old ivy-clad Hotel de Haro at Roche Harbor and gaze out at the trellised, cobblestoned waterfront and yacht-dotted bay, you will—it's a ringer for The Village, the show's setting. The resort evolved from the company town that John McMillin built a century ago for his lime mill, once the largest west of the Mississippi. The hotel attracted such notables as Teddy Roosevelt. It has seen some renovation since his time, but one visitor remarked that the rooms "seem to have been glued together with repeated applications of wallpaper," and the angles of some of the floors and walls remind one of *The Cabinet of Dr. Caligari*. Still, the 105-year-old hotel has a terrific view, and if it's too quaint for you, you can try the cottages or the new suburban-style condos. The hotel rooms with private baths (only four) have the best views. There's plenty to do at Roche Harbor. A sign with multiple arrows reads "Airport, Mausoleum,

Swimming Pool, Tennis, Snack Bar," and there's moorage for 200 boats, plus a private airfield with service from Sea-Tac and Bellingham, a chapel, a grocery, swell gardens, a yacht-side restaurant (That's been improving lately), and regular entertainment in the lounge.

Westwinds Bed & Breakfast
2 miles from Lime Kiln Whale Watch Park, (206) 378-5283, 4909 H Hannah Highlands, Friday Harbor, WA 98250 Expensive; MC, V; checks OK

Westwinds commands what may easily be the most magnificent view on all of the San Juan Islands. Unfortunately, too few people will enjoy the 10 acres of mountainside abundant with deer and quail. This private paradise remains a one-bedroom facility, even though the property itself has recently been doubled in size. Owners Chris Durbin and Gayle Rollins have built an extraordinary glass-and-wood home that uses the setting to optimal advantage: look from your cathedral-ceilinged bedroom, private bath, patio, living room, or virtually any seat in the house, and you're likely to feel in possession of a large part of the world (or at least the Strait of Juan de Fuca and the Olympic Mountains). Breakfast is almost as majestic. Particularly popular with honeymoon couples (privacy is never an issue), this bed and breakfast is to be enjoyed whatever the occasion, whatever the season.

Blair House Bed and Breakfast Inn
4 blocks up Spring to Blair, (206) 378-5907 345 Blair Avenue, Friday Harbor, WA 98250 Moderate; AE, MC, V; checks OK

Believe it or not, it's a country retreat—four blocks from the ferry (which is actually very convenient if you happen to arrive late). Owners Jane Benson and Jeff Zander have tastefully decorated their early 1900s home in pastels, floral prints, and antique furnishings, without overdoing the frou-frou, so just about anyone can feel comfortable here. Most of the six rooms have their own bath; the one-bedroom cottage is fully equipped. A bountiful morning meal featuring home-baked coffee cakes, fresh fruit, and other delights is included, and on sunny days breakfast may be taken to the attractive poolside patio. Since the salt water is too cold for leisurely swimming, the heated pool is a definite attraction. You share the parlor, equipped with a VCR (tape rentals nearby), as well as a huge, old-fashioned wraparound verandah. The owners are both attentive and businesslike, striking the perfect balance between warm hospitality and invisibility.

Moon & Sixpence Bed & Breakfast
3½ miles from the ferry dock on Beaverton Valley Rd, (206) 378-4138, 3021 Beaverton Valley Rd, Friday Harbor, WA 98250

Moon & Sixpence is a classic country B&B with an artsy flourish (witness the nod to Somerset Maugham in the name). Charlie and Evelyn Tuller's big, sunny farmhouse in the middle of San Juan Island is done up brightly but tastefully in a gamut of folk arts, from family heirlooms and Pennsylvania Dutch to Eskimo prints and Navajo rugs. A one-bedroom cabin is also an option, but has no running water; the new attraction is the Lookout—a converted water tower with exposed post-

Moderate; no credit cards; checks OK

and-beam construction, a reading loft, bathroom, and views out of all four sides. Evelyn is more than glad to give a tour of her weaving studio out back, and maybe even show you a flip or two of the shuttle. Breakfast is a more-than-substantial meal, and the bread is freshly baked. The farm pond is a dandy spot for picnics, barbecues, or just counting the clouds.

San Juan Inn
A half block from the ferry at 50 Spring St, (206) 378-2070 Mail: PO Box 776, Friday Harbor, WA 98250 Moderate; MC, V; checks OK

Formerly the San Juan Hotel, this nicely restored little place near the ferry has ten antique-filled guest rooms with a tidy, old-fashioned feeling. Continental breakfast is served in the parlor, a cozy room with an 1870 marble-top buffet, an old parlor stove with isinglass doors, and a complete view of Friday Harbor. The Inn changed hands in June of 1990, but the entertaining resident cat, Abigail, is still around. No smoking.

Tucker House
1½ blocks from the ferry on B St, (206) 378-2783 260 B St, Friday Harbor, WA 98250 Moderate; AE, MC, V; checks OK

On a quiet street a few blocks from downtown Friday Harbor and the ferry dock, this B&B offers a total of six rooms: three pleasant-but-plain rooms in the somewhat-cramped main house and three more elegant cottage-type quarters in back (one with space for four, two with kitchens, all with private baths and fireplaces). Each opens onto a peaceful enclosed yard, deck, and hot tub—a nice chance to get away from it all without driving halfway across the island. Breakfast (if you're lucky, it'll include cinnamon bread) is served in the solarium.

Wharfside Bed & Breakfast
On the K dock in Friday Harbor, (206) 378-5661 Mail: PO Box 1212, Friday Harbor, WA 98250 Moderate; no credit cards; checks OK

If nothing lulls you to sleep like the gentle lap of the waves, the Wharfside's the B&B for you. It's this region's first realization of the European tradition of floating inns. Two guest rooms have been installed on the 60-foot sailboat *Jacquelyn*, both very nicely finished with full amenities and that compact precision that only living on a boat can inspire. The fore cabin has a double bed and sleeping berths for kids or extras. When the weather's good, you can enjoy the huge breakfast on deck and watch the local fishermen gather their nets. And what other B&B can you hire for a sail around the islands?

LA CONNER

La Conner was founded in 1867 by John Conner, a trading-post operator, who named the town after his wife, L(ouisa) A. Conner. Much of what you see today was originally built before the railroads arrived in the late 1880s, when the fishing and farming communities of Puget Sound traded almost entirely by water. In an

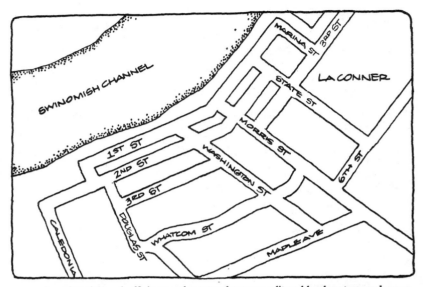

age of conformity and efficiency, the town became a literal backwater, and something of a haven for nonconformists (Wobblies, WWII COs, McCarthy-era escapees, beatniks, hippies and bikers), always with a fair smattering of artists and writers including Mark Tobey, Morris Graves, Guy Anderson, and Tom Robbins.

This long-standing "live and let live" attitude of the town has allowed the neighboring Native American Swinomish community to contribute to the exceptional cultural richness of La Conner. Even the merchants here have created a unique atmosphere, an American bazaar; **Chez la Zoom, Originals in Gold, Cottons, Nasty Jack's,** and the **Dinghy Baby. Cafe Pojante** espresso bar in the loft above **Skagit Bay Books** is where most of the town's intelligentsia congregate.

Tillinghast Seed Co., at the entrance of town, is the oldest operating retail and mail-order seed store in the Northwest (since 1885); it has (in addition to seeds) a wonderful nursery, florist shop, and general store. (206) 466-3329. **Go Outside** is a small but choice garden and garden accessory store; (206) 466-4836.

Gaches Mansion, on Second Street overlooking the main drag, is an wonderful example of American Victorian architecture, with a widow's walk that looks out on the entire Skagit Valley. It is filled with period furnishings, and a small museum of Northwest art occupies the second floor. Open weekends; (206) 466-4288.

Sea King Products is building up a solid reputation. Sunday brunch is especially enjoyable; (206) 466-4444.

RESTAURANTS

Barkley's of La Conner
2nd and Washington,
(206) 466-4261
205 Washington,
La Conner
Moderate; full bar; AE,
MC, V; checks OK
Lunch, dinner every day

★★

We admire this place for, if nothing else, its ability to maintain an even keel through a turmoil of ownership. Now that it has landed in the hands of Rose Garner, who has successfully carried on the commendable menu of former chef Michael Hood, we suspect Rose will soon move beyond those established guidelines and develop a restaurant more of her own. Until then, expect good renditions of pastas, seafoods, and steaks—

nothing outrageously inventive, but competently prepared. It's an accommodating place: locals like the hobbit-like pub; others prefer the modestly elegant restaurant. The result? A restaurant that caters to your mood rather than imposing its own on you.

The Black Swan
1st and Washington,
(206) 466-3040
505 S 1st St, La Conner
Expensive (upstairs)/
Inexpensive (downstairs);
beer and wine; MC, V;
checks OK
Dinner Thurs-Mon

There was a time when folks came from far and wide with an almost cultish devotion to The Black Swan for culinary transport. Unfortunately, for a few years now the performance of this flagship of the starfleet of small Northwest dinner houses has not been all that reliable. The broiled salmon fillet, basted with fresh lime and pistachio herb butter, was overdone and dry and the Pirate Stew, bristling with myriad aquatic denizens, was interesting but uninspired. The formal upstairs dining room is cramped, nine small tables in one small room, hence the intimate acquaintance with other people's food and conversation. Service is a weak point. It is not entirely clear whether chef/owner Martin Hahn has lost his focus. He *is* definitely operating on two different levels: the dining room upstairs and an informal, less-expensive bistro downstairs. For the time being, your money is better spent at the vinyl-topped tables of the street-level cafe.

Calico Cupboard
South end of the line on
1st, (206) 466-4451
720 S 1st, La Conner
Inexpensive; beer and
wine; no credit cards;
checks OK
Breakfast, lunch every
day

It's awfully cute—Laura Ashley meets Laura Ingalls Wilder—but the bakery is the reason to go, turning out excellent carrot muffins, pecan tarts, shortbread, raspberry bars, currant scones, apple Danish, and much more. Our advice for avoiding the weekend crowds is to buy your goodies from the take-out counter of the bakery and then find a sunny bench by the water. Hearty waffle and omelet breakfasts are offered, but let's face it, most folks come here for the pastries. Lunches run to sandwiches on homemade bread, salads, and terrific soups.

La Conner Seafood & Prime Rib House
Next door to Skagit Bay
Books on the waterfront,
(206) 466-4014
614 1st St, La Conner
Moderate; full bar; AE,
DC, MC, V; checks OK
Lunch, dinner every day

Every weekend, those in the know drop in to get their names on the waiting list and pop out again for another 20 minutes of window-shopping. Their reward is excellent seafood (pasta with fresh Dungeness crab or baby Rock Point oysters sautéed with fresh fennel), and the young are happy with fish and chips. In warm weather, diners flee the split-level dining room of channel-view tables for the ample outdoor seating on the deck.

LODGINGS

Downey House
3½ miles southeast of La

Just three miles out of La Conner, Downey House has perfect access to the tulip fields in spring. It's a lovely,

Conner, (206) 466-3207
1880 Chilberg Rd,
La Conner, WA 98257
Moderate; MC, V;
checks OK

neat, tidy place with five guest rooms (three with baths) and Victorian appointments. Jim and Kay Frey have lived in the house for 25 years and share their love of the Skagit Valley and its lore with guests. There's a hot tub out back, and in the evenings they serve guests warm wild blackberry pie with ice cream. The full breakfast may include sourdough pancakes, omelets, or fruit-topped crêpes. Reserve now for tulip season.

The Heron in La Conner

On the edge of town at 117
Maple St, (206) 466-4626
Mail: PO Box 716,
La Conner, WA 98257
Moderate; AE, MC, V;
checks OK

The Heron is the prettiest hostelry in town, with 11 rooms done in jewelry-box fashion. We like those that show a little individuality, like the Antiques Room with its lovely furnishings and an old claw-footed tub, or the View Suite with its gas fireplace and view of Mount Baker. All rooms have private baths and TVs. There's also a bridal suite with a two-person Jacuzzi. Downstairs is an elegant living room with wing chairs and lush carpeting, along with a formal dining room in which you can eat your continental breakfast. Out back you may barbecue in the stone fire pit or slump in the sun or the hot tub.

Hotel Planter

End of the line on the
south end of 1st St,
(206) 466-4710
715 S 1st St,
Mail: PO Box 702,
La Conner, WA 98257
Moderate; AE, MC, V;
checks OK

The most famous (and infamous) characters of La Conner's colorful past once inhabited this end of the town. They drank at the raucous Nevada Tavern, ate at the steamy Planter Cafe, and slept one floor above in the Hotel Planter. The first two landmarks have long since been replaced by more genteel shops and galleries, but the 85-year-old Hotel Planter is up and running again. In 1988, owner Don Hoskins used his connoisseur's eye and artisan's care to create a style that is a tasteful blend of past (original woodwork staircase and entrance) and present (private baths and armoire-hidden TVs in every room). Six rooms face the waterfront; others, including a special bridal suite with Jacuzzi, overlook a Renaissance garden courtyard (with a hot tub reserved for hotel guests only). The staff, well-versed on the Skagit Valley, are exemplary. Complimentary coffee is always available, but the Planter has no dining room.

Rainbow Inn

½ mile east of town,
(206) 466-4578
1075 Chilberg Rd,
La Conner
Mail: PO Box 1600, La
Conner, WA 98257
Moderate; MC, V;
checks OK

On Chilberg Road on the way into La Conner sits an elegant turn-of-the-century farmhouse, the Rainbow Inn, amidst acres of Skagit Valley flatlands. From the eight guest rooms you get sweeping views of the region you came to see: lush pastures, Mount Baker, the Olympics. Inside is pretty too: most of the furnishings are American country-pine, consistent with the farmhouse, and some of the baths have claw-footed tubs. Downstairs are plenty of lingering zones, from the parlor with its wood-burning ceramic fireplace to the hot tub on the back deck. Owners Herb and

Marianne Horen serve a three-course breakfast on an enchanting French-windowed front porch.

White Swan Guest House
*6 miles southeast of La Conner, (206) 445-6805
Mail: 1388 Moore Rd, Mount Vernon, WA 98273
Moderate; MC, V; checks OK*

Walk into the house Peter Goldfarb's house and you'll think you've entered your grandmother's place: Peter has tossed handmade quilts on the beds, has installed lace curtains around the windows, and often has cookies in the oven. There are three gaily painted guest rooms with an odd assortment of antiques (two with queen beds, one with a king); they share two baths down the hall. Pamper yourself with a soak in the large claw-footed tub, or curl up on the pink sofa in front of the wood stove. A charming, romantic guest house out back provides an additional and especially private accommodation. Peter serves a breakfast of freshly baked scones or muffins, fruit from his garden, and coffee. Bring binoculars for bird watching and bikes for easy touring around the flat farmlands of Fir Island.

La Conner Country Inn
*2nd and Morris, (206) 466-3101
107 2nd St, La Conner
Mail: PO Box 573, La Conner, WA 98257
Moderate; AE, MC, V; checks OK*

This is not an intimate and personally run B&B, nor is it a historic small hotel like the Planter. And despite its name, the La Conner Country Inn is not even a country inn—it's more of a classy motel with 28 spacious rooms with gas fireplaces. Breakfasts are a complimentary and served in the library, where an enormous fieldstone fireplace and comfortable furniture beckon you and a good book. Recent reports of store-bought sweet rolls and slips on the upkeep (dirty windows and mysterious mid-day absences at the front desk) make us wonder if they've been concentrating too much on the opening of the 40-room La Conner Channel Lodge. The lodge, which will be under the same ownership and management as the Country Inn (same phone number for reservations, too), was still under construction at press time.

MOUNT VERNON

Mount Vernon is a rare working town: one in which there are more good restaurants and bookstores than taverns and churches. It is the Big City to residents of surrounding Skagit and Island counties, and a college town to a surprising number of local folk, even though Skagit Valley College is but a blip on the very outskirts of town.

The classy old town center of Mount Vernon heroically survived the terrible winter floods of 1990, the worst river flooding since the town was founded 101 years prior. The Mount Vernon Mall was not so lucky, virtually wiped out that same year by the opening of the Cascade Mall in neighboring Burlington.

To travelers on I-5 it is little more than a blur except during the spring when the lush farm lands are brilliantly swathed in daffodils (March 15–April 15), tulips (April 1–May 10), and irises (May 15–June 15). The pastoral countryside is flat and ideal for bicyclists, except for the gridlock that occurs on the small farm lanes during the **Tulip Festival** (usually early April). Mount Vernon is really all about fresh food and beautiful flowers, products of surrounding Skagit Valley farms. For information on the many harvest festivals (June is Strawberry Month, September Apple Month, and October Redleaf Month) call the Chamber of Commerce, (206) 424-3510.

Little Mountain Park has a terrific picnic spot plus a knockout vista of the valley (look for migratory trumpeter swans in February). On the other end of the spectrum **The Chuck Wagon Drive Inn** offers 50 different kinds of burgers, electric trains, and the largest collection of ceramic whiskey bottle cowboys in the free world.

RESTAURANTS

Wildflowers
3 minutes east of I-5 from
College Way exit,
(206) 424-9724
2001 E College Way,
Mount Vernon
Expensive; full bar; MC,
V; checks OK
Lunch Wed-Fri, dinner
Tues-Sun

Without doubt, chef David Day and owner Michele Kjosen have created a restaurant worthy of considerable attention. And attention *is* the secret—attention to the smallest detail, in the kitchen, on the plate, in the surrounding ambience. It begins with Michele's attention to her guests, which verges on excessive but never crosses the line. Without her help we might have overlooked a marvelous entrée hidden on the menu under "salads": char-grilled prawns radiating atop a mound of brown rice and pecans, with lightly sautéed fresh orange slices in cilantro-cumin beurre blanc. Inspirations such as this come on a daily basis. Chef Day has succeeded in nurturing his wildflowers to full bloom year-round.

The Longfellow Cafe
In the historic Granary
Building, (206) 336-3684
120-B N 1st St,
Mount Vernon
Expensive; beer and wine;
MC, V; local checks only
Lunch Mon-Sat, dinner
Tues-Sat

★★

Local people fill The Longfellow Cafe because they have come to expect good food. With high volume, high ceilings, and high expectations, chef/owner Peter Barnard also has a creative, playful twist or two to lavish on us. The "steamers" with lemon dill butter off the daily-special blackboard were a mélange of butter clams, blue mussels, and pink singing scallops, all locally harvested and wonderfully prepared. The cafe features an excellent selection of wines by the glass, including vintage port, and a nice variety of beers. This brother and sister team, Peter and Annye Barnard, have worked hard to warm up the cavernous old brick granary, now a showcase of Skagit Valley produce and their solid culinary talents. The adjacent bookstore (Scott's) makes a happy ending.

Pacioni's Pizzeria
In old downtown Mount
Vernon, (206) 336-3314
606 1st St,
Mount Vernon
Inexpensive; beer and
wine; no credit cards,
checks OK

Wafts of fresh bread, fresh herbs, and fresh espresso tug at passersby. As the first weeks of opening turn into months, fewer pass by. They congregate at the red-and-white-checkered tables, enjoy a friendly glass of red wine, and savor the pungency of pizza. Young owners Dave and Paula Alberts have thrown their hearts into this restaurant as impressively as Dave throws the pizza dough into the air (remember the mad Italian baker in *Moonstruck?*). Paula (nèe Pacioni) is the

Continental breakfast, lunch, dinner Tues-Sat

keeper of family secrets, but we'll let you in on our favorite pie, the tri-color pizza (pesto, ricotta, and Roma tomatoes). All ingredients are fresh (even the biscotti are baked here), and *everything* is made to order. Pacioni's is showing signs of becoming one of the most gregarious spots in the Skagit Valley.

Cafe Europa
In old downtown Mount Vernon, (206) 336-3933
516 S 1st St, Mount Vernon
Inexpensive; beer and wine; no credit cards; checks OK
Lunch, dinner every day

This is one of the busiest lunch spots in town. The sandwich fillings are as good as their homemade bread, and with Greek salads, Polish sausage, and Swiss pastries, Cafe Europa lives up to its name. At the busiest times we've encountered unkempt tables and soiled floors, an unfortunate by-product of popularity. The entrance might be imposingly elegant, but inside the atmosphere is decidedly pleasant and informal. So is the service. Begging and bribery will not help. Kari and Ken Vonnegut will not sell any of the bread they bake until the restaurant's about to close.

STANWOOD

Stanwood is a sleepy little farm center with a Scandinavian heritage, a Midwestern air, and one good reason for a few minutes' sightseeing. Years ago, local daughter Martha Anderson started working at *rosemaling*, traditional Norwegian "flower painting," and teaching it to her fellow Stanwoodians. Now they've embellished many everyday businesses with charming rosemaled signs—not for tourist show as in Leavenworth, but out of an authentic impulse to express their heritage and make Main Street pretty.

Pilchuck School. Founded in 1971 by glass artist Dale Chihuly and Seattle art patrons John Hauberg and Anne Gould Hauberg, Pilchuck is an internationally renowned glass art school. Students live and study on this campus, situated in the midst of a country tree farm. An open house twice each summer gives folks a chance to see craftspeople at work; call first for times and directions. Summer: (206) 445-3111; winter: (206) 621-8422.

CAMANO ISLAND
LODGINGS

Willcox House
1 mile west of Stanwood
(206) 629-4746
1462 Larkspur Lane, Camano Island, WA 98292
Moderate; no credit cards; checks OK

The clapboard house looks like a remodeled Victorian with its turrets and wraparound porch, but it was built just a few years ago. Out of 60 windows you get fine views of Skagit Bay, and in clear weather you can see Mount Baker from the meadowlike lawn. Four guest rooms are decorated with antiques and brass and iron beds. Only one has a private bath. The Captain's Room that adjoins the turret is a wonderfully sunny spot to read. The morning's meal might be an omelet of local wild mushrooms, muffins, fruit, juice, and coffee.

EVERETT

Enormous regional population growth is forcing this sleeping bear to wake up and plant some roses. Progress is slow, but at least it is moving. Hanging flower baskets now decorate the main boulevard downtown, a retail complex **Colby Square** is in the works, as are the plans for a city-financed performing arts theater. The city is experiencing new pride as it readies itself for the arrival of the Navy later this decade.

The **Everett Giants** are an exciting Class A minor-league baseball affiliate of the San Francisco Giants. Games are played outdoors, tickets are cheap, and the ballpark food isn't bad. Call (206) 258-3673 for tickets and information.

The **Boeing 747/767 plant**, in South Everett on Highway 526, offers free 90-minute tours of the world's largest plant (measured in volume). No children under 10; (206) 342-4801.

Heritage Flour Mills boasts Washington's largest stone grinding mill. Tours of the mill, located at 2925 Chestnut Street, and the adjacent country store are regularly scheduled Tuesday through Friday, (206) 258-1582. **Marina Village** is a small but pleasant shopping center/restaurant complex on Port Gardner Bay. A ferry shuttle service runs from mid-July to September to Jetty Island, for beachcombing and bird watching; schedules vary with the tide.

RESTAURANTS

Passport
Hewitt Ave between Oakes and Lombard,
(206) 259-5037
1909 Hewitt Ave,
Everett
Moderate; full bar; MC, V; local checks only
Lunch Mon-Fri, dinner Mon-Sat

Passport is your ticket to good food in Everett. In August 1990, owners/chefs Lil Miller and Nan Wilkinson began an ambitious dream to bring the world (at least, a culinary taste of the world) to this old mill town. Believe it or not, they pull it off. If the menu's unfamiliar, just choose something, anything. It is all good: the freshly cured Scandinavian gravlax, the spicy Brazilian coconut shrimp, the outstanding Greek steak salad, and the hot-and-sour Indonesian salad with plenty of fresh seafood. In addition to a good wine list and full bar, fresh-dripped Sumatra coffee is served European style in a bowl. Desserts are good but anticlimactic. Scribble your thoughts on the butcher-papered tables.

The Sisters
8 blocks west of Broadway, in the Everett Public Market,
(206) 252-0480
2804 Grand St,
Everett
Inexpensive; no alcohol; MC, V; checks OK
Breakfast, lunch Mon-Fri

This place is as popular as it is funky. Soups such as mulligatawny, gazpacho, or just plain old beef barley can be outstanding. Salads are also consumer-friendly. Sandwiches range from average deli stuff to very healthful concoctions, including a vegetarian burger made with chopped cashews and sunflower seeds. Among the usual morning fare are some delights—the blueberry or pecan hotcakes; granola with yogurt and blueberry sauce; or scrambled eggs with bacon, onion, cottage cheese (or cheese of choice), sprouts, and salsa, wrapped in flour tortillas. Fresh-squeezed lemonade and strawberry lemonade are available year-round. A slice of blackberry pie weighs 10.5 ounces.

LODGINGS

Marina Village Inn
Take exit 193 off I-5 onto
Pacific Ave, turn right on
W Marine View Dr to
waterfront,
(206) 259-4040
1728 W Marine View Dr,
Everett, WA 98201
Expensive; AE, DC, MC,
V; no checks

Waterfront accommodations are a surprising rarity on Puget Sound, making this 28-room inn on Port Gardner Bay all the more attractive. It offers all the sophistication of a big-city hotel without the parking problems and convention crowds, and is therefore becoming increasingly popular with corporate executives. Best to book rooms a month or more in advance.

Rooms in the old inn are very contemporary and stylish (we've actually picked up decorating tips), featuring oak chests of drawers, tasteful art and lamps, refrigerators, hand-crafted ceramic sinks, color satellite TVs, extension phones in the bathrooms, and trouser presses; some rooms have notably comfy couches and easy chairs. Four of the rooms have Jacuzzis; most have telescopes for gazing out over the water. Be sure to book a room on the harbor side; sea lions might be lollygagging in the sun on the nearby jetty. A new addition features 11 rooms, all with harbor views and Jacuzzis and some with decks. The only visible drawback here is the lack of room service.

SNOHOMISH

This small community, formerly an active lumber town, now bills itself as the "Antique Capital of the Northwest." It certainly has plenty of antique shops filling the downtown historic district; the **Star Center Mall** is the largest, with 165 antique dealers from all over the area; 829 2nd St, (206) 568-2131.

In addition to antiquing, get a lift in a **hot air balloon** at Harvey Field, (206) 568-3025, which also offers scenic flights, (206) 259-2944, and skydiving opportunities, (206) 568-5960.

RESTAURANTS

Sweet Life Cafe
1st and B on the 2nd floor
of Marks Bldg,
(206) 568-3554
1024 1st St, Snohomish
Moderate; beer and wine;
MC, V; checks OK
Breakfast Sat-Sun, lunch
Tues-Sun, dinner
Wed-Sat

What began as a coffeehouse (reportedly the first of its kind in Snohomish County) has become the town's favorite restaurant. It's now located on the second floor of the old brick Marks Building, where owners Dennis Lebow and Paula Inmon have maintained the classic coffeehouse appeal with secondhand mismatched tables, classical jazz on the sound system, and a separate room devoted to overstuffed couches and reading material. The counter servers at lunch are friendly and lightning-fast (weekends can get quite busy), ladeling up generous bowls of ginger-carrot soup or making a roasted turkey and cranberry sandwich on hand-sliced five-grain bread. Dinners slow down a bit and the food takes a different approach. The nine nightly entrées change weekly but might include a lamb stew spiked with North African spices and dried figs and served over orzo, grilled fresh Alaskan white salmon with an orange sauce, or perhaps a vegetarian ravioli with grilled vegetables. The light and dark chocolate mousse confirms it is, indeed, a sweet life.

LODGINGS

Iverson House
*2 blocks north of
old Snohomish,
(206) 568-3825
312 Ave D, Snohomish,
WA 98290
Moderate; MC, V;
checks OK*

There's a gracious, tranquil atmosphere about this classic Edwardian bed and breakfast (formerly the Noris House), even though it's on the main drag into Snohomish's historic shopping district. New hosts Fred and Laura Hines have maintained its reputation for wonderful breakfasts, served in an elegant Mission-style dining room. They'll try to adapt the meal to guests' needs. There are now four suites available, although only two rooms are rented per evening (exceptions made for families or special occasions); each is decorated in the style of a different era. No smoking.

MUKILTEO

Unfortunately, Mukilteo is probably best known for the traffic congestion caused by the Whidbey Island ferry ((206) 355-7308). There are, however, a small state park and a historic lighthouse worth seeing. You can also stroll along the waterfront and fish off the docks.

RESTAURANTS

Charles at Smugglers Cove
*At intersection of Hwys
525 and 526,
(206) 347-2700
8310 53rd Ave W,
Mukilteo
Moderate; full bar; AE,
MC, V; local checks only
Lunch Tues-Fri, dinner
Mon-Sat*

★★★

The smugglers were none other than Al Capone and associates, who built this mansion in 1929 as a speakeasy and distillery complete with a secret tunnel to the docks below. (Mukilteo was Snohomish County's first port city.) Charles is the owner's father. Chef Claude Faure and partner Janet Kingma have turned this Northwest landmark building into an elegant French restaurant. There are two floors; for best atmosphere, reserve a table downstairs, where the country-French ambience is more appealing. The veal medallions with chanterelles and the sweetbreads were fork-tender, each in a delectable wine-based sauce and served with steamed vegetables. Portions were ample and rich; every vegetable bore its own sauce (too many sauces on the plate). Entrées come à la carte, but for an extra $6.50 you can get a dinner salad and dessert (worth the extra)—baked Alaska or chocolate mousse. Much of Charles's business is from nearby Boeing, and accordingly, weeknights tend to be busier than weekends. There's a small terrace with a view of the Sound, or ask for a table in the back with the same vantage.

WHIDBEY ISLAND

With the recent Supreme Court declaration of New York's Long Island as a peninsula, Captain Whidbey's namesake landfall now qualifies as the longest island in the U.S. During the 1980s, Island County (which includes Whidbey and Camano islands) experienced the second-highest population growth rate in the state. Whidbey's largest employer is still government (since the Navy base was spared by the Federal budget in 1991), then retail trade, then services. Whidbey boasts pretty villages, viewpoint parks, sandy beaches, and some lovely rolling farmland. It makes for a particularly nice family-outing day, during which you can combine browsing, varied sightseeing, and sun. Whidbey's flat, relatively untrafficked roads make it great for biking. At press time, there was talk about a proposed bike-only route around the island; call the Island County Planning Department, (206) 679-7339, or the Central Whidbey Chamber of Commerce, (206) 678-5434, for details. A new bus-and-boat service scheduled to start summer 1991 will be taking tourists from Seattle to and from Whidbey via Everett; call Mosquito Fleet Enterprises, (206) 321-0506 or (800) 235-0506.

WHIDBEY ISLAND: CLINTON

You won't find a manicured course or even a clubhouse at **Island Greens** (3890 East French Road, Clinton, (206) 321-6042) but the par-three, nine-hole course is challenging, the location is scenic, and fees are an amazingly low ($5 per person). This is an "alternative" golf course built on former farmland and maintained with minimal pesticides and fertilizers. Course fees and rental charges are paid on an honor system.

LODGINGS

Home by the Sea
6 miles north of Clinton on Useless Bay,
(206) 221-2964
2388 E Sunlight Beach Rd, Clinton, WA 98236
Expensive; MC, V; checks OK

Home by the Sea captures a relaxed beach-house mood better than most other B&Bs on the island, situated as it is right on the driftwood-strewn beach of Useless Bay. The main house, a modern split-level with two upstairs suites, features a hot tub on the deck right outside the door. Other alternatives are a Nordic cottage on the shores of Lone Lake, a Swiss chalet in the woods (for two adults only), the Chanterelle Cottage nearby, and a lovely Cape Cod cottage (good for families) just up the street from Home central. Two new cottages include the Camaii Beach cabin and French Road Farm. All cottages come with full kitchens, fireplaces, and basket breakfasts, and some cottages are equipped with new Jacuzzis. 2-night minimum stay.

Lovely Cottage
From Clinton go 1 mile, left on Cultus Rd to Lovely Rd,
(206) 321-6592
4130 E Lovely Rd, Clinton, WA 98236

It happens to be on Lovely Rd, it also happens to be quite lovely. On a bluff above Possession Beach, it's a very private place. Below (via a steep staircase) is miles of undeveloped beach. Owner Lori Adams, an Alaska Airlines pilot, knows well what people want on a getaway: down comforter on the bed, lots of pillows, and lots of time together (or alone, if you're one). Pack

Expensive; no credit cards; checks OK

a picnic; the deck (equipped with a barbecue, inside there's a full kitchen too) is a favorite spot at sunset. The vegetable garden is yours to forage in. The bathroom has the essentials you may have forgotten, right down to the hair dryer and an extra toothbrush. Breakfast is ready when you are, and so is the hot tub.

WHIDBEY ISLAND: LANGLEY

The nicest town on Whidbey evinces small-town virtues. The tidy downtown strip along 1st Street provides all a visitor could want: espresso, ice cream, benches overlooking Saratoga Passage. The arts and crafts festival takes place over the Fourth of July weekend, the Island County Fair in mid-August; (206) 321-4677. The residents like to attend first-run movies at the **Clyde Theatre** ($3.50), drink pitchers of ale at the **Dog House Backdoor Tavern**, and swap stories with Josh Hauser at **Moonraker Books**. **Islandesign Interiors** and **Virginia's Antiques** are among the best shops for home furnishings; the **Star Store** and **Annie Steffen's** provide great upscale general mercantile and woven wearables, respectively. You'll find rare reading material, baseball cards, sheet music, and collectable coins at **Madhatter's Old Books** (107 First St, (206) 221-2356).
  Public fishing. The small boat harbor has a 160-foot public fishing pier.

RESTAURANTS

Cafe Langley
At the south end of town, (206) 221-3090 113 1st St, Langley Moderate; beer and wine; AE, MC, V; checks OK Lunch, dinner every day (closed Wed in winter)

Witness the long waiting line on weekend nights and you'll know that owners Shant and Arshavir Garibyan have created a Whidbey appetite for Middle Eastern standards such as lamb shish kabobs, perfect, creamy hummus scooped with warm, chewy pita bread, and savory, utterly satisfying Mediterranean seafood stew packed with scallops, salmon, mussels, and shrimp in a cumin-rich tomato sauce. The menu includes some Northwest infusions such as Dungeness crab cakes and Whidbey's own Penn Cove mussels steamed in olive oil, garlic, and vermouth. The dozen-or-so daily specials often venture beyond the Middle Eastern theme (perhaps a light, clear tortilla soup with tomato and mushroom). The vegetarian entrées do not quite measure up to the rest of the fare. The desserts, such as the ultrarich Russian cream with a raspberry sauce, do.

Star Bistro
Above the Star Store on 1st, (206) 221-2627 201½ 1st St, Langley Moderate; full bar; AE, MC, V, checks OK

Art Deco is not exactly what you'd expect in Langley, but nibbling Penn Cove mussels in the late afternoon on a sun-splashed deck is a favorite pastime at this somewhat trendy black, white, and red bistro. Located on the second floor of the Star Store, this fun eatery serves up generous plates of good food: Caesar salads, a burger with onions, peppers, bacon, and cheese, and a shrimp and scallop linguine with a tangy sauce of mustard, mushroom, tomato, cream, and sherry.

When the place gets hopping (usually on hot summer days), it can get erratic in quality and service.

LODGINGS

Inn at Langley
At the edge of town at 400 1st, (206) 221-3033
Mail: PO Box 835, Langley, WA 98260
Expensive; beer and wine; AE, MC, V; checks OK
Continental breakfast Mon-Wed, dinner Fri-Sun (by reservation only)

Paul and Pam Schell's first private venture since Paul left Cornerstone Development (the Alexis in Seattle) is one of Whidbey's finest. Architect Alan Grainger designed the building in a marriage of three themes: Frank Lloyd Wright's style, Northwest ruggedness, and Pacific Rim tranquillity. For the most part, it works—fabulously. Inside this rough-hewn, cedar-shingled building (whose size is disguised by the clever design) are 24 rooms finely decorated with an eye for pleasing detail: quiet shades of tan and gray (a tad austere for some tastes), simple Asian furnishings, trimmings of three different woods, and a quarry-tiled bathroom (in a brown hue reminiscent of beach stones) with hooks made from alder twigs. Adjacent is a Jacuzzi from which you can watch the boat traffic on Saratoga Passage and the flicker of your fireplace through the translucent shoji-style sliding screen. All this opens onto a private shrubbery-lined balcony with cushioned bench seats overlooking Saratoga Passage. We prefer the upper-level rooms; others are approached by a dark concrete stairwell. The small conference room (equipped with up-to-the-minute business necessities) has the expansive view of the Passage that the dining room (above the parking lot) lacks. Friendly and gracious, Sandy Nogel arranges for all needs.

In a country-style kitchen, chef Steve Nogal serves a five-course weekend dinners at 7pm ($38). Dinners are a fresh Northwest harvest with inventive touches. Portions are way too large, so one can easily end up uncomfortably stuffed. Most opt to dine with other guests at the large center table, where conversation can be lively and service is slightly more attentive. Reservations are required, and don't be late: dinner starts in the lobby with a glass of sherry and a tour of the wine cellar. Sunday suppers, more homestyle fare, are very popular, especially with locals (and visitors in no particular rush to get home); these prix-fixe dinners begin at 6pm (four courses $29.95).

Eagle's Nest Inn
Bed & Breakfast
Follow 2nd St until it becomes Saratoga Rd,
(206) 321-3313
236 E Saratoga Rd, Langley, WA 8260

This funky, four-story, octagonal home makes the most of its view overlooking Saratoga Passage, Camano Island, and Mount Baker. The entire third and fourth stories are for guests, including a living room with a library of books, videotapes, and CDs. The adjacent balcony offers a Jacuzzi. A snack counter with coffee, tea, and drinks is open for guests, as is the "bottomless" cookie jar. Each of the four rooms offers a pretty, spotlessly clean setting with floral-printed

Moderate; MC, V;
checks OK

quilts and a private bath. The best is the Eagles' Nest, an eight-sided penthouse suite rimmed with windows (and a balcony) giving a 360-degree view of the water and the surrounding forest. For less extravagance, stay one floor below in the balconied Saratoga Room. Breakfast is served either in the dining room or on the large deck, weather permitting. Nancy will happily try to accommodate your breakfast wishes, but if you leave the choice up to her you'll dine on a feast of baked apples with whipped cream, followed by crisp-sweet French toast and scrambled eggs with turkey sausage.

Log Castle
1½ miles west of Langley
on Saratoga,
(206) 321-5483
3273 E Saratoga Rd,
Langley, WA 98260
Moderate; MC, V;
checks OK

This is the house that Jack built—literally—and whenever he's home from his job as state senator, Jack Metcalf builds on it some more, to his wife Norma's newest designs. As a result, the beachside castle has a slightly unfinished air about it—which shouldn't in the slightest detract from what can be a distinctly unusual experience. Every log tells a story (ask Norma about the log-end floor entrance, the branded-log table, the hollow-log sink), and the place can feel quite cozy on a winter evening. The loft suite comes with an antique ship's stove; two rooms on the other side of the house are built into a turret and feature remarkable views. Each room has its own bath. Breakfast usually includes Norma's homemade bread. The Metcalfs possess a genuine gift for the art of hospitality.

Whidbey Inn
At 106 1st St,
(206) 221-7115
Mail: PO Box 156,
Langley, WA 98260
Expensive; no credit
cards; checks OK

Formerly the Whidbey House, Richard Francisco's B&B clings to Langley's bluff and offers six sparkling guest rooms that look out onto the grand sweep of beach and bay below. The three downstairs rooms ($95-$105) are country-Victorian dreams of furnishing; three top-floor suites ($130-$145) capitalize best on the view and have fireplaces. One of these has a walkway to an atmospheric gazebo on stilts outside. Look one way, out to sea, and you feel wonderfully isolated; turn the other way, into town, and you have an old-fashioned sense of small-town belonging. A simple and filling breakfast-in-a-basket is delivered to your room.

Richard has bought an old Victorian house just down the road and recently opened Francisco's Italian Cuisine, (206) 221-2728. It's not quite as relaxed as islanders would like it to be, and one suggests that with a few more more bicycles hanging from the walls this could become the cozy, Italian restaurant chef Thomas Cartè deserves.

Lone Lake
Cottage & Breakfast
5½ miles from the Clinton
ferry, off Hwy 525 on S
Bayview, (206) 321-5325

You can't take your room out for a spin on Lone Lake anymore, but Delores Meeks' place is still one of the most unique B&Bs around. One of the three lodgings is *The Queen Whidbey* a beamed-ceiling stern-wheeler that has been permanently moored on the lake since its

5206 S Bayview Rd,
Langley, WA 98260
Expensive; no credit
cards; checks OK

maker, Delores's husband Ward Meeks, passed away. ("No one else knew how to run it.") However, guests staying on board the *Queen* now enjoy the same extras found in the two lakeside cottages: fireplace, VCR, CD player, and a private shoji-screened deck with Jacuzzi and barbecue grill. The one-bedroom Terrace Cottage is nicest; it looks into the domed top of an aviary housing some 300 rare birds from around the world. In addition, there are exotic ducks, pheasant, quail, peacocks, and swans in an outdoor pen. Each room has a full kitchen stocked with breakfast makings, plus seasonings for the barbecue should you get lucky and land a trout or two from the lake. Guests are welcome to use the canoes, rowboat, and bikes.

WHIDBEY ISLAND: FREELAND

Just a serviceable little town, but it does have the one good bakery on the island, an essential spot for picnic supplies: **The Island Bakery.** The seven-grain breads are very good. Main Street, (206) 321-6282.

LODGINGS

Cliff House
Bush Point Rd to
Windmill Rd,
(206) 321-1566
5440 Windmill Rd,
Freeland, WA 98249
Expensive; no credit
cards; checks OK

Seattle architect Arne Bystrom designed this dramatic house, which makes an extraordinary getaway. The home on a cliff above Admiralty Inlet is full of light from lofty windows, centering on a 30-foot-high atrium (open to the weather) and a sunken fireplace. For $265 a night ($365 for two couples) you have use of the entire house, with two large loft bedroom suites and a kitchen for cooking your meals. The house is strikingly decorated with an interesting arrangement of Oriental rugs, modern art, and Indian baskets and is set amid 13 acres of woods with hammocks, bench chairs, and a platform deck with a hot tub built high on the cliff. The elfish one-bedroom Sea Cliff Cottage goes for $135 a night. Peggy Moore sets the country kitchen table (in both houses) with a continental breakfast.

WHIDBEY ISLAND: GREENBANK

Here on the narrowest part of the island, stop by **Whidbeys Greenbank Farm,** at one time the largest loganberry farm in the country. After a short self-guided tour, sample Whidbeys Loganberry Liqueur. Lots of pretty picnicking spots.

RESTAURANTS

Whidbey Fish
Market & Cafe
On Hwy 525,

The big colorful murals of sea creatures are not just another roadside attraction. Inside this cafe on Highway 525 (you can't miss it) is some of the best seafood in the area. Owners Thom and Jan Gunn put tiny Green-bank on the map when they expanded their retail fresh-fish business into something of a communal dining experience. Mondays are an all-you-can-eat fish feed, a local fave. This is its own kind of roadhouse; expect a little funk and lots of good vibrations.

LODGINGS

Guest House Bed & Breakfast Cottages
1 mile south of Greenbank off Hwy 525 on E Christenson Rd,
(206) 678-3115
835 E Christenson Rd, Greenbank, WA 98253
Expensive; AE, MC, V; checks OK

We love this place, partly for all its alternatives. You can stay in the $85 Wildflower Suite farmhouse (closest to the swimming pool and hot tub), a pricier log-cabin cottage ($125), the one-bedroom carriage house ($125), or the new Kentucky Pine Cottage ($175). All have kitchens, baths, and VCRs. But our favorite—everybody's favorite—is the $225-a-night lodge cabin. Full of antiques but built in 1979, the lodge combines the old (a wood stove next to the breakfast nook, a hammock and picnic tables outside by the pond) with the new (two-person Jacuzzi, remote control TV, dishwasher) to a most appealing effect. Perched at the edge of a lovely pond and ringed by trees, the two-story home features a broad deck and views of the Cascades and the Sound from the loft bedroom. Breakfast makings are left in the fully equipped kitchens.

WHIDBEY ISLAND: COUPEVILLE

The second-oldest incorporated town in the state dates back to 1852, when farming commenced on the fertile isle. It was founded by sea captain Thomas Coupe, whose home still stands on Front Street. A fort was built in 1855 after some Indian scares, and part of it, the Alexander Blockhouse on Front Street, is open for touring. Amid the growing pressures of development, the town has set itself a strict agenda of historical preservation.

Coupeville's downtown consists of half a dozen souvenir and antique shops; however, more noteworthy is pioneer memorabilia in **Island County Historical Museum** (which opened in 1989).

Coupeville's first bike shop and rental, **All Island Bicycles** (302 N Main, (206) 678-3351), sells, rents, and repairs bikes and equipment. An extra bike lane follows Engle Road three miles south of Coupeville to **Fort Casey**, a decommissioned fort with splendid gun mounts, beaches, and commanding bluffs. The magnificent bluff and beach at the 17,000-acre **Ebey's Landing** and **Fort Ebey State Park** are good places to explore. The **Keystone ferry**, connecting Whidbey to Port Townsend, leaves from Admiralty Head, just south.

LODGINGS

Captain Whidbey Inn

*Off Madrona Way on W
Captain Whidbey Inn Rd,
(206) 678-4097
2072 W Captain Whidbey
Inn Rd, Coupeville,
WA 98239
Moderate; full bar; AE,
DC, MC, V; checks OK
Breakfast, lunch, dinner
every day (lunch Sat-Sun
only during winter)*

The old inn, dating back to 1907 and built from madrona logs, nestles picturesquely in the woods overlooking Penn Cove: a lovable place with some serious quirks. The lodge has 12 upstairs rooms (two suites) and two shared bathrooms; there are four sparsely furnished cottages with fireplaces and baths, two with separate bedrooms, plus 13 lagoon rooms—the best choices—with private baths and verandahs. The problem is that the walls are so thin they seem to talk, and sniffle, and sneeze. The public rooms—a dining room with creaky wooden floors that seem to slope toward the sea, the deck (when the weather's warm), a cozy bar, a well-stocked library, a folksy fireplace room—are quite attractive. In the past, the restaurant has suffered from a constant turnover of chefs; under the direction of current chef Ken Floyd, the food is still uneven. Stay with simple preparations off the very limited menu and you'll do well here (fresh Penn Cove mussels—you're looking at the mussel beds/pens—steamed in ginger, soy, and garlic, or the pasta primavera with just-steamed veggies in a zesty marinara sauce). Dessert (Washington apple cake, warmed and served with cream cheese topping) almost made up for the flaws of dinner.

Colonel Crockett Farm

*Follow signs to Fort
Casey off Hwy 20,
(206) 678-3711
1012 S Fort Casey Rd,
Coupeville, WA 98239
Moderate; MC, V; checks
OK*

From the skinny, winding road, Colonel Crockett's looks like a genuine 40-acre farm with its large fields and cluster of faded red-painted barns—until you spot the Mercedeses and BMWs parked in the guest area outside the farmhouse. This was the island's first B&B and also claims to be the oldest home on the island still in use. You can't beat the setting overlooking Admiralty Inlet (Bob and Beulah Whitlow have a telescope, if you ask). Trouble is, there have been reports of religious overtones (morning prayer at breakfast). Our favorites of the five guest rooms are the big Crockett Room with a Victorian claw-footed tub and a canopy bed, and the white-and-lavender Davis Room that opens off the smart oak-paneled English library. Breakfast is taken downstairs in the dining room. Four resident cats roam the large, well-manicured yard of blooming shrubs and century-old trees. Crockett Lake is a bird sanctuary.

Fort Casey Inn

*2 miles west of
Coupeville,
(206) 678-8792
1124 S Engle Rd,
Coupeville,
WA 98239*

Built in 1909 as officers' quarters for nearby Fort Casey, this neat row of nine houses now offers no-frills accommodations with a military theme. Each is divided into two duplexes, each with two bedrooms, a living room with small fireplace, private bath and kitchen stocked with breakfast makings. Rooms are plain but comfortable, with original stamped-tin ceilings. Decor consists mostly of tied-rag rugs, old photographs of

Moderate; AE, MC, V;
checks OK

soldiers, renditions of early U.S. presidents, plus military emblems on everything including the bathtub. The recently restored Garrison Hall, which now offers a small reception area with its own private bedroom and bath, can be rented for weddings or private parties. Unlike most B&Bs on Whidbey, Fort Casey welcomes kids—and is truly a fun place to explore. Gina Martin can tell you anything you need to know about the nearby Fort Casey State Park, the bird sanctuary at Crockett Lake, or nearby Ebey's Landing National Historic Reserve just north.

Inn at Penn Cove

Take Hwy 20 from
Deception Pass or Hwy
525 from the ferry,
(206) 678-8000
702 N Main St,
Coupeville, WA 98239
Moderate; AE, MC, V;
checks OK

They haven't always been painted carnation pink, but the 1887 and 1891 homes that make up this inn have been familiar sights in Coupeville for over a century. Not on Main Street, mind you; Jim and Barbara Cinney moved one of them here in 1990 and have since transformed the two homes into a gracious inn. The three guest rooms in the main house are prettily furnished, if slightly overdecorated (lots of frills and the occasional stuffed animal). The swankest room, Desiree's, has a king-size bed, its own mini-parlor with a view of Penn Cove and sometimes Mount Baker, and a double Jacuzzi. Until renovations are complete in the second home, we recommend staying in the main house, where you can pad downstairs to play the piano or check out the Cinneys' extensive classic-movie collection. Early visits show a few kinks still need to be worked out—late risers might get cold showers. Breakfasts, though, are a great send-off, with blueberry and oat-bran muffins, fruit salad topped with granola, and a light spinach quiche.

WHIDBEY ISLAND: OAK HARBOR

Whidbey's largest city is dominated by the Whidbey Island Naval Air Station, a big air base for tactical electronic warfare squadrons. For the most part, Oak Harbor is engulfed in new military and retired military folk.

An interesting stop is **Lavender Heart**, which manufactures floral gifts on a 12-acre former holly farm. From the Hendersons' gift store, you can peek at the impressive 1000-square foot impressive production facility; 3 miles south of Deception Pass at 4233 N DeGraff Rd, (206) 675-3987.

Deception Pass. The beautiful, treacherous gorge has a lovely, if usually crowded, state park with 2,300 acres of prime camping land, forests, and beach. The pass can also be toured from the water by the Mosquito Fleet (800) 235-0506. **Strom's Shrimp/Fountain and Grill**, just north of the pass, sells fresh seafood and shrimp for your cookout. They also grill up a mean oyster burger to go. (206) 293-2531.

RESTAURANTS

Lucy's Mi Casita
On the main drag of Oak
Harbor, (206) 675-4800
1380 W Pioneer Way,
Oak Harbor
Inexpensive; full bar;AE,
MC, V; local checks only
Lunch, dinner every day

Locals keep coming back for the fresh, homemade food and lively atmosphere of Lucy and Al Enriquez's comfortable—if somewhat tacky—Mexican restaurant. The dining room is decorated with a hodgepodge of cutouts of flamenco dancers, beer ads, and "curtains" formed by strings of crimped beer-bottle caps; upstairs is a lounge with a balcony. The large menu includes fajitas, chimichangas, and chiles rellenos, plus a few specialties from Lucy's home town of Chihuahua such as entomatadas—a tortilla topped with tomato sauce, cheese, and onion.

LODGINGS

Auld Holland Inn
8 miles south of Deception
Pass on State Rd 20,
(206) 675-2288
5681 State Rd 20, Oak
Harbor, WA 98277
Moderate; full bar; AE,
DC, MC, V; checks OK
Dinner every day (Mon-
Sat in winter)

A half mile north of Oak Harbor, this newish motel is just fine, if a shade close to the highway. Some upper-story rooms have antiques, and there's a tennis court, a hot tub, and a pool. Prices are good. The adjacent restaurant, Kasteel Franssen, has quite a regal, European feel about it and a solid reputation amongst locals. There's a big gas fireplace, tapestry-upholstered dining chairs, and a lively piano bar. Appetizers are the best bet here, especially the pâté maison and the North Sea herring with capers and onion. Eighty-year-old chef Jean Paul Combettes has a creative way with seafood (if sometimes oversauced); be sure to ask what's fresh. Combettes' chowder has won numerous awards.

VASHON ISLAND

Faintly countercultural, this bucolic isle is a short ferry ride away from Seattle (take the Fauntleroy ferry) or Tacoma. It's a wonderful place to explore by bicycle, although the first long hill up from the ferry dock is a killer. Few beaches are open to the public.

Unlike Bainbridge, its northern neighbor, Vashon Island employs many of its own in island-based companies that market their goods both locally and nationally; many of these offer tours (it's a good idea to call ahead): **K-2 Skis, Inc.,** (206) 463-3631; **S.B.C,** (popularly known as Seattle's Best Coffee), Island Highway, (206) 463-3932; **Maury Island Farms,** with berries and preserves, at 99th and 204th on Island Highway, (206) 463-9659; **Island Spring, Inc.,** with locally made tofu, (206) 463-9848. **Wax Orchards** on 131st SW, north of 232nd is no longer open for tours, but you can stop by and pick up some fresh preserves, fruit syrups, and apple cider. **The Country Store and Farm** is an old-fashioned general store stocking most of the island-made products, along with natural-fiber apparel, housewares, sundries, dried herbs, and gardening supplies; (206) 463-3655.

RESTAURANTS

Cafe Tosca
Downtown Vashon,

With the hearty exception of Sound Food, there simply wasn't a great place to eat on the island. Nowadays,

(206) 463-2125
9924 SW Bank Rd,
Vashon Island
Moderate; beer and wine;
MC, V; checks OK
Lunch, dinner Tues-Sun

visitors vie with locals for tables at ex-Bronxite George Green's excellent new bistro. The bread is divine, the pasta is fresh (imported from Cardini's in Everett), and virgin olive oil reigns supremo. Everyone comes for the capellini pomidoro (fresh angel hair pasta with tomatoes, olive oil, garlic, and basil), scampi with olive oil and lemon, and the special puttanesca—a spicy mountain of linguine, kalamata olives, capers, anchovies, tomatoes, and peppers. And many a cold weather lunch has been made of a big bowl of Cafe Tosca classic minestrone and a glass of good red. Per dolci? The cheesecake is deliciously homemade, the torta Tosca rich with butter and almond flour, the caffè dark roast Italian, of course. If only you could return home by gondola.

Sound Food Restaurant

7 miles south of the ferry
on Island Hwy,
(206) 463-3565
20312 99th Ave SW,
Vashon Island
Moderate; beer and wine;
MC, V; checks OK
Breakfast Mon-Fri,
lunch, dinner every day;
brunch Sat-Sun

It's a delightfully mellow place, an airy room with wood floors, fresh flowers and, in summer, pretty wisteria overhanging the windows. The restaurant started out as a hangout for the island's artsy population, but lately mainlanders have been coming over, drawn by the honest cooking and excellent ingredients. The weekend rushes result in interminably long waits for waiter, water, and menus—but you'd have to be pretty mean of spirit to let anything annoy you here. Weekend brunches are especially popular: potato pancakes, crêpes, French toast, whole-wheat waffles, blintzes with fresh fruit toppings, omelets—perhaps with asparagus and ham, and topped with Mornay sauce. Lunches offer healthful soups, salads, and sandwiches made from their own bread. Dinners may include bay scallops poached with sherry and baked with leeks in a light cream sauce, or a garden-vegetable linguine, or spicy Mexican meatballs. An incredible array of fresh-baked goods—seven-grain bread, sprouted wheat bread, cinnamon rolls, cheese Danish, muffins, cookies (try the snickerdoodles), wonderful pies—offered for consumption on the spot or to take home. Live a little—do both. Good espresso, too.

LODGINGS

The Shepherd's Loft

Corner of 63rd SW and
Luana Beach Rd,
(206) 463-2544
23226 63rd Ave SW,
Vashon, WA 98070
Moderate; no credit cards;
checks OK

This guest cottage high on Maury Island (which is really attached to Vashon) will accommodate two for $55 and up to four for $60. Kids are welcome. Hosts David and Mary Cooper don't do breakfast, but you can cook your own in the complete kitchen. Wander outside; there really are sheep, and a wonderful view of the water on a clear day.

PUYALLUP

At the head of the fertile Puyallup Valley, this frontier farm town serves as a major gateway to Mount Rainier. While much of the bulb, rhubarb, and berry farmland continues to be cultivated, a great part of it has been malled and auto-row-ravaged around the edges. Avoid the fast-food strip to the south and head east up the valley to Sumner, White River, Orting, Wilkeson, and Carbonado.

Ezra Meeker Mansion is the finest original pioneer mansion left in Washington. Its builder and first occupant, Ezra Meeker, came west in an oxcart in 1852, introduced hops to the Puyallup Valley, and later became known as the "hops king of the world." The lavish 17-room Italianate house (built 1890) is complete with fireplaces, carved cherrywood staircases, and ornate brass doorknobs, and now stands beautifully restored in the rear parking lot of a Main Street furniture store; 312 Spring St, (206) 848-1770. Open Wednesday through Sunday, 1 to 4pm, March through mid-December.

Puyallup is big on old-time seasonal celebrations, and it's home for two of the biggest in the Northwest: the **Daffodil Festival and Parade** in early April and the **Western Washington Fair** better known as the **Puyallup Fair**, in September. Beginning the Friday after Labor Day, over one million people "do the Puyallup." One of the nation's biggest fairs; call (206) 845-1771. **Puyallup Downtown Farmers' Market** is held every Saturday starting at 9am, June through September, at Pioneer Park.

RESTAURANTS

Balsano's
Between Pioneer and E Main, (206) 845-4222
127 15th SE, Puyallup
Moderate; beer and wine; MC, V; checks OK
Lunch Tues-Fri, dinner Tues-Sun

Since Italian meals usually begin in the marketplace, it makes sense that there's an enjoyable Italian restaurant in the fertile Puyallup Valley. This ex–drive-in, just a short detour off I-5 on the northern outskirts of Puyallup, is still a pleasant surprise. The menu's filled with enjoyable and unusual regional dishes. Try a dish of tender lemon chicken and artichoke hearts (native to Sicily), or a homemade Sicilian sausage of coarsely chopped pork and fennel seeds. Lunches are very reasonable, and there are special suggestions at all meals for children. Would-be gourmets should inquire about cooking and wine-tasting classes.

TACOMA

Sided by Commencement Bay and the Tacoma Narrows and backed by Mount Rainier, this city is undergoing a cultural and psychological renaissance that is dramatically changing both its landscape and its self-image. Having begun finally to shed its industrial past and recover its natural beauty, Tacoma is returning to the Seattle orbit it left over a century ago. No longer is it a blue-collar town courting heavy industry. It is now a growing urban center with a thriving cultural core.

A city once famous for its hostility to art is now a home to the arts. From the McCarver Street Bookstore in Old Town, to the waterfront's avant-garde public-arts project, "Trestle: Ancient," to city-subsidized artists' housing in the historic warehouse district, the arts are breaking out all over.

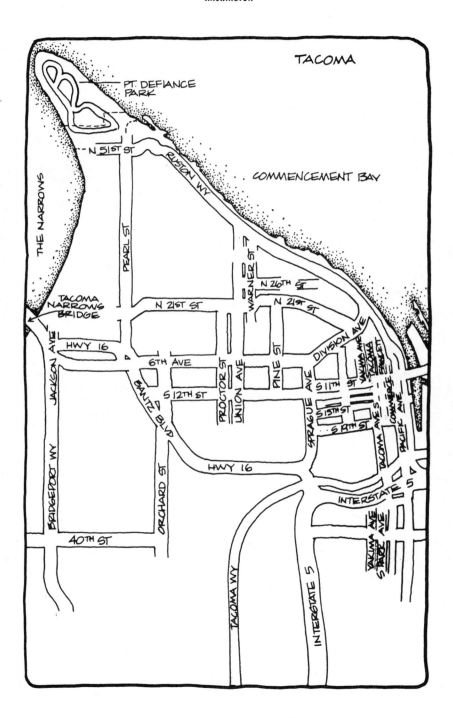

TACOMA

PT. DEFIANCE PARK

COMMENCEMENT BAY

THE NARROWS

N 51ST ST

RUSTON WY

PEARL ST

WARNER ST

N 26TH ST

N 21ST ST

N 21ST ST

TACOMA NARROWS BRIDGE

JACKSON AVE

HWY 16

6TH AVE

PROCTOR ST

UNION AVE

PINE ST

DIVISION AVE

YAKIMA AVE

S 11TH ST

TACOMA AVE

COMMERCE ST

PACIFIC AVE

SPRAGUE AVE

S 12TH ST

S 15TH ST

S 19TH ST

BRIDGEPORT WY

GANTZ BLVD

ORCHARD ST

HWY 16

INTERSTATE 5

40TH ST

TACOMA WY

INTERSTATE 5

YAKIMA AVE

STADIUM AVE

Tacoma has also fervently embraced the idea of preservation. Its downtown warehouse district is being converted from industrial use to residential and commercial functions without destroying the historic buildings. The University of Washington is about to begin construction of a branch campus there which will use many of the old warehouses now standing empty. The stately homes and cobblestone streets in the north end are often used as living sets for Hollywood's moviemakers, and students still fill the turreted chateau of Stadium High School. Old City Hall, with its Renaissance clock and bell tower, the Romanesque First Presbyterian Church, the rococo Pythian Lodge, and the one-of-a-kind copper-domed Union Depot (now being restored, while next to it a new State Historical Museum is about to be built) are historical and architectural buffs' delights. The Ruston Way waterfront, a six-mile mix of parks and restaurants, is thronged with people in any weather.

Pantages Center (901 Broadway Plaza), the restored 1,100-seat Pantages Theatre, originally designed in 1918 by B. Marcus Priteca, is the focal point of the some reviving downtown cultural life—dance, music, and stage presentations; (206) 591-5894. The **Rialto Theatre** will soon be reopening for smaller performance groups. **Tacoma Actors Guild** (1323 S Yakima) is Tacoma's thriving professional theater, offering an ambitious and successful blend of American classics and Northwest premieres, (206) 272-2145). In the fall of 1993, TAG will join the Pantages and the Rialto downtown in a new home at the Commerce Street level atop the park-covered transit center.

Tacoma Art Museum (12th at Pacific) is housed in a former downtown bank. This small museum has paintings by Renoir, Degas, and Pissarro, as well as a collection of contemporary American prints, (206) 272-4258. The **Washington State Historical Museum** (315 N Stadium Way) has some valuable Native American artifacts, including canoes, baskets, and masks from British Columbia and Puget Sound; early Tacoma memorabilia includes arresting photographs; (206) 593-2830. The Historical Museum's projected move in 1995 will take it to a new residence near the railroad depot on Pacific Avenue.

The University of Puget Sound in the north end (with its downtown law school) and **Pacific Lutheran University** in the south not only are major educational institutions but also provide a variety of cultural programs and art events open to the public.

OTHER THINGS TO DO

Point Defiance Park is situated at the west side of Tacoma; its 500 acres of untouched forest jut out into Puget Sound. Aside from its many other attractions, this park is one of the most dramatically sited and creatively planned city parks in the country. The wooded five-mile drive and hiking trails open up now and then for sweeping views of the water, Vashon Island, Gig Harbor, and the Olympic Mountains beyond. There are rose, rhododendron, Japanese, and Northwest native gardens, a railroad village with a working steam engine, a reconstruction of Fort Nisqually (originally built in 1833), a museum, a swimming beach, and the much-acclaimed zoo/aquarium. Watching the almost-continuous play of seals, sea lions, and the white Beluga whale from an underwater vantage point is a rare treat, (206) 591-5335. **Wright Park** at Division and I streets is a serene, in-city park with many trees, a duck-filled lake, and a beautifully maintained, fragrant conservatory, built of glass and steel in 1890. One of the area's largest estates and the former home of the late Corydon and Eulalie Wagner is now **Lakewold Gardens**, (12221 Gravelly Lake Drive SW; (206) 584-3360), a 10-acre estate garden on Gravelly Lake. The gracefully landscaped grounds opened to the public in May 1989. Reservations are required (open April through September); admission is $5 for adults, $4 for seniors.

The **Tacoma Dome**, the world's largest wooden dome, is the site of many entertainment and trade shows as well as a sports center. The dazzling neon sculpture by Stephen Antonakos provides a dramatic background for events such as the **Tacoma Stars'** indoor soccer games, championship ice-skating competitions, and many other regional activities. Ticket information, (206) 272-6817. **Freight House Square** (the old Milwaukee Railroad freight house), just downhill from the Dome, houses a popular central dining commons, surrounded by take-out restaurants selling everything from Jamaican jerked chicken to Korean noodles and oversized cinnamon rolls.

Fans who like their baseball played outdoors in a first-class ballpark arrive in enthusiastic droves at **Cheney Stadium** to watch the **Tacoma Tigers**, the Triple-A farm team of the Oakland A's, (206) 752-7707.

Fishing/boating: with the waters of South Puget Sound lapping at virtually half of Tacoma's city limits, it is to be expected that many Tacomans and visitors choose to spend their leisure time afloat or on the dock. There are two fishing piers jutting out from Ruston Way and public launches and boat rentals at Point Defiance.

RESTAURANTS

Pacific Rim

Corner of 9th and A,
1 block north of Pacific,
(206) 627-1009
100 S 9th, Tacoma
Expensive; full bar; AE,
MC, V; checks OK
Breakfast, lunch Mon-
Fri, dinner Tues-Sat
(reservations required)

Finally, Tacoma as a restaurant of national repute—one that can be compared to Seattle's best. Owner Bill Nevins courageously chose a site in the nearly nonticking heart of downtown Tacoma, albeit in a beautifully renovated two-story 1908 bank structure complete with marble façade and close to the Pantages Theater and the Sheraton Hotel. The restaurant works because its authentic approach is a natural for this port city—the foods of the Pacific Rim which drift into the Mediterranean on occasion. Most of the dishes are impressively stylish and exploding with flavor: a tasty, thick chunk of grilled salmon came one time with a tongue-tingling cucumber-wasabe butter and another time with a dollop of cinnamon butter. On the side was an extravagant olio of wild and domestic rice laced with shreds of brandy-soaked apricots and soft-roasted nuts. Many regular patrons choose as their main course a selection of appetizers, which invariably includes the seafood sausage served with a cognac cream sauce. Desserts are wonderful. The upstairs dining area provides a more subdued atmosphere, especially on weekends, than the narrow downstairs with its open kitchen and beautiful Italian marble and mahogany bar. Live music Wednesday through Saturday nights is played at the foot of the stairs in the lounge and filters up to the dining room. Service is competent and swift.

C.J. Shenanigan's

Take City Center exit off
I-5 and follow Schuster
Pkwy onto Ruston Way,

With the increasing number of diners looking for both good food and great views, the many restaurants bordering scenic Commencement Bay are booming. C.I. Shenanigan's is one of the best of the formula restau-

(206) 752-8811
3017 Ruston Way,
Tacoma
Moderate; full bar; AE,
DC, MC, V;
local checks only
Lunch, dinner every day,
brunch Sun

rants, and in good weather, even a sardine can't wiggle in without a reservation. The classy bar specializes in oysters on the half shell, which, with fried artichoke hearts, fresh, peelable shrimp, and a bottle of dry white wine, make a perfect way to while away a sunny afternoon on the deck. Seafood dominates both the lunch and dinner menus. While there are plenty of fancier seafood dishes, a favorite is the Fisherman's Feast, a heaping serving of clams, salmon, and prawns. Those with really gargantuan appetites will finish with mud pie—a mile-high creation (well, almost) of ice cream, cookies, fudge, whipped cream, and nuts. Subtle it is not. Good it is.

Fujiya
Between Broadway and
Market on Court C, near
the Sheraton Hotel,
(206) 627-5319
1125 Court C, Tacoma
Moderate; beer and wine;
AE, MC, V; checks OK
Lunch Mon-Fri, dinner
Mon-Sat

The Fujiya continues to be one of downtown Tacoma's more distinguished and popular eating spots, particularly for lunch. It does not take reservations, so come early if you want to be seated right away. Owner/sushi chef Masahiro Endo is a master of his craft; sit at the sushi bar, experience his often brilliant compositions of sea-briny ingredients, and watch a great performance as well. A top choice to begin a meal is gyoza. Gyoza come both fried and steamed, but the texture and flavor of the savory pork filling are more apparent in the latter. The real test of a Japanese kitchen is the tempura: here the seafood and vegetables are done to just the right golden-crisp stage.

Lessie's Southern Kitchen
6th and Division,
(206) 627-4282
1716 6th Avenue,
Tacoma
Inexpensive; no alcohol;
no credit cards; checks
OK
Breakfast, lunch, dinner
Mon-Sat (closes at 7pm)

There is no better place to abandon restraint than this comfortable cafe on this busy five-way corner. The thin, light corncakes alone are worth the trip. It's a place for those with a hankering for smothered pork chops or liver with lots of lovely onions. Or, perhaps, crusty fried chicken and barbecued ribs. Lessie, who hails from southern Alabama, dishes these all up with "sides" of yams, greens, grits, and black-eyed peas, and finishes the meal with the likes of bread pudding or sweet potato pie. Butterfish with eggs, home-fries and biscuits, and of course, a side order of corncakes, can start your day—or finish it, but what better way to go?

Pacific
Corner of 9th and Pacific,
(206) 572-3651
823 Pacific Ave, Tacoma
Inexpensive; no alcohol;
no credit cards;
checks OK
Lunch, dinner Mon-Sat

Expert techniques employing subtle contrasts produced understated Asian works of art. The same factors apply to the food of this Vietnamese addition to Tacoma's growing group of ethnic restaurants. What this family-run restaurant lacks in atmosphere, it recovers in displaying the great skill required to create the complex dishes of Vietnam. To start off, there is an addictive spring roll wrapped in butterfly wing–thin sheets of rice paper and served with a spicy peanut dip. One favorite Vietnamese special is *banh xeo*, a culinary gymnastic feat to eat. This large, eggy crêpe filled with tangled shreds of pork, shrimp, and bean sprouts, the eater then stuffs it with crisp basil, cilantro, and leaf lettuce, rolls it up, and dips it in a fish sauce. Don't be shy; if you need help, ask for it. No alcoholic beverages are served, but the French influence comes through with little pots of coffee brewed individually at your table and poured over ice.

Stanley and Seaforts Steak, Chop, and Fish House

City Center exit off I-5 to 38th, right on Pacific Ave, right on 34th,
(206) 473-7300
115 E 34th St, Tacoma
Moderate; full bar; AE, MC, V; checks OK
Lunch Mon-Fri, dinner every day

You can see it from I-5, flanked by two dramatically lit bridges, but it's still tough to find—overlooking the city and Commencement Bay. Every customer in the stepped-down dining room has a panoramic view of the city, the harbor, and, on a clear day, the Olympics. The food and service are of good quality. The standouts are still the seafood dishes, such as roasted prawns with garlic, and albacore tuna or swordfish grilled over mesquite, but the sirloin or lamb or sesame chicken are also good choices. Try a fresh berry sherbet or a piece of Key lime pie for dessert. The spacious bar features a comprehensive and distinctive selection of Scotch whiskies; since it sports the same view as the dining room, it's not surprising that it is a favorite spot to watch the sun go down.

Bimbo's

15th and Pacific,
(206) 383-5800
1516 Pacific Ave,
Tacoma
Inexpensive; full bar;AE, MC, V; local checks only
Lunch Mon-Sat, dinner every day

Since 1921, Tacomans have been flocking to this lower-Pacific Avenue Italian restaurant, where very little has changed either architecturally or gastronomically. The area around it, although its upgrading is being spurred on by the restoration of the Union Depot across the street, is still dismal. Forget the environs. Members of the original owners' family are still cooking their native Tuscan recipes, with emphasis on quality of raw materials and simple preparation. The homemade ravioli and the pasta with clams are both show-offs—the accompanying sauces, not exactly light on the oil, provide the impetus for repeated visits. The lemony tomato sauce alone will make you return, and now it's available to go—by the pint.

Engine House #9

6th and Pine,
(206) 272-3435
611 N Pine St,
Tacoma
Inexpensive; beer and wine; no credit cards; checks OK
Lunch, dinner every day

For connoisseurs of taverns, this former firehouse, listed on the National Register of Historic Places and complete with hoses, ladders, rescue nets, and brass fire pole, is a definite winner. It offers close to 50 brands of quality draft and bottled beer and ale, including the rare Xingu from the jungles of Brazil. Closer to home, Engine House #9 has now recreated Tacoma's original beer, Tacoma Brew, once the premier label of the Pacific Brewery (converted to a soap factory during Prohibition). An eatery it is too, specializing in such world-roving dishes as bangers and onions, soft tacos, and excellent pizzas. On Fridays, gourmet pizza night finds such esoteric toppings as lamb, eggplant, and pesto. The daily soups and specials are consistently good. A limited menu is served until midnight.

Harbor Lights

*City Center exit and
follow Schuster Pkwy to
Ruston Way,
(206) 752-8600
2761 Ruston Way,
Tacoma
Moderate; full bar; AE,
DC, MC, V; checks OK
Lunch Mon-Sat, dinner
every day*

Tacoma's pioneer Ruston Way waterfront restaurant still packs them in. Nothing trendy here. Decor is circa 1950, with glass floats, a stuffed marlin, and a giant lobster. The main concession to progress is a new, glassed-in sun deck. Up-to-the-minute it may not be, but that doesn't seem to bother the seafood fans who regularly crowd into the noisy dining room to consume buckets of steamed clams and plates of Columbia River smelt in season. Grilled fillet of sole is done to perfection here. The halibut and chips are the best around, as are the crisp hash browns. The usual complaint is that portions are so gargantuan that only a trencherman can clean the plate. Reservations are essential—unless you don't *mind* waiting.

Katie Downs

*Take City Center exit off
I-5, follow Schuster Pkwy
onto Ruston Way,
(206) 756-0771
3211 Ruston Way,
Tacoma
Inexpensive; beer and
wine; MC, V; checks OK
Lunch, dinner every day*

This attractively designed tavern and restaurant rates two superlatives—it has probably the most unusual pizza to be found in the south Puget Sound region, and, built above Commencement Bay, it's way up there on the view ratings. Place your order at the food counter for one of their deep dish pizzas. Do get an order of fresh steamer clams to tide you over as you wait for your pizza. Watch the ever-changing activity on the waterfront, with sea lions, hydrofoil fire boats, freighters, and sailboats all vying for attention. One caution: don't expect a quiet, restful dinner, particularly on weekends. This place is noisy, boisterous, and fun. It now delivers locally.

Le Snack Cafe Espresso

*4th and Tacoma,
(206) 272-5937
322 Tacoma Ave S,
Tacoma
Inexpensive; beer and
wine; MC, V;
local checks only
Lunch Mon-Fri, dinner
Thurs-Fri, brunch Sat*

This tiny place near Wright Park, once a Bavarian restaurant with a meat-laden menu, reopened in 1989 with new owners and a lighter menu. The "tunafish sandwich" is definitely not the lunch-box standard, but a special serving of grilled tuna on your choice of bread—succulent is not too strong a term. Entrée-sized salads, gourmet burgers (no fries, though), and pastas round out the menu. A good place for a light and tasty meal.

The Lobster Shop

*Off Dash Point Rd,
(206) 927-1513
6912 Soundview Dr NE,
Dash Point, Tacoma*

The Lobster Shop South

*City Center exit off I-5,
Schuster Pkwy to Ruston,
(206) 759-2165*

The original Lobster Shop, situated out on Dash Point, is a welcome change from the increasing number of pricey, slick eateries blossoming along the local waterfront. This sea-weathered (and nonsmoking) restaurant, tucked away next to a small public beach, is one where we particularly like to spend a blustery winter or fall evening. In the comfortable and intimate surroundings you can eat a superb grilled salmon. No wonder those who crave simply prepared, fresh seafood flock here. There is a good selection of beer and wine, although the owners never bothered to put in a bar.

4013 Ruston Way,
Tacoma
Moderate; full bar; AE,
DC, MC, V; checks OK
Dinner every day; Sunday
brunch at Ruston Way
location

The larger, swankier Lobster Shop South on the Ruston Way waterfront has a distinctly different atmosphere and menu. It provides good seafood dishes and a full bar, but has not half the personality of the original. No problem here about lighting up.

Osaka
Take 84th St exit off I-5,
(206) 588-0627
8602 S Tacoma Way,
Tacoma
Moderate; full bar; MC,
V; checks OK
Lunch, dinner every day

The influx of Asian restaurants to Tacoma's south side is barely keeping pace with the demand. Osaka is one of the best. It's similar in decor to a number of Japanese places—crisply clean and uncluttered—but with a rare warmth. All of the staff go out of their way to make you welcome, and owner/sushi chef D.Y. Kim is no exception. If you sit at the sushi bar, you'll often find extra gift portions gracing your plate, maybe of lightly smoked mackerel (called *saba*). D.Y. loves to introduce customers to the almost infinite shapes, colors, and textures of his medium. There is always one more thing to try, such as his special handroll made with crunchy salmon skin and a bit of everything else. It isn't hard to consume an exorbitant amount (and later, be surprised by an equally exorbitant bill); if money's a concern, ask for prices as you go along.

Rose Room (Sheraton Tacoma Hotel)
Between 13th and
15th on Broadway,
(206) 572-3200
1320 Broadway Plaza,
Tacoma
Expensive; full bar; AE,
DC, MC, V;
local checks only
Lunch Mon-Fri, dinner
Mon-Sat, brunch Sun

For a special-night-out-on-the-town restaurant, the Rose Room is still exciting, the ingredients still of the highest quality and delightfully presented, but the important test—the taste—just doesn't come through. Flavors often obliterate, instead of complement, each other, such as a cloyingly sweet apricot-coriander sauce on a definitely chewy piece of duck. Some mistakes may just be careless (a warm shrimp and mango salad was icebox-cold); some dishes are just bad (a pathetic oyster stew). Many entrées are good (a grilled lamb and fennel sausage was superb). There are still the special touches, such as coffee served on a silver tray with shaved chocolate and cinnamon. All in all, this elegant dining room with a gorgeous setting high above Tacoma offering a panoramic view of the mountains and Puget Sound is to be recommended.

Antique Sandwich Company
Corner of 51st and N
Pearl, 2 blocks south of
Point Defiance Park,
(206) 752-4069
5102 N Pearl, Tacoma
Inexpensive; no alcohol;
no credit cards;
checks OK
Breakfast, lunch, dinner
every day

A visit here is a little like returning to a storybook grandma's house. Plastic bears filled with honey adorn the shared tables; a roomy couch usually has several students curled up on it studying and eating; and everyone just generally has a good time. On the way to Point Defiance Park, it's also a favorite luncheon gathering place for the diaper set and their parents. Toys abound on a carpet-covered platform, which doubles as a stage when the folk or classical music concerts begin. Peanut-butter and jelly sandwiches with bananas and fresh-fruit milk shakes share the menu with big-people food such as hearty homemade soups, quiches, and a variety of other tasty sandwiches. The clam chowder is still, hands-down, the best in town. There is excellent coffee from your choice of beans. Tuesday is open-mike night, when locals perform. No smoking.

Boat House Grill

In Point Defiance Park, just west of the ferry dock, (206) 756-7336 5910 N Waterfront Dr, Tacoma Inexpensive; beer and wine; MC, V; local checks only Breakfast, lunch, dinner every day

Long closed following destruction by fire, the landmark Boathouse at Point Defiance Park has been totally rebuilt and is managed by the Metropolitan Park District of Tacoma. A wraparound deck over the water provides intimate views of nearby Gig Harbor and Vashon Island. Sometimes seals and sea lions perform here, almost more than in the nearby zoo. This is a cheery place, tastefully decorated and highlighted by a series of old photos from Tacoma's waterfront past. The food is plain and simple, but it's just fine. It starts at 6am with a fisherman's-style breakfast. They even serve biscuits with real country-style gravy. For lunch, stick with the fish and old favorites like liver and onions and chicken-fried steak. The soups are always a good bet, as are the flaky-crust pies. It's a good place for families, with kid-sized portions and special diet foods.

O'Shea's

Commerce and 9th, (206) 383-8855 786 Commerce, Tacoma Inexpensive; no alcohol; AE, MC, V; local checks only Breakfast, lunch Mon-Fri

Although the printed menu varies from week to week, the lineup of customers does not. They return for the daily hot specials, soups, salads, and sandwiches. Filled croissants add variety and show off imaginative culinary skill. Breakfasts range from simple oatmeal to eggs Benedict, with special breads, muffins, and scones to jump-start the day. The bakery also supplies diet-destroying pastries, but they're worth every cent and calorie. The only problem here: what may delight you one day may not appear again for months.

Ya Shu Yuen

Between Park and Yakima on 38th, (206) 473-1180 757 S 38th St, Tacoma Inexpensive; beer and wine; MC, V; no checks Lunch Tues-Sun, dinner Tues-Sat

Through the thicket of plastic strawberry vines and red-tasseled lamps lies the small family-run restaurant that almost all Tacoma fans of Chinese food have on their list of favorites. They come for the spring rolls, with their delicate casings and stuffing of crunchy vegetables; for the chicken with a plum sauce; or for the almost-crisp dry-braised beef. The Mandarin/Sichuan menu is limited, but what this place has it does well; the spicy dishes are properly piquant and the others strong with individual flavors.

LODGINGS

Sheraton Tacoma Hotel

Take City Center exit off I-5; between 13th and 15th on Broadway,

The Sheraton Tacoma Hotel, with its elegant decor, 319 rooms, and two restaurants, has filled a real need in Tacoma. Adjacent to the massive Tacoma Convention Center, it's most suitable for conventions. Most

(206) 572-3200
1320 Broadway Plaza,
Tacoma, WA 98402
Expensive; AE, DC, MC,
V; checks OK

rooms look out over Commencement Bay or have a view of Mount Rainier. The more expensive concierge rooms on the 24th and 25th floors include a continental breakfast and early-evening hors d'oeuvres. Guests can eat either at the Wintergarden, attractively situated off the mezzanine balcony, or on top of the hotel in the scenic Rose Room (see review). The Music Room on the side of the lobby offers a restful place for afternoon tea or drinks, and Elliott's bar offers a plentiful array of appetizers to placate the after-work customers.

GIG HARBOR

By land and water, weekend vacationers flock to the small fishing community of Gig Harbor. It's still home port for an active commercial fishing fleet, and the good anchorage and various moorage docks also attract gunwale-to-gunwale pleasure craft. There are many interesting shops and galleries for browsing, and when the clouds break, Mount Rainier holds court for all. There's an annual arts festival in mid-July.

Nearby, **Kopachuck State Park** is a popular destination, as are **Penrose Point** and **RFK state parks** on the Key Peninsula, all with numerous beaches for clam digging. (Purdy Spit and Maple Hollow Park are the most accessible spots.) At **Minter Creek State Hatchery** the public can watch the various developmental stages of over four million coho salmon.

Performance Circle (6615 38th Ave NW, (206) 851-7529), Gig Harbor's resident theater group, mounts seven enjoyable productions from July to March, with summer shows staged outside in the meadow at Celebrations, 9916 Peacock Hill Avenue NW. Theatergoers bring picnics and blankets, watching the shows beneath the stars. It's turning into a wonderful small-town custom. Celebrations is open for meals (brunch is especially abundant).

RESTAURANTS

Tides Tavern
Harborview and
Soundview,
(206) 858-3982
2925 Harborview Dr,
Gig Harbor
Inexpensive; beer and
wine; MC, V; checks OK
Lunch, dinner every day

While the locals still claim this as theirs (after all, it was the General Store for decades), on sunny days and weekends boaters, bikers, and the "over the bridge" crowd come in droves. Even a family of otters lives under the deck. When the sun is out, you have to scramble for a table on the deck, but wherever you sit you will enjoy the hearty sandwiches, burgers, and pizzas. The double shrimp salad is a local favorite. Owner Pete Stanley is planning to enlarge the kitchen and provide table service (you now place your own order at the bar), but promises the spirit of this old tavern won't go, even though the pool tables might have to, as they command the best view.

W.B. Scotts Restaurant
Corner of Harborview
and Pioneer,
(206) 858-6163

Gig Harbor, sadly, still lacks a restaurant commensurate with its location, but W.B.'s offers the best quality and service in town. Not on the water, but on the main street, this attractive restaurant does good

3108 Harborview Dr,
Gig Harbor
Moderate; full bar; AE,
DC, MC, V; checks OK
Breakfast, lunch, dinner
every day

things to its numerous seafood and chicken dishes, like adding a crunchy walnut crust to a piece of flaky halibut. The chicken in the justly popular fajitas manages to stay moist and imbued with flavor. At lunch, satisfy yourself with a hot seafood salad or choose from among the six types of hamburgers, served with a tangle of fried potato frizzies. A piano bar (with a lounge menu served after 2pm) brings in the after-dinner crowd.

LODGINGS

The Pillars
Take the first Gig Harbor
exit off Hwy 16,
(206) 851-6644
6606 Soundview Dr,
Gig Harbor, WA 98335
Expensive; MC, V;
checks OK

From the windows of this landmark Gig Harbor house overlooking Puget Sound you can see Colvos Passage, Vashon Island, and Mount Rainier. It's a newly opened guest house with all three guest rooms beautifully decorated, large private baths, and separate reading areas furnished with writing desks and telephones. An added bonus is the covered, heated swimming pool and Jacuzzi. Breakfasts feature home-baked breads and muffins. No smoking. No children (except by special arrangement) or pets.

No Cabbages B&B
On the east side of the
harbor; call for directions,
(206) 858-7797
7712 Goodman Dr NW,
Gig Harbor, WA 98332
Inexpensive; no credit
cards; checks OK

If you are looking for an unstructured and relaxed environment in an old, well-loved beach house with a friendly, laid-back hostess who happens to be an accomplished cook, No Cabbages may be perfect for you. After reluctantly getting out of your bed—which has an intimate view of the harbor—you might start the day with a large glass of freshly squeezed orange juice, a Brie and green apple omelet, and all the freshly ground coffee you can drink. There is boating, and it's a superb place for bird watching—great blue herons nest nearby, and there are always a clutter of gulls, terns, grebes, ducks, and cormorants. The knotty-pine interior is filled with Northwest arts and crafts; the two guest rooms (with shared bath) have a separate entrance.

STEILACOOM

Once an Indian village and later Washington Territory's second incorporated town (1854), Steilacoom today is a quiet village of old trees and houses, with no vestige of its heyday, when a trolley line ran from Bair's drugstore to Tacoma. October's **Apple Squeeze Festival** and mid-summer's **Salmon Bake**, with canoe and kayak races, are popular drawing cards.

The **Steilacoom Tribal Museum** is located in a turn-of-the-century church overlooking the South Sound islands and the entire Olympic Mountain range. Ferries run to Anderson Island, with restricted runs to McNeil Island (a state penitentiary); call the Pierce County Public Works Department for more information; (206) 591-7250.

RESTAURANTS

ER Rogers
*Corner of Commercial
and Wilkes, off
Steilacoom Blvd,
(206) 582-0280
1702 Commercial St,
Steilacoom
Moderate; full bar; MC,
V; checks OK
Dinner every day, brunch
Sun*

View restaurants on Puget Sound are not novelties, but views like this one are still exceptional, particularly when seen from a restored Queen Anne–style home built about 100 years ago. The halibut baked in parchment paper is noteworthy, but the Steilacoom special prime rib, first roasted, then sliced and quickly seared, is still tops. You can't beat the huge Sunday buffet brunch, with its large selection of seafood: oysters on the half shell, cold poached salmon, flavorful smoked salmon, cracked crab, pickled herring, steamed clams, and fettuccine with shrimp. There is a beautiful upstairs bar with a widow's walk just wide enough for one row of tables. Fresh flowers appear in unexpected places, and chamber music plays softly in the background.

**Bair Drug
and Hardware Store**
*Lafayette and Wilkes,
(206) 588-9668
1617 Lafayette St,
Steilacoom
Inexpensive; beer and
wine; AE, MC, V; local
checks only
Breakfast, lunch
Tues- Sun*

Side orders of nostalgia are presented gratis when you step into Bair's. Except for the customers, little has changed since it was built—in 1895. Products your grandparents might have used—cigars, washtubs, perfume and apple peelers—are still on display. Old post office boxes mask the bakery, which turns out pies and pastries such as flaky apple dumplings; the potbelly stove warms customers in the winter. Best of all, there is a 1906 soda fountain, where you can still get a sarsaparilla, a Green River, or a real ice cream soda.

ANDERSON ISLAND

LODGINGS

Anderson House on Oro Bay
*Head south from ferry for
3½ miles to head of Oro
Bay, (206) 884-4088
12024 Eckenstam-
Johnson Rd, Anderson
Island, WA 98303
Moderate; MC, V;
checks OK*

Anderson Island, for the moment, is still one of the best-kept secrets on Puget Sound. A short ferry ride from Steilacoom, and a few miles from the ferry dock is a large red house surrounded by 200 acres of woods. The house has four large bedrooms, some with private bath, beautifully furnished with antiques (many have been in this pioneer family since 1840). Since hosts Randy and B. Anderson stay next door at grandfather's home, guests have the run of the house. The two-bedroom cottage next door is good for small groups. Full farm breakfasts feature breads hot from the oven, fruit pizzas and other treats. Since this is isolated country—no stores or restaurants—the Anderson's will also serve lunch or dinner, perhaps a seven-course Greek meal; Randy's an excellent chef. Available on a weekly basis is a remodeled cedar fishing cabin (wood stove–heated) that sleeps eight, located on outer Amsterdam Bay. Truly a hideaway (no children, no pets, no smoking). A short bike ride from the Anderson

House brings you to the west side of the island, where your own mile-long secluded beach is backed by old-growth forest and has a dramatic view of the Olympics.

OLYMPIA

The capitol's centerpiece is the classic dome of the Washington State Legislative Building. Lavishly fitted out with bronze and marble, this striking Romanesque structure houses the offices of the Governor and other state executives. The State Senate and House of Representatives meet here in annual sessions that can be viewed by visitors.

Just opposite the Legislative Building rises the pillared Temple of Justice, seat of the State Supreme Court. To the west is the red brick Governor's Mansion, open to visitors on Wednesday afternoons from 1pm to 2:45pm. Reservations must be made in advance, (206) 586-TOUR.

Handsomest of the newer state buildings is Paul Thiry's squarish State Library, directly behind the Legislative Building. Open to the public during business hours, it boasts a unique nonobjective mural by Washington's best-known painter, the late Mark Tobey and artifacts from the state's early history. At 211 West 21st Avenue, the State Capitol Museum, (206) 753-2580, permanent exhibit includes an outstanding collection of western Washington Indian baskets.

Downtown, on 7th Avenue between Washington and Franklin streets, is the restored Old Capitol, whose pointed towers and high-arched windows suggest a late medieval chateau. In another part of the downtown, just off the Plum Street exit from I-5, and adjacent to City Hall, is the newly installed Yashiro Japanese Garden, which honors one of Olympia's sister cities.

There is also a triad of colleges here: The Evergreen State College (TESC), west of Olympia, on Cooper Point; St. Martin's, a Benedictine monastery and college in adjacent Lacey; and South Puget Sound Community College, just across Highway 101. Though TESC is relatively new, its innovative educational policies have already won national praise. It offers a regular schedule of plays, films, and experimental theater, as well as special events like its annual February Tribute to Asia. Its library and pool are public; (206) 866-6000, ext. 6128.

In Olympia proper, the Washington Center for the Performing Arts (on Washington Street between 5th Avenue and Legion Way) has brought new life to the downtown. In the same block is the Marianne Partlow Gallery, a leading outlet for contemporary painting and sculpture. Across 5th Avenue, the Capitol Theatre provides a showcase for the offerings of the active Olympia Film Society as well as for locally produced plays and musicals. Toward the harbor, at the corner of North Capitol Way and West Thurston Street, is the lively Olympia Farmer's Market, which displays produce, flowers, and crafts from all over the South Sound; open Thursday through Sunday during the growing season.

Wholly different in character is West 4th Avenue between Columbia and Water streets, a hangout for students and ex-students, artists and would-be-artists, gays, lesbians, and counterculture members. Increasingly, Percival Landing (a new waterfront park) is becoming a community focal point, the site of harbor festivals of all kinds. The historic heart of the whole area (Olympia, Lacey, and Tumwater) is Tumwater Falls, where the Deschutes River flows into Capitol Lake. Established here today is the chief local industry, the Tumwater Division of the Pabst Brewing Company with free daily tours.

The area's finest nature preserve lies well outside the city limits. This is the relatively unspoiled **Nisqually Delta**—outlet of a river that rises on a Mount Rainier glacier and enters the Sound just north of Olympia. Take exit 115 off I-5 and follow the signs to the **Nisqually National Wildlife Refuge.** From here, a 5-mile hiking trail follows an old dike around the delta, a wetland alive with bird life. Just south, a rookery of great blue herons occupies the treetops.

RESTAURANTS

Bristol House
Off Evergreen Park Dr,
(206) 352-9494
2401 Bristol Ct SW,
Olympia
Moderate; full bar; MC,
V; checks OK
Breakfast Sun-Fri, lunch
Mon-Fri, dinner
Tues-Sat

Adolf Schmidt (of the Olympia Brewery founding family) is owner and chef at this cheerful place, located in the rapidly developing professional office area south of the Thurston County courthouse. His menu has greatly expanded in the past two years. His Bacardi Beef may be the best steak available in town, and he offers such unusual creations as curried prawns served with mushrooms, raisins, and grapes. An excellent dessert is chocolate mousse prepared with either Grand Marnier or creme de cacao. The wine list is conservative but sufficiently comprehensive. Go at dinner if you want to take full advantage of the chef's ingenuity; lunches are adequate, but relatively uninspired. Service is fast and professional. Overseeing all this, with an appropriately no-nonsense mien, is a gold-framed portrait of an avuncular Schmidt ancestor who looks as though he would tolerate no inefficiency.

Fleur de Lys
1 block east of Plum St,
(206) 754-6208
901 E Legion Way,
Olympia
Moderate; beer and wine;
MC, V; checks OK
Lunch Tues-Fri, dinner
Fri-Sat

Owner/chef Jim Jones offers his traditional continental cuisine in this friendly, unpretentious country-style restaurant. Both lunch and dinner menus are unusually large. Seafood frittata and chicken sauté sec with port wine and mushrooms are available at lunch, and salmon en croute, topped with crab in flaky pastry, and raspberry chicken at dinner. Star selections are the beef Wellington and the Grand Marnier souffle. Special care has been taken with the wine list; Jones offers several French wines, as well as selections from Washington and California. Over the years, Jones hasn't varied his menu much, but since he offers so many choices, his regular patrons are well satisfied.

Gardner's Seafood
and Pasta
North on Capitol Way to
Thurston,
(206) 786-8466
111 W Thurston St,
Olympia
Moderate; beer and wine;
AE, MC, V; checks OK
Dinner Tues-Sat

Loyal Gardner's fans consider that this small place, across from the Farmer's Market, serves the best seafood in Olympia. Here the rambunctious geoduck has been thoroughly tamed. A true Puget Sound specialty is an appetizer of a dozen Calm Cove Olympia oysters, each the size of a quarter, served on the half shell. Interesting soups include rock shrimp with dill; a variety of pastas are available with or without seafood. A Dungeness crab casserole is sauteed with bacon, green onions, mushrooms, Chablis, and cream and topped with mozzarella and Cheddar cheeses. Connoisseurs of ice cream won't want to pass up Gardner's homemade product. Because of the restaurant's small size and popularity, early reservations are advisable.

La Petite Maison

1 block south of Division and Harrison,
(206) 943-8812
2005 Ascension Ave NW,
Olympia
Moderate; beer and wine;
MC, V; checks OK
Lunch Mon-Fri, dinner Tues-Sat

This tiny, converted 1890s farmhouse—now overshadowed by a beetling new office building— is a quiet, elegant refuge for Olympians seeking imaginative, skillfully prepared Northwest cuisine. Among its specialty appetizers are steamed Kamiche clams and mussels, and delicate and flavorful Dungeness crab cakes served with a dill sauce. Entrées include perfectly sautéed medallions of pork with tangy Dijon mustard sauce and fresh poached petrale sole stuffed with salmon mousse. The tender sautéed venison comes with a rich juniper-berry sauce. In spring or summer, it's pleasant to sit on the restaurant's glassed-in porch—though the view of over-trafficked Division Street outside may make you long for the days when this place was truly a farm.

Seven Gables

¾ mile north of the 4th Ave bridge,
(206) 352-2349
1205 W Bay Dr, Olympia
Moderate; beer and wine;
MC, V; checks OK
Dinner Tues-Sat, brunch Sun

Visually, this dinner house is the most striking restaurant in Olympia, occupying as it does the fine old Carpenter Gothic residence built by the city's turn-of-the-century mayor, George B. Lane. The site takes full advantage of a splendid Mount Rainier view, and the surrounding gardens are tended with loving care by owner Sally Parke. The menu includes numerous steaks, including steak Neptune, a filet of tenderloin stuffed with crab and served with hollandaise sauce. Among seafood dishes are Indienne crab and prawns, or Dungeness crab and prawns sauteed with pea pods and chutney in a curry cream sauce. A daily special might be tilapia, a flavorful freshwater white fish, sautéed in sherry and topped with brandied pecans.

Ben Moore's

On 4th Ave, east of Columbia,
(206) 357-7527
112 4th Ave, Olympia
Inexpensive; full bar;AE,
MC, V; checks OK
Breakfast, lunch, dinner Mon-Sat

Ben Moore's plain exterior, which looks as though it hasn't changed much since the time of the New Deal, should not succeed in hiding from anyone that behind it there holds sway one of the most talented chefs in the area. Mike Murphy is in charge, and if you order any of his prawn, oyster, or steak dinners, you'll get a lot to eat, and none of it is likely to disappoint. Prices are out of a bygone era; the costliest complete dinner is a New York steak with prawns at $13.95.

Budd Bay Cafe

Between A and B on Columbia,
(206) 357-6963
525 N Columbia St,
Olympia
Moderate; full bar; AE,
DC, MC, V; checks OK

There's no doubt about it: the Budd Bay Cafe, with its long row of tables looking out across Budd Inlet, has suddenly become the preferred after-hours haunt of many of today's legislators, lobbyists, and state-government movers and shakers. Restaurateur John Senner is on hand most of the time, seeing that everyone is satisfied. Don't look for elaborate dishes here; the menu (steaks, sandwiches, pasta, salads, seafood)

Breakfast Sat, lunch Mon-Sat, dinner every day, brunch Sun

is designed for boaters and people to whom good talk matters more than haute cuisine. It's also more expensive than many places in town. Sunday brunch features eggs Benedict and oysters on the half shell, either fresh or baked with pesto. The bar is pleasant and lively, and there's a long list of specialty beers. This place has become such a scene that you wonder what people were doing before it opened.

Chattery Down

Across from the Capitol Theatre, (206) 352-9301 209 5th Ave E, Olympia Moderate; beer and wine; AE, MC, V; checks OK Breakfast, lunch, dinner Mon-Sat

This small dining room which began as an annex to Ann Buck's gift shop next door has proven so successful that it's almost taken over the whole place. For lunch, there are homemade breads, interesting soups like lemon broccoli bisque, and salads. Many patrons prefer Fridays, when an oyster dish is always on the menu— angels on horseback, oyster stew, or chowder. Or Saturday mornings when a full breakfast is served instead of the weekday continental fare. Dinner specials change daily, but might include paupiettes of sole stuffed with spinach and salmon mousse or steak and prawns Monique, served in a dill cream sauce. Lighter dinners are offered at a lighter price; vegetarian dishes too. Some patrons (many single) come in only for the appetizers, such as oysters Rockefeller or baked Brie with pesto. High tea Wednesdays and Saturdays.

Falls Terrace

Across the Deschutes River from the Olympia Brewery, (206) 943-7830 106 Deschutes Way, Tumwater Moderate; full bar; AE, DC, MC, V; checks OK Lunch, dinner every day

It would be hard to find an Olympian who hasn't had at least one meal at this longtime Tumwater institution; anyone wanting to eat at regular hours should get reservations. Part of the reason for its popularity is its splendid setting, overlooking the Tumwater Falls of the Deschutes River. There's a wide variety of steak, lamb and chicken dishes, along with a fried version of the delectable Olympia oysters (we prefer them raw). The menu also includes a bouillabaisse, containing prawns, lobster, salmon, crab and clams. Ice cream desserts are featured; apple strudel cream is essentially a generously portioned version of pie à la mode. The wine list is not for connoisseurs, but Irish coffee is available as an after-dinner drink. The adjacent bar, one of the most agreeable drinking spots in town.

Mark's After Five

Near Washington Center for the Performing Arts, (206) 786-8448 204 E 5th, Olympia Moderate; beer and wine; MC, V; checks OK Dinner Tues-Sat

This is an understated, low-key dinner restaurant which in a relatively short time has attracted a loyal following of regulars. Its short, deceptively simple menu consists of seafood, steak, and combinations of the two. There's often a fresh catch of the day (like sautéed rock cod) alongside an offering of prawns and oysters. The calamari, sautéed in butter and white wine, is fresh and simple. The beef mushroom soup is excellent, the wine list limited, and service courteous.

The Spar

1 block east of Capitol Way, (206) 357-6444
114 E 4th Ave,
Olympia
Inexpensive; AE, MC, V; checks OK
Breakfast, lunch, dinner every day

Above the restaurant's old-fashioned booths are blown-up Darius Kinsey photos of teams of old-time loggers beaming over unbelievably mammoth trees they've just brought to earth. Indeed, some 60-odd years ago, the Spar used to be known as a workingman's hangout. Today it's wholly classless, with a volatile mixture of students, attorneys, businesspeople, artists, politicians, fishermen, tourists, and leisured retirees. The Spar's robust milk shakes, thick turkey sandwiches, and homemade bread pudding are all locally acclaimed, as is its water, which comes from its own artesian well. Willapa Bay oysters or fresh salmon from the Farmer's Market are sometimes available; the prime rib dinner is popular on weekends. Conversations at the long, J-shaped counter range from state house scandals to the probable origin of the galaxies.

Touch of Europe

Just north of the Capitol grounds, (206) 754-5152
1023 Capitol Way S,
Olympia
Moderate; beer and wine; AE, MC, V; checks OK
Lunch Mon-Fri, dinner Mon-Sat

Srecko-Felix Korpar is a fervent Croatian national whose food has a strong Dalmatian flavor. Dinner is usually more interesting than lunch: calamari Dubrovnik, a Greek salad, and many variations on the schnitzel theme. Agramar veal honors the German name for the Croatian city of Zagreb. It consists of four pieces of tender Provimi veal stuffed with ham and cheese. The house clam chowder is red and spicy. Like some of their European counterparts, the waitstaff are helpful with suggestions. The wine list is impressively topped by Dom Perignon, though the decor is an incongrous and unsuccessful American Art Deco. The dinner music—Chopin mazurkas, Beethoven sonatas—sounds just right.

Tug's Restaurant and Bar

Off Harrison at
W Bay Dr,
(206) 352-2261
2100 W Bay Dr, Olympia
Moderate; full bar; AE, MC, V; local checks OK
Lunch Mon-Fri, dinner every day

Tug's is located at Olympia's West Bay Marina where many of the area's finest sailing craft are moored. The peak of Mount Rainier is just visible to the west; to the north are the crests of the Olympics. Though steak and prime rib are on the menu here, seafood is emphasized; a special might be baked sole fillets wrapped around a mixture of cream cheese, Parmesan, and bay shrimp. On the regular menu is a seafood salad, including scallops, Dungeness crab, and shrimp; there's also a smoked salmon and scallop fettuccine tossed in a whiskey cream sauce. Salads are available in half portions.

Urban Onion

Legion and Washington,
(206) 943-9242
116 Legion Way, Olympia
Moderate; beer and wine; AE, MC, V; checks OK
Breakfast, lunch, dinner every day

The site of many a power lunch for Olympia's rising breed of feminist politicians, the Urban Onion retains a faint flavor of the counterculture of the '60s. A signature dish is an especially satisfying lentil soup. The Mexican chicken grilled with mushrooms is also outstanding. Breakfasts include a hefty huevos rancheros. The Urban Onion has recently expanded into the lobby of the former Olympian Hotel, and meeting space is available.

Wagner's European Bakery and Cafe

*Capitol Way and Union,
(206) 357-7268
1013 S Capitol Way,
Olympia
Moderate; no alcohol; no
credit cards; checks OK
Continental breakfast,
lunch Mon-Sat*

Almost as *echt deutsch* as an opera by that other well-known Wagner is the formidable collection of pastries regularly produced by Rudi Wagner's bakery, which effortlessly fabricates stuff like apricot squares, raspberry mousse tortes, pig's ears, cream horns, several species of doughnuts, and all kinds of fresh-baked breads. Toothsome Black Forest tortes whirl temptingly in a display case. An attached cafe, featuring light breakfast and lunch, has expanded to serve many more customers. German-born Wagner, chief baker as well as owner, gets new ideas on trips back to Europe.

LODGINGS

Harbinger Inn

*1 mile north of State St,
(206) 754-0389
1136 E Bay Dr, Olympia,
WA 98506
Moderate; AE, MC, V;
checks OK*

Occupying a restored 1910 mansion, this B&B offers Edwardian furnishings, a fine outlook over Budd Inlet and the distant Olympic mountains, and four choice guest rooms (two with views, two without). Nicest is the two-room suite on the view side, which has its own bath (all other rooms share); but rooms on the back side are farther from the street, with only the sound of a small-artesian-fed waterfall to disturb the tranquillity. The inn is situated near excellent routes for bicycle riding, and complimentary bicycles are available. A light breakfast of fresh fruit and home-baked pastry is served. Under new owners Terrell and Marisa Williams, the place remains pleasant and well maintained, with a bright garden in front to welcome you.

Westwater Inn

*Exit 104 from I-5,
(206) 943-4000
2300 Evergreen Park Dr,
Olympia, WA 98802
Moderate; full bar; AE,
DC, MC, V; checks OK
Lunch Mon-Fri, dinner
Mon-Sat, brunch Sun*

Few urban hotels around Puget Sound take such striking advantage of the Northwest's natural beauty as this one, dramatically perched on a high bluff above Capitol Lake, with much greenery in view, and the Capitol dome—illuminated by night—rising to the north. There are fairly large rooms, a heated outdoor pool (seasonal), a year-round Jacuzzi, and an entertainment lounge presenting live music Tuesday through Saturday nights. Some rooms can be noisy, so it's advisable to request one on the water side. Meals are served at an almost continuously operated coffee shop, and at Ceazans, a restaurant with as scenic an outlook as any in town. A Sunday brunch concentrates on an impressive variety of desserts.

TENINO

Wolf Haven (3111 Offut Lake Road, (206)264-4695) is an educational research facility that teaches wolf appreciation and studies the question of whether to reintroduce them into the wild. The public is invited to see the wolves or join them in a "howl in."

RESTAURANTS

Alice's Restaurant
Call for directions,
(206) 264-2887
19248 Johnson Creek Rd
SE, Tenino
Moderate; beer and wine;
AE, DC, MC, V;
checks OK
Dinner Wed-Sun

Just getting there is half the fun. For the modern, freeway-frazzled driver, it's like going back into a vanished epoch to take old Highway 99 from Olympia to Tenino, and then to turn right into the unspoiled reaches of the remote Skookumchuck Valley. Located in a fine turn-of-the century farmhouse on a lively little creek, Alice's serves hearty dinners, all including crudités, creamy peanut-butter soup, a green salad, trout, an entrée, and choice of dessert. The price of each entrée determines the price of dinner (baked ham with pineapple glaze, fresh oysters, a selection of game dishes, perhaps quail, and even catfish). In conjunction with the restaurant, Ann and Vincent de Bellis operate the Johnson Creek Winery. (You will be invited for a pre-dinner tour and tasting when you call for reservations.) Advance reservations are required.

YELM

RESTAURANTS

Arnold's Country Inn
Across from the Thriftway
Shopping Center,
(206) 458-3977
717 Yelm Ave E, Yelm
Moderate; full bar; AE,
MC, V; checks OK
Breakfast Sat-Sun,
lunch, dinner Tues-Sun

Long known as one of Olympia's most accomplished chefs, Arnold Ball has established his latest restaurant just outside Yelm on the road leading from the state Capitol to Northwest Trek (see Eatonville section) and Mount Rainier. Steaks and meat dishes dominate here. But besides steak Diane, there are familiar Arnold's specialties such as chicken sautéed with raspberry brandy, roast ducking à l'orange, and traditional escargots. Arnold is careful with small details: his rolls baked on the premises are warm and delicious, as are his fine pies. His wine list is adequate, but many patrons are happy to drive all the way from Olympia just for the food.

WASHINGTON

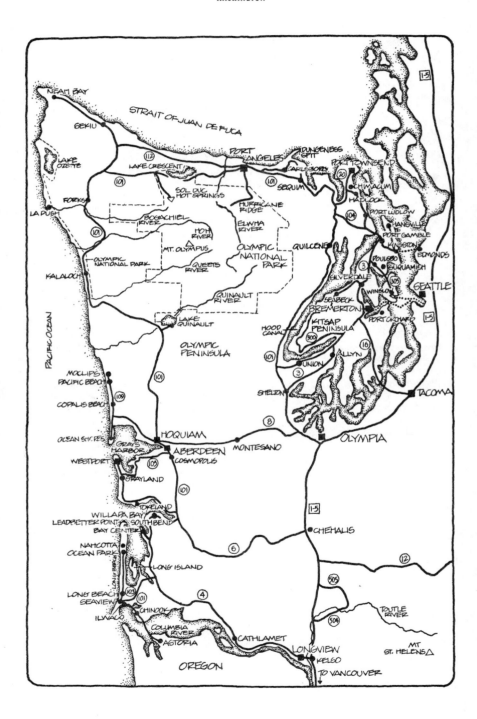

OLYMPIC PENINSULA

The Kitsap Peninsula north to the Hood Canal Bridge, then west along the Juan de Fuca shore of the Olympic Peninsula and southward along the Pacific Coast to Ocean Shores.

BREMERTON

Bremerton, as even many residents will admit, can seem a pretty dismal place. Its first reason for existing is its huge U.S. Naval Shipyard; and the Trident nuclear submarine base, across the Kitsap Peninsula in Bangor, has brought frenetic boom to the entire area. Bremerton sometimes seems built of tough sailors' taverns at the center and endless roadside sprawl at the edges. The town has found a new tourist identity since it lost its ace, the battleship **USS Missouri**— but the **USS Nimitz** will most likely be moored here until the Everett Naval Base is complete. Some lesser, older warships are still here to be seen from outside the shipyard fences. The **Bremerton Naval Museum**, near the ferry terminal, tells of shipbuilding history back to bowsprit-and-sail days; (206) 479-7447, closed Mondays. A foot ferry (walk-on only) runs the Seattle-Bremerton route on weekdays; call the Bremerton terminal for schedule, (206) 478-4902.

RESTAURANTS

Boat Shed
East side of Manette Bridge, on the water,
(206) 377-2600
101 Shore Dr, Bremerton
Inexpensive; full bar;
MC, V; local checks only
Lunch Mon-Sat, dinner every day

A mile from the ferry landing is this nautical place, not far from the road but perched grandly out over the water. The food runs to seafood, sandwiches, and salads; at lunchtime you wait in a long line to look at the menu (during which you should commission one member of your party to grab a table on the deck), but the line moves fast and the hearty food is worth it. Try the Skipjack Sandwich, with three kinds of cheese, red onions, and chopped olives in hot pita bread. The nachos, perhaps the most generously bedecked in the region, are also the *best* in the region.

LODGINGS

Willcox House
9 miles south of Seabeck,
(206) 830-4492
2390 Tekiu Rd,
Bremerton, WA 98312
Expensive; MC, V;
checks OK

Seventeen miles west of Bremerton, this Art Deco manse on 242-mile-long Hood Canal is surprisingly polished. It was originally the lavish home of Colonel Julian and Constance Willcox (and their eight servants;) later it became a school for boys, and for a few years it was an adult retreat. Three years ago Philip and Cecilia Hughes opened it as Hood Canal's first inn. Other inns have since followed, but this large 1936 octagonal red-tiled house with an unusual copper roof is the Canal's most opulent. The entryway—once faux marble—is softened with a padded white silk, the living room is paneled in walnut with a large copper fireplace, and the library (our favorite room here) looks out over the colorful garden and unheated saltwater lap pool. The five bedrooms (all with baths en suite, two with Jacuzzis, one with a fireplace) are impressive. Hope for a stormy night and reserve the lavish Mrs. Constance Willcox's Room with its stone fireplace. After one of Cecilia's satisfying breakfasts, the rest of the day (and the oyster-laden beach) is yours. That is, until teatime (once a month) or dinner (Saturdays only); both by reservation only. It's a half-hour drive from the Bremerton ferry, though some prefer to take a seaplane right to the Hughes' dock.

PORT ORCHARD

Fifteen minutes by car from Bremerton, a wander through this charming port makes for a fine afternoon jaunt. **Olde Central Antique Mall** on Bay Street is full of pottery, stained-glass, and crafts shops, antique shops and restaurants.

ALLYN

RESTAURANTS

Bellagamba's Restaurant and Lounge
On Lakeland Dr in the main clubhouse; look for signs; (206) 275-2871 Lakeland Village Golf Course, Allyn
Moderate; full bar; MC, V; checks OK
Lunch, dinner Wed-Sun (winter hours may vary)

This romantic downstairs restaurant has its roots in the original Bellagamba's in Shelton. It's a charming sliver of a space, with an intimate loft and a serene outlook onto a pond and a lake beyond. The menu includes a few each of fish, pasta, beef, and chicken entrées. But, Gentle Diner, choose wisely: you are in the heart of shellfish country, with impeccably fresh oysters and steamed mussels that have surely been plucked off the beach that morning. With dinners come big baked spuds, wild rice, or fettuccine; a basket of warm, yeasty bread; pedestrian shrimp-and-lettuce salads with excellent homemade dressings; and side plates of stir-fried zucchini. The wine list (and their willingness to uncork any white to try by the glass) impressed us. Have dessert.

UNION

RESTAURANTS

Victoria's
¼ mile west of Alderbrook Inn on Hwy 106,
(206) 898-4400

Inside a large A-frame adorned with wooden beams and log-style walls, this dining room makes up in charm for any misgivings we may have about the food. An open fireplace sets off a view of Hood Canal beyond; outside

E 6791 Hwy 106, Union
Moderate; full bar; MC,
V; checks OK
Breakfast Sat-Sun,
lunch, dinner every day

is a beautiful garden-terrace with a stream running alongside—quite idyllic. Its culinary aspirations, while high, do not quite measure up to the setting. The local seafood is the safest bet, and often the freshest—even though the chef's talents stem from Northern Italy.

SHELTON

RESTAURANTS

Cafe Luna
In the Mercantile Mall at
3rd and Railroad,
(206) 427-8709
221 W Railroad St,
Shelton
Moderate; beer and wine;
no credit cards;
checks OK
Dinner Thurs-Sun

Here's a place you'd never expect to find this far out on the Peninsula. This pretty little gray-green Art Deco restaurant with its silvery fingernail new moons hanging from ceiling and glued to walls is an oasis in this tough lumber town. Evening pastas are excellent. The salads are carefully executed and delicious; the rest of the menu is filled with various Mediterranean dishes, from North African to Spanish to Middle Eastern. For dessert, try the perfect chocolate mousse, generously filling a tulip glass and prettily topped with a flying spiral of orange peel. No smoking.

SILVERDALE

RESTAURANTS

Yacht Club Broiler
From 305 take Silverdale
exit, first right into town,
then left on Bayshore,
(206) 698-1601
9226 Bayshore Dr,
Silverdale
Moderate; full bar; MC,
V; checks OK
Lunch, dinner every day,
brunch Sun

In an office building on Dyes Inlet is Silverdale's swankiest restaurant, opened a few years ago by Brett Hayfield (of Bremerton's Boat Shed), Andy Graham, and Alan Quick. The tables aren't packed every night, the prices are a bit more than locals would like, and there's no actual yacht club in sight (though it *is* on the water). For dinner you select from the specials sheet: perhaps roast duckling in a raspberry brandy sauce, or baked halibut, with a lightly breaded crunch, surrounded with a subtle vermouth-cream demiglace. The deck is a good spot for lunches and after-work appetizers (try the prawns and scallops in a black bean, garlic, and cream sauce). Each day Graham selects about a dozen wines by the glass from the extensive list of over 90 bottlings. Desserts are refreshingly simple; the IBC Root Beer Float is a great way to go.

LODGINGS

Silverdale on the Bay
Resort Hotel
Silverdale Way and
Bucklin Hill Rd,

Inside, tasteful design highlights serene views over Dyes Inlet. Each view room has a private balcony, remote-control TV, and clock radio; mini-suites are the best. Extras establish it as the resort it aspires to be;

(206) 698-1000
3073 Bucklin Hill Rd,
Silverdale,
WA 98383
Moderate; full bar; AE,
DC, MC, V; checks OK
Breakfast, lunch, dinner
every day

an indoor lap pool with sliding glass doors that open onto a large brick sun deck (where you can sip cool drinks all afternoon if you'd like), a sauna, weight room, pool tables, video game room, boat dock, and convention facilities. The Mariner Restaurant offers white-linened tables, professional service, and expertly prepared dinners that aren't too pricey. Young, conscientiously trained hands toss the Caesar salads at tableside and light the flambés—showy food that sometimes misses the mark but is often pleasing.

POULSBO

This attractive small community that hugs a fine harbor wears its Scandinavian heritage on its sleeve. Somehow, the heavy dose of heritage comes across in good taste and with good cheer.

Sluys Bakery is surely a diabolical initiative by the League of Scandinavian Dentists. Inside you'll find sweets galore, (*too* sweet, some say) in manifestations that can barely be imagined. As well as the Nordic goodies, Sluys bakes bread that is estimably healthful. A local specialty, Poulsbo Bread, is distributed nationally; there are also various Scandinavian loaves; 18924 Front Street NE, (206) 779-2798.

At the end of a pier on Fjord Drive in the Liberty Bay Marina is **Marie's Wild & Woolly**, selling quality yarns. It's the only shop we know of with a knitting deck looking out on the marina; (206) 779-3222.

Lemolo Custom Meats is particularly well known for its curing and smoking of hams, bacon, jerky, and salmon; there's a full range of locally raised meat; 17166 Lemolo Shore Drive, 1.5 miles out of Poulsbo towards Seattle, (206) 779-2447.

LODGINGS

Manor Farm Inn
½ hour from Winslow
ferry dock off Hwy 3 on
Big Valley Rd,
(206) 779-4628
26069 Big Valley Rd NE,
Poulsbo, WA 98370
Expensive; MC, V; local
checks only
Breakfast, dinner
every day

A lavish retreat in the middle of nowhere, Manor Farm is a working farm with horses, sheep, dairy cows, chickens, and a trout pond—a beguiling mix of the raw and the cultivated that succeeds in spoiling even the city-bred. Englishman Robin Hughes, a former veterinarian, and his wife Jill, a Los Angeles native, are the proprietors who run a superlative accommodation and pour heart and soul into the food. There are eight bright, airy guest rooms (two have fireplaces; most have private baths), and a hot tub bubbles in what is maybe a too-central location (at the entrance to the restaurant). Best are the cottages. The farm cottage is across the road, with vaulted ceilings, French country-pine antiques, down comforters, and Robin's own watercolors. A newer addition is the beach house on Hood Canal with two-plus bedrooms, plenty of decks, and an inviting hot tub. Adjacent to the farmhouse is a 50-person conference center. Future plans include a larger conference area, spa facility, tennis courts and, ideally, a winery. Our advice is to visit before the place is overrun, and book early.

Breakfast happens twice at Manor Farm: first a tray of hot scones and orange juice is left at your door; then (for non-guests as well), at 9am, there are fresh fruit, oatmeal folded with whipped cream, eggs from the farm chickens, and rashers of bacon. (Ample, but too simple for the $12 prix fixe.) Dinner is even more of an event: a one-seating (6:30pm) six-course affair that begins with sherry and hors d'oeuvres in the lovely drawing room, where Robin Hughes will announce chef Rob Harris's evening's preparations. You proceed to the dining room for soup, salad, and appetizer. The entrée might be a sautéed chicken breast fragrant with rosemary, or perhaps halibut with papaya and honey. The finish is dessert, port, coffee—a proper finale for what aspires to be a proper English meal. The result is food that's pleasant, but nothing special; prix fixe is $40 Fridays and Saturday and $30 other nights (with only four courses). Wine and service not included.

SUQUAMISH

In Suquamish on the Port Madison Indian Reservation (follow the signs past Agate Pass), the **Suquamish Museum** in the Tribal Center is devoted to studying and displaying Puget Sound Salish Indian culture; (206) 598-3311. **Chief Sealth's grave** can be found nearby, on the grounds of St. Peter's Catholic Mission Church. Twin dugout canoes rest on a log frame over the stone, which reads, "The firm friend of the whites, and for him the city of Seattle was named."

PORT GAMBLE

Built in the mid-19th century by the Pope & Talbot timber people, who traveled here by clipper ship from Maine, this is the essence of the company town. Everything is company-owned and -maintained, and the dozen or so Victorian houses are beauties and in splendid repair. The town, which was modeled on a New England village, also boasts a lovely church, a vital and well-stocked company store, and a historical museum—down the steps and in back of the store—that is a gem. An ideal presentation of a community's society and industrial heritage, it was designed by Alec James, who designed the displays for the Royal Provincial Museum in Victoria. The lumber mill, incidentally, is still in operation and proves to be an interesting sight. Unfortunately, a grand hotel that sat on a splendid bluff overlooking the water was razed in the 1960s; the hotel's splendid lobby is re-created in the museum. For more information, call (206) 297-3341.

HANSVILLE

Just beyond the unassuming fishing town of Hansville are a couple of the prettiest, most accessible, and least explored beaches on the peninsula. To the east is **Point No Point**, marked by a lighthouse and great for kids and families, as there's a parking lot just steps away. Follow the road from Hansville to the west and you'll come across **Cape Foulweather**. The short trail through the woods is tough to find, so look for the Nature Conservancy sign on the south side of the road.

QUILCENE

RESTAURANTS

Loggers Landing
At the south end of town on Hwy 101,
(206) 765-3161
30281 Hwy 101 S,
Quilcene
Inexpensive; beer and wine; MC, V; local checks only
Breakfast, lunch, dinner every day

It's easy to be thrown off by this modest building and its cement floors. From behind the counter comes a clam chowder fragrant with large pieces of tender bivalve, snippets of bacon, inch-square cubes of potato, and secret seasoning. Or join the forest workers, who use this place as their mess hall, for the logger's breakfast ($7.95): OJ, a hefty 8-ounce steak, hash browns, three eggs, toast, and coffee refills. The place is packed with locals, and the service is no-nonsense friendly.

The Timber House
About ½ mile south of Quilcene on Hwy 101,
(206) 765-3339
Hwy 101 S,
Quilcene
Moderate; full bar; MC, V; checks OK
Lunch, dinner Wed-Mon

The Timber House, a charming place, resembles nothing so much as a large and rough-hewn hunting lodge. Although the menu is not without more pretentious items, the local seafood is the thing to go for. Quilcene oysters come from right down the road, and there's much more from the waters around the Sound. Sautéed Dungeness crab is a winner, as are the scallops Timber House, sautéed with mushrooms and onions and bathed in a Mornay sauce. Even the deep-fried selections that make up the Captain's Plate are nicely done and not oven-battered.

PORT LUDLOW

LODGINGS

The Resort at Port Ludlow
6 miles north of the Hood Canal Bridge on the west side, (206) 437-2222
9483 Oak Bay Rd, Port Ludlow, WA 98365

While you're dining at the Harbormaster Restaurant, imagine the same view being enjoyed by old Cyrus Walker—Pope & Talbot's legendary 1880s sawmill manager. His "biggest damn cabin on the Sound" (actually a splendid Victorian manse) once occupied this site with its eye-filling Olympic peaks, teardrop bay, and rolling, timber-covered hills. Now 148 units, indoor

Expensive; AE, DC, MC, V; checks OK

and outdoor pools, a marina, seven tennis courts, a championship golf course, hiking and cycling trails, and a hidden waterfall fill the 1,500 developed acres. All of the individually decorated suites have fireplaces, kitchens, and private decks; many include views of the water. The suites with lofts are grand, but other rooms boast outlooks just as lovely onto the countryside. Port Ludlow also hosts a good number of conventions; at other resorts, these usually prove to be the kiss of death for a romantic weekend, but here a feeling of spaciousness acts as a serene buffer. In the Harbormaster, Northwest salmon and Dungeness crab are our dinner recommendations. Lunches are nothing much, but the breakfast fried potatoes and seafood omelets are treats.

CHIMACUM

RESTAURANTS

The Chimacum Cafe
9 miles south of Port Townsend,
(206) 732-4631
4900 Rhododendron Dr,
Chimacum
Inexpensive; no alcohol;
MC, V; checks OK
Breakfast, lunch, dinner
every day

Sunny atmosphere and cheerful help have created a fiercely loyal, mostly local, clientele who'll argue with anyone who denies this place serves the best diner food on the Peninsula. Draws are the succulent homemade pies and farm-style meals, including special Sunday chicken dinners with gravy made the old-fashioned way. Friday clam chowder is a knockout.

PORT TOWNSEND

Riding high until the 1890s, the city fell flat when the Union Pacific failed to hook up the town with its transcontinental rail system. Lucky city, for people's energies aimed in other directions, and dozens of Victorian houses and commercial structures were spared. Though the area's economy is still fragile, these buildings are the pride of the region and a reason in themselves for a visit.

Architecture. The town's charm can be quickly taken in on a walking tour of Water Street, an agreeable stretch of ornate old brick-and-stone buildings mostly erected about the same time Seattle's Pioneer Square was being rebuilt from the fire of 1889 (and in some cases by the same architects). Pick up a tour map from the Visitor's Center at 2437 E Sims Way, (206) 385-2722, to check out the town's mansions. Notable are the Daniel Logan House (Taylor and Lawrence), with an iron roof crest; Bartlett House (end of Polk Street on the bluff) with its famous mansard roof; and the Ann Starrett Mansion (Adams and Clay), with a bed and breakfast in its 1890 Stick-style architecture (see review). Buildings open for public tours are the Jefferson County Courthouse (Washington and Jefferson), with its clock tower and fantasy-castle appearance; City Hall (Water and Madison), with a fine museum, a jail, a restored Victorian hearse, and every

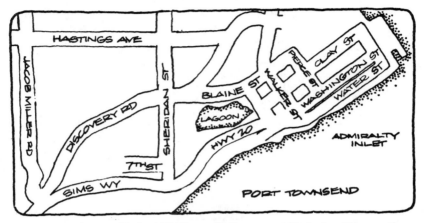

imaginable whatnot; Rothschild House (Jefferson and Taylor), with an antique rose garden and period rooms with breathtaking views; and the Commanding Officer's House at Fort Worden (see review).

Chetzemoka Park, in the northeast corner of town, has a charming gazebo, picnic tables, tall firs, and a grassy slope down to the beach; you can also gobble up blackberries here during the fall.

Events. Old homes can be toured the first weekend in May and the third weekend in September—always worth doing. **The Rhododendron Festival** in May, with a parade and crowning of the queen, is the oldest festival in town. The **Centrum Summer Arts Festival**, (206) 385-3102, one of the most successful cultural programs in the state, with dance, fiddle tunes, chamber music, a writers' conference, jazz, and theater performances, runs at Fort Worden from June to September. The **Wooden Boat Festival**, (206) 385-3628, first weekend in September, is a charming bit of creative anachronism. The **Poverty Playhouse** provides film and live productions (from theater to storytelling) every weekend throughout the year. There are suggested donations, but if you can't afford a ticket, you'll get in free; 419 Washington, (206) 385-5923.

Wandering. On Water Street you'll find colorful shops. **Earthenworks** deals in ceramic and graphic arts; **Captain's Gallery** has an amazing selection of pricey kaleidoscopes; **Imprint Book Store** is a superior bookshop, well stocked with classics, best sellers, regional books, and a great selection of contemporary verse; **Phoenix Rising** offers all angles of New Age culture, from self-help and astrology books to crystals and aromatic oils. The best ice-cream cone can be had at **Elevated Ice Cream**, the best pastry at **Bread & Roses Bakery**, and the best antique selection at **Port Townsend Antique Mall**, 802 Washington, where about 40 antique merchants have convened under one roof. For a nip with the natives, head for **Back Alley Tavern** for live music and local color, or the historic **Town Tavern**, where the pool tables, the huge bar, and the owner's great taste in music draw an interesting assortment of people. Finally, check out the retail revitalization of uptown Port Townsend at **Aldrich's** (Lawrence and Tyler), an authentic 1890s general store come to life with an upscale twist.

The Victoria Clipper runs daily from Seattle and Friday Harbor; call for reservations toll-free (800) 888-2535 or (206) 448-5000.

RESTAURANTS

Cafe Piccolo
*On Hwy 20 about a mile
outside of town,*
(206) 385-1403
3040 Hwy 20,
Port Townsend
Moderate; beer and wine;
MC, V; checks OK
Dinner every day

In a welcome change from menus saturated with Port Townsend funk, Cafe Piccolo opts for the simple preparations and fresh ingredients of Italian food. Owner Farnham Hogue brought 20 years of cooking experience up from San Francisco, assessed the local dining scene, and opened his "little cafe" with the help of his wife Nancy and sister (and partner) Patricia Hodge. Hogue's menu borrows flavors and textures from all over the Italian boot, from a wonderfully marinated *bistecca alla fiorentina* to Sicilian fisherman's stew. There's a selection of pizzas (they're meant to be one-person, but they're *huge*) in different combinations. Pastas are nicely prepared, with a judicious choice of ingredients.

Chula's Bar and Grill
In the Marina district,
(206) 385-7474
2330 Washington St,
Port Townsend
Moderate; full bar; AE,
MC, V; checks OK
*Lunch Mon-Fri, dinner
every day*

Families dress up in their embroidered blouses and bolo ties to eat at this evolving Southwestern eatery. An acidy purple, yellow, and peach mural (painted by a native Texan) unrolls along one wall, but this is no screaming tequila joint. A guitarist in the corner strums mellow renditions of easy-listening tunes, and service is young but pleasant. Chips and good, piquant salsa arrive promptly at the table; potent margaritas come in three sizes. Texans Eric and Dawn Dobson combine regional Mexican recipes with local ingredients (most notably, fresh seafood) and a healthy dose of innovation; some of the specials hint of Caribbean and Asian influences. On one visit, an achingly tender swordfish steak came prettily (and successfully) crisscrossed with three different sauces—cilantro cream, black bean, and mild ancho—and accompanied by little vegetable dim sum. For the less adventurous, there are a number of solid renditions of the Mexican standards.

Fountain Cafe
*At the Port Townsend
fountain steps,*
(206) 385-1364
920 Washington St,
Port Townsend
Moderate; beer and wine;
MC, V; checks OK
Lunch, dinner every day

Locals are proud to bring their out-of-town guests here. And they'll line up several deep in the cozy storefront dining room to inspect quirky local art on the walls and wait for a table. Chances are they've come for the oysters, on the menu in a variety of preparations, including pan-fried, or one of the fresh (but uninspired) pasta-and-shellfish dishes. Things can get spicy—our oysters diablo with black squid-ink linguine was downright satanic—and someone in the kitchen has a penchant for pepper. But the wine list is good. And you'd have to be loony not to try the loganberry fool for dessert. Service is courteous even with patrons queued in front.

The Landfall
North end of Water St,
(206) 385-5814
412 Water St,

This funky neighborhood standby, with its octagonal boathouse-style add-on and a wood stove for warming up Point Hudson winters, is frequented for its burgers and fish and chips. But the nicely seasoned cod and

Port Townsend
Moderate; beer and wine;
no credit cards;
checks OK
Breakfast, lunch every
day, dinner Wed-Sun

tender grilled salmon, with flavorful brown rice on the side, are also highly respectable. So are the prices. The menu features some Mexican selections. A typical Port Townsend touch: restrooms are out back.

Salal Cafe
Quincy and Water,
(206) 385-6532
634 Water St,
Port Townsend
Moderate; beer and wine;
no credit cards; local
checks only
Breakfast, lunch Wed-
Sun, dinner Wed-Sat

Breakfasts are justly famous here, with a couple of morning newspapers circulating and locals trading stories back in the solarium. The omelets are legendary—we like the avocado with homemade salsa and the spinach and feta cheese—and cheese blintzes, oyster scrambles, and tofu dishes are satisfying. The lunch menu—plus a couple of specials—doubles as the dinner menu, but the light, cheerful atmosphere here is really more fitting for the morning meal.

Silverwater Cafe
On Quincy St, near the
old ferry dock,
(206) 385-6448
126 Quincy St,
Port Townsend
Moderate; beer and wine;
MC, V; local checks only
Lunch Mon-Sat, dinner
every day, brunch Sun

Port Townsend's New Age slant is captured inside the four walls of the Silverwater Cafe. Light music floats through the air, colorful banners with mystical symbols decorate the walls, and meals are approached from a holistic, healthy angle. The Silverwater favors simple, fairly light preparations, which usually include rice, lots of veggies, and a couple of unusual ingredients (a tarragon pesto, for example, on a warm shellfish salad). The fish selections are what draw the raves here (Canterbury oysters, salmon, and an additional daily fresh shellfish), but there are chicken and beef entrées and a couple of wholesome standbys (stir-fry, pasta primavera) for vegetarians. Desserts deviate from the peaceful example set by dinner and the atmosphere; a chocolate espresso cheesecake was a zinger.

Khu Larb Thai
Off Water St on Adams,
(206) 385-5023
225 Adams St,
Port Townsend
Inexpensive; beer and
wine; MC, V; local
checks only
Lunch, dinner every day

Locals rave about this authentic Thai spot—Port Townsend's only southeast Asian fare in its eclectic dining scene—but warn first-timers to be wary of blithely adding hotness. The no-MSG meals can be prepared from one star (mild) to five stars (extremely hot) to Thai hot, which is simply "not recommended." There's sure to be something on the nearly-50-item menu for everyone. A calm, pleasant place with accommodating service and intriguing silverware.

LODGINGS

The James House

*Corner of Washington
and Harrison,*
(206) 385-1238
*1238 Washington St, Port
Townsend, WA 98368*
*Moderate; MC, V; checks
OK*

The legendary Bogarts are gone, but everything's still up to snuff at the James House—arguably one of the most pleasant places to stay in the state. This fine Victorian B&B now rests in the competent hands of Carol McGough and Anne Tiernan, who are still improving it, continually freshening the rooms and the pretty garden. All 12 rooms are beautifully furnished in antiques; those in the front of the house have the best views out across the water. Not all rooms have private baths, but the shared facilities are spacious and well equipped. The main floor has two sumptuous adjoining parlors, each with a fireplace and plenty of stimulating reading material. Guests can look forward to fresh fruit, granola, homemade baked goods, and quiche or eggs at breakfast, either at the big table in the formal dining room or in the kitchen with its antique cookstove.

Hastings House/Old Consulate Inn

*At the intersection of
Washington and Walker
on the bluff,*
(206) 385-6753
*313 Walker St, Port
Townsend, WA 98368*
*Expensive; MC, V;
checks OK*

One of the most photographed Victorians in these parts, this former German consulate is one of the most comfortable and nonstuffy, with its wraparound porch and Sound views. Finishing touches are being made by owners Rob and Joanna Jackson, who most recently turned a dirt basement (where prior to World War I German seamen used to wait for safe passage home) into a cozily dark pool-and-cards room with a working wood stove. All of the immaculate rooms have private baths; most are closet-sized (from their former incarnations as, well, closets), but guests in the Master Suite can soak and admire a gracious view at the same time. The third floor Tower Suite, with a sweeping bay view and dripping with lace, is a honeymooner's dream. Mammoth, 7-course breakfasts—over which Joanna will be more than delighted to wittily recount the inn's history—are made only with natural ingredients and include a heavenly liqueur cake at the end.

Heritage House

*Corner of Washington
and Pierce,*
(206) 385-6800
*305 Pierce St, Port
Townsend, WA 98368*
*Moderate; MC, V;
checks OK*

An immaculate yard welcomes visitors to this hillcrest Victorian B&B. The sprightly variety of refinished antiques matches guest rooms with names like Lilac and Morning Glory. Four of the six rooms have private baths; the Peach Blossom has an oak-and-tin clawfooted bathtub that folds away when not in use. Relax in the evenings on the porch swing, in the mornings over breakfasts of decadent French toast with fresh fruit. Children over eight are permitted, but pets are not. Views over the North Sound and the business district come close to rivaling those of Heritage's venerable neighbor, the James House.

Ann Starrett Mansion

Corner of Clay and

The most opulent Victorian in Port Townsend, this 1889 multigabled Queen Anne hybrid appears to have

Adams, (206) 385-3205
744 Clay St, Port
Townsend, WA 98368
Moderate; AE, MC, V;
checks OK

thrived under the ownership of Edel and Bob Sokol. The spiral stairway, octagonal tower, and "scandalous" ceiling fresco (the Four Seasons, complete with unclad winter maiden) are visually stunning. All rooms are antique-furnished and have high ceilings and lovely decorating touches. But all in all, it's not as impressive as it sounds, and not everyone feels comfortable here. The color scheme may throw the artistically inclined for a loop. The Drawing Room (with a tin claw-footed bathtub) opens to fabulous views of the Sound and Mount Baker, while the new, romantic Gable Suite, which occupies the whole third floor, has a skylight (also with a knockout view) and ample seating area. The less-expensive brick Carriage Room (billed as being on Carriage House Level) feels more like a basement room, with old carriage doors and a sleigh bed. Breakfasts, served in stately Victorian splendor, are a dieter's nightmare; Sunday breakfast is a chocoholic's dream. The house is open for tours from noon until three o'clock, which may be disgruntling for those who like their privacy.

Fort Worden
1 mile north of
Port Townsend,
(206) 385-4730
Mail: PO Box 574, Fort
Worden State Park
Conference Center, Port
Townsend, WA 98368
Moderate; no credit cards;
checks OK

Fort Worden was one of three artillery posts built at the turn of the century to guard the entrances of Puget Sound. The troops have since marched away, and the massive gun mounts on the bluff have been stripped of their iron, but the beautifully situated fort has become a state park, a conference center, the site of the splendid Centrum arts festival, and an unusual place to stay.

Twenty-four former officers' quarters, nobly proportioned structures dating back to 1904, front the old parade ground. These houses, including a few duplexes with period reproductions, have been made into decent lodgings. They are wonderfully spacious, each has a complete kitchen, and the rates are bargains—from $55 for one bedroom to $180 for a house with six bedrooms. Reservations should be made well in advance (the office recommends a year to the day). A picturesque lighthouse adjoins the primitive beach; the hill and parade ground where scenes for the film *An Officer and a Gentleman* were shot inspire some great imagining. The adventuresome find the maze of empty bunkers an endless source of delight, and the summer festival lends an enlightened note to it all.

Lizzie's
Near the corner of Lincoln
and Pierce in the historic
district, (206) 385-4168

Lizzie, the wife of a tugboat captain, put the deed of this model of Victorian excess in her own name; her name now graces a B&B as well as a line of lotions and sweet bubble baths created by friendly owners Patti and Bill Wickline. Breakfast, served in a huge, cheerful farm kitchen, can turn into a friendly kaffeeklatsch; a soak in the tub in the black-and-white corner bath-

731 Pierce St, Port
Townsend, WA 98368
Moderate; MC, V;
checks OK

room—especially if the sun is slanting in—is a Victorian treat. There are views from half of the eight bedrooms, and flowered decor. Two parlors, once frequented by former boardinghouse tenants, seem to have been plucked from the past; in one you'll even find a vintage stereoscope and a basket of photos to look at.

Palace Hotel
Near the corner of Water
and Tyler,
(206) 385-0773
1002 Water St, Port
Townsend, WA 98368
Moderate; AE, MC, V;
checks OK

Right downtown, this 1889 Romanesque building places visitors in the midst of Port Townsend's shopping and gawking district. Shops, eateries, and rare examples of Victorian seaport architecture are everywhere. The 15 rooms retain the ex-bordello atmosphere; Marie's (the venerable madame of the house until the mid-1930s) Room is decorated in the original shades of burgundy and forest green. Prices are within most budgets, ranging from $54 to $95. The Skogman family has added a new lobby, so check-in is a little less confusing, and hopes to add a Victorian teahouse and restaurant upstairs. Warning: long flights of stairs, though handsome reminders of another era, are a challenge to the infirm or impatient guest.

Ravenscroft Inn
Corner of Quincy and
Clay on the bluff,
(206) 385-2784
533 Quincy St, Port
Townsend, WA 98368
Moderate; MC, V;
checks OK

It's set apart from other Port Townsend bed and breakfasts by virtue of its vintage: this airy inn was built in 1987. New owners Leah Hammar and John Ranney brought 16,000 pounds of antiques with them when they arrived at Ravenscroft, but have managed to keep the place free from clutter, which makes this the perfect option for the visitor weary of Port Townsend's unremitting Victoriana. Seven immaculate rooms are currently available, all with private bath and nice touches (fireplaces, heated towel racks). An attic suite is currently underway, with plans for window seats, a teak-covered soaking tub, and sleeping arrangements for four. Breakfast is served on separate tables adjacent to the huge kitchen; plates and coffee cups are kept full under the watchful eyes of Leah and John.

SEQUIM

Until about 16 years ago, Sequim (pronounced *skwim*) was one of Washington's best-kept secrets. The town sits smack in the middle of the "rain shadow" cast by the Olympic Mountains: cacti grow wild here, the sun shines, glaciated mountains border New England–style saltwater coves, and the fishing's just fine. Now Sequim's been discovered and is growing. Farms have become subdivisions and golf courses sprout in what used to be grainfields. Retirees form the bulk of the new population, and their influence colors Sequim's transformation from a quiet cultural community into a semisuburban town. Peninsula Partners (Mitsubishi Corporation, Lowe Enterprises Northwest, and Shimizu Corporation) has been laying the groundwork for the establishment of a huge—and controversial—Cape Discovery Resort.

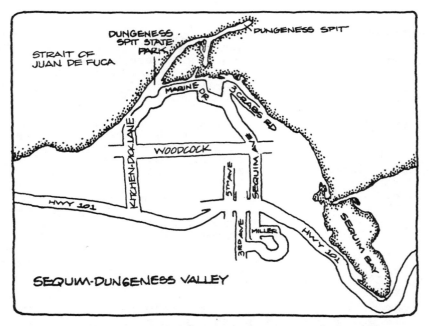

Cedarbrook Herb Farm (open March through Christmas, 9am to 5pm daily) has a vast range of herb plants, scented geraniums, and fresh-cut herbs. The owners have cultivated many unusual items, such as salad burnet and elephant garlic. Good gift shop. 986 Sequim Ave S, (206) 683-7733.

Olympic Game Farm breeds endangered species and raises a line of beasts for Hollywood; a nice drive-through, 5 miles north of Sequim in Dungeness, (206) 683-4295.

Dungeness Spit, six miles northwest, is a national wildlife refuge for birds (though duck hunting is allowed in season) and the longest sandspit in the country (a favorite spot for horseback riders during the off season). The driftwood displays are extraordinary and the winds are often good for kite-flying. Call (206) 683-5847 for camping information.

Two wineries are in the vicinity: **Lost Mountain Winery** offers tours and tastings when they're open, 3142 Lost Mountain Road, (206) 683-5229; **Neuharth Winery** is open daily for tastings in summer (winter hours vary), 148 Still Road, (206) 683-9652.

RESTAURANTS

Casoni's

1½ miles west of Sequim on Hwy 101 at Carlsborg Junction, (206) 683-2415 104 Hooker Rd, Sequim Moderate; full bar; AE, DC, MC, V; checks OK Dinner Wed-Sun (every day in summer)

★

The popularity of Casoni's sparkling-clean Italian restaurant is undeniable. Perhaps it's the lingering memory of the fresh pasta served alongside veal Marsala, or perhaps it's the gray-haired warmth of Mama Casoni herself that keeps diners returning for more. The tender calamari and the very fresh salads with homemade dressing are enough to bring us back, though we're still wary of the overpowering sauces which are sometimes too much for Mama's delicate noodles. The delectable desserts, such as the peanut-butter–chocolate-chip cheesecake, are another area in which Mama goes too far.

Oak Table Cafe
1 block south of Hwy 101
at 3rd and Bell,
(206) 683-2179
292 W Bell St, Sequim
Inexpensive; no alcohol;
no credit cards;
checks OK
Breakfast every day,
lunch Mon-Fri

There's good news for fans of the Oak Table's breakfasts: a new room has expanded the restaurant's seating area, so weekend waits for huge omelets, fresh-fruit crêpes, or legendary, gigantic, puffy apple pancakes are considerably lessened. Service is friendly and efficient—the coffee keeps coming—and the cream is the real thing. Lunches are lighter, with quiches, sandwiches, and seafood salads. It's noisy and boisterous and chatty. Espresso is served all day.

Hiway 101 Diner
Hwy 101, Sequim,
(206) 683-3388
392 W Washington,
Sequim
Inexpensive; beer and
wine; no credit cards;
checks OK
Breakfast, lunch, dinner
every day

It's not as aggressively kitschy as, say, the Beeliner Diner in Seattle, but for the laid-back folks in sunny Sequim, that's just fine. The retro-'50s theme extends to the back end of the '56 T-bird (which is actually a CD player stocked with 2,400 selections) and a healthy dose of neon, but they don't push it much further than that: this is just a diner, and a pretty good one at that. Breakfasts are standard omelets and combination fare, but it's in the burger-and-pizza area that this place really shines. Burgers are juicy, two-fisted events loaded with your choice of toppings (the Nifty Fifty, a fully dressed quarter pounder, is quite popular), and a chicken breast sandwich was uncommonly moist and tender. Pizzas come Chicago style with all sorts of toppings. Service is a gamble; one waitress ignored her tables while another provided toys to distract hungry children.

Three Crabs
Turn north from Hwy 101
onto Sequim Ave, head 5
miles toward the beach,
(206) 683-4264
101 Three Crabs Rd,
Sequim
Moderate; full bar; MC,
V; checks OK
Lunch, dinner every day

A trip to Dungeness Spit is not complete without a stop at Three Crabs. The Dungeness crab is one of the major culinary delights of the Northwest, and this modest place right on the beach is the place where many pay tribute to the sweet, flavorful creature. Unfortunately, the reputation here way outclasses the reality. A dated overfondness for deep-fried seafood—not even the salmon escapes breading—and lack of regard for the food's presentation (limp, tired dyed-apple-ring garnishes) leave us wondering about the weekend hordes. Order the whole, crack-it-yourself Dungeness crab (they get it all year round) and try for a table overlooking the bay. Pies are baked on the premises.

LODGINGS

Juan de Fuca Cottages
7 miles north of Sequim,

You can't go wrong at any of these charming and comfortable (although pricey for what you get) cabins: four

(206) 683-4433
561 Marine Dr,
Sequim, WA 98382
Moderate; no credit cards;
checks OK

overlook Dungeness Spit, one overlooks the Olympics, and a two-bedroom suite has both views. Each is equipped with kitchen utensils, a TV, a clock radio, and reading material; outside is the spit, begging for beach walks and clam hunts. Two-night minimum stay on weekends.

Groveland Cottage
Follow signs from Sequim
to Three Crabs,
(206) 683-3565
1673 Sequim Dungeness
Way, Dungeness,
WA 98382
Moderate; MC, V;
checks OK

Simone Nichol's place is only a spit away from Dungeness, and the rooms have that comfortable salty-air feel of a comfortable old beach house, plus fair weather that's almost a guarantee. This 90-year-old building has four cheerful rooms upstairs (with cheerful names to match) and—it comes with the territory—a gift and food store below (but look carefully—you can find some pretty jewelry and fragrant, locally-made potpourris among the t-shirts). Avoid the dark one-room cottage out back with its awkward approach through the cluttered yard. The place fills up in the summer with guests addicted to Simone's amenities, such as receiving the newspaper and coffee in your room before her four-course breakfast.

PORT ANGELES

Hardly a tourist trap, the town offers a fine, broad harbor and one interesting architectural artifact, the Clallam County Museum. Built in the Georgian style in 1914 as the county courthouse, the building makes a strong, distinctive statement (except for an incongruous, ultramodern added-on wing). Its collections tell a low-key story of local history and industry. Lincoln and 4th, (206) 452-7831

Port Angeles is the jumping-off point to both Victoria (via the privately owned Black Ball Ferry, (206) 457-4491) and the north (and most popular) end of **Olympic National Park**. The park fills the interior of the Peninsula. The often-inclement weather ensures a low human population and large numbers of elk, deer, bear, and (on the highest crags) mountain goats. Follow the signs to the visitors' center, (206) 452-0330, and stop in for an orientation to the area. Then drive 17 miles along winding precipices to an expansive view that few mountains with twice the altitude can offer (the Olympics make only the 6,000–8,000–foot range). **Hurricane Ridge**, with restrooms and snack facilities, sits among spectacular vistas. The best time to see wildflowers is after mid-July; in winter there is good cross-country skiing and a Poma-only downhill area (weekends only). It is always wise to check current road conditions by calling a 24-hour recorded message, (206) 452-9235, before you set out.

If you prefer the low road to the high, for a more relaxing form of recreation you'll find the Elwha natural hot springs in the backcountry west of Port Angeles. Call the visitors' center for hiking and camping information: (206) 452-0330.

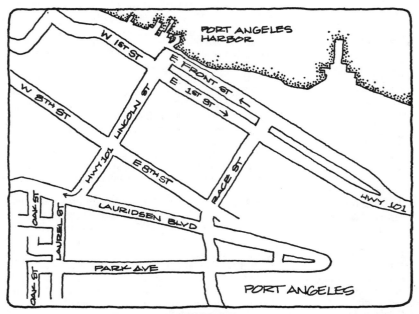

RESTAURANTS

C'est Si Bon

4 miles east of Port Angeles on Hwy 101, (206) 452-8888 2300 Hwy 101 E, Port Angeles Expensive; full bar; AE, DC, MC, V; no checks Dinner Tues-Sun

An odd place to find such an affected French restaurant—just east of Port Angeles on Highway 101—the room is pleasant (if a bit *too* precious) with tables set with crisp linens and polished silver, and large windows overlooking the rose garden. The menu is classical French (escargots au Pernod, coquilles St. Jacques, tournedos royal) with a few specials including a delectable sturgeon or succulent veal Normande prepared with apples and calvados. It's especially busy on Saturday nights, which continually overwhelms the staff (and makes for very slow service). The background music is most annoying.

China First

Between Eunice and Francis, (206) 457-1647 633 E 1st St, Port Angeles Inexpensive; full bar; MC, V; local checks only Lunch Tues-Fri and Sun, dinner every day

China First won't seem like much more than a typical Chinese joint on the main road out of Port Angeles, but Khoan Vong, a Vietnamese chef trained in Hong Kong, whips up some exceptional fish selections with remarkable flair. We left our table by the little carp-filled pool raving about tender stir-fried oysters with black beans and spicy sautéed squid; the lemon duck and marinated barbecued pork ribs were outstanding as well. Unfortunately, most customers order the standard combinations, which are, well, standard, but at least not swimming in grease and a nice amount of food for the price. Service is quite slow; the restaurant is large, and there is only one chef behind the grill.

First Street Haven

1st and Laurel, next to the Toggery, (206) 457-0352
107 E 1st St,
Port Angeles
Inexpensive; no alcohol; no credit cards; checks OK
Breakfast, lunch Mon-Sat, brunch Sun

It's just a skinny slot of a restaurant, easily missed among the storefronts if you're not paying attention, but it's the best place in Port Angeles for informal breakfasts and lunches. Fresh and unusual salads with homemade dressings, hearty sandwiches, pastas, and quiche constitute the menu, with pleasing arrangements of fresh fruit on the side. We've heard great things about the chili and fajitas. Expertly made espresso and their own coffee blend are fine jumpstarters, especially with a fresh blueberry muffin or sour-cream coffee cake. Prices are reasonable, service friendly and attentive, the air smoke-free.

The Coffee House Restaurant and Gallery

1st and Lincoln,
(206) 452-1459
118 E 1st St,
Port Angeles
Inexpensive; no alcohol; no credit cards; local checks only
Breakfast, lunch, early dinner Mon-Sat

Port Angeles' countercultural minority calls this urban place home: the bulletin board lists all the alternative events that the newspaper skips, and the menu lists adventurous, mostly vegetarian, fare and eclectic espresso drinks (which most peninsula restaurants skip). There's some form of entertainment—music or poetry readings—here every Friday night and some Saturdays and there's always local art on the walls. We like their original sandwiches (try the Middle Eastern), the sweet-potato biscuits, and other inventions, including the vegetable cream-cheese turnover and the homemade fresh fruit pockets. Hang out with a cup of caffeine and a sweet, sumptuous truffle or two. No smoking—this *is* an art gallery.

LODGINGS

Lake Crescent Lodge

20 miles west of Port Angeles on Hwy 101,
(206) 928-3211
Mail: HC 62, Box 11,
Port Angeles, WA 98362
Moderate; AE, DC, MC, V; checks OK
Closed mid-Nov-April

Some places never change, and in the case of Lake Crescent Lodge, it's a good thing. The lodgings are comfortable and well worn, but well kept up. The main building has a grand verandah (marvelous for reading or for afternoon tea) overlooking the placid, enormous, mountain-girt lake, and the cabins have nice porches. The service is just fine: eager college kids having a nice summer. Fishing (for a fighting *crescenti* trout, found only in this lake), hiking, evening nature programs, and boating are the main activities. The food is merely adequate, but the bar is above average.

We recommend staying in the motel rooms or in one of the cabins that have fireplaces; the main lodge is, as they say, rustic—a euphemism that means, among other things, the bathroom is down the hall—and noisy.

Tudor Inn

11th and Oak,
(206) 452-3138
1108 S Oak St, Port

One of the best-looking buildings in town, a completely restored Tudor-style bed and breakfast, is located 12 blocks from the ferry terminal in an unassuming neighborhood. Owners Jane and Jerry Glass are friendly

Angeles, WA 98362
Moderate; MC, V;
checks OK

hosts and well versed in Port Angeles political and cultural life; even their popular cat, Toby, is a character. Their house boasts a well-stocked library, fireplace, crisp linens, and antique touches here and there. The rooms are quite small (the Glasses are in the process of adding a private bath to each one), but the best one has wonderful views of both the Strait of Juan de Fuca and the Olympics. Breakfast is usually English traditional (bacon, eggs, muffins, fresh fruit juice, and coffee), although Mrs. Glass will surprise her guests occasionally with treats such as sourdough pancakes. Other pluses include transportation to and from the ferry dock and the airport (with advance notice), afternoon tea, winter ski packages, and hosts who really know the town.

Pond Motel

½ mile west of city limits,
(206) 452-8422
196 Hwy 101 W, Port
Angeles, WA 98362
Inexpensive; MC, V;
checks OK

Six rooms overlook an acre-big pond where bufflehead ducks and mallards float by and two pet rainbow trout occasionally stir the serene water. Frank and Jo Kelly, the friendly owners of this unassuming arrangement, are gradually relandscaping the area; pretty little meadows and quiet moments show up unexpectedly here and there. The rooms are clean and spare—and very reasonably priced. There are two single rooms (dark, but sort of cozy) next to the office, and two bigger rooms equipped with vintage '40s kitchenettes. There's occasional noise from Highway 101, which runs right by, but the *place* is so quiet, it hardly seems to matter.

SOL DUC HOT SPRINGS
LODGINGS

Sol Duc Hot Springs Resort

12 miles off Hwy 101,
between Port Angeles
and Forks,
(206) 327-3583
Mail: PO Box 2169, Port
Angeles, WA 98362
Moderate; AE, MC, V;
checks OK
Breakfast, lunch, dinner
every day

This 1910 family resort is still the old Sol Duc but with a paint job, bathrooms in each of the 32 minimal cabins (some with kitchens, some without), and three re-tiled hot sulfur pools (98 to 106 degrees). There is also a chlorinated pool, and a staff masseuse to work out post-swim kinks. The area offers plenty of hiking and fishing. Families still flock around the poolside deli, but now, with chef Lonny Ritter behind the line, the dining room is a refuge from the fast food around the pool: you'll find Dungeness crab with fresh mushrooms, grapes, green onions, and Stilton cheese, for example. Camping facilities and RV hookups are also available, and you don't have to be a guest to use the hot springs ($4.35 a day). Open mid-May to the end of September.

SEKIU

Right about here you begin to think you really are getting away from it all: the road's getting small and snaky, and the coast has enough primitive ruggedness to make it seem uninhabitable. The little towns stay alive on lumbering and fishing. The season for salmon is April through October.

LODGINGS

Van Riper's Resort
Corner of Front and Rice on the main street,
(206) 963-2334
Mail: PO Box 246,
Sekiu, WA 98381
Inexpensive; MC, V;
checks OK

The only waterfront hotel in Sekiu, Van Riper's is family-owned and -operated, friendly, low-key, and comfortable. The protected moorage of Clallam Bay draws picturesque fishing boats, so views from 6 of the 11 rooms are great. The best room is the Penthouse Suite: it sleeps six, has a complete kitchen and three walls of windows, and goes for just $65. Other rooms are smaller and cheaper, some with thin walls.

NEAH BAY

The little town of Neah Bay, located on the Makah Indian Reservation, was the site of an 18th-century Spanish settlement. It offers some fine fishing (charters are available and fishing permits may be obtained from the tribal council), but it is most famous for its museum and research center, housing some of the finest artifacts from the magnificent archaeological dig nearby at **Lake Ozette**. The Makah Indian fishing village there was obliterated suddenly by a mudslide over 500 years ago. The clay soil sealed the contents of the houses, retarding the decay of a wealth of wooden and woven items. Discovered in 1970, the village has yielded some 55,000 artifacts. Unfortunately, the dig was closed in 1981 as a result of budget cuts, but signs still direct you to the 3-mile hike to the lake (20 miles from Neah Bay).

The **Makah Cultural and Research Center** displays photomurals from pictures taken by Edward S. Curtis in the early 1900s, dioramas, a life-size replica of the longhouse that was the center of village life, and whaling, sealing, and fishing canoes. Seasonal displays reveal the pattern of life in the village, and artifacts include seal harpoons, clubs, nets, hooks, baskets, and barbs. A cedar carving of a whale fin inlaid with 700 sea-otter teeth is one of the most prized possessions; (206) 645-2711.

Cape Flattery, the northwesternmost point of mainland America, is supposedly the most perfect "land's end" in the United States, with the longest unbroken expanse of water before it. It can be reached by a short trail that leads to a viewpoint of Tatoosh Island.

Point of Arches, south of Neah Bay, is lovely formation of offshore rocks which make a grand display of foam and tidepools from Shi Shi beach. Unfortunately, at the moment the north access to the beach is closed (it's private property in the process of being logged). There are other ways to access Shi Shi, but they're extremely difficult to get to. Before you venture out there, contact the Parks Department to find out if the access is open: (206) 452-4501 or (206) 963-2725. Three miles south of Neah Bay, **Hobuck Ocean Beach Park** offers pleasant camping facilities; (206) 645-2422.

FORKS

RESTAURANTS

South North Garden
North end of town, 100 yards off Main St (Hwy 101) behind totem pole, (206) 374-9779
Sol Duc Way, Forks
Inexpensive; beer and wine; MC, V; local checks only
Lunch, dinner Tues-Sun

A surprisingly good Chinese restaurant in the middle of logging country: the restaurant expanded into the space next door in 1989 and continues to be popular, especially considering its remoteness. The food includes standard Cantonese and Sichuan dishes, which the chef will spice up if you ask. The won ton soup was made with a flavorful chicken stock. Mongolian beef was a generous serving of tender, spicy beef strips. Hot pepper diced chicken (kung pao chicken) was an excellent example of that popular dish.

LODGINGS

Misty Valley Inn
Mile marker 195 on Hwy 101, (206) 374-9389
Mail: RR 1, Box 5407, Forks, WA 98331
Inexpensive; MC, V; checks OK

If guests can walk away from Rachel Bennett's breakfast table, she hasn't done her job. Hospitality is the key to this lovely contemporary home with three guest rooms, decorated in English, Irish, and French styles (all share a bath). In summer she opens up the Dutch Room—the master suite with private bath. There's a baby grand piano in the living room, Nintendo in the family room, and a deck (where breakfast is sometimes served) overlooking the Sol Duc Valley. Rachel's breakfast might include waffles, French toast, or apple soufflé, or she is happy to honor special requests. The Inn is on Highway 101, but set off from the road by a large screen of trees and shrubs.

Miller Tree Inn
6th St and E Division, (206) 374-6806
Mail: PO Box 953, Forks, WA 98331
Inexpensive; MC, V; checks OK

A large, attractive house, Miller Tree Inn was one of the original homesteads in Forks. Conveniently located a few blocks east of Highway 101, it's popular with hikers and fisherfolk. The six rooms are attractive, if a bit small, with comfortable furnishings. Two have private baths. Breakfast is served in the big farmhouse kitchen. The atmosphere is relaxed and friendly—kids and well-behaved pets are welcome. At $50 a couple (summer rate) the price is at least as good as the motel down the road.

Olympic Suites
¼ mile north of town on Hwy 101, (800) 262-3433 or (206) 374-5400
Mail: Rt 1, Box 1500, Forks, WA 98331
Inexpensive; AE, DC, MC, V; checks OK

This former condominium complex (Calawah Estates) at the north end of town offers spacious one- and two-bedroom suites with fully equipped kitchens, living rooms with TV, and very reasonable prices. It's especially well suited for backpackers or fisherfolk who need a base of operations. The decor is standard motel, but the suites are large and clean and, in Forks, the kitchens are a welcome addition.

308

WASHINGTON

LA PUSH

The town is a Quillayute Indian village noted for its rugged seascape, fine kite-flying, salmon charter boats, and Indian fishing by canoe. Offshore stacks of rocks give the coastline its haunting appeal. One of the finest beach walks in the world is the 16-mile stretch south from Third Beach to the Hoh River Road; trailheads to the beaches are along the highway coming into La Push. Be sure to stop in at the ranger station in nearby Mora to get a backcountry use permit and tide tables; (206) 374-5460. Due to extreme tide changes, it's easy to get stranded on the beaches if you're not careful.

LODGINGS

La Push Ocean Park Resort
La Push Road,
(206) 374-5267
Mail: PO Box 67, La
Push, WA 98350
Moderate; MC, V;
checks OK

Most of the cabins have been remodeled, so if you request one of these you can count on a clean one. Most of the front row of cabins have queen-size mattresses and new ovens and refrigerators (good thing, since there's no restaurant in La Push). Front row cabins also have their own well-stocked fireplaces (numbers 36 and 37 have huge stone fireplaces). The water (laden with harmless sulfur) tastes even worse than we remembered. By all means, if you plan to drink or cook, bring your own water or purchase bottled water in the convenience store across the street. The motel units on the top floor have nice views but thin walls; all have balconies overlooking the beach. Skip the townhouses. The campers' cabins, about as rustic as you can find on the coast, are small A-frame structures with wood stoves and toilets (and showers in a couple); you lug your wood from the woodshed and shower in the communal washroom. The beach, the main reason for going to La Push, is beautiful, and just beyond the driftwood logs.

KALALOCH

The attraction here is the beach, wide and wild, with bleached white logs crazily pitched on the slate-gray sand. The road from the Hoh River to Kalaloch hugs the coast and offers magnificent vistas if the weather isn't too foggy. A good way to learn about the area is to take one of the guided walks and talks conducted out of the ranger station; summer only, (206) 962-2283. You can see whales offshore during fall and spring.

Rain forests. These shaggy regions lie along the Bogachiel, Hoh, Queets, and Quinault rivers, all within easy drives from Kalaloch. The Hoh, 25 miles north, has a nice visitors' center, (206) 374-6925, and many moss-hung trails leading into the mountains. There are self-guided nature hikes, lots of wildlife to spy, and some of the most amazing greenery you're likely to see anywhere. Some of the world's largest Douglas fir, Sitka spruce, and red cedar are in the area, reachable by trails of varying difficulty. You can find out details in the Hoh ranger station. Rainfall in these parts reaches 140 inches annually.

LODGINGS

Kalaloch Lodge
Hwy 101, Kalaloch,
(206) 962-2271
Mail: HC 80, Box 1100,
Forks, WA 98331
Moderate; AE, MC, V;
no checks

Note that Kalaloch Lodge is quite impossible to get into on short notice during the summer; long stays may require reservations half a year in advance. The attractions are obvious: a wonderful beach, cabins dotted around the bluff, a wide variety of accommodations (the lodge, cabins, duplex units, and a modern motel). This formerly family-owned resort is now run by ARA (the same organization that took over Lake Quinault a short while ago). The rooms in the lodge, which allows no cooking, are quite good—bright, clean, and quiet—and rooms 1, 6, 7, and 8 have ocean views at prices from $48-$68. Sea Crest House is the modern motel, set amid wind-bent trees; rooms 407 to 409 have glass doors that open onto decks with ocean views, while suites 401, 405, 406, and 410 have fireplaces and more space (the tab runs about $90). The old cabins can be rather tacky and hard to keep warm; the 21 new log cabins are a bit expensive, but they have nice facilities (except for the annoying practice of not providing eating utensils in the kitchenettes). Six duplexes on the bluff all feature ocean views, for $85 a night. Two-day minimum stays on weekends; pets allowed in cabins only. The mediocre food in the dining room rarely matches the splendid ocean view.

LAKE QUINAULT

The lake, dammed by a glacial moraine, is carved into a lovely valley in the Olympic Range. The coast-hugging highway comes inland to the lake at this point, affording the traveler the easiest penetration to the mountains. You are near a mossy rain forest, the fishing for trout and salmon is memorable, and the ranger station can provide tips on hiking or nature study.

Big Acre is a grove of enormous old-growth trees, an easy hike from the lodge. **Enchanted Valley** is a 10-mile hike into the fabulous old forests, with a 1930s log chalet at the end of the trail.

LODGINGS

Lake Quinault Lodge
S Shore Rd, Lake
Quinault,
(206) 288-2571 or
(800) 562-6672
Mail: PO Box 7,
Quinault, WA 98575
Expensive; AE, MC, V;
no checks

A massive cedar-shingled structure, the lodge was built in 1926 in a gentle arc around the sweeping lawns that descend to the lake. The public rooms are done up like Grandma's sun porch in wicker and antiques, but the gift shop seems inappropriately large. There's a big fireplace in the lobby, the dining room overlooks the lawns, and the rustic bar is lively at night. You can stay in the main building, where there are nice (small) rooms, but only half of them with a view of the lake; all have private baths (but the towels look a little ratty) and go for between $78-$85. The adjoining wing has balconies and queen-size beds in each unit; the decor is tacky, including plasticky fireplaces; they run $99. Summer reservations take about two months' advance notice. Amenities consist of a sauna, an indoor heated pool, a Jacuzzi, a game room, canoes and rowboats for touring the lake, and well-maintained trails for hiking or running. Reports are varied on food in the dining room (but it seems to be on an upswing these days): stick with simpler items—waffles for breakfast, seafood for dinner—and brown-bag it when you can. There are often too many conventioneers around (mainly in the winter months), drawn by the spalike features of the resort, but somehow the old place manages to exude some of the quiet elegance of its past.

MOCLIPS

LODGINGS

Ocean Crest Resort
18 miles north of Ocean Shores, (206) 276-4465
Mail: Hwy 109,
Moclips, WA 98562
Moderate; AE, MC, V;
checks OK

Nestled in a magnificent stand of spruce on a bluff high above one of the nicest stretches of beach on the Olympic Peninsula, the Ocean Crest has always offered rooms with memorable views (and some with kitchens). Now there's a handsome wing featuring modern units done up in smart cedar paneling, with fireplaces and European-style showers. The ocean views from these rooms are even better. A handsome recreation center is just across the road, with a swimming pool, sauna, Jacuzzi, weight rooms, tanning beds, and massages. They'll sell you a vinyl swimsuit if you forgot to bring yours. An annex a quarter mile down the road offers two apartments with complete kitchens, porches, and two bedrooms each ($84 for two, $4.50 per child). Maids are hard pressed to trek the extra distance and may need to be requested.

Access to the beach is along a winding walkway through a lovely wooded ravine. There are few views on the Northwest coast outside of Cannon Beach that can rival the panorama from the dining room at the Ocean Crest. For many, the best news here is that the Ocean Crest's food is now consistently excellent, with prompt and friendly service. Breakfasts, especially, are outstanding. The lunch and dinner menus feature fresh, expertly cooked seafood. One floor above, there's a cozy bar, furnished with Northwest Coast Indian artifacts and offering the same view.

PACIFIC BEACH

LODGINGS

Sandpiper
Rt 109, 1½ miles south of Pacific Beach,
(206) 276-4580
Mail: PO Box A,
Pacific Beach, WA 98571
Moderate; MC, V;
checks OK

★★

Here's the place to vacation with four other couples, or to bring the kids, the grandparents, and the family dog: miles of beach and a fleet of kites and volleyball players. The resort consists of two four-story complexes containing large, fully equipped suites—usually a sitting room with a dining area and a fireplace, a compact kitchen, a small porch, and a bedroom and bath. There are splendid views of the beach (and a childrens' play area) from every deck. Penthouse units have an extra bedroom and cathedral ceilings. We prefer the rooms in the older complex (the northern one), since they are a tad larger. There are also five cottages, and one-room studios are available too. This resort knows enough not to try to compete with the draws of the Pacific: there's no pool, no TV, no restaurant, no in-room telephones, no video machines—but the gift shop does sell board games, kites, and sand buckets. Prices remain very good, too: about $54 to $85 for most doubles. Minimum stays are imposed on weekends and summers, and reservations usually take months to get. Housekeeping drops by every day to see if you need anything (but you'll need to pay extra for logs for the fireplace); otherwise you're on your own... just like home.

COPALIS BEACH

LODGINGS

Iron Springs Resort
Rt 109, 3 miles north of Copalis Beach,
(206) 276-4230
Mail: PO Box 207,
Copalis Beach,
WA 98535
Moderate; AE, MC, V;
checks OK

★

Friendly owners maintain this complex of cabins along a well-forested bluff, overlooking a beautiful stretch of beach. Some cabins are quite old and spacious—and amiably dowdy: light bulbs can be dim, and the sun can beat its way through the roof in the summer. Decor is mid-century chartreuse and orange, but each cottage has its own fireplace. Other cabins are newer, with vast view patios (number 8) and beautiful corner windows (number 14). Number 6 is the only one with no view; newer (and quite spiffy) are those numbered 22 to 27. The beach is especially fine here, with a river meeting its destiny with the surf just south of the resort. The heated pool is covered for year-round use, and Olive Little's famous clam chowder and cinnamon rolls are still available. As a family place, where nobody's kids and pets seem to bother other people, Iron Springs is at its best. It's also a great clamming spot. Three-day minimum stays are imposed in the summer, two-day minimum stays on weekends after Labor Day.

OCEAN SHORES

As the big, silly gate to the city might indicate, Ocean Shores would like to become Atlantic City West. Big-time gambling has not yet been approved by the legislature, so the town has to make do with casino-style gambling most Saturday nights at the Ocean Shores Inn right by the main beach.

A good way to avoid downtown altogether is to reserve one of the private beach houses that owners occasionally put up for rent. Most, located a few miles away from the hotels, are on the beach, and boast fireplaces, kitchens, and room for six to eight. The homes rent for $100 to $200 a night, with a two-night minimum on weekends and a three-night minimum over holidays. Winter rates are lower, and there are weekly rates, too. Reservations need to be made weeks in advance; (206) 289-2430 or toll-free (800) 562-8612 in Washington only. The same numbers can also take motel reservations. For charter fishing arrangements, call Ocean Shores Harbors, Inc. at (206) 289-3391.

RESTAURANTS

The Misfit

Second floor, Ocean Shores Golf Club,
(206) 289-3376
160 Albatross St NE,
Ocean Shores
Moderate; full bar; MC,
V; local checks only
Lunch, dinner every day
(closed Mon in winter)

The Misfit still is, but that's good news. It sticks out because it's so good. Not since the late and lamented Onion Patch of the early '80s has Ocean Shores had such an excellent restaurant. Tim McClelland, an enterprising ex-cop who also operates a drive-in and the Homeport, a family-style restaurant here, adopted the Misfit in 1990. He redecorated, installed a long and ambitious menu (including escargots, black-tipped shark, Quinault salmon, and apricot chicken with bourbon and pecans), and demanded consistency. It's a warm and relaxing place overlooking the golf course and the distant dunes. The chairs are comfortable, the service attentive. The homemade clam chowder is wonderful, and they even know how to cook vegetables. A good wine list, too.

LODGINGS

The Grey Gull

In town on Ocean Shores Blvd, (206) 289-3381
Mail: PO Box 1417,
Ocean Shores, WA 98569
Expensive; AE, DC, MC,
V; local checks only

This condominium-resort looks like a ski lodge (a rather odd style here on the beach), with jagged angles, handsome cladding, and a front door to strain the mightiest triceps. There are 36 condominium units, facing the ocean at a broad stretch of the beach (although not all have views; prices are calibrated accordingly), each outfitted with a balcony, fireplace, kitchen, and attractive furnishings. The resort has a pool, a sauna, and a spa. You are right on the beach, the main plus, and the lodge has been built with an eye for good Northwest architecture. Prices for the suites get fairly steep, but there are smaller rooms, and you can save money by doing your own cooking in the full kitchens.

SOUTHWEST WASHINGTON

A clockwise route: southward on the southern half of I-5, west along the Columbia River, north along the Long Beach Peninsula and the south coast, and eastward again at Grays Harbor.

CHEHALIS

RESTAURANTS

Mary McCrank's
Jackson Hwy, 4 miles south of Chehalis,
(206) 748-3662
2923 Jackson Hwy, Chehalis
Inexpensive; beer and wine; MC, V; checks OK
Lunch Tues-Sat, dinner Tues-Sun

Take a break from I-5: this dinner house, in business since 1935, is one of the nicest stops you can make along the freeway corridor. The restaurant occupies a large home, with fireplaces in some of the dining rooms, windows overlooking the garden, lawns and stream, and armchairs scattered around the comfy rooms. The food is all homemade and prices are very low. Dinner starts with breads, jams, and an outstanding tray of homemade relishes. Offerings include fried chicken, chicken with dumplings, pork chops, steaks, and other country fixings. Grilled chicken livers and onions are a local favorite. A glorious pie comes for dessert: never turn down the sour-cream raisin if it's offered. Your girth may have widened, but your wallet will only be out $13 (tops) per person.

LONGVIEW

Longview may seem to be nothing but a lumber-exporting town, but it has the unusual distinction of having been a totally planned community, ever since R.A. Long appeared in 1918 and hired Kansas City planners to make a town for his sawmill workers. **Lake Sacajawea Park**, a lovely stretch of green alongside a necklace of ponds, is the best evidence of this design. The town also is the jumping-off point for southwest Washington's biggest natural draw: Mount St. Helens.

RESTAURANTS

Henri's
45th and Ocean Beach,
(206) 425-7970
4545 Ocean Beach Hwy,

The Longview big shots all come here for lunch, when the large place can be fun and reliable; at dinner, when the pretension level rises and the number of customers dips, things can be rather lonely and the food not really

See page 286 for a map that includes Southwest Washington.

Longview
Moderate; full bar; AE,
MC, V; checks OK
Lunch Mon-Fri, dinner
Mon-Sat

worth the money. Still, the steaks are perfectly good, you can have some nice seafood bisques, and the rack of lamb with béarnaise is quite tasty. There is a fancy wine room, into which guests are escorted by owner Henry Paul, who learned how to do this kind of thing years ago at Seattle's Golden Lion. Service and decor are only passable.

LODGINGS

Monticello Hotel
Larch and 17th,
(206) 425-9900
1405 17th Ave,
Longview, WA 98632
Inexpensive; AE, MC, V;
no checks
Breakfast, lunch, dinner
every day

It fronts onto Civic Center Park with an impressive facade of brick and terra cotta, obviously the heart of town. But the 1923 edifice has suffered a loss of confidence over the years; now the hotel rooms are rented out as senior housing and offices, and the public rooms are showing their age. However, four executive suites have recently opened in the old hotel, and you can stay in a motel-like wing to one side, where the rooms are perfectly standard but the cost is low (around $43 for a double). The dining room, still spiffy, is quite the place to be seen in Longview. In short, there are no better places to stay among the plug-ordinary motels.

MOUNT ST. HELENS

The tempermental **Mount St. Helens** simmers about two hours south of Seattle off I-5. On a clear day it is well worth the trip to see the 8,365-foot remains, as well as the mountain's regrowth since the incredible eruption of May 18, 1980 (it's 1,300 feet shorter than before the blast). The US Forest Service's wood-and-glass visitors' center (3029 Spirit Lake Highway, Castle Rock, WA, (206) 274-6644; or (206) 274-4038 for weather conditions) sits in a stand of timber in the Gifford Pinchot National Forest, near Silver Lake. On clear days the view of the mountain is stunning, either with the naked eye or through one of the center's telescopes. The center commemorates the blast with excellent exhibits, a walk-through volcano, hundreds of historical and modern photos, geological and anthropological surveys, and a film documenting the destruction and rebirth. A network of trails, some for wheelchairs, are good for short, scenic strolls.

To get there, take exit 49 from I-5 and travel 5 miles east on Highway 504. Or for the better view from the north, the side on which the blast carved out a crater 2 miles across and half a mile deep, from I-5 turn east on Route 12 into Randall, then take Route 25 to connect with 26, which will lead you to **Windy Ridge**; park at the end of the road (closed winters). Many of the trails have been created or reconstructed to allow further exploration. The big thrills are to see the volcano from the air, which can be arranged with any of the numerous charter companies in the nearby towns of Kelso and Longview, or to climb it. Most climbers take one of two trails (Butte Camp or Monitor Ridge) up the south face—more of a rugged hike than real alpine climbing, but an ice axe is still recommended. The all-day climb (8 miles round trip) is ideal for novice alpinists: the only big dangers are some loose-rock cliffs and the unstable edge around the crater. In winter you can ski down. Permits are required mid-May through October, and only 100 are given out each day (for free). *Everyone* must register with the Forest Service headquarters in Amboy; (206) 247-5473 or (206) 247-5800. A small percentage of the permits are dispensed each day at the trailhead on a first-come, first-served basis, but don't count on it; arrive early. Fines *are* doled out—at the top.

VANCOUVER

Vancouver, long known as the bedroom community of Portland, is coming into its own with the advent of new industry. Among the modest tourist attractions is the Northwest's oldest apple tree (in Old Apple Tree Park, east of I-5 on Columbia Way). Locals claim that it was planted in 1829 by a member of the Hudson's Bay Company.

Fort Vancouver was the major settlement of the Hudson's Bay Company from the 1820s to the 1860s, when it passed to the Americans. The stockade wall and some of the buildings have been reconstructed, and the visitors' center has a decent museum; 1501 E Evergreen Boulevard, (206) 696-7655. On your way to Officers' Row, you'll pass the active military post, **Vancouver Barracks**. The Heritage Trust of Clark County gives walking tours of the restored officers' quarters nearby; (206) 699-2359.

Clark County Historical Museum reconstructs pioneer stores and businesses; 1511 Main Street at 16th, (206) 695-4681. **Covington House** is the oldest log house (1846) in the state; 4201 Main Street, (206) 695-6750.

Ridgefield Wildlife Refuge, 3 miles west of I-5 exit 14, has nature trails leading to the bird refuge on the lowlands of the Columbia River; (206) 887-3883.

RESTAURANTS

Hidden House
*Corner of 13th and Main
in downtown Vancouver,
(206) 696-2847
100 W 13th St,
Vancouver
Moderate; beer and wine;
AE, MC, V; checks OK
Lunch Mon-Fri, dinner
Tues-Sun*

The Hiddens, a leading family in these parts since 1870, made their money with a brick factory. Their handsome (brick, of course) home was opened by Susan Courtney as a restaurant in 1976, and she has succeeded in turning it into a reliable place for an intimate dinner. You are offered an interesting combination of small-city standards (pasta primavera, scampi, tenderloin), and gourmet dishes such as roast pork loin medallions with plum sauce and hazelnuts. The lunch menu changes every 10 days, providing loyal customers with new combinations of beef, chicken, fish, or salad dishes. A "beggar's banquet" of soup, salad, and homemade poppy seed or banana bread is a midday favorite. If you call ahead, Courtney and her conscientious longtime staff will prepare special orders such as an unusual Indonesian chicken dish. There's an extensive Northwest wine list.

Pinot Ganache
*Corner of Washington
and Evergreen,
(206) 695-7786
1004 Washington St,
Vancouver
Moderate; beer and wine;*

Downtown Vancouver, forever struggling to buff up its image, shows off a glimmer of sophistication at Pinot Ganache. The interior is slick (and not just by Vancouver standards), with well-spaced tables and a cart of fresh flowers. The best thing about dinner is dessert: a brandied espresso chocolate mousse, chocolate decadence with white chocolate mousse, and a hazelnut tof-

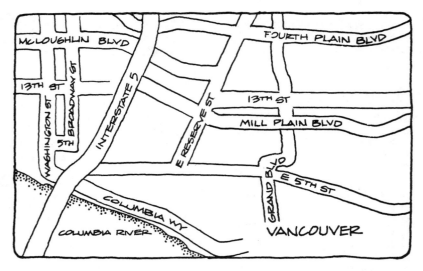

AE, MC, V; checks OK
Lunch, dinner Mon-Sat

fee cake. Beforehand, try the juicy sirloin burger with sautéed onions and mushrooms, the Djakarta (fried jasmine rice with prawns, chicken, and Oriental vegetables tossed with soy sauce) or the special charbroiled ahi with sun-dried tomato–rosemary butter. It's a popular enough place to demand minimum charges at peak hours. The place brightens in summer, when pink geraniums bloom in the sidewalk cafe.

DeCicco's Italian Ristorante
Between Grant and
Franklin streets,
(206) 693-3252
611 W 11th St,
Vancouver
Inexpensive; no alcohol;
AE, MC, V; checks OK
Breakfast, lunch
Mon-Fri

Some come here for the homemade almond biscotti to be dipped into Torrefazione coffee, others like the outdoor seating that lends this little Italian cafe in Vancouver a more European air. Lunch is refreshingly unpretentious—seafood pasta or spinach lasagna; a focaccia sandwich; and an array of fresh, imaginative salads (rigatoni, roasted eggplant, or an Oriental offering with angel hair pasta, fresh snow peas, chicken, and ginger). Nothing exceeds $6. Arrive early as there's not always enough food to last until the 4:30pm closing time.

Juliano's Pizzeria
South on 164th Ave to
Fishers Mercantile
Shopping Center,
(206) 254-1286
16209 SE McGillivray
Blvd, Vancouver
Inexpensive; beer and
wine; MC, V; local
checks only
Dinner every day

Steve Juliano, a Brooklyn-born but as Italian as any vintage immigrant, brings to Vancouver suburbs what he knows best: pizza to break your mama's heart—handmade, hand-thrown dough, thick to extra-thin with generous piles of fresh vegetables and meats and portions of whole-milk mozzarella and Romano cheeses. One of the most sought after is the "Jerry G," named for the Grateful Dead's Jerry Garcia, Juliano's hero, and is loaded with sausage, onion, and green pepper. The atmosphere is about as tasteful as Coney Island (video machines, Muhammad Ali posters, laundry-sink bathrooms); unfortunately, you can't get these delectable pizzas to go.

Tyrone's Patisserie
Downtown Vancouver between Broadway and Main St, (206) 699-1212
106 E Evergreen Blvd, Vancouver
Inexpensive; no alcohol; MC, V; checks OK
Breakfast, lunch Mon-Fri

Gary Galland has had a good thing going for several years in his downtown patisserie, although few other than loyal locals know about it. He cooks up curries, pastas, fresh soups, croissant sandwiches, and generous salads. His place is open for a 40-cent cup of fresh coffee, gargantuan bran and carrot muffins, and even two scrambled eggs with diced ham for breakfast. Come midday, this counter-top restaurant on a lazy downtown Vancouver boulevard has a choice of fresh bargains: try the whole wheat fettuccine finished with pine nuts, garlic, and fresh zucchini and carrots, the artichoke-hazelnut soup, or the hearty ratatouille served with a buttery croissant. Around town, Galland's reputation rests as solidly on his fudge cake as on his stewardship of jazz—his place often doubles as an afternoon getaway for Northwest musicians.

Who-Song and Larry's Cantina
Take the Camas exit off I-5, go east 1 mile, turn right at light,
(206) 695-1198
111 E Columbia Way, Vancouver
Moderate; full bar; AE, DC, MC, V; local checks only
Lunch, dinner every day

If you wondered, wandering around downtown Vancouver, where all the *people* were: this is the place. The entire basketball team is packing in enchiladas by your side, families are rounding the large buffet with dedicated zeal, there's lots of chat to make you feel part of a large, homey party. Jolly menu patter is a bit of a delusion: Larry's actually back East, in his 80s, and Who-Song is a fictitious figure lending only his name to the spot—the place is yet another link in the vast El Torito chain. Mexican buffet ($5.45) is no great shakes (tired taco shells, etc.), but there are great margaritas and swift service (free corn chips and salsa before you draw a breath). A jolly cantina away from the hubbub lets you nibble nachos with your Corona and watch the grain ships force the Vancouver-Portland bridge to open.

LODGINGS

Red Lion Inn at the Quay
Under the I-5 bridge on the Columbia River,
(206) 694-8341, toll-free (800) 547-8010
100 Columbia St, Vancouver, WA 98660
Expensive; full bar; AE, DC, MC, V; checks OK
Breakfast, lunch, dinner every day

You'll know you're in a hotel dining room, but the food at the Quay is not half bad. It's wisest to opt for seafood: the ambitious menu offers more than a dozen sorts, including Willapa oysters, razor clams, Oregon scallops, halibut, haddock, snapper, and sole, all cooked to your specifications. Most tables offer handsome views of the Columbia and the Oregon shore. All the rooms have just been remodeled to the Red Lion standard. Be sure to request a room overlooking the river.

CATHLAMET

Cathlamet, seat of Wahkiakum County, is an old-style river town, tied almost as closely to the Columbia as Mark Twain's Hannibal was to the Mississippi. Although hunting is good in this area, fishing is everyone's recreation—in season, for trout, salmon, and steelhead, all year round for the Columbia's mammoth, caviar-bearing sturgeon. Nearby **Puget Island**, reachable by bridge, is flat dairyland, ideal for cycling; a tiny ferry can take you from there directly across to Oregon. Wahkiakum County is the sort of place where nostalgia buffs discover round barns and covered bridges, and it's refreshingly free from late-20th-century schlock. You can camp right on the river beach at **Skamokawa Vista Park** (say Ska-MOCK-away).

LODGINGS

Country Keeper

Just off SR 4, on Main St,
north end of town,
(206) 795-3030
61 Main St,
Cathlamet, WA 98612
Inexpensive; MC, V;
checks OK

It's not exactly in the country (Main Street, Cathlamet is more exact) but it's certainly a keeper. This former town library is an immaculate 1907 mansion—original decorative hardwood floors, Oriental rugs, light fixtures, and all. It's handsomely furnished with period pieces and glass work by owner Terry Beaston (a gracious man who taught art in Australia for 15 years). Each room is decorated with prints by the artist for whom it's named (Degas, Monet, Chagall, Van Gogh, Renoir). As a tribute to the mansion's former incarnation, the comfortable bedrooms are filled with books. A patio with a distant view of the Columbia invites long afternoon visits in summer.

Our Place

Take Welcome Slough Rd
off Hwy 409,
(206) 849-4328
305 N Welcome Slough
Rd, Cathlamet,
WA 98612
Inexpensive; no credit
cards; checks OK

A net shack (but cozy and refurbished) on the shore of picturesque Puget Island has been polished into a comfortable, rustic bed and breakfast. Owners ElRose and Everett Groves live in the fisherman's house next door. Perfect for families or couples seeking privacy, there's a fully equipped kitchen, bath, wood stove, double bed on the main floor, three-person loft above, and a stretch of beach outside for long, meditative tromps. The house is stocked with plenty of games and surrounded by lots of greenery. Very private.

CHINOOK

Nestled on the shores of Baker Bay, part of the broad Columbia River estuary, Chinook was formerly a salmon fish-trapping center (and once reportedly had the highest income per capita in the *country*). The too-efficient fish traps were outlawed earlier this century. Most of the thousands of wooden pilings visible in the bay at low tide are all that remains of these harvesting contraptions.

Nearby, on Scarborough Hill, **Fort Columbia State Park** is a collection of restored turn-of-the-century wooden buildings that once housed soldiers guarding the mouth of the Columbia River from the threat of foreign invasion. The former commander's house is now a military museum; foreboding concrete bunkers once held huge cannons. The park also claims some of the area's largest rhododendron bushes. Open daily, mid-May to September, but hours vary; (206) 777-8221.

RESTAURANTS

The Sanctuary
Hwy 101 and Hazel,
(206) 777-8380
Chinook,
Moderate; full bar; AE,
MC, V; local checks only
Lunch Wed-Sun, dinner
every day (days vary
in winter)

You dine in a deified setting, an old Methodist church, complete with pump organ, stained-glass windows, statues of angelic cherubs watching over you—even pews to sit in, for God's sake. Amid the finery, owner/chef Joanne Leech serves an eclectic array of food, from steak and seafood to *svenska kottbullar* (Swedish meatballs) and *fiskekaker* (Scandinavian fish-cakes). The Sanctuary's strength lies in Leech's imaginative preparations and use of sauces, marinades, and other homemade accoutrements. The shrimp and chicken, sautéed in a marinade of Madeira, ginger, garlic, and cranberries, is worth trying; so is seafood fettuccine with a cilantro pesto-and-cream cheese sauce featuring chock full of baby shrimp and scallops. For dessert, homemade sherbet—blackberry one time, lemon another—is, er, heavenly. Light lunches are served in the herb house.

LONG BEACH PENINSULA

The slender finger of land dividing Willapa Bay from the Pacific is famous for its 37-mile-long flat stretch of public beach; its gentle marine climate; its exhibition kite-flying; its cranberry bogs, clamming, and rhododendrons; and for its food, which is unequaled by any like-sized area on the Northwest Coast.

Willapa Bay's **Long Island**, reachable only by boat, harbors a 274-acre old-growth cedar grove. Some trees are over 200 feet tall, with trunks 11 feet in diameter. Campsites are available. The island is part of the **Willapa National Wildlife Refuge**, with headquarters on Highway 101, 10 miles north of Seaview; (206) 484-3482.

LONG BEACH PENINSULA: ILWACO

Named after a Chinook Indian chief, Ilwaco is best known as the sport-fishing hub of the lower Columbia River. Two popular sport-fishing operators are Hobo Charters, (206) 642-2300, and Coho Charters, (206) 642-3333.

The **Ilwaco Heritage Museum** offers a look at southwest Washington history, including a scale-model glimpse of the Peninsula in the 1920s; 115 SE Lake Street, in the Convention Center, (206) 642-3446.

Fort Canby State Park covers 2,000 acres stretching from North Head south to Cape Disappointment at the Columbia's mouth. Good surf fishing and wave watching can be had from the North Jetty, 2 miles of massive boulders separating the ocean and river, with an observation platform for good views. The park also includes hiking and biking trails and 250 campsites; open all year, (206) 642-3078.

Also in the park is the **Lewis and Clark Interpretive Center**, which depicts the explorers' journey from St. Louis to the Pacific, explains the history of Cape Disappointment and North Head lighthouses, and enjoys the best view of the Columbia River bar—a great storm-watching spot. The lighthouses are not open to the public, but may be approached on foot; (206) 642-3029.

LODGINGS

Inn at Ilwaco
Off 4th at 120 Williams St NE, (206) 642-8686
Mail: PO Box 922, Ilwaco, WA 98624-0922
Moderate; MC, V; checks OK

Located atop a quiet dead-end street overlooking the town of Ilwaco, this bed and breakfast is housed in the old Ilwaco Presbyterian Church. The church has been converted into a performing arts center (but still a good place for a wedding), the Sunday school into nine guest rooms (seven with private bath), all very new yet rich with a sense of history and grace: plush bedding, lacy curtains, original wood floors, some even with window seats. One caveat for privacy seekers—the walls are quite thin. There's a room with two twins, ideal for the kids. In the large public room, guests take their ample continental breakfast, read the morning papers on comfortable furnishings, or tickle the ivories. Innkeeper Judy Clements provides first-rate hospitality.

LONG BEACH PENINSULA: SEAVIEW

RESTAURANTS

The Shoalwater (in The Shelburne Inn)
Pacific Hwy 103 and N 45th, (206) 642-4142
In the Shelburne Inn, Seaview
Expensive; full bar; AE, DC, MC, V; local checks only
Dinner every day

Few folks familiar with the southwest Washington dining scene would argue the Shoalwater's number-one ranking on the coast. Amidst an elegantly understated, nonsmoking atmosphere, owners Ann and Tony Kischner, chef Cheri Walker, and sous-chef Jerry Branham combine their appreciation for the Northwest's finest foodstuffs with skillful preparation and an artful touch to produce memorable meals. The fresh seafood is generally your best choice, especially if it is locally harvested. Start out with the innkeeper's mussel chowder, or sautéed Dungeness crab cakes served with a tangy red pepper mayonnaise. The foods' flavors combined with eye-catching aesthetics—the diverse colors and textures—alert you to the kitchen's expertise. Entrées might include poached Willapa Bay oysters, pan-fried cod in orange, lime, and cranberry sauce, Oregon quail in raspberry sauce, and salmon with a cran-blueberry mustard butter sauce—tantalizing examples of what can be accomplished here. While most are excellent, there are a few quibbles, a baked marlin special was too tough and not very flavorful (we should have opted for fish from local waters). The wine list, with over 400 selections, is superlative. As are the desserts, skillfully crafted by Ann Kischner; the bread pudding is perfection, and anything with cranberries is sure to please.

42nd Street Cafe

42nd St and Pacific Hwy, (206) 642-2323
Seaview
Inexpensive; beer and wine; MC, V; checks OK
Lunch Wed-Sat, dinner Wed-Mon

The 42nd Street Cafe is not a cafe at all, but rather a house transformed into an Americana-style restaurant that's warm, unpretentious, and smells good. In fact, the eating experience here is akin to a crowded family reunion. Tables are so closely packed you feel although you could reach around and tap the woman behind you—is it Aunt Martha?—and inquire about her latest baking exploits. Everyone appreciates a good deal and that's what you get here. Nothing fancy, just good food at bargain prices. Dinners, which include soup, salad, homemade bread (with corn relish and cranberry conserves), *and* dessert. The food? It's American Gothic (country-fried steak, pot roast, and fried chicken with overcooked veggies) joined by Peninsula favorites (oysters, often heavily breaded, and halibut). All selections are served on diner china. There's an expansive (and inexpensive) array of wine, mostly Washington vintages. Desserts are straightforward and sweet.

The Heron and Beaver Pub

Pacific Hwy 103 and N 45th, (206) 642-4142
In the Shelburne Inn, Seaview
Moderate; full bar; AE, DC, MC, V; local checks only
Lunch, dinner every day

There's a feeling of serendipity here. Your table at the Shoalwater, across the foyer, won't be available for a while, and you're not keen on leaning against the waiting-room wall. You discover this attractive, pint-sized pub with handsome dark woodwork and stained-glass windows. If only it wasn't so small. Just think of it as cozy as you sip something with a head on it, select from the excellent wine list, or savor a single-malt scotch. Light meals are also available—pasta, pâté, sandwiches, soup, and a delectable cheese fondue—all prepared under the discriminating eye of the Shoalwater's Tony Kischner. You might even decide to stay.

LODGINGS

The Shelburne Inn

Pacific Hwy 103 and N 45th, (206) 642-2442
Mail: PO Box 250, Seaview, WA 98644
Expensive; AE, MC, V; checks OK

You can't really hear the ocean from here, and you certainly can't see it. But you most definitely can feel the allure of the sea throughout the historic Shelburne, a creaky but dignified structure approaching its 100th birthday. Don't expect the modern amenities (sauna, Jacuzzis etc) that have become de rigeur at so many chic hideaways. There's also a busy highway out front, with a well-lit supermarket across the way. Consequently, east-side rooms can something less than restful. Request one of the comfortably decorated (and more expensive) west-side rooms. They're bright and cheerful, with antiqued interiors, private baths, and cozy homespun quilts covering queen-size beds. Upstairs on the third floor (now relieved of summer heat by a skylight/vent) are more moderately priced ($69), with lots of tongue-and-groove woodwork and floors with a gentle slant. Breakfasts are superb. Innkeepers David Campiche and Laurie Anderson whip up surprising morning meals of razor-clam cakes or scrambled eggs with smoked salmon, chives (from the herb garden out front), and Gruyère cheese. The Shoalwater (see review) is the dinner restaurant.

Sou'wester Lodge
1½ blocks southwest of Seaview's traffic light,
(206) 642-2542
Mail: PO Box 102,
Seaview, WA 98644
Inexpensive; MC, V;
checks OK

★

Those who appreciate good conversation, a sense of humor, and rambling lodgings on the beach will find Leonard and Miriam Atkins's humble, old-fashioned resort just what the doctor ordered. The 1892 main structure was built as a summer home for U.S. Senator Henry Winslow Corbett, of the well-known Portland family. Also on the premises are fully equipped cabins and a collection of classic trailers. The hosts are as much a draw as the unspoiled beach resort. Originally from South Africa, they came to Long Beach by way of Israel and Chicago. The view from the lodge's balcony—across windswept, grassy dunes to the sea—is enough to keep them here permanently. Interesting books and periodicals clutter the living room, which also occasionally hosts lectures, chamber-music concerts, and informal (but stimulating) conversations. Leonard has deemed this joint the official outpost of the "B & (MYOD)B club"—Bed and (Make Your Own Damn) Breakfast.

LONG BEACH PENINSULA: LONG BEACH

Long Beach, the town, boasts a half-mile-long elevated boardwalk, stretching between S 10th and Bolstad streets, that is accessible by wheelchairs, baby strollers, and, of course, by foot.

Kite lovers can visit the **Long Beach World Kite Museum** and Hall of Fame, 3rd and N Pacific Highway, (206) 642-4020; or purchase kites at Ocean Kites, 511 S Pacific, (206) 642-2229. August's **International Kite Festival** brings hundreds of soaring creations to the skies. The entire Peninsula swells with visitors for this event, so plan ahead; (206) 642-2400. Milton York Candy Company, on the main drag, purveys chocolates and ice cream, (206) 642-2352. Pasttimes Coffee and Collectibles, a coffeehouse with chessboards, lots of reading material, and a congenial owner, offers respite from Long Beach's bustling streets, (206) 642-8303. Clark's Nursery grows fields of rhododendrons, (206) 642-2241.

RESTAURANTS

The Lightship Restaurant and Columbia Bar
Between 10th St and the beach, (206) 642-3252
At Nendel's Inn on 10th,
Long Beach
Moderate; full bar; AE,

Housed on the top floor of a boxy Nendel's Inn with bare drywall everywhere, the Lightship restaurant looks like just another poor-quality, high-priced, oceanfront eatery, the type of establishment that seems to proliferate wherever land and sea meet. A tenement like slow elevator ride to the third floor, artificial flowers, an open kitchen, and window tables reserved

DC, MC, V; checks OK
Breakfast, lunch, dinner
every day

for groups of four or more reinforce the negative impression. Disregard all that, for the food makes it all worthwhile. A basket of warm and chewy sourdough bread and an outstanding Dijon dressing on the simple salad show attention to gustatory (if not decorative) detail. Main courses are ample and include fish, fowl, beef, and pasta selections. Pan-fried Willapa Bay oysters are served either lightly floured or heavily dusted with herbed cornmeal. Linguine is fresh, the sauces herby and flavorful. Actually, after a few bites of anything on the menu, you get the impression that owners Ann and Tony Kischner (of Shoalwater Restaurant fame) make certain that the Lightship, whose kitchen is under the direction of chef Francis Schafer (former sous-chef at the Shoalwater), is not just another view restaurant. For dessert, try the fruit cobbler of the day or the Columbia Bar Sludge Pie, a top-heavy concoction of chocolate-cookie crust and vanilla and chocolate ice cream smothered in caramel sauce.

Although it's billed as a family restaurant with kids' courses, Sunday brunch, and an ample noontime menu, we think the Lightship's prices are out of range for many families.

My Mom's Pie Kitchen
Pacific Hwy and 12th St,
(206) 642-2342
Long Beach
Inexpensive; no alcohol;
MC, V; checks OK
Lunch Tues-Sun

The name says it all. This is a small, nondescript establishment that serves a host of homemade pies. Banana cream, pecan, sour-cream raisin, rhubarb, raspberry, and a myriad of other concoctions are offered, depending on the time of year (and what ingredients are available) and, in some cases, the time of day. Arrive too late, and baker Jeanne McLaughlin might be sold out of your favorite. A few other items are offered, such as an okay clam chowder and a crab quiche. The place is becoming increasingly popular with the summer hordes.

LONG BEACH PENINSULA: OCEAN PARK

Ocean Park, a tranquil retirement community, offers a quiet beach, and **Potrimpos Gallery** in a restored Victorian house with Eric Wiegardt seascapes; Bay Avenue between Sandridge Road and Pacific Highway, (206) 665-5976.

At the end of the Ocean Park beach approach is **Kopa Wecoma** (no phone), a great place to stop for a good burger or fish 'n' chips in between volleyball games or foot-tingling forays into the cold Pacific. On summer evenings, there's often a line (and lots of wind), so bring a coat.

LODGINGS

Klipsan Beach Cottages
Hwy 103, 2 miles south of
Ocean Park,
(206) 665-4888

In an area justly known for its fine marine views and spectacular Maytime rhododendrons, it's remarkable that so few lodgings have bothered with landscaping. This cozy operation, a row of nine small, separate,

22617 Pacific Hwy,
Ocean Park, WA 98640
Moderate; MC, V;
checks OK

well-maintained older cottages, is an exception; it stands facing the ocean in a parklike setting of pine trees and clipped lawns. Since these are individually owned condominiums, interior decoration schemes can vary widely, but all of the units have fully equipped kitchens and bed linens. Charges range from $65 for a one-bedroom cottage to $95 for three bedrooms. All cottages have broad decks with outlooks over the grass to the sea. They all feature fireplaces, for which wood is furnished. Guests may bring children, but no pets.

LONG BEACH PENINSULA: NAHCOTTA

Nahcotta has become almost synonymous with oysters. The best place to pick up a few dozen is at **Jolly Roger Seafoods**, across from The Ark; (206) 665-4111.

RESTAURANTS

The Ark
On the old Nahcotta dock,
next to the oyster fleet,
(206) 665-4133
273rd and Sandridge Rd,
Nahcotta
Expensive; full bar; AE,
MC, V; local checks only
Dinner Tues-Sun, brunch
Sun (closed Tues
in winter)

The Ark is a paradox. The restaurant with the picture-perfect setting on Willapa Bay has drawn acclaim from far and wide. Restaurant reviewers from up and down the West Coast have practically enshrined the place with frequent praise; The Ark now basks in its almost legendary reputation among Northwest gastronomes. If you hit it right, The Ark will fulfill your food fantasies and be everything you expected. Trouble is, not every night is good. It all adds up to a gamble you shouldn't have to take at a restaurant of this repute. Based on our numerous experiences at The Ark, we recommend you stick with the simple preparations featuring local and regional ingredients. This culinary approach, after all, is what made owners Nanci Main and Jimella Lucas famous in the first place. Uncomplicated meat dishes, such as a recent special of veal medallions with green peppercorn sauce, will also fulfill your expectations. And shellfish aficionados shouldn't miss with The Ark oyster feed, an unlimited serving of Willapa Bay bivalves lightly breaded and pan-fried. When the dessert tray rolls around, however, throw caution to the wind. Unless you're counting calories, you can't go wrong.

LODGINGS

Moby Dick Hotel
South of Bay Ave
on Sandridge Rd,
(206) 665-4543
Sandridge Rd, Nahcotta,
WA 98637
Moderate; V; checks OK

Fritzi and Edward Cohen of the Tabard Inn in Washington, DC first spied the Moby Dick from a window table of The Ark. The hotel, originally built in 1929 by a railroad conductor from his gold-prospecting money, is now under their careful ownership. It's quite beachy with a couple of spacious public rooms, ten small and simple bedrooms, and a rambling bayfront (loaded with oysters). Full breakfasts include a choice of the hotel's own garden produce and oysters (in season).

LONG BEACH PENINSULA: OYSTERVILLE

Oysterville dates to 1854 and features a distinctive row of shoreside homes, sur-rounded by stately cedars and spruce trees. (Follow Sandridge Road north to the Oysterville sign.) Also known for bivalves, **Oysterville Sea Farms**, at the old can-nery in Oysterville, sells 'em by the dozen (open weekends, year-round).

Leadbetter Point State Park occupies the northernmost tip of the peninsula and is a bird-watcher's paradise, a stopover site for over 100 species. Hiking trails abound (3 miles north of Oysterville on Stackpole Road).

BAY CENTER

RESTAURANTS

Blue Heron Inn
1 mile west of Hwy 101,
12 miles southwest of
South Bend,
(206) 875-5130
Water St, Bay Center
Inexpensive; beer and
wine; MC, V; checks OK
Breakfast, lunch, dinner
every day

The 1-mile detour to the fishing village of Bay Center on pristine Willapa Bay is worth your while for the scenery alone—all the better if you're hungry, particu-larly if it's breakfast time. The Blue Heron Inn is a gen-uine roadside attraction, with oyster omelets and tasty fish 'n' chips, checkered oilcloth on the tables, and Elvis on the jukebox. The cooler near the cash register of-fers fresh oysters and crab to go, plus smoked and pickled salmon. A new ventilation system has alleviated the smoke problem, and on the whole this is a cozy place with a nice staff and nice prices.

SOUTH BEND

The sleepy Pacific County seat perches picturesquely on the low bluffs that ring the inside curve of the north arm of Willapa Bay. The outsized **County Court-house** two blocks south of US 101 atop "Quality Hill" rules over the town like a medieval castle. On Highway 101 just north of town, **H & H Cafe** is the place to stop for transcendent pie, in rhubarb, blackberry, or four other flavors and fresh-baked daily by the owner (or her granddaughter).

RESTAURANTS

Boondocks
Hwy 101, (206) 875-5155
1015 W Robert Bush Dr,
South Bend
Moderate; full bar; MC,
V; checks OK
Breakfast, lunch, dinner
every day

★

South Bend, the historic county seat of Pacific County, bills itself as "The Oyster Capital of the World." That's a classic bit of boosterism, but the oysters *are* world-class, and this pretty little town is coming out of its shell. Boondocks is right on the waterfront, with an outdoor deck and a fine view, not to mention pan-fried fresh Willapa Bay oysters and razor clams. The deli-cious Hangtown fry is a crowd-pleaser at breakfast, and the dinner menu now features combination plates and blackened prime rib.

TOKELAND

Set on the long peninsula reaching into northern Willapa Bay, this crabbing community named after 19th-century Chief Toke is the loneliest part of the southwest coast, where the omnipresent tackiness of contemporary resort life is least apparent. Pick up a container of crabmeat and some cocktail sauce from **Nelson Crab** (open daily 9am-5pm) to enjoy on a driftwood log at the beach across the street, or bring a crab trap and try your luck off the pier at **Toke Point** (warning: seals steal bait).

LODGINGS

Tokeland Hotel
*Kindred Ave and
Hotel Rd,
(206) 267-7006
100 Hotel Rd,
Tokeland, WA 98590
Moderate; beer and wine;
AE, MC, V; local
checks only
Breakfast everyday, lunch
Mon-Sat, dinner
every day*

This chaste, century-old structure teetered for several years on the edge of genteel collapse until its rescue by two couples who aim to fully restore "the oldest resort hotel in Washington." As of this writing there is still plenty of finish work to be done, although 12 of the inn's 17 bedrooms are open. Rooms, some with views of Willapa Bay, are somewhat spartan, and bathrooms are shared. The creaky-floored restaurant is often filled with folks from the surrounding community, who take advantage of reasonable prices, large helpings, and a peaceful setting. Breakfast (included in the price of a room) offers ample choices for everyone, including kids with a yen for pigs in a blanket. Lunches are decent; dinner entrées include steak, chicken, and local seafood, ably prepared.

GRAYLAND

RESTAURANTS

The Dunes
*Right off Hwy 105 at the
sign of the giant razor
clam, (206) 267-1441
783 Dunes Rd, Grayland
Moderate; beer and wine;
AE, MC, V; checks OK
Breakfast, lunch, dinner
every day (winter
hours vary)*

Follow the bumpy gravel road a quarter of a mile down to the dunes. You will discover a funky kind of place that's as comfortable as an old windbreaker: a beachcomber's hideaway, eclectically decorated with shells, ship models, stained glass, and blooming begonias. The main dining room is always warm and wonderful, with a fireplace in the middle and linen-draped oak tables. Unfortunately, the non-smoking section is upstairs. Families are everywhere, especially on Sunday mornings, dressed in their Sunday best or their Eddie Bauer gear. The restaurant offers a front-row seat on the ocean just beyond the dunes, and you won't find fresher seafood—clams, salmon, crab, and oysters.

GRAYS HARBOR

Nature's abundance in the area around the estuary continues to help support the economies of its communities, including timber milling and shipping operations in

Aberdeen and Hoquiam, charter fishing, whale watching, crabbing and clam digging in Westport, and cranberry bogging in Grayland. The wild beauty of the expansive bay and the obvious attractions of the coastal beaches draw retirees, tourists, surfers, and migrating shorebirds.

A half million Arctic-bound shorebirds migrate from as far south as Argentina and congregate on the tidal mudflats at the wildlife refuge of **Bowerman Basin** each spring from about mid-April through the first week of May. At high tide, the birds rise in unison in thick flocks that shiver through the air, twisting and turning, before settling back onto their feeding grounds. There are trails through the marsh (located just beyond the Hoquiam airport). Be sure to wear boots. For more information and peak migratory days, call the Grays Harbor National Wildlife Refuge, (206) 753-9467.

WESTPORT

For a small coastal town that regularly endures the flood tide of tourists out to catch The Big One, the city of Westport remains surprisingly friendly and scenic. Most fisherfolk rise early and join the almost-comically hasty 6am exodus from the breakwater to cross the dreaded bar and head for the open sea. The short **salmon-fishing** season has changed charter-boat marketing, so many now feature whale-watching cruises as well. **Gray whales** migrate off the coast March through May on their way toward Arctic feeding waters, where they fatten up for the trip back down to their breeding lagoons in Baja come fall (when waters are too rough to go out and greet them). Breakfast cafes are open by 5am, some much earlier (especially those down by the docks).

You can drop by and pick up a bushel of Brady's Oysters (a shack at water's edge) or take home some great chorizo, kielbasa, or beef jerky, all made on premises of **Bay City Sausage Company.**

Charter rates vary little from company to company. Some of the **best charters** include Cachalot, (206) 268-0323; Gull, toll-free (800) 562-0175 or (206) 268-9186; Deep Sea, toll-free (800) 562-0151 or (206) 268-9300; Westport, toll-free (800) 562-0157 or (206) 268-9120; Islander, toll-free (800) 562-0147 or (206) 268-9166; Ocean, toll-free (800) 562-0105 or (206) 268-9144; Northwest Educational Tours, (206) 268-9150; Travis, (206) 268-9140. (Toll-free numbers are in operation only during the season.)

Things quiet down until the 3:30pm return of the fleets. You can explore the town during this lull, or head for the expansive beaches—open for driving, jogging, clamming, or picnicking—along the coast from Grayland to Westport. **Surfers** can be found year-round hoping to catch their own Big One at the jetty in Westhaven State Park.

RESTAURANTS

Arthur's
Westhaven and Cove,
(206) 268-9292
2681 Westhaven Dr,
Westport
Moderate; beer and wine;
MC, V; checks OK
Lunch, dinner Tues-Sun

Arthur Lawrence, former chef at the landmark Islander (now under new owners after 28 years) across the street, operates this cheery spot that offers good seafood, steaks, prime rib, and pasta. You can rationalize dessert by vowing to climb the viewing tower opposite the cafe, where there's a panorama of the Grays Harbor channel.

Constantin's

½ block from the dock,
(206) 268-0550
320 E Dock St, Westport
Moderate; beer and wine;
AE, MC, V; local
checks only
Lunch, dinner Wed-Mon
(call for winter hours)

Constantin "Dino" Kontogonis, who came to Westport in 1987 "to get away from Seattle," is a Greek with a gift for cooking. Beware only of calories—and garlic. From behind the plastic grapes emerges some chewy, fresh pita bread. Use it to scoop up dollops of skordalia, a delicious garlic-potato-almond dip. A mixed grill combines marinated lamb chop, prawns, and chicken for a Greek spin on the surf-and-turf concept (the lamb was undercooked for our tastes). You're only a stone's throw from the Westport docks, so there's fresh seafood, such as a recent red snapper special (unexpectedly breaded and fried). Desserts are uninspired. A joint venture with the wine shop next door provides Constantin's with an inexhaustible wine list and over three dozen varieties of beer.

LODGINGS

Glenacres Inn

1 block north of
the stoplight at
222 N Montesano,
(206) 268-9391
Mail: PO Box 1246,
Westport, WA 98595
Moderate; MC, V;
checks OK

Turn-of-the-century entrepreneuse Minnie Armstrong ran a horse 'n' buggy service from the docks of Westport to her bed and breakfast, long before B&Bs became the latest thing in charming accommodations. Now it's back in service—a gabled gem with lots of lodging alternatives and a hot tub, no less. In addition to the five plush bedrooms (all with private baths), there are three simpler "deck" rooms and four cottages on the property, ranging from the two-bedroom Chickadee ($65-$80) to the Rainbird, which sleeps 11 ($110-$170). Full breakfast is included.

The Chateau Westport

W Hancock and S Surf
streets, (206) 268-9101
Mail: PO Box 349,
Westport, WA 98595
Moderate; AE, DC, MC,
V; no checks

This is considered the fanciest motel lodging in Westport—though it bears no resemblance to any chateau we know. Prices for the 108 units range up from $59; indoor pool and hot tub are available. Studio units have fireplaces and can be rented alone (with a queen-size hideabed) or in conjunction with adjoining bedrooms to form a suite. It's not the quietest place, and the continental breakfast is nothing to get excited about, but the ocean views are magnificent; those from the third and fourth floors are best.

COSMOPOLIS

LODGINGS

Cooney Mansion

Follow C St to 5th,
(206) 533-0602
802 E 5th St,
Cosmopolis, WA 98537

For many years this 1908 manse housed timber tycoon Neil Cooney, his servants, and his out-of-town guests. There's a very masculine feel to the place (Cooney was a bachelor): spruce wainscoting in the living room, large windows with dark wooden frames, heavy furniture throughout. There are five rooms, each with private bath. A clubby feel prevails: from the deck on the

Moderate; MC, V;
no checks

★★

second floor you can sit and watch golfers on the public course next door, and you see tennis courts as you head up the driveway (they are part of Mill Creek Park but are available for guests' use). In the morning, owner George Barker prepares a substantial breakfast, including eggs Benedict or perhaps the Cooney omelet.

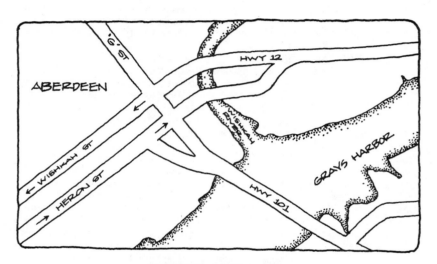

ABERDEEN/HOQUIAM

With the timber industry in slow decline, these old Siamese-twin lumber towns are in transition, as they have been since the sawmilling and shipping glory days of the early 1900s. At the **Grays Harbor Historical Seaport** (east side of Aberdeen; (206) 532-8611) you can tour a replica of Captain Gray's *Lady Washington*, a 105-foot floating museum offering afternoon and evening cruises in summer around Grays Harbor.

Hoquiam's Castle gives tours of the 20-room mansion, built for a prominent lumberman in 1897; 515 Chenault Avenue, Hoquiam, (206) 533-2005.

Polson Park is a fine house by Arthur Loveless, with a rose garden; 1611 Riverside Avenue, Hoquiam, (206) 533-5862.

RESTAURANTS

Parma

On Heron, 1 block west of Broadway,
(206) 533-0956
116 W Heron St,
Aberdeen
Moderate; beer and wine;

Fortunately for Aberdeen, French-Italian chef Pierre Gabelli loves rain and doesn't like cities. Few urban trattorias can match his excellent pastas and gnocchi—all of it made fresh daily. The place is as spotless as it was when it was Misty's. Gabelli named his restaurant after his birthplace—the northern Italian city where Parmesan cheese was also born. The spaghetti *arrab-*

MC, V; checks OK
Lunch Tues-Fri and Sun,
dinner Tues-Sun

biata with fresh tomatoes, olives, peppers, and hot spices made a huge hit with Governor Booth Gardner. The fresh-baked bread is wonderfully chewy, and there's a mondo selection of beers and ales, including several Northwest microbrews on tap. The espresso machine is always on. An Italian logger would pronounce it "great ciao."

Billy's Bar and Grill
Corner of Heron and G,
(206) 533-7144
322 E Heron St,
Aberdeen
Inexpensive; full bar;AE,
DC, MC, V; local checks
Lunch, dinner every day

The best little whorehouse in town used to be right across the street from this historic pub, and the walls at Billy's sport some original artwork that recalls Aberdeen's bawdy past. The place is named after the infamous Billy Gohl, who terrorized the Aberdeen waterfront in 1907. Billy shanghaied sailors and robbed loggers, consigning their bodies to the murky Wishkah River through a trapdoor in a saloon only a block away from the present-day Billy's—where you get a square-deal meal and an honest drink without much damage to your pocketbook. The thick burgers and ranch fries are popular with everyone.

Bridges
1st and G,
(206) 532-6563
112 N G St, Aberdeen
Moderate; full bar; AE,
DC, MC, V; local
checks only
Lunch, dinner every day

Sonny Bridges started out with a corner cafe and kept expanding his horizons, both in space and in taste. An extensive remodel produced an airy, pastel restaurant with casual class. The diverse menu features fresh seafood, including razor clams and salmon, plus prime rib and pasta. Bridges is bolder now, offering some tasty Cajun-style specials, albeit with few surprises. The bar is first-class, with Northwest wines, beers, and espresso drinks. The staff, as always, is extraordinarily professional.

The Levee Street
7th and Levee,
(206) 532-1959
709 Levee St, Hoquiam
Moderate; full bar; MC,
V; checks OK
Dinner Tues-Sat

With a new riverside park, a centennial dock, and some handsome new office buildings, Hoquiam is rediscovering its picturesque waterfront. Roy Ann Taylor spent 12 years as a cook at a logging camp, serving up "acres of flapjacks and mounds of meat and potatoes." But apart from good food and generous portions, her newly redecorated restaurant has nothing in common with a cookhouse. There are plum-colored carpets, soft music, and a great view of swooping seagulls and tugboats. The menu is now more adventuresome, everything from "Raging Bull"—a logger-size portion of medium rare prime rib coated with a port and peppercorn sauce—to salmon fresh from the docks, veal Marsala, and bouillabaisse. Chewy homemade bread sticks accompany the soups and salads.

LODGINGS

Lytle House
Bed & Breakfast
Head west on Emerson,

In 1900, when Robert Lytle built what was to become Hoquiam's big architectural landmark, Hoquiam's Castle, his brother Joseph erected a smaller version

*turn right on Grant, go 3
blocks, (206) 533-2320
509 Chenault,
Hoquiam, WA 98550
Moderate; MC, V;
checks OK*

next door. This has become Lytle House with the almost-requisite Victorian embellishments throughout. The front parlor feels too formal to hunker down in a big chair for reading, but there are more than enough parlors for all and the seven guest rooms are spacious enough. On the second floor the Windsor Room has a small library, an antique wood stove, and a balcony overlooking the town. Guests share the bathrooms, with huge claw-footed tubs that remind you how long it once took to draw a bath. Goldfish luxuriate in a tub of their own in a third-floor bath, honest. Breakfasts are ample. Owners Robert and Dayna Bencala—he an antique furniture refinisher and she an Air Force helicopter mechanic—are B&B hosts of the best kind: genuinely hospitable yet unobtrusive.

MONTESANO

RESTAURANTS

Savory Faire
*Take Montesano exit off
Hwy 12, (206) 249-3701
135 S Main St,
Montesano
Inexpensive; no alcohol;
AE, MC, V; checks OK
Breakfast, lunch
Mon-Sat*

This is a charming place a block away from the handsome and historic Grays Harbor County Courthouse (whose murals have been freshly restored). The restaurant grew out of Candi Bachtell's popular cooking classes at Montesano's ambitious Community School. Breakfasts are wonderful: omelets, country-fried potatoes, and homemade breads. At lunchtime, she can elevate a French dip sandwich to a veritable event. Customers crane their necks to admire the food at the next table as they peruse the menu and sniff the aromas from Candi's ovens. An outdoor patio is available for fair-weather seating. Fresh-baked breads, rolls and cakes, pasta, and specialty coffees are available for take-out. If a glass of fresh lemonade fails to do the trick, take a dip in Lake Sylvia at the north end of town.

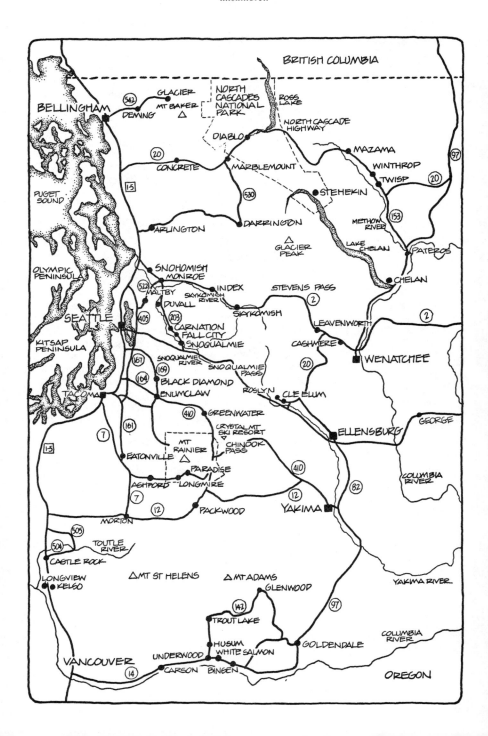

WASHINGTON CASCADES

Easterly crossings, starting in the north from Deming to Mount Baker, then Concrete to the Methow Valley along the North Cascades Highway. Farther south the "Cascade Loop": eastward along Highway 2 to Cashmere on Route 2, south to Cle Elum, westward again on I-90, then north through dairy country to Duvall. Then two Mount Rainier approaches—Maple Valley to Chinook Pass; Eatonville to Ashford—followed by a southward route through the heart of the Cascades and a short easterly jog along the Columbia River.

DEMING

RESTAURANTS

Deming Tavern
Off Mount Baker Hwy at Deming Rd and 1st St,
(206) 592-5282
5016 Deming Rd,
Deming
Moderate; beer and wine;
no credit cards;
checks OK
Lunch, dinner every day

In operation since 1922, this is one of the few real steak houses left hereabouts. It's not a fancy place, but everyone (a mix of loggers, suburbanites, and Bellingham city slickers) comes for the steak. You can get a tender, well-aged 6-ounce tenderloin for $8.50, a 16-ouncer for $14.50. The ultimate challenge here: you can have a 72-ounce steak, with a baked potato and spaghetti, for *free*—provided you can eat the whole thing in half an hour. If you can't, it's $36.95. Reserve in advance. So far, everyone has paid up. Twelve beers on tap.

Carol's Coffee Cup
1½ miles east of Deming
at Mount Baker Hwy,
(206) 592-5641
5414 Mount Baker Hwy,
Deming
Inexpensive; no alcohol;
MC, V; checks OK
Breakfast, lunch, dinner
every day

Carol's is a local institution: a pleasant little hamburger joint/bakery/cafe, long a favorite with loggers, skiers, and hikers. The hamburgers are fine, but the big cinnamon rolls and homemade pies are best. Be prepared for a long wait on summer weekends and during the peak of the Koma Kulshan (Mount Baker) ski season.

LODGINGS

The Logs
18 miles east of Deming
on Mount Baker Hwy, 30
miles east of Bellingham,
(206) 599-2711
9002 Mount Baker Hwy,
Deming, WA 98244

When we last checked, there was still a lot of damage from the floods to be cleaned up (the water came up to the cabins' doors, the pool was filled with silt, and there were lots of downed trees), but they were working hard to clean up the place. Despite the flood, in July when the streams run clear the trout begin to bite and bushes are laden with blueberries, and in winter no place could be cozier. Five log cabins (built by owner

Moderate; no credit cards; checks OK

Rod Ohlsen) are hidden in dense stands of alder and fir at the confluence of the Nooksack River and Canyon Creek. Cabins are spare and the twin beds are bunks, but the necessities are there: a large fireplace (built from river cobbles and slabs of Nooksack stone) complete with firewood; a couple of small bedrooms; a large, fully equipped kitchen. Cabins sleep up to 10; pets are okay.

GLACIER

RESTAURANTS

Innisfree

31 miles east of Bellingham on Mount Baker Hwy, (206) 599-2373 9393 Mount Baker Hwy, Glacier Moderate; beer and wine; MC, V; checks OK Dinner Thurs-Mon (summer), Fri-Sun (winter)

★★

Discriminating folks are lured from Seattle and Vancouver to Fred and Lynn Berman's special treatment and food at Innisfree. The Bermans are organic farmers, and they opened the restaurant as a reliable outlet for their produce. Over the years they've honed their cooking skills to the point of excellence. The menu is simple (only four entrées per night—a vegetarian dish, a meat or poultry, a fresh local fish) but intriguing. This cuisine is pure, ever-changing Northwest eclectic: Nooksack Valley fowl, beef, and veal; halibut with strawberry butter. Our salad was a little too watery, but the butternut apple soup was delicate, the bread was fresh and warm, and the finisher, tart local blueberries with the Bermans' homemade kefir (from a culture they brought back from Norway), was exceptionally flavorful. You can sit in the new area up front but it's better to wait for a seat in the dining room. They open up in early afternoon and will happily serve a steaming bowl of soup or other light dishes. It's probably not a place for everyone (the food is unsalted; no smoking is allowed), but for a getaway evening in Washington's own North Woods, you can't do better.

Milano's Market and Deli

Mount Baker Hwy in Glacier, (206) 599-2863 9990 Mount Baker Hwy, Glacier Moderate; beer and wine; MC, V; checks OK Lunch, dinner every day, breakfast Sat-Sun (closed Tuesdays in winter)

Popular with locals and carbo-loading hikers and skiers alike. This tiny, clean restaurant is really three: a deli (with meats and sandwiches), a casual Italian restaurant (with hearty pastas and a good, well-priced wine selection), and a nice place for dessert and coffee. The pasta is made fresh daily and stars in dishes ranging from two different lasagnes to a filling chicken Gorgonzola to a slew of wonderful raviolis (including a woodsy porcini mushroom ravioli in a delicate, herby marinara). Hot and cold sandwiches are noble concoctions. The deck outside boasts a panoramic vista of Mount Baker and Church Mountain.

MOUNT BAKER

Mount Baker, 56 miles east of Bellingham, has good downhill slopes but is equally noted as a cross-country skiing destination. It's open daily from mid-November through December; Friday, Saturday, and Sunday and some select "holiday weeks" during the remaining season (the longest in the state). The mountain never lacks for snow, and runs are predominantly intermediate, with bowls, meadows, and trails. Call (206) 734-6771 or (206) 671-0211.

Hiking in the area is extensive and beautiful, especially in the late summer when the foliage is turning, the wild blueberries are ripe, and the days are hot and dry. The end of the road (which in winter doubles as the Mount Baker ski resort) is a jump-off point for some easy day hikes and spectacular views of both Mount Baker and the most photographed mountain in the world, the geographically eccentric **Mount Shuksan.** For trail and weather conditions call the Glacier Public Service Center, (206) 599-2714.

CONCRETE

LODGINGS

Cascade Mountain Inn
5 miles west of Concrete,
off Hwy 20,
(206) 826-4333
3840 Pioneer Ln,
Concrete-Birdsview,
WA 98237
Moderate; MC, V;
checks OK

Here's one of the few bed and breakfasts that began life as an inn, not as a residence. Ingrid and Gerhard Meyer celebrated their retirement by building this spacious log inn on 10 acres in the Upper Skagit Valley, near where hundreds of bald eagles gather in the winter. There are six immaculate guest rooms, each named after a different country where the Meyers have lived; in the German room, piles of down gently pillow you to sleep. Breakfast is served in a cozy dining room or on the patio with its calming views of the North Cascades. The convivial Meyers will pack you a picnic for your jaunt into the surrounding countryside—they're close to both Baker Lake and the North Cascades National Park—if you'd like. A lovely place.

MARBLEMOUNT

Eagle watching. Hundreds of bald eagles perch along the Skagit River from December through March. The best area to view these scavengers is along Route 20 between Rockport and Marblemount (bring your binoculars). You'll be able to spy a number from the road; however, the best way to view them is from the river; call **Downstream River Runners,** (206) 483-0335; **Northern Wilderness River Riders,** (206) 448-RAFT; or **Orion Expeditions,** (206) 322-9130. The adventuresome may want to canoe downriver from Marblemount to Rockport (an easy 8 miles); the river appears tame but can be deceptively swift.

RESTAURANTS

Mountain Song Restaurant
In the middle of town on

Even if you have to serve yourself now, this restaurant makes for a nourishing stop along the North Cascades

Hwy 20, (206) 873-2461
Hwy 20, Marblemount
Moderate; beer and wine;
AE, MC, V; checks OK
Breakfast, lunch, dinner
every day (days vary
in winter)

Highway. Homemade breads and organically grown vegetables become big sandwiches; soups, salads, and quiches round out the menu along with pasta, chicken, and fish on the specials list (but never anything deep-fried). For dessert, try a slice of fresh berry pie. Northwest microbreweries and vintners are well represented. The feeling is rustic and faintly counter-cultural, with a wood stove and hanging plants inside, a pleasant, tree-ringed garden outside. No smoking.

DIABLO

Since the only road access to Ross Lake is south from Hope, B.C., the best way to get to the southern end of the lake—save by a 3½-mile hike—is on the Seattle City Light tugboat from Diablo. Here Seattle City Light built an outpost for crews building and servicing the dams on the river. The tugboat leaves twice daily (8:30am and 3pm) and the ride is a few bucks round trip; (206) 684-3112.

Worth visiting are the dams themselves, built by a visionary engineer named James Delmage Ross. **Skagit Tours** offer 3½-hour journeys through the Skagit Project, including an informative slide presentation, a ride up an antique incline railway to Diablo Dam, then a boat ride along the gorge of the Skagit to Ross Dam, a construction of daring engineering in its day. Afterward there is a lavish chicken dinner back in Diablo. Six miles down the road in Newhalem are inspirational walks to the grave of Ross and to Ladder Creek Falls, with plantings gathered from around the world. Tours are arranged through Seattle City Light, 1015 3rd Ave, Seattle, WA 98104, (206) 684-3030; summer only.

MAZAMA

LODGINGS

Mazama Country Inn
14 miles west of
Winthrop,
(509) 996-2681, toll-free
(800) 843-7951
Mail: PO Box 223,
Mazama, WA 98833
Moderate; beer and wine,
MC, V; checks OK
Breakfast, lunch, dinner
every day

With a view of the North Cascades from nearly every window, this spacious 6,000-square-foot lodge makes a splendid year-round destination (especially for horse-back riding and cross-country skiing), with ten good-sized rooms of wood construction with cedar beams (an attached wing offers four additional rooms). Some of the guest rooms have lofts that can be a bit stuffy in the summer, but each has a private bath, thick comforters on the beds, and futonlike pads that can be rolled out for extra guests. The four rooms behind the sauna have individual decks, two with views of Goat Peak and two looking out into the woods. Prices are reasonable, and many winter packages include three meals. Although the kitchen works at serving big, family-style meals in the winter, summers are à la carte with about ten entrées to choose from (salmon to prime rib to spaghetti). Pasta remains the best choice for dinner. Meals for non-guests require reservations.

The original inn, a converted ranchhouse, lacks the charm of the new one. The six rooms there (which share two baths) are used only during busy periods (or rented to groups). Families might want to try one of the two cabins that sleep up to six, especially since children under 13 are discouraged in the quiet lodge during the winter.

WINTHROP

Stroll through this Western-motif town and stop in at the **Shafer Museum,** housed in pioneer Guy Waring's 1897 log cabin on the hill behind the main street. Exhibits tell of the area's early history and include old cars, a stagecoach, and horse-drawn vehicles. It is said that Waring's Harvard classmate Owen Wister came to visit in the 1880s and found some of the material for *The Virginian* here.

Winthrop's rendezvous with destiny appears to be drawing near (although we've been saying this for years now), as Early Winters' downhill ski resort faces yet another "last" challenge from opponents. Meanwhile, there is plenty to do here for the outdoor enthusiast. The valley offers fine whitewater rafting, spectacular hiking in the North Cascades, horseback riding, fishing, and cross-country or helicopter skiing (call Central Reservations for more information; see below). An excellent blues festival in the summer brings in such talents as John Mayall and the Bluesbreakers and Mick Taylor (see Calendar).

Methow Valley Central Reservations is a booking service for the whole valley—Mazama to Pateros—as well as a good source of information on things to see and do and on current ski conditions. Write PO Box 505, Winthrop, WA 98862, or call toll-free (800) 422-3048 or (509) 996-2148. For road and pass conditions, call (509) 976-ROAD or (206) 434-ROAD.

The Methow Valley Touring Association keeps the valley's excellent cross-country ski trails groomed and available to visitors. Write to the association at PO Box 327, Winthrop, WA, 98862, or phone Central Reservations for conditions.

Hut-to-Hut Skiing offers miles of cross-country ski trails connecting with three spartan huts in the Rendezvous Hills. Each hut bunks up to eight people and comes equipped with a wood stove and a propane cookstove. Open for day skiers—a warm, dry lunch stop. For Rendezvous Huts information, call the Central Reservations office listed above.

RESTAURANTS

Duck Brand Cantina and Hotel
On the main street,
(509) 996-2192
248 Riverside Ave,
Winthrop
Inexpensive; beer and wine; AE, MC, V; local checks only
Breakfast, lunch, dinner every day

★

Built to replicate a frontier-style hotel, Duck Brand is a local favorite for good meals at good prices. The menu ranges from bulging burritos to fettuccine to sprout-laden sandwiches on whole-grain breads. The smooth homemade salsa has plenty of zip. Try a wedge of fudgy brownie or a three-inch-thick slice of fabulous berry pie. The American-style breakfasts are consistantly good and feature giant whole-wheat cinnamon rolls, homemade muffins (raspberry are great) and wonderful cheesy Spanish potatoes. An in-house bakery is slated to open soon. Upstairs, the Duck

Brand Hotel has six homey, sparsely-furnished rooms, but the price is right (around $49 for two).

LODGINGS

Sun Mountain Lodge
9 miles southwest of Winthrop on Patterson Lake Rd, (509) 996-2211 Mail: PO Box 1000, Winthrop, WA 98862 Expensive; full bar; AE, MC, V; checks OK Breakfast, lunch, dinner every day

When the European-based Haub family took over this resort, they made a few changes—$20 million worth so far. The location has always been dramatic, set on a hill high above the pristine Methow Valley and backed by the North Cascades. Now, at the end of the construction phase of the remodel, the massive timber-and-stone resort is equally impressive. Ask for one of the rooms in the 28 Gardner unit. They are dressed in natural colors, from the hand-painted bedspreads to the bent-willow headboards. Each new room has a gas fireplace (only those in the suites burn wood) and a view of the spectacular Methow Valley. Rooms in the main lodge are more standard. In addition there are eight rustic cabins available just down the hill at Patterson Lake. In winter, over 50 miles of well-groomed cross-country trails make this a haven for Nordic skiers (with 150 miles available throughout the valley). Expert instructors are available for skiers of any level. Close by are a heated pool (summers only), a hot tub, and tennis courts. In summer there are also guided nature hikes through the wilderness, brisk breakfast trail rides, and outfitter pack trips as well. The restaurant now offers a great table to every guest, whether it's a warm spot by the massive stone fireplace or a window table with a sweeping view of the valley. Chef Jack Hanes, formerly of Salishan Lodge fame, has brought in a Southwest influence and a welcome upgrade to the food.

The Farmhouse Inn
709 Hwy 20, (509) 996-2191 Mail: PO Box 118, Winthrop, WA 98862 Inexpensive; AE, MC, V; checks OK

A restored farmhouse, this bed and breakfast a quarter mile outside Winthrop has lots of charm but not enough floor space. You're best off with room Number 6, a two-bedroom suite with private bath; or Numbers 1 and 2, with private baths and queen-size beds. The other three rooms are too small (about as big as the bed), and they share baths. The beds are soft. There's a hot tub and very limited cable TV. Continental breakfast and registration are at the Duck Brand Hotel, about a 10-minute walk from the Inn.

METHOW

RESTAURANTS

Methow Cafe
Middle of town, (509) 923-2228 Hwy 153, Methow

Besides the Post Office, this is the only business in town, but even if Pat Luft *had* competition we think he'd still have a loyal following. In summer, river rafters pile into the cozy Cafe; in winter, it's packed

*Inexpensive; beer and
wine; no credit cards;
checks OK
Lunch, dinner Wed-Sun
(days vary in winter)*

with locals and cross-country skiers. For the most part, the food is the same year-round—hearty fare with names like the Steelheader Breakfast (two eggs, two oversized buttermilk pancakes, and thick strips of bacon from nearby smokehouse, Wenatchee Pack) and the McFarland Creek sandwich (grilled ham and turkey with Monterey jack and Cheddar cheeses). Nothing fussy, just good food—and since Luft hired Susie Lamoreux to woman the kitchen, he's learned to spell vermicelli. Visit awhile and they'll talk about the beavers that felled a dozen poplars on a nearby creek, or the best trails for skiing or hiking on any given day.

PATEROS

LODGINGS

Amy's Manor

*5 miles north of Pateros
on Hwy 153,
(509) 923-2334
Mail: PO Box 411,
Pateros, WA 98846
Moderate; MC, V;
checks OK*

★★

Orchardists Barb and Rodney Nickell opened their enchanting four-bedroom home as a B&B a few years ago to keep it in the family. Built in 1928, the manor is dramatically situated at the foot of the Cascades overlooking the Methow River, and the rooms are country-quaint, with patchwork quilts tossed over rocking chairs and comfortable beds. The 170-acre estate has a small farm where chickens and rabbits wander freely. A continental-plus breakfast is served, (something easy but filling, says Barb) such as fresh fruit and waffles.

MONROE

RESTAURANTS

Ixtapa

*Main and Lewis,
(206) 794-8484
118 E Main St, Monroe
Inexpensive; full bar;AE,
MC, V; checks OK
Lunch, dinner every day*

Ixtapa is a nice find on an otherwise sleepy main street in Anytown, USA. The richly spiced shredded beef, with its hints of cloves and cumin, is a big hit at Ixtapa. Chorizo here is upstaged by that shredded beef and the chile verde. Chiles rellenos are not as light and fluffy as they should be, but the sizzling fajitas—chicken or beef—come with a good array of condiments. Be prepared to wait in line, but don't despair—the service is fast, particularly if you're willing to sit at the counter. There's another outlet in Snohomish; (206) 568-4522.

INDEX

RESTAURANTS

Bush House Country Inn

1 mile north of Hwy 2,

First established during the mining boom of 1889, the inn has operated on and off (and up and down) over the

(206) 793-2312
300 5th St, Index
Inexpensive; full bar;AE,
MC, V; local checks only
Breakfast, lunch, dinner
every day, brunch Sun

years. The improving restaurant has a nice country charm, with a big stone fireplace in the middle. The menu features fresh fish, aged beef, Washington fryers, and fresh fruits and vegetables. Portions are generous (the main-course salad was enough to feed the proverbial army). The fresh vegetable and dip appetizer, the New York steak, and a pork Marsala are all quite good. But it's the fresh-out-of-the-oven blackberry cobbler for which we'd stop again. Sunday brunch has become quite popular and includes fresh fruits, waffles, old-time favorites like biscuits with gravy, assorted meats, omelets made to order, and a variety of home-baked pastries and rolls. Friendly service. The 11 rooms are still small, clean, and unmemorable, the view alpine. There are only two shared baths, but the third-floor suite (which sleeps six) has its own bath. It's all very country—especially the plumbing. The price is fair ($35; $65 for the suite).

LEAVENWORTH

A railroad-yard-and-sawmill town that lost its industry, Leavenworth, with its stunning alpine setting in the Cascade Mountains, decided 30 years ago to recast itself as a Bavarian-style town with tourism as its primary industry. The architecture in the city center features some excellent craftsmanship in the Bavarian mode. Popular festivals are the Autumn Leaf Festival the last weekend in September and the first weekend in October, the Christmas Lighting Festival the first two Saturdays in December, and the Mai Fest the second weekend in May.

Shopping. We recommend browsers head to The Clock Shop, with an impressive display of new and antique clocks, 721 Front Street; the Gingerbread Factory, for authentic decorated gingerbread cookies and a delightful village of gingerbread houses, 828 Commercial St; Images and Sounds for distinctly non-Bavarian posters, prints and notecards, 9th and Commercial; The Black Swan and Ugly Duckling, for boutique fashions and children's wear, 827 Front Street; the Blue Heron, for original artwork and limited edition prints, 905 Commercial Street; Village Books, for an excellent collection of books about the Northwest, books by Northwest authors, and cookbooks, 215 9th Street; and Country Things, for folk art, antiques, furniture, tinware and linens, 221 8th Street. Oberland Bakery and Cafe relies largely on whole-grain breads but also does a great raspberry Danish. The restaurant's spare, but they also serve hearty soups and sandwiches on their substantial breads; 703 Front Street, (509) 548-7216.

Other attractions include **Homefires Bakery**, where visitors can see the German-style, wood-fired oven (the nine-grain bread is the thing to get, but don't pass up the dark German rye bread) and during fair weather can sit at the picnic table on the lawn and have cinnamon rolls and coffee; 13013 Bayne Road (off Icicle Road).

Outdoor activities include river rafting on the Wenatchee; fishing and hiking at Icicle Creek; touring the national fish hatchery on Icicle Creek to watch the Chinook salmon run (June and July) and spawn (August and September), 12790 Fish Hatchery Road (off Icicle Road), (509) 548-7641; golfing at the scenic 18-hole Leavenworth Golf Club, (509) 548-7267; downhill skiing at Stevens Pass,

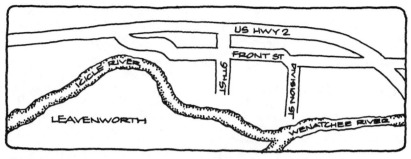

(206) 973-2441, or Mission Ridge, (509) 663-6543; fabulous cross-country skiing around the area, at the golf course, on Icicle Road just past the Fish Hatchery, or at the Leavenworth Nordic Center, (509) 548-7864; horseback riding at Eagle Creek Ranch, (509) 548-7798; sleigh rides behind Belgian draft horses at Red-Tail Canyon Farm, (509) 548-4512; walking along the river on a new city center trail system which leads via wheelchair-accessible ramps to Blackbird Island; mountain biking with rentals available at Icicle Bicycle at the Leavenworth Nordic Center, (509) 548-4566 or (509) 548-7864; and rock climbing in the new **Peshastin Pinnacles State Park** just 10 miles east of Leavenworth (no camping, just climbing).

Scottish Lakes Snomad Camps, eight miles into the backcountry west of Leavenworth, is a cluster of primitive plywood cabins at the edge of the Alpine Lakes Wilderness Area. It's most popular for backcountry skiers, but open (and less expensive) for hikers come summer. You can ski up the 8 miles or be carted up in a snowmobile and ski home the 3,800-foot descent; PO Box 312, Leavenworth, WA 98826; (509) 548-7330, by reservations only.

RESTAURANTS

Terrace Bistro
*On the corner of 8th and
the alley between
Commercial and Front,
(509) 548-4193
200 8th St, Leavenworth
Moderate; full bar; MC,
V; checks OK
Lunch, dinner every day*

Hands down, locals will tell you, this is the place for dinner in Leavenworth. For one reason: this second-floor eatery leaves the German food alone (okay, there is *one* wiener schnitzel on the menu). At the bistro, favorites are chicken Jerusalem (chicken breasts grilled with bread crumbs, parsley, basil, Parmesan cheese, and served with artichoke sauce) and tortellini with shrimp. The medallions of pork tenderloin sautéed in a brandied cream sauce were rich and tender. As the name implies, there's a terrace for fair-weather dining. The meal is unhurried and it's easy to linger over coffee and dessert. Service is attentive and hospitable though the atmosphere and presentation are a bit heavy handed; reservations recommended.

Walt's Other Place
*Commercial St,
(206) 548-6125
820 Commercial St,
Leavenworth
Moderate; beer and wine;
MC, V; checks OK*

Locals frequented the Terrace Bistro so often that Walt Wilmouth opened a second restaurant just so they wouldn't have to go to the same restaurant two nights in a row. Turns out we're not the only ones who actually prefer the downscaled atmosphere of this place to the more affected Terrrace. On ground level (just down from the Terrace Bistro), this place is smaller

Dinner every day

and simpler in decor and menu. The prices are lower (where they should be), and the food, primarily unfussy Italian and Greek, is just as good. Service is slow.

Gustav's Onion Dome Tavern
On Hwy 2 at the west end of town, (509) 548-4509
617 Hwy 2, Leavenworth
Inexpensive; beer and wine; MC, V; checks OK
Lunch, dinner every day

Popular with the outdoors crowd, which picks Gustav's as the place to drop by for good burgers and a beer. There's a patio on the roof now, so in fair weather you can sit under colorful umbrellas and take in the panorama of the town. For a change from Leavenworth's ubiquitous German fare, Gustav's offers homemade fries and onion rings with its burgers and a good selection of imported beers. Because it's a tavern, you must be 21 to patronize Gustav's.

Reiner's Gasthaus
Across from the gazebo, (509) 548-5111
829 Front St, Leavenworth
Inexpensive, beer and wine; MC, V; checks OK
Lunch, dinner every day

For the quintessential Bavarian culinary experience in Leavenworth, Reiner's is the place. The menu offers Austrian and Hungarian specialties as well. The smoked Bavarian-style farmer's sausage with sauerkraut and German rye bread is a safe selection for the uninitiated. More adventuresome eaters can try the homemade dumplings (boiled liver, egg, and bread) served with melted cheese for lunch; or the schnitzel topped with paprika sauce or the Hungarian goulash for dinner. Seating is European style (which means tables are sometimes shared); service is prompt and knowledgeable. Because it's located on the second floor at the back of the buildings on Front Street, the views of the town from the restaurant are slim (although a tiny balcony seats a few patrons in good weather). There's a wide selection of imported wines and beers. Have dessert somewhere else.

LODGINGS

Pine River Ranch
1½ miles off Hwy 2 on Hwy 207, (509) 763-3959
19668 Hwy 207, Leavenworth, WA 98826
Moderate; MC, V; checks OK

One mile from Lake Wenatchee, this 35-acre former dairy farm is a comfortable place to stay—that is, if you like to be followed around by a goat, nuzzled by a horse, pecked by the rooster, or tricked by Daisy, the dog who likes to play dead. We wouldn't really call it a ranch, but there are four nice rooms here; try for the Wildflower room with French doors to a private deck and, reportedly (though it wasn't in yet at press time). In winter, Mike Zenk grooms a leisurely cross-country ski trail through much of the valley's 200 acres. Summers there are plenty of biking opportunities and day hikes as well. Groups of six to eight may choose to rent the 1950s-style house next door with a deck and hot tub ($85 for two; $15 per each extra) but don't expect a lot of atmosphere or many extras. (Is it too much to expect a lampshade in the bedroom?)

Run of the River
1 mile east of Hwy 2 at

Built on the bank of the Icicle River, this log-construction bed and breakfast boasts such solitude and comfort

9308 E Leavenworth Rd,
(509) 548-7171
Mail: PO Box 285,
Leavenworth, WA 98826
Moderate; AE, MC, V;
checks OK

that you may want to spend the entire day on the deck, reading or watching the wildlife in the refuge across the river. Hosts Monty and Karen Turner run Leavenworth's finest B&B. There are four rooms, each with private bath, TV (cable), and terrycloth robes; one has a Jacuzzi. The rooms facing the river have commanding views of the mountains. The Tumwater suite on the ground level has an extra room with a Jacuzzi, a wood stove, and deck access. Others have their own decks and loft nooks with southern exposure; all are furnished in country pine. Hearty breakfasts such as yogurt and fruit, juice, eggs, French toast, and baked apples are served. There's a Jacuzzi on the deck near the river, a large-screen TV in the living room, and mountain bikes available for off-road explorations. This is an excellent getaway for adults. No smoking whatsoever.

Haus Lorelei Inn

2 blocks off Commercial
on Division,
(509) 548-5726
347 Division St,
Leavenworth, WA 98826
Moderate; no credit cards;
checks OK

Here's a rarity: a bed and breakfast that not only welcomes kids but is run by four of them (and their mom). The two-acre site, surrounded by towering pines and flanking the Icicle River, is only two blocks from Leavenworth's main street and provides many activities for the younger guests. Elisabeth Saunders and her children offer six bedrooms furnished in comfortable European tradition, four with private baths. Each of the rooms affords gorgeous views of the Cascades; at night you can hear the river rushing over the boulders. During the summer months, guests eat on the screened sun porch and may use the private tennis court. There's a hot tub, and a short walk away there's a sandy swimming beach.

Haus Rohrbach Pension

About 1 mile off of Ski
Hill Dr, (509) 548-7024
12882 Ranger Rd,
Leavenworth, WA 98826
Moderate; AE, MC, V;
checks OK

It's a true European pension, with alpine architecture, bathrooms down the hall, gracious hosts, and breakfast included with the room. The lodge is tucked into the base of Tumwater Mountain, so it has a nearly Bavarian view over the valley farmland back toward town and the snow-clad mountains. Most of the rooms open onto a flower-decked balcony facing this direction, and the delicious, ample breakfast is served on a large deck with the same majestic vista. The rooms are a bit thin of wall, decorated rather austerely, and feature very firm platform beds; those on the uppermost floor facing the valley have the most light and appeal. The Alm Haus, which sleeps six, is a good deal at $100 a night. Bring the kids—there's a swimming pool, a sled hill out back, and an ice-cream parlor in the basement. Sometimes a naturalist will drop by to give an evening talk.

Mountain Home Lodge

Mountain Home Rd off
E Leavenworth Rd
and Hwy 2,

There's a lot to do here. Miles of tracked cross-country ski trails leave from the back door; you can snowshoe and sled, and there's a 1,700-foot toboggan run. Cross-country ski rentals are available at the lodge. There's a

(509) 548-7077
Mail: PO Box 687,
Leavenworth, WA 98826
Expensive; AE, MC, V;
checks OK

Jacuzzi on the deck overlooking a broad meadow and the mountains across the valley. Summer activities include hiking, horseshoe pitching, badminton, swimming, and tennis. And that's a good thing because there aren't many places to gather when the weather's not cooperating except the sheepskin-covered couches in front of the fireplace adjacent to the dining area. The nine rooms themselves are very plain (almost motel-ish), and noise still travels from bedroom to bedroom. No children.

Straightforward meals are included in the price during the winter and are available at an additional cost in the summer. Winter weekend reservations should be made a few months ahead of time. In the winter, a heated snow-cat will pick you up from the parking lot at Duncan Orchard Fruit Stand, just east of Leavenworth. In the summer, Mountain Home is accessible over three miles of dirt road, appropriately labeled primitive.

Mrs. Anderson's Lodging House
Just off the center of town at 917 Commercial St,
(509) 548-6173
Mail: PO Box 254,
Leavenworth, WA 98826
Moderate; DC, MC, V;
checks OK

The newest lodging alternative in Leavenworth is also the oldest: the revivified Mrs. Anderson's Lodging House, which originally opened in 1903 as a boarding-house for sawmill workers. Though it's been through other incarnations since that time, this 10-room inn right in the center of Leavenworth has charm to spare and very friendly operators. It's basic—rooms are minimally, crisply furnished, boardinghouse style—but sparkling clean, with pristine whitewashed walls. It's a bargain: the two that share baths cost $40 and $45; the rest, with private baths, average $57 a night. (All prices include breakfast of fruit compote, granola, muffins, tea, and coffee.) We fancy the room upstairs with the deck facing town, or the room with the splendid view of the North Cascades. Large groups would do well to inquire about Mrs. Anderson's holiday townhouse, two blocks away.

River Chalet
4½ miles west of Leavenworth off Hwy 2,
(509) 663-7676
1131 Monroe St,
Wenatchee, WA 98801
Expensive; no credit cards; checks OK

An ideal vacation spot for groups of couples, this contemporary guest house on the east side of Leavenworth gives the visitor a real feel for the Northwest. It's right on the Wenatchee River, and large windows look out over mountains. Three bedrooms sleep 12 comfortably (but slumber parties of 22 sleeping-baggers have occurred); wood stoves keep you warm. Outside there's a hot tub. In winter there's ample skiing all around, and a large kitchen makes gourmet collaborations a pleasure. Cost is $200 for four. Catering can be arranged on request.

Enzian Motor Inn
On the north side of Hwy 2 in the center of town,
(509)548-5269

This is the best hotel/motel place in town. Built by former contractor Bob Johnson and his son, Robert, it is now owned by the father/son team and their wives. Equal parts owner and contractor, they were meticu-

590 Hwy 2, Leavenworth,
WA 98826
Moderate; AE, DC, MC,
V; checks OK

lous about detail throughout. Stair rails and ceiling beams are hand-carved by a true Bavarian woodworker. The suites offer in-room spas and fireplaces; even the standard rooms are tasteful and a cut above most "motor inns." Breakfast (included with the price of a room) is served in the large fourth floor breakfast solarium. During the summer the older Johnson plays the alpenhorn on the balcony outside the dining room.

CASHMERE

If you're not in a Bavarian mood, this little orchard town gives cross-mountain travelers an alternative to stopping in Leavenworth. The main street has put up Western storefronts; the town's bordered by river and railroad.

Chelan County Historical Society and Pioneer Village has an extensive collection of Indian artifacts and archaeological material; the adjoining pioneer village puts 19 old buildings, carefully restored and equipped, into a nostalgic grouping. 600 Cottage Avenue, (509) 782-3230.

Aplets and Cotlets. These confections, made with local fruit and walnuts from an old Armenian recipe, have been produced for decades; you can tour the plant at Liberty Orchards and (of course) consume a few samples. 117 Mission Street, (509) 782-2191.

RESTAURANTS

The Pewter Pot
Downtown Cashmere in
the business district,
(509) 782-2036
124½ Cottage Ave,
Cashmere
Moderate; beer and wine;
MC, V; checks OK
Lunch, dinner Tues-Sat

Here you can get Early American food such as apple-country chicken topped with owner Kristi Biornstad's own apple-cider sauce, Plymouth turkey dinner, and New England boiled dinner. Desserts are tasty. Although her restaurant's short on atmosphere, Biornstad tries hard to serve dishes that reflect the area, using local ingredients. Try one of the daily specials. But if you try dinner, arrive early; the place closes promptly at 8pm even on Saturdays.

LODGINGS

Cashmere Country Inn
Off Hwy 2, follow
Division to Pioneer,
(509) 782-4212
5801 Pioneer Ave,
Cashmere, WA 98815
Moderate; AE, MC, V;
checks OK

A village whose tourist effort has heretofore been centered squarely on the Aplets and Cotlets factory now has a first-class country inn to broaden its allure. Seattle expatriates Patti and Dale Swanson are consummate innkeepers: energetic but never intrusive, full of enthusiasm about the area, genuinely concerned for the well-being of their guests, and possessors of excellent (if slightly floral) decorating taste. The four-guestroom farmhouse was remodeled and fitted out with a keen eye for aesthetics and detail, and there are a couple of large public rooms just for guests. That's important, because the pretty guest rooms—two with private baths, two with shared—are small. Breakfasts here don't taste like an innkeeper's duty as much as an accomplished cook's delight. Patti might whip up wine-stewed cherries with orange juice and a sour-cream egg bake, or perhaps homemade apple-pear juice and delicate lemon crêpes, served with lemon syrup and decorated with nasturtiums from her garden. She'll also do a candlelit five-course dinner on request, which we haven't had a chance to sample but have every reason to suspect would be lovely.

THORP

LODGINGS

Circle H Holiday Ranch
Exit 101 off I-90,
(509) 964-2000
Mail: Rt 1, Box 175,
Thorp, WA 98946
Expensive; AE, MC, V;
checks OK

Sweeping views of the Kittitas Valley and the Cascade foothills and a small herd of saddle horses are the big draw to the Circle H, located an easy hour and a half from Seattle. The sprawling, modern ranch house was bought out of bankruptcy from an agriculture baron who hit hard times. Jim and Betsy Ogden (who moved from New York three years ago) converted ranch hand bunkhouses into two-room suites, decorated with the overflow from Betsy's collection of Westernalia. Each suite sleeps four and contains a kitchenette and bath; books, puzzles, and playing cards fill the shelves, but no phones or TVs (there's a big-screen TV in the day room). Meals, included in the price of your stay, are served family style in the summer (breakfast only in the winter). The pine board interiors of the cabins are whitewashed, and Indian-design blankets cover the beds. The Tonto and Lone Ranger suites are back-to-back with a connecting door, as are the Roy Rogers and Dale Evans cabins, to accommodate bigger families.

The corral supports a small menagerie, from a family of angora rabbits to burros. Oliver, the ranch collie, playfully herds guests around the landscaped grounds. The Ogdens welcome young hands to help with ranch chores, while others opt for a trail ride on one of the 15 horses. The 100,000-acre L.T. Murray Wildlife Area backs up to the ranch and is prime for hiking, biking, and riding (bring your own horse, if you like). The nearby Yakima River provides quality fly-fishing and lazy-day river rafting.

CLE ELUM

Easy access·brings travelers from the freeway to Cle Elum, a former coal-mining town now undergoing a modest rediscovery.

Cle Elum Bakery is a longtime local institution, doing as much business these days with travelers as with locals. From one of the last brick-hearth ovens in the Northwest come delicious torchetti, cinnamon rolls, and great old-fashioned cake doughnuts. Closed Sundays. First and Peoh, (509) 674-2233.

Cle Elum Historical Telephone Museum. Open Memorial Day to Labor Day only, this museum incorporates the area's original phone system, which was operating well into the 1960s; 1st and Wright, (509) 674-5702.

RESTAURANTS

Mama Vallone's Steak House & Inn
On the main drag at the west end of town,
(509) 674-5174
302 W 1st St, Cle Elum
Moderate; full bar; AE, DC, MC, V; checks OK
Dinner everyday, lunch Sun

Talk to the regulars and they'll tell you about the warm welcomes, great steaks, and good homemade pasta at Mama Vallone's. It's definitely the best Cle Elum has to offer, but it never seems to live up to its rumored reputation. Our chicken breast in marinara sauce was fine, but the pork scalloppine, a special the day of our visit, was disappointingly underseasoned. One of the big deals is bagna cauda, a "hot bath" of garlic, anchovy, olive oil, and butter into which you dip strips of steak, chicken breast, or your favorite seafood. Or simply order steak, the tastiest version of which tosses Sicilian-spiced steak slices over homemade fettuccine. Wines are only okay; service (you're cared for by several members of the staff) is exceptional. Upstairs there are two bedrooms with private baths, decorated in antique reproductions, that rent for $55 a night.

LODGINGS

The Moore House
Adjacent to Iron Horse State Park at 526 Marie St, (509) 674-5939 or toll-free (800) 22-TWAIN
Mail: PO Box 2861, South Cle Elum, WA 98943
Moderate; AE, MC, V; checks OK

It's a winner. Named for owners Connie and Monty Moore, who lovingly restored the structure, this bed and breakfast was originally built in 1913 to house transient employees of the Chicago, Milwaukee, St. Paul & Pacific Railroad. Now on the National Register of Historic Places, the bunkhouse with 10 guest rooms is light and airy, and pleasantly furnished with reproduction antiques. Four of the rooms have their own baths; the others share two and a half immaculately clean baths. Throughout the house the railroad motif is evident: rooms are named for men who actually stayed in the house decades ago, and railroad memorabilia—vintage photographs, model trains, schedules, and other artifacts—is displayed in the hallways and the public rooms. Two cabooses in the side yard are fully equipped with bathes, fridges, queen beds, and private sundecks. Included in the reasonable price (rooms range from $41-$95) is an ample breakfast, and should you feel the spirit, there's an outdoor hot tub that the Moores will rev up for your use.

Hidden Valley Guest Ranch
Off SR 970 at milepost 8, Hidden Valley Rd,
(509) 857-2322
Mail: HC 61, Box 2060, Cle Elum, WA 98922

A short hour from Seattle is the state's oldest dude ranch. Owners Bruce and Matt Coe have brought a little pride of ownership back to this pastoral 700 acres. The nine cabins are still quite rustic and thin of wall (the ones with the fireplaces are the best in the winter), but miles of wildflower-lined trails, horseback riding, nearby trout fishing, a pool, a hot tub, and splendid

Moderate; MC, V; checks OK

cross-country skiing terrain make up for the basic accommodations. There is a kitchen in each cabin but no utensils or cookware. This really not a problem unless you like to snack; all meals, included in the package price, are taken in the cookhouse, a dining room serving country-style buffets (open to the public by reservation). Here you'll also find treats like cookies and lemonade throughout the day. On Sunday mornings they load up the chuck wagon with blueberry pancakes, muffins, and wrangler-style coffee for a hearty breakfast out in the fields. We're talkin' country, so don't forget the bug repellent.

ROSLYN

Until recently Roslyn was just a sleepy reminder of its rough-and-tough days as a thriving coal-mining town, but today it's the locale where the new TV series *Northern Exposure* is filmed. The TV production is beginning to do for this town what *Twin Peaks* did to Snoqualmie.

Modest turn-of-the-century homes have become weekend places for city folk, and the former mortuary is now a video store and movie theater, but the main intersection still offers a cross-section of the town's character: the historic Northwestern Improvement Company building (which once housed the company store) occupies one corner, while the old brick bank across the way still operates behind the original brass bars and oak counters.

An old stone tavern, inexplicably called **The Brick**, has a water-fed brass spittoon running the length of the bar; (509) 649-2643. Down the road, behind the town's junkyard, you'll find **Carek's Market**, one of the state's better purveyors of fine meats and sausages. Notable are the Polish sausage, the pepperoni, and the jerky; 4 South A Street, (509) 649-2333.

RESTAURANTS

Roslyn Cafe

2nd and Pennsylvania, (509) 649-2763
28 Pennsylvania Ave, Roslyn
Inexpensive; beer and wine; AE, MC, V; local checks only
Breakfast Sat-Sun, lunch, dinner Tues-Sun (winter hours vary)

The Roslyn Cafe (under the new ownership of Peter Skiba) remains the kind of funky eatery that every picturesque, slightly chic town like Roslyn should have. It's an old building with high ceilings, a short bar that is now a counter, neon in the window, hard chairs, a jukebox with original 78s—full of a sense of different types belonging. Dinners try to be a bit more fancy—grilled halibut with dill sauce, Chinese pepper steak. But really, it's best earlier in the day, when you can get really good burgers, a fine corn chowder, or a super Philadelphia steak sandwich at lunch. Breakfast is also worth the side trip (but it begins a little later than what we call normal breakfast hours): bacon and eggs, blueberry shortstacks, homemade fried potatoes, gooey cinnamon rolls, and huevos rancheros. The help was gratifyingly spacey, and the patrons—all the politically correct types—were filling up before heading back to Seattle on a Sunday afternoon.

Village Pizza
Main and Pennsylvania,
(509) 649-2992
6 Pennsylvania Ave,
Roslyn
Inexpensive; beer and
wine; no credit cards;
checks OK
Dinner every day

You've found the local hangout, run by a real couple of characters, Nan and Darrel Harris, a mother/daughter team from San Francisco. Their urban literary passions (they'll have copies of the *New York Review of Books* and *Architectural Digest* arrayed on the tables) are well in evidence. This is good pizza too, some bordering on *molto delizioso* (the pungent fresh garlic pizza is out of this world). Interesting toppings include mild green chiles, sauerkraut, and cashews (not all at once), all of which are inexplicably popular. Everyone is here—gangs of wild children with their bicycles piled outside, longhairs, local ranchers, yuppies—peacefully coexisting, which is perhaps the biggest tribute to the Harrises and their pizza.

SNOQUALMIE

This lovely country, where the dairyland folds into the mountains, was once best known for its falls. Today, it's familiar to most as the setting for *Twin Peaks*. The series is over but the town's diner still serves Twin Peaks pie, and Peakers can still purchase a T-shirt almost anywhere (even at the bank). The 268-foot **Snoqualmie Falls** just up the road is, as it has always been, a thundering spectacle. There is an observation deck; better is to take a picnic down the 1-mile trail to the base of the falls.

Puget Sound Railway is a volunteer-operated steam-locomotive that runs Saturdays and Sundays from April through October, up to Snoqualmie Falls gorge. There's also a good railroad museum. Call Snoqualmie Depot for schedule, (206) 746-0425.

The **Snoqualmie Winery**, now under the new ownership of Stimson Lane, reopened in early 1991 after a brief closure. It is a splendid stop on the way through the Cascades, with tours, tastings, and a marvelous view; 1000 Winery Road, (206) 888-4000.

Snoqualmie Pass. The four ski areas (Alpental, Snoqualmie, Ski Acres, and Hyak), all now under the same ownership (with a free shuttle that runs between the areas), offer the closest downhill and cross-country skiing for Seattle buffs. Alpental is the most challenging, Snoqualmie (with one of the largest ski schools in the country) has excellent instruction for beginners through racers, Ski Acres has some challenging bump runs, and the smallest of the four, Hyak, is a favored spot for downhill telemark skiers, with lit, groomed cross-country tracks and many kilometers of trails. In summer, the relatively low-lying transmountain route is a good starting point for many hikes.

LODGINGS

The Salish Lodge
Exit 27 off I-90, follow
signs to Snoqualmie
Falls, (206) 888-2556
37807 SE Fall City Rd,
Snoqualmie, WA 98065
Expensive; full bar; AE,

The falls may be the initial draw. But since you really can't see much of them from the rooms, it's a good thing the owners have rebuilt a lodge with rooms that are as much as a selling point as the falls themselves. Each room is designed in a tempered country motif: light, clean-lined wooden furnishings, pillowed window seats (or balconies in some), flagstone fireplaces (and a

DC, MC, V; checks OK
Breakfast, lunch Mon-
Fri, dinner every day,
brunch every day

woodbox full of split wood and kindling), and a cedar armoire. The details are covered here: TV cleverly concealed, bathrobes and even a telephone in the bathroom. Jacuzzis are separated from the bedrooms with a swinging window to invite the full effect of fire. Still, it's tough to book a room with a great view. There are only 8 (out of 91) with a falls view; most have views of the upper river (and the power plant). The rooftop open-ceiling hot tub is another nice feature. For the most part, the inn hosts honeymooners, second-honey-mooners, and small business conferences (there are two banquet rooms downstairs and every detail is well attended to). It's a good getaway, but there's not much to do besides falls-gazing.

The five-course brunch—filling but disappointing—lives on. We prefer the dining room for dinner (rather than brunch) these days. Window tables overlooking the falls are separated by curtains for privacy. Our dinner began with terrine of smoked duck with brandied melons, ringed with mustard sauce—an unusual but successful combination. This was followed by an exquisite pumpkin crab bisque, thick with morsels of succulent crabmeat. Our entrées were simple but well prepared: choucroute of "Puget Sound" (salmon, scallops, and shrimp on sauerkraut) and sea scallops on creamy polenta with tomato sauce. Aside from the sauerkraut, there were few signs of any vegetables; for the price (starting at $18 a plate) we expected at least a few greens. The wine list is almost legendary (some say overwhelming), but the sommelier is friendly and helpful. It is almost as difficult to choose from the impressive dessert selection (we suggest the chocolate mousse cake in raspberry sauce). The chocolate truffles with the check are a nice touch.

FALL CITY

RESTAURANTS

The Herbfarm

3 miles off I-90 from exit
22, (206) 784-2222
32804 Issaquah-Fall City
Rd, Fall City
Expensive; wine only;
MC, V; checks OK
Lunch Fri-Sun (late
April-Dec only)

What began as a front-yard wheelbarrow filled with a few extra herbs for sale has become, among many other things, a trustworthy little haven of gourmandize. Whether more attention is lavished upon the herbs grown here, the gourmet preparations they give rise to, or the few patrons lucky enough to get a reservation is difficult to say. It's much easier to claim that no other restaurant works with such devotion and delight to transform a midday meal into a memorable occasion.

Plan to spend two hours or more tasting, learning, and talking about what you have eaten. Each meal is served to no more than 24 people, and generally starts with a short tour of the 17 herbal theme gardens. Except for the introduction and a brief question-and-answer session, the education happens tableside, as the proprietors come around with plants for guests to sniff and sample.

The Herbfarm's menu changes according to the current yields of the gardens and chef Jerry Traunfeld makes every attempt to gather other ingredients as close to home as possible. Our mid-spring meal began with chive oil–drizzled raviolis of herb-smoked black cod wrapped in greens and garnished with sturgeon caviar. This was followed by two extraordinary soups—morel mushroom with caraway, and wild stinging nettle with lovage—served in the same bowl, topped with swirls of créme fraiche and tiny cheese puffs. Tulip petals enveloped a sorbet which followed. Extraordinarily tender herb-encrusted medallions of Ellensburg lamb in a garlic-and-grainy-mustard sauce formed the heart of our meal. A memorable salad contained dozens of ingredients, including the blossoms of several edible flowers and a hard-boiled quail egg. Dessert was a delightful and unusual trilogy of faux eggs including an angelica-and-ginger soufflé cooked in a hen's egg, geranium ice cream with a "yolk" of saffron ice cream, and a white chocolate sauce with an apricot mousse. So easy to enjoy this place; so tough to get a reservation.

CARNATION

Twenty-five miles northeast of Seattle is the home of the **Carnation Research Farm**, where self-guided tours let you glimpse several stages in the pasteurizing process. Kids love it; (206) 788-1511. Closed Sunday and during the winter.

At **MacDonald Memorial Park**, meandering trails and an old-fashioned suspension bridge across the Tolt River provide a great family picnic setting; Fall City Road and NE 40th Street.

Biking. The Cascade Bicycle Club sponsors rides all over the region. The Carnation-North Bend ride leaves from MacDonald-Tolt River Park and winds its way up to Snoqualmie Falls, the Herbfarm in Fall City, and George's Bakery in North Bend. Free to anyone who wants to ride; call (206) 522-BIKE.

Remlinger Farms. The sky's the limit for your favorite fruits and vegetables at this U-pick farm. The Strawberry Festival in mid-June starts off the season. Throughout the summer you can choose from the best in raspberries, apples, corn, and grapes. The kids, young and old alike, love tromping through the fields in search of the perfect jack-o'-lantern-to-be in October. Call (206) 333-4135 or (206) 451-8740 for more information.

RESTAURANTS

The Original Brown Bag Restaurant and Bakery
On the main drag,

Now back in the family of the original owners, The Brown Bag still fills Carnation's air with the sweet fragrance of fresh cinnamon rolls and breads. The historic

(206) 333-6100
4366 Tolt Ave (Hwy 203),
Carnation
Inexpensive; no alcohol;
no credit cards;
checks OK
Breakfast, lunch
Tues-Sun

1913 building (spruced up with a coat of paint and wallpaper) holds only ten tables (plus six outdoors for the overflow), and gets pretty packed on weekends. Alex and Allison Awaski serve up wholesome and hearty soups and sandwiches to the teeming mobs.

LODGINGS

Idyl Inn on the River
From the middle of town,
go east on Entwhistle for 2
miles, look for signs,
(206) 333-4262
4548 Tolt River Rd,
Carnation, WA 98014
Moderate; DC, MC, V;
checks OK

A half hour from Bellevue, this inn on a 7-acre organic farm along a secluded bend of the Tolt River seems worlds away. Host Trivia Sebik obviously appreciates the environment and has done much to ensure that guests feel the same. The large common rooms have a commanding view and so do of the swift-moving river, and so do two of the three guest rooms. Each has its own bathroom but our favorite is the south suite (sleeps four), with one of the best views and a private steam room. There's an indoor pool and solarium with a hot tub and sauna. The Inn provides plenty of space for small gatherings of up to 18 people, but there's also room for privacy. Landscaping is minimal; nonetheless, a stroll by the river, with stops by the duck pond, the birdhouse, and two gazebos, is pleasant. The kitchen is available for communal use—except in the morning, when you might expect perhaps a frittata and an arrangement of fresh fruit, baked goods, and cheeses.

BLACK DIAMOND

Black Diamond Bakery boasts the last wood-fired brick oven in the area. The bread that comes out of it is excellent: 26 different kinds, including raisin, cinnamon, sour rye, potato, seven-grain, honey-wheat, and garlic French. They offer doughnuts and cookies too (and recently a number of deli sandwich specials), but it's the bread that draws lines of people. To get there, take the Maple Valley exit from I-405; at Black Diamond turn right at the big white Old Town sign; at the next stop sign veer left; the bakery is on the right (32805 Railroad Avenue, (206) 886-2741); closed Monday.

ENUMCLAW

Stop in at the Lindon Bookstore (1522 Cole St, Enumclaw; (206)825-1388) for a large well-thought selection of books and an espresso machine.

RESTAURANTS

Baumgartner's
On Hwy 410 ½ block west of The Pickle Factory,
(206) 825-1067
1008 E Roosevelt,
Enumclaw
Inexpensive; beer and wine; MC, V; checks OK
Lunch every day

Stop here to collect picnic supplies for a trip to Mount Rainier, or sit at a pink-draped table in the atrium for an early supper after a day at the mountain. It's a full delicatessen with a range of European sausages and cheeses, coffee beans, teas, and spices, and even hand-dipped ice creams and Boehm's chocolates. The friendly staff make up delectable sandwich combinations on fresh bread and croissants (they're huge). Try Marsha's special with your pick of cheese, meat and avocado, green peppers, lettuce, tomato, sprouts, mustard and a pickle on a poor-boy roll with ham, pastrami, salami, Swiss, Provolone, and the works. The freshly baked desserts have made a name for themselves: raspberry tarts filled with a heavenly white chocolate-almond mousse, German chocolate cake, and a slew of cheesecakes—the chef's specialty.

GREENWATER

RESTAURANTS

Naches Tavern
North side of the highway,
(206) 663-2267
Hwy 410, Greenwater
Inexpensive; beer and wine; no credit cards; no checks
Lunch, dinner every day

Now *this* is the way to do a country tavern. The fireplace is as long as a wall and roars all winter long to warm the Crystal Mountain après-ski crowd. The food is bountiful, homemade, and modestly priced—deepfried mushrooms, chili, burgers, pizza, four-scoop milk shakes. There's a countrified jukebox, pool tables, a lending library (take a book, leave a book) of yellowing paperbacks, and furniture so comfortable that the stuffing is coming out. It's not pretty—Big Don, the "chef," wouldn't want it pretty—but he's a gracious host and a no-nonsense barkeep. The group assembled is a peaceable mix of skiers, hunters, loggers, and locals—depends on the season. Bring your own good company, play a little cribbage, stroke the roving house pets, nod off in front of the hearth.

CRYSTAL MOUNTAIN

The ski resort is the best in the state, with runs for beginners and experts, plus fine cross-country touring; (206) 664-2265 and (206) 634-3771. Less well known and less used are the summer facilities. You can ride the chair lift and catch a grand view of Mount Rainier and other peaks; rent condominiums with full kitchens, balconies, or other facilities from Crystal Mountain Reservations, (206) 663-2558 or toll-free (800) 852-1444; play tennis; and go horseback riding from Crystal Mountain Corral, (206) 663-2589. Other than that, there's just a grocery store, a sports shop, and Rafters, the bar-and-buffet restaurant atop

Crystal's lodge. In summer, the Summit House offers weekend dinners. Off Highway 410 just west of Chinook Pass.

ELBE

The advent of the Morton Dinner Train (and an enterprising restaurateur) has turned this onetime sawmill town into more of a museum (some say graveyard) for antique cabooses. The **Morton Dinner Train** ($45 per person; (206) 569-2588) is a 4-hour, 40-mile round-trip train ride from Elbe to Morton. Passengers travel through gorgeous scenery and over an old-fashioned trestle in a restored passenger train, circa 1920. The dinner (shrimp cocktail, prime rib, and the works) is surprisingly good, and the conductor is well versed in the area's lore. (Dinner time varies, so call for information.)

You don't get dinner on the hour-long **Mount Rainier Scenic Railroad** ($6.75 adults, $3.75 children, 7 days a week at 11:00, 1:15, and 3:30, summers only; (206) 569-2588,) but the scenery (to Mineral and back) is equally attractive. Two years ago, the **Mount Rainier Railroad Dining Company** (54106 Mountain Hwy, (206) 569-2505) opened two stationary cabooses: one a dining room (steak's the thing), the other a bar and dance floor—for those who want to get sidetracked.

EATONVILLE

Northwest Trek is a "zoo" where animals roam free while people tour the 600-acre grounds in small, open-air trams. The 5-mile tour passes by a large collection of native wildlife, with all kinds of Northwest beasts from caribou to mink. The buffalo herd steals the show. The whole tour is impressive for kids ($3.50) and adults ($5.75) alike; you can also combine your visit with breakfast at the in-park food service concession, the Fir Bough. Open daily February through October, weekends only the rest of the year. Group rates available. Seventeen miles south of Puyallup on Route 161, (206) 832-6116.

LODGINGS

Old Mill House Bed and Breakfast
Off Hwy 161 (called Michelle Ave in town) at 116 Oak St,
(206) 832-6506
Mail: PO Box 543, Eatonville, WA 98328
Moderate; MC, V; checks OK

A 1920s mill baron's mansion in an unassuming neighborhood is now a delightful B&B, recreated in the flair of the period—there's even a Prohibition-era bar (and dance floor) accessible through a secret panel in a bookcase. The enormous mauve, gray, and ice-green Isadora Duncan Suite resonates with the free spirit of this dancer—private his-and-hers dressing rooms, a prettily tiled bath with a tub and a shower (boasting seven shower heads), and a king-size bed. The three other rooms share a bath and have equal character (Will Rogers, Bessie Smith, and F. Scott Fitzgerald). The latter comes with an ongoing novel penned by guests (reportedly *full* of cliff-hangers).

ASHFORD

Wellspring is a privately operated, judiciously situated hot tub/sauna/massage center, where the tub is nestled into a sylvan glade surrounded by evergreens. Perfect after a day on the Hill. 2¼ miles east of Ashford on Kernahan Road. Call ahead to schedule a massage, (206) 569-2514.

RESTAURANTS

Wild Berry Restaurant
4 miles east of Ashford,
(206) 569-2628
37720 Hwy 706 E,
Ashford
Inexpensive; beer and
wine; MC, V; checks OK
Lunch, dinner every day,
breakfast Sat-Sun
(breakfast every day
July-Aug)

Decorated in self-proclaimed "mountain yuppie" style, this place, a mile from the Nisqually entrance to Mount Rainier National Park is the perfect spot for hearty mountain fare—and lots of it—that tastes surprisingly good. Chicken crêpes, big pizzas, rainbow trout, huge sandwiches, and excellent homemade wild blackberry pie; absolutely no grease. The seasonal breakfast skips the fried eggs in favor of quiche, yogurt, and granola. Everything (including beer and wine) is available to take out.

There's a log cabin for rent (sleeps up to eight) across the way, equipped with full kitchen facilities, claw-footed tub, and wood stove. Perfect for cross-country skiing groups.

LODGINGS

Alexander's Country Inn
4 miles east of Ashford on
Hwy 706,
(206) 569-2300, toll-free
(800) 654-7615
37515 Rt 706 East,
Ashford, WA 98304
Moderate; beer and wine;
MC, V; checks OK
Lunch, dinner every day
(weekends only in winter)

★★

This quaint country inn has gained such a following that it now rivals the mountain itself as the best reason to visit Ashford. First opened in 1912 by lumberman Alexander Mesler as a hotel, it's owned by Gerald Harnish and Bernadette Ronan, who have lovingly restored the rambling inn to much of its early grandeur.

Best is the Tower Room: a lofted suite in the turret of the manor. A large wheelchair-accessible suite has been added on the second floor—very private, with its own deck. Most of the bathrooms are shared, but they're large, modern, and immaculate. Indeed, this blending of old and new is the real genius here; it feels turn-of-the-century, but the comforts such as carpeted rooms and a new outdoor Jacuzzi, with a view of Heron Pond, are pure 1990s. Full breakfast is included.

The dining room, open to guests and non-guests alike, is your best bet in these parts for a fine meal. We've heard that the artichoke soup is exquisite in texture and taste; and we'll vouch for the orange roughy and the scampi. Our fresh trout—caught out back in the holding pond, pan-fried quickly, and then filleted at the table—was perfect; and the beef stroganoff was a satisfying ending to an active day. During the summer, get a table on the brick patio, ideal for summer dining.

Mountain Meadows Inn
and B&B

Logger-turned-innkeeper Chad Darrah saved this 1910 mill superintendent's home from fading away in the

¼ mile west of Ashford at 28912 Rt 706 E, (206) 569-2788 Mail: PO Box 291, Ashford, WA 98304 Moderate; MC, V; checks OK

ghost town of National, Washington. It is now situated near a trout pond on 14 acres of landscaped grounds in Ashford. There are three large guest rooms (each has its own bath) filled with antiques, books, and extensive train memorabilia—everything from model Lionels to full-size lanterns. Nothing kitschy here; trains are Darrah's passion (he's also the conductor on the local scenic train). There's a VCR with rare train footage in the living room, if you're so inclined, and a player piano if you're not. If you need more space, ask about the guest house with two studio apartments. Full breakfasts of homemade sausage and muffins baked in a wood stove are fuel enough for a locomotive.

Nisqually Lodge
Hyw 7 to Rt 706, 5 miles from park entrance, (206) 569-8804 31609 Rt 706, Ashford Moderate; AE, DC, MC, V; no checks

Reasonably priced and clean, this new lodge just a few miles before the west entrance to Mount Rainier offers welcome respite from the train-memorabilia theme that's pervading the area. This two-story lodge (owned by the same folk who run the Cowlitz River Lodge in Packwood and the Seasons Motel in nearby Morton) is well visited—returnees like the stone fireplace in the pinewood lounge and the hot tub outside (though we hear reports about the thin walls). Coffee and doughnuts for breakfast. If it's a view that you want, book a room at the Cowlitz (13069 US Hwy 12, Packwood, (206) 494-4444).

MOUNT RAINIER

The majestic mountain is the abiding symbol of natural grandeur in the Northwest and one of the most awesome mountains in the world. Its cone rises 14,410 feet above sea level, thousands of feet higher than the other peaks in the Cascade Range. The best way to appreciate the mountain is to explore its flanks: 300 miles of back country and self-guiding nature trails lead to ancient forests, dozens of massive glaciers, waterfalls, and alpine meadows, lush with wildflowers during its short summer. Chinook and Cayuse passes are closed in winter; you can take the loop trip or the road to Sunrise only between late May and October. The road from Longmire to Paradise remains open during daylight winter hours. It is advisable to carry tire chains and a shovel during winter, and it is always wise to check current road and weather conditions by calling a 24-hour information service: (206) 569-2211. Obligatory backcountry use permits for overnight stays can be obtained from any of the ranger stations.

   Climbing the mountain. There are two ways to do it: with **Rainier Mountaineering**, the concessionaire guide service, or in your own party. Unless you are qualified to do it on your own—and this is a big, difficult, and dangerous mountain on which many people have been killed—you must climb with the guide service. (Call Paradise (206) 569-2227 in the summer, Tacoma (206) 627-6242 in the winter.) If you plan to climb with your own party, you must register at one of the ranger stations in Mount Rainier National Park, (206) 569-2211. They will make sure you have adequate experience and the proper equipment, and will inform you of routes, avalanche conditions, and weather forecast. You also must check in with them when you get back down. Generally, the best time to climb the mountain is from late June through early September.

Longmire. A few miles inside the southwestern border of the park, the little village of Longmire has a simple inn (see review), a small wildlife museum with plant and animal displays, a hiking information center, and a cross-country skiing rental outlet. It also has the only place that sells gas in the park.

Paradise. At 5,400 feet, Paradise is the most popular destination point on the mountain. On the way to this paved parking lot and visitors' center, you'll catch wonderful views of Narada Falls and Nisqually Glacier. The visitors' center, housed in a flying saucer–like building, has a standard cafeteria and gift shop, extensive nature exhibits and films, and a superb view of the mountain from its observation deck. Depending on the season, you could picnic (our advice is to bring your own) among the wildflowers, explore some of the trails (the rangers offer guided walks), let the kids slide on inner tubes in the snow-play area, try a little cross-country skiing, or even take a guided snowshoe tromp. The ice caves, three miles northeast of Paradise, still exist but entering the deteriorating caves has become extremely dangerous.

Sunrise. Open only during the summer months, the visitor center at Sunrise (6,400 feet) is the closest you can drive to the peak. The old lodge here has no overnight accommodations, but it does offer a snack bar and exhibits about the mountain. Dozens of trails lead from here, such as the short one leading to a magnificent viewpoint of Emmons Glacier Canyon.

LODGINGS

Paradise Inn
Hwy 706 to Paradise in Mount Rainier National Park, (206) 569-2291; reservations (206) 569-2413 Mail: PO Box 108, Ashford, WA 98304 Moderate; full bar; MC, V; checks OK Breakfast, lunch, dinner every day

The hotel at Paradise, just above the visitors' center, is a massive, old-fashioned 1917 lodge, full of exposed beams, log furniture, and American Indian rugs. Unlike the modest inn at Longmire, the Paradise Inn has 125 rooms, a comfortable full-service dining room, a small, smoky bar, and a lobby with two big stone fireplaces. The greatest advantage to staying here, however, is the proximity to the summit; the rooms are nothing grand, the bathrooms can be antiquated, and the expensive meals in the restaurant tend toward routine beef and frozen seafood dishes. Open late May to October only.

National Park Inn
Off Hwy 706, 6 miles inside southwest (Nisqually) entrance to park at Longmire, (206) 569-2411 or (206) 569-2275 Mail: PO Box 108, Ashford, WA 98304 Moderate; full bar; MC, V; checks OK Breakfast, lunch, dinner every day

After 14 months of remodeling, the small hotel at Longmire, 6 miles inside the western border of the park, has reopened. The rooms are still quite basic (no TVs, phones, or room service and no smoking anywhere) but they're clean and functional (especially in the new east wing). Some of the 25 rooms face the mountain, but the small windows don't really offer much of a view. Only about half, at $65, have private baths. The new lounge is very inviting, with a stone fireplace and plenty of comfortable seats that encourage a sociable visit (fortunately, they moved the gift shop to the building next door). The food is adequate, although most come first for the plethora of outdoor activities just steps away. Open year-round.

MOUNT ADAMS

Mount Adams and its surrounding area are a natural splendor largely overlooked by visitors from Portland and Seattle, who seldom venture in from the Columbia Gorge. Besides climbing to the summit of the 12,276-foot mountain—greater in mass than any of the five major volcanic peaks in the Northwest—hikers and skiers can explore miles of wilderness trails in the Mount Adams Wilderness Area and the Gifford Pinchot National Forest.

Volcanic activity long ago left the area honeycombed with caves and lava tubes, including the **Ice Caves** near Trout Lake with stalactites and stalagmites formed by dripping ice. To the southwest of Trout Lake is **Big Lava Bed**, a 12,500-acre lava field filled with cracks, crevasses, rock piles, and unusual lava formations. Contact the Mount Adams Ranger Station in Trout Lake, (509) 395-2501, to register for ascents and for information on area activities.

In the warm months, Klickitat County is a land of abundance: morel mushrooms in the Simcoe Mountains (April-June), wildflowers in the Bird Creek Meadows (part of the only area of the Yakima Indian Reservation open to the public) in late July, and wild huckleberries—reputedly the best in the state—in and around the Indian Heaven Wilderness (mid-August to mid-September).

TROUT LAKE

LODGINGS

Mio Amore Pensione
Just off Hwy 141, take a sharp right onto Little Mountain Rd,
(509) 395-2264
Mail: PO Box 208, Trout Lake, WA 98650
Moderate; MC, V; checks OK

It looks like the International Embassy of Trout Lake from the road with all those flags in the front yard, but they're actually part of the welcome mat: proprietors Tom and Jill Westbrook fly the flags of their guests' countries during their stays. The restored 1904 farmhouse sits alongside Trout Lake Creek, with a view of Mount Adams from the Jacuzzi. The inside is decorated with memorabilia collected from spots around the world. Our only quibble is that everything here is a little *too* precious (even more so with the gift shop of local and imported crafts nearby). Bedrooms are small, but the Venus Room is the most spacious—and the priciest—with a private bath and a two-seat sitting room with a view of Mount Adams. The converted stone icehouse in the corner of the yard is quiet and rustic, and it sleeps four.

Breakfast includes a bountiful array of Jill's award-winning baked goods, with a hot dish such as French toast soaked in Grand Marnier. Tom, a trained chef, will prepare a dinner (the entrée is chosen by the first person to make a reservation) for $20 extra (including appetizer, dessert, coffee, and wine). You don't need to be a pensione guest to sample these savories, but you do need a reservation.

GLENWOOD

LODGINGS

Flying L Ranch
Off Trout Lake-Glenwood Rd on Flying L Ln, (509) 364-3488
25 Flying L Ln, Glenwood, WA 98619
Moderate; AE, MC, V; Checks OK

★

For 40-odd years the Lloyd family has owned and operated the 160-acre Flying L Ranch, which they opened to guests in 1960. The current host, Darvel Lloyd, is well known in these parts for his active involvement in establishing hiking trails and other outdoor activities. The pace here is relaxed. You'll feel quite comfortable putting on some classical music and curling up with an old issue of *National Geographic* by the lava fireplace in the main lodge's spacious living room or watching the evening fall over Mount Adams from the hot tub in the new gazebo. The bedrooms, named after Old West notables or cowhands, are nothing fancy—but we love 'em that way. Those in the main lodge have shared baths (the Charles Russell and the George Fletcher have fireplaces); those in the adjacent guest house are less charming but face The Mountain. Two cabins back in the woods offer the most privacy. As you dive into your huckleberry pancakes in the cookhouse at breakfast, think about ways to spend the day: bicycling the back roads around Glenwood (three-speeds for rent), bird watching at Conboy Lake National Wildlife Refuge, or skiing groomed trails. For lunch and dinner you'll have to bring your own food to prepare in one of the two well-equipped, wood-heated kitchens. And if you bring your own horse, the Flying L will provide a corral and a tack room.

COLUMBIA RIVER GORGE

When windsurfing took off, the town of Hood River was poised to go along for the ride. The folks on the Washington side of the Gorge, though, had no grand tourism plan, and they stuck to logging and milling. This is why, a local waitress explains, crossing the Hood River–White Salmon bridge is "like going back 20 years." But while the protected waters across the Columbia make Hood River an ideal spot for beginning windsurfers, the wind "really pulls" on the Washington side. Here the hottest boardheads circumvent rocky shores and industrial areas to surf off points in the road like **Swell City** and **Doug's Beach**. To find them, follow the streams of vans and wagons piled high with boards and masts. See also Columbia River Gorge entry in the Oregon chapter.

If you've found a place that you think is a best place, send in the report form at the back of this book. If you're unhappy with one of the places, let us know why. We depend on reader input.

CARSON

LODGINGS

Carson Hot Mineral Springs Resort
On Windriver Hwy, 2 miles from the junction of Hwy 14 and Carson,
(509) 427-8292
Mail: PO Box 370, Carson, WA 98610
Inexpensive; MC, V; checks OK

Carson Hot Springs is attempting to put a little bit of the resort back into their name. Last year they opened a nine-hole golf course and a modest clubhouse, and at press time were preparing to unveil the remaining nine. The old resort on Windriver Road outside of Stevenson is still rustic and a little bit eccentric, reminiscent of days when the sickly "took the waters" to improve their health. Current bathhouse talk ranges from rheumatism and arthritis to the day's windsurfing feats on the Gorge. The 1897 resort consists of two charming white clapboard structures—one, the 9-room hotel and restaurant; the other, the hot mineral baths—and 13 very well-worn cabins. But we do recommend the hot mineral bath ($5), after which you're swathed in towels and blankets for a short rest. Massages ($12 per half-hour, more in evenings and on weekends) are available to complete the bliss, but reserve these well in advance. Don't expect as healthy a treatment from the restaurant; it serves standard soups, salads, steaks, and some seafood— mostly fried.

HUSUM

LODGINGS

Orchard Hill Inn
2 miles up Oak Ridge Rd out of Husum, Milepost 2,
(509) 493-3024
199 Oak Ridge Rd, White Salmon, WA 98672
Moderate; MC, V; Checks OK

★★

You're asked to leave your shoes by the doormat (and they might even get a shine) at this B&B on 13 acres that revels in its setting, overlooking pear and apple orchards and the White Salmon River valley. The three bedrooms, decorated with family antiques, offer refreshing respite. Two bathrooms—one with a whirlpool bath—are shared. The bunkhouse out back has its own bath and sleeps six. A full sideboard breakfast includes homemade breads, huckleberry bran muffins, baked apples, eggs, and local produce. Children are welcome at Orchard Hill and have a place of their own in a two-story tree house in front; hosts James and Pamela Tindall will even supply parents with a list of local babysitters. There's pitch-and-chip golf at the inn, and a nine-hole course at nearby Husum Hills.

BINGEN

RESTAURANTS

Fidel's
1 mile east of Singing Bridge (toll bridge) on

This Mexican restaurant seems transplanted straight from California; in fact, Fidel and Martha Montanez and

Hwy 14, (509) 493-1017
120 E Stuben St, Bingen
Inexpensive; full bar;
MC, V; checks OK
Lunch, dinner every day
(call ahead in winter)

their family recipes recently arrived from San Diego. Lively Mexican music sets the mood. Enormous margaritas go with the warm chips and disappointing salsa. The menu is surprisingly varied, offering carne asada, a chili verde, a chili colorado, and machaca (a shredded beef omelet). Portions are generous; a plate of chorizo con huevos (mild) with rice and beans is big enough for two. The chile relleno is encased in a thick layer of egg whites so that it resembles a big pillow on your plate, and is bathed in a delicious spicy sauce. Tables and chairs are big and comfortable, service is friendly and efficient. It's a place that everybody loves.

GOLDENDALE

Maryhill Museum, a stately Palladian mansion, perches rather obtrusively upon the barren Columbia River benchlands. Constructed in 1917 by the eccentric Sam Hill, son-in-law of railroad tycoon James J. Hill, Maryhill began as the European-inspired dream home for Hill and his wife Mary, but became instead what it is today: a fine art museum. With one of the largest collections of Rodin sculptures in the world, a whole floor of classic French and American paintings and glasswork, unique exhibitions such as chess sets and Romanian folk textiles, and splendid Northwest tribal art, the museum makes for quite an interesting visit. A cafe serves espresso, pastries, and sandwiches; peacocks roam the lovely landscaped grounds. Highway 14, 13 miles south of Goldendale, (509) 773-3733. Up the road is another of Sam Hill's bizarre creations: a not-quite-lifesize replica of Stonehenge, built to honor World War I veterans.

Goldendale Observatory, on a hill overlooking town (20 minutes north of Goldendale on US 97), was a popular spot when Halley's comet dropped in. Through high-powered telescopes you get incredible celestial views through unpolluted skies. Open daily and some evenings; call ahead on weekends or in the wintertime, (509) 773-3141.

LODGINGS

Three Creeks Lodge
18 miles north of the
Columbia River on Hwy
97, (509) 773-4026
2120 Hwy 97,
Goldendale, WA 98620
Moderate; full bar; AE,
MC, V; checks OK
Breakfast, lunch Mon-
Sat; dinner every day;
brunch Sun (call for
winter hours)

Changes in ownership have taken their toll on the Three Creeks Lodge, set down to meet no obvious demand in the Simcoe Mountains on the Satus Pass road to Yakima. It is a collection of vaulted-ceiling cedar chalets, some with wood-burning fireplaces and private spas, scattered throughout the beautiful backwoods wilderness. You fish in summer and go on sleigh rides in winter. The place capitalizes on the romance of seclusion, yet the simple fourplex creekhouses with thin walls between units make televisions a bother. The dining room in the main lodge makes splendid use of its situation at the confluence of three creeks, with glass and cedar walls that seem to bring the trees inside. But the beauty of the place ends here. Food is decent but overpriced. Stay in a chalet with a kitchen.

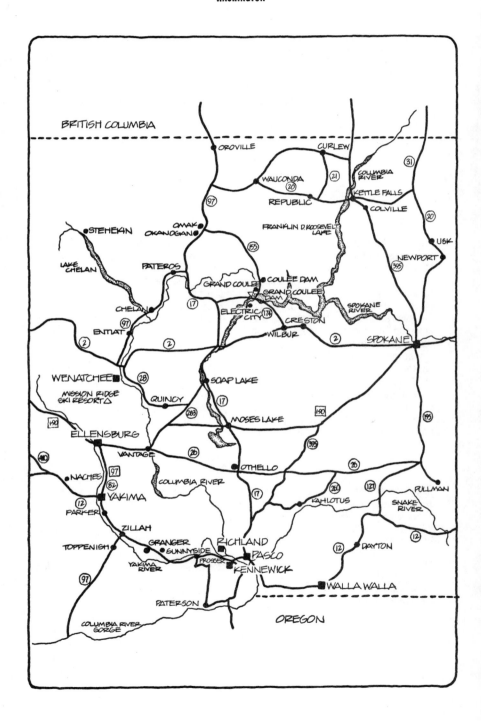

EASTERN WASHINGTON

An eastward route along I-90, Ellensburg to Spokane, then a northwesterly arc through the northeast corner of the state to the Okanogan and Colville national forests. The Wenatchee loop begins in Okanogan and continues clockwise through Grand Coulee, Soap Lake, and north again to Wenatchee and Chelan (and Stehekin, accessible from Chelan). Finally, an eastward drive along the bottom of the state—Yakima to Pullman.

ELLENSBURG

If you get away from the tourist ghetto by the freeway, as you should, this college-and-cowboy town projects a pleasant ease. Its famous Labor Day rodeo, now in its sixth decade, draws many for its slice-of-life view of rural America.

Architecture. Ellensburg has more than its share of interesting buildings. The downtown area was rebuilt after a devastating fire in 1889. Among the handsome structures still standing are the Davidson Building, on the corner of Pearl and 4th, and the Masonic Temple, with its intriguing asymmetrical facade. Off on the fringes of town, at 3rd and Wenas, is a prime example of the Great American Train Station, built late in the last century for the Northern Pacific. Art Deco is represented by the Liberty Theater, at 5th and Pine, and by the Valley Cafe, whose interior is prime. For modern architecture, turn to the campus of Central Washington University, which displays Fred Bassetti's library and dormitory compound and Kirk/Wallace/McKinley's fine-arts complex. Close to the campus along 9th Street are tree-lined blocks of attractive turn-of-the-century homes.

Arts. Sarah Spurgeon Gallery, on 14th Street in the fine-arts complex at Central, presents regional and national exhibits in all media, Monday-Friday 8am-5pm, October-May, (509) 963-2665. Summer Theatre, a university/community funded summer stock season, is performed by the Laughing Horse Company, a hodgepodge of student, pro, and semipro actors. Plays are staged in another architectural gem: the new Tower Theater on the Central campus, (509) 963-1766. Community Art Gallery, 408½ N Pearl, (509) 925-2670, has nice quarters in an old building, displays good contemporary art, and sells local crafts; open noon to 5pm Tuesday-Saturday.

Olmstead Place, 4 miles east of town on Squaw Creek Trail Road (off I-90), is a cottonwood log cabin from an 1875 cattle ranch now coming back to life; tours Thursday-Monday, 8am to 5pm, (509) 925-1943.

Yakima River. There are fine canoe and raft trips to be made through the deep gorges, and the river is one of the finest trout streams in the country; Highway 821, south of town, follows the gorge. Information about floats and river trips: (509) 925-3137.

Mills Saddle 'n Togs, 4th and Main, (509) 962-2312, has been outfitting riders and cowboy types for as long as anyone can remember.

RESTAURANTS

The Valley Cafe
Near the corner of 3rd and Main,
(509) 925-3050
105 W 3rd, Ellensburg
Moderate; beer and wine;
AE, DC, MC, V;
checks OK
Breakfast Fri-Sun,
lunch, dinner every day

This 1930s-built bistro, with mahogany booths and back bar, would be an oasis anywhere—but is especially so in cow country. People traveling on business to Ellensburg arrange to arrive around lunchtime just to eat at this airy Art Deco spot (be aware that the service can, at times, be quite slow). Salads are the choice at lunch. For breakfast you'll find variations on Mexican huevos, adaptations of the crépe, and an all-American meal. Italian concoctions and fresh seafood compose most of the no-red-meat dinner menu: tortellini and chicken sauté, coho salmon grilled in herb butter, and cheese-filled tortes. There's a choice list of Washington wines, and there are some bracing espresso drinks. Service, though it tends to favor regulars, has on recent visits been quite efficient. If you're just passing through (and require faster service), there's a take-out branch next door.

Giovanni's on Pearl
1 block east of Main in the historic district,
(509) 962-2260
402 N Pearl, Ellensburg
Moderate; full bar; AE,
MC, V; checks OK
Lunch, dinner Tues-Sat

Welsh-born owner John Herbert started in the food and hotel business at age 12 in his parents' hotel in the Isle of Jersey. He landed here a few years ago and took over the fledging Carriage House, and Ellensburg is all the better for it. The prime rib is gone (replaced by the oft-requested Ellensburg lamb) but there's a good sampling of fish and, recently, lotsa pasta. A recent chef's special featured chicken breast baked in puff pastry with basil leaves and dried mushrooms. Candlelight, flowers on the tables, and green chintz tablecloths with a slight English country air add to a fresh and relaxing atmosphere. The college-bound servers are knowledgeable and prompt. The outstanding desserts (blackberry cobbler and Dutch apple pie) are made by a former employee in her nearby farmhouse.

VANTAGE

Situated on a splendid stretch of the Columbia, Vantage has nothing much in the way of food, but the view from the parking lot of the A&W surpasses that of all other known root-beer stands.

Ginkgo Petrified Forest State Park has an interpretive center—open daily in summer, 10am to 6pm (by appointment only otherwise) (509) 856-2700— that takes you back to the age of dinosaurs; then you can go prospecting for your own finds. It's a lovely spot for a picnic, by the way.

GEORGE

The naturally terraced amphitheater looking west over the Columbia Gorge at **Champs de Brionne Winery** offers a spectacular summer-evening setting for musical performances and attracts thousands of people with big-name performers such as Bob Dylan, Bonnie Raitt, and the late Stevie Ray Vaughan, who gave one of his last concerts here; concert information is given at (206) 244-4005, winery info at (509) 785-6685. You can bring a picnic, but any wine must be purchased on the premises. Arrive early; the one country road leading to George is not fit for crowds of this kind.

MOSES LAKE

It's the RV capital of the state, with many campers and boaters attracted by the fishing and hunting around the lakes. The anglers come for trout and perch. You can rent a boat, then motor out to a sandy island in Potholes Reservoir for a picnic or camping.

SPOKANE

The friendly city by Spokane Falls is far more attractive to visit than is generally recognized. It is full of notable old buildings, marvelous parks, and splendid vistas, and the compact downtown is most pleasant for strolling. The gold rush of the 1880s brought it wealth and the railroads brought it people.

Architecture. The three blocks on W Riverside Avenue between Jefferson and Lincoln contain a wealth of handsome structures in the City Beautiful mode—doubtless the loveliest three blocks around. The **Spokane County Courthouse,** north of the Spokane River on W Broadway, is a Loire Valley clone built in 1895 by Willis A. Ritchie.

Old homes. Tour Overbluff Drive to see the small palaces of the upper crust, and Cliff Drive or Sumner Avenue on the South Hill to view some splendid older homes. Browne's Addition, west of downtown, is full of late-Victorian homes.

Parks. Riverfront Park is the pleasant green heart of the old city. Developed from old railroad yards by Expo '74, the park is now an airy place full of meandering paved paths, with entertainments ranging from ice skating to an IMAX theater. The 1909 carousel is a local landmark, hand-carved by master builder Charles Looff. The music is too loud for children under about four (and most adults), but older kids love riding the animal menagerie. **Manito Park,** at Grand Boulevard and 18th, has a spendidly splashable duck pond and theme gardens. **Finch Arboretum** (west of downtown Spokane), a pleasant picnic site, hosts a modest but attractive collection of trees and shrubs among ravines and a stream. For a panoramic vista of Spokane, visit **Cliff Park** at 13th and Grove.

Nature. Two natural areas just a couple of miles outside Spokane's city limits offer excellent places to hike and see birds and wildlife: the **Little Spokane Natural Area,** (509) 456-4730, and the **Spokane Fish Hatchery,** (509) 625-5169. The fishery is at 2927 W Waikiki Road; for the Natural Area, look for the Indian Rock Paintings parking lot on Rutter Parkway. The **Dishman Hills Natural Area,** a 460-acre preserve in the Spokane Valley has a network of trails and mixed wildlife habitats. Just 45 minutes south of Spokane you'll find the 15,000-acre **Turnbull National Wildlife Refuge** especially interesting during fall and spring migration. Take I-90 west, exit at Cheney; (509) 235-4723.

Culture. Soviet-born conductor Vakhtang Jordania has been working with the **Spokane Symphony** since June 1991; programs, including a pops series, are lively and innovative. An annual free Labor Day concert in Comstock Park draws thou-

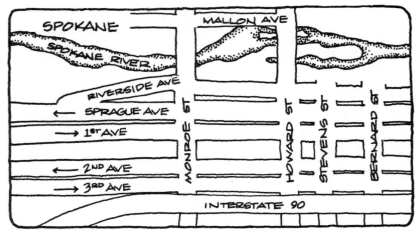

sands of picnicking spectators; (509) 326-3136. **The Spokane Civic Theatre,** 1020 N Howard, offers a mixed bag of amateur performances each season; the **Interplayers Ensemble Theatre,** 174 S Howard, is a young professional company with a full season. Riverfront Park often hosts concerts of jazz, bluegrass, and popular music during the summer; call (509) 456-5512 for information.

Museums. The Museum of Native American Cultures, 200 E Cataldo, (509) 326-4550, contains one of the most comprehensive collections of Indian artifacts and archives in the country, housed in a tepee-shaped building. Nearby is **Crosby Library,** on the Gonzaga University campus, 502 E Boone, the crooner's gift to his alma mater, with lots of gold records, an Oscar, and other memorabilia; Bing grew up in the house a block away at 508 E Sharp. **Cheney Cowles Memorial Museum** displays pioneer and mining relics, 2316 W 1st Avenue, (509) 456-3931.

Sports. Golf is very good here and there are numerous courses. Indian Canyon, (509) 747-5353, and Hangman Valley, (509) 448-1212, two of the most beautiful public courses in the nation, have recently attracted a number of professional tournaments. Spokane's parks and hilly roads and the new Centennial Trail (flanking the river from downtown to the Idaho border) offer great **bicycle riding. Runners** will find themselves in good company especially during Spokane's annual Bloomsday Run (see calendar), held during the lilac season on the first Sunday in May. The good **ski areas** nearby are 49 Degrees North, 58 miles north of Spokane, (509) 935-6649, a good place for beginners; Mount Spokane, 31 miles north on Highway 206, (509) 238-6281, with fair facilities and some challenging runs; Schweitzer Mountain Resort in Sandpoint, Idaho, (208) 263-9555, with excellent facilities for family skiing; and the country's newest destination ski resort, Silver Mountain at Kellogg, Idaho, (208) 783-1113.

RESTAURANTS

Milford's Fish House and Oyster Bar
Corner of Broadway and Monroe, (509) 326-7251
719 N Monroe St,

Spokane's oldest fish house offers simple decor— exposed brick, red-and-white-checkered tablecloths, a few green plants—and good food at reasonable prices. Check the fresh list, updated daily, for best bets, and don't hesitate to ask the waiter for recommendations.

Spokane
Moderate; full bar; AE,
MC, V; local checks only
Dinner every day

Fresh salmon, baked or poached, is available in season, and the halibut is always a winner. On the weekend, service can be slow, especially in the trendy Oyster Bar. Reservations are a must unless you can wait.

Moreland's

2 blocks north of Riverside
on Main and Howard at
skywalk level,
(509) 747-9830
216 N Howard St,
Spokane
Inexpensive; full bar;AE,
MC, V; checks OK
Lunch Mon-Sat, dinner
Tues-Sat

As you enter the historic Bennett Block building, your nose leads you to Moreland's, furnished with oak, exposed brick, brass, and lacy doilies, the design of which has been repeated in the etched windows. Cafeteria-style lunches feature a consistently good soup or casserole option, and picnic specials offer combinations of fruits, cheeses, salmon pâté, and breads. Premium wines are available by the glass, and the selection constitutes a revolving tour of the Northwest. Dinner at Moreland's is always a treat; the specials based on lamb and pork are a welcome sight-and-savory in this steak town.

Auntie's Bookstore and Cafe

Between Washington and
Bernard, (509) 838-0206
313 W Riverside Ave,
Spokane
Inexpensive; no alcohol;
MC, V; checks OK
Breakfast, dinner Mon-
Sat, lunch every day

This cheerful cafe-in-a-bookstore (new and used) makes a great place to settle with a cup of coffee and a good read. The nonsmoking atmosphere is so inviting, in fact, that many lingerers fall prey to the vigilant meter maid. Soups, salads, pasta salads, and dessert are all made daily from scratch—the thick and hearty lentil soup is an obvious favorite. On a chilly day, try the melted cheese and mushroom sandwich, spiced with a mild salsa. Breakfasts consist of muffins, cinnamon rolls, or bagels, and espresso.

Clinkerdagger's

Off Monroe in Flour Mill,
(509) 328-5965
621 W Mallon Ave,
Spokane
Moderate; full bar; AE,
DC, MC, V; local
checks only
Lunch Mon-Sat, dinner
every day

Clinkerdagger's has broadened its menu from the basic chicken and steak selection to include more Northwest-oriented dishes, but in the end, it's the basic but well-handled (and attractively presented) food that wins us over. When fresh seafood is available, there might be four or five specials featuring fish and lobster. Expect a lengthy wait in the bar, even with reservations. In the spring, when the Spokane River is rushing by, the views from the window tables are exciting.

The Downtown Onion

On Riverside at Bernard,
(509) 747-3852
302 W Riverside Ave,
Spokane
Inexpensive; full bar;AE,

The magnificent old bar harks back to the days when the building that houses this eatery was a fine hotel, the St. Regis. Some of the furnishings—the pressed-tin ceiling, the wood dividers—are also relics from the original hotel. The Onion set the standard in Spokane for gourmet hamburgers, and they're still local classics. The beer selection would be outstanding anywhere;

MC, V; checks OK
Lunch, dinner every day

fruit daiquiris are a specialty. (The huckleberry daiquiris—and the other huckleberry offerings such as huckleberry layer cake and huckleberry milk shakes— are available year-round.) A young, informal crowd dominates on most nights, especially on Monday nights during NFL season. Don't take a booth in the sunroom addition if you want to be part of the chaos. Service is attentive. The same menu is served at the North Onion at 7522 N Division, (509) 428-6100.

Niko's Greek & Middle Eastern Restaurant
2 blocks off Sprague, (509) 928-9590
321 S Dishman-Mica Rd, Spokane
Inexpensive; beer and wine; AE, MC, V; local checks only
Lunch Mon-Fri, dinner Mon-Sat

Niko's is deservedly popular locally for traditional Greek food, much of which is homemade in this modest taverna-style restaurant. Lamb is especially well treated here, and the garlicky, smooth hummus can be ordered as an entrée at lunch with a plate of vegetables or pita. Several Indian entrées have been added to the dinner menu, most notably the *keema mater*, chunky beef with yogurt and Indian spices served with pita. The Greek salads have plenty of salty, strong feta and Greek olives; the baklava is loaded with honey and nuts between layers of phyllo (there's also a chocolava—and 12 other pastries). Thursday is belly-dancing night. Reports from Niko II at W 725 Riverside Avenue, (509) 624-7444, have not been as favorable.

Patsy Clark's
15 blocks west of downtown at 2nd and Hemlock, (509) 838-8300
2208 W 2nd Ave, Spokane
Expensive; full bar; AE, DC, MC, V; local checks only
Lunch Mon-Fri, dinner every day, brunch Sun

Patrick F. Clark, "Patsy" to his friends, arrived in America in 1870 at the age of 20, and by the time he was 40 he was a millionaire many times over, thanks to the success of Montana's Anaconda Mine. Naturally anxious to display his success, he instructed architect Kirtland Cutter to build him the finest mansion he could conceive—never mind the cost. Marble was shipped in from Italy, wood carvings and clocks from England, a mural from France, and a spectacular stained-glass window (with more than 4,000 pieces) standing 14 feet tall from Tiffany's of New York. Locally, the restaurant isn't famous for its entrées (the kitchen has been cutting corners with the quality of its ingredients); rather, we like Patsy's for formal occasions. An elegant spot it is, and you *should* find some excuse to go by, even if it's only for a drink (the wine list is one of the best in the area). The bar, located in the mansion's original wood-paneled dining room is relaxing and luxurious. Drinks on the second-story verandah can be pleasant on a summer evening. Sunday brunch—a memorable experience based on the sheer quantity of the offerings—requires reservations.

Spezia
On Francis just west of Division, (509) 467-2149
420 W Francis St, Spokane

A remodeled auto parts store is now a restaurant with recessed lighting, faux granite columns, and an exposed kitchen that lends an air of contemporary European sophistication. The recipes are authentic Italian: antipasto, pasta primavera, and more unusual dishes

Moderate; beer and wine; AE, MC, V; checks OK Lunch Mon-Fri, dinner every day

★

Thai Cafe

Sprague at Washington, (509) 838-4783 410 W Sprague Ave, Spokane Inexpensive; Thai beer only; no credit cards; local checks only Lunch Mon-Fri, dinner Mon-Sat

★

Azar's Restaurant

Monroe and Jackson, (509) 326-7171 2501 N Monroe, Spokane Inexpensive; no alcohol; MC, V; local checks only Breakfast, lunch every day, dinner Mon-Sat

Coyote Cafe

Corner of 3rd and Wall, (509) 747-8800 702 W 3rd Ave, Spokane Inexpensive; beer, wine, and tequila; MC, V; checks OK Lunch, dinner every day

Europa Pizzeria and Bakery

North side of the railroad trestle downtown, next to the Magic Lantern Theater, (509) 455-4051 125 S Wall St, Spokane Inexpensive; beer and wine; MC, V; checks OK

(fettuccine with pesto, goat cheese, and pine nuts) are good choices. Less adventuresome eaters won't go wrong with the pizza. The small nonsmoking section is sandwiched between the kitchen (where grilling is done over peachwood) and a generous smoking section.

You won't just stumble into this ethnic oasis in the eastern Washington desert. Its location off the beaten track of the downtown skywalk system keeps this Thai restaurant exclusive to those in the know. A waft of curry greets patrons at the door; and you'll find curry seasonings, along with coconut milk and peanuts, in most of the entrées. If you ask, the cooks will spice the dishes to the degree of hotness you want; but be aware that "medium" is hot by the standards of most American palates. We've yet to be disappointed with any of the 12 chicken selections. If you can't decide, try the *pra ram long song*—chicken with peanut sauce, served on a bed of fresh spinach. And don't miss the Thai desserts—black rice pudding over ice cream or warm bananas in coconut milk.

The chrome doesn't shine at this Lebanese eatery, formerly an A&W, but those who seek out ethnic food know that more effort is put into Azar's food than into its atmosphere. Close your eyes—and you won't be disappointed. Everything is fresh; if you can't decide, try the gyros, which, although it's unusual because it's made with beef and lamb, is especially tasty, as is the falafel sandwich. Breakfasts here are basic, lunches and dinners feature more interesting fare. The original Azar's (3818 N Nevada St, (509) 487-0132) has the same menu and equally good food but an even less-appealing atmosphere.

The walls of this Mexican place are covered with offbeat art, and the service is prompt and relentlessly cheerful. If you want to be in and out in 20 minutes, that's no problem. Food includes reasonably priced, standard south-of-the-border fare—tacos and burritos, refried beans and fajitas—all of which are enhanced by the large, icy margaritas. Try the grilled chicken tacos.

Exposed brick walls and bare wood give this place a certain Old World charm, and the relaxed atmosphere attracts good-tempered students from adjacent downtown college branch campuses. The food fits collegiate needs well: Yugoslavian pizzas (on homemade crust) and large, fresh calzones, which can be overwhelming as a midday meal. Dinner specials often feature Slavic fare, and there's lasagne. Counter service

Lunch Mon-Fri (Mon-Sat in summer), dinner Mon-Sat

has been replaced with a cheerful waitstaff that gives good advice and keeps the pace relaxed (sometimes too much so) enough for you to feel entirely comfortable settling in with a beer and a book.

Lindaman's Gourmet-to-Go, Inc.
South on Stevens to Grand Blvd,
(509) 838-3000
1235 S Grand Blvd,
Spokane
Moderate; beer and wine;
AE, MC, V; checks OK
Breakfast, lunch, dinner Mon-Sat

The cafe, housed in a former grocery store, still offers some interesting casseroles, good salads (like the romaine and feta with garlicky croutons), and a solid array of (mostly chocolate) desserts. Generally, though, the food (boldly served on paper plates) suffers from a lack of attention and imagination. By evening, some of the dishes seem to suffer from sitting in warming trays too long, and the soups lack substance. The menu changes daily, although you might encounter some regular items. Breakfast is simple: fresh muffins and scones, quiche and scrambled eggs, and good, strong coffee served in real mugs, or the usual offering of espresso, lattes, or cappuccino. Take-out is as popular here as eating in.

LODGINGS

Waverly Place
Take Division St exit off I-90 and head north to Waverly Pl,
(509) 328-1856
709 W Waverly Place,
Spokane, WA 99205
Moderate; AE, MC, V;
checks OK

Across the street from what was once a racetrack, Waverly Place retains the elegance of the Victorian era. The track is now Corbin Park, a lovely oval with a couple of tennis courts, a tree canopy, and plenty of places to walk. Guests at this bed and breakfast can sit on the broad porch overlooking the park and sip lemonade. There are three guest rooms: The Skinner Suite (named for the man who built the house, Harry J. Skinner), recently redecorated with all oak furnishings—including a sleigh bed— and a private bath; Anna's Room, with a window seat overlooking the park; and the Mill Street Room with its big brass bed. The last two rooms share a bath. Fresh fruit, Swedish pancakes with huckleberry sauce, sausage, and coffee are a sample of the breakfast fare.

Cavanaugh's Inn at the Park
Off Division,
(509) 326-8000 toll-free
(800) 843-4667
303 W N River Dr,
Spokane, WA 99201
Expensive, AE, DC, MC, V; checks OK

This hotel on the bank of the river across from Riverfront Park has 266 rooms, many with southern views of downtown Spokane (and a few of the hydropower weir). The spacious lobby is the center of the main building, and all seven stories of rooms open out to it; it can be noisy, so specify a quiet corner room or perhaps one in the new wing at the east end of the hotel, away from the lobby and busy Washington Street. The attractive Windows on the Seasons restaurant overlooks the river, but the food is perfunctory. The lounge has comedy on Wednesday nights.

WestCoast Ridpath Hotel
In the heart of downtown,
(509) 838-2711 toll-free

The 340 rooms, recently renovated, are pleasant and spacious, and those in the tower overlook the city. The downtown location is as convenient as they come. This

(800) 426-0670
515 W Sprague Ave,
Spokane, WA 99204
Moderate; AE, DC, MC,
V; checks OK

place is popular with conventioneers and tourists, and some of the public areas can be crowded, but the mood here is always convivial. The rooftop restaurant, Ankeny's, boasts a grand view of Spokane. At night, when all is glittering and reflected repeatedly by the smoked glass and mirrors of the interior decor, the effect can be dazzling, glitzy, or just plain bewildering. The food is somewhat predictable; the Sunday brunch is a buffet; the Silver Grill, a coffee shop, provides more low-key fare. The bar has live music every night but Sunday and really hops on Fridays and Saturdays.

Sheraton Spokane Hotel
Next to the Opera House,
(509) 455-9600
322 N Spokane Falls Ct,
Spokane, WA 99201
Moderate; AE, DC, MC,
V; checks OK

Right on the riverfront next to the Convention Center, the Agricultural Trade Center, and the Opera House, this large hotel occupies an ideal location for visitors to downtown Spokane. The main shopping district and Riverfront Park are within an easy walk. This 15-year-old-plus hotel was showing signs of old age, but the current $5 million remodel should help. Nonetheless, the rooms are airy and pleasant, many with attractive river views, and the corner rooms are spacious indeed. The bathrooms are large and very clean. The pool is enclosed in a greenhouse atrium—cozy in the winter. The staff is courteous and helpful, the rates modest.

COLVILLE

The Colville River Valley has tiny farming communities, but outdoor recreation—fishing and cross-country skiing, primarily—is beginning to draw many to the pristine area. Highway 20 from Colville to Tonasket was dedicated last year as a National Scenic Byway. It climbs over, amazingly, the highest pass in Washington.

Hale's Ales is a microbrewery which welcomes visitors after 5pm, when the day's brewing work is done (call ahead). There are wall taps for the brews: Hale's pale ale, bitter, and porter, Moss Bay ale, and seasonal specialties. They also retail by the keg; 410 N Washington, (509) 684-6503.

KETTLE FALLS

LODGINGS

My Parent's Estate
7 miles past downtown
Colville on Hwy 395,
(509) 738-6220
Mail: PO Box 724,
Kettle Falls, WA 99141
Moderate; no credit cards;
checks OK

This 118-year-old house has also been a mission school, an abbess's home in a Dominican convent, a home for troubled boys, and a private residence; it's now a quiet haven in the woods. The 49-acre estate on the Colville River boasts a gym, a barn, a chicken coop, a caretaker's house, and a cemetery; more modern additions include a Jacuzzi and private baths. Hosts Al and Bev Parent are proud of their home; Bev's arts and crafts collection is displayed around the house, and Al is always eager to take guests on a historical tour of the grounds. The three guest rooms encourage quiet country relaxation, with comforters on the queen-size beds, refinished vanities, and antique washbasins. The lofty living room is dominated by a floor-to-ceiling stone fireplace. There's cross-country skiing in the winter; in more temperate months guests can float the Colville River, which flows by the estate, hike, or play in the water at nearby Franklin D. Roosevelt Lake.

CURLEW

RESTAURANTS

The Riverside Restaurant and Lounge
On the main drag, on the river, (509) 779-4813
813 River St, Curlew
Moderate; full bar; MC, V; checks OK
Dinner Wed-Sun

Curlew's downtown cafe has gained quite a reputation among backcountry hikers and mountain climbers. The setting is pleasant, comfortable, and funky: wooden tables and chairs and a wooden bar, all of them looking more or less handmade. The dining room has a large wood stove. There's a lovely view of the river, the produce is fresh, and the food is fairly simple but always good: fresh prawns in homemade beer batter or all-American thick sirloins, accompanied by steamed vegetables. Weekend fare includes prime rib; there's usually great cheesecake.

WAUCONDA

RESTAURANTS

The Wauconda Cafe, General Store and Post Office
The only place in town, (509) 486-4010
2432 Hwy 20, Wauconda
Inexpensive; beer and wine; MC, V; local checks only
Breakfast and lunch every day, dinner Mon-Sat

If you want atmosphere, here it is in this small general store cum gas station cum post office cum restaurant. A lunch counter with a few booths is squeezed between the general store and the dining room. It's a popular hangout for the local folk, both rancher types and counterculturalists. The view is out across the rolling meadows so typical of the Okanogan Highlands, with a few weatherbeaten barns enhancing the horizon and wildflowers in the spring. Cindy and Dean Dyer have added a couple of items to the menu in the last year, but the food remains homemade and simple: tasty burgers, milk shakes, sandwiches, and homemade soups for lunch; sautéed prawns, prime rib, and big salads for dinner. Breads and desserts are homemade.

OROVILLE

RESTAURANTS

Don Ernesto's
Main and Central,
(509) 476-2339
1511 Main St, Oroville
Inexpensive; no alcohol;
AE, DC, MC, V;
checks OK
Lunch, dinner every day

The extensive hand-colored and -embellished menus give you an idea of the extra care taken at this oasis of good Mexican food, now located in the old Orada Theater. They still serve a long menu of tacos, enchiladas, burritos, and so forth, plus tamales, menudo, and chile verde, all well prepared. There's mainstream American food (fish'n'chips, chicken sticks), but stick to the Mexican theme and order fried ice cream for dessert. The swimming pool–sized margaritas are for now a thing of the past; Ernesto's lounge has become an alcohol-free haven where teens and others can relax or enjoy the live music on Saturday nights.

LODGINGS

Sun Cove Resort
11 miles southwest of
Oroville on Wannacut
Lake, (509) 476-2223
Mail: Rt 2, Box 1294,
Oroville, WA 98844
Moderate; MC, V;
checks OK

John and Marge Donoghue run this cozy lakefront hideaway that's both comfortable and away from it all. Reasonably priced cabins are squeaky clean and fully stocked with kitchen utensils (even soap for the dishes), bedding, and linens. Ten of these rustic cabins sleep four each comfortably. There are also two- and three-bedroom cottages for families of six or eight in which a one-week minimum stay is required. You'll undoubtedly want to stay longer, though. There's excellent rainbow trout fishing in 2-mile-long Wannacut Lake, swimming in a heated pool, kayaking, canoeing, a game and toy center for youngsters, even a small library and a tanning center. Horseback riding is available at extra cost. The Donoghues also run the store and snack bar, which makes scrumptious pies. If there's a drawback, it's the dusty, narrow drive in to the resort—but that's a small price to pay for such seclusion. John and Marge think of the resort as their extended family, and children are more than welcome.

OMAK

The famous—and controversial—Suicide Race is the climax of the Omak Stampede the second weekend each August. At the end of each of the four rodeos that take place over the three-day weekend, a torrent of horses and riders pours down a steep embankment, across the Okanogan River, and into the arena. No one's ever been killed during the races since the event started in 1933, but plenty of horses have broken their legs. You can watch the purely macho competition from the Stampede Grounds at Omak's Eastside Park.

Indian tribes from all over the Pacific Northwest gather here during the Stampede to celebrate their heritage. A tepee Indian village is constructed, and traditional games and dances are performed.

RESTAURANTS

Breadline Cafe
Ash and 1st,
(509) 826-5836
102 S Ash St, Omak
Inexpensive; beer and
wine; AE, MC, V;
checks OK
Breakfast, lunch Mon-
Sat, dinner Tues-Sat

Here in the heart of steak and Stampede country, the Breadline offers a choice of fare. In the front of an old bottling-works building, owner Paula Chambers has expanded her eatery to include a low-tech bistro/nightclub offering full dinners and live music—from small folk bands to big-name blues artists like Charlie Musselwhite. The country-style menu includes steak and scampi, Cajun chicken, and pasta dishes. We like the big, informal, cheerfully cluttered cafe in the back. Here, the food takes a more New Age twist: homestyle breakfasts and creative lunches with daily specials. You watch the whole-grain bread come out of the oven as your hearty sandwich or salad is prepared. The Washington's Best salad combines lettuce, smoked salmon, tomato, and cucumber in a unique cranberry dressing (especially tasty), served with a hot wholegrain roll. Hot apple fritters with cream maple sauce finish you off.

OKANOGAN
LODGINGS

U and I Motel
Off Hwy 97 on old 97 at
838 2nd Ave N,
(509) 422-2920
Mail: PO Box 549,
Okanogan, WA 98840
Inexpensive; MC, V; no
checks

The name suits this family-run place's folksiness. It's not much to look at from its front on the old back road between Okanogan and Omak, but a closer look uncovers a more-than-usually-pleasant little nook for hiding away from it all. The two-room cabinettes are less than spacious, but they're clean and cozily done up in rustic paneling. They are a deal, starting at $28, as are one-roomers with a double bed for $22. Best of all, the whole back yard of the motel is a grassy lawn and flower garden fronting on the tranquil Okanogan. Grab a deck chair, cast a fishing line, and watch the river flow. Pets okay.

COULEE DAM
LODGINGS

Coulee House Motel
Birch and Roosevelt,
(509) 633-1101
110 Roosevelt Way,
Coulee Dam, WA 99116
Moderate; AE, DC, MC,
V; no checks

With a great view of the dam, this motel has decent amenities—pool, sauna, and refrigerators in some of the large, clean rooms, to name a few. At night you can sit on the tiny lanai outside your room (smoking or non) and watch the new animated laser light show (summers only) over the dam as the water cascades past.

GRAND COULEE

Grand, yes—this is a wonderful area from which to appreciate the outsized dimensions of the landscape and the geological forces that made it. The Columbia, as it slices through central Washington, has an eerie power: the water rushes by in silky strength through enormous chasms. The river, the second largest in the nation, traverses a valley of staggering scale; in prehistoric times glacier-fed water created a river with the largest flow of water ever known.

Grand Coulee Dam is one of the largest structures on the earth—tall as a 46-story building, with a spillway twice the height of Niagara and a length as great as a dozen city blocks. The dam, completed in 1941, was originally intended more to irrigate the desert than to produce electricity; so much power was generated, however, that the dam became a magnet for the nation's aluminum industry. The north-face extension (completed in 1975) was designed by Marcel Breuer, a great practitioner of the International Style, and the heroic scale of the concrete is quite magnificent. There are daily self-guided tours of the dam; hours vary according to season and famous laser light show: (509) 633-9265.

Eccentric inventor Emil Gehrke amassed an oddly compelling **windmill collection** at North Dam Park on Highway 155 between Electric City and Grand Coulee. Four hardhats tilted sideways catch the wind, cups and saucers twirl around a central teapot—it's whimsical and fascinating.

Houseboating. Until two years ago, Lake Roosevelt was untapped by the RV-on-pontoons fleet. Now there are 40 houseboats available to explore the 150-mile-long lake, and most book up early for the summer. The sun's almost guaranteed, and all you need to bring is food, bed linens, and your bathing suit; boats are moored at Kelly Ferry Marina, 14 miles north of Wilbur, 1-800-648-LAKE.

CRESTON

RESTAURANTS

Deb's Cafe
Hwy 2, (509) 636-3345
600 Watson, Creston
Inexpensive; full bar;
MC, V; local checks only
Breakfast, lunch, dinner
every day

The glory days of Deb Cobenhaver, a world-champion rodeo rider back in the mid-1950s, are kept in a kind of time capsule here. Outside there is a wooden porch, like a stage-set saloon; inside, the place is strewn with trophies, photos, and saddles. Cowboy-hatted men and women shoot pool in the bar or line up at the lunch counter.

The main cafe opens at 5am for its hearty breakfasts with homemade cinnamon rolls; at lunch there are a few decent sandwiches, served with home-cut fries; dinner is steaks—natch—and on Saturday nights they grill your steak out back. There's also an all-you-can-eat barbecued rib special with salad bar, and great Western music.

SOAP LAKE

Early settlers named the lake for its unusually high alkali content, which gives the water a soapy feel.

Dry Falls, off Route 17 north of town, is the place where the torrential Columbia once crashed over falls 3 miles wide and 400 feet high; an interpretive center (Wednesday-Sunday, 10-6, summer) explains the local geology, which has been compared to surface features of Mars. From this lookout, you can also see Sun Lakes, which are actually puddles left by the ancient Columbia. It's RV territory, but the waters are prime spots for swimming and fishing; (509) 632-5583.

LODGINGS

Notaras Lodge
236 E Main St,
(509) 246-0462
Mail: PO Box 987,
Soap Lake, WA 98851
Moderate; MC, V;
checks OK

On the shores of Soap Lake, you can stay in the Norma Zimmer Room (the bubble lady on the Lawrence Welk Show) complete with a jukebox or the Bonnie Guitar Honeymoon Suite (named for a local country-and-Western celeb whose own guitar is memorialized in an epoxied table along with other souvenirs of the singer's career). Such memorabilia are owner Marina Romary's passion; the Western Nostalgia Room boasts a real pool table as well as a whirlpool. The healing waters of Soap Lake are available to guests on tap in the bathrooms (eight of which have Jacuzzis). Ms. Romary also owns the nearby Don's Restaurant (14 Canna St, (509) 246-1217) a popular steak, seafood, and Greek eatery, where man-sized meals are served in a dark, slightly seamy interior.

WENATCHEE

You're in the heart of apple country, with an Apple Blossom Festival the first part of May. **Ohme Gardens**, 3 miles north on Route 97, is a 600-foot-high promontory transformed into an Edenic retreat, with a fastidiously created natural alpine ecosystem patterned after high mountain country. Splendid views of the valley and the Columbia River, (509) 662-5785.

Mission Ridge, 13 miles southwest on Squilchuck Road, offers some of the best powder snow in the region, served by four chair lifts (cross-country skiing too), (509) 663-7631. On the third Sunday in April, the Ridge-to-River Pentathlon is an impressive sporting event.

Rocky Reach Dam, 6 miles north on Route 97, offers a beautiful picnic and playground area (locals marry on the well-kept grounds), plus a fish-viewing room. Inside the dam are two large galleries devoted to the history of the region.

RESTAURANTS

John Horan House
Restaurant
South on Easy St to
Horan, (509) 663-0018
2 Horan Rd, Wenatchee
Moderate; full bar; AE,
MC, V; checks OK
Dinner Tues-Sat

Many of the orchards that surrounded the house built by Wenatchee pioneer Mike Horan, the "Apple King," are gone. Yet the roundabout drive to the house near the confluence of the Wenatchee and Columbia rivers sets the tone for an evening that harks back to more gracious times. New owners John and Inga Peters serve dinner as they would at home for friends. The fireplace is ablaze on chilly nights, and they like to greet regulars by name. The couple brightened the main dining room while keeping the original Horan family furnishings and portraits. Upstairs they converted three bedrooms into intimate dining rooms for private parties. The prix-fixe menu now offers hearty country dishes such as cassoulet and roast pork with glazed onions; lighter eaters can order entrées á la carte or choose from several pasta dishes. This isn't the place to come if you are in a hurry. Sometimes the leisurely service can stretch out to be a bit slow, but if you're settled in with chef Joe Gapan's burnt cream-dessert, you won't even notice.

New Orleans Kitchen

*Just before the East
Wenatchee bridge on
Mission, (509) 663-3167
928 S Mission St,
Wenatchee
Moderate; beer and wine;
no credit cards;
checks OK
Dinner Wed-Sat*

Lots of flavor here—and it's not all in the food. You can select Creole, Cajun, or classic French eats from the extensive menu offered in this ramshackle restaurant in Wenatchee's south end. Oysters Bienville is a good choice for a starter, although the blackened prime rib comes with its own spicy "bones" as an appetizer. Catfish and specials like crab-stuffed quail are prepared with equal expertise. For dessert, Fudge, Fudge, Fudge (chocolate spoon cake with layers of fudge poured onto vanilla ice cream, whipped cream, and pecans) is unbelievable. It's a get-to-know-your-neighbor atmosphere, and if Jim Swickard doesn't pour the wine fast enough, he doesn't mind if you do it yourself. Reservations are a good idea.

The Windmill

*1½ blocks west of Miller,
on the main thoroughfare,
(509) 663-3478
1501 N Wenatchee Ave,
Wenatchee
Moderate; beer and wine;
AE, MC, V; checks OK
Dinner Tues-Sat (Mon-
Sat in summer)*

A constantly changing number on a blackboard keeps track of the steaks sold at this celebrated steak house. On our last visit it was 219,478. That's not the number of steaks sold since The Windmill opened 69 years ago, that's since January, 1982, when Pat and Linda Jackson took over as owners, and we haven't heard of even one that wasn't terrific. Waitresses here don't come and go—they stay and stay, sporting pins that proudly declare the number of years they've served. The meals, too, are time-tested and classic. They start you off with bread sticks and a relish tray, a lettuce salad, and a bottle of wine. There are seafood and pork chops, but don't be a fool—order the well-aged, perfectly cooked steak! Ritual dictates that you finish with a piece of one of the magnificent pies, baked fresh daily. It's our favorite steakhouse in the whole Northwest; beware of long waits.

Steven's at Mission Square

*1 block off Wenatchee at
2nd and Mission,
(509) 663-6573
218 N Mission St,
Wenatchee
Moderate; full bar; AE,
MC, V; checks OK*

Steven's is a handsome place where Wenatchee's premier chef Steve Gordon serves Northwest cuisine with a few international excursions. The split-level dining room with potted plants is elegant in a trendy sort of way; full-length mirrors reflect the well-dressed clientele. Pasta and seafood dishes are served here with pride and a flourish, from fettuccine with asparagus and prosciutto to apricot-honey-mustard

Lunch Mon-Fri, dinner
every day

chicken with sweet basil on a bed of spinach, pecans, and Bermuda onions. We've had best luck with the specials (East Coast scallops sautéed with red and green bell peppers, artichoke hearts, and scallions, in a tomato sauce). Bread is freshly baked and warm, and desserts are first-rate, especially rich triangles of chocolate-peanut-butter ice cream pie or chocolate hazelnut cheesecake.

Tequila's
On Wenatchee Avenue
south of 9th,
(509) 662-7239
800 N Wenatchee Ave,
Wenatchee
Inexpensive; full bar;
MC, V; checks OK
Lunch, dinner every day

Go ahead, salvage your high school Spanish; the friendly staff may even give you a few extra lessons. Tequila's takes Mexican food one step beyond the norm. Onions, pepper, and cilantro spice the fresh salsa. The baskets of warm tortilla chips are refilled often. Margaritas are generous and the refried beans have never seen the inside of a can. Best is any dish with the excellent carnitas or the tangy verde sauce. Or try the sizzling fajitas. It's all priced as if you were south of the border and you'll leave mui feliz.

Visconti's Italian Restaurant
At the west end of town on
Wenatchee,
(509) 662-5013
1737 N Wenatchee,
Wenatchee
Inexpensive; beer and
wine; AE, DC, MC, V;
checks OK
Lunch Mon-Fri, dinner
every day

Owner Mark Mecham's Sicilian grandmother taught him how to cook; he named the restaurant in her honor. This is a come-as-you-are place where Mecham or his wife Candy will greet you at the door. All the standards are on the menu, from spaghetti to Caesars to thick slabs of lasagne. Fresh garlic and herbs permeate each generously sized dish. Try the mostaccioli (a tube-shaped noodle) with Italian sausage and mushroom sauce. Many wines are available by the glass and Mecham will offer sips to those unsure of the choice. Reports on dessert are good, especially the chocolate espresso cheesecake; we've haven't yet had room to try them. There's another branch in Leavenworth at 217 8th St, (509) 782-0204.

Golden East
Across the Columbia
River and up Grant Rd,
(509) 884-1510
230 Grant Rd,
East Wenatchee
Inexpensive; beer and
wine; MC, V;
local checks only
Lunch, dinner Tues-Sun

A remodeled bank is now a vault of red vinyl booths, paper lanterns, and Chinese food. George Chang and his wife Marisa prepare both Cantonese and more potent Sichuan favorites (even so, you might need to tell them you like it hot). Chang trained and worked in Seattle before going east to seek his fortune. He has a light hand with oil and favors cook-to-order preparation. The combination plates are fine, but you'll do better to order moo shu pork with tender rice pancakes or chicken with cashews, soul-warming with hot peppers. Ask for a window table with a view of the Wenatchee River and Mission Ridge beyond.

LODGINGS

The Chieftain
On Wenatchee off 9th,

The motels all line up along Wenatchee Avenue, but this one stands out for its dependable quality year after

(509) 663-8141, toll-free
(800) 572-4456
1005 N Wenatchee Ave,
Wenatchee, WA 98801
Moderate; full bar, AE,
DC, MC, V; checks OK
Breakfast, lunch, dinner
every day

year (since 1928). It's popular with the locals, who come for "executive lunches," brunches after church on Sunday, or the famous prime rib in the evening. Guests will note that rooms are larger than those of the Chieftain's cousins down the pike. Ask for rooms in the newer wing, the "executive rooms," and you'll be surprised what spacious quarters you've got for about $51. There's a swimming pool, a hot tub, and a helicopter pad (which doubles as a basketball court). You can bring your pet with advance notice. Ugly views.

WestCoast Wenatchee Center Hotel
Center of town on Wenatchee,
(509) 662-1234
201 N Wenatchee Ave,
Wenatchee, WA 98801
Moderate; AE, DC, MC, V; checks OK

The newest hotel has a new name, and it's the nicest one on the strip, with its view of the city and the Columbia River. It's elegant, but not overdone for this city. The nine-story hotel has three floors designated nonsmoking, with a total of 146 large, moderately priced rooms. A restaurant on the top floor is open for breakfast, lunch, and dinner, and the city's convention center is next door, connected by a sky bridge. The outdoor pool is great under the hot Wenatchee sun. Also available are an indoor pool, a Jacuzzi, and a weight room.

CHELAN

This resort area is blessed with the springtime perfume of apple blossoms, a 55-mile lake thrusting like a fjord into tall mountains, 300 days a year of sunshine, and good skiing, hunting, fishing, hiking, and sailing. It's been trying to live up to its touristic potential since C.C. Campbell built his hotel here in 1901, but with mixed success so far. Now that time-share condos are springing up near the golf course and B&Bs are blooming near the cross-country trails, the amenities are improving. No one need improve the scenery.

The top attraction is the cruise up the lake on an old-fashioned tour boat, *The Lady of the Lake* or the newer *Lady Express*. The lake is never more than 2 miles wide (it's also one of the deepest in the world), so you have a sense of slicing right into the Cascades. At Stehekin, the head of the lake, you can check out craft shops, take a bus tour, eat a barbecue lunch, and get back on board for the return voyage. The tour boat departs Chelan at 8:30am daily in summer, three or four days a week off season, and returns in the late afternoon; rates are $21 per person round trip; kids 6-11 years are half price. No reservations needed. The faster *Lady Express* shortens the daily trip to just over two hours, with a one hour stop in Stehekin before heading back; round trip tickets are $38, and reservations are suggested. More info: The Lake Chelan Boat Company, (509) 682-2224. Or you can fly up to Stehekin, tour the valley, and be back the same day: Chelan Airways, (509) 682-5555.

Chelan Butte Lookout, 9 miles west of Chelan, provides a view of the lake, the Columbia, and the orchard-blanketed countryside.

Sports. Echo Valley, northeast of Chelan, offers rope tows and a Poma lift on gentle slopes; Lake Chelan Golf Course, (509) 682-5421 for tee times, is an attractive, sporting course near town; fishing for steelhead, rainbow, cutthroats, and Chinooks is very good, with remote, smaller lakes particularly desirable.

One thousand feet above Lake Chelan sits **Bear Mountain Ranch**, a 5,000-acre estate with 50 kilometers of tracked and skating trails for cross-country skiers. There's a warming hut with picnic tables and ski videos, and what are wheatfields in the summer provide gentle slopes for beginning telemarkers. Bigger plans are in the works, but for now you just go here to ski. Open for two weeks at Christmas, and weekends December through mid-March; (509) 682-5444.

Nostalgia. St. Andrew's Church, downtown Chelan, is a log edifice, reputedly designed by Stanford White in 1898, and still in service; from the Chelan Museum (Woodin Avenue, 1-4pm in summer) you can learn about other restored houses nearby, such as the old Lucas Homestead.

RESTAURANTS

Goochi's Restaurant
Across Woodin from Campbell's Lodge,
(509) 682-2436
104 E Woodin, Chelan
Inexpensive; full bar;AE, MC, V; local checks only
Lunch, dinner every day, brunch Sat-Sun

After years of abuse as a tavern in the historic Lakeview Hotel building, this pretty space with its huge antique cherrywood back bar is now a smart stop for lunch or dinner. Classic rock 'n' roll plays on CDs and neon sculpture decorates the cedar-planked walls. Burgers and pasta selections are popular with children; for the adults, however, the restaurant strives for a slight twist on the usual, offering black-eyed peas in lieu of potatoes or rice pilaf. A moist chicken breast may come with a tart lemon-thyme cream sauce. Soups (such as cream of green pepper) are often light and flavorful. Chelan's Riverfront Park, just around the corner, is good for a postprandial stroll.

River Park Dining
By the log church near the old bridge,
(509) 682-5626
114 E Woodin, Chelan
Inexpensive; beer and wine; MC, V; checks OK
Lunch Mon-Sat; dinner Thurs-Fri (winter), Tues-Sat (summer)

This five-year-old restaurant is brand new since a fire a few years ago. They're still serving their famous hearty lunches (the veggie sandwich is a meal of avocado, cream cheese, sprouts, tomato, and almonds; ditto the enormous baked potatoes, notably the mushroom-and-cheese-filled baker). Dinner includes such things as glazed salmon and sassy grilled chicken. Every Friday is prime rib night. The terrace is enclosed now for year-round use, and the best views are from the second-floor sun room.

LODGINGS

Campbell's Lodge
104 E Woodin, Chelan,
(509) 682-2561
Mail: PO Box 278, Chelan, WA 98816
Expensive; full bar, AE, DC, MC, V; checks OK
Breakfast, lunch, dinner every day

Chelan's venerable resort, whose history goes back to 1901 and includes the recent absorption of its rival to the north, Cannon's, continues to be the most popular place for visitors with its prime lakeside properties and 148 rooms, many with kitchenettes. Among the facilities you'll find three heated pools and an outdoor Jacuzzi, a sandy beach, and moorage, should you arrive by boat. A new convention center can service up to 250 people. The most dependable restaurant at the Lake is here: Campbell House Restaurant. The menu changes frequently, but you can usually start the day with pumpkin-apple bread (and fresh strawberries in season), stop in for a spicy Cajun chicken sandwich lunch, or dine upstairs on informal Italian fare like flavorful cioppino or garlicky prawns and pasta. Reservations here, as at the lodge, are not always easy to get.

Mary Kay's Romantic Whaley Mansion
415 3rd, Chelan,
(509) 682-5735
Mail: Rt 1, Box 693,
Chelan, WA 98816
Expensive; AE, DC, MC, V; checks OK

Mary Kay offers a romantic return to the Victorian Age in this historic Chelan home, built in 1911. Overstuffed beds, lace and ruffles, handmade French wallpapers, Belgian velvets, and lots of pink create a paradise for those who like that kind of stuff. Each of the 11 rooms has a private bath attached, and you can ask for a room with a view of the lake. Our brunch (included with room) featured raspberry ice garnished with fresh raspberries marinated in Chambord, topped with Chantilly cream; brioche; eggs Florentine with Italian sausage; and strawberry mousse in baked meringue shells. Mary Kay caters to every want (she's even been known to purchase a negligée for a forgetful honeymooner). A good-bye hug and a hand-dipped chocolate seem to be part of the stay.

Darnell's Resort Motel
Off Manson Hwy at 901
Spader Bay Rd,
(509) 682-2015
Mail: PO Box 506,
Chelan, WA 98816
Expensive; AE, MC, V; checks OK

Situated right on the shore of the lake, this is a resort especially suited to families. Newly refurbished bedroom suites are large and attractive and all have views ($75-$145 for suite a for four). Lots of amenities are included with the price of the room: putting green, heated swimming pool, sauna, hot tub, exercise room, shuffleboard, volleyball, badminton, tennis, barbecues, bicycles, rowboats, and canoes. Down the road from Campbell's and the center of town, Darnell's is removed from the seasonal hurly-burly.

Kelly's Resort
14 miles uplake on the
south shore,
(509) 687-3220
Mail: Rt 1, Box 119,
Chelan, WA 98816
Expensive; MC, V; checks OK

Kelly-owned for about 45 years, this resort is a favorite for families because it is right on the shore and not right in town. The original ten fully-equipped cabins are set back in the woods; they're dark and rustic (request for the one above the volleyball courts, it has the most sun), but they're great for those on a budget ($79 for three) and families seeking a playground. But we prefer one of the four new condo units on the lake (from the lower units you can walk right off the deck into the lake). There's a nice deck near the grocery store (a good spot to have a beer) and a knotty-pine common area with a ping-pong table and a fireplace. A very friendly spot.

STEHEKIN

A passage to Stehekin, a little community at the head of Lake Chelan, is like traveling to another world, where there is no telephone service. This jumping-off point for exploring the rugged and remote North Cascades National Park can be reached only by a four-hour *Lady of the Lake* boat trip or the faster *Lady Express* (daily from mid-April to mid-October, less frequently in winter), (509) 682-2224; by Chelan Airways float plane, (509) 682-5555; by hiking (write Chelan Ranger District, PO Box 189, Chelan, WA 98816); or by private boat. The boat and the plane will take you to Stehekin from the town of Chelan. For a shorter boat ride, catch the *Lady* uplake at Field's Point.

Exploring the area is the prime reason for coming here. There are several day hikes, including a lovely one along the lake shore and another along a stream through the Buckner Orchard, and many more splendid backcountry trails for the serious backpacker. In winter there are some fine touring opportunities for cross-country skiers or snowshoe enthusiasts, although the town pretty much shuts down then. The ranger station at Chelan (open year-round), (509) 682-2576, is an excellent source of information for these activities. A National Park Service shuttle bus provides transportation from Stehekin to trailheads, campgrounds, fishing holes, and scenic areas mid-May to mid-October (for information call either (206) 856-5700 or (509) 682-2549). There are also bicycle and boat rentals at the North Cascades Lodge.

Stehekin Valley Ranch. The Courtney family picks you up at Stehekin in an old bus and takes you to the farthest end of the valley for seclusion and hearty family-style meals at their ranch. Open in the summer months, their rustic tent-cabins offer a place to bunk and just the basics (a kerosene lamp, showers in the main building), plus hearty, simple food at a decent price ($49 per night per person). **Cascade Corrals**, also run by the family, arranges horseback rides and mountain pack trips; (509) 682-4677 or write Stehekin Valley Ranch, Box 36, Stehekin, WA 98852.

The **Stehekin Pastry Company**, fills the void the Honey Bear Bakery left when the bakery migrated to Seattle; this spot is a local favorite for sweet desserts and rich conversation.

LODGINGS

Silver Bay Inn

Take the Lady of the Lake *to Stehekin,*
(509) 682-2212
Mail: PO Box 43,
Stehekin, WA 98852
Moderate; no credit cards;
checks OK

The Silver Bay Inn, located where the Stehekin River flows into Lake Chelan, is a wonderful retreat for those who want to explore the Stehekin Valley. Friendly Kathy and Randall Dinwiddie welcome their guests to this passive solar home with hikes and stories only the locals know. At breakfast you may find fresh fruit with Devonshire cream, along with an apple pancake, or scrambled eggs with cashews, or orange French toast with blueberries. And if you're there at the right time, Kathy might serve a piece of warm blueberry cake with a scoop of Randall's homemade ice cream in the evening while you relax on the deck.

The setting is spectacular: 700 feet of waterfront with a broad green lawn rolling down to the lake. The main house has a master suite (with a two-night minimum to ensure you'll take time to enjoy yourself) decorated in antiques, with a separate sitting room, two view decks, a soaking tub, and a faraway view. Two separate lakeside cabins are remarkably convenient (dishwasher, microwave, all linens) and sleep four and six. Bicycles and the family car are available.

North Cascades Lodge
Boat landing, Stehekin,
(509) 682-4711
Mail: PO Box 1779,
Chelan, WA 98816
Moderate; MC, V;
checks OK

A rustic resort with a range of accommodations: choose the lodge itself (the larger rooms are much better) or a unit with a kitchenette. Suites in simple A-frames or cottages are available for larger parties and are booked early in the season. A hot tub is now available for lodge guests. The lodge, overlooking the lake, tends to be swarming with tourists who arrive for lunch each day when the *Lady of the Lake* steams up to the dock and sandwiches are mass-produced in the restaurant. Breakfasts and dinners are more relaxed. In the evening there is a varied salad bar, freshly baked bread, steaks, chicken, and seafood. A longtime favorite, the Veggie Potato, filled with vegetables and topped with cheese, sour cream, and mushrooms, is still on the menu. The chef might prepare your catch if you've been lucky fishing in the local waters. Supplies, which must come from Chelan, are sometimes short.

YAKIMA WINE COUNTRY

If your last visit to the Napa Valley recalled rush-hour traffic on the freeway to Disneyland, you may be ready for the less traveled, more organic pleasures of the Yakima wine country. Get off the freeway at virtually any point between Union and the Tri-Cities and you'll find a scene of unspoiled pastoral splendor. Vineyards and orchards follow the meandering Yakima River. Cattle graze the pastures. And the small towns scattered here and there provide constant surprises and unexpected small pleasures. The burgeoning wine industry (there are close to two dozen wineries in the valley, and more on the way) has encouraged small businesses to go after the tourist trade, and each year brings more restaurants, galleries, and bed and breakfasts to the verdant valley. Warm welcomes in the shops and tasting rooms are genuine; they really are glad to see you.

Since vineyards were first planted about two decades ago, the valley's unique weather patterns—warm days, cool nights, with seemingly more daylight than down in Napa—have encouraged winemakers to develop new approaches to winemaking. A Northwest style has emerged; bright fruit flavors underscored by crisp acids. The white wines are mostly dry (even the rieslings tend that way) and firmer than their counterparts in California, while the reds are rich and textured, with the structure of fine Bordeaux. Prices are low, and wineries often sell special bottlings unavailable elsewhere.

The Yakima Valley Wine Growers Association (PO Box 39, Grandview, WA 98930) publishes a useful brochure that lists member wineries along with tasting room hours, easy-to-follow maps, and a bit of history. Big or small, all offer a taste of what's new and a chance to chat about the vintage in the most relaxed circumstances. Here's a quick rundown, as you head east from Yakima. **Thurston Wolfe**, 27 N Front, Yakima, (509) 452-0335, dessert wine specialists, including a Sauternes-style "Sweet Rebecca" and a landmark Zinfandel port. **Staton Hills**, 71 Gangl Road, Wapato, (509) 877-2112, in an attractive building, with a view of Union Gap, picnic grounds. **Vin de l'Ouest Winery**, 101 Toppenish Avenue, Toppenish, (509) 865-5002, a gallery/tasting room in a town dominated by antique shops and wild-West murals. **Bonair Winery**, 500 S Bonair Road, Zillah,

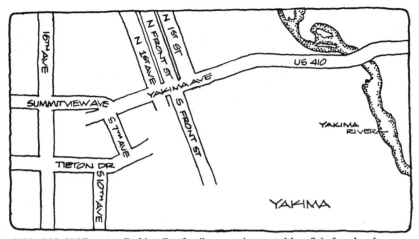

(509) 829-6027, a small, friendly, family-run winery, with a flair for chardonnay. **Hyatt Vineyards Winery,** 2020 Gilbert Road, Zillah, (509) 829-6333, fine dry white wines and a lovely view. **Zillah Oakes Winery,** Zillah, (509) 829-6990, off-dry white wines, gift shop, and a tasting room with a Victorian motif, faces right on the highway. **Covey Run,** 1500 Vintage Road, Zillah, (509) 829-6235, one of the larger wineries, expansive tasting room, picnic grounds, view, and a full line of well-made wines, particularly rieslings. **Portteus Vineyards,** 5201 Highland Drive, Zillah, (509) 829-6970, new, family-owned with estate-bottled reds—cabernet, merlot, and Lemberger. **Horizon's Edge Winery,** 4530 E Zillah Drive, Zillah, (509) 829-6401, another spectacular view and good lineup of wines. **Cascade Crest Estates,** 111 E Lincoln Avenue, Sunnyside, (509) 839-9463, large selection of pleasant wines in a no-frills facility. **Eaton Hill Winery,** 530 Gurley Road, Granger, (509) 854-2508, new winery and B&B in a restored homestead and cannery, all white wines so far. **Stewart Vineyards,** 1711 Cherry Hill Road, Granger, (509) 854-1882, one of the oldest vineyards in the state, rieslings and cabernets are worth noting. **Tucker Cellars,** Sunnyside, (509) 837-8701, a family enterprise offering an extensive selection of Yakima valley fruit and produce as well as wines. Excellent tours at **Chateau Ste. Michelle,** W 5th & Avenue B, Grandview, (509) 882-3928; where the state's biggest winery set up shop in the late '60s, and the highly regarded reds are still made here, in a facility dating back to the repeal of Prohibition. **Yakima River Winery,** Prosser, (509) 786-2805, riverside location, full-blown reds and superb dessert wines. **Pontin del Roza,** Prosser, (509) 786-4449, family-owned and operated. **Hinzerling Winery,** 1520 Sheridan, Prosser, (509) 786-2163, one of the state's pioneering wineries, now under new ownership; look for tannic reds and fine late harvest "Die Sonne" gewürztraminer. **Chinook Wines,** Prosser, (509) 786-2725, a charming, intimate setting in which small quantities of some of Washington's best wines are produced. Don't miss the merlot. The **Hogue Cellars,** Wine Country Road, Prosser, (509) 786-4557, spectacularly successful family enterprise making superb whites and cellarworthy reds; look for "Reserve" wines. **Oakwood Cellars,** Benton City, (509) 588-5332, one of the newest additions to the growing number of wineries in the vicinity of Red Mountain. **Kiona Vineyards Winery,** Benton City, (509) 588-6716, a small estate winery, the first to plant on Red Mountain, making remarkable cabernet, Lemberger, and dry and sweet rieslings. **Blackwood Can-**

yon, Benton City, (509) 588-6249, just up the road from Kiona, a no-frills facility making controversial but distinctive wines; the late-harvest wines are excellent. **Columbia Crest Winery,** Paterson, (509) 875-2061, off the beaten track a half hour south of Prosser, this impressive facility showcases sophisticated winemaking on a grand scale. Ten miles west at Canoe Ridge is the planned site of **Chalone Inc.**'s proposed new winery. **Mercer Ranch Vineyards,** 522 Alderdale Road (17 miles west of Paterson), (509) 894-4741, a drive through wide-open dryland wheat country along the banks of the Columbia leads to this red wine specialist, located on an old ranch in the Horse Heaven Hills. Nearby **Crow Butte State Park** makes a nice picnic stop.

YAKIMA

Irrigation (first tried by the Indians and missionaries here in the 1850s) has made this desert bloom with grapes, apples, mint, asparagus, and hops. The town also blooms with small conventions.

Front Street Historical District includes a 22-car train that houses shops and restaurants, and the renovated Pacific Fruit Exchange Building, which holds a local farmers' market.

The Greenway Bike Path winds along the Yakima River for 4.6 miles. Start out in Sherman Park on Nob Hill and go to the Selah Gap. Along the way, look for bald eagles and blue herons, or pick out a fishing hole; (509) 453-8280.

The Wine Cellar is a fine place to sample local vintages and orient yourself for a more extended foray into the wine country. Lenore Lambert, the owner, is a good source for local lore. Food products sold; 5 N Front Street, (509) 248-3590.

Interurban Trolley. A restored 1906 trolley provides summer-evening and weekend rides around Yakima. Call (509) 575-1700 for schedules.

Horse racing. Yakima Meadows has live races November-March, and beams Longacres Park races by satellite April-September weekends. It's a dandy place to see small-town, old-West racing. 1301 S 10th, (509) 248-3920.

Yakima Valley Museum has handsome pioneer pieces, plus a collection from Yakima's most famous native son, Justice William O. Douglas. 2105 Tieton Drive, (509) 248-0747 open Wed-Sun.

RESTAURANTS

Gasperetti's Restaurant
6 blocks south of the N Front St exit off I-82,
(509) 248-0628
1013 N 1st St, Yakima
Moderate; full bar; AE, MC, V; checks OK
Lunch Tues-Fri, dinner Tues-Sat

Almost a quarter-century after its beginning, John Gasperetti's Northern Italian restaurant continues to be one of the most innovative establishments in the region. You feel comfortable here in this intimate, leisurely, and friendly place—even if it's your first visit. Originally a family-style restaurant, the place still offers spaghetti with meat sauce on the left side of the menu, but the daily fresh sheet on the right side displays the real skill of chef Brad Patterson. No matter which side you order from, don't pass up the onion rings—cut very thin, stacked very high, and served very hot.

The restaurant, too, is double-sided. Those in the know head to the room on the right; first-time patrons may find themselves shunted to the more austere left-hand room. Either way, you'll find pastas made fresh daily with seasonal sauces—light tomato cream, fresh pesto, rabbit with Chianti. You might want to split an appetizer of roasted garlic and Rollingstone chèvre, or asparagus vinaigrette. The light touch extends to both the pastas (try the ravioli and lemon butter) and the meat dishes such as Provimi veal finished with garlic, rosemary, lemon, and capers or pan-fried filet mignon with a Gorgonzola and Marsala sauce. And save room for dessert—fresh berries in season; praline cheesecake; something chocolaty; or the pick of a dessert cart with delicacies ranging from light to ultrarich. The wine list (one of the best in the Valley) offers excellent bottlings of Washington wines, including many hard-to-find reds. Service is informed, attentive, anticipating, and unobtrusive. There's a smaller menu (but a nice sampling) now offered for lunch. The location, on a busy street, is a little less desirable.

Birchfield Manor

Take exit 34 off Hwy 24, head east 2 miles, then south on Birchfield, (509) 452-1960
2018 Birchfield Rd, Yakima
Expensive; wine only; AE, MC, V; checks OK
Dinner Thurs-Sat

All in all, Birchfield Manor offers elegant French country dining. When you arrive for your appointed seating, owners Wil and Sandy Masset greet you at the door and show you to your table in the large living room of this antique-filled historic home. Meals here are preceded by their reputation, which is taken *very* seriously. Young children are not welcome, lest they disturb others' enjoyment of the evening. Wil's European training as a chef produces an ambitious, imaginative meal. If only the ambience were more pleasing. It's the kind of place that deserves candles; instead, the bad lighting produces a gloomy effect. That said, Birchfield Manor is one of a kind in Central Washington, and therefore worth visiting when you're in the mood for a formal evening. Of the four entrées, we selected the double breast of chicken Florentine and the bouillabaisse; the latter, although the serving was small, was everything a *patron* from Marseilles hoped. Washington wines are featured, and the courses—dutifully explained by a friendly waitperson—are both individualistic and complementary to each other. The Massets have moved across the road to allow for five B&B rooms upstairs ($55-$85 with baths). In contrast to the dark color scheme of the restaurant, bright colors and continental appointments fill each bedroom. An outdoor pool and hot tub are for guest use only.

The Greystone Restaurant

Corner of Front and Yakima, (509) 248-9801
5 N Front St, Yakima
Moderate; full bar; AE, MC, V; checks OK
Dinner Tues-Sat

Here amid turn-of-the-century decor in the historic Lund Building, Yakima's young professionals relax and dine. Owners Gayla Games-Hopkins and Nancy Beveridge-Camper, who took over in 1983, have developed a menu that draws on family recipes and new creations by chef Steven Woods. Seasonal entrées are thoughtfully chosen and carefully prepared: excellent veal in caper cream sauce, pork tenderloin in a port and green peppercorn sauce, Yakima apple-and-sausage-stuffed breast of chicken in a brandy cream sauce. The best deal is to order off the cafe menu in the comfortable lounge—same food, just less expensive. The staff is friendly and helpful. A well-chosen wine list emphasizes regional vintages, with some fine selections from California and Europe, as well as several good wines by the glass. Desserts are all homemade and change with the seasons—shortcake with fresh rhubarb sauce, local cheeses, and fresh fruits. The piano bar swings.

Ichiban
*1st St exit from I-82,
(509) 248-2585
1010 N 1st Ave, Yakima
Moderate; full bar; MC,
V; local checks only
Lunch Tues-Fri, dinner
Tues-Sat*

In their new location complete with sushi bar, Joe and Susan Sugimoto's authentic Japanese restaurant continues to be a Central Washington treat. The sushi (fresh ingredients come over from Seattle) selection is small but outstanding, and the tempura coating is light and crisp. *Nebemono* (single-pot items) are a specialty, and the menu offers a wide variety of sukiyaki, donburi, curry dishes (as hot as you wish), and assorted udon. A short drive from downtown Yakima, but worth the extra mile or two.

The Blue Ox
*1 block north of Yakima
Ave, (509) 248-5930
15 N 6th St, Yakima
Expensive; full bar, AE,
MC, V; local checks only
Dinner Mon-Sat*

White linens, fresh flowers—and just homey enough to be a very comfortable restaurant. Several favorable reports have crossed our desks rating the steaks as some of the best in the area. With no less than 18 steak choices (from an aged top sirloin to a Chateaubriand—for two—carved at tableside), you probably won't go wrong. It's located in a large blue house near the center of town; the wine list stands up to the high expectations of the region.

The Brewery Pub
*Head west on Yakima,
turn right on Front,
(509) 575-2922
32 N Front St, Yakima
Inexpensive; beer; MC,V;
checks OK
Lunch, dinner every day*

Bert Grant, one of the creators of the Northwest's boom in microbreweries, has brought back full-flavored, fresh, locally made ales, stouts, and hard cider. In 1990 he moved the brew pub next door into the old train station. Small experimental batches are now brewed here while the bulk of the beer is made at the original location across the street (open for tours by reservation only). It's a popular place (especially on weekends) that serves up a British pub menu to accompany the ales. (Only Grant's brews are served.) Homemade soups and Mexican food occasionally appear at lunch. A good place to meet friendly residents.

Deli de Pasta
*½ block off Yakima on N
Front St, (509) 453-0571
7 N Front St, Yakima
Inexpensive; beer and
wine; AE, MC, V;*

The North Front Street area is a comfortable blend of the old, the funky, and the hip. A half block south of Grant's, this intimate Italian cafe is quite popular with the locals. Owners Bob and Diane Traner have a flair for decor, making simple touches (red wooden chairs, red tablecloths, white linen napkins) seem somehow extraordinary. Fresh pastas and sauces, made on the premises, can be mixed and matched to suit your

checks OK
Lunch, dinner Mon-Sat

mood. The kitchen doesn't consistently deliver the goods—a crisp salad, served with a flavorful garlicky dressing, accompanied slightly chewy pasta with a timid lemon sauce. Still, the service is friendly, the coffee's fine, and the congenial atmosphere makes up for the kitchen's occasional shortcomings. The wine list needs a little work (especially in this territory).

Maria's Cafe

Between Nob Hill and
Mead Ave,
(509) 452-6440
1514 S 1st, Yakima
Inexpensive; no alcohol;
no credit cards;
checks OK
Lunch, dinner Mon-Sat

For 10 years Denver-born Maria Layman ran a simple, whitewashed roadhouse in Parker just on the edge of the Yakima Indian Reservation. She was recently forced to move her whole operation to a new location in Yakima. The new spot, situated on a busy strip of auto dealers and used-furniture warehouses, lacks the visual charm of the original. But that's okay—her tender bite-sized Mexicana steak and her homemade salsa, one of the hottest in Yakima County, still remain the same. Maria, who learned to cook from her Mexican parents, has expanded the menu to include fiery chorizo, tender chimichangas, and sizzling beef and chicken fajitas. Quaff a beer at Grant's, for it's the only thing Maria's lacks—though a liquor license may be in her future.

Santiago's

Close to the intersection of
1st and Yakima,
(509) 453-1644
111 E Yakima Ave,
Yakima
Inexpensive; full bar;
MC, V; checks OK
Lunch, dinner every day

The high ceiling, huge murals, and Southwestern art are festive—if the effect is somewhat overdesigned. Still, the price of the Mexican offerings is right, and the taste is quite good. The chalupas and the tacos Santiago (with beef, guacamole, and two kinds of cheese) are especially popular. Steak picado (their version of fajitas) was on the menu long before the sizzling sirloin strips became chic at every other Mexican restaurant. Owners Jar and Debra Arcand are especially proud of their all-Washington list of wines, every one of them available by the glass.

Haleaina

Corner of N 16th and
Hwy 12, (509) 248-1965
1406 N 16th Ave, Yakima
Moderate; full bar; AE,
MC, V; checks OK
Lunch Mon-Fri, dinner
Mon-Sat, brunch Sun

On the edge of manmade Lake Aspen, in a business park complex, Haleaina ("restaurant" in Hawaiian) presents a menu inspired by Polynesian and Asian cuisines. A buffet is now served at lunch and dinner. The menu lists such standbys as almond chicken and teriyaki niku (marinated beef on skewers) but also tries its hand at classical presentations like mahi mahi baked in parchment paper or broiled lamb chops. But it's the ample portions of Polynesian food that keep people coming back.

LODGINGS

The Tudor Guest House

32nd and Tieton,
(509) 452-8112
3111 Tieton Dr,
Yakima, WA 98902

This stately Tudor mansion was built in 1929 by a prominent Yakima philanthropist, whose standards of quality are evident throughout the house. Oriental carpets cover hardwood floors, leaded-glass windows look out onto the gardens and well-maintained grounds, and

Moderate; MC, V;
checks OK

graceful archways lead into many of the rooms. Each room is tastefully decorated with beautifully restored antiques. The five guest rooms ($55-$75 for a double), all on the second floor, share three spacious bathrooms. The mansion is peaceful and sedate, and so tends to attract mature customers. The home has three working fireplaces, one in a guest room, the others a back-to-back affair in the large living room/morning room, where breakfast is served. Summer use of the formal garden and lawn is encouraged.

Rio Mirada Motor Inn
Exit 33 off I-82,
(509) 457-4444
1603 Terrace Heights Dr,
Yakima, WA 98901
Moderate; AE, DC, MC,
V; local checks only

Just off the I-82 freeway and right next to the shimmering Yakima River, this Best Western motel doesn't look like much from the road. A peek inside reveals 96 attractive rooms, each with a small balcony and a view of the river ($49-$61). Most rooms have tiny refrigerators and a few have kitchenettes. For exercise there's an outdoor heated pool, an indoor exercise room with a Jacuzzi, and a recently expanded 7-mile path along the riverbank. All the rooms have recently been updated, and the convenience and views are worth the stay. The staff could use some orientation about the sights and events in the Yakima area.

TOPPENISH

Western artist Fred Oldfield was raised here, and returns occasionally at the request of the Toppenish Mural Society, (509) 865-2619, to lead a mural-painting posse. As a result, the whole town is an art gallery, with 10 large walls covered with murals and more planned. Clusters of Western shops, antique stores, and galleries make strolling and shopping pleasant, and there are rodeos scheduled throughout the summer months. Recently a new winery, **Vin de l'Ouest**, has opened a tasting room in the Vineyard Gallery.

Yakima Nation Cultural Center, located on ancestral grounds, houses an Indian museum and reference library, plus a gift shop, a Native American restaurant, a commercial movie/performing arts theater, and the 76-foot-tall Winter Lodge, for conventions and banquets. Open every day (closed Jan-Feb). On Fort Road off Highway 97, Toppenish, (509) 865-2800. **Fort Simcoe** was built in 1856, and its Gothic Revival officers' quarters still stand in desolate grandeur; 28 miles west of Toppenish on Route 220.

ZILLAH

RESTAURANTS

El Ranchito
Exit 54 off I-82, follow the
signs, (509) 829-5880
1319 E 1st Ave, Zillah
Inexpensive; no alcohol;

Here in hops- and fruit-growing country, where many Mexican-Americans live, is a jolly tortilla factory-cum-cafeteria that makes a perfect midday stop. You eat in the large dining area or in the cool, flower-shaded patio during the summer. After lunch you can browse in the

no credit cards;
checks OK
Breakfast, lunch, dinner
every day

gift shop, a mini-mercado with Mexican pottery, rugs, and hard-to-find Mexican peppers, spices, canned goods, very fresh tortilla chips, and even south-of-the-border medicines. The authentic food is ordered á la carte. The smooth burritos, tasty nachos, and especially the *barbacoa*, a mild, slow-barbecued mound of mushy beef served in a tortilla shell or a burrito, are generous and recommended. There is a Mexican bakery on the premises, but no cerveza.

SUNNYSIDE

RESTAURANTS

Taqueria La Fogata
In Sunnyside,
(509) 839-9019
1300 Yakima Valley Hwy,
Sunnyside
Inexpensive; no credit
cards; checks OK
Breakfast, lunch, dinner
Wed-Mon

A small, simple roadside Mexican taqueria doing a lot of things right. The clientele is clearly local, the help clearly Mexican, and the menu expansive enough to include specialties such as pozole (Michoacán stew of pork back and feet and hominy) and menudo (Michoacán tripe and cow's-feet stew in a spicy sauce) along with all the usual tacos and burritos. Prices are prehistoric, the service friendly, the smells sublime.

LODGINGS

Sunnyside Inn Bed and
Breakfast
Exit 63 or 69 off I-82,
(509) 839-5557
800 E Edison Ave,
Sunnyside, WA 98944
Inexpensive; no alcohol,
AE, MC, V; checks OK
Dinner Fri-Sat,
reservations required

A brand new favorite with business travelers and doctors visiting the hospital nearby. The eight bedrooms in this 1919 home are huge, four have outside entrances, and all come with phones, cable TV, air conditioning, and private baths with pedestal sinks and double Jacuzzi tubs. The bathrooms alone are bigger than most bedrooms. On the main floor, ask for the Jean room (king-size bed, outside entrance) or the Karen room (gas fireplace). Upstairs, the cheerful Viola room is decorated in peach, and the Lola room features a pleasant sun porch. For those who like the friendliness of B&B's but need their fair share of privacy, this place is a godsend. Breakfast is a bountiful affair of blueberry pancakes, warmed syrups, fruit, and classical music.

On weekend evenings, the Sunnyside Inn offers a prix-fixe gourmet dinner ($18 for guests, $30 for non-guests) prepared by former Waldorf-Astoria chef James Graves. Call for reservations.

Books in the Best Places *series read like personal guidebooks, but our evaluations are based on numerous reports from local experts. Final judgments are made by the editors. Our inspectors never identify themselves (except over the phone) and never accept free meals or other favors. You can help too, by sending us a report.*

GRANDVIEW

RESTAURANTS

Dykstra House Restaurant
Exit 73 off I-82; 1½ miles on Wine Country Rd,
(509) 882-2082
114 Birch Ave,
Grandview
Moderate; beer and wine;
AE, MC, V; checks OK
Lunch Mon-Fri, dinner
Fri-Sat

Who can resist a restaurant that features bread made from hand-ground whole wheat grown in the Horse Heaven Hills? Rich desserts and a few choice Washington State wines complement this mansion's simple menu. If you go with an open mind, you won't be disappointed. Chef Judy Nagle cooks by whim, so the menu changes daily (though Fridays are always Italian). The tasty French onion soup gets high praise. Proprietor Linda Williams takes the time to make visitors feel at home in the gray stone 1914 home of Grandview's former mayor and in the town at large. Local groups often reserve the upstairs for meetings or parties. Reservations are required for Saturday dinner, at which time there is a choice of two entrées only. A screened front porch is used for summer meals.

PROSSER

RESTAURANTS

The Blue Goose
Exit 80 off I-82,
(509) 786-1774
306 7th St, Prosser
Inexpensive; full bar;AE,
MC, V; local checks only
Breakfast, lunch, dinner
every day

Wine-country visitors will get a fast start with chef Ed Sebens' hearty breakfasts. An early-bird dinner menu (4pm-6pm) and special Sunday dishes such as breaded veal and teriyaki chicken help make this off-the-beaten-path restaurant a treat; the generous servings of pasta can be a bit oversauced. Washington wines are featured, and the waitpersons have been given special training about the nuances of local wineries. The completed expansion includes a new patio.

LODGINGS

Wine Country Inn Bed & Breakfast
Exit 80 off I-82, near bridge in Prosser,
(509) 786-2855
104 6th St,
Prosser, WA 99350
Inexpensive; beer and wine, MC, V; checks OK
Dinner Fri-Sat

A welcome addition to the limited overnight options in Prosser, this riverside home has three rooms up and one down, with attached restaurant and gift shop. The river winds lazily by the front door and the restaurant, from which owners/innkeepers Chris Flodin and Audrey Zuniga turn out terrific country breakfasts and ample, hearty fixed-price dinners (weekends only, by reservation only). The thin-walled rooms are clean and comfortable, but the upstairs rooms share a single, cramped bathroom with a claw-footed tub, (the downstairs room has its own bath). A new deck and gazebo open onto the river, with outside restaurant seating on warm summer nights. No smoking, pets, or children, please.

TRI-CITIES WINE COUNTRY

The Tri-Cities wine country is the hub of the huge Columbia Valley viticultural appellation, which includes both the Yakima Valley and Walla Walla Valley appellations within its borders. Here its three principal rivers (Columbia, Snake, and Yakima) converge. A few miles to the west, at Red Mountain, the Yakima Valley wineries begin; and a few miles to the east is the small cluster of Walla Walla Valley wineries. The Tri-Cities Visitor & Convention Bureau, (509) 735-8486, can provide up-to-date wine touring maps and tasting room schedules, and visitors will find some of the state's oldest wineries and vineyards located nearby (reportedly, 90 percent of the state's vineyards are located within a 50-mile radius of Red Mountain). In the immediate area are **Bookwalter Winery**, 2708 Commercial Avenue, Pasco, (509) 547-8571, a small facility located just off the cloverleaf joining Highway 395 and I-82; **Gordon Brothers Cellars**, 531 Levey Road, Pasco, (509) 547-6224, one of the state's best vineyards, with a special flair for merlot and a nice view of the Snake River; **Preston Wine Cellars**, 502 E Vineyard Drive, Pasco, (509) 545-1990, a large, family-owned enterprise with an expansive tasting room and park; and **Quarry Lake Vintners**, 2520 Commercial Avenue, Pasco, (509) 547-7307, another big operation, whose success is built on the excellent Balcom & Moe Farms vineyard. Southwest of Tri-Cities is Stimson Lane's $25-million third winery called **Columbia Crest Winery**, Highway 221, Paterson, (509) 875-2061.

TRI-CITIES: RICHLAND

Richland was once a secret city, hidden away while the atomic bomb workers did their thing in the 1940s; now "the Atomic City" is the second largest of the Tri-Cities. However, as nuclear reactors close and the controversy over hazardous waste continues, civic leaders are working hard on industrial diversification.

Hanford Science Center tells a bit of the saga of atomic energy; the energy displays are quite instructive; 825 Jadwin Avenue, (509) 376-6374.

Howard Amon Park, along the bank of the Columbia, makes a very nice spot for picnics, tennis, golf, jogging, or just ambling.

RESTAURANTS

The Emerald of Siam
William and Jadwin,
(509) 946-9328
1314 Jadwin Ave,
Richland
Inexpensive; beer and
wine; MC, V; local
checks only
Lunch Mon-Fri, dinner
Mon-Sat

One of the most authentic Thai restaurants in the Northwest is improbably located in a converted drugstore in a Richland shopping center. Floor space has been considerably expanded in the last year and the place now includes a cultural center for visiting school groups, a display of Thai handicrafts for sale, and an Oriental grocery. Thai-born Ravadi Quinn and her family have created something of the feel of a small Southeast Asian restaurant, and they are serving delicious native recipes. The curries, satays, and noodles all get high marks. Thai salad, a favorite in Asia, is a good bet. Weekday buffet lunches are popular. Ravadi's many projects include occasional cooking classes and her own cookbook, *The Joy of Thai Cooking*.

Giacci's
Corner of George
Washington and Lee,
(509) 946-4855
94 Lee Blvd, Richland
Inexpensive; beer and
wine; no credit cards;
local checks only
Lunch Mon-Sat, dinner
Fri-Sat

In Richland's oldest building (1906), wonderful aromas waft from the busy kitchen and Puccini arias float through the air. Good salads and Italian sandwiches are the weekday lunch offerings at this attractive deli/restaurant in Richland. Unfortunately, the two-night-a-week dinner is rather ordinary (too much marinara sauce on the spinach ravioli and the veal Parmigiana made these two dishes taste identical). Still, you'll finish on a fine note if you add a glass of Chianti and one of their excellent desserts. No espresso. Outdoor tables in summer.

Gaslight Restaurant and Bar
At the first main
intersection on George
Washington,
(509) 946-1900
99 Lee Blvd, Richland
Inexpensive; full bar;
MC, V; local checks only
Lunch, dinner every day

The Gaslight was here long before Shakey's and Pizza Hut, and for a long time it was the only place to get pizza in Richland. It looks like just another tavern on the outside, and the image is not dispelled by the giant TV screen inside, but it has evolved into a place where everybody goes to get a good pizza and super potato skins. There's the usual excess of period brass lamp fixtures and Gay Nineties mirrors, but there are also cozy booths and an outdoor deck that overlooks the Columbia River.

LODGINGS

Red Lion Hanford House
Take Richland exit off
I-82 to George
Washington,
(509) 946-7611
802 George Washington
Way, Richland,
WA 99352
Moderate; AE, DC, MC,
V; checks OK

Since this is a prime Richland social center, you'll notice a great deal of pro-nuclear activity, but do not be dissuaded: this is the place to stay in the Tri-Cities, with large rooms overlooking an attractive courtyard and a dandy pool for lazing in the broiling sun. What used to be the Columbia rushing by is now Lake Wallula, transformed by the construction of McNary Dam. The best rooms are those overlooking the lake/river (odd-numbered rooms 169–187 and 269–287). The lounge is pleasant; the popular dining room serves standard Red Lion fare.

TRI-CITIES: PASCO

This was the first of the Tri-Cities, a railroad town started in 1884.

Columbia Basin Community College, near the airport, puts on shows and lectures; the Performing Arts Building (design: Brooks/Hensley/Creager) is a splendid, virtually windowless building in the Brutalist mode.

LODGINGS

Red Lion Inn
Take 20th St exit off Hwy
395, (509) 547-0701
2525 N 20th St,
Pasco, WA 99301

The large, sprawling motel (281 rooms) in half-timbered style has several notable attractions. There is a nice outdoor pool, surrounded by the rooms, and a new exercise facility, and the 18-hole municipal golf course is right alongside, making the motel appear to

Moderate; AE, DC, MC, V; checks OK
Breakfast, lunch, dinner every day

be set in a park even though it's right on the freeway. It's exceptionally convenient to the Tri-Cities airport and Columbia Basin Community College. Local residents like the dining room for "dressy" occasions. The room is big and dark (perhaps so that the blue flaming desserts and coffees can be seen clear across it) and the menu is very eclectic—usually a bad sign. Here we're proven wrong; this is one of the few restaurants in Eastern Washington that really knows how to cook seafood, *and* duck, *and* beef. The service is unpolished but eager to please. Given the location, the wine list could be a bit more adventurous.

TRI-CITIES: KENNEWICK

RESTAURANTS

The Blue Moon
½ of a block from Washington,
(509) 582-6598
21 W Canal Dr,
Kennewick
Expensive; wine only;
MC, V; checks OK
Dinner Fri-Sat

Owners Linda, Dale, and Dean Shepard opened this first-class restaurant in the Tri-Cities as an adjunct to their catering business. Diners enjoy a seven-course meal at one seating (7:00pm Fri, 7:30pm Sat) in quiet and attractive surroundings (private parties of 10 or more can book Tues-Thurs). You get a prix-fixe ($28) menu with choice of entrée. The lobster bisque is full-flavored, rich, and spicy. After a good Caesar salad, a tasty cabernet sorbet cleanses the palate. Entrée selections include rack of lamb Provençal, Cajun blackened catfish, tournedos Blue Moon, sautéed pork Dijon, and breast of chicken Grand Marnier. The wine list is composed entirely of local bottlings. Reservations are essential. A gem.

LODGINGS

Quality Inn on Clover Island
Columbia Dr and Washington,
(509) 586-0541
435 Clover Island,
Kennewick, WA 99336
Inexpensive; AE, DC,
MC, V; checks OK

It's actually on an island, and thus offers wonderful river views from many of its 150 rooms. Otherwise, even under its new ownership (Quality Inn) there's not much to distinguish it from its Red Lion and Holiday Inn cousins except its comparatively inexpensive rates. Avoid dining here.

TOUCHET

RESTAURANTS

Alkali Flats Cafe
Center of Touchet, State
Hwy 12, (509) 394-2310
Touchet

Larry and Anna Edwards host the Walla Walla Valley's early risers—ranchers, farmers, vintners—with bountiful old-fashioned breakfasts. Lunches consist of specials, thick soups, Dagwood sandwiches, and more

Inexpensive; no alcohol; no credit cards; checks OK

Breakfast, lunch Mon-Sat, dinner once a month

mom-style cooking. Dinners ($12.50), served one Friday each month, often commemorate such events such as St. Patrick's Day or Octoberfest. It's just a doublewide trailer in the middle of expanses of wheat, asparagus fields, horse ranches, and vineyards, but Alkali Flats Cafe in downtown Touchet (pronounced TWO-she) is the place to be.

KAHLOTUS

RESTAURANTS

Tom's Inn-Digestion (aka Tom's Place)

In Kahlotus, 45 miles north of Pasco on Hwy 395, (509) 282-3324 Kahlotus

Inexpensive; beer and wine; no credit cards; local checks only

Breakfast, lunch, dinner every day

Tiny, remote Kahlotus, population 250, has only one commercial establishment. This is it. On one side, groceries are sold, and on the other, beer, wine, and very good hamburgers are served. Breakfasts are popular. Owner Tom Keene is something of a pack rat, and an amazing collection of curious items hang from the ceiling. While the general focus of these is barnyard/outhouse, there are probably artifacts to interest more sedate scholars.

WALLA WALLA

The valley of the Walla Walla is an important historical area: Lewis and Clark came by in 1805, fur trappers set up a fort in 1818, and in 1836 Marcus Whitman built a medical mission west of the present town where he and his wife, Narcissa, were murdered by Indians in the famous massacre of 1847. The town itself was founded in 1858 and has grown into a pleasant vale with fecund wheatlands all around and a pretty private college anchoring the city.

Whitman Mission, 7 miles west, off Highway 12, sketches out the story of the mission and the massacre; there aren't any historic buildings, but the simple outline of the mission in the ground is strangely affecting.

Fort Walla Walla Museum in Fort Walla Walla Park on the west edge of town has a collection of old buildings and pioneer artifacts. Call (509) 525-7703 for tour hours; open summer only.

Whitman College. The lovely campus is worth a stroll, and Memorial Building, an 1899 Romanesque Revival structure, is worth admiring for architecture; (509) 527-5176. The campus puts on lots of plays, some in the wonderfully funky Harper Joy Theatre, a wooden playhouse; Penrose Library has a strong collection of Northwest materials; and there are some summer workshops.

Old houses. Kirkman House Museum, listed on the National Register of Historic Places, is a fine period-home museum; 214 N Colville St, (509) 529-4373. Mature trees and Colonial architecture lend a New England feeling to Catherine Street, S Palouse Street, and W Birch Street. Pioneer Park on E Alder Street is a good example of the urban park style of 80 years ago, and was designed by the Olmstead brothers, the landscape architects whose father created New York City's Central Park and Seattle's Lake Washington Boulevard.

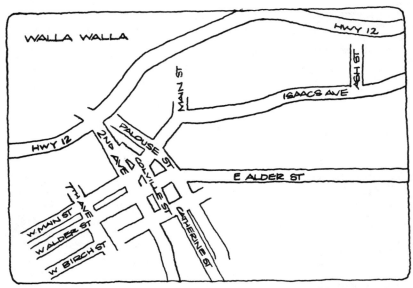

Onions and shallots. Walla Walla Sweets are splendid, truly sweet onions, great for sandwiches; here you can get the "number ones", with thin skins. For information on the onion festival, call the Chamber of Commerce, (509) 525-0850. More recently, the fertile lands of the Walla Walla Valley have enabled the Robison Ranch to become the country's top grower of colossal French shallots—larger and more flavorful than most. Robinson's is located at the end of N 4th Street in Walla Walla; open to the public for tours, (509) 525-6589.

Local food products. Ascolano's, a specialty food store located in the restored Northern Pacific Depot, 416 N 2nd, has almost all of the Walla Walla Valley wines, and at reasonable prices. It also stocks some fine and unusual local grocery selections such as barley mustard from Dayton and jars of pickled peppers, asparagus, and cherries from the Robison Ranch.

Wines. Walla Walla is home of some of the state's most brilliant wineries. Most notable is **Woodward Canyon**, Lowden, (509) 525-4129, which produced a cabernet in 1987 that was judged one of the top ten in the world by *Wine Spectator*. Others are **L'Ecole No. 41**, Lowden, (509) 525-0940; **Leonetti Cellars**, Walla Walla, (509) 525-1428; **Waterbrook Winery**, Lowden, (509) 522-1918; **Seven Hills Winery**, (509) 529-3331), with production facilities over the state line in Milton-Freewater, Oregon, (503) 938-7710; and **Biscuit Ridge**, (509) 529-4986, with a Waitsburg address but actually located just outside Dixie.

RESTAURANTS

Merchants Ltd.
Take 2nd St exit off Hwy 12, turn left on Main,
(509) 525-0900
21 E Main St,
Walla Walla
Moderate; beer and wine;

It's a cluttered New York–style deli, with tempting culinary merchandise piled ceiling-high on broad shelves, a deli counter loaded with breads, cheeses, sausages, salads, caviar, and such, and a glass-fronted bakery from which enticing smells waft into the rooms. The homemade soups are deservedly popular. There are tables inside, or you might sit out front at a

MC, V; checks OK
Breakfast, lunch Mon-
at until 6pm; dinner Wed
until 8pm

sidewalk table and watch Walla Walla waltz by. Upstairs is a more sedate dining room, where the food is quite good. Lunch is served buffet style Tues-Fri (as is Wednesday dinner, featuring spaghetti). Excellent wine list.

The Whitman Inn

Take 2nd St exit from
Hwy 12, (509) 525-2200
107 N 2nd St,
Walla Walla
Moderate; full bar; AE,
DC, MC, V; local
checks only
Breakfast, lunch, dinner
Mon-Sat, brunch Sun

We're getting quite used to changes at the Whitman. Although the menu is still devoted to such country classics as Salisbury steak and sautéed liver and onions, new items have appeared. Chef David Ferguson now offers fresh seafood selections, salads, and Oriental stir-fries. The house specialty is prime rib. These dishes are well prepared and reasonably priced. The once-dreary rooms have been brightened; the bar has recently been enlarged and now features live music Tuesday through Saturday evenings.

The Ice-burg Drive-In

Corner of W Birch and
9th, (509) 529-1793
616 W Birch St,
Walla Walla
Inexpensive; no alcohol;
no credit cards;
checks OK
Lunch, dinner every day

Some say the hamburgers served at this back-street drive-in are the best in the nation, but let's just say they're strong contenders for the title in the Pacific Northwest. Owner Alan Jones is dedicated to using strictly fresh ingredients, and each burger is grilled to order. Terrific French fries and thick milk shakes (some made with seasonal fruits) are accompaniments. You can eat at a wooden picnic table or take your meal to one of Walla Walla's pretty parks. Order by phone to avoid a long wait in the car line.

Jacobi's Cafe

Take 2nd St exit off Hwy
12 to the old Burlington
Northern Depot,
(509) 525-2677
416 N 2nd St,
Walla Walla
Inexpensive; beer and
wine; MC, V; checks OK
Lunch, dinner every day

In a town with many beautiful old buildings, it is surprising that there isn't more interest in historic preservation and restoration; thus Jacobi's, in the former Northern Pacific Depot, is a welcome addition. Although this isn't the spot for a quiet dinner (old railroad stations seem to echo from their hardwood floors to their ceilings), the food (deli salads and pizza) is quite good. New owners Vince and Kelle Cannone are staying on the right track by adding a dining car.

Pastime Cafe

Half a block east of
the courthouse,
(509) 525-0873
215 W Main St,
Walla Walla
Inexpensive; full bar; no
credit cards; checks OK
Breakfast, lunch, dinner
Mon-Sat

Very little has changed since this Walla Walla institution opened in 1927. It is still run by descendants of the original owners, the Fazzari family, which pleases Walla Walla's large Italian population. They come for the homemade pasta and the best lasagne in town and don't seem to mind that everything's just a touch underseasoned. Experienced patrons skip the vegetables—usually pale canned peas. It's strictly a 1930s atmosphere, complete with card room.

LODGINGS

Best Western Pony Soldier Motor Inn
2nd St exit off Hwy 12,
(509) 529-4360
325 E Main St,
Walla Walla, WA 99362
Moderate; AE, DC, MC,
V; checks OK

It's just another Best Western motel, but its proximity to Whitman College makes it very popular. When there's an event at the college, book early. There's a pleasant swimming pool courtyard, and continental breakfast is included in the room price. A fitness room containing Jacuzzis, saunas, and such has been added. You can bring your poodle, but more proletarian dogs (particularly those with long hair) are not welcome.

DAYTON

RESTAURANTS

Patit Creek Restaurant
On Hwy 12 at north end
of town, (509) 382-2625
725 E Dayton Ave,
Dayton
Moderate; beer and wine;
MC, V; local checks only
Lunch Tues-Fri, dinner
Tues-Sat

Bruce and Heather Hiebert have achieved the seemingly impossible: they've turned a small rural cafe into an excellent regional restaurant. Serving good food to the locals (both conservative farmers and more liberal college types) has been an experience—at times frustrating and educational—but the effort has paid off. There is now a steady and very appreciative clientele who don't mind driving long distances to eat superbly roasted meat at Patit Creek. The menu has been expanded to feature more regional dishes and changes in the fall and spring. Appetizers are notable, particularly the smoked salmon cheesecake (non-sweet) and the chèvre-stuffed dates wrapped in bacon and broiled. Bruce uses only the freshest vegetables and herbs. In the spring, fresh morel mushrooms are offered in a different entrée each night. A little later in the season, he'll wander into the hills in search of extraordinarily sweet wild onions to use in some of his sauces. Try the steak in green peppercorn sauce. The wine list is short but carefully chosen including some of the fine Walla Walla Valley wines. Heather's homemade pies and desserts provide a proper conclusion to such delightful fare. Reservations are crucial on weekends. Urbanites may sneer at fine food being served in a room with such folksy decor. A small gripe that easily disappears shortly after the first bite.

PULLMAN

Pullman's population swells in the fall with Washington State University students, while the permanent residents are a mix of wheat farmers and university faculty. The largest of the Palouse towns, Pullman retains some of its cowpoke image but covets an international reputation as a university town. The central business district consists mostly of one main street crowded with shops and some restaurants. There is abundant free parking just off the main street. Browsers might

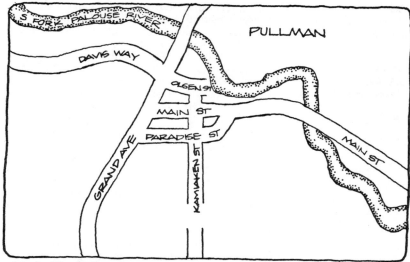

visit the **Nica Gallery** for an excellent representation of Eastern Washington artists, 125 NE Olson; **Bruised Books** for used books that sometimes include hard-to-find first editions, 105 N Grand; **The Combine** for pastries, espresso, ice cream, and teas and herbs, 215 E Main; and the **Sport Shack**, 460 E Main, for an amazing array of fishing lures.

Washington State University. The campus is expanding constantly. The Fine Arts Center is a showcase with a spacious gallery that attracts exhibits by notable artists. Martin Stadium, home of the WSU Cougar football team, can now hold Pac-10 Conference–sized crowds; the baseball team plays on the new Bailey Field near Beasley Performing Arts Coliseum, which houses both the basketball team and frequent rock concerts. Visitors might want to drop by Ferdinands, located in Troy Hall and open weekdays only, which offers ice cream, milk shakes, and Cougar Gold cheese, made from milk and cream from WSU's own dairy herd, (509) 335-4014.

Kamiak Butte, 13 miles north on Route 24, offers a good place for a picnic and nice overlooks of the rolling wheat country.

Steptoe Butte. About 30 miles north of Pullman on Highway 195, this geologic leftover towers above the Palouse and affords an impressive view of the Palouse or great stargazing.

RESTAURANTS

The Seasons
On the hill about half a block off Grand,
(509) 334-1410
215 SE Paradise St,
Pullman
Moderate; beer and wine;
AE, DC, MC, V;
checks OK
Dinner Tues-Sun

No doubt Pullman's finest dining experience. This elegant eatery occupies a renovated old house atop a flower-covered cliff, where a winding wooden staircase leads diners to the front door. The interesting menu changes often, and dinner is presented in a proper and elegant fashion; chicken and seafood are good choices. Salad dressings are made on the premises and salads are served with scrumptious homemade breads such as whole-wheat with cornmeal, poppyseeds, and sesame seeds. Offerings from the dessert tray are worth saving room for.

Swilly's

1 block east of Grand,
(509) 334-3395
200 NE Kamiaken St,
Pullman
Moderate; beer and wine;
AE, MC, V; checks OK
Lunch, dinner Mon-Sat

This eatery is located in what in the 1920s was Pullman's railroad depot. It flanks the Palouse River and sports a small outdoor cafe in good weather. Across the street is one of the 20 artesian wells, drilled between 1890 and 1909, that were the deciding factor in locating a state college in Pullman. Inside, the warmth of the hardwood floors, the exposed brick walls, and the rich smell of espresso invite lingering. Works by area artists, all for sale, decorate the walls. Swilly's boasts fresh local ingredients, right down to cream from a nearby dairy and bread from a local bakery. Diners will find a separate calzone menu (billed as "the freshest and finest in the Palouse"). The regular menu (which changes seasonally) offers pastas with tempting ingredients such as marinated artichoke hearts, a lemon-caper combination, or an Oriental fish sauce. For lunch, a chicken curry sandwich with apples and Indian curry mayonnaise was served on sourdough bread. Swilly's has a modest selection of imported and local beers and a wine list with a good representation of Washington wines. Plan to spend enough time to enjoy a second cup of caffe latte.

Hilltop Steakhouse

At the city limits off Hwy
195, (509) 334-2555
Davis Way, Pullman
Moderate; full bar; AE,
DC, MC, V; checks OK
Lunch Mon-Fri, dinner
every day, brunch Sun

This motel and restaurant has probably the best steaks in Pullman, family-style chicken dinners Sunday afternoons, Sunday brunch, and a wonderful view of the university and surrounding hills. The food is consistently good, albeit standard, fare.

LODGINGS

Paradise Creek Quality Inn

¼ mile east of the WSU
campus near the junction
of Hwy 270 and Johnson,
(509) 332-0500 or toll-
free (800) 669-3212
1050 SE Johnson Ave,
Pullman, WA 99163
Moderate; AE, DC, MC,
V; checks OK

Just far enough off Highway 270 to afford guests quiet nights away from traffic noise, this motel is also within easy walking distance of the WSU campus. It's situated over the meandering creek for which it's named.

BRITISH COLUMBIA

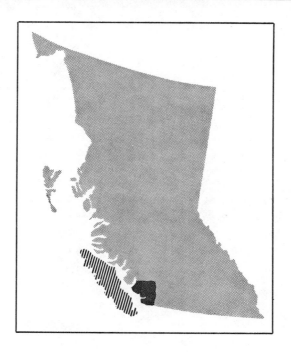

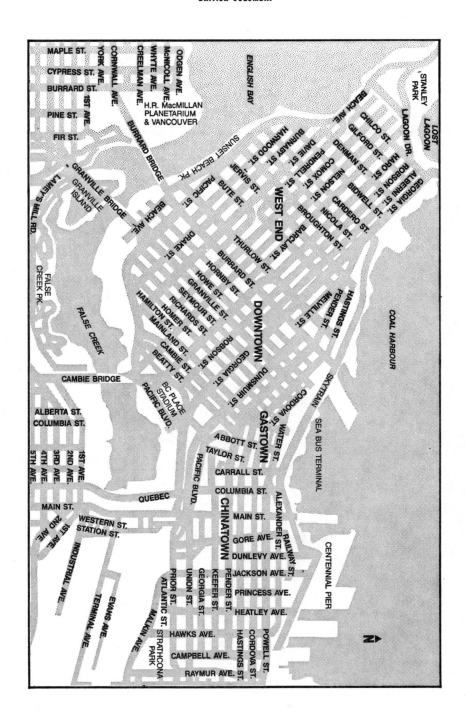

VANCOUVER AND ENVIRONS

Including the suburbs: West Vancouver; North Vancouver; Surrey; Richmond; and Ladner to the south.

Vancouver has long touted itself as Canada's gateway to the Pacific Rim. But only when Hong Kong billionaire Li Ka-shing scooped up the old EXPO site, two hundred acres of prime development land, did the realization sink in that the city was also becoming the Pacific Rim's gateway to Canada. The new arrivals, especially those from Hong Kong, have taken advantage of immigration regulations designed to lure investors and have bought up more than billions of dollars worth of real estate since 1985.

Yet Vancouver has always accepted the waves of immigrants that have broken on its shores. Indeed, the city seems living proof that a benign environment will produce an easygoing disposition. Despite a stiffening of the work ethic of late, this is still a place of leisure and relaxed enjoyment, where the office population thins out noticeably on Friday afternoons.

Glance away from the opulence of the shops as you saunter along Robson and you will see why; at the end of a side street lap the peaceful waters of Burrard Inlet. Beyond, the mountains on the north shore glitter with snow for half the year. Vancouver, residents are fond of saying, is one of the few cities in the world where you can go skiing and sailing on the same day. How remarkable, then, that it should also be one of the few where, sitting outside a Neapolitan cafe, you can eavesdrop on an impassioned argument in Hungarian and see graffiti in Khmer.

Vancouver's chameleon identity is that of home to the children of the dispossessed, whether they be Scottish Highlanders or Hmong tribespeople. To the sculptors and the screenwriters, the dancers, jugglers, retired war correspondents and exiled aristocrats, to the drifters and dreamers who have settled here in such disproportionate numbers, this is as close to the Promised Land as it's possible to get.

THE ARTS

Visual Arts. Francis Rattenbury's elegant old courthouse is now the Vancouver Art Gallery, which holds more than 20 major exhibitions a year and whose permanent collection includes works by Goya, Carr, Gainsborough, and Picasso (750

Wondering about our standards? We rate establishments on value, performance measured against the place's goals, uniqueness, enjoyability, loyalty of clientele, cleanliness, excellence and ambition of the cooking, and professionalism of the service. For an explanation of the star system, see "How to Use This Book."

Hornby, (604) 682-4668). Many of the city's commercial galleries are located on the dozen blocks just south of the Granville Bridge, and Granville Island, site of the Emily Carr College of Art and Design, has a number of potteries and craft studios. The avant-garde is most often found on the east side of the city, at spaces such as Grunt Gallery (209 E Sixth, (604) 875-9516) and Pitt International Galleries (36 Powell Street, (604) 681-6740). The Museum of Anthropology at the University of British Columbia (UBC, 6393 Northwest Marine Drive, (604) 228-5087) has an extensive collection of Indian cultures of coastal British Columbia (including an impressive collection of totem poles) as well as artifacts from Africa to the Orient.

Music. Thanks to vigorous fund-raising by the musicians and their supporters and injections of government cash, the Vancouver Symphony Orchestra is back on its feet after a couple of bumpy years. The main season starts in October at the Orpheum, an old vaudeville theatre (884 Granville). The Vancouver Opera Association puts on four productions a year at the Queen Elizabeth Theatre (630 Hamilton): the program is a balance of popular and experimental. For information about any musical event, call Ticketmaster (604) 280-4444.

Theatre. The Vancouver Playhouse is heading away from recycled Broadway hits, American musicals, and thrillers and entering the world of contemporary theatre; in the Vancouver Playhouse off of Hamilton and Dunsmuir, (604) 872-6622. The Arts Club is a commercial theatre with three locations and, usually, less production panache than the Playhouse; Granville Island, (604) 687-1644. Contemporary theatre in Vancouver is largely centered in the VECC—Vancouver East Cultural Center, 1895 Venables Street, (604) 254-9578.

OTHER THINGS TO DO

Parks and Gardens. The city is blessed with a climate—very similar to Britain's—well-suited for flowers and greenery. Take a walk through the quiet forest in the heart of Stanley Park. The western edge is rimmed by three swimming beaches; you'll find tennis courts, a rose garden, an aquarium, and kiddie attractions on the southern fringes. Also great for kids is Science World British Columbia, across town at the old EXPO site. Here, hands-on exhibits, films, and working models will keep families busy for hours; 1455 Quebec Street, (604) 687-7832. At Queen Elizabeth Park, dramatic winding paths, sunken gardens, and waterfalls skirt the Bloedel Conservatory, (604) 872-5513, (stop in for lunch at Seasons). The University of British Columbia campus boasts three superb gardens—the Botanical Garden, Nitobe Memorial Gardens, and Totem Park—along with a top-drawer Sunday-tea setting at Cecil Green Park House, 6251 Cecil Green Park Road, (604) 228-6289. The new Chinese Classical Garden within Dr. Sun Yat-Sen Park (E Pender and Carrall streets), is a spectacular model of the Oriental garden complex with pavilions and water-walkways. Near Queen Elizabeth Park, the VanDusen Botanical Garden stretches over 55 acres. Each part of the garden offers flora from different regions of the world, as well as those native to the Pacific coast. Open every day, year round; 5251 Oak Street, (604) 266-7194.

Shopping Vancouver has always been bursting with storefronts. Robson Street has a pleasant, European feel with few high rises, colorful awnings, and a proliferation of delicatessens, boutiques, and restaurants. Downtown is full of outstanding shops. In poor weather, head underground for the Pacific Centre and Vancouver Center malls, with shops like Eatons, The Bay, Birks, Woodward's, and Marks & Spencer. At Granville Island Public Market on the south shore of False Creek, you can get everything from just-caught salmon to packages of fresh herbs to fine unpasteurized lager (at the Granville Brewery) to a wonderful array of fresh produce in late summer. Or visit the lesser-known public market at Lonsdale Quay in North Vancouver with two levels of shops and produce right at the North Shore sea-bus terminal. It's a 15-minute sea-bus ride ($1.75) from the terminal near Canada Place across Burrard Inlet. Gastown is a restored 1890s precinct, once touristy, now anchored by some really good shops of more use to locals. Book Alley, the 300 and 400 blocks of West Pender, has bookstores specializing in everything from cookbooks to radical politics to science fiction.

Nightlife. On a warm summer night, the music spilling out from Vancouver's clubs and bars will range from down-and-dirty R&B at the suitably raunchy Yale Hotel (1300 Granville, (604) 681-9253) and the sprung-floored Commodore Ballroom (870 Granville, (604) 681-7838) through local bands at the Town Pump (66 Water, (604) 683-6695) and disco thump at Richard's on Richards, the yuppie meat market (1036 Richards, (604) 687-6794), to swing at the Hot Jazz Society (2120 Main, (604) 873-4131). The Railway Club (579 Dunsmuir, (604) 681-1625) has a remarkably varied membership and presents consistently good music, whether jazz or rock. Top names perform at BC Place Stadium (777 Pacific Blvd South, (604) 669-2300). To find out who's playing where, pick up a copy of the *Georgia Straight* or Thursday's *Vancouver Sun*. Jazz fiends can call the Jazz Hotline (604) 682-0706).

Sports. The Vancouver Canucks, who usually make the NHL playoffs but haven't made the finals since 1982, are the obvious draw when they play (Pacific Coliseum, (604) 280-4400). The Vancouver 86ers, the local soccer team, has a devoted following especially since their 1988 Canadian championship (1126 Douglas, in Burnaby; (604) 299-0086). The BC Lions haven't had a very good track record in the past but the 1991 season stirred up some hopeful fans (BC Place, (604) 669-2709. Visiting baseball enthusiasts should try to catch a Vancouver Canadians game at the Nat Bailey Stadium, a venue of which many locals have fond memories (Queen Elizabeth Park, (604) 872-5232). But most Vancouverites would rather play than watch. Golf, sailing, hefting weights, exploring the local creeks and inlets by any kind of boat you can name—the city has first-rate facilities for these activities and many more. For information, contact Sport, BC (1367 West Broadway, (604) 737-3000).

Ethnic Vancouver. The oldest and biggest of Vancouver's ethnic communities is Chinatown. The 200 block of East Pender is the main market area; to get started, try Yuen Fong for teas or the Dollar Market for barbecued pork or duck. More recently, a growing number of Asians are moving into Richmond as evidenced by the increasing number of outstanding Chinese restaurants and the New Aberdeen Centre where you can get ginseng in bulk, durian from Thailand, and eat home-style Chinese food while you bowl. Italian commercial and cultural life thrives in the distinctive neighborhood around Commercial Drive, east of downtown. A second, less discovered Italian district is on Little Italy's northern border—the 2300 to 2500 blocks of East Hastings. Vancouver's 60,000 East Indian immigrants have established their own shopping area called the Punjabi Market in south Vancouver at 49th and Main streets, where you can bargain for spices, chutney, and sweets. Vancouver's longest-established group of ethnic inhabitants, the Greeks, live and shop west of the intersection of MacDonald and West Broadway.

RESTAURANTS

Bishop's
Corner of Yew and
Fourth, (604) 738-2025

Bishop's is Vancouver's most highly regarded restaurant. The fashionable dining crowd may flirt with the newer places, but in the end it is to Bishop's that they

*2183 W Fourth Ave,
Vancouver
Expensive; full bar; AE,
DC, MC, V; no checks
Lunch Mon-Fri, dinner
every day*

remain faithful. The reason for this lies less with the food (which is excellent) than with their devotion to owner John Bishop himself, whom many consider to be a personal friend. A man who truly understands the art of hospitality, Bishop's treats all his customers, whether they are first-time visitors or a twice-a-week regulars, to a welcome that is gracious and sincerely warm. In this he is assisted by the most professionally polished young restaurant staff in the city. The minimalist decor enhances the visual impact of the food in much the way a plain frame and matting set off a painting. Bishop's cuisine borrows the best ideas from many different cuisines. One of our favorite dishes was the tandoori chicken marinated in yogurt and cumin then oven roasted and served with mango chutney, Marsala-marinated raisins, roasted tomatoes and basmati rice. Everything bears the Bishop trademark of light, subtly complex flavors and bright, graphic color. A typical dinner begins with a basket of homemade braided curry bread; or a small plate of tidbits appearing at the table. Then it's on to the appetizers—which might include a delicate, savory potage like sweet potato, orange and ginger soup, or a wild turkey sausage accented with North African spices on local greens with a balsamic vinaigrette. Entrées are an uncomplicated listing: a couple of fish-of-the-day selections, and several meat- or chicken-based dishes. You can't go wrong with any of them. The tender lamb is always excellent as is daily fish (recently halibut roasted with basil and sweet cicely butter). Desserts are not to be missed. The papaya flan in a macadamia crust is heavenly, easily the most talked-about dessert in Vancouver.

**Dynasty Restaurant
(Ramada Renaissance
Hotel)**
*Between Thurlow and
Burrard, (604) 691-2788
1133 W Hastings St,
Vancouver
Moderate; full bar; AE,
DC, MC, V; no checks
Lunch, dinner Tues-Sun*

This is arguably the best Cantonese in Vancouver and arguably among the finest restaurants in the entire Pacific Northwest. Excellent food, decor, and service combine for an unsurpassed dining experience. In creating the first Chinese hotel dining room in North America, the New World Group spared no expense. The visual details, meticulously maintained, from the fluid white walls and beautifully etched glass partitions that divide the room into intimate alcoves to the delicate china and silver utensils, combine to create a serene and elegant atmosphere. To ensure freshness, dim sum—from the traditional shrimp dumplings to unusual shrimp and mango rolls—is prepared to order. Open for over two years now, the restaurant is on firm ground with master chef Lam Kam Shing's creative and cosmopolitan style, which includes an emphasis on local products; the fried salmon in champagne sauce is one of the best preparations of salmon around. Another specialty is the famous roasted suckling pig. If in doubt, rely on the well-trained staff, which also serves a formidable banquet in the hotel ballroom. The adequate wine list and the well-stocked port and brandy cart are rare commodities among Chinese restaurants.

Le Crocodile

Corner of Robson and
Thurlow, (604) 669-4298
818 Thurlow St,
Vancouver
Expensive; full
bar; AE, MC, V;
no checks
Lunch Mon-Fri,
dinner Mon-Sat

The best French food in the city can be found at Le Crocodile. Forget your preconceptions of heavy, overly sauced, overly fussed-over food. We are talking about honest, regional French cooking—country-style ingredients cooked with elegance and presented with flair. Chef/owner Michel Jacob named the bistro-style restaurant after his favorite restaurant in his hometown of Strasbourg, and there are many clues to his Franco-Germanic culinary heritage on the menu: an Alsatian onion tart, almost jammy with its rich concentration of onions; a perfect round of warm goat cheese nestling in a bed of greens; and an authentic tarte Tatin for dessert. Entrées are consistently hearty, richly flavored, and tastefully presented. Meats are mostly grilled or lightly pan-sautéed, augmented with light sauces redolent of fresh herbs, flavored mustards, or wine. We've had excellent grilled calf liver with spinach butter, roast leg of lamb in a mint and orange sauce, and garlicky baked mussels—all uncomplicated but exquisite-tasting dishes. The best desserts are the traditional ones: a tangy lemon tart, a soothing crème brulée, and of course the aforementioned tarte Tatin. The restaurant, being small, has an attractive, cozy atmosphere, but conversation is unlikely to escape the ears of your neighbor close by.

Tojo's

Broadway and Willow,
(604) 872-8050
777 West Broadway,
Vancouver
Moderate; full bar; AE,
MC, V; no checks
Dinner Mon-Sat

Tojo Hidekazu is the heart of Tojo's and he certainly has his share of devotees. Upstairs in a flashy green glass building, Tojo's is a pleasantly spacious restaurant, with a view out to the mountains, plenty of table seating and six tatami rooms. The sushi bar seats ten isn't big enough for his devoted patrons, but ten people is the most Tojo likes to tend at one time. A brilliant sushi chef, endlessly innovative, surgically precise and committed to fresh ingredients. Show an interest in the food, and if the restaurant isn't frantically busy, Tojo will offer you a bit of this and that from the kitchen: Tojo tuna, special beef (very thin beef wrapped around asparagus and shrimp). Getting to be a regular is not difficult, and it's highly recommended. Tojo's hot kitchen is mostly out in the open. Japanese menu standards like tempura and teriyaki are always reliable and daily specials usually superb: pine mushroom soup in October and November; wonderfully satisfying deep-fried tofu covered with seasonal stir-fried vegetables from October to May, cherry blossoms with scallops in April and May, and homemade egg tofu in the summer. Plum wine and fresh orange pieces finish the meal.

Caffe de Medici

*Between Burrard and
Thurlow,
(604) 669-9322
1025 Robson St,
Vancouver
Expensive; full
bar; AE, DC, MC, V; no
checks
Lunch Mon-Fri,
dinner every day*

Caffe de Medici features patrician decor: high molded ceilings, serene portraits of members of the 15th-century Medici clan, chairs and drapery in Renaissance green against the crisp white of the table linen, and walls the color of zabaglione (and now room for more happy diners). Waiters have the polish of kindly diplomats; no matter which one is assigned to your table, they all seem to look after you. Businesslike by day, romantic by night—the mood changes, but the quality of the Northern Italian food does not. The antipasto is beautifully presented here: a bright collage of marinated eggplant, artichoke hearts, peppers, olives, squid, and Italian cold meats. The *bresaola della Valtellina* (air-dried beef, thinly sliced and marinated in olive oil, lemon, and pepper) is well worth trying. Pasta dishes are flat-out magnifico—a slightly chewy plateful of tortellini alla panna comes so rich with cheese you'll never order any of the others. Although it's mostly a Florentine restaurant (with a knockout version of beefsteak marinated in red wine and olive oil), we've also sampled a Venetian-style fish soup, brimming over with fresh fish and shellfish, and a Roman-style rack of lamb. For dessert, stick with the zabaglione alla Medici, a concoction of egg yolks whipped with Marsala, brandy, and sugar into a heady, aromatic froth.

Chartwell (Four Seasons)

*Corner of W Georgia and
Howe, (604) 689-9333
791 W Georgia St,
Vancouver
Expensive; full bar; AE,
DC, MC, V; no checks
Lunch Mon-Fri, dinner
every day*

Chartwell, named after the famous abode of Sir Winston Churchill, evokes an upper-class English men's club atmosphere. Its dark, wood-paneled walls, leather and brocade chairs, stiff white napery and large paintings give the illusion of tapestry wall hangings. The service, under the watchful eye of manager Angelo Cecconi, is attentive and very unselfconscious. Two years ago, chef Wolfgang Von Weiser, took over after the departure of stellar former chef Kerry Sear (now at the Four Seasons in Seattle). Von Weiser, more tame with inventions, has worked hard to maintain such high standards we've come to expect from the Four Seasons. In between each course is a little surprise, perhaps a salmon paté on a tiny biscuit, a light consommé with Marsala, or wafer-thin almond crisps. Unfortunately, recent meals have fallen short of perfection. Starters are a bit precious, two brussel sprout leaves, one topped with gently smoked salmon and the other with minced tomato and bacon and a light sesame dressing. The sweetbread served atop a creamy fettucine, was pan-fried in too much egg batter for the tiny serving. The venison with steeped cranberries was savory but not as tender as we would have liked. More enticing was the pumpkin ravioli with cinnamon chive butter which came alongside the delicately herb-smoked snapper. A smoker is part of the kitchen equip ment, and the resulting dishes are among the best choices on the menu.

At Chartwell dessert is a must: pastry chef Kurt Ebert and his staff are the best in the business. One of their most seductive creations is an elegant pouf of hot espresso-Kahlua souffle.

Hoshi Sushi
Golden Gate Centre,
Suite 203,
(604) 689-0877
645 Main St,
Vancouver
Moderate; full bar; AE,
MC, V; no checks
Dinner every day

One of the few redeeming features of the ugly Golden Gate Centre on the fringe of Chinatown is Tsutomu Hoshi's very Japanese restaurant. Tucked upstairs in its relatively obscure location, Hoshi Sushi is powered strictly by Hoshi-san's reputation from his 18 years' experience in restaurants in Tokyo and 11 years at the Aki Restaurant in Vancouver (one of the city's first Japanese restaurants). Making head or tail out of the extensive list of specials can be amusing, with the young Japanese waitstaff eager to practice their English while explaining it. Efforts are generally rewarded when one samples seasonal delicacies like the steamed monkfish livers with wasabe and ponzu or the crisp tempura of soft-shelled crab with its accompanying daikon, green onion, and soy dipping sauce. The chef's superior technique and total dedication to quality and freshness are evident throughout. Utter simplicity is the key here.

Il Barino
In Yaletown at Mainland
and Helmcken,
(604) 687-1116
1116 Mainland St,
Vancouver
Moderate; full bar; AE,
DC, MC, V; no checks
Lunch Mon-Fri, dinner
Mon-Sat

A truly great Tuscan-style restaurant, even an ultra-elegant one, presents food that is fresh, earthy, and so ripe with sensuality it makes you want to roll up your Armani sleeves, tear a chunk off a loaf of crusty bread, and start paddling in the olive oil. Il Barino falls short of feeling authentically rustic. Patrons are not encouraged to get their hands sticky with olive oil and the fashionably dressed clientele seem entirely too self-conscious. Never mind the focaccia, there's plenty better on which to fill up. Starters are especially good: tangy baked chèvre in a hazelnut vinaigrette, smooth grilled-eggplant salad. The grilled wild mushrooms aren't always wild but they are delicious. Pastas are excellent. Try the linguine with a light lemon sauce and grilled chicken tenderloin, the cappelletti with sweet butter, hazelnuts, and Parmesan, or the spaghettini with grilled scallops and chiles. Entrées with their subtly fused bold and robust flavors exhibit true competence in the kitchen: Australian rack of lamb in a savory rosemary and garlic sauce, a grilled duck breast with raspberries. The wine list is a well-considered roster of food compatibility, mostly Italian and American wines. If you cannot make up your mind, ask the knowledgeable staff for advice. If you don't smoke come with a large group (for they tend to seat small parties way in the back against the wall). Desserts are good (made by a local caterer) but only the tiramisu is made on the premises.

Imperial Chinese Seafood Restaurant
Burrard and Hastings,
(604) 688-8191
355 Burrard St,
Vancouver
Moderate; full bar; AE,
MC, V; no checks
Lunch, dinner every day

Regal Meridian
Granville and 6th,
(604) 261-8886
8298 Granville St,
Vancouver

The Imperial and its sister restaurant, the Regal Meridian, are aptly named; they may lay claim to being the two most opulent Chinese dining rooms in Vancouver. Located in the majestic Marine Building with two-story high windows, the Imperial commands a view of Burrard Inlet and the northshore mountains. There's a feeling of being in a grand ballroom of eras past; a central staircase leads to the balustrade-lined mezzanine and the luxurious private rooms where diplomatic dignitaries and famous rock stars dine in style and privacy. The food is equally polished: wonderful deep-fried soy-marinated prawns, a rich and silky braised Sui Choy in Fu Yu (fermented bean curds). If it weren't for a bit of unevenness in the service and a few minor glitches (too few crêpes with the Peking duck, overcooked crab steamed in a fresh, aromatic broth), this could be a perfect restaurant. A very busy place for a dim sum lunch.

Kirin Mandarin Restaurant
Alberni St at Bute,
(604) 682-8833
1166 Alberni St,
Vancouver
Expensive; full bar; AE,
MC, V; no checks
Lunch, dinner every day

Kirin Seafood Restaurant
In City Square, on
Cambie, (604) 879-8038
201-555 W 12th Ave,
Vancouver

Kirin's postmodern decor—high ceilings, slate green walls, black lacquer trim—is all oriented around the two-story-high mystical beast that is the restaurant's namesake. The food is consistently good, and the selections read like a book spanning the culinary regions of China: Cantonese, Sichuan, Shanghai, and Beijing. Remarkably, most of the vastly different regional cuisines are authentic and well executed. Live lobsters and crabs alone can be ordered in 11 different preparations. Try the red bean pie for dessert: a thin crêpe folded around a sweet bean filling and fried to a fluffy crisp. There's valet parking and Western-style service, which is attentive though sometimes bordering on haughty and a tad aggressive. A second, equally fine outpost has opened in the City Square, this time with more of a focus on seafood and a view of the city.

Le Club (Le Meridien Hotel)
Corner of Smithe and
Burrard, (604) 682-5511
845 Burrard St,
Vancouver
Expensive; full bar; AE,
DC, MC, V; no checks
Dinner Mon-Sat

Regardless of the name change the genteel ambience is still there; French-accented young waiters glide smoothly to and fro against a plush background of beige fabric walls, handsome oil paintings, cabinets displaying antique china, mirrors, and dried flower arrangements. French chef Olivier Chaleil still presides in the kitchen, composing gourmet extravaganzas with as light a hand as this haute cuisine will allow. The menu is intriguing, if limited. Soup, for instance, is a sweet garlic and bread potage with parsleyed snails in cream. Raves go to the lobster salad—mixed seasonal greens, generous pieces of lobster, all covered with a warm champagne vinaigrette coulis. But the appetizer of the evening should be the tartare of eggplant and mussels with a caviar of salmon and ground fish. The roasted farm-raised duckling in a not-too-sweet star anise and honey marinadeand star anise is succulent and fork-tender. The chef offers the farm-raised Oregon tilapia on lentil-

and-rosemary cream or a light tomato cream sauce. For $30 you can get the table d'hôte, a four-course meal. The crème brulée with raspberries is a perfect example of what this dessert can be. The wine list is excellent, and surprisingly complete for a province that has difficulty assembling good lists.

Le Gavroche

Across from the Westin Hotel, (604) 685-3924 1616 Alberni St, Vancouver Expensive; full bar; AE, DC, MC, V; no checks Lunch Mon-Fri, dinner Mon-Sat

Going to Le Gavroche for dinner is like stepping into the past: in this pretty French restaurant in an old Vancouver house, a woman dining with a man gets a menu without prices; Caesar salad is prepared with ceremony at tableside; and waiters still give excellent, unobtrusive service. The food at Le Gavroche is much more modern: cream and butter are used sparingly. A long, luxurious meal (punctuated by small surprises like the tiny puff-pastry savory, a scoop of palate-clearing sherbet) doesn't necessarily mean a day of remorse to follow. Try steamed mussels served with a saffron, white wine, and cream sauce or the homemade rabbit pâté with quince purée. The large menu features the usual fish, meat, and game dishes, often not as interesting as the many daily specials: moist, tender smoked pheasant breast resting on an intensely flavorful puree of celeriac, shallots, and wine with a light truffle sauce. Owners Jean-Luc Bertrand is especially fond of Bordeaux and hunts out little-known finds; waiters can be counted on for good recommendations.

Phnom Penh Restaurant

Close to Chinatown, Main and Georgia, (604) 682-5777 244 E Georgia St, Vancouver Inexpensive; full bar; MC, V; no checks Lunch, dinner Wed-Mon

Once touted as the best-kept secret in Vancouver, Phnom Penh has recently won a steady stream of accolades, from local magazine polls to Julia Child. This restaurant is steadily improving at every step. The menu has expanded from its original rice and noodle dishes to the cuisines of China, Vietnam, and Cambodia. Hot and sour soup with sablefish is richly flavored, redolent of lime and purple basil. An excellent appetizer of marinated beef sliced carpaccio-thin was seared rare and dressed with nuoc cham (a spicy, fishy sauce). A masterpiece is the hot, velvety steamed rice paste, covered with sautéed baby shrimp in prawn roe and tender slivers of salted pork. Butterfly prawns with lemon-pepper dip were crisp and vibrant, and chicken salad with cabbage was a refreshing twist on a pedestrian vegetable. Service is knowledgeable and projects a feeling of gentle hospitality. A new location has opened at 955 W Broadway.

Szechuan Chongqing Restaurant

Victoria and Broadway, (604) 254-7434 2495 Victoria Dr, Vancouver

The outside of the building still resembles a shoebox, but inside, new furniture, lamps, and wall coverings brighten up the place. The food is still the best Szechuan fare in the city. Mrs. Wong manages the front and Mr. Wong rules the kitchen. Consistency is the key: rich brown sauces, heavy on the garlic, lots of

Inexpensive; full bar;AE, MC, V; no checks
Lunch, dinner every day

explosive red peppers, and wheat (not rice) as the principal starch. Favorites include a big bowl of noodle soup in a rich peanutty broth accented with red chiles, green onions, and crushed peanuts or #56 Chongqing Chicken, tender morsels in a hot and garlicky brown sauce served on a bed of crisp deep-fried spinach. The seafood specials are reliably good, and the hot-pot dishes—strips of meat and vegetables to cook at your own table in a pot of blistering hot broth—are fun for groups. Order a sliced roll (one easily feeds two) to mop up all the sauces. It's a popular spot, and the crowds are not handled very well. So make a reservation, particularly on Sunday evenings, when large family groups converge unannounced on the restaurant and claim every seat in sight.

Vassilis Taverna
Near MacDonald and Broadway,
(604) 733-3231
2884 W Broadway,
Vancouver
Moderate; full bar; AE, DC, MC, V; no checks
Lunch Tues-Fri, dinner Tues-Sun

Since 1977, Vassilis has been consistently perfect—a family-run, moderately priced restaurant doing outstanding ethnic cooking. In summer, the restaurant's front opens onto the sidewalk. Inside, the decor is catalogue Greek, right down to the paper placemats with their maps of the Greek islands. The menu has just enough originality, just enough comforting traditionalism. Start with a huge plate of very light calamari—the region's best—or the saganaki, Greek kefalotiri cheese fried in oil and sprinkled with lemon juice. The house specialty is perfectly juicy kotopoulo: chicken pounded flat, seasoned simply with lemon juice, garlic, and oregano, and then barbecued. The lamb fricassee, in a casserole of artichoke hearts and broad beans, is falling-off-the-bone tender. The Greek salad is a sufficient meal in itself or side it with a succulent pile of quick-fried baby smelts. Try to fit in one last treat: a honey-sweet piece of baklava or the truly luscious navarino. Little money spent, but much enriched.

The William Tell
(Georgian Court Hotel)
Across from BC Place Stadium, (604) 688-3504
765 Beatty St,
Vancouver
Expensive; full bar; AE, DC, MC, V; no checks
Lunch Mon-Fri, dinner every day, brunch Sunday

The William Tell is elegant, jackets required type of place with old-world cuisine. Owner Erwin Doebeli is the consummate restaurateur. All evening Doebeli seems to be here, there, and everywhere, greeting arrivals at the door with enthusiasm, dispensing bread from a large wicker tray like one of the busboys, or whipping up a mean cafe diablo with a flamboyance that alone makes the expensive tab bearable. New chef Pierre DuBrulle, who founded La Gavroche, maintains the tradition of French perfectionism set so solidly by Lars Jorgensen while adding his own style. Among the appetizers are Swiss-style air-dried beef or British Columbia-style smoked salmon. The soup, cream of fiddlehead, was an excellent use of this rare fern; though the sweetbread fricassee with prawns and chanterelles came in a disappointing sauce. The free-range chicken with leeks and morels was a savory concoction. We recommend the strong-flavored barbarie duck pan-fried in a juniper gin sauce or the Chateaubriand carved à table. As a rule, the desserts prepared to order in the kitchen (some, like the showy cherries jubilee, are prepared at your table). The wine cellar is one of this restaurant's most rewarding features; ask to see the "reserved wine menu" for a listing of its most special contents.

Accord

27th and Main,
(604) 876-6110
4298 Main St, Vancouver
Moderate; wine and beer;
MC, V; no checks
Dinner every day

Behind those impenetrable white Venetian blinds, it serves excellent Cantonese seafood—try the live shrimp, when available, steamed in the shell and brought to the table with a spicy soy-based dipping sauce, or the beef tenderloin teppan with peppercorn sauce (essentially pepper steak with a Chinese accent). The menu includes a handful of Chiu Chow specialties, the food of most of Southeast Asia's Chinese immigrants. Open until 2am weekdays, 3am on weekends—perfect for those evenings when the '50s come back and the only thing that will do is Chinese food.

Alma Street Cafe

Broadway and Alma,
(604) 222-2244
2505 Alma St, Vancouver
Moderate; full bar; AE,
MC, V; local checks only
Breakfast, lunch, dinner
every day, brunch
Sat-Sun

An original neighborhood sort of place with a lively atmosphere, Alma Street manages quite successfully to offer something for everyone. It's open all day; the food is imaginative, reasonably priced, and homemade. From 8am on weekdays and during the popular weekend brunches, a central display table is loaded with fresh breakfast buns and baked goods, and you can choose from honest breakfast fare like omelets, hot cereal, or pancakes. New chef Sue Janda is experimenting with local ingredients in the kitchen and turning out dishes that people are ordering like crazy—a recent trout stuffed with shrimp hijiki and seaweed and glazed with a sesame-soy-lemon sauce was a big hit. For the vegetarian, the tofu selections are quite inventive. Baked goods are available to take home, and the desserts are wonderful. Live jazz often.

The Avenue Grill

West Blvd and 41st,
(604) 266-8183
2114 W 41st Ave,
Vancouver
Moderate; full bar; MC,
V; checks OK
Breakfast Mon-Fri,
lunch Mon-Sat, dinner
every day, brunch
Sat-Sun

A few years ago this dowager was rejuvenated into a California girl. Everything fits the California bistro formula: pastel peach-and-mint decor; glass blocks; a palm tree named "Larry"; and a light, trendy menu with nouveau California-French-Asian-Italian influences. Recently, the Grill has bettered the formula by making a concerted effort at purchasing locally grown products. Very popular with the neighborhood Kerrisdale crowd, and a fun place to be during the two-week culinary festivals (garlic and hot pepper, for example). The most imaginative food is offered during these theme weeks, though the regular menu is beginning to show signs of consistent ingenuity.

Bandi's
Between Beach and
Pacific on Howe,
(604) 685-3391
1427 Howe St,
Vancouver
Moderate; full bar; AE,
MC, V; no checks
Lunch Mon-Fri, dinner
every day

This is the sort of place we would like to see at Whistler. After a cold day on the ski slopes, nothing would be more comforting than a warm bellyful of the robust country food of Hungary. At Bandi's, chef/owner Bandi Rinkhy produces authentic cuisine, with maître d' and co-owner Kader Karaa's sense of humor providing the dash of paprika. The peasant bread (deep-fried and puffy) comes with a side dish of raw (not roasted) garlic; goulash soup is presented in a little kettle set over a portable flame; and the *paraszt sonka* (smoked farmer's ham with fresh horseradish and green onions) is served in large, hearty portions. *Uborkasalata* (cucumber with sour cream dressing) may be the only concession to a timid palate. Desserts are mostly rich, sweet crêpes.

Bruno's Restaurant
41st and Granville,
(604) 266-3210
5701 Granville St,
Vancouver
Moderate; full bar; AE,
MC, V; no checks
Lunch Mon-Fri, dinner
Mon-Sat

This was the first in a series of three Bruno Born-owned restaurants (he has since sold Zeppo's). It's located at one of Vancouver's busiest intersections. but is definitely a neighbourhood restaurant—a long, narrow, comfortably upholstered, tables-slightly-too-close-together sort of place, extremely popular with the local Kerrisdale residents. Watch for the blackboard at the entrance listing the daily specials as well as wines available by the glass, and don't miss Born's rich-tasting baked rabbit if it's available. Once you're seated, the waiter will bring you a tiny dish of salmon mousse and another of herb butter, to enjoy with a selection of house breads while you peruse the menu. The menu items are conservative but masterfully prepared. Best are the fresh veal kidneys Dijon, sautéed in a mustard cream sauce and dotted with green and pink peppercorns; a rustic chicken with caramelized garlic; and a satisfying pork tenderloin with an apple stuffing, placed on a brandy sauce and sprinkled with roasted pecans.

Chez Thierry
Robson between Bidwell
and Cardero,
(604) 688-0919
1674 Robson St,
Vancouver
Moderate; full bar; AE,
DC, MC, V; no checks
Dinner every day

The quintessential neighborhood restaurant—small and warmed by the sunny good nature of owner Thierry Damilano, a transplanted Frenchman (and avid windsurfer) who rolls out the red carpet for regulars and grants newcomers a more reserved but nonetheless polite welcome. Chef François Launay leaves experimentation to the nouveaux chefs and instead prepares simple, traditionally based meals without a lot of ornamentation. The house pâté is good but not outstanding; try a watercress and smoked salmon salad instead, or the impossibly melting chicken mousse, served warm in port sauce. A find: fresh tuna grilled with artichoke, garlic, and fresh tomato. Red snapper is poached and served in a bright yellow saffron sauce with sweet red peppers. Chocolate desserts are rich and just bitter enough; the tarte Tatin is superb, served upside down and flamed with Calvados. The wine list is carefully chosen and every wine district of France is represented. For an unusual show, order a bottle of champagne and ask Damilano to open it for you. His favorite party trick is slashing off corks with a military saber, his record being 80 in one evening.

Chiyoda
Burrard and Alberni,
(604) 688-5050
1050 Alberni St,
Vancouver
Moderate; full bar; AE,
MC, V; no checks
Lunch Mon-Fri, dinner
every day

In a town full of sushi restaurants with robata grills on the side, Chiyoda is a robata restaurant with a sushi bar. Built on a generous scale, Chiyoda was meticulously designed (right down to the graceful little beer glasses) in Japan. Robata selections are arranged in wicker baskets on a layer of ice that separates the customer's side of the bar from the cook's side. Order from the simple menu: it lists a score of dishes, including snapper, squid, oysters, scallops, eggplant, and Japanese mushrooms, with no space wasted on adjectives. The cook prepares your choices and hands the finished dishes over the bar on the end of a long wooden paddle. Seafood is excellent, but don't miss a foray into cross-cultural world of robata—cooked garlic, potatoes, and corn.

Delilah's
Corner of Haro and
Gilford, (604) 687-3424
1906 Haro St, Vancouver
Moderate; full bar; MC,
V; no checks
Dinner every day

It really doesn't matter what you eat here, the place is a giggle. Tucked away under the old Buchan Hotel and resembling nothing so much as the salon of a 19th-century bordello (oversized red plush banquettes, painted cherubs on the ceiling), this is a hip little spot catering to young West Enders, some of whom seem challenged to live up to the decor. Food comes in small portions but is good and reasonably priced. Your menu is your bill; just check off your selections and hand it to your waiter. The carrot and ginger soup is a good choice, and so is the pepper-studded rib eye steak with burnt onions in a red-wine demiglace. There's a decent wine list, but the house specialties are the 32 varieties of martinis, which you shake (or stir) yourself. Expect a wait—it's a popular neighborhood drop-in, and reservations are accepted only for groups of six plus.

El Mariachi
Between Robson and
Georgia on Denman,
(604) 683-4982
735 Denman St,
Vancouver
Moderate; full bar;
AE, MC, V; no checks
Dinner Tues-Sun

El Mariachi serves the most authentic Mexican food in the city. Sure, you can have enchiladas, but husband-and-wife team Arcelia and Giovanni Vagge (she's Mexican, he's Italian—which may explain the dash of Parmesan on the refried beans) offer much more. Try crab-stuffed puff-pastry tortillas, sole in coriander sauce, or prawns cooked with smokey-tasting chipotle peppers. Of the chicken dishes, the *mole poblano* is best; the mole sauce is made from 28 ingredients, including nine types of nuts, four peppers, and bitter chocolate. It's a thick and hauntingly spicy concoction.

Il Giardino di Umberto

Pacific and Hornby,
(604) 669-2422
1382 Hornby St,
Vancouver
Expensive; full bar; AE,
DC, MC, V; no checks
Lunch Mon-Fri, dinner
Mon-Sat

In the ongoing debate over which of Umberto Menghi's five Vancouver restaurants is the best, Il Giardino continues to hold the lead. Certainly it is the most romantically attractive, with its Tuscan-villa decor: high ceilings, tiled floors, winking candlelight, and vine-draped terrace for dining alfresco (no better place in summer). The emphasis is on pasta and game with an "Italian nuova" elegance: farm-raised pheasant with roasted-pepper stuffing and port wine sauce, tender veal with a mélange of lightly grilled wild mushrooms. An accompanying slice of pan-roasted polenta added a comforting homey touch. Be warned: the prices on the specials are in their own category. For dessert, go for the tiramisu—the best version of this pick-me-up in town.

Jean-Pierre's Restaurant

Opposite the Hyatt,
(604) 669-0360
1055 Dunsmuir St, Plaza
Level, Vancouver
Moderate; full bar; AE,
DC, MC, V; no checks
Breakfast, lunch Mon-
Fri, dinner Mon-Sat

Located in the heart of the business district, Jean-Pierre's tony ivory-and-rose-colored dining room with outdoor terrace is a magnet to the town's power lunchers. Hence, owner Jean-Pierre Bachellerie's dinner trade is all gravy, which gives him license to innovate and to pass on a few good deals to his customers. On Thursday nights he offers his French provincial dinner—a four-course set menu. The rest of the week, the dinner menu concentrates on French-accented seafood specialties, spit-roasted meats, and traditional entrées like Chateaubriand with three sauces, rack of lamb, veal kidneys à la moutarde, and sole amandine. Jean-Pierre's is also one of the few French restaurants to serve breakfast, and morning can be one of the nicest times to be there.

Kilimanjaro

2 blocks east of Sky Train
station in Gastown,
(604) 681-9913
332 Water St, Vancouver
Moderate; full bar; AE,
DC, MC, V; no checks
Lunch Mon-Fri, (bistro
open every day for lunch)
dinner every day

Like East Africa itself, Amyn Sunderji's place is an intriguing melting pot: African masks and batiks mix with the deep pink walls, French provincial prints, and the swirling ceiling fans of the location's former tenants to create the atmosphere of a chic Nairobi restaurant. Try the coconut fish soup, a recipe from Zanzibar of amazing complexity and depth; a Swahili specialty of curried goat; the famous prawns piri piri; or the uniquely African (specifically, Zairean) combination of chicken in ho-ho peppers, palm oil, and garlic. "Burning spear," lamb served flaming on a sword in honor of Jomo Kenyatta, is the house specialty. The samosas (stuffed savory pastries) are the best in town. Desserts bring a fittingly exotic finale, from a rich homemade saffron ice cream topped with Frangelico to a safari mango mousse. A smaller bistro downstairs is appealing for lunches, late-night snacks, or private parties.

La Brochette

A 5-minute walk east of
downtown, in Gastown,

Sit near the antique French *tourne-broche* and you get theater with your dinner as chef/owner Dagobert Niemann does his intricate ballet of stoking the hard-

(604) 684-0631
52 Alexander St,
Vancouver
Moderate; full bar;
AE, V; no checks
Dinner Mon-Sat (closed
Mon in summer)

wood fires, putting racks of lamb and duck breasts on the rotisserie, sautéing vegetables, and arranging plates. Downstairs is quieter and has an attractive bar, with seating on wide benches around a huge stone fireplace. Especially good here are duck breast with gin and juniper berries and Fraser Valley duckling. Fresh local vegetables in various preparations (potatoes mashed with a hint of blueberry; spinach mousse) appear with the main course. The wine list has some superb (if pricey) selections, including a fair number of California reds.

Landmark Hot Pot House
On Cambie near Queen
Elizabeth Park,
(604) 872-2868
4023 Cambie St,
Vancouver
Moderate; full bar; MC,
V; no checks
Dinner every day

Hot potting—traditionally for the warming of body and soul on long wintry nights—seems to have transcended its seasonal limits and is emerging as the latest Chinese culinary trend. In the Landmark, the center of each table is cut out for the built-in natural gas stove and its settings, which include a personal strainer and chopsticks. The trilingual menus are simply lists of available ingredients and prices. The rest is up to you. We ordered the Duo Soup Base of satay and chicken broth and merrily experimented with platters of fish, chicken, beef, dumplings, vegetables, and noodles. This is heartwarming, healthy food at its simplest, embellished only by the chef's exquisite knifework and perfect presentation.

Malinee's Thai Food
Between Arbutus and
Yew on W 4th,
(604) 737-0097
2153 W 4th Ave,
Vancouver
Moderate; full bar; AE,
DC, MC, V;
no checks
Dinner every day

The exterior, still bearing signs of its former life as a Greek restaurant, isn't impressive, but inside there's a serene room with Bangkok-style tablecloths, linen napkins, and good quality china and flatware. Co-owners Ted Hamilton and Stephen Bianchin work the front, offering diners a sophisticated knowledge of Thai food gained during two years in Bangkok. Chef Kem Thong works behind the line, creating authentic northeast Thailand fare—something she began doing in Bangkok at the age of 12. Daily specials, carefully explained, are almost always worth ordering. From the regular menu, choose the attractive well-balanced appetizer assortment: clams or mussels, basil/shrimp stir-fry, satay chicken, spring rolls, and cashew nuts spiced with red peppers. Western desserts are available—ice cream, or the cake of the day—for those who don't want cassava root in coconut cream at the end of a meal.

Mocha Cafe
W Broadway at
Granville,
(604) 734-5274
1521 W Broadway,
Vancouver

Mocha Cafe used to be a busy little lunch-only restaurant serving great muffins, soups, salads and sandwiches. New owner Don McDougall was hesitant to make changes on Mocha's popular lunchtime menu, so instead, he breaks loose at dinner time. Now it's a good, small non-smoking neighborhood restaurant where you might find fresh Florida rock shrimp with saffron and cream, a designer pizza, lamb chops with

Moderate; wine and beer;
MC, V; no checks
Breakfast, lunch, dinner
Mon-Fri

blueberry sauce, or a creamy agnolotti with chicken, rosemary and mushrooms. And there have been numerous accolades on the oyster stew and Cheddar cheese bread. He likes salads that make a statement—like Belgian endive, with impeccably fresh walnuts and blue cheese. The wine list is a careful collection of moderately priced British Columbia, Washington and California wines; 10 or so are available by the glass.

Montri's Thai Restaurant

W 4th and Trafalgar,
(604) 738-9888
2611 W 4th, Vancouver
Moderate; full bar; AE,
DC, MC, V; no checks
Dinner every day

Montri Rattanaraj is from southern Thailand. Several decades ago, he started traveling the world as a waiter, cook, and maître d', including a stint at the Roof in the Hotel Vancouver in 1973. Rattanaraj now runs certainly the most elegant, and arguably the best, Thai restaurant in the Lower Mainland. He changed the white tablecloths of the former Angelica's space to pink, added a few Thai masks and carvings for atmosphere, and left the rest untouched. Then he unveiled a menu that draws on his southern Thai background: Montri's Thai *gai-yang*, chicken marinated in coconut milk and broiled, is a close cousin to the chicken sold on the beach at Puhket. Have it with *som-tam*, a green papaya salad served with sticky rice and wedges of raw cabbage. The cabbage and the rice are coolants, and you'll need them. Familiar Thai dishes (Panang beef, garlic prawns, and a devil's hot pad spinach) are done well here too. Ask for help in menu planning; Rattanaraj is happy to advise.

Passionate Pizza

W 7th Ave and Hemlock,
(604) 733-4411
1387 W 7th Ave,
Vancouver
Inexpensive; no alcohol;
MC, V; local checks only
Lunch Mon-Fri, dinner
every day

Passionate Pizza is the best takeout gourmet pizza in Vancouver. And you don't have to order their Wolfgang Puck (mozzarella, smoked bacon, sweet red peppers, red onions, feta and Asiago cheese and eggplant) to see why. For one thing, Passionate is the only pizza joint given to topping its home-delivered pizzas with sprigs of fresh basil. The crust is traditional: white, crisp in the thin places, chewy in the thick ones, drizzled with good olive oil and adorned with bits of baked-on cheese. Vegetarians can do well here: the Granville Island Gourmet is mozzarella and Gorgonzola, caramelized onions, pine nuts and roast garlic. Passionate's Caesar salad has strips of sun-dried tomatoes and giant capers hiding among the romaine leaves and croutons; they'll even deliver cheesecake and Italian ice cream. Slices available if you eat in or pick up.

Piccolo Mondo

On Thurlow one block
south of Robson,
(604) 688-1633
850 Thurlow St,
Vancouver
Moderate; full bar; AE,
MC, V; no checks
Lunch Mon-Fri, dinner
Mon-Sat

A few people think it is the best Italian restaurant in the city, but others are yet to be convinced. Service is uneven—sometimes warm and accommodating, at other times unfriendly and self-impressed. Certainly the food remains the most consistent factor, well-prepared, country-style food. The kitchen has a "real man" attitude towards garlic, onions, and olive oil and a

Bianco Nero
W Georgia St and Richards,
(604) 682-6376
475 W Georgia St, Vancouver

macho disregard for presentation. Too many dishes come heaped onto the plate like Mount Vesuvius. The choices are just as overwhelming and the Xeroxed sheet of daily specials is so crammed they hardly seem special. You will find every type of Italian dish imaginable, plus some surprises, such as sole in aquavit with Danish caviar (from chef Gildo Casadei's days as a chef in Sweden). We can enthusiastically recommend the radicchio alla griglia (an appetizer of radicchio, studded with garlic cloves, oven-broiled, and splashed with olive oil, lemon juice, and salt); the tortellini alla nonna (homemade tortellini in a delicate mustard cream sauce) and the osso bucco (veal shank bones cooked to the meltdown point in a sauce of tomatoes and saffron). Avoid the watery risotto. This is the place for lovers of Italian wine; Piccolo Mondo has the most comprehensive and most sophisticated selection in Canada. Casadei's second downtown location, Bianco Nero, opened almost two years ago and offers virtually the same menu in a jazzed up black-and-white atmosphere.

The Pink Pearl
Hastings and Clark,
(604) 253-4316
1132 E Hastings St, Vancouver
Moderate; full bar; AE, MC, V; no checks
Lunch, dinner every day

Royal Mandarin
In the Royal Centre mall, next to the Hyatt Regency,
(604) 669-8383
1088 Melville St, Vancouver

At 650 seats, the Pink Pearl is the certainly the biggest Chinese restaurant in Vancouver. Fresh seafood tanks out front are a clue that the Cantonese menu is especially strong on seafood. The crab sauteed with five spices is not the expected star-anise taste, but a spectacularly good take on a dish sometimes translated as "crab with peppery salt," crisp, chile-hot and salty on the outside, moist on the inside. Pink Pearl serves an excellent dim sum every day (be sure to arrive early on weekends to avoid the lineups). Cart jockeys always seem to have time to smile and wait for you to make your selections among such dishes as sticky rice wrapped in a lotus leaf, stuffed dumplings, and fried white turnip cakes. The table-clearing system makes an amusing scene. The "tablecloth" is actually a stack of thick white plastic sheets; when you finish eating, a waiter will grab the corners of the top sheet, with a quick flip, scoop everything up, dishes and all, and haul the mess away—a great place for kids. An equally large second location opened downtown in March 1991.

The Prow
Northern tip of Canada Place on Burrard St,
(604) 684-1339
999 Canada Place, Suite 100, Vancouver
Expensive; full bar; AE, DC, MC, V; no checks
Lunch every day (Mon-Fri in winter), dinner every day, brunch Sun

To eschew view restaurants as nothing more than stunning showcases for mediocre food is to miss out on restaurants like The Prow. Its location at the bow of the cruise ship–shaped Vancouver Convention Centre affords it one of the most arresting outlooks in this view-rich city, but the creations of chef Denis Blais—accompanied by selections from an award-winning wine list—easily hold their own. His appetizers range from the traditional (Caesar salad) to the nouvelle (ginger prawns in black bean sauce with watercress tempura). A range of culinary influences is exhibited in the menu—a little Italian (roasted half duck with blackberry port sauce, served with Gorgonzola polenta), a little Oriental (a sizzling clay pot of marinated beef, straw mushrooms, Oriental greens, and chiles with broad noodles and sake). We recommend the mahi mahi, pan-fried and draped with an amazing grapefruit and sorrel yogurt sauce, or halibut (in season) with hazelnuts and ginger crème fraîche. By all means reserve a window seat with that endless view of Burrard Inlet, but bring along a sweater; window tables can be drafty.

Raintree
Corner of Alberni and
Cardero, (604) 688-5570
1630 Alberni St,
Vancouver
Moderate; full bar; AE,
MC, V; no checks
Lunch Mon-Fri, dinner
every day, brunch Sun

The Raintree heavily markets itself as a Northwest Coast restaurant. On the whole, this place has great potential but sometimes it seems as if much of the hype is driven by their public relations director than the clientele. The concrete-walled space is prettied with huge flower arrangements, decorated with a simple sophistication and, provided you are seated facing the right way, offers a spectacular view of the North Shore skyline. Chef Rebecca Dawson departed at presstime and was replaced by Eric Rogers. We can't vouch for his creations yet but in the past there have been many wonderful entrees: the wild spring salmon with a tart rhubarb sauce is a melt-in-your-mouth luxury; the Washington rack of lamb in a crust of mustard and herbs with garlic zinfandel sauce is savory and suc-culent. Others, like the smoked black cod, lack inspira-tion. Recently, service has been annoyingly slow and forgetful. Desserts include a heaping Okanagan apple pie with cheddar cheese or chocolate bread pudding. The wine list echoes the Northwest Coast theme, with wines from British Columbia, Washington, Oregon, and California.

Raku Kushiyaki
10th and Trimble,
(604) 222-8188
4422 W 10th Ave,
Vancouver
Inexpensive; full bar;
MC, V; checks OK
Lunch Thurs-Fri, dinner
Tues-Sat

Perhaps being so firmly in the orbit of the University of British Columbia accounts for Raku's pleasantly in-tellectual air. It's not just the quirky blond pine tables cut into rhomboids or the pebbles serving as chopstick rests. The food here is a witty, friendly, challenging cross-cultural mix that's as experimental and successful as the Japanese themselves. The menu bounces from Japan to Italy and points between with cheerful ir-reverence: salmon with Chinese pesto, confit of duck with mango chutney, black cod kasuzuke, stir-fried broccoli de rabe with shiitake mushrooms. In com-parison, the traditional Japanese offerings seem or-dinary. Trevor Hooper and Laurie Robertson modeled Raku on a venerable institution, the sake bar. In Japan, you go to sake bars for serious drinking and many small, inexpensive plates (similar to tapas); here, most are below $4. Raku stocks four brands of sake. If you're unfamiliar with them, try a taster-glass cold—the flavors are more distinct when sake is unheated.

Rubina Tandoori
Near the corner of
Victoria Dr and
Kingsway,
(604) 874-3621
1962 Kingsway,
Vancouver
Moderate; full bar; AE,
MC, V; no checks
Lunch Mon-Fri, dinner
Mon-Sat

Son Shaffeen Jamal is the amiable maître d'; mother Krishna cooks the authentic East Indian fare. Rubina's menu is built around tandoori dishes, South Indian seafood, Punjabi and Mogul dishes, and many more. Tandoori breads are especially good here. Try the fish masala, a dry curry with potatoes, or any of the dishes that include the Rubina's homemade cheese called paneer. If the coconut barfi (a puddinglike dessert) is still warm, it's delicious. Rubina has separate smoking and nonsmoking rooms. Nonsmokers get the older and funkier room, smokers get the newer, plusher one. Whom do they prefer?

Santa Fe Cafe
Between Fir and Pine on
W 4th, (604) 738-8777
1688 W 4th Ave,
Vancouver
Moderate; beer, wine and
Cognac; AE, MC, V;
no checks
Lunch Mon-Fri, dinner
every day

A bright box of a room with tables too close together, an open kitchen, and a changing gallery of striking art for sale, it doesn't look particularly Southwestern. Foodwise, it sticks pretty close to the chiles-and-salsa theme (with some Cajun and Californian influences thrown in). Hong Kong–born and California-trained owner Eddie Cheung offers both a typed menu of regular items and a handwritten sheet of daily specials. On the regular menu rest our favorites: the crab chimichanga, a neat tortilla package encasing spicy crab in New Mexico–style red and green chile sauce; an unclassical Caesar salad; and the homemade Yucatan sausages, stuffed with pork and chicken, seasoned with allspice, cumin, jalapeño, and parsley. Grilled fish is a familiar choice on the specials list; the corn and crab chowder is a welcome one. Side dishes and desserts show less imagination, but then, no one else in town dares make Southwestern cuisine this good.

Sawasdee Thai Restaurant
Corner of Main and 27th,
(604) 876-4030
4250 Main St, Vancouver
Moderate; full bar; MC,
V; no checks
Dinner Tues-Sun

The oldest of Vancouver's Thai restaurants has aged well. Sawasdee doesn't offer the most sophisticated Thai food you can eat in Vancouver, but it might be the most fun place to go. The authentic Thai feel, mostly supplied by the staff, is of genuine happiness. The *mee krob* appetizer—crisp noodles with shrimp, bean sprouts, dried tofu, and shredded red cabbage—will be either too sweet or addictive, depending on your taste. Seafood is very reliable: try the clams with green pepper, onions, and fresh basil in a rich brown sauce, or the prawns sautéed with garlic, broccoli, and black pepper, fragrant with just-cracked peppercorns. The Granville Street Sawasdee (2145 Granville Street, 604 737-8222) is not as good as the original location.

Shijo Japanese Restaurant
West of Burrard on
W 4th, (604) 732-4676
1926 W 4th Ave,
Vancouver
Moderate; full bar; AE,
MC, V; no checks

With its uncluttered modern design (short on Japanese restaurant clichés and long on comfort), Shijo is a pleasant sushi bar, with excellent sushi and robata food.

Lunch Mon-Fri, dinner every day

with a light miso sauce, or the "shiitake foilyaki," shiitake mushrooms sprinkled with lemony ponzu sauce and cooked in foil. Wow. Orange sherbet, served in a hollowed-out orange, is a refreshing end to the meal.

Tai Chi Hin

Smithe and Burrard,
(604) 682-1888
888 Burrard St,
Vancouver
Moderate; full bar; AE,
V; checks OK
Lunch, dinner every day

Tai Chi Hin was one of the first restaurants in Vancouver to set a high standard for the growing number of Chinese restaurants. It is still among the best. Here the decor is postmodern: glass-block and pastel. New-wave music plays on the sound system, and the tuxedoed waiters give the same polished service as Swiss hotel school graduates. The look is so glamorous, it makes the food appear to be more expensive than it actually is. We recommend the fried smoked duck (served in crisp chunks with coriander and dumplings); the crab and white asparagus soup; and the garlic eel in a smooth brown sauce. The rock cod comes to your table live in a plastic case for your pre-meal inspection (though you're welcome to skip the preview). For something special, the Peking duck does not need to be ordered in advance, but the Beggar's Chicken does. It comes as a whole stuffed chicken, wrapped in lotus leaves, and baked inside a two-inch coating of dough (the original recipe called for river clay). A dramatically different dish, ask them to remove the rock-hard crust at the table—it's fun to watch.

Tandoori King

E 65th and Fraser,
(604) 327-8900
689 E 65th, Vancouver
Inexpensive; full bar;AE,
MC, V; no checks
Lunch, dinner Tues-Sat

The very pink Tandoori King gets a zero for decor, and service—while friendly—is quite slow. None of that really matters here, because this East Indian restaurant devotes its attention to two large clay tandoori ovens set into metal boxes in the kitchen. Tandoori breads (especially the house naan stuffed with tandoori chicken) are spectacular, as is the smokey eggplant, roasted whole over the wood fire in the tandoor before being mashed and seasoned. Chicken tikka and lamb tikka, both boneless cubes of meat, come tender and fresh to dip in mint chutney. Don't miss the pakora appetizers on your way to the meats. These bites of cauliflower, chicken, fish, or shrimp, coated in a batter made from chickpea flour and deep-fried, are rarely made so well. Finish the meal with homemade mango or pistachio ice cream. Take-out and delivery available.

The Teahouse Restaurant at Ferguson Point

Enter the park from
Georgia St follow road to
Ferguson Pt,
(604) 669-3281
Stanley Park, Vancouver

This is one of the loveliest places to eat in Vancouver, and certainly the one most in demand on Mother's Day. In the original section, the soft peach-and-leaf-green decor is that of an English country home; the newer glassed-in wings look out over the water and garden, giving you the feeling of dining in a conservatory. If only the food could rise to the setting. The ingredients are certainly of the best quality, but the menu is domi-

Moderate; full bar; AE, MC, V; no checks
Lunch, dinner every day, brunch Sat-Sun

nated by old-fashioned, vaguely French continental entries (with a few recent innovations). The simple dishes can be the best: the lamb chops are cooked perfectly medium rare, the fish of the day is grilled simply and well. Vegetables get the attention they deserve.

With the exception of the rarely-seen-nowadays baked Alaska, the desserts tend toward the same teahouse-tourist mode but, with the sun setting and the prospect of a walk along the seawall before you, perhaps you could forgive this restaurant almost anything. Weekend brunches are popular, and reservations are necessary at all times.

Tio Pepe

Commercial Dr,
(604) 254-8999
1134 Commercial Dr, Vancouver
Inexpensive; wine and beer; MC, V; no checks
Dinner Mon-Sat (in summer)
Lunch Mon-Fri, dinner Mon-Sat (in winter)

Tio Pepe is a shoebox of a restaurant, one long, narrow room crammed full of tables, with the kitchen at the back. Chef-owner José Trejo and wife Eileen keep the prices are low, and the excellent food is unlike any other Mexican food in town. At Tio Pepe you can get lamb—skewered, charbroiled, marinated in wine and spices—with a haunting taste of oranges. The grilled pork steak is marinated in red achiote, chile paste and spices; the black turtle beans have a luxurious, velvety texture. Pascaya con huevo, date-palm shoots fried in an egg batter and served with tomato sauce is an unusual appetizer, with a pleasantly astringent taste. The food is flavorful without being too spicy: a mildness which is typical of the Yucatan cook's subtle hand with spices. You'll find on your table a bottle of habañero hot sauce, distilled from hottest peppers known to man.

Umberto al Porto

In Gastown near the steam clock,
(604) 683-8376
321 Water St, Vancouver
Moderate; full bar; AE, DC, MC, V; no checks
Lunch Mon-Fri, dinner Mon-Sat

Large parties order wine by the magnum and take the empty one home for their change collections; more serious students of Italian wine come to the basement of a Gastown warehouse to choose from pages of listings, divided by region. Umberto's least expensive restaurant, Al Porto has a lively, color-splashed decor and good pasta (in spite of the fact that Menghi gives this place very little attention). We recommend the antipasto plate or the excellent carpaccio as a starter, and suggest you then move right into pasta. A good but seasonal entrée is the salmon.

Villa del Lupo

On Hamilton between Robson and Smithe,
(604) 688-7436
869 Hamilton, Vancouver
Moderate; full bar; AE, DC, MC, V; no checks
Lunch Mon-Fri, dinner every day

No strangers to Italian food, Julio Gonzales, and Vince and Mike Piccolo, who befriended each other during various stints at a number of Vancouver's better Italian restaurants (Caffe de Medici, Il Giardino di Umberto, and Il Barino) opened their own restaurant in early 1991. The former Le Napolean restaurant is now a simple elegant space with white walls and forest green trim. Upstairs there's a private dining room for larger parties. There are nice touches like plump blackberries and large homemade croutons on the salad della casa. We've devoured luscious homemade ravioli with eggplant and veal in a light buttery cream sauce, smooth cannelloni ripieni stuffed with chicken, mushrooms, ricotta and parmesan, and an excellent penne del contadino with roasted peppers, tomatoes, fresh basil and parmesan cheese. Finish the meal with a piece of white chocolate mousse pie. It's a good place for a pre- or post-show meal. Service is efficient and well-informed. The "house of the wolf" is on its way to the front of the pack of the city's Italian restaurants.

Water Street Cafe

Water St and Cambie,
(604) 689-2832
300 Water St, Vancouver
Moderate; full bar;
MC, V; no checks
Lunch, dinner every day

Across the street from Gastown's steam-powered clock, this small corner cafe is a delightful find, especially when you can sit outside at the sidewalk tables (best to call ahead and reserve one at lunch). The menu's not long but, lunch or dinner, there's always something that's exactly right: a citrus-and-sour prawn and papaya salad with plenty of both on top of a bed of tender baby lettuce, a true-to-Italy puttanesca, crab-and-Pacific shrimp cakes with a salsa picante, and meltingly-delicious carpaccio. The special penne was perfectly balanced with bites of tenderloin in a just-spicy cream sauce with sundried tomatoes and basil. The superb waitstaff matches the whole feel of the place: intelligent, friendly and even a bit witty. The two rooms upstairs (one seats 12, the other 45) are used for private parties.

The Amorous Oyster

Corner of 16th and Oak,
(604) 732-5916
3236 Oak St, Vancouver
Moderate; beer and wine;
AE, MC, V; no checks
Lunch Mon-Fri, dinner
every day

It calls itself "a casually elegant bistro," but we consider it more of an Australian seafood house. Oysters are the reigning delicacy, with as many as eight variations on a given day (from the classic oysters Rockefeller to the exotic oysters in green-chile pesto). But the selective menu is suffused with the love of fresh food that owner/chef Sue Adams brought with her from Australia, and the wine list (all available by the glass, half-liter, or bottle) is especially strong on down-under entries. Fresh daily offerings are chalked up on a large blackboard. Try the Limey lime mousse for dessert.

Beijing

Corner of Smithe and
Hornby, (604) 688-7788
865 Hornby St,
Vancouver
Moderate; full bar; AE,
DC, MC, V; no checks
Lunch, dinner
every day

The Beijing broke ground in Vancouver as the first upscale downtown Chinese restaurant. By now its competitors have long surpassed it in both food and decor, but Beijing's food is still good. Seafood dishes are outstanding, especially the abalone, the sea cucumbers with mushrooms, and the geoduck stewed in onion-redolent broth. Lovers of hotness will not be disappointed, provided they choose wisely.

Bodhi Vegetarian Restaurant

The deli showcases "pork", "squid", and "braised beef", but the restaurant is 100 percent vegetarian.

Off Main at Hastings,
(604) 682-2666
337 E Hastings St,
Vancouver
Inexpensive; no alcohol;
MC, V; no checks
Lunch, dinner Wed-Mon

These "savage" terms are merely masks for the elaborate and ingenious simulations crafted out of soy products and wheat gluten. Each of the 130-plus dishes is excellent, and not just for the few Buddhists who wander in: steamed or Swatow-style dumplings or the fluffy Lo-Hon buns, all regular dim sum items. For dinner try the cleansing mixture of vegetables with winter melon soup, mock abalone in black bean sauce, crisp vegetarian duck, and the unique salt and chile bean curd. An enlightening place, even for carnivores.

The Cannery

East on Hastings, left on
Victoria Dr, right on
Commissioner,
(604) 254-9606
2205 Commissioner St,
Vancouver
Expensive; full bar; AE,
DC, MC, V; no checks
Lunch Mon-Fri, dinner
every day

Who says you can't eat the view? From the Cannery's upstairs tables, amid old beams and lobster pots, the vista of the industrial end of Burrard Inlet is one of the best in the city. Fresh fish is barbecued or poached quite carefully, and vegetables are treated with respect. It's a difficult place to find, but easy to digest.

Owner Bud Kanke has just opened The Fish House in Stanley Park—a great location for after-tennis drinks and appetizers on the deck, (604) 681-7275.

English Bay Cafe

Corner of Beach and
Denman, across from the
beach, (604) 669-2225
1795 Beach Ave,
Vancouver
Moderate; full bar; AE,
DC, MC, V; no checks
Lunch Mon-Sat, dinner
every day, brunch Sun

Anyone who wants to eat while the glow spreads over English Bay is well advised to choose the English Bay Cafe. Downstairs is a bistro featuring light everything: a salads/sandwiches/light entrées menu and light music every night. Upstairs, where the view of the water doesn't battle the foreground interference of Beach Avenue traffic, the kitchen is more serious. It offers seafood, pasta, and other continental specialties, which might include a marinated rack of lamb or a combination of veal scalloppine and prawns. Brunches are very popular. Mid-May to mid-September, there's patio seating when it does not rain, with a separate barbecue menu of grilled fish, ribs, and burgers. Finding parking around here is very difficult, so we always spring for the cafe's $3.50 valet parking service (free at lunch and Sunday brunch). In the evening, there's often a jazz trio playing downstairs in the bistro.

Ezogiku Noodle Cafe

Robson at Bidwell,
(604) 687-7565
1684 Robson St,
Vancouver
Inexpensive; no alcohol;
no credit cards; no checks
Lunch, dinner every day

If it weren't for the word "noodle" in its name, one would expect to find a trendy espresso-and-pastry bar here. But no, ramen dishes are the order of the day in this spot. There are only ten seats at the counter and four at the window. The menu offers ramen in regular (pork) broth, miso, or soya, a fried rice dish, a fried noodle dish, gyoza, and that's all. Ezogiku's size and focus is the secret to the large bowls of perfectly cooked chewy noodles in rich steaming broth. Do what the old master in the movie *Tampopo* instructed: study, sniff, and savor. Found here, as nowhere else, is Zen in the art of noodle-making. After ten lessons you get one for free. Almost always a wait.

Greenhut
Vietnamese Cuisine
Across from the main gates of Granville Market, (604) 736-9688
1500 W 2nd Ave, Vancouver
Moderate; full bar; AE, DC, MC, V; no checks
Lunch Mon-Sat, dinner every day

On the revitalized approach to Granville Island is a restaurant which emphasizes the French end of the Vietnamese spectrum. Here you can get escargots, frogs' legs, chicken grand'mère farci (a boneless chicken stuffed with meats, vegetables, and seafood), and a rack of lamb; but don't ignore the more characteristically Vietnamese dishes. One of the best is the hot and sour seafood soup, its sourness provided by tamarind rather than the usual vinegar. Desserts are worth trying, especially the banana "cake," a warm, custardy bread pudding made with coconut milk. Many of the Vietnamese restaurant clichés have been left behind in this bright upstairs room with its pink faux-marble columns and clever posters. There's another, more traditionally decorated Greenhut on Robson (1429 Robson Street, 604 688-3688), and a third at 2143 W 41st Avenue, (604) 261-0688.

Hermitage
Between Burrard and Thurlow on the Robson, (604) 689-3237
115-1025 Robson St, Vancouver
Moderate; full bar; AE, DC, MC, V; checks OK
Lunch Mon-Fri, dinner every day

Vancouver doesn't need another French restaurant—but it's a pity there isn't more attention being paid to this deserving little place. Owner Hervé Martin brings a great deal of worldly expertise to his venture. Try as he might to create a casual bistro atmosphere, the food wants to be big-hotel grand. Hervé is a master with the saucepan, creating artistically appealing dishes napped in richly flavorful sauces: lamb medallions in a subtle but delicious papaya cream sauce or a boneless breast of duck is flambéed with Armagnac. Most of the problems here were with the service. The prawns came with a good tart raspberry sauce (we expected pomegrante, and were not alerted to the change). Another slip came at dessert when the raspberry soufflé we ordered appeared in the form of a mediocre raspberry sorbet. Nonetheless, the courtyard is a pleasant place to dine in the summer.

Kam's Garden Restaurant
South of Hastings on Main, (604) 669-5488
509 Main St, Vancouver
Inexpensive; no alcohol; no credit cards; no checks
Lunch, dinner every day

In one of the steamy windows that fronts this plain, boxy room are hung some of the best barbecued ducks and pork in the city—freshly cooked, ready to top bowls of rice, noodles, or congee (or be taken home). In the other window, noodles are tossed on wire strainers in and out of cauldrons of boiling broth, then spooned into bowls and topped with wonton or meatballs. The individually cooked bowls of congee with beef and sliced fish, the best Chinese curries in Vancouver, the daily slow-cooked soup—a bargain at one dollar, and the wonderful black-pepper beef chow mein are some of the reasons the legal beagles who work at the nearby Provincial Courthouse choose this no non-sense tea-in-a-glass place as their noontime haunt.

Kamei Sushi
*Thurlow and Robson
(and branches),
(604) 684-4823
811 Thurlow St,
Vancouver
Moderate; full bar; AE,
DC, MC, V; no checks
Lunch Mon-Fri, dinner
every day*

Kamei Sushi just keeps growing. Now at five locations (the original, two on West Broadway, one in Burnaby, one in Richmond), Kamei may not be the best Japanese restaurant in town, but its simple, Westernized dishes certainly make it one of the most popular. The Thurlow Street location is particularly lively at night when the theaters empty out. If you go earlier, try for a seat at the sushi bar so you can watch the antics of the sushi chefs. Combination platters contain all the standards (tuna, salmon, octopus, abalone, salmon roe); or try the red snapper *usuzukui*, thinly sliced and fanned prettily upon the plate with a citrus sauce.

Koji Japanese Restaurant
*Corner of Hornby and
Georgia, (604) 685-7355
630 Hornby St,
Vancouver
Moderate; full bar; AE,
DC, MC, V; no checks
Breakfast everyday, lunch
Mon-Fri, dinner
every day*

Koji wins the landscaping award for the most beautiful garden in a downtown Vancouver restaurant: an island of pine trees and river rocks on a patio several stories above Hornby Street. The best seats in this bank-building outlet (there's another Koji, this one with a view of False Creek, on West Broadway) are the non-smoking seats by the windows looking out on the garden, or at the sushi and robata bars. The rest is a crowded, smoky room often full of Japanese tourists. Sushi is not the best in town. Selections from the robata grill are dependable; the grilled shiitake mushrooms, topped with bonito flakes and tiny filaments of dry seaweed, are sublime. The Japanese boxed lunch might contain chicken kara-age; superb smoked black cod; prawn and vegetable tempura; two or three small salads; rice with black sesame seeds; pickled vegetables; miso soup; and fresh fruit—for around $10. Finish with green tea ice cream.

La Bodega
*½ block north of Granville
St Bridge, between Davie
and Drake,
(604) 684-8815
1277 Howe St, Vancouver
Inexpensive; full bar; AE,
DC, MC, V; no checks
Lunch Mon-Fri, dinner
Mon-Sat*

The Bodega is, in theory, just the bar and tapas lounge of the Chateau Madrid restaurant upstairs. But the dark, cozy, red-bricked cellar with its oddly endearing bull's head mounted on the wall is, in fact, a busy restaurant in its own right. Along with the night's specials, diners can order from a standard dozen hot tapas and 15 or so soups, salads, vegetables, and cold tapas plates. *Patatas bravas* (fried potatoes with a spicy dressing) are essential, along with clams marinera, prawns in garlic oil, slices of chorizo sausage and, ah, the white bean salad with herb dressing.

Las Tapas
*Between Robson and
Georgia on Cambie,
(604) 669-1624*

The elegant fast food of Spain is offered here in this sunny tiled and whitewashed room, where those in search of delicately spiced and marinated lamb, chicken livers, or charbroiled eggplant mingle over big glasses of earthy Spanish wine. We like the intensely spicy

760 Cambie St,
Vancouver
Inexpensive; full bar;
MC, V; no checks
Lunch Mon-Fri, dinner
every day

chorizo, chunks of crusty bread to dip in the little pans of garlicky shrimp, and the calamari (particularly good with the sauce that accompanies the potatoes). Most dishes come in three sizes—small, medium, and large—so you can indulge in a big way with familiar favorites and have an experimental taste of something new. Close to the Queen Elizabeth Theatre, Las Tapas is an excellent spot for a quick preconcert meal.

**Monterey Lounge & Grill
(Pacific Palisades Hotel)**
Robson St and Jervis,
(604) 684-1277
1277 Robson St,
Vancouver
Expensive; full bar; AE,
DC, MC, V; no checks
Breakfast, lunch, dinner
every day

Chef Anne Milne, who made such memorable waves at Cafe Splash, Bishop's, and the Bedford in Victoria, returned from a trip through Thailand to chef the new Monterey Grill. The restaurant itself is an odd space looking out over the hotel's courtyard. So we prefer to dine in the comfortable lounge where jazz pianists tickle ivory six nights a week or at the sidewalk tables (heated on cool days). In the first few months of business, Milne has not yet achieved what we know can, but she's well on her way. Appetizers such as the crab cakes with a citrus salsa were light and flavorful; the smoked scalloped wontons did not work as well as the crab cakes. Best are simple dishes like the skillet-roasted chicken breast filled with shiitake mushrooms, spinach, and bacon or the spiral pasta with pancetta, pinenuts, roasted garlic, roasted tomatos, and radicchio. The sundried cherries marinated in grappa made an excellent sauce for the well-cooked duck but we would have liked the duck more crispy. With the opening of the roof garden, with its cedar planters full of herbs, vegetables and edible flowers for Milne's use, we expect things can only get better. The service is excellent; the wine list needs a little more time.

**Moutai Mandarin
Restaurant**
Davie at Denman,
(604) 681-2288
1710 Davie, Vancouver
Inexpensive; full bar;AE,
DC, MC, V; no checks
Lunch, dinner every day

Lisa and James Wong are second-generation restaurateurs who modeled the menu at their new Moutai Mandarin restaurant on the menu at their parents' well-patronized Szechuan Chongqing at Broadway and Victoria. Now West Enders don't have to leave their territory to get good versions of Szechuan Chongqing favorites like green beans with pork (whole green beans sautéed with already-cooked ground pork, and plenty of chile pepper). We particularly like the specials: spicy black-bean-sauce clams and the blistering stir-fry with tiger prawns called *dai ching*. Moutai's shiny, acid-green tabletops and arborite trim in a pattern of big black, white, and gray pebbles has a cheeky punk swagger that's miles removed from either red-dragon tacky or Hong Kong slick, the city's two dominant Chinese restaurant styles. A tropical fish tank divides the room into two tiny sections (smoking and non).

Nazarre BBQ Chicken
Commercial and
Kitchener,

This place was bombed by animal rights activists a couple of years ago, but it's back and as good as ever.

(604) 251-1844
1408 Commercial Dr,
Vancouver
Inexpensive; no alcohol;
no credit cards;
checks OK
Lunch, dinner
every day

Rubber chickens decorate the storefront, but you'll find only tender barbecued chicken on your plate. French-born, Mexican-raised owner Gerry Moutal bastes them in a mixture of rum and spices while in the rotisserie. The chickens drip their juices onto potatoes roasting below. This duo then comes with a choice of mild, hot, extra hot, or hot garlic sauce. You can eat in, at one of four rickety tables, or take out.

New Seoul

E Broadway and
Commercial,
(604) 872-1922
1682 E Broadway,
Vancouver
Inexpensive; full bar;
MC, V; no checks
Lunch Mon-Fri, dinner
every day

Some of the best Korean food in Vancouver comes from this unprepossessing restaurant squeezed between a blank-faced drugstore and a Chinese movie theater. Every table has a gas barbecue. Customers cook their own marinated beef, pork, chicken, and prawns while nibbling on the dozen or so side dishes included with the entrée: bean sprouts; zucchini in garlic and chile; shredded daikon; and, of course, the Korean national pickle, spicy, chilled kimchi. Stick with the barbecue; tempura dishes can be leaden. The New Seoul is too busy to encourage loitering over coffee and dessert, so you can avoid that temptation.

Noor Mahal

Between 27th and 28th on
Fraser, (604) 873-9263
4354 Fraser St,
Vancouver
Inexpensive; full bar;
MC, V; no checks
Dinner every day

A haven for big appetites on small budgets, the Noor Mahal is also one of the very few restaurants in Vancouver that specialize in the snack foods of southern India. Decor is basic truck-stop, with an overlay of spectacular beaded chandeliers and flashy Indian art. A television set in the corner plays Indian movies and soap operas. The Noor Mahal's specialty is the *dosa*: a large, light, lacy crêpe made from a batter of rice and wheat flour, then stuffed with a variety of fillings (choose from 14, including chicken and spinach or homemade cheese) and served with coconut chutney and a bowl of thick, flavorful lentil soup. Order a mango milk shake to cool the flames of an extra-hot curry, or one of the garishly colored but flavorful homemade ice creams.

Nyala Restaurant

Near the corner of W 4th
and MacDonald,
(604) 731-7899
2930 W 4th Ave,
Vancouver
Inexpensive; full bar;
AE, DC, MC, V;
no checks
Lunch, dinner
every day

Many people are unaware that Ethiopia, like other African nations, has a cuisine all its own. Vancouver is home to two family-run restaurants which offer good representations of this underappreciated exotic cuisine (the other's Lalibela Ethiopian Cuisine, 2090 Alma Street, (604) 732-1454, and it's just as good). The food is served in traditional Ethiopian style—no knives, forks, or spoons. The injera (a big plate-sized flat bread with a honeycomb texture) is all the utensil you need. Just tear off a little bread, fold it around bite-size portions of food, and pop the whole thing into your mouth. The food, mostly soft stew or currylike preparations of savory beef, lamb, chicken, fish, or vegetables, is served communally at each table on a large metal platter accompanied by an assortment of condiments (spicy sautéed cabbage, golden herbed bulgur wheat, gingered lentil purée). It's impolite to use your left hand.

Olympia Fish Market & Oyster Co.
Robson and Thurlow,
(604) 685-0716
1094 Robson St,
Vancouver
Inexpensive; no alcohol;
V; checks OK
Lunch, dinner every day

Five years ago, Robson Street fish merchant Carlo Sorace decided that what the street really needed was a good place to get fish 'n' chips. His store is still a functioning fish store, but push on into the back, where you'll find one of the contenders for top fish 'n' chips in the Lower Mainland. Whatever is on special in the fish store is the day's special at the fish 'n' chips bar, which really means scallops, catfish, or calamari, along with the standard halibut and cod. Eat in at one of 10 stools at the counter or take out. Soft drinks include Chinotto and root beer.

Pho Hoang
20th and Main,
(604) 874-0810
3610 Main St, Vancouver
Inexpensive; no alcohol;
no credit cards;
no checks
Lunch, dinner Fri-Wed

Vietnam's counterpart to the hamburger, *pho* is a quick lunch, dinner, or snack. Pho Hoang has been packing in crowds at its modest location on Main Street for the past four years. A bowl of fragrant broth with rice noodles and your choice of flank, rump, brisket, tripe, or a dozen other beef cuts and combinations, it is accompanied by a plate of bean sprouts, fresh basil, lime, and hot chile peppers for individually tailored soup. A cup of strong Vietnamese coffee, filter-brewed at the table, is the only other thing you need.

Quilicum West Coast Native Indian Restaurant
Between Bidwell and
Denman on Davie,
(604) 681-7044
1724 Davie St,
Vancouver
Moderate; full bar; AE,
MC, V; no checks
Lunch Mon-Fri, dinner
every day

The original Northwest Coast restaurant, Quilicum serves what qualifies as "roots food" for enthusiasts of the region's cuisine: native Indian specialties. Downstairs in the Davie Street longhouse, among totem poles, Indian masks, and art (available for purchase), diners consume alder-grilled salmon and local vegetables from hand-carved ceremonial bowls. Our favorite is a dish called *succulent parts*: the tail, head, neck, and belly of the salmon. Accompaniments include rice with seaweed, a dish of baked sweet potato and hazelnuts, and sweet bannock bread. Other unusuals include steamed herring roe on a bed of kelp, caribou stew, and big bowls of oolichan grease, prepared from the oil of a native fish. Although it sounds like novelty food, there is sincerity in the kitchen, and results can be superior.

Settebello
Between Thurlow and
Bute on Robson St,
(604) 681-7377
1131 Robson St,
Vancouver
Inexpensive; full bar;AE,
DC, MC, V; no checks
Lunch, dinner every day

Like much of the new Robson Street, Settebello sometimes seems overly impressed with its own casual sophistication. The name of Umberto Menghi's seventh restaurant means "beautiful seven" (from an Italian card game), and it's a departure from his other establishments in its attempt to cash in on the "grazing" trend of the city's younger dining crowd. Settebello is best on sunny days, as a respite from shopping, when you can sit out on the rooftop patio nibbling at pasta or a collection of Italian tapas-style dishes. Try the salsiccia pizza (cooked in a wood-burning oven): hot Italian sausage, spinach, sun-dried tomatoes, and chile peppers. For purists there's the classic Settebello: tomatoes, mozzarella, basil, and olive oil. Too bad the food is inconsistent, and the service a little too casual.

Sophie's Cosmic Cafe

W 4th and Arbutus,
(604) 732-6810
2095 W 4th, Vancouver
Inexpensive; beer and
wine; MC, V; no checks
Breakfast, lunch, dinner
every day

Greek-born Jimmy Dikeakos, his brother Christos, and sister-in-law Sophie purchased the old Arbutus Cafe three years ago with the intention of keeping the diner decor and improving on the food. As the food got better and the crowds bigger, Sophie brightened up the place with her collections of kids' colorful lunch boxes and hats once stashed in her attic. It's a fun place to be and an even better place to eat. Breakfast (try the great mash of Mexican eggs with sausage, peppers, onions spiced with salsa poured from a wine bottle) is served right through lunch. The big spicy burgers are midday favorites and the blackened salmon burger is getting raves. Dinners run a similar line with the addition of chicken enchiladas, ribs, cosmic pastas (prawns and vegetables), or lamb chops. Great shakes.

Splendido

On Robson between Bute
and Thurlow,
(604) 685-2717
1145 Robson, Vancouver
Moderate; full bar; AE,
DC, MC, V; no checks
Lunch, dinner every day

Umberto Menghi's newest restaurant is located in the former second-floor Milieu space. It's terracotta floor and peach-stucco walls with small colorful bicycle and windsurfing figurines set a nice tone. Early reports on the rabbit are excellent; it's on the menu served with bitter greens but also is prepared as a special too. One recent meal, it came marinated as an appetizer on top of wide nicely spiced lasagna noodles. The risotto is a little to heavy. It's large windows open onto bustling Robson Street, a great place to watch the Robson scene. The new Foccacia Deli downstairs, (604) 685-2718, serves good Italian sandwiches and espresso.

The Topanga Cafe

1 block west of
MacDonald,
(604) 733-3713
2904 W 4th Ave,
Vancouver
Inexpensive; full bar;
MC, V; no checks
Lunch, dinner
Mon-Sat

The name comes from LA's Topanga Canyon and reflects the westernized Mexican fare that can best be described as "Mexicali." It's a plain, soulful little place with a few wooden tables and a closet-sized kitchen. The only decorative touch is provided by a multitude of menu covers, hand-colored by restaurant patrons and hung on the walls. It is so popular with the Kitsilano neighborhood crowd, with lineups at the door such a regular feature that other restaurants have opened in the vicinity hoping to catch some of the overflow. The food never changes; portions are generous, prices low, and quality high. Chicken enchiladas are made with moist, tender breast meat, beef dishes with shredded beef (not hamburger), and the pork tenderloin taco is stuffed with large chunks of pork. Extra-garlicky salsa and home-fried tortilla chips could satisfy any vaquero.

Tropica Malaysian Cuisine
Denman at Davie,
(604) 682-1887
1096 Denman,
Vancouver
Moderate; full bar; AE,
DC, MC, V; no checks
Lunch, dinner every day

Until Tropica opened—in prime restaurant territory a block away from English Bay—the only Malaysian restaurant in town was a truck stop in a dilapidated minimall on Kingsway. Now we may eat our satay under techy little spotlights in the embrace of sponge-painted walls on Denman. Despite the location and the illustrated menu, Tropica offers authentic fare. Try the spicy spinach for its pungent, characteristic savor of dried shrimp and fish sauce. Less fiery is the Hainan chicken, a super-tender steamed chicken. *Rendang lembu,* a subtle beef curry with its heat cut by coconut milk is (even at one star) quite hot. Avoid the prawns—they're big, but the results are uneven. Two rice dishes stand out on the menu: a luxurious coconut rice and a warm, porridgey sweet-black-rice pudding—the latter is served in Bali as breakfast and makes a soothing late-morning meal here too.

Vong's Kitchen
Corner of Fraser and E
44th, (604) 327-4627
5989 Fraser St,
Vancouver
Inexpensive; no alcohol;
no credit cards; no checks
Dinner Wed-Sun

With new upscale Chinese restaurants cropping up all over the city, one could get positively nostalgic about Vong's. It seems to have been around forever: the same tiny place on unfashionable Fraser Street, same steamy windows and kitchen-table decor inside. If you are serious about food and not into making impressions, then Vong's is the choice. The place is owned and run by the Vong family who prepare each dish with loving attention: chile sauce prawns and atomic rice (rich broth is poured on top of the crisp-cooked rice and vegetables, producing a loud, sizzling racket). Although the execution of some dishes can be inconsistent, milder palates will enjoy the jade chicken (on spinach) or the orange beef. Your bill is accompanied by deep-fried banana fritters. If you don't plan on arriving before 6pm, reservations are essential—even then, be prepared to wait for your table. It's worth it.

Zeppo's Trattoria
1½ blocks west of
Burrard, (604) 737-7444
1967 W Broadway,
Vancouver
Moderate; full bar; AE,
MC, V; no checks
Lunch Mon-Fri, dinner
every day

When well-known local chef Bruno Born opened this salmon-and-sage-colored trattoria three years ago, it quickly became a noisy and popular hangout for the city's eat-around crowd. Born has since sold the establishment to concentrate on his French restaurant (Le Coq d'Or) down the street. It remains to be seen whether the regulars will move along too. Chef Tim Johnstone continues his pleasant, if somewhat unfocused, Italian fare, which always starts with decent focaccia bread and a small pot of pâté. The cold and the hot antipasto platter—with its tempting assortment of grilled vegetables, duck sausage, shrimp in phyllo, deep-fried smelt—is one of the more interesting starters. Pastas are the most reliable entrée—in particular, a penne melanzane in a spicy tomato sauce of eggplant, prosciutto, and brandy and the rich conchiglie pasta with scallops, spinach, and pine nuts. Jazz piano plays on the weekends. Skip the desserts. Service is pleasant and attentive.

Japanese Deli House
Powell and Gore,
(604) 681-6484
381 Powell St,
Vancouver
Inexpensive; beer only;
no credit cards; no checks
Lunch, dinner Tues-Sun

W 1st Ave near Burrard
1815 W 1st Ave,
(604) 734-5858
Vancouver
Inexpensive; beer only;
MC, V; no checks
Lunch, dinner Tues-Sun

This is the bargain beauty of the sushi crowd, right in the middle of old Japantown. Although Powell Street has never recovered from the forced relocation of Japanese citizens during the Second World War, it still has Japanese grocery and fish stores worth visiting. The Deli is an old high-ceilinged room with big windows, arborite-topped tables and an all-you-can-eat philosophy applied to sushi. Start with eight pieces of nigiri sushi, four pieces of maki and soup for $8.95; if you can eat more than that, it's yours for free. Quality is surprisingly good, especially if you arrive early: sushi is made in quantity at 11am for the 11:30 opening. Dinner only until 8pm weekdays, 6pm on weekends. A new Kitsilano branch opened at press time.

Woodlands Natural Cuisine
W Broadway and
Trafalgar,
(604) 733-5411
2582 W Broadway,
Vancouver
Inexpensive; beer and
wine; MC, V; no checks
Breakfast, lunch, dinner
every day

Five minutes from downtown Vancouver, this restaurant goes well beyond the usual limitations of vegetarian dining. In fact, the menu is almost international. We enjoyed a moist and filling eggplant moussaka with a special cream topping and textured soy beneath. The honey-glazed baked tofu over basmati rice was delicious. Fukumeni was a Japanese-style stir-fry over thread noodles. The dal was mild yet flavorful and the salads outstanding. You select from the buffet and pay by weight (dieters take note). There is a separate dining room for dinner service.

Le Coq d'Or
W Broadway and Trutch,
(604) 733-0035
3205 W Broadway,
Vancouver
Moderate; full bar; MC,
V; no checks
Breakfast, lunch Tues-
Fri, dinner Tues-Sat,
brunch Sat-Sun

unrated

Bruno Born's brand new establishment is striving for the same appeal of his former restaurant, Zeppo's (a popular Italian hangout for the city's eat-around crowd), but this time in the mood of a true French bistro. The "golden rooster" is a sun-splashed place that's somehow both country French and urban chic with tall windows, rich mustard-colored walls, elegant reddish wood back bar, and a few sidewalk tables. There's an earnestness here. The eggplant and roasted red pepper appetizer baked with goat cheese was nearly enough for dinner. The oysters are fresh and presented with shallot vinegar. Meals are simple and well executed: perhaps a half chicken roasted with fresh herbs, caramelized garlic and lemon. The extra thick pork chop was moist; now if only he'd learn how to make really great frites.

LODGINGS

The Four Seasons
Howe and W Georgia,

After leaving your car in the porte cochère, you take an escalator up to a lively and elegant lobby, filled with

*(604) 689-9333, toll-free
(800) 268-6282
791 W Georgia St,
Vancouver, BC V6C 2T4
Expensive; AE, DC, MC,
V; no checks*

marble, plants, and people. The rooms, with $14 million worth of new furnishings, come in three color schemes: terracotta, beauvais (a regal rose), and black and white; the last is the most stunning. Furnishings are tasteful without being ostentatious, and the many small amenities that are offered as a matter of course—outstanding 24-hour room service, terrycloth robes, hair dryers, VCRs (with rentals from reception desk), complimentary newspapers, fresh flowers—make this place a refined and welcome refuge. Evening tea service, slippers, and traditional *yukatas* on arrival are given to Japanese tourists; however, these are not exclusive to the Japanese. If you would like the same, just ask. Aside from the split-level suites (there are two of them), our favorite rooms are those on a corner above the 20th floor. There are 24 floors of rooms, 8 of which are smoking floors. There's a big deck off the spa with an indoor/outdoor pool, a Jacuzzi, and a sauna. The atriumlike Garden Lounge, off to one side, provides a bosky retreat for cocktails and conversation and serves an excellent buffet brunch on Sundays. An informal restaurant, Seasons Cafe, opens into the rotunda of the Pacific Centre mall; in summer, light lunches and fruit drinks are served around the outdoor swimming pool. The formal dining room, Chartwell (see review), is a first-class restaurant.

Le Meridien
*Corner of Smithe and
Burrard,
(604) 682-5511, toll-free
(800) 543-4300
845 Burrard St,
Vancouver, BC V6Z 2K6
Expensive; AE, DC, MC,
V; no checks*

Le Meridien is the most elegant hotel in Vancouver. The large pinkish stone building holds the refined, patrician decor that you would expect in an aristocratic European hostelry. Built just prior to EXPO '86, the place is fairly big—397 rooms and 47 suites—and well suited to its address, close to the Vancouver Art Gallery and the fashionable browsing district of Robson Street. The lobby—decorated in soft shades of coffee and peach, with Asian-inspired rosewood furniture and dramatic flower arrangements in glazed pottery urns—sets the tone for the whole place. The ample-sized rooms are soothing spaces with city views out of floor-to-ceiling windows (ask to face north for the best views). Prices in season are high—$185 to $240 for a standard-size double, up to $1000 for the presidential two-bedroom suite—but regardless of the size they *all* include twice-daily maid service, fresh flowers, shoeshine, a downtown limousine at your disposal, an umbrella, and membership in Le Spa (a fitness and beauty and tanning salon complete with indoor and outdoor pool and sun deck). Of the restaurants, the dark, polished, publike Gerard Lounge is the current after-work gathering place for locals; Cafe Fleuri offers a good breakfast, pleasant Sunday brunches, and weekend chocolate buffets; and Le Club (formerly Gerard) is now a continental restaurant (see review). A business center (complete with stock market TVs, computer workstations, and a bar) was in the works at press time.

Delta Place

Dunsmuir and Howe,
(604) 687-1122, toll-free
(800) 268-1133
645 Howe St, Vancouver,
BC V6C 2Y9
Expensive; AE, DC, MC,
V; no checks

Original owners, Mandarin International, spared no expense with design and fixtures (the standard rooms, with large baths and extra amenities, are labeled deluxe). All the extras—wool carpeting, solid oak cabinetry, marble shower stalls, cast-iron bathtubs, balconies off most rooms, a health club (sauna equipped with a color TV, towels on ice, and racquetball *and* squash courts)—tipped the scales, and Mandarin had to sell. Now that it's owned by a local investment group (and managed by Delta), business has picked up a bit. Summer rates hover at around $225. Located in the center of Vancouver's financial district, Delta Place has ample facilities for the business traveler (boardrooms, secretarial services, and fax, among others).

The Georgian Court Hotel

Cambie and Beatty,
(604) 682-5555, toll-free
(800) 663-1155
773 Beatty St,
Vancouver, BC V6B 2M4
Expensive; AE, DC, MC,
V; checks OK

This exclusive, brick-clad hotel, just across the street from BC Place, combines the business amenities traditionally associated with a "name" hotel with the luxury and personality of a small one. Exceptional meeting facilities, three phones in each room, a health club (with whirlpool, sauna, and exercise room), and its prime location are practical advantages. The amiable lobby is small and appealing, in tasteful green with peach and gray accents. Doubles (starting at about $115 a night) and one- and two-bedroom suites (from $140 to $350) are smartly furnished with mahogany, antiques, and Audubon prints—more reminiscent of a fine home than of a hotel. For these prices, however, we'd expect a little more precision: sounds of the heating system found their way into our room on a recent visit, and the bathroom was curiously understocked with towels. Perhaps the biggest plus is the city's best continental restaurant, the William Tell, just down the stairs (see review). Rigney's is a casual, less pricey alternative.

Pacific Palisades

Between Bute and Jervis
on Robson,
(604) 688-0461
1277 Robson St,
Vancouver, BC V6E 1C4
Expensive; AE, DC, MC,
V; no checks

The tri-tower complex (owned by Shangri-La International) takes up an entire city block of the ultra-fashionable Robson Street. It was formerly an apartment complex (long-term rates are still available), and the rooms are some of the most spacious in the city. Call them suites, as every one has a kitchenette (no stoves, just microwaves) and is supplied with thoughtful extras such as umbrellas, hair dryers, and robes. Reserve a room above the fourth floor and you'll be guaranteed a choice of view. There's a courtyard with a health center (pool, sauna, weight room, whirlpool, masseuse, and table tennis), where pick-up badminton or barbecues might be held in the summer. Or rent a mountain bike and work out in Stanley Park. Businesspeople will appreciate the business center, with a number of small meeting rooms, a fax machine, and computers; you can even rent a cellular phone.

Live jazz is often heard in the comfortable Monterey Lounge (with pleasant sidewalk tables)—a good place to meet for a drink before dinner at the Monterey Grill (see review).

Pan Pacific Hotel
At the north foot of Burrard St, across from Stanley Park,
(604) 662-8111, toll-free (800) 663-1515 in Canada, in the U.S.
(800) 937-1515
300-999 Canada Pl, Vancouver, BC V6C 3B5
Expensive; AE, DC, MC, V; no checks

As part of Canada Place in the heart of Vancouver's harborfront, the Japan-based Tokyu Corporation's 507-room hotel stands in all its white-sail magnificence overlooking the docking cruise ships and the whole expanse of the inner harbor. The five signature sails (made to resemble a flotilla of sailboats racing up Burrard Inlet) have attracted a lot of attention, but that's not always a good thing: the entrance is a bit awkward (past Vancouver's Trade and Convention Centre, then up two escalators to the reservation desk), and the big atrium space leans more toward a tourist attraction than a first-class hotel. Rooms are smallish but some of the prettiest in town, with bird's-eye maple armoires and marble bathrooms (shower early, there's not always enough hot water for everyone). All have views— on the west side toward Stanley Park and the Lion's Gate Bridge, and on the east looking over the city; Ask for a corner room (any room ending with "10") and you'll even have a view from the bathtub. Suites are spacious and lovely. Service is first-rate, and health facilities are endless: an outdoor lap pool (heated to 86 degrees) and hot tub, saunas, a running track, high-tech exercise equipment, indoor hot and cold pools, squash and racquetball courts and, in keeping with the hotel's Asian connection, shiatsu massage.

The main floor features the Cascades Lounge with its marvelous water outlooks, the five enormous sculptured sails poised on the outside deck, and a waterfall. Other restaurants (all overpriced due to the hotel's popularity with conventioneers) are Cafe Pacifica, a casual place serving continental cuisine and dim sum lunches; Suntory, with Japanese food; and the Five Sails, a French restaurant.

Ramada Renaissance Hotel
Above Burrard Inlet between Butte and Thurlow, (604) 689-9211
1133 W Hastings St, Vancouver, BC V6E 3T3
Expensive; full bar; AE, DC, MC, V; no checks
Lunch, dinner Tues-Sun

A 15-million-dollar renovation completely erased any hints that this waterfront hotel was ever a Holiday Inn. Hong Kong–based New World Development brought its level up to that of the better hotels in the city. A wave-like design (the hotel is just above Coal Harbour) is carried throughout the hotel—from the confetti-patterned rug in the lobby to the contoured hallways (leading to the meeting rooms) to the rotating dining room (Vistas) on the top floor. The rooms are standard hotel size; however, they include unusual features such as heated bathroom floors and hair dryers, even in the most inexpensive. Ask for a room with a view of the

North Shore, and if you want extra-special treatment, request a room on the exclusive 18th floor.

A ballroom is one of the few in the city, with a spectacular entryway with a view of the harbor. A pool, sauna, workout room, and sun deck are on the fourth floor. Dynasty restaurant is one of the finest Chinese restaurants in the city (see review).

Coast Plaza Hotel
At Stanley Park,
(604) 688-7711, toll-free
(800) 663-1144
1733 Comox St,
Vancouver, BC V6G 1P6
Expensive; AE, DC, MC,
V; checks OK

This tall hotel, located in a pleasant residential neighborhood, has seen a few owners and a few names. It is currently being operated by the Coast Hotel chain. The pastel lobby and the rooms have recently been upgraded. Because this was originally an apartment building, rooms are larger than average and have individual balconies with wonderful views. All have mini-bars and some have kitchens. Upstairs floors constitute Limited Edition, a private businesspersons' territory where guest rooms have more personal service. All guests enjoy membership privileges in the newly renovated Olympic Athletic Club next door—*the* place to play squash in Vancouver. Breakfast and lunch are served in the Brasserie, dinner of West Coast fare at Windows on the Bay. The location—a few steps from English Bay and not far from the Zoo and Aquarium—makes this a good choice for families with kids.

English Bay Inn
1 block from English Bay
on Comox at Chilco,
(604) 683-8002
1968 Comox St,
Vancouver, BC V6G 1R4
Expensive; MC, V; checks
OK

Last April, Bob Chapin exchanged teaching English for innkeeping on English Bay, and he has already rounded up a whole new class of devotees. His Tudor house is tiny in comparison to the other places of this caliber; however, Chapin's impeccable taste measures up on every level. Most of the five rooms echo Chapin's passion for 18th- and 19th-century history with Louis Phillipe sleigh beds, antique armoires, and paisley-patterned down comforters. The two-level suite with a fireplace in the top-floor bedroom is, no doubt, the best. But a stay in any of the other four rooms (all with small bathrooms) is no less exquisite. Two rooms open out to the small cloister-like garden out back. Complimentary robes, phones in each room, tea upon arrival, and sherry at bedtime are nice thoughts. A formal breakfast is served upstairs in the dining room, often warmed with a fire. You're only steps away from English Bay and Stanley Park (bring your tennis racquet and bike). With a little more time to settle in, ever-accommodating Chapin's small inn should earn a third star.

Granville Island Hotel
and Marina
Far east corner of
Granville Island,

The Granville Island Hotel is a bold combination of an old stucco building (now pink) and a dramatic new complex of glass and corrugated iron, the latter reminiscent of Granville Island's industrial past. A glass atrium, ex-

(604) 683-7373,
toll-free (800) 663-1840
1253 Johnston St,
Vancouver, BC V6H 3R9
Expensive; AE, DC, MC,
V; no checks

tending toward the water like the bow of a ship, splits the building down the middle and lets in a stream of natural light all the way to the first floor. A whimsical, brightly colored sculpture, the Cyrus P. Windless Kite Flying Machine, fills the atrium space in the lobby. The small 54-room hotel has a lot to recommend it: the custom-furnished rooms are decorated in muted tones with light wood accents, and some have shutters that open onto small balconies. Avoid rooms that face the atrium: the nightclub can make for a sleepless night. Prices range from $140 for a double to $250 for a one-bedroom suite. Boats can hook up to the dock and connect with the hotel's television and telephone system, power and water lines, and even use its room service. There are two new restaurants here: the casual Pelican Pub and Grill and the more formal Pelican Bay.

Hyatt Regency
Burrard and Georgia,
(604) 687-6543, toll-free
(800) 233-1234
655 Burrard St,
Vancouver, BC V6C 2R7
Expensive; AE, DC, MC,
V; checks OK

Located in the city's core, the Hyatt is popular for conventions and business meetings, with over 25,000 square feet dedicated to this purpose. But this is also a good spot for the vacationer: one block to Robson Street shopping, a 15-minute walk to Stanley Park. Harborside rooms with a terrific view onto busy Burrard Inlet and the surrounding mountains run $170 to $260. Suites cost $425 to $725. Each room comes with its own electronic safe. A fitness club and pool round out the amenities. Cafes and lounges abound, but most noteworthy is the casual Fish & Company, which under chef Othmar Steinhart is earning a reputation as one of the best seafood restaurants in town.

Ming Court
Davie and Thurlow,
(604) 685-1311, toll-free
(800) 663-685-1311
1160 Davie St,
Vancouver, BC V6E 1N1
Expensive; AE, DC, MC,
V; checks OK

Recently purchased by Mainami Canada, the former Miramar is lovely and coolly sophisticated. The marble lobby is all pastels—peach and dusty rose—and the garden court lounge is particularly fine. Rooms are large and nicely furnished; each has a balcony, and from ours, on the 18th floor, there was an incomparable view of English Bay and the islands beyond. Extras include sauna, outdoor swimming pool, exercise room, and secretarial services. Prices are competitive. You're a 15-to-20-minute walk from the hub of the city, but the lively street life right outside your door in Vancouver's West End is a show in itself. Free parking is available for guests.

The Sylvia
Beach and Gilford,
(604) 681-9321
1154 Gilford St,
Vancouver, BC V6G 2P6
Moderate; AE, DC, MC,
V; checks OK

This charming and rather shabby brick landmark, completely covered with ivy, offers one of the best locations in the city: right on English Bay in the heart of the West End. Families with children especially enjoy its proximity to the beaches and playgrounds of Stanley Park, but the major attraction is its incredibly low prices (especially for Vancouver). Doubles run $53 to $77, triples (an extra bedroom for the kids) are $72 to

$85, and suites are $70 to $120. Children under 18 traveling with a parent stay free. Avoid the cheaper rooms, which tend toward the tacky—opt for a room with a view of the bay or for one of the 16 newer rooms, which are pleasant and slightly less dowdy, although somewhat characterless. Ask to see the room first; the difference in price doesn't necessarily mean much difference in rooms here. The English Bay–view bar can get rowdy in the evenings with neighborhood apartment dwellers. The new dining room, Sylvia's, offers great sunset-watching but mediocre food.

The Wedgewood Hotel

On Hornby between Smithe and Robson, (604) 689-7777, toll-free (800) 663-0666 845 Hornby St, Vancouver, BC V6Z 1V1 Expensive; AE, DC, MC, V; no checks

Veteran hotelier Eleni Skalbania virtually custom-ordered this hostelry, which emerged like a butterfly out of the dilapidated Mayfair in the center of town. Skalbania exudes a tangible presence here, with her effort and care stamped on almost every facet of the operation. Businesspeople may prefer the corporate atmosphere of the bigger properties, but the Wedgewood is the place Vancouverites recommend to their friends. Doormen usher you into a lobby decorated handsomely with antiques and Oriental fixtures. There are 94 bedrooms; the suites are decorated in shades of dusty rose and cool green, and many of them include fireplaces. Doubles start at $160. All the rooms have flower-decked patios, remote-control TVs, stocked mini-bars, and morning newspaper delivery. Recent reports indicate that careless service can be a problem here—curious for such a small place run by such an exacting taskmaster. Guests enjoy membership privileges at the Chancery Squash Club next door. The former Wedgewood Room restaurant is now a meeting room for 100. In the Bacchus Ristorante, the 150-seat oyster bar and bistro serves rusticiana (country-style) cuisine created from local, organically grown foods.

Westin Bayshore

Georgia and Cardero, just south of Stanley Park, (604) 682-3377, toll-free (800) 228-3000 1601 W Georgia St, Vancouver, BC V6G 2V4 Expensive; AE, DC, MC, V; checks OK

The setting is grand: gaze out over a small harbor, with Stanley Park beyond and the mountains beyond that. The city is behind you, but as you look north from your room you're at the edge of Stanley Park's wilderness. A great round pool fills up the courtyard, so in the summer you can sunbathe in this secluded setting. Or you can rent a boat (or a bike) for a little tour, or go jogging in Stanley Park. There is also an indoor pool for the cooler months. Problem is, the rooms are small and the staff doesn't go to any extra effort to justify the high price of a room. If you've a boat, moorage at the nearby marina is cheap and allows for full use of the hotel facilities and room service. The Garden Restaurant, a pleasant, open area facing the pool, serves modest breakfasts, lunches, and suppers. The big-deal restaurant is Trader Vic's.

Hotel Georgia

Howe and Georgia,
(604) 682-5566, *toll-free*
(800) 663-1111
801 W Georgia St,
Vancouver, BC V6C 1P7
Expensive; AE, DC, MC,
V; no checks

It may not have the flash of some of the newer hotels in town, but this old, familiar face in the center of downtown has pleasant rooms adorned with new oak furniture and done in a calming jewel-toned palette. In all, it's a unpretentious place. The Cavalier Grill features a casual breakfast and lunch menu as well as fine dining in the evening; two other popular spots are the Night Court Lounge and the raucous George V pub, with sing-alongs Thursday-Saturday evenings and authentic pub lunches.

Hotel Vancouver

Georgia and Burrard,
(604) 684-3131, *toll-free*
(800) 268-9143
900 W Georgia St,
Vancouver, BC V6C 2W6
Expensive; AE, DC, MC,
V; checks OK

Built in the French chateau style favored by the Canadian railways, this grand hotel comes complete with a steep green copper roof, BC stone exterior, menacing gargoyles and griffins, and rich ornamentation. Even so, the dowager has been made into a convention hotel, owned and managed by Canadian Pacific. Its location is about as central as you can get, near the big stores, the Law Courts complex, and the Vancouver Art Museum. The 508 rooms are moderately sized, sophisticated, and quiet; and service is good. A brand-new health club adds a modern touch to the old place. Dining is not the high point of staying here, but the Roof Restaurant and Lounge has a grand view; it is one of the very few places in town that still offers the dinner dance. The Timber Club, with decor designed to honor BC's timber industry, is a favorite haunt of lunching businessmen, and Griffin is a good spot for breakfast.

West End Guest House

1 block south of Robson,
between Jervis and
Broughton,
(604) 681-2889
1362 Haro St,
Vancouver, BC V6E 1G2
Moderate; MC, V;
no checks

Here's an alternative to the big expensive hotels: a quasi-Victorian home nestled amid the newer and larger architecture of the last few decades. The place is bright pink, so you can't miss it. At press time, a change of ownership made us uncertain about the future of this well-established bed-and-breakfast, but for the moment Vancouverite Evan Penner seems to be handling his new business fairly smoothly. There are seven bedrooms, all with private baths, ranging in price from $84 to $120 for a double, depending on size. Most have writing tables and queen beds. Each wears a different theme: Oriental, Laura Ashley, or Old Master (in stately blues). The living room is comfortable, if its collection of furnishings is somewhat odd. Breakfast is filling enough; on one recent stay it was hot and cold cereals, quiche, and fruit.

Waterfront Centre Hotel

Across the street from
Canada Place,
(604) 691-1991; *toll-free*
in Canada
(800) 268-9411 *or in the*
U.S. (800) 828-7447

Vancouver's newest hotel (just opening as we go to press) may well become the city's finest. Although it's situated behind the Pan Pacific its pie-shaped design allows equal views of Burrard Inlet and the northshore mountains. There are 489 guest rooms and a good 75-percent of them have water views. Of the tastefully decorated standard rooms, the corner ones are the

900 Canada Place Way,
Vancouver, BC V6C 3K2
Expensive; full bar; AE,
DC, MC, V; checks OK
Breakfast, lunch, dinner
every day

unrated

best, with two walls of windows. The Royal Suite comprises two floors with views from every room (including the closet and the bathrooms with Jacuzzi). Ten rooms on the business class level open onto the terrace level, a nice feature if privacy isn't a factor. Around the corner on the terrace level is an outdoor heated pool and spa with a whirlpool and steam room. For personalized service (private check in, concierge, lounge, shoeshine, and complimentary hors d'oeurves, newspapers and continental breakfast) request the Entrée Gold floor. The hotel is well-suited to host meetings of any size (there's over 20,000-square-feet of meeting space from small boardrooms with kitchen facilities to expansive ballrooms) but at first peek it does not feel like a convention hotel. The Herons Restaurant and Lounge is on the main floor.

GREATER VANCOUVER: WEST VANCOUVER

RESTAURANTS

West Vancouver Seafood Grill
22nd and Marine,
(604) 922-3312
2168 Marine Dr,
West Vancouver
Moderate; full bar; AE,
MC, V; no checks
Dinner Tues-Sun,
brunch Sun

The former Chesa Seafood Restaurant was purchased by its former manager Gary Chalk, his wife Diana, and Gail Schmidt. The name's different, the rest is essentially the same: very reliable seafood from a warm leek salad with Belgian endive and scallops to a stir-fried spinach fettuccine with black beans, tomatoes, and a generous serving of crabmeat. Daily specials are even better: you might try a salmon fillet stuffed with scallop mousse and served on sorrel sauce. No entrée costs more than $10; only one wine on the list breaks the $20 barrier. And the warm chocolate sauce served with ice cream is addictive. At night, don't sit by the windows—the fluorescent streetlights can be annoying.

La Toque Blanche
On Marine near Keith,
(604) 926-1006
4368 Marine Dr,
West Vancouver
Moderate; full bar; AE,
MC, V; checks OK
Dinner Tues-Sun

In a small strip mall on the way to Horseshoe Bay you can find the sort of things you'd forgotten you used to love: chicken cordon bleu, pork loin en croûte, profiteroles with chocolate sauce. The veal medallions come in a creamy anise sauce, the noisettes of lamb with crushed mustard seeds and Burgundy sauce. Desserts are good too: soufflé glace pistachio with Benedictine sauce; charlotte russe with raspberry sauce and a bit of grappa hidden in the middle. The decor—mirrors and cedar—is simple (an interior designer would probably say period '70s), and the entrance is actually around the back where the cars are parked.

Salmon House on the Hill
21st St exit off Hwy 1 W,
(604) 926-3212

Every Vancouverite's favorite place to take the out-of-towners (the location, high on a hill in West Vancouver, offers a superb panoramic view of the downtown

2229 Folkestone Way,
West Vancouver
Moderate; full bar; AE,
MC, V; no checks
Lunch, dinner every day,
brunch Sun

skyline) has a menu with a not-too-exclusive emphasis on the West Coast Indian theme. Salmon, barbecued over green alder wood to infuse it with a delicate smokey flavor, remains the house specialty (and deservedly so), but other items, such as the West Coast shrimp and salmon wontons and the Alaska black cod, are worth investigating.

LODGINGS

The Park Royal Hotel
6th and Clyde,
(604) 926-5511
540 Clyde Ave, West
Vancouver, BC V7T 2J7
Expensive; AE, DC, MC,
V; checks OK

Every city should have a hotel like this one (only 10 minutes from downtown): 30 spacious units surrounded by a couple of acres of lovely gardens and a walking path along the Capilano River. There's more: a rollicking English pub in the basement, a fine dining room, and a garden lounge (The Terrace) with gazebo for drinks and lunch. It's tough to get a reservation here. If you do make it, ask for one of the 11 ivy-clad riverside rooms, overlooking the gardens and the river (even though reservations in these rooms cannot be guaranteed); rooms facing the parking lot are somewhat noisy. Prices range from $105 to $225 for a double and include a morning newspaper and tea and coffee with your wake-up call. A note of caution to light sleepers: the pub tends to be quite noisy into the night. The Tudor Room serves continental fare, and host Mario Corsi will take good care of you.

GREATER VANCOUVER: NORTH VANCOUVER

RESTAURANTS

Cafe Norte
In the Edgemont Village,
(604) 255-1188
3108 Edgemont Blvd,
North Vancouver
Moderate; full bar; MC,
V; no checks
Lunch Mon-Sat, dinner
every day

Cafe Norte is cheerfully loud, with tables squeezed together around the central fireplace. You can get enchiladas, fajitas, and burritos, of course, but the imaginative Mexican menu includes San Pedro pizza, smoked turkey quesadillas, and blue-corn tortillas filled with spinach. Daily specials are even more out of the ordinary. The black beans served with the entrées, or in a smokey chipotle chile dip, are as rich as chocolate and, because they're made without lard, less heavy than refried beans. Pint-sized tacos, pizzas, and hot dogs are available for "little amigos." The Mexican curios will keep your eyes diverted during what is usually a bit of a wait for your food. There's a patio outside.

Cafe Roma
Semisch and Esplanade,
(604) 984-0274
60 Semisch St, North
Vancouver

Owner Antonio Corsi (also of the Park Royal Hotel and Corsi Trattoria) has rejected trendiness to create a big, casual, family sort of place with food that a real Italian can recognize. A very good focaccia bread appears at your elbow while you contemplate the menu, which has been shortened recently and changed frequently. Some

Moderate; full bar; AE, DC, MC, V; no checks Lunch Mon-Fri, dinner every day

of the pasta dishes, like the ultraspicy spaghetti trasteverini (with a sauce of minced chicken, black beans, garlic, and pepperoncini) are rarely seen outside the old country. There are several choices of Italian designer pizza, as well as many nicely prepared fish and meat dishes. A light meal? Opt for the halibut cooked on a slate with fresh herbs and olive oil. In a quandary? Eight ˙tasting menus allow you to sample several pastas, pizzas, or entrées. The deck is choice in summer, with its wide-open view south across Burrard Inlet to Vancouver.

Corsi Trattoria

Across from the Lonsdale Market, (604) 987-9910 1 Lonsdale St, North Vancouver Moderate; full bar; AE, DC, MC, V; no checks Lunch Mon-Fri, dinner every day

Mario Corsi, owner of the Park Royal Hotel and restaurant, and his brother have owned this trattoria at the bottom of Lonsdale Avenue since before there was even a thought of the sea-bus terminal and the Lonsdale Quay Public Market (now just blocks away). Their family ran a trattoria in Italy, so they know what it's all about. The 20-odd pastas are all homemade, with the specialty being *rotolo*: tubes of pasta stuffed with veal, spinach, and ricotta and topped with cream and tomato sauces. Another good choice is the *trenette al salmone affumicata* (pasta with smoked salmon, cream, olives, and tomatoes). Adventurous eaters might try the Roman food orgy (for a minimum of two big appetites): four pastas, mixed salad, a platter of lamb, veal, and prawns, coffee, and dessert. Those who can't resist a challenge should take on the spaghetti trasteverini (labeled "for Italians only"), loaded with garlic, hot peppers, chicken, black beans, and olive oil. It's good, but prepare to be a social outcast for the rest of the week.

La Cucina Italiana

Marine Dr and McGowan, (604) 986-1334 1509 Marine Dr, North Vancouver Moderate; full bar; AE, MC, V; no checks Dinner Mon-Sat

La Cucina is a contemplative Italian restaurant, stuck rather incongruously in the middle of North Vancouver's strip of car dealerships and video shops. The little white stucco building looks as though it might dispense Greek fast food, but inside, it's pretty and elegant, with Italian opera playing at exactly the right volume. When it's available, try bresaola—air-dried beef imported from Switzerland—as an appetizer, or the cold antipasto. Pastas range from traditional spaghetti with tomato and meat sauce to fettuccine with squid and sweet red peppers. Fish specials are usually good; or try pollo alla diavola, a grilled chicken breast with black-pepper-crusted skin. Don't leave without sampling the homemade ice cream.

The Tomahawk

Marine Dr and Philip, (604) 988-2612 1550 Philip Ave, North Vancouver

Part museum of Indian kitsch, part tourist trap, and part restaurant, the Tomahawk, now in its 65th year, must be the original inspiration for all those hokey, totem-pole theme restaurants on highway intersections across North America. In Vancouver, it's an institution, deservedly famous for its hungry-man-sized meals.

Inexpensive; no alcohol;
AE, MC, V; no checks
Breakfast, lunch, dinner
every day

The Yukon Breakfast, for instance, gives you five slices of Yukon-style bacon, two eggs, hash browns, and toast for $6.50. At lunch there are several hamburger platters (named after Indian chiefs), sandwiches, fried chicken, fish 'n' chips, and even oysters on toast to choose from. The pies (lemon meringue, Dutch apple, banana cream) are homemade on the premises, and they will even wrap one up in a box to go. For children there is a special breakfast menu for braves and princesses.

GREATER VANCOUVER: RICHMOND
RESTAURANTS

Maple Garden Restaurant
North of Richmond on
Garden City Rd,
(604) 278-2323
135-4751 Garden City,
Richmond
Moderate; full bar; AE,
MC, V; no checks
Lunch, dinner every day

The suburb of Richmond, east of the Vancouver International Airport, is fast becoming the hub of Chinese culinary activities. Maple Garden offers the ubiquitous postmodern decor of gleaming brass and marble, well-appointed VIP dining rooms, and banks of live seafood tanks, much like any upscale downtown dining room, but the service is less haughty (and quite attentive). On a recent visit our feast included sweet prawns dipped in fresh light soy with chile, and crab baked in a hot pot with ginger and scallions, served over cellophane noodles. Maple Garden is also one of Vancouver's favored dim sum restaurants, and the demand is such that freshness is never a concern. Try their shark's fin soup dumpling, which is possibly the best around, rich and slightly smokey from the unusual addition of Chinese sausage. Be sure to finish off with a bowl of warm, silky-soft bean curd served from a traditional wooden bucket—a sweet revelation.

Sun Sui Wah
Seafood Restaurant
In Alderbridge Plaza,
(604) 273-8208
4940 No 3 Rd, Richmond
Moderate; full bar; MC,
V; no checks
Lunch, dinner every day

After opening a test restaurant on Main Street, this Hong Kong restaurant chain's research team decided they were in friendly waters and went ahead with their 400-seat expansion in the demographically fertile market of Richmond. The new restaurant is full most nights of the week, and its food has a proven track record. Simon Chan and his chefs have brought with them specialties and preparations that are tried and true and ordered: crisp, tender roasted squab, deftly steamed scallops on silky bean curd topped with creamy-crunchy tobikko (flying fish roe) sauce, and steamed rock cod slices interweaved with paper-thin slices of ham and fleshy mushrooms and presented on a fresh lotus leaf. Their mastery of contrast is also demonstrated in their ingenious execution of a platter of deep-fried "milk"—fragrant, sweet coconut contained in a fluffy crust. With only a few minor lapses in service, their success is richly deserved.

Carrianna Restaurant
*Garden City Rd and
Alexandra Rd,
(604) 270-8233
8511 Alexandra Rd,
Richmond
Moderate; full bar; AE,
MC, V; no checks
Lunch, dinner every day*

The Lower Mainland's best answer for a genuine Chiu Chow restaurant boasts VIP rooms and all the amenities that seem necessary to attract today's Chinese gastronome. True to the tradition of the Chiu Chow region in China, every meal is preceded and concluded with the ritualistic offering of thimble-sized cups of Kung Fu tea. At lunch, a small menu of à la carte dim sum selections is offered, from dumplings filled with pork, shrimp, bamboo shoots, and peanuts to mouthwatering fried dumplings with garlic chives and shrimp—both are widely imitated, but we've found none better. Other unique items include the fragrant classic double-boiled soup made from fresh duck and dried lemons, and a whole steamed salmon on a heated platter bathed in stock and heaped with fresh ginger, cilantro, and scallions. Service is friendly and attentive. Given time, one of Richmond's newest restaurants may soon become one of Vancouver's finest.

Steveston Seafood House
*Corner of Moncton and
No 1 Rd, (604) 271-5252
3951 Moncton St,
Richmond
Moderate; full bar; AE,
MC, V; local checks only
Dinner every day*

Appropriately located near the Fraser River and the fishing docks, the Steveston Seafood House continues to earn its reputation as "that great little seafood place in Richmond." The decor is funky-rec-room, with a nautical motif featuring overhead nets, glass floats, and those corny little made-from-seashells knickknacks. Simply prepared and generously served on large fish-shaped plates, the seafood delivers all it promises. You are safe with any of the house specialties—even ones with names like Jonathan Livingston Seafood (a mixed seafood platter)—but we have been most pleased with the simple dishes like the moist, meaty pan-fried halibut with lemon butter. It isn't cheap, but on a nice day it's worth the 30-minute drive from Vancouver.

LODGINGS

Delta River Inn
*On Cessna Dr before
airport, (604) 278-1241,
toll-free (800) 268-1133
in Canada,
(800) 877-1133 in US
3500 Cessna Dr,
Richmond, BC V7B 1C7
Expensive; AE, DC, MC,
V; checks OK*

This big (416 units) hotel is near the airport, but you can get a room overlooking the Fraser River and a small marina if you'd rather not gaze at jets. Prices range from $130 to $150; rooms are comfortable and spacious. The 10-story hotel has plenty of facilities: a nearby jogging trail, a sauna, and summer barbecues for lunch around the pool. In its main dining room, the Pier, chef Ron Gibbs serves up French cuisine.

GREATER VANCOUVER: LADNER
RESTAURANTS

La Belle Auberge
Corner of 48A and 48th,
(604) 946-7717
4856 48th Ave, Ladner
Expensive; full bar; AE,
MC, V; no checks
Dinner every day

If this were Europe and not Canada, every afternoon would see the parking lot filled with Mercedes Benzes and Peugeots that had brought their owners out from the big city for a long, leisurely lunch in the country. Here in North America, though, we don't like to be too far from our office towers during the day, so La Belle Auberge is open only for dinner; and only on the weekends does it really draw the Vancouver crowd. Locating his restaurant in an old, shuttered Victorian manse in Ladner, owner Bruno Marti seeks to preserve and enshrine the cuisine of the traditional French school. Marti (who became well known to Vancouverites as a member of the gold medal–winning team at the '84 Culinary Olympics) is the chef, and his wife oversees the operation of the dining room. You'll find the menu predictable—rack of lamb, milk-fed veal, and some game dishes—but superb. The duckling in blueberry sauce is, deservedly, his most popular dish. It's a nice stop on the way to the Tsawwassen ferry, but allow enough time to relax and enjoy.

Uncle Herbert's
Fish & Chip Shop
Next to Delta Museum at
Delta and Bridge,
(604) 946-8222
4866 Delta St, Ladner
Inexpensive; beer and
wine; MC, V;
no checks
Lunch Tues-Sat, dinner
Tues-Sun

This British-style fish 'n' chips house was resurrected after a fire a few years ago. Good thing too; most of them in this country are long on photographs of the royals but short on the necessities: fresh potatoes and super-fresh fish. At the new Uncle Herbert's, owner Ken Mertens has crafted an old English village-street atmosphere, with differently styled rooms lining either side of a main "avenue." The walls in one room are covered with tea-towels from every English town big enough to print one, and the Royal Green Room is stocked with royal memorabilia dating back to George V. But the fish (lingcod or halibut) and chips are top quality, and no older than yesterday. The roster of pub food includes English pork pies, Scotch eggs, sausage rolls, New England clam chowder, and Yorkshire fishcakes (two slices of large potato with fish between them, like a sandwich, battered and deep-fried). Ken imports as many English beers as he can get.

GREATER VANCOUVER: NEW WESTMINSTER
RESTAURANTS

Boua Thai Restaurant
Kingsway at Salisbury,
(604) 526-3712
7090 Kingsway,

Boua Thai is a small, family-run Thai restaurant out on the far reaches of Kingsway. The window treatment still speaks loudly of its former incarnation as a Greek taverna, but portraits of the Thai royal family now

New Westminster
Moderate; full bar; AE,
MC, V; no checks
Lunch Sun-Fri, dinner
every day

preside over the dining room, which is decorated with Thai artifacts such as an electric incense burner. The attraction here is fresh and authentic Thai food: *yum pla mugh* (squid salad), or *gang panang nuea*, a beef curry cooked in coconut milk with roasted chile-pepper paste, lemon grass, coriander root, Kaffir lime, garlic and shallots. So far, the only disappointment is a dish called "vegetables in chili paste"—an undistinguished stir-fry sporting tired bits of canned baby corn.

GREATER VANCOUVER: GRANVILLE ISLAND
RESTAURANTS

Bridges Seafood Restaurant
Across from Granville
Island Market,
(604) 687-4400
1696 Duranleau St,
Vancouver
Moderate; full bar; AE,
MC, V; checks OK
Lunch, dinner every day,
brunch Sun

On a warm sunny afternoon or a sultry summer evening, the most popular grazing spot in the city is at Granville Island on Bridges' outdoor deck. If the fare here were downright bad, it wouldn't matter much; the star of the show is not food but downtown Vancouver, its glittering towers making an irresistible light show across the waters of False Creek. The Burrard and Granville bridges dominate the view (hence the name), and fresh yields from the market just across the street dominate the menu. There are four places to eat here: the deck; the pub for drinks and appetizers; the bistro for light informal meals (where flavors are not very subtle); and the upstairs dining room, where more ambitious offerings make up the menu.

Isadora's
On Granville
Island, (604) 681-8816
1540 Old Bridge St,
Vancouver
Inexpensive; full bar;
MC, V; no checks
Breakfast, lunch, dinner
every day, brunch
Sat-Sun

Parents with young kids bless Isadora's on Granville Island for its children's menu (clown-faced pizzas and grilled cheese with potato chips), its in-house play area, and its tables next to the outdoor water park in the summer. Isadora's wholesome menu also features more grown-up items such as smoked salmon, stuffed croissants, salads, burgers, and plenty of choices for vegetarians. Open at 7am weekdays for early-morning business meetings over good coffee, Isadora's is busiest at Sunday brunch. Service is generally slow.

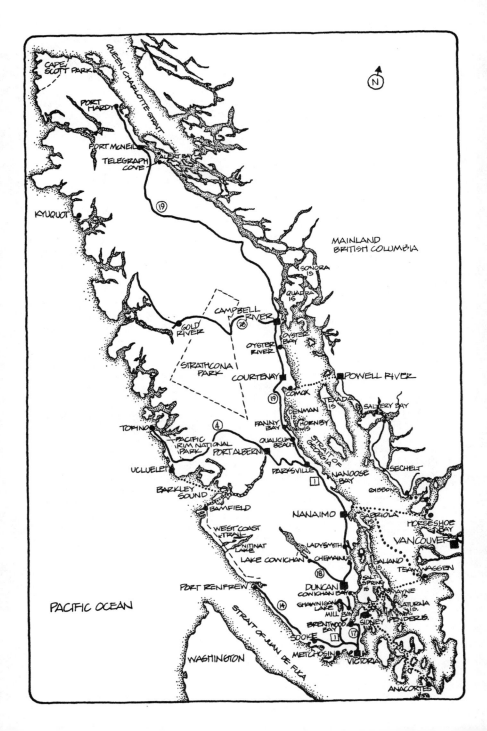

VANCOUVER ISLAND

From Victoria and environs—westward to Sooke, northward to Sidney—up-island along the east coast to Parksville. From there a short jog inland to Port Alberni (and access to west coast towns); then back to Qualicum Beach and north along the coast to Port Hardy. Finally, the Gulf Islands, north to south.

VICTORIA

Romantic as Victoria may be, with its delightful natural harbor and the Olympic Mountains of Washington State on the horizon, the provincial capital of British Columbia is less a museum piece nowadays than it is a tourist mecca. Visitors pour in to gawk at huge sculptured gardens and London-style double-decker buses, to shop for Irish linens and Harris tweeds, sip afternoon tea and soak up what they believe is the last light of British imperialism to set on the Western hemisphere. Raves in the travel press have brought a new crop of younger residents to upset Victoria's reputation as a peaceful but dull sanctuary for retiring civil servants from eastern Canada. The quality and variety of restaurants is improving as a result, and no longer are Victoria's streets silent after 10pm.

Getting There. Ferries: The last direct car ferry service from Seattle was discontinued in November of 1990; however, the passenger-only **Victoria Clipper**, a jet-propelled catamaran, makes its 2½-hour voyages up and back thrice daily, all year round ($79 round trip). The good seats on the upper deck by windows go quickly, so board early; (604) 382-8100 or (206)448-5000. Other ferry services **from Washington** to the Victoria area leave from Anacortes (destination Sidney, 27 kilometers north of Victoria), one of the most scenic routes in the Pacific Northwest; (206) 464-6400 or (604) 381-1551, $31.25 round trip in summer or $26.05 in winter; and from Port Angeles (via the privately run Black Ball ferry), a 1½-hour voyage (year-round) on which cars are allowed but for which no reservations are taken (call a day in advance to find out how long the wait will be); (206) 457-4491 or (604) 386-2202, $48 round trip car and driver. Ferries **from British Columbia** depart from Tsawwassen (destination Swartz Bay, 32 kilometers north of Victoria) every hour from 7am to 10pm in summer, following a scenic route through the Gulf Islands; $48 round trip car and driver; call BC Ferries at (604) 386-3431.

Air transportation. Seaplane. The fastest link from Seattle (Lake Union) to Victoria (Inner Harbour), is provided several times daily for about $120 round trip on Lake Union Air, toll-free (800) 826-1890. You can also fly from Vancouver via Air BC (604) 688-5515 or Helijet Airways (604) 273-1414.

Attractions. First stop should be Tourism Victoria, a well-staffed office dispensing useful information on the sights, 812 Wharf Street, (604) 382-2127. The **Royal British Columbia Museum** is one of the finest of its kind in the country, offering dramatic dioramas of natural BC landscapes and full-scale reconstructions of Victorian storefronts. Of particular interest is the Northwest Coast Indian exhibit, rich with spiritual and cultural artifacts. Open every day, Belleville and Government, (604) 387-3701. The **Art Gallery of Greater Victoria** houses one of the world's finest collections of Oriental art (including the only Shinto shrine in North

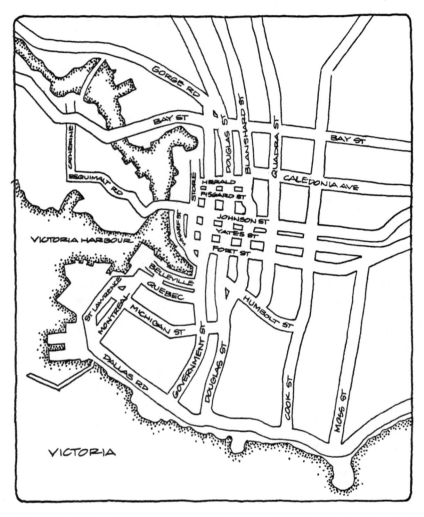

America), with special historical and contemporary exhibits on display throughout the year. Open every day, 1040 Moss Street, (604) 384-4101. **McPherson Playhouse,** a former Pantages vaudeville house done up with baroque trappings, offers evening entertainment througout the summer. The box office, (604) 386-6121, also has information about plays and concerts at the Royal Theatre and other sites. The free *Monday Magazine* offers the city's best weekly calendar of events. Spreading out over 184 acres, **Beacon Hill Park** provides splendid views of the water, but the real interest here is in the landscaping (much of it left wild) and the hand-holding couples who stroll the walkways and give retirement a good name. A lovely spot to get away from the shopping mania downtown. **Crystal Garden** is a turn-of-the-century swimming-pool building converted into a glass conservatory with a tropical theme (lush greenery, live flamingos and macaws)

and a palm terrace tea room that is preferable to its counterpart at the Empress. It's a fine place to spend a rainy day; admission is $6. Open every day, 713 Douglas Street, (604) 381-1213. Just across the street is the **Victoria Conference Centre**, linked to the Empress by a beautifully restored conservatory and accommodating 1,500 delegates. **Butchart Gardens**, 21 kilometers north, shows what can be done with dug-out limestone quarries (with help from a small army of Chinese workers). The 50 acres of gardens are beautifully manicured, lovely displays in many international styles; they're lighted after dark. Take the time to look beyond the profusion of blooms to the landscape structure and its relationship to the setting of rocky bays and tree-covered mountains. In the summer it's best to go late in the afternoon, after the busloads of tourists have left. Concerts, fireworks summer evenings, a surprisingly good afternoon tea, and light meals provide diversions. Open every day, (604) 652-5256. **Craigdarroch Castle** puts you back into an era of unfettered wealth and ostentation. Vancouver Island coal tycoon Robert Dunsmuir built this 19th-century mansion to induce a Scottish wife to live in faraway Victoria. Open every day, 1050 Joan Crescent, (604) 592-5323. **Victoria heritage homes.** You can visit five of the better restored old-Victoria homes (604) 387-4697: Helmcken House, behind Thunderbird Park, east of BC Royal Museum; Point Ellice House, at Bay Street and Pleasant Street; Craigflower Manor, 110 Island Highway; Craigflower Schoolhouse (Admirals and Gorge Road West), and Carr House, at Government and Simcoe. Admission to all four is $3.25. The **Esquimalt and Nanaimo (E&N) Railway** leaves early in the morning from a mock-Victorian station near the Johnson Street bridge and heads up-island to towns with fine resorts. The trip is slow but scenic; no food service. For an autoless vacation, take the ferry to Victoria and the train from there. Call Via Rail, (604) 383-4324 or toll-free (800) 665-0200.

Specialty Shopping. For British woolens, suits, and toiletries, the downtown area north from the Empress on Government Street is the place to shop. **George Straith Ltd** is the best of the clothing stores, and you can be measured for a suit here that will be tailored in England; **Piccadilly Shopper British Woolens** specializes in good-quality women's clothes; **W & J Wilson Clothiers** for English wool suits and women's clothes; **Sasquatch Trading Company, Ltd** offers some of the best of the Cowichan sweaters; **EA Morris Tobacconist, Ltd.** for a very proper, Victorian mix of fine pipes and tobaccos; **Campbell's British Shop**, with its unique British collectibles and imports; **Munro's** books, a monumental 19th-century bank-building-turned-bookstore, with a thoughtful selection of books; **Murchie's Teas and Coffee**, with the city's best selection of specially blended teas and coffees; and **Roger's Chocolates** and the **English Sweet Shop** for chocolates, almond brittle, blackcurrant pastilles, marzipan bars, Pontefract cakes, and more, and **Bernard Callebaut Chocolaterie** for picture-perfect chocolates in the Belgian style. Farther north, on Yates and lower Johnson streets, are the trendier shops and designer boutiques. Market Square is a restored 19th-century courtyard surrounded by a jumble of shops, restaurants, and offices on three floors. A few blocks farther on at Fisgard Street, the entrance to Victoria's small and seemingly shrinking **Chinatown** is marked by the splendid, lion-bedecked Gate of Harmonious Interest. Visit the tiny shops and studios on Fan Tan Alley and check out Morley Co. Ltd, a Chinese grocery. **Antique hunters** should head east of downtown, up Fort Street to Antique Row—block after block of shops, the best of which are The Connoisseurs Shop and David Robinson, Ltd, with excellent 18th-century English pieces. Visit **Bastion Square** for sidewalk restaurants, galleries, the Maritime Museum, the alleged location of Victoria's old gallows, and a great gardener's shop called Dig This; Trounce Alley for upscale clothing; and Windsor Court for boutiques and gifts.

RESTAURANTS

Da Tandoor Restaurant
Fort and Vancouver,
(604) 384-6333
1010 Fort St, Victoria
Inexpensive; full bar;
MC, V; no checks
Lunch Tues-Fri, dinner
Tues-Sun

Da Tandoor (no connection with Vancouver's similiarly named establishment) elevates Indian cuisine to its finest degree. A sweet roselike aroma (not an acrid incense) blends with the fragrance of clay pot–cooked foods and exotic spices. The resulting gastronomic perfume raises expectations that are not only met but surpassed. If you're in unfamiliar territory try the *murgh shorba*, a mild but flavorful chicken soup seasoned with garlic, ginger, cinnamon, cardamom, and other Indian spices, or the Tandoor Special with chicken, butter chicken, lamb curry, pulao, dal, raita, and a large flat round of nan, a leavened bread of fine flour baked on the tandoor. When your order is placed, popadums, the gossamer tortilla-sized bread made from chick-pea flour, arrive at your table. A glass of sweet (but not too) lassi, flavored with rose water, is an ideal foil for the tableful of strange and wonderful flavors.

Herald Street Caffe
Government and Herald,
1 block past Chinatown,
(604) 381-1441
546 Herald St, Victoria
Moderate; full bar; MC,
V; no checks
·Lunch Wed-Sat, dinner
every day, brunch Sun

It has the energy, noise level, and modest prices of a bistro, but it is one of Victoria's best restaurants. The Herald Street Caffe opened to waiting lines its first night; the only thing that has changed in the ensuing decade is that the food keeps getting better and the lines longer. The creative energy and talents of the three partners, Greg Hays (wine), Mark Finnigan (kitchen), and Helen Bell (desserts and bread) indicate that improvements, however subtle, will continue to be made on a daily basis. Pasta, bread, and desserts are made in-house. Our favorite dish is pasta puttanesca, especially on the days when it is made with fresh albacore tuna. But the sautéed ginger chicken (finished with double cream, rice wine, and chile flakes, and served with apple chutney and toasted sesame seeds) and the grilled lemon veal chop never fail to delight. The wine list has the best selection of West Coast wines on the Island at reasonable prices. The satisfying dessert list includes a lemon pie and an apple crumble dessert that are so popular there's been talk of a dessert-only extension. Service is tops—most of the waitstaff has been in place for five or more years. The biggest disappointment is not getting in. Dinner reservations are essential. But Herald Street keeps late hours (till midnight), and it's one of the best places in town to people-watch while having an after-concert snack and espresso.

Cecconi's Pizzeria
and Trattoria
Shelbourne and N Dairy
Rd, across from Hillside
Mall, (604) 592-0454

Victoria's first wood-oven pizzas can sometimes be a little too L.A.—smoked fresh asparagus with hollandaise sauce—but for the most part they are the best in town. Bruschetta al pomodoro is a generous serving of chewy bread rubbed with garlic and topped with

3201 Shelbourne,
Victoria
Moderate; full bar; MC,
V; no checks
Lunch Mon-Sat, dinner
every day

chopped tomatoes. The waitstaff is slightly on the cocky side of confident about its food, but in a charming way and is quick to bring a chunk of Reggiano Parmesan to grate over everything but drinks and dessert. Made-on-premises pastas are excellent, especially the *fettuccine pesto di pollo grigliata*, creamy pesto with grilled chicken, and the *rotini alla baresse*, hot Italian sausage, peppers, onions and tomatoes. Cheesecake is big in Victoria and you will find some of the best here.

Chez Daniel

Estevan and Beach, past
Sea Land,
(604) 592-7424
2524 Estevan Ave,
Victoria
Expensive; full bar, MC,
V; checks OK
Dinner Tues-Sat (Mon-
Sat in summer)

In a city overpopulated with mediocre French restaurants, this small exception, tucked a long way off the tourist track in Oak Bay, stands out. It's been around a long time, and quality here has a reputation for being consistently high, thanks to the attention of chef Daniel Rigollet. Rumor has it that Rigollet is not always in the kitchen, but we've yet to miss him. The decor is pleasant, and the food and the thoughtful wine list need no improvement. The expensive menu, though conservative-French in approach, is wide-ranging in flavor: salmon in vermouth and cream sauce, fresh young rabbit, New York steak with peppercorns, duck in a fine chestnut sauce. The food can be very rich, but the accompaniment of crisply cooked vegetables is a good antidote. A few nouvelle touches find their way into some presentations: tender pieces of lamb cooked just enough, sauced in reduced cream, and finished with shreds of fresh ginger, and chicken breast wrapped around fresh thyme, quickly roasted and served with pan juices. Service ranges from understandably slow (this type of food takes a while to prepare) to condescending. Plan to make an evening of it.

La Petite Colombe

Off Government, 2 blocks
north of the Empress
Hotel, (604) 383-3234
604 Broughton, Victoria
Moderate; full bar; AE,
DC, MC, V; no checks
Dinner Mon-Sat

The menu is simple and French. Our favorites are the veal crêpes and the filet of beef with green peppercorn sauce. Crab crêpes served with a zesty sauce are also popular. But the most popular entrée is tiger prawns served in a very light cream-cheese sauce lightly influenced by Triple Sec. The sorbets top our list among dessert choices. Try the pear sorbet with kiwi and strawberries, accompanied by three brilliant sauces: raspberry, apricot, and a coconut concoction with a hint of almond. The chef is Japanese and recent reports say he's a little heavy-handed with the MSG.

Metropolitan Diner

Between Herald and
Fisgard, (604) 381-1512
1715 Government St,
Victoria

A diner in name only, this is a small, stylish restaurant with an out-of-the-ordinary menu. How about a salad that combines charbroiled and shredded beef marinated in oyster sauce and tossed with lemon grass, mint, garlic, bean sprouts, and roasted sweet peppers, or a pizza with Castiollo blue cheese with sliced green apple and caramelized onion? This kind of thing can get out of

*Moderate; full bar; MC,
V; no checks
Lunch Mon-Fri, dinner
every day*

hand, but here it works. The pan-fried oysters in our Caesar salad were tender and lightly breaded, and our chilled melon, mint, and tomato soup was an unusual but delicate blend of flavors. Service is chummy if somewhat harassed, but everyone's having a good time. The Metropolitan is a great après-theater/concert place for lovers of desserts and espresso or steamed drinks.

San Remo Restaurant
*Quadra and Hillside,
(604) 384-5255
2709 Quadra, Victoria
Inexpensive; full bar;AE,
MC, V; no checks
Lunch Mon-Sat, dinner
every day*

One fourth of the menu is pizza, the rest is Greek (and we wish the menu weighed even more heavily on the Greek side). The pita bread is the best we've found, perfect for dipping tzatziki or hummus. The *saganaki,* pan-fried goat cheese flamed at your table with brandy and lemon, is an exciting dish (especially for your close-by neighbors). Flavor is great, but the texture comes off a bit rubbery. Dino's dinner platter for two ($34) gets you moussaka, lamb chops, chicken souvlaki, calamari, spinach pie, tzatziki, Greek salad, rice, and fresh veggies.

Siam
*Government and
Johnson, (604) 383-9911
1314 Government St,
Victoria
Moderate; full bar; AE,
MC, V; no checks
Lunch Mon-Sat, dinner
every day*

By far the best Asian food in town is the Thai food found here. Lemongrass, peanuts, chiles, lemons and limes season 54 menu selections that range from mild to painful, but the flavors all work and the presentations are almost too pretty to eat. Almost. Many of the menu entries indicate the style of cooking and list ingredients, then offer a choice of meats. Especially good are the Siam Curry (red curry with coconut milk, bamboo shoots, sweet basil, and choice of meats) and the Siam Delight (sautéed bamboo shoots, black mushrooms, straw mushrooms, peanuts, baby corn, chile, and your choice of meat). You might not always be understood (and sometimes you'll be misunderstood). But the waitresses try hard and that's part of the charm. Siam's interior is upscale and immaculate.

Spinnakers Brew Pub
*Travel west over the
Johnson St Bridge to
Catherine,
(604) 386-2739
308 Catherine St,
Victoria
Inexpensive; full bar,
MC, V; no checks
Breakfast, lunch, dinner
every day*

Spinnakers has everything a decent pub should have: excellent cottage-brewed draft ales; a cheerful, noisy atmosphere; a great waterfront view; friendly staff; a dart board; hearty, casual food; and no minors. Although a recent expansion alleviated some of the crowding problem, it's good to come early. A restaurant seating 125 replaced the pub on the ground floor and a new pub that seats 65 (at half the decibels) was installed on the second floor. Cod and salmon have joined halibut as options for fish 'n' chips. Burgers, pot pies, and the Mt. Tolmie Dark beer are exemplary. The bartender's job seems to be to educate drinkers on the local microbrews as much as to serve them, especially when you ask for a taste of each.

Szechuan

Across from the Memorial
Arena parking lot,
(604) 384-5651
853 Caledonia Ave,
Victoria
Moderate; full bar, AE,
MC, V; no checks
Lunch, dinner Tues-Sun

Joseph Wong turns out some excellent dishes, particularly if you let him know in advance that you like spicy food. Try the Pon Pon chicken as an appetizer—a tender chicken breast with thick sesame sauce. For the main course we recommend the very crisp whole rock cod, served with hot bean, sweet-and-sour, or fermented rice sauce, or the spicy chicken with a hot garlic-soy sauce, mandarin pork, and shrimp. Decor is generic Chinese restaurant. Service is lightning-fast (and a good thing, since Szechuan is located right across from the Memorial Arena). But even if there's no hockey game or rock concert, it's best to order in relays; otherwise, the dishes won't come in any particular sequence.

Yoshi Sushi

In Gateway Village Mall
just outside of town on
Hwy 17, (604) 383-6900
601 Vernon Ave, Victoria
Moderate; full bar; AE,
MC, V; no checks
Lunch Mon-Sat, dinner
every day

Yoshi makes sushi. Whether you sit at the sushi bar, at the robata bar, or in one of the 12 tatami rooms, you'll get consistently excellent service and very fresh traditional Japanese food. The shabu shabu (sliced beef and vegetables in a delicate broth) is a good alternative to sushi. All of the entrées (including tempura, teriyaki, sukiyaki) are preceded by miso soup, sunomono, and an appetizer of yakitori or sushi.

Barb's Place

At Fisherman's Wharf,
(604) 384-6515
310 St Lawrence St,
Victoria
Inexpensive; no alcohol;
no credit cards; no checks
Breakfast, lunch, dinner
every day

You can't top Barb's atmosphere: the fishing fleet bobs nearby as you sit at open-air picnic tables eating your fish 'n' chips out of a greasy piece of newspaper. The fish is fine, tender halibut encased in crisp batter, and the chips are fried with the skins on. Help yourself to vinegar and ketchup from large vats on the counter.

Blethering Place

Oak Bay and Monterey,
(604) 598-1413
2250 Oak Bay, Victoria
Inexpensive; beer and
wine; AE, MC, V; local
checks only
Breakfast, lunch, dinner,
tea every day

"Blethering" is Scottish for voluble, senseless talking. What could be bordering on too precious works well here, and kids love it. This is the closest thing to a proper tea we've found in Victoria. It's a good place to settle in for a pot of tea, Devonshire cream and scones, and a bit of conversation. Afternoon tea can be ordered as a package for $6.95 or item by item. Breakfast, lunch, and dinner all run together; breakfast is served until 4pm, the "day" menu is served until 4:30, and dinner comes along about that time. Farmhouse English food is excellent, most of it fitting into the "comfort food" category. Owner Ken Agate also owns the

Teddy Bear's Picnic next door. Minimum purchases in Blethering Place will qualify one for a Bear discount.

Camille's
Fort and Langley in Bastion Square,
(604) 381-3433
45 Bastion Square, Victoria
Moderate; full bar; MC, V; no checks
Dinner Tues-Sat

The basement location has a sunny garden that adds an unexpected warmth. Cuisine, self-described as "West Coast," takes advantage of fresh local produce, rabbit, and lamb. For starters, the salmon cakes with pineapple-ginger coulis were a hit, but the drunken chicken, an anglicized sushi roll, wasn't. There's a succulent prawn and papaya brochette and a vegetarian red pepper curry. This new place has yet to hit its stride (some of the dishes can be too dry), but there is a lot of potential here.

Chez Pierre
Yates and Wharf,
(604) 388-7711
512 Yates St, Victoria
Moderate; full bar; AE, MC, V; no checks
Dinner Mon-Sat

Jean-Pierre Mercier has been operating this small, rustic downtown restaurant long enough to render it the oldest French restaurant in Victoria. To a standard menu of French classics—tournedos, veal in cream and mushroom sauce, duck à l'orange, rack of lamb—chef Gilbert Leclair has added fresh seafood, including mussels and scallops on the half shell served with a cream and white wine sauce, a wonderful dish. Tourists pack the place—so reservations are necessary.

Demitasse
Corner of Blanshard and Johnson, (604) 386-4442
1320 Blanshard St, Victoria
Inexpensive; no alcohol; MC; no checks
Breakfast, lunch, dinner every day

Finding an excellent cup of espresso in Victoria, the land of tea, is a spiritual experience for those used to jump-starting their day with a caffeine hit. So, it's no wonder that since it opened in 1981, Demitasse, with its good selection of coffees (by the cup and by the bag), has become a favorite haunt of the committed local caffeine-and-croissant set. Lunch is popular, with homemade soup (try the borscht), thick sandwiches, and excellent desserts, but the real Demitasse fan comes for breakfast. Don't miss the hot almond croissant; or try a plain one filled with steam-scrambled eggs with cheese. For spare change you can add such goodies as avocado, artichoke hearts, and smoked sausage. Pleasant service and quiet, tasteful decor make this tiny coffee shop a winner.

Futaba
Quadra and Pandora,
(604) 381-6141
1420 Quadra St, Victoria
Moderate; full bar, MC, V; no checks
Lunch Mon-Fri, dinner every day

A curious sort of Japanese restaurant without tatami rooms or kimono-clad waitresses, the recently relocated Futaba is nevertheless a good place to try some Japanese dishes that you won't find anywhere else in Victoria. The appetizers are the most interesting and varied selections, as the sushi bar is only okay. We constructed a satisfying meal of herb- and garlic-flavored vegetarian dumplings, deep-fried tofu with sesame sauce, and teriyaki salmon. Futaba serves only brown rice. In fact, the whole menu has a distinctly vegetarian, health-food tone.

Jag's

Across from Hudson's
Bay Company,
(604) 388-5247
1724 Douglas, Victoria
Moderate; full bar; MC,
V; checks OK
Lunch Tues-Fri, dinner
Tues-Sat

This is a beautiful restaurant in the wrong place. It has a great kitchen, but it is too far from the harbor for foot traffic, and the no-parking block it sits on presents imagined rather then real access problems. Nevertheless, this new place deserves much more patronage than it has received to date. Once you're inside, the natural light from the skylight, the mauve, royal blue, and teal color scheme, fresh flowers, and light jazz work their magic. Although the menu is limited, the food is up to the environment: a sobering tomato soup with a splash of gin and basil cream, ravioli stuffed with fresh spinach and ricotta with a creamy pesto. For dinner, the basil-crusted veal steak with port jus is worth a return trip.

Six Mile Pub

Colwood exit off Island
Hwy, (604) 478-3121
494 Island Hwy, Victoria
Inexpensive; full bar;
MC, V; no checks
Lunch, dinner every day

This jolly pub-restaurant at the Sooke turnoff boasts the longest-established liquor license in British Columbia and a fiercely loyal clientele that continues to crowd the place. It has a dark, smoky Tudor interior, so we like it best on a sunny day when you can select a courtyard table under a patio umbrella. You stand in line to order your delicious beer accompaniments from a takeout window: garlicky Caesar salad with big homemade croutons; mammoth savory roast beef sandwiches au jus served on slabs of fresh French bread; and rich French onion soup. Lots of international beers.

John's Place

Douglas and Pandora,
(604) 389-0711
723 Pandora Ave,
Victoria

It's clear that breakfast is serious business at John's. Okay, so maybe this little place is a bit chi-chi, a tad too "in" for everybody's taste. It still serves up some of the fluffiest Belgian waffles in town (more than 160,000 in the last eight years) and innovative omelets (try a lamb, feta cheese, and mushroom combination) that are accompanied by satisfyingly thick wedges of potato. Lunch has its attractions too: lots of real food (good burgers, huevos rancheros, and pies) in real portions. Desserts are mammoth. A smoky place even in the nonsmoking section.

Pagliacci's

Between Fort and
Broughton on Broad near
Eaton Centre,
(604) 386-1662
1011 Broad St,
Victoria
Moderate; full bar; MC,
V; checks OK
Lunch Mon-Sat, dinner
every day, brunch Sun

Owner Howie Siegel is a mile-a-minute talker and first-rate eccentric who drifted into Victoria a few years ago from New York via Los Angeles and Lasqueti Island. He bought the old Red Swing tearoom, turned it into a Jewish-flavored Italian restaurant, and quickly created what has become a popular Victoria institution. Howie is a movie buff who names his fresh, hearty salads after such mediagenic types as Veronica Lake, and saddles entrées with punny monikers like "Last Chicken in Paris." Photos of Hollywood stars and wannabes decorate the strange orange walls, with big-band hits casting a vague presence over the din of chatter in this small establishment. Service can be slow, and the food is modest (chicken Marsala tossed with tri-colored fettuccine) but reasonably priced. An already crowded restaurant is packed even tighter when some tables are pushed together to make room for live music. Go for the Sunday brunch and you might meet the whole Siegel family, including Howie's own Jewish mama.

The Re-bar
On Johnson between Wharf and Government,
(604) 361-9223
549 Johnson St, Victoria
Inexpensive; no alcohol;
no cards; local checks only
Breakfast, lunch, dinner
Mon-Sat (closes at 6pm)

Victoria's counterpart to Seattle's techy and trendy Gravity Bar, The Re-bar caters to an allegedly health-conscious crowd that's big on almond burgers and bee pollen. Fortunately, most of what you'll find on the photocopied menu is tasty and filling enough to make you forget that you're sitting in a room decorated with corrugated metal walls. Especially good and spicy are the bean and cheese enchiladas, served with multi-vegetable and sprout salad. Also worth ordering is the cream of asparagus soup, which comes with homemade-tasting corn muffins. The shots of wheat-grass juice, a thick green liquid that's squeezed from young shoots raised on the premises, are supposed to cure a plethora of digestive ills.

Soho Village Bistro
Gladstone and Fernwood,
(604) 384-3344
1311 Gladstone, Victoria
Inexpensive; full bar;
MC, V; no checks
Dinner every day

This is the late-night eatery for the mobile crowd: it's five minutes from downtown by car. You won't find burgers and fries. What you will find is falafel, souvlaki, and the Haight Ash-Burger—a light patty of tofu, almonds, pumpkin seeds, and Asian spices. Turn on, tune in, and drop $6.95. Steaks come with basmati rice or baked potato; the most expensive one costs about $13. The energy here is measured in megawatts. Now if they would just find some parking nearby.

LODGINGS

Abigail's
Vancouver and McClure,
(604) 388-5363
906 McClure St, Victoria,
BC V8V 3E7
Expensive; MC, V;
checks OK

The feminine counterpart of the Edwardian Beaconsfield, just two blocks away, the Tudor Abigail's is all gables and gardens and crystal chandeliers, with three floors of odd-shaped rooms, each with a shiny-tiled bathroom. Not a lavish detail is missed: guest rooms are decorated in restrained tones (rose, peach, periwinkle, mint); crystal goblets sit in each room; the halls smell faintly of good coffee and beautiful women. Practicalities, too, are all well in place—there are electrical outlets wherever you might need them, a light shines in the shower, the walls are well soundproofed (light sleepers, however, may want to request a room as far from noisy Quadra Street as possible). In short, Abigail's combines the beauty of the Old World with the comforts of the New. Third-floor guest rooms are grandest: the Foxglove Room has a canopy bed, and a few of the bathrooms are equipped with Jacuzzis. Breakfast is served from 8am to 9:30am in the sunny downstairs dining room. The sitting room is inviting in the sort of way that makes one want to linger, with a glass of port and a hand of whist, after a day of traipsing about Victoria.

The Beaconsfield

Vancouver and Humboldt,
(604) 384-4044
998 Humboldt St,
Victoria, BC V8V 2Z8
Expensive; MC, V;
checks OK

Of all the imitation England spots, this is the best. The Beaconsfield opened its Edwardian gates in 1984 and since then has quietly and capably assumed its place at the forefront of Victoria's accommodations. Tree-lined Humboldt Street is closer to the hub of downtown than its quiet demeanor would suggest, so the Beaconsfield's location here just a block and a half from Beacon Park is prime. It's meant to convey a sense of romance and hideaway and does, with 12 antique-filled bedrooms, all with private baths and down comforters. The Attic Room occupies the entire top floor, features its own Jacuzzi and wet bar, and is exceedingly private. Lillie's Room is a little more feminine, with inlaid mahogany pieces and an unusual wood-enclosed period bathtub. The antiques are offset by rediscovered "modernities" such as steam-heated towel racks. Public areas are elegantly crafted, with so much dark, gleaming mahogany that one can feel a bit cloistered on a sunny day, but this is easily remedied in the sun room/conservatory. The place is so popular for breakfast that you sign up for your morning meal when you check in.

Holland House Inn

2 blocks behind the
Parliament buildings, at
Government and
Michigan,
(604) 384-6644
595 Michigan St,
Victoria, BC V8V 1S7
Expensive; AE, DC, MC,
V; checks OK

The house is a modern beauty (just the antidote to the endless Olde England theme so prevalent in Victoria), decked with rose trellises and a picket fence outside, skylights and stark white walls inside. Fine art and sculpture, many of the pieces by owner Lance Olsen, fill the 10 sparkling guest rooms. The result is startlingly chic and about as avant-garde as you're likely to find in Quaintville. The Lilac Room has an intriguing Art Deco–inspired headboard. Rooms 20 and 30 have fireplaces, the former with a unique lace-draped bed. All of the rooms have immaculate private baths (the fixtures in room 11 are equipped for wheelchair access); all but one of the rooms have their own balconies or patios. This is consistent with the inn's other orientation, a healthy one: Olsen's wife, Robin Birsner, is an occupational therapist. No smoking in the rooms, natch. Owners and the managers are always at the ready with hospitality, but the service is never fawning. A full breakfast can be had anywhere from the Gallery to your balcony. Most of the art is for sale.

Laurel Point Inn

On the west side of Inner
Harbour, (604) 386-8721
680 Montreal St,

A massive brick-and-glass ziggurat addition now overlooks the harbor; inside there's a subtle Oriental touch. The angular construction of the lodge means that all of the rooms have good views of the harbor or the ship channel. Rooms on each floor can be connected to form two-room suites, a particularly nice touch if you are

Victoria, BC V8V 1Z8
Expensive; AE, MC, V;
no checks

traveling with children. A standard now runs about $125. Junior suites, $195, make up most of the new pyramid-shaped addition. These spacious rooms have the niftiest bathrooms—floors and walls entirely of marble and extremely comfortable bathtubs. A separate shower graces each of the new rooms. The channel-side rooms offer the best view of the comings and goings of boats and seaplanes and the Japanese garden at channel's edge, completed in 1991. The dining room is a wicker-and-fern place called Cafe Laurel with better-than-adequate food. Sunday brunch is the best in town. Underground parking is adjacent to the hotel. Reservations are tough to make, and the front desk and bell staff are poorly trained or nonexistent. When these areas are given the same degree of attention that the rest of the hotel has received, Laurel Point Inn will be as close to perfect as you will find in the city.

The Prior House

St Charles and Rockland,
(604) 592-8847
620 St Charles, Victoria,
BC V8S 3N7
Expensive; MC, V;
checks OK

No imitation here: this grand, tranquil B&B occupies an English mansion built during the Edwardian period for the King's representative in British Columbia. It is in a quiet neighborhood about 1½ miles from downtown. Four of the five rooms have fireplaces and views of water, and all rooms have private baths. The Lieutenant Governor's suite, with a luxurious Jacuzzi bath, gold fixtures, crystal chandeliers, and a view of the strait and the Olympic Range, is $190. The newly finished Windsor Room, the only room without a fireplace, occupies the entire top floor and rents for $150. Innkeeper Candis Cooperrider fixes lavish breakfasts every morning—maybe a mushroom-Gruyère omelet, cottage fries, and a baked apple. No-smoking premises. Well-behaved children welcome.

The Bedford

½ block north of Fort St,
(604) 384-6835 or toll
free (800) 665-6500
1140 Government St,
Victoria, BC V8W 1Y2
Expensive; AE, MC, V;
no checks

The liveried doorman is gone, but the carefully maintained flower boxes, thick and pillowy bed quilts, private Jacuzzis, and a dozen rooms with fireplaces are still here. In a renovation that proved frogs can still become princes, Victoria's reigning dukes of hospitality, Bill McKechnie and Stuart Lloyd (who masterminded the Beaconsfield and Abigail's), transformed what used to be downtown's shoddiest hotel, The Alhambra, into a small showcase of European elegance and then sold the place in the fall of 1988 to Heathwood Resorts Ltd. Most of the 40 rooms don't boast much of a view, and they're pricey ($135-$185 in season), but the hotel's central location—smack in the middle of the shopping district—is hard to beat. There's no room service, and afternoon tea is an extra $11.95, but a continental breakfast is included in the price.

The Haterleigh

*Take Belleville west to
Pendray until it dead
ends, (604) 384-9995
243 Kingston St, Victoria,
BC V8V 1V5
Expensive; MC, V;
checks OK*

The Haterleigh House was built in 1901 by Thomas Hooper, an architect who designed many of Victoria's Victorian homes. Owner Mary Lane Anderson went to great lengths to preserve (and in many cases, restore) the original character of the home. Fine curved, stained-glass windows grace the parlor; plaster moldings were recast from molds made from sections of existing molding. All six rooms are now complete, each with private bath. Four have large Jacuzzi whirlpool tubs. Stay on a Friday night and you'll get one night free. Vegetarian breakfasts are generous, leaning toward homemade breads and pancakes and lots of fruit.

Oak Bay Beach Hotel

*Near the corner of Oak
Bay Ave and Beach Dr,
(604) 598-4556
1175 Beach Dr, Victoria,
BC V8S 2N2
Expensive; AE, DC, MC,
V; no checks*

Presiding over the Haro Strait, this Tudor-style hotel is the loveliest—and most British—part of Anglophile Victoria, a nice place to stay if you want to be removed from downtown. Even so, it's a very busy spot—especially its bars. Yet it still evokes another world: handsome antiques dot the comfortable public rooms, and the private rooms, lavishly furnished, are full of nooks and gables. The best rooms are those with private balconies and a view of the sea, but the price runs up to about $170. Full breakfast for two is included. For a special treat, take lunch on the hotel's yacht.

The dining room is prettily done, overlooking the gardens, but isn't up to the rest of the place. Opt for the Snug—quite possibly the coziest bar in the whole city—where you can sit before the fire. For more status assurance, walk across the street and play a round at Victoria Golf Club, a Scottish-style links with windswept holes dramatically bordered by the sea. And don't forget the hotel's afternoon tea—a proper affair where you will feel more than a wee bit conspicuous dressed in jeans.

Victoria Regent Hotel

*Corner of Yates and
Wharf, (604) 386-2211
1234 Wharf St, Victoria,
BC V8W 3H9
Expensive; AE, DC, MC,
V; checks OK*

For those with a taste for very luxurious condo living, the modern Victoria Regent is a posh apartment hotel with grandstand views of the harbor from the north. Don't let the unadorned exterior put you off. Inside, huge, nicely decorated one- and two-bedroom suites range from $175 to $285 per night for two people (but double up with another couple and the price is more within reach, especially if you do your own cooking). Each apartment has a living room, dining room, deck, and kitchen, and most have two bedrooms and two bathrooms. All are furnished with quiet taste, and most have views of city and harbor. A restaurant, Alex's Place, has been recently added, and full room service is now available.

The Captain's Palace

*2 blocks west of the
Empress Hotel,
(604) 388-9191*

What was once a charming one-guest-room B&B with a mediocre restaurant is now a charming 16-guest-room B&B (in three Victorian houses) with a mediocre res-

309 Belleville St,
Victoria, BC V8V 1X2
Expensive; AE, DC, MC,
V; no checks

taurant. The B&B outgrew the original handsome 1897 mansion near the harbor and spread into the adjacent property, where the quarters are newer and decorated in florals and muted pastels. Some have balconies; all have private baths—some with cute claw-footed tubs. Early morning coffee is brought to your door before the orange-blossom-special breakfast. High season prices range from $125 to $175, the latter offering views of the water and Beacon Hill Park.

Craigmyle Guest House

1½ km up Fort St from
city center; look for the
castle, (604) 595-5411
1037 Craigdarroch Rd,
Victoria, BC V8S 2A5
Moderate; MC, V;
no checks

Built as a guest house early in the century, the Craigmyle stands next to Craigdarroch Castle (a grand, well-preserved mansion). Recently, the whole place has been recarpeted—but more important, the excellent mattresses are new too. Best rooms are those with views of the neighborhood castle. A large breakfast with homemade preserves and good coffee is served in the dining room, and the main lounge features traditional wainscoting, lofty ceilings, an enormous fireplace, and (on our visit) annoying easy-listening music. Rooms are quite reasonable ($50 for a single, $70 for a double), but you're 1½ kilometers from city center. We appreciated the quiet neighborhood.

The Empress

Between Humboldt and
Belleville,
(604) 384-8111 or toll
free (800) 828-7447 from
US; tollfree
(800) 268-9411 from
Canada
721 Government St,
Victoria, BC V8W 1W5
Expensive; AE, DC, MC,
V; checks OK

The hotel that once stood as the quiet, ivy-clad dowager of the Inner Harbour has gone through a $45 million facelift. A separate guest entrance pavilion has been added, the Palm Court and the Crystal Ballroom have been polished up, and 50 new rooms have been added, bringing the total to 470. The grounds have been landscaped, and a restored conservatory at the rear of the hotel connects it to the new Victoria Conference Centre. Unfortunately, the attitude of the place was not much improved: many of the rooms received little or no attention, and you pay a lot for the view. On our last visit, we had to endure a cold shower (as did most of the hotel), go without coffee because decaf was not served in the lobby dessert bar, and wake up at 5am due to a short in the fire alarm. The valet parking staff is unreliable. Nevertheless, the Empress is the most notable landmark in town and is worth a stroll (you might even want to take the excellent historic tour). High tea is served daily by reservation; it may be overpriced, but it's still the best value at the Empress.

Heritage House

Hwy 1 north, right on
McKenzie, left to 1100
Burnside Rd W,
(604) 479-0892
Mail: 3808 Heritage Ln,
Victoria, BC V8Z 7A7
Moderate; MC, V;
no checks

Sandra and Larry Gray have completely remodeled this 1910 beauty 5 kilometers from the center of town. The five rooms (soon to be six) have been redecorated to the original Craftsman style of the house. They're still enchanting, and the bright Garden Room, with its three walls of windows, is still a favorite. The four bathrooms are shared. Downstairs, the fireplace parlor makes a cozy place to linger; in warm weather, a wraparound porch provides ample seating for garden appreciators (the garden is splendid). Gourmet breakfasts consist of several courses, and—if you're lucky—Sandra's much-praised salmon quiche. Two-day minimum stay; no kids, pets, or smoking.

Huntingdon Manor Inn
Downtown across from the harbor,
(604) 381-3456
330 Quebec St, Victoria,
BC V8V 1W3
Expensive; AE, DC, MC, V; no checks

A comfortable antique-furnished parlor with a blazing log fireplace and an indoor whirlpool and sauna make for a pleasant stay at the Huntington. Unfortunately, it's behind the very touristy stuff near the harbor and views can be rather odd. Rooms are nicely furnished, some with four-poster beds, and the spacious two-story gallery suites have bedroom lofts. This is a full-service hotel including room service, but some rooms have full kitchen facilities. Kids under 12 stay free in their parents' suite.

The Coast Victoria (Harbourside Hotel)
Between Laurel Point and Fisherman's Wharf,
(604) 360-1211
146 Kingston St, Victoria,
BC V8V 1V4
Expensive; AE, DC, MC, V; checks OK

unrated

The Coast Victoria, which was just opening at press time, features Victoria's only indoor/outdoor pool. Rooms view the Olympic Mountains, the Strait of Juan de Fuca, and the Inner Harbour. Other features are underground parking, whirlpool, sauna, exercise and steam rooms, and a 42-slip marina. The 132 air-conditioned rooms range in price from $138 to $178. Suites come in different sizes and run $195 to $475.

SOOKE

This relatively undiscovered area, half an hour west of Victoria, offers spectacular beach scenery and seclusion. The road at Port Renfrew peters out into the famous **West Coast Trail**, one of the greatest (and most demanding) hikes in the Northwest (see Pacific Rim National Park in Ucluelet). **Botanical Beach**, just south of Port Renfrew, has exceptionally low tides in the early summer that expose miles of sealife and sculpted sandstone. The entire coast has excellent parks, with trails to the beach or into the forest and good waves for surfers.

Royal Roads Military College, on the road to Sooke, is a Dunsmuir family castle turned military college; the beautiful grounds are open to the public each day 10am-4pm; call (604) 363-4660.

East Sooke Park, a wilderness park, offers hiking trails in the forest, spectacular views, and good swimming beaches.

Sooke Region Museum mounts some interesting displays of logging and pioneer equipment, Indian artifacts, and a fully restored historic cottage showing turn-of-the-century lifestyles. The museum also sponsors BC's largest juried fine arts show, held every August in the Sooke Arena. Museum open daily; call (604) 642-6351 for more information.

Between Sooke and Port Renfrew are dozens of trails leading down to ocean beaches (Mirror Creek is a favorite), all of which offer fine beachcombing possibilities. Ask at the Sooke Region Museum for details.

Lester B. Pearson College of the Pacific, on Pedder Bay, has been open since 1974 with a two-year program to foster international understanding; the setting and the architecture are both worth seeing; call (604) 478-5591.

RESTAURANTS

Sooke Harbour House
At the very end of Whiffen Spit Rd, (604) 642-3421
1528 Whiffen Spit Rd, Sooke
Expensive; full bar; MC, V; checks OK
Dinner every day

At the end of the road in a modest Sooke neighborhood, this white clapboard farmhouse gives little indication that it is one of British Columbia's finest inns. Over the past 12 years, owners Sinclair and Frederica Philip, along with their team of four chefs, have gained national attention for their rare dedication to the freshest natural ingredients, blended with a good deal of energy and flashes of searing innovation using utterly fresh free-swimming scallops, octopus, sea urchins, whelks, and red rock crabs. Meats all come from local farmers, and gardens around the property yield some 200 varieties of herbs year-round. With such expectations, there are bound to be a few critics. Recent reports of blandness (a fennel, leek, and sea-urchin soup was flavorless; the pink swimming scallops steamed in seaweed, miso, and apple cider somehow lacked the earthiness of the seaweed, the salt of the miso, or the punch of the cider), attentive but curt service, and insultingly high prices leave us wondering if the chefs are working too hard with unusual ingredients and not spending enough time on the execution.

The original 1931 inn (with the light and airy dining room) is complemented by three spectacular suites and a graciously designed second house just steps away. Each room is singular: the Victor Newman longhouse room creates a theme rich in the spirit of the Northwest, with a vaulted ceiling, native American accoutrements, and an enormous bathtub positioned before a breathtaking view; the Herb Garden Room, in shades of mint and parsley, opens out through French doors onto a private patio. Views, decks (or patios), and artful extras such as bouquets of fresh flowers in every room, a decanter of fine port, and terrycloth bathrobes are a given. Breakfast in your room and an inventive light lunch are included in the cost of a night's stay.

Good Life Bookstore and Cafe
In downtown Sooke, (604) 642-6821
2113 Otterr Point Rd, Sooke
Moderate; beer and wine; MC, V; checks OK

The good life is, indeed, good food served among books. It's a funky establishment with a mishmash of furnishings in an old house where the former living room is now the dining room and a couple of the bedrooms, a bookstore. Locals will tell you the food is not anything fancy but it's quite good and well priced. Breakfast is just coffee and muffins (eggs, only if Phippen is not too busy). Lunches usually entail two soups

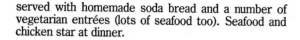

Lunch Tues-Sun, dinner Tues-Sat

served with homemade soda bread and a number of vegetarian entrées (lots of seafood too). Seafood and chicken star at dinner.

Margison House
In the center of Sooke Village, look for signs, (604) 642-3620 6605 Sooke Rd, Sooke Inexpensive; beer and wine; V; local checks only Lunch, tea Thurs-Sun (May through September)

An elegant cottage just off the highway in downtown Sooke serves up the best afternoon tea in these parts, along with light lunches of seafood chowder, raisin scones, sausage rolls, and the like. The view is fine, the grounds are pretty, and amiable owner Sylvia Hallgren has a charming B&B cottage next door with a bathroom and full kitchen. Ms. Hallgren stocks the fridge with freshly laid eggs and breakfast goodies from her garden.

LODGINGS

Malahat Farm
15 minutes west of Sooke off West Coast Rd at Anderson Rd, (604) 642-6868 Mail: RR2, Sooke, BC V0S 1N0 Moderate; no credit cards; checks OK

Diana Clare's 45-acre "gentleman's farm" is a perfect escape for any city slicker longing for a little taste of the country. From the charming upstairs rooms, you can keep an eye on the well-grazed fields of Herefords (with a solitary Angus bull), sheep, and chickens. The two grand downstairs rooms have fireplaces but lack the farm view of the upstairs ones. Diana lives in the cottage next door, but in the morning she comes over to prepare a farmhand's breakfast including an abundant spread of which virtually everything—muffins, blackberry jam, granola, grilled potatoes, honey, and eggs—comes from the farm. The tranquil setting provides sweet rejuvenation, but if you're inclined for exploring, Diana is a wealth of local knowledge and will point out the best walks, loan you a good mountain bike, and even pack you a thermos of coffee and muffins to go.

Point No Point Resort
Hwy 14, 24 kilometers west of Sooke, (604) 646-2020 West Coast Rd, RR2, Sooke, BC V0S 1N0 Expensive; no credit cards; checks OK

The Soderberg family owns a mile of beach and 40 acres of wild, undeveloped, quintessentially Northwest coastline facing the Strait of Juan de Fuca and west to the Pacific. They rent 15 cabins ($58-94 for two) among the trees on or near the cliffside, catering to those who eschew TV and telephones and seek remote beauty and tranquillity (only cabins 3 and 4 allow pets). Four new cabins hang right over the water. The only distractions here are the crashing of the rolling swells and the crackle of the fireplace. Firewood is supplied, but stop on the way to Point No Point and buy your own food. The cabins are rustic (and some are quite dark) but they're clean—besides, you're really here for the coast. Trail access to the shoreline promotes a relaxed appreciation of the area, including tidepools with all manner of marine life to discover. Afternoon tea (with mediocre pastries) and light, soup-and-sandwich lunches are served in a dining room that is both worn and convivial.

Ocean Wilderness
10 minutes west of Sooke,
(604) 646-2116
109 West Coast Rd,
Sooke, BC V0S 1N0
Expensive; MV, V;
checks OK

This log cabin is still very new (the landscaping needs some time to settle in) but it's a good choice if you want to leave pretensions behind. The rooms are big (and so are the bathrooms) and filled with an odd assortment of furnishings. Best are the upstairs suites each with its own balcony. Captain Bill and Marion Paine added a full wing onto their house and opened their seven-room B&B in the summer of 1990. The location, set back in a cove with a nice trail to the beach, couldn't be better. There's a separate Jacuzzi in its own Japanese-style enclosed building (reserved soakings).

BRENTWOOD BAY

LODGINGS

Amaryllis Lodge and Marina
Follow the signs to the
Brentwood/Mill Bay ferry
terminal, (604) 652-9828
7212 Peden Ln,
Brentwood Bay,
BC V0S 1A0
Moderate; MC, V;
checks OK

You could almost walk to Butchart Gardens from this four-room bed and breakfast on Brentwood Bay (formerly the Little Thistle, now with a less prickly name). The best room, though small, is upstairs with its own deck. You'll find '50s architecture, dainty flowered wallpaper, and spanking-new shared baths. Downstairs at the Marina you can rent an 18-foot covered boat for a day of fishing. Start your day with a full breakfast served up by owners Patricia and Brandt McKay, who are also planning to open a soup-salad-sandwich–type cafe nearby. No smoking.

Brentwood Bay Bed &
Breakfast
Corner of Stelly and W
Saanich, (604) 652-2012
7247 W Saanich Road,
Brentwood Bay, BC
V0S 1A0
Moderate; no credit cards;
checks OK

Inside this restored Victorian you'll find seven guest rooms (soon to be nine) with antique furniture, glossy wood floors, lace curtains, colorful braided rugs, and hand-crafted coverlets. There's also a cottage (summers only), a suite designed especially for the handicapped wtih a kitchenette and a full bath. Most rooms have en suite bathrooms. Ask for a room away from the fairly busy highway. Owner Evelyn Hardy serves spicy sausage and pear cobbler for breakfast in a glassed-in sun porch. No smoking. Future plans include a few more guest rooms, a honeymoon suite in the garret overlooking the bay, *and* a chapel in the restored barn.

SIDNEY

RESTAURANTS

Deep Cove Chalet
40 kilometers north of Victoria on the Trans-Canada Hwy,
(604) 656-3541
11190 Chalet Rd, Sidney
Expensive; full bar; AE, DC, MC, V; checks OK
Lunch, dinner Tues-Sun

Scrupulously manicured lawn rolls down to the cove. Even in winter the fragrance of an extravagant English flower arrangement greets you at the door. The service is professional without being stuffy, although sometimes it can be forgetful (especially on busy Saturday nights). Pierre Koffel is one of the most gifted chefs on Vancouver Island—and one of the most entertaining. He's not above taking on whatever task needs attention in the Chalet: on any given night he might be spied clearing a table, ceremoniously decanting a bottle of wine, or greeting a guest with the warmest of welcomes. As eccentric as he is, regulars know he's a stickler for freshness and quality. The wine list is thoughtful, with lots of high-priced California bottlings. The traditional menu has a light contemporary touch. You may choose from a prix-fixe menu which ranges in price from $28 to $70. Or you can put together your own meal, starting with a splendid avocado salad with perfectly cooked scallops and prawns dressed in an intense curry vinaigrette and continuing to lamb roasted in mustard sauce, exquisite in flavor and texture. Finish your meal with classic crêpes Suzettes, prepared with a flourish at your table—an appropriate Koffel finale.

Cafe Mozart
Downtown Sidney, between 2nd and 3rd,
(604) 655-1554
2470 Beacon Ave, Sidney
Moderate; beer and wine; MC, V; local checks only
Lunch Mon-Sat, dinner Mon-Sat

James and Marietta Hamilton have a fascination with Mozart; they even married on the day of his death (well, a couple of hundred years later). So it's not surprising that they (with their Austrian ties and their Swiss training) named their small European cafe after him. It's a bit stark, with lots of shiny black furniture and a few framed posters of Germany on the wall, but reports on the food have been consistently good. Two outstanding dishes include the humanely raised veal schnitzel topped with smoked ham in a cheese cream sauce and the prawns with garlic and saffron in a pastry shell. Desserts might be an aromatic rose petal sorbet or a delightful crème caramel. Guess who's playing on the stereo?

The Latch
3.2 kilometers out of Sidney on Harbor Rd,
(604) 656-6622
2328 Harbor Rd, Sidney
Moderate; full bar; AE, DC, MC, V; checks OK
Lunch Mon-Fri, dinner every day

The Latch—rough logs outside, refined wood paneling inside—was built for the provincial lieutenant governor in 1926 and converted to a tranquil restaurant half a century later. Fancy dining rooms feature views of the peerless gardens and the harbor yachts. This is one of the Saanich Peninsula's most accessible dress-up restaurants. In summer, the Latch bustles with an international clientele who expect good food and usually get it. Locals prefer winter, when the food might not be up to par but the price is down: a prix-fixe four-course dinner is $14.95. The entrées are dependable and sometimes superb (coquilles St. Jacques chock full of tender scallops and shrimp; a succulent full rack of lamb). The wine list offers selections from Summerland, British Columbia, to Wyndham, Australia, with a half dozen or so offered by the glass.

Blue Peter Pub and Restaurant
3 kilometers north of Sidney on Harbour Rd,
(604) 656-4551
2270 Harbour Rd, Sidney
Inexpensive; full bar;
MC, V; no checks
Lunch, dinner Tues-Fri

Blue Peter is the international flag yachtsmen use to signal their ship is about to sail. There are plenty of boats here, but the sailors are often found moored to the deck of this pub. The food is as comfortable and as considerate as the place itself: salmon and spinach wrapped in phyllo dough, tangy Caesar salad, garlic-ginger prawns. Other expected pub items include tasty burgers, clubhouse sandwiches, and fish 'n' chips. A lovely interpretation of a beachfront home, with petunias and nasturtiums, this place is especially inviting on warm summer eves when the sun sets sail over the marina.

Pelicano's Cafe and Bakery
At new Port of Sydney Marina, (604) 655-4116
1B-9851 Seaport Pl,
Sidney
Inexpensive; no alcohol;
MC, V; no checks
Breakfast, lunch, dinner every day

A quick cafeteria-style bakery, espresso, and salad nook that is overwhelmingly popular because it fills a niche (in fact, at press time they were scheduled to quadruple the amount of seating): inexpensive lunch (prices top out at $5.95) with a view of the water. The food runs from muffins that aren't too heavy or sweet to meat pies, sausage rolls, and a harvest of good salads. The menu also includes a new selection of fresh pasta dishes. In the summertime the crowds overflow onto the deck.

MALAHAT

LODGINGS

The Aerie
Trans-Canada Hwy and look for signs,
(604) 743-4055
Mail: PO Box 108,
Malahat, BC V0R 2L0
Expensive; full bar; MC,
V; no checks
Breakfast, dinner every day

Maria and Leo Schuster's new 12-room guest house roosts on a hill they built (yes, the hill) to look out over the Saanich Inlet's Finleyson Arm. On a nice day Mount Baker looms to the east, and the Olympics spread out across the south; at night, the lights from Port Angeles glimmer in the distance. The building is impressive, with nooks and crannies, odd angles and arched doorways (and a couple of resident carpenter ants). Some rooms have private decks and/or built-in Jacuzzis and fireplaces; most have excellent views (the most plush of these rooms weigh in at a hefty $290 per night). Unfortunately, you can still hear the cars from the Trans-Canada Highway from your deck and the gardens need a few years to fill out. Prepare yourself for a formal getaway (not a place to come with the kids) popular with newlyweds.

Meals, cooked by Leo (originally of Innsbruck, Austria), are many coursed, highly sauced, and accompanied by perfectly prepared vegetables: poached salmon (though lacking the sea asparagus the menu promised) was cooked through yet moist; black-tiger shrimp—accompanied by angel-hair pasta and basil—were firm, each one a fresh burst of flavor. Desserts—such as port-marinated local strawberries with chocolate or chilled cheese soufflé with raspberry sauce—are not to be missed. An excellent complimentary breakfast is especially bountiful on Sunday—eggs benedict with smoked salmon and creamed mushrooms are just the beginning of the feast (which attracts a dressy crowd). Presentation is unfailingly pleasing; the piano player is a nice thought, though sometimes intrusive. Ask for a window table in advance.

Amenities here are not always what they seem: the exercise room boasts only a sauna and a hot tub; the "outdoor trails" are a good distance down the road. A tennis court and fitness walk are in the works.

MILL BAY

LODGINGS

Pine Lodge Farm Bed & Breakfast
Merideth and Mutter Rds, (604) 743-4083
3191 Mutter Rd, Mill Bay, BC V0R 2P0
Moderate; MC, V; checks OK

The word "farm" may be misleading. This is a classy country inn. When former antique dealers Cliff and Barbara Clarke retired eight years ago, they built their dream house—a sprawling knotty-pine affair—on 30 acres overlooking Satellite Channel and the Gulf Islands. Now that retirement has set in, it sometimes seems that the Clarkes aren't always as into running their home as an inn as they used to be. Still, it's an impressive place. The living room is appointed with rich Oriental rugs, plush velveteen turn-of-the-century furniture, and intricately carved wooden chests dating back as far as the 1700s. The fieldstone fireplace acts as a centerpiece, unless there's someone around who knows how to play the organ or piano (there's one of each). Each of the seven smallish rooms (all with private baths; rooms 1 and 7 have full views) opens up onto a balcony that wraps around the massive two-story living room. Privacy seekers can opt for a cabin down the drive which includes two bedrooms and a hot tub. Breakfast eggs are courtesy of the hens kept on the property and, in season, there are berries from the garden. Trails meander through the farm.

SHAWNIGAN LAKE

In summer, Shawnigan Lake is the favored swimming hole in the area. A good spot to get a lunch to go is **Jalna's Diner** in Shawnigan Village, serving huge pieces of fish on a mountain of fries, or a hamburger in the shape of a hot dog.

RESTAURANTS

Jaeger House Inn
*Shawnigan/Mill Bay Rd
off Trans-Canada Hwy 1
to 6.4 km to Renfrew,
(604) 743-3515
2460 Renfrew Rd,
Shawnigan Lake
Moderate; full bar; MC,
V; no checks
Lunch, dinner every day*

An informal pub-style eatery in a massive building, with a big stone fireplace and a new outdoor garden. The 65-item menu is just as substantial, with a German standby like a mushroom-laden veal cutlet with brown gravy side by side with teriyaki chicken and seafood casserole. It's still good, though, and situated on the skirt of pretty Shawnigan Lake.

COWICHAN BAY

RESTAURANTS

The Bluenose
*40 kilometers north of
Victoria, (604) 748-2841
1765 Cowichan Bay Rd,
Cowichan Bay
Moderate; full bar; AE,
MC, V; no checks
Breakfast, lunch (coffee
shop), dinner (restaurant)
every day*

Have breakfast or lunch at the coffee shop—either indoors at its horseshoe-shaped counter or out on the deck, where one waitress handles the whole place with savvy. For dinner, the restaurant is the local favorite in Cowichan Bay, with a menu of steaks and seafood (go for the seafood—ask the waitress to tell you what's fresh) and a great water view. Check out the Wooden Boat Society's museum next door.

LODGINGS

Caterham Bed & Breakfast
*First Cowichan Bay
turnoff on Trans-Canada
Hwy 1 N, (604) 748-6410
2075 Cowichan Bay Rd,
Cowichan Bay,
BC V0R 1N0
Moderate; V; checks OK*

Don't be discouraged by the Astroturfed stairs. Inside you'll find three comfortable rooms furnished in over-done Laura Ashley style (the canopied beds are a little girl's dream). Ask for one of the two rooms facing the bay. Claire Killick, with years of experience in the hotel industry, serves a full English breakfast and offers little boats you can row in the bay.

Inn at the Water Resort
*Watch for signs to
Cowichan Bay from*

The offending brick edifice with HOTEL lettered boldly across the top belies the dandy suites inside, all with

Trans-Canada Hwy 101,
(604) 748-6222
1681 Botwood Lane,
Cowichan Bay,
BC V0R 1N0
Moderate; AE, DC, MC,
V; checks OK

views over picturesque Cowichan Bay. Originally built as a timeshare property, it's composed of 56 modern units, each of which has a bedroom, living room, bath, and (usually) an unfurnished kitchen. Swim in the indoor heated pool, play tennis on nearby grass courts, or enjoy the Jacuzzi and sauna.

DUNCAN

The Native Heritage Centre is a must-see for aficionados of Native American arts and crafts. Permanent exhibits include Cowichan sweaters, which are hand-knit in one piece with unique patterns, usually from homespun wools. In the summer, the Centre features an open-air carving shed, where a native carver whittles away at a traditional 12- to 20-foot totem pole; each pole interprets a traditional design in the carver's own artistic language. There are, at present, 66 such totem poles in Duncan, both downtown and along a beautiful half-kilometer section of the Trans-Canada Highway. Stop at one of the pull-outs along the way for stunning views of the Saanich Peninsula and Salt Spring Island. (Native Heritage Centre, 200 Cowichan Way, (604) 746-8119. Call for hours.)

RESTAURANTS

The Inglenook
8 kilometers north of
Duncan, (604) 746-4031
7621 Trans-Canada
Hwy, Duncan
Moderate; full bar; MC,
V; local checks only
Dinner Wed-Sun

The traveler may well have grown a little weary of Vancouver Island's fascination with restaurants in Tudor houses, but under the new ownership of Jeannette and Eberhard Hahn (who've brightened the place up and expanded the menu) this one's a notch or two above the standard: roast rack of lamb, oysters coquille, New York steak with Pernod, crab, shrimp, and scallops. The dessert list showcases the apple strudel, of course. There's a cozy library that calls for an after-dinner brandy.

Arbutus Cafe
Kenneth and Jubilee,
(604) 746-5443
195 Kenneth St, Duncan
Inexpensive; beer and
wine; MC, V; no checks
Lunch Mon-Sat, dinner
Mon-Fri

This small vinyl and formica-tabletop corner cafe packs in the locals. They come for real home cooking with a twist; surprisingly spicy vegetarian curry and steaming espressos are as voraciously devoured as the burgers and rich cream pies. Nothing on the menu steps over the $9 mark. Service is young and upbeat; the radio blares from the kitchen. Everyone knows each other and their musical tastes.

LODGINGS

Grove Hall Estate
Turn east at first set of
lights in Duncan,
continue to Lake Road, go
north 1.6 kilometers,

It's all very secluded: it's not always open and there isn't a sign out front. Captain Frank and Judy Oliver want it that way. Tough for the curious, but an un-

(604) 746-6152
6159 Lakes Rd, Duncan,
BC V9L 4J6
Moderate; no credit cards;
checks OK

disturbed retreat for guests. Seventeen wooded acres surround this 1912 Tudor-style manse near Lake Quamichan. From the outside it looks as if there would be far more than three rooms—until you see the size of the rooms. Each room has an Oriental theme (Indonesian, Malaysian, Thai), magnificent rugs (you're provided with slippers), and no bath. The master bedroom, decorated with pieces from Jakarta and Bali, expands into a sitting area and then onto a balcony. There are two and a half baths in the mansion. Play tennis on the private court or games in the billiards room, or stroll along the quiet lakefront. Just remember: call ahead.

The Quamichan Inn
Just east of Duncan,
(604) 746-7028
1478 Maple Bay Rd,
Duncan, BC, V9L 4T6
Moderate; full bar; MC,
V; checks OK
Dinner every day

Set in the midst of several acres of lawn and garden, this comfortable turn-of-the-century home has been nicely transformed into a bed-and-breakfast-cum-dinner house for boaters moored at the nearby marinas. Each of the guest rooms has its own bath. Morning begins with an English hunt breakfast (sausages, mushrooms, bacon and eggs). Dinner might include roast Salt Spring Island lamb, Indian curry, or roast prime rib with Yorkshire pudding. There are Fanny Bay oysters, locally produced clams, and wines from France to California. A seasonal dessert might be a Pavlova made from raspberries, whipped cream, and meringue; there's always homemade ice cream. You can drink after-dinner coffee in the garden among wisteria, fuchsias, and dahlias. The proprietors of Quamichan Inn will pick you up at Maple Bay or Genoa Bay and return you when dinner's over.

Fairburn Farm Inn
11.2 kilometers south of
Duncan at 3310 Jackson
Rd, (604) 746-4637
Mail: RR 7, Duncan,
BC V9L 4W4
Expensive; no credit
cards; checks OK

Once it was an Irish millionaire's country estate, now it's a 130-acre organic farm and country inn; you're literally at the end of the road here. The aged farmhouse occupies a sloping dale, and the working-farm orientation is the charm of the place, especially for families. Six large guest rooms feature comfortable furniture and new, private baths with Jacuzzi tubs. There's also a cottage in summer that will house six comfortably. Guests are welcome to use two downstairs parlors (family reunions often book Fairburn) and to roam the grounds, where a sheepdog minds the lambs and a creek flows idly by. The bed comes with a hearty breakfast that always begins with porridge. For a more replete vacation, you can include three meals with the cost of a night's stay. In this modern-day Eden you can witness a stunning example of how it is still possible to live off the land: most everything you eat is organically home-grown.

CHEMAINUS

Faced with the shutdown of its mill in 1981, this logging town bucked up and hired artists to come paint murals all over everything telling the story of the town. It's now a tourist attraction, and what it lacks in inspired art it more than makes up for in good old-fashioned small-town chutzpah.

LADYSMITH

RESTAURANTS

Crow and Gate Neighbourhood Pub
About 12.8 kilometers south of Nanaimo,
(604) 722-3731
2313 Yellow Point Rd,
Ladysmith
Inexpensive; full bar;
MC, V; no checks
Lunch, dinner every day

This magnificent English country pub makes a nice destination for a lazy afternoon. It is set back from the road, with a rose-arbor entrance, a back-yard patio, a duck pond, and a noisy peacock. The homesick fellow who built it remembered the English original well, recreating it scrupulously from beamed ceiling to Oriental rugs, with a blazing hearth and a dartboard. The pub food is top-notch, especially the pasties encased in flaky crusts, the steak-and-kidney pie, and the buttery Yorkshire pudding. The staff is chatty, the draughts are foamy, and at night everyone's having a ruddy good time.

LODGINGS

Yellow Point Lodge
Yellow Point Road, 14.4 kilometers east of Ladysmith,
(604) 245-7422
Mail: RR3, Ladysmith, BC V0R 2E0
Expensive; MC, V; checks OK

On a rocky promontory overhung with tall trees is Yellow Point Lodge, perhaps the most serene of all the classic British Columbia resorts. It's creaky and delightful. The hours still pass with six meals a day—of standard but wholesome quality—as if you were on a cruise ship. In truth, it's a little more like summer camp for grown-ups (though it's popular year-round): you eat family style at shared tables in the lodge, with no kids under 16 to detract from the mood. Many of the good-sized rooms have private baths. Rooms 4 and 5 have balconies. You'll want a cabin, however; the best are the small white beach cabins with wood stoves and delightful beds with tree-trunk bases. There are two kinds of cabins: those on the beach (the Cliff Cabin is most remote, and the nicest) and the field cabins (Eve's is the most private). And there are the very popular beach barracks, ramshackle quarters with thin walls, built right on the shoreline rocks, with a "tree shower."

Best of all is the site: two good tennis courts, a huge seawater pool, 130 acres of meadow and forest for strolling, a hot tub, a sauna, windsurfing gear, a classic 32-foot boat for picnic cruising, and big slabs of rock jutting into the sea for sunbathing.

Mañana Lodge

4760 Branton-Page Rd,
4.8 kilometers east of
Ladysmith,
(604) 245-2312
Mail: RR1, Ladysmith,
BC V0R 2E0
Moderate; MC, V;
no checks

Mañana Lodge is permeated with the atmosphere of an old family beach house; the shaved logs are reminiscent of a Maine lodge. Under the new ownership the place has been spruced up a bit: there are now four small guest rooms (two with their own baths); the best faces the harbor. The price includes not only breakfast, but a decanter of sherry for your room. The dining room serves a full breakfast, but better is the delightful deck for a summer's-eve beer. The view of Ladysmith Harbor might include a glimpse of a bald eagle or a docking seaplane.

Inn of the Sea

3600 Yellow Point Road,
14.4 kilometers east of
Ladysmith,
(604) 245-2211
Mail: RR3, Ladysmith,
BC V0R 2E0
Moderate; AE, MC, V;
no checks

Inn of the Sea's nicest feature is the scenery, especially the long stretch of beach along Stewart Channel. Deluxe suites have fireplaces, kitchens, and balconies; large parties can request rooms that connect vertically via a spiral staircase. Many of the rooms are smaller than standard, and there have been recent grumblings about less-than-clean rooms. In the dining room, chefs arrive and depart almost as often as guests, so play it safe: cook in your own suite. You can play tennis, or swim in the large heated pool at the water's edge. A pier out front allows for boat moorage, with water and power hookup.

NANAIMO

This former coal-mining town is emerging into something very different. It now has a clean, accessible waterfront, cultural festivals in the summer, a university campus with a marvelous view, and vastly improved dining. Of the new attractions, Nanaimo claims itself as the home of North America's first (and only) bridge built specifically for bungee jumpers. You can watch ($5) or jump ($95) from this 140-foot bridge above the Nanaimo River; contact Bungy Zone, (604) 755-6728. Or for $3, ferry over to the **Dinghy Dock Pub**, a very nautical floating bar off Protection Island. Other attractions are: **the Bastion**, one of the few Hudson's Bay Company forts still standing, was built in 1853 as protection against marauding Haida Indians. There's a cannon firing every day at noon in the summer. **The Nanaimo Centennial Museum**, 100 Cameron Road, (604) 753-1821, has a to-scale replica of a coal mine entrance, among other displays.

Wandering. The waterfront promenade extends from the downtown harbor, past the modern seaplane terminal and through Swy-a-lana Lagoon Park (Canada's only manmade tidal lagoon), over the new pedestrian bridge, by the Nanaimo Yacht Club, as far as the BC Ferry Terminal. The **Bastion Street Bookstore**, 76 Bastion Street, (604) 753-3011, houses an impressive collection of children's books, natural history texts, guidebooks, and Canadian authors. On nearby Commercial Street, the Scotch Bakery concocts the namesake **Nanaimo bar**. Several companies offer wildlife and harbor tours; **Bastion City Wildlife Cruises**, (604) 754-8474, provides informative commentary, fresh fruit and baked goodies too.

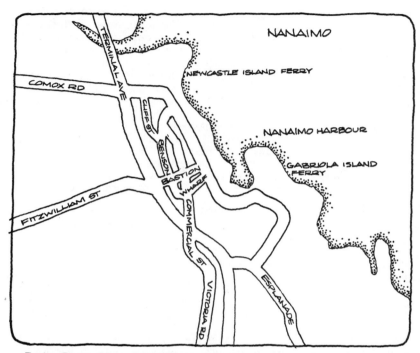

Parks: **Pipers Lagoon**, northeast of downtown, includes a spit that extends into the Strait of Georgia backed by sheer bluffs for bird watching. **Newcastle Island**, (604) 753-5811, is an autoless wilderness island reached by ferries that leave hourly from behind the civic arena; it has a long shoreline trail, a trail for the handicapped, and some fine old-growth timber.

Golf. Nanaimo and the area to the north have seen the proliferation of new or recently upgraded golf courses. Most noteworthy is the **Nanaimo Golf Club**, 5 kilometers north of the city, a demanding 18-hole course with beautiful views of the water, (604) 758-6332. Others include Pryde Vista Golf Club in Nanaimo, (604) 753-6188; FairWinds at Nanoose, (604) 468-7766; and Morning Star, (604) 248-2244, and EagleCrest, (604) 752-9744, near Qualicum.

Gabriola Island. A 20-minute ferry ride from Nanaimo will take you to this rural spot (see Gulf Islands).

RESTAURANTS

Old Mahle House
Corner of Cedar at Hemer Rd, (604) 722-3621
Site 01-6, RR 4, Nanaimo
Moderate; full bar; MC, V; local checks OK
Dinner Wed-Sun

It's intimate: three elegant, airy rooms done in a country motif seat 55 people. The affable and intelligent owners, Delbert Horrocks and Maureen Loucks, emphasize fresh, locally produced ingredients. A dozen daily specials fill a whiteboard: thick savory carrot-and-ginger soup; homemade pasta tossed with salmon and cream, capers and scallions providing a tart counterpoint; or a succulent beef tenderloin in a green peppercorn sauce. The regular menu competes with fresh-caught prawns in zesty tarragon sauce or boneless lamb loin from Australia. End the meal with one of a battery of homemade desserts—the silken chocolate banana cheesecake alone was worth the drive. Visit during the summer months, or attend one of the monthly four-course dinners with six excellent wines included in the meal (about $45) and you could possibly encounter a 3-star evening.

Gina's Cafe
1 block up from the waterfront,
(604) 753-5411
47 Skinner St, Nanaimo
Inexpensive; full bar;
MC, V; checks OK
Lunch Mon-Fri, dinner every day

Gina's is a comfortable place with all the down-home ambience of a Tex-Mex roadside cafe. A healthy, imaginative menu reflects the Korfields' vegetarian leanings. We enjoyed the daily special, a ricotta and spinach enchilada lavishly smothered in salsa, and barely managed dessert—a fruit burrito topped with ice cream.

Maffeo's
Prideau and Wentworth,
(604) 753-0377
538 Wentworth, Nanaimo
Moderate; full bar; AE,
MC, V; no checks
Lunch Mon-Fri, dinner every day

A favorite of Nanaimo-ites, this was once the home of former mayor Pete Maffeo and now houses Nanaimo's most *real* Italian restaurant. A deli occupies the main floor: made-on-the-premises pasta and Italian cheeses and meats. (Where else on the island are you going to find authentic prosciutto or cappocolla?) You dine upstairs in one of the two rooms prettied with antiques: pastas are well done here, and the cioppino with a dash of saffron is a local favorite.

The Grotto
On the waterfront next to the BC ferries,
(604) 753-3303
1511 Stewart Ave,
Nanaimo
Inexpensive; full bar;AE,
MC, V; no checks
Dinner Mon-Sat

The Grotto, a Nanaimo perennial for over 30 years, has completely outgrown its wharfish name. Its ample menu has many proven favorites—fresh salmon and Zum Zum (a seafood platter)—and cafe entrées such as gourmet burgers, veal, and pasta dishes.

LODGINGS

Coast Bastion Inn
Bastion St and Island Hwy, (604) 753-6601 or toll-free (800) 663-1144
11 Bastion St, Nanaimo,
BC V9R 2Z9
Expensive; AE, DC, MC,
V; no checks

All 179 rooms of this swanky hotel have views of the restored Hudson's Bay fort; all are tastefully styled in postmodern hues. There are a new, formal meeting room and a trio of formula eateries— the family-style Cutters Cafe, the Offshore Lounge, and Sargent O'Flaherty, a New York–style deli. A sauna, a hot tub, and a cool tub make the Bastion a self-sustaining entity. It's right in the middle of things downtown.

The Dorchester Hotel
Church and Front St,
(604) 754-6835
70 Church St, Nanaimo,
BC V9R 5H4
Moderate; AE, MC, V;
no checks
Breakfast, lunch, dinner
every day

It was built in the late 1880s on the site of an opera house and the residence of a coal baron, but there's little hint of the past at this newly refurbished Nanaimo landmark. That's partly because the original third floor, with its archways and detailing, was removed sometime during the '50s (after a fire) and was replaced with utilitarian block architecture. The rooms are tastefully decorated; many have lovely views of the harbor and the Bastion. One really nice touch: there's a library on the second floor, complete with an extensive collection of old *National Geographics*. The lobby is light and airy, with a fireplace and complimentary newspapers; the restaurant, Café Casablanca, offers good food at surprisingly reasonable rates for a hotel (and a view too). It is popular with locals, who venture in for the smoked-on-the-premises scallops with saffron and lime or the rack of lamb with whole hazelnuts and blackberry demiglace. Service is extremely on the ball; the wine list is touted even in Vancouver.

PARKSVILLE

The town offers good sandy beaches, lovely picnic sites on Cameron Lake, Englishman River Falls and Little Qualicum Falls, and fine fishing. **MacMillan Nature Park**, 32 kilometers west of Parksville on Route 4 heading for Port Alberni, has preserved Cathedral Grove, a haunting old-growth forest of Douglas firs and cedars ranging up to 200 feet high and 1,000 years old. The annual **Brant Festival** is held in April (see Calendar).

LODGINGS

Tigh-Na-Mara Hotel
2 kilometers south of
Parksville on Island
Hwy, (604) 248-2072
Mail: 1095 E Island
Hwy, Parksville,
BC V0R 2S0
Moderate; AE, DC; MC,
V; local checks only

Owners Jackie and Joe Hirsch's complex of rustic log cottages is no longer so rustic, and always busy. They've acquired more acreage and, last year, added a condominium (all units have views of the Strait of Georgia and some have their own Jacuzzis). The 40 or so log cabins are spread among the now-22 acres of natural arbutus and fir. The 12 suites in the lodge are surprisingly cozy, and although none has a view, each has a fireplace, fridge, and full bath, and a few have their own kitchens. Reports on the log-cabin restaurant have been favorable. With the indoor pool and Jacuzzi, outdoor tennis courts, volleyball, and 700 feet of beachfront, you'll have no problem working up an appetite.

PORT ALBERNI

The *Lady Rose* departs from the Harbor Quay at the end of Argyle Street in Port Alberni and voyages to Bamfield on Tuesdays, Thursdays, and Saturdays, with special Sunday trips during July and August. Round-trip fare is $30. June 1 to September 20, she sails for Ucluelet on Mondays, Wednesdays, and Fridays. Besides being a better way to reach these remote towns than over rough roads, the four-hour cruise down Alberni Inlet and through the Broken Islands Group is breathtaking. Breakfast and lunch are served. (604) 723-8313. Or take along a loaf of cheese bread from The Flour Shop, (604) 723-1105.

BAMFIELD

Bamfield is a tiny fishing village heavily populated by marine biologists. The *Lady Rose* from Port Alberni comes on Tuesdays, Thursdays, and Saturdays (and Sundays in summer). You are advised to take the boat rather than the bumpy, dirt road, which has some frightening logging traffic. For hikers, it's the end (or the start) of a five- to six-day beach trek along the **West Coast Trail** from Port Renfrew (see Pacific Rim National Park under Ucluelet). It is one of the premier places for finding a wilderness beach all to yourself, all week long. Photographers, bring your cameras. In Bamfield you can rent boats for fishing or exploring the islands.

Whale watching. During March and April, pods of migrating gray whales can be seen off the coast: book whale-watching trips through Ocean Pacific Whale Charters Ltd., Box 590, Tofino, BC V0R 2Z0, (604) 725-3919, or SeaSmoke Sailing Charter & Tours, Box 483, Alert Bay, BC V0N 1A0, (604) 974-5225.

LODGINGS

McKay Bay Lodge
On the west side of the harbor, across from Lady Rose *dock,*
(604) 728-3323
Mail: PO Box 116, Bamfield, BC V0R 1B0
Expensive; V; local checks only

In July and August a lot of fisherfolk book into Bamfield's newest lodge. But fishing is not the sole reason Cheryl and Brian McKay opened their lodge across the harbor from the *Lady Rose* dock. There's lots to do here besides search for that king-sized salmon: hiking, beachcombing, scuba diving, whale watching. There are seven guest rooms in this large wooden lodge, a comfortable living room with a fireplace, and a lounge with a TV in back. The best rooms are those upstairs and up front. Dinners often consist of a lot of fresh seafood (in abundance in these parts); full meal packages are available, and suggested, unless you're into foraging.

UCLUELET

Pacific Rim National Park, the first National Marine Park in Canada, comprises three separate areas—Long Beach, the Broken Islands Group, and the West Coast Trail—each conceived as a "platform" from which visitors can experience the power of the Pacific Ocean. Long Beach, an 11-kilometer expanse of sand and rock outcrops backed by forest and mountains, can be reached by car from Port Alberni over a winding mountain highway. The Broken Islands Group—more than 100 in all, at the entrance to Barkley Sound—are accessible only by boat. This area is famous for sea lions, seals, and whales, and is very popular with fishermen, skindivers, and kayakers. The West Coast Trail is a rugged 72-kilometer stretch that was once a lifesaving trail for shipwrecked sailors. It can be traveled only on foot, and it's a strenuous but spectacular five- to six-day hike for hardy and experienced backpackers. For more information on the park, go to the information center at the park entrance on Highway 4, or call (604) 726-4212, Pacific Rim National Park, Box 280, Ucluelet, BC V0R 3A0.

The **Wickaninnish Interpretive Center** has interesting oceanic exhibits and an expansive view: (604) 726-7333, 10 kilometers north of Ucluelet off Highway 4. The same building houses The Wickaninnish Inn (see review).

RESTAURANTS

The Wickaninnish Inn
*10 kilometers north of Ucluelet in Pacific Rim National Park,
(604) 726-7706, Ucluelet
Moderate; full bar; AE, MC, V; checks OK
Lunch, dinner every day
(closed mid-October through mid-March)*

It's a dramatic setting on an otherwise untouched 3-kilometer-long beach, in a dramatic building with glass on three sides, a beam-and-stone interior, and a rock fireplace setting off white linen tablecloths and pastel-cushioned chairs. We'd recommend it for the food too. It's owned by Oak Bay Marine Group (Painter's Lodge in Campbell River) and what they do, at least, is usually well done—from the Wickaninnish salad with a raspberry vinaigrette to a saffron-laced bouillabaisse, fresh halibut with pesto, or tender veal draped in a savory blackcurrant and mushroom sauce. The popular chowder is heavily clammed. The wine list even includes a few selections difficult to find in British Columbia.

Whale's Tale
*Behind the Thornton Motel, 4 blocks from downtown,
(604) 726-4621
1861 Peninsula Rd, Ucluelet
Moderate; full bar; AE, MC, V; local checks only
Dinner every day
(Feb-Oct)*

Perhaps because it doesn't have a view, locals regard this as the best dinner house in town. Built on pilings that sway on windy evenings, the Whale's Tale is intimate and quiet. Fresh, simply cooked seafood is on the menu; we found the halibut, sautéed in butter, to be refreshingly clear-tasting.

LODGINGS

Bed & Breakfast at Burley's
*1078 Helen St and Marine Dr,
(604) 726-4444
Mail: PO Box 550, Ucluelet, BC V0R 3A0
Inexpensive; MC, V; checks OK*

Located on the inlet of Hi-Focus Island, linked by causeway to Ucluelet proper and boasting spectacular scenery, this B&B has six bedrooms and a large living room. Hosts Michelline Riley and Ron Burley (he used to be the mayor of Ucluelet; now he's the coroner) fix simple morning meals and stay out of your way. No children under 10. A rowboat and a canoe are available free to guests to take out in the inlet.

Canadian Princess Fishing Resort

A retired 235-foot survey ship in the Ucluelet Boat Basin has been converted to 30 cabins for lodging and a

In the boat basin,
(604) 726-7771
Mail: PO Box 939,
Ucluelet, BC V0R 3A0
Moderate; full bar; AE,
MC, V; no checks
Breakfast, lunch, dinner
every day

below-decks dining room for meals. The accommodations are comfortable but not at all luxurious: the small cabins have from one to six berths and share washrooms. If you want something a little more spacious, ask for the captain's cabin with adjoining bathroom. The nautical gear has been left in place—the ship's mast goes right through the dining room—but the conversion is rather spiffy. The newer 46 shoreside units, a little roomier and more modern, are for dry-land sailors. The galley serves reasonable food, with steaks and seafood predominating, and opens at 4:30am for breakfast during the fishing season. A small ship's bar and a roomier stern lounge are pleasant places; there's a fine supply of cold beer. The *Canadian Princess*, with ten charter boats, serves as a base for fishermen who flock to the Barkley Sound area.

TOFINO

Literally at the end of the road on the west coast of Vancouver Island, Tofino, once a timber and fishing town, is quietly becoming a favored destination for Northwest and European travelers alike. Local environmentalists and artists have banded together to suspend destruction of one of the last virgin timberlands on the west coast of Vancouver Island and halt the rapid development for which the area is prime. It boasts miles of sandy beaches, islands of old-growth cedar, migrating whales (March-April, September-October), natural hot springs, colonies of sea lions, and a temperate climate.

Neophyte paddlers should contact the **Tofino Sea-Kayaking Company** for guided day trips with an experienced boater and naturalist; or explore the wilds of the west coast with one of the eight charter **water taxi companies** (which are as available as their four-wheeled counterparts in New York City); or contact the seaplane company, **Tofino Air Lines**, to venture out to the sea lion caves or other remote places on the west coast of Vancouver Island.

Galleries. There are two excellent galleries in town, Roy Henry Vickers' hand-hewn longhouse called **Eagle Aerie Gallery** and the newer **House of Himwista**, both native-run.

RESTAURANTS

Alley Way Cafe
Behind bank,
(604) 725-3105
Mail: Box 439, Tofino
Inexpensive; no alcohol;
no credit cards; local
checks only
Lunch, dinner every day
(usually closed for a few
months in winter)

Christina Delano-Stephens thinks the way of life in Tofino is the closest thing to her Latin-American roots she'll ever see in Canada. Five years ago, Christina livened up a little sun-filled house with some pink and turquoise paint, put two picnic tables outside and cactus-shaped balloons in the window, and opened one of the most heart-filled spots north of Victoria. Today, Vancouver Island's only organic restaurant outside of Victoria is thriving with a menu that just won't stop growing, as there's nothing she or the locals want to drop. The litany above the counter is getting stuffed with extraordinary vegetarian burritos, clam burgers, organic rice salad with onions, parsley, and carrot, excellent enchiladas and, if you're lucky, pickled geoduck. Or try the cornmeal squares with seaweed and cheese. The huevos verdes for breakfast are quite popular. And all, *all*, right down to the mayonnaise on the clam burgers, is made by Christina herself.

Blue Heron Dining Room at the Weigh West Motel
Just south of town on the west side of Rt 4, behind the Chevron station,
(604) 725-4266
634 Campbell St, Tofino
Moderate; full bar; AE, DC, MC, V; local checks only
Breakfast, lunch, dinner every day

This is the motel that locals recommend. Not necessarily for the rooms; most venture here for the restaurant and bar. The Blue Heron restaurant in the Weigh West Motel is not perfect, and the supportive locals know it—and forgive it. The view is an immediate hit: a working marina backed by Meares Island, where old-growth forests grow and bald eagles nest. At least once during your meal the restaurant's long-winged namesake will probably swoop by your window. You can get the same view from the bar. Dinner's a bit less striking: a Caesar salad generously doctored with crab and avocado, a tender charbroiled steak au poivre, and an overcooked halibut fillet (billed as halibut steak). The motel is neither on the beach nor right in town, but its 63 rooms are clean and well-equipped. Reserve a room with a kitchen: they're the ones with the views, and the refrigerator will come in handy for lunch.

Common Loaf Bake Shop
Just behind the bank,
(604) 725-3915
180 First St, Tofino
Inexpensive; no alcohol; no credit cards; no checks
Breakfast, lunch, dinner every day (in winter, baked goods only)

A town meeting place where save-the-whale buttons are at the cash register and save-the-trees pleas on the bulletin board has moved to a new location, but the rest of the place (the wonderful cheese buns and healthful peasant bread) has stayed the same. Come summer, the bread dough becomes pizza dough and it's the busiest nook in town. A fabulous seafood combo pizza is topped with smoked sockeye salmon, shrimp, and mushrooms; a European version has beer sausage and cheese. Service is young and easily distracted.

LODGINGS

Chesterman's Beach Bed and Breakfast
1345 Chesterman's Beach Road; call ahead for directions,
(604) 725-3726
Mail: PO Box 72, Tofino, BC V0R 2Z0
Expensive; V; checks OK

With its location on Chesterman's Beach, you can't go wrong: miles of beach which stretch out at low tide to nearby islands, with ever-changing tidepools. Joan Dublanko designed her home around driftwood and travelers. Each space is different and very much your own: a romantic nook with a comfortable bed, small bath, and a beach-view sun deck (Joan brings hot muffins and fruit in the morning; you make coffee); a separate one-bedroom cabin with a kitchen, living room, and bath (no view, sleeps up to four); or the main floor of the house with its own entrance, two bedrooms, kitchen, bath, and sauna. Showers should be quick: the hot water sometimes runs low. In the evening, you can have beach bonfires long into the night.

Paddler's Inn Bed and Breakfast

Just above the Front St dock at 322 Main St, (604) 725-4222 Mail: PO Box 620, Tofino, BC V0R 2Z0 Inexpensive; MC, V; no checks

Ahh, simplicity. White 100% cotton sheets, down comforters, clean-lined Scandinavian-style furnishings. The five rooms in Tofino's original hotel are as basic and lovely as Tofino itself: no phones, no TVs, no distractions but the ocean breeze and friendly conversation. Owner Dorothy Baert (whom you'll often find in her Tofino Sea-Kayaking Company downstairs) comes in to cook you a fitting breakfast in the kitchen—and lets you take over for dinner. Check-in is at the kayak shop.

Vargas Island Inn

3 miles by water taxi from Tofino, (604) 755-0329 or (604) 725-3309 Mail: Box 267, Tofino, BC V0R 2Z0 Inexpensive; V; checks OK

The doorjambs aren't all square and perhaps it's not all up to code, but what the heck, you're a couple of hours by kayak or a half-hour by skiff from Tofino on an island all to yourself. There are a few sacrifices: there aren't any showers, refrigerators, or chefs (though owner Marilyn Buckle is an expert on cookies and crab). But that's a small price to pay to be so far from civilization and so close to the warmth of a living-room fireplace, sipping tea in the wood-furnace-heated kitchen or sleeping in absolute silence. Upstairs, there are five modest rooms. What more? There's a woodburning sauna, a hobbit-like A-frame nearby (great—and cheap—for groups of six or so), not too mention all the crab or cod you (and the Buckles) happen to catch.

Ocean Village Beach Resort

4 kilometers south of Tofino at 555 Hellesen Dr; look for signs, (604) 725-3755 Mail: PO Box 490, Tofino, BC V0R 2Z0 Moderate; MC, V; no checks

It's too bad this motel—like all the other large motels on the Esowista peninsula—doesn't live up to its setting: a mile of marvelous beach with a tiny island reached by sandbar at low tide, and secluded rocky coves a short walk away where you can gather mussels. Just north of Pacific Rim National Park, it's the best of the three big on-the-beach resorts. Ocean Village has three rows of cedar-shake housekeeping units (51 total), each accommodating a family of four for $75-$91 a night. The rounded A-frames ("gothic arches") are a bit odd but very well equipped; all face the beach and those glorious northern-summer sunsets. The heated indoor pool and hot tub are nice in cool weather. In summer, minimum stay is two days.

QUALICUM BEACH

RESTAURANTS

Old Dutch Inn

110 Island Hwy, Qualicum Beach, (604) 752-6914 Mail: PO Box 1240,

It's a funny place, a motel and dining room done in a Dutch motif with a spectacular view of the expansive Qualicum Bay. The 36 rooms that make up the hotel portion of the inn are comfortable enough; some feature views, but be aware that there's a major thorough-

Qualicum Beach,
BC V0R 2T0
Moderate; full bar; MC,
V; no checks
Breakfast, lunch, dinner
every day

fare between the motel and the beach. The real draw is the Dutch cuisine. We liked the *uitsmyter*—an open-faced sandwich topped with Dutch smoked ham and Gouda cheese—and the *lekkervekje*—Dutch-style fresh fish 'n' chips. The food can be a little pricier than that of competitors, but it's consistently praised.

FANNY BAY

RESTAURANTS

The Fanny Bay Inn
In the center of town—you
can't miss it,
(604) 335-2323
7480 Island Hwy,
Fanny Bay
Inexpensive; full bar; V;
no checks
Lunch, dinner every day

Ever wonder what a real roadhouse looks like? It's called the "FBI," an unassuming haunt with Ma-and-Pa vibes, a fine fireplace, the obligatory collection of tankards, a dartboard, and hearty pub fare. Low-key and lovely. Stop in for a pint and darts at this classic slice of Canadiana.

COURTENAY/COMOX

The Comox Valley has skiing in winter, water sports in summer, the best restaurants around, and scenic access to Powell River on the Sunshine Coast via the *Queen of Sidney*, which leaves four times daily from Comox, (604) 339-3310. Cross-country and downhill skiers flock to a pair of surprisingly decent hills: **Mt. Washington**, where four chair lifts operate over 140 days of the year and there are 29 kilometers of cross-country tracks, (604) 338-1387; and **Forbidden Plateau**—named for an Indian tale—a half hour from downtown Courtenay, (604) 334-4744.

RESTAURANTS

La Crémaillère
Take 17th St Bridge road
off Island Hwy,
(604) 338-8131
975 Comox Rd,
Courtenay
Moderate; full bar; AE,
MC, V; no checks
Lunch Wed-Fri, dinner
Wed-Sun

One of the few area restaurants capable of answering the challenge of The Old House, La Crémaillère, a two-story Tudor with a charming Puntledge River view, relies on the culinary skills of Michel Hubert, a menu that transforms the region's delicacies into fine French cuisine, and an ambience that offers more intimacy than the bigger restaurant down the road. Start your meal with huîtres Rockefeller (using local oysters) or an extraordinarily delicate pheasant pâté. Enjoy your dinner in a plush private dining room for two if you like. The emphasis on regional products stops at the wine cellar—La Crémaillère features an excellent selection of French wines.

The Old House Restaurant

Turn right on 17th from Island Hwy north, take the first right before the bridge, (604) 338-5406
1760 Riverside Ln, Courtenay
Moderate; full bar; AE, DC, MC, V; checks OK
Lunch, dinner every day, brunch Sun

A carefully restored pioneer home is set amid lovely trees and colorful flower gardens. Cedar shakes cover the outside; inside, the exposed heavy beams, large stone fireplace, copperware, and old porcelain combine to create an air of simple, rough-hewn charm. The Old House was one of the first restaurants in the area to divide into distinct formal and casual areas (others following suit, competently). It features—upstairs—linen, fresh flowers, a pricier, more innovative menu, and—downstairs—a more informal restaurant with a latticed deck and simpler fare: sandwiches, salads, pastas (which are also served upstairs at lunch). Both levels are extremely popular, placing heavy burdens on a generally competent serving crew; lunch can be disastrously slow. The upstairs menu changes every six months, reflecting the freshest of local seafood, fruit, vegetables, meat, and herbs. Recently we've encountered signs of skimping on quality, but we've still enjoyed fine lunches of beef pie made with dark beer and lots of vegetables or house pâté with fruit chutney. Dinner's invention may yield veal timbales stuffed with sweetbreads or roasted pecan chicken with peaches and apricot tarragon sauce. You'll also do well with time-tested French classics: a savory quenelle of escargots, milk-fed veal medallions with basil and wild mushrooms, a full-bodied pepper steak. The wine list is well chosen.

Michael McLaughlin's latest addition is Stan's (1760 Riverside Ln, (604) 338-0050) in the hand-crafted wood cottage next door with a few tables and glass cases filled with torta rustica, chicken and shrimp pasties, a smorgasbord of salads, and desserts (including their own homemade chocolates).

The Homestead

Near the corner of Cumberland and Fitzgerald,
(604) 338-6612
932 Fitzgerald Ave, Courtenay
Moderate; full bar; MC, V; checks OK
Lunch, dinner Tues-Sat

Margaret and John Bowie, charming former owners of the popular Moorings in Comox, have resurfaced in Courtenay. The Homestead is an unassuming restaurant (it's right behind the bus terminal) that's developed a following in town amongst folks who say it's like dining in the home of friends. They crowd the place at lunchtime, then return for dinner. The Bowies maintain generous portions and a light, informal atmosphere fragrant with the scent of home-baked breads. Try the chicken Alexander, enlivened with fresh herbs, or the fresh fish entrées. At Christmas there's fresh glögg.

LODGINGS

Greystone Manor

5 kilometers south of Courtenay on Island Hwy, watch for signs,

Conveniently close to the booming ski scene at Mount Washington and Forbidden Plateau, mid-way between boaters' havens of Nanaimo and Campbell River, this elegant four-room B&B is a welcome alternative to a

(604) 338-1422
Mail: 4014 Haas Rd, Site
684/C2, Courtenay,
BC V9N 8H9
Inexpensive; no credit
cards; checks OK

night in a featureless Island Highway hotel. Authentic Victoriana and other splendid period furnishings and a lawn that gently slopes to an unobstructed view of the water are just some of Greystone's winning attributes. Owners Mike and Mo Shipton serve a hearty breakfast—fresh fruit, homemade muffins, fruit pancakes, or quiche—from 7:30am to 9am.

Kingfisher Beach Resort
4330 S Island Hwy, 8
kilometers south of
Courtenay,
(604) 338-1323
Mail: RR6, Site 672,
Courtenay, BC V9N 8H9
Moderate; AE, DC, MC,
V; no checks

Set off the highway among a grove of trees, five minutes south of Courtenay, this motel with its clean lines, cedar-shake roof, and white stucco walls is pleasing to the eye after the dozens of run-of-the-mill places that line the route. The lobby invites with a large fireplace, skylight, and hanging plants; and the rooms are spacious, with striking, simple furnishings, refrigerators, and decks overlooking the heated pool and the Strait of Georgia. Diversions include a tennis court, sauna, and whirlpool.

OYSTER BAY

RESTAURANTS

Gourmet-by-the-Sea
14.4 kilometers south of
Campbell River on
Discovery Bay,
(604) 923-5234
4378 S Island Hwy,
Oyster Bay
Moderate; full bar; AE,
DC, MC, V; no checks
Dinner Wed-Sun
(Oct-May)

They've surprised us with a strong comeback since the place was razed by a fire in 1986. The new incarnation is larger than the old—and all tables look out to the same magnificent view. A bistro section is a nice addition, with four or five lighter specials; the main dining room offers 14 or so entrées.

Chef Michel Rabu has made a name for himself with townspeople and travelers alike, who return for the fresh leeks wrapped in prosciutto and a cheese sauce, a simple watercress salad sprinkled with a lovely raspberry vinaigrette, and a mousseline of scallops in a sauce of puréed lobster reduced in whipping cream and accented with Cognac. His seafood specialties are utterly fresh—don't miss his bouillabaisse.

LODGINGS

Bennett's Point Resort
4383 S Island Hwy,
watch for signs,
(604) 923-4281
Mail: RR1, Site 113,
Campbell River, BC
V9W 3S4
Inexpensive; AE, MC, V;
checks OK

The 27-unit motel has all the necessary facilities but no pretensions to elegance. It is set on a beautiful wooded point that lends itself to beachcombing and barbecues, as well as boating and salmon fishing. There are an indoor pool, tennis court, a Jacuzzi and sauna, and some kitchenettes. The owners are very helpful. Gourmet-by-the-Sea is right next door.

CAMPBELL RIVER

A town of over 16,000 people, Campbell River is big as Island cities go. It's completely ringed with shopping malls, yet the city center still looks and feels as it undoubtedly did in the '50s. Here you'll find some of the best fishing outfitters on the island, and during the Salmon Festival in July, the town is abuzz with famous and ordinary fisherfolk. For information on the region's wealth of short trails and dive sites, call the Chamber of Commerce, (604) 286-0764.

Strathcona Provincial Park, to the west, is a park of superlatives. It has Canada's highest waterfall and Vancouver Island's highest mountain and offers a wide variety of landscapes to explore, including alpine meadows and lakes and large forests of virgin cedar and Douglas fir. Easily accessible by road (take Highway 28 from Campbell River), the park has campgrounds and boat-launching facilities at Buttle Lake, and a surprisingly deluxe lakeside accommodation, **Strathcona Park Lodge** (see review). The park also has fine trout lakes and an extensive trail system for backpacking.

RESTAURANTS

Koto
*Behind the Bank of BC
building, (604) 286-1422
80 10th Ave,
Campbell River
Moderate; full bar; AE,
MC, V; no checks
Lunch Tues-Fri, dinner
Tues-Sat*

It makes sense: a very fresh sushi bar smack in the middle of fishing country. Still, it's tough to find essential Japanese ingredients where most people opt for loggers' cuisine. In his pleasant Campbell River restaurant, Takeo Maeda (Tony) is single-handedly turning that around. Locals are becoming familiar with (and fond of) his sushi specialties and other Japanese fare from teriyaki to sukiyaki. It's a nice meal, especially if you pull into town late. There's only one sushi chef—so when it's busy (especially in summer) the service can be slow.

Royal Coachman Inn
*2nd and Dogwood,
(604) 286-0231
84 Dogwood St,
Campbell River
Inexpensive; full bar;AE,
MC, V; no checks
Lunch, dinner every day*

We like everything about this place, from the hearth bearing soccer trophies to the savory aroma of the soup du jour (if it's French onion, order it) to the practiced pouring arm of the bartender. A steady stream of regulars crowds the Coachman from lunch into the wee hours, and chef George Saunders meets demands with a small, hard-working kitchen staff of three. A blackboard menu changes daily. Meals include surprisingly ambitious dishes that you don't expect to see in a pub: crêpes, schnitzel cordon bleu, sole topped with asparagus, shrimp, and hollandaise. Tuesday and Saturday nights are prime rib nights—come early.

LODGINGS

Painter's Lodge
*1625 McDonald Rd and
Island Hwy, 4 kilometers
north of Campbell River,
(604) 286-1102*

You'd never know this was a 60-year-old fishing lodge. Due to a fire in 1985, the place is brand-spanking new. Old photos of big-name types and their award-winning fish line the plush lobby, lounge, and dark Tyee pub, where unkempt fishermen seem almost out of place—but aren't. Pandemonium breaks out at 4am as the seaplanes and 50 Boston whalers zoom in to pick up the

Mail: Box 460, Campbell River, BC V9W 5C1
Moderate; AE, MC, V; no checks

anglers and shatter any non-fisherman's sleep. Packages run from $259-$419 a night, which includes eight hours of fishing. Painter's is a growing resort with now four buildings (in addition to the main lodge) totaling 80 rooms and more in the works. Best are rooms in the main lodge (no longer for anglers only), with two steps down into the bedroom and a porch overlooking Discovery Passage and Quadra Island. In the evening, appetizers in the lounge are our choice: try the moist smoked salmon marinated in a honey-mustardseed-and-lime vinaigrette. Dinners are inconsistent and service incompetent.

Strathcona Park Lodge
At the edge of Strathcona Park, 44.8 kilometers west of Campbell River, (604) 286-8206
Mail: PO Box 2160, Campbell River, BC V9W 5C9
Moderate; full bar; MC, V; checks OK

A week-in-the-woods experience: canoeing, day hikes, lake play. Stay in one of the attractive cabins with kitchens or one of the modest motel units—we think they're a bit overpriced for what you get, but you couldn't ask for a better location. There are lots of outdoor activities (including rock-climbing and rope courses), perfect for families seeking fresh-air fun. Family-style buffet meals at strictly regulated hours feature healthful food—plenty of vegetables and limited amounts of red meat. Don't be late.

GOLD RIVER

The *Uchuck III* will take you for a magnificent 10-hour chug from Gold River along Vancouver Island's broken western coastline to the remote settlement of Kyuquot. You spend the night at a bed and breakfast and return the next day ($145 all-inclusive); PO Box 57, Gold River, BC V0P 1G0; (604) 283-2325. Book these tours well in advance.

PORT McNEILL

The major asset of this remote spot is proximity to all things wild and wonderful—great boating, diving, whale watching, salmon fishing, and tidepooling.

The U'mista Cultural Centre in Alert Bay, an inspiring Kwakiutl museum, is a short ferry ride from Port McNeill. This one examines cultural origins and potlatch traditions. Seasonal hours, closed Sundays, (604) 974-5403.

Whale watching is superior (July through October only) from Telegraph Cove, 16 kilometers south of Port McNeill. Stubbs Island Charters, (604) 928-3185, takes groups out for morning and afternoon cruises to view the cetaceans on their migration down Johnstone Strait, and can accommodate groups of five or more in a cluster of modest harborfront cabins; two suites are suitable for couples.

RESTAURANTS

The Cookhouse
*In Pioneer Mall on Hwy
19, (604) 956-4933
Port McNeill
Moderate; full bar; MC,
V; local checks only
Lunch, dinner Tues-Sat*

The minimalism of Port McNeill makes the polished amenities of The Cookhouse shine all the brighter. Located in Pioneer Mall, Walter and Sue Schinner's elegant restaurant and carry-out deli/bakery feature tasty continental fare prepared on the spot in a central kitchen midway between deli counter and dining room. The Schinners' subtle Eastern European influence is most evident in dishes like chicken Budapest or chicken à la brochette in a light lemon-hazelnut sauce. More traditional fare served on brown stoneware includes Chateaubriand, filet mignon, crab béarnaise, and veal Oscar. Eat hearty—it could very well be your last high-quality feast before plunging into the North Country.

PORT HARDY

You'll feel as though you're on the edge of the world in Port Hardy—venture any farther north and you'll have to go by boat. It's a town full of loggers, fishermen, miners, and travelers stopping long enough to catch the 15-hour ferry to Prince Rupert, (604) 949-6722. The boat leaves every other day in summer and once a week in the winter.

The famous Edward S. Curtis film "In the Land of the War Canoes" was filmed in nearby **Fort Rupert,** still one of the best places to purchase authentic Native American art.

Cape Scott Park. An hour and a half's drive on a dirt road west of Port Hardy and then a short hike on a rickety boardwalk through old-growth forest bring you to spectacular San Josef Bay. For exact directions or information on other hikes at the northernmost tip of the island, contact the Chamber of Commerce, (604) 949-7622.

THE GULF ISLANDS

The Gulf Islands, a 240-kilometer string of small islands in the Strait of Georgia, are British Columbia's more remote version of the American San Juans to the south. Similar in geography and philosophy, the Gulf Islands also enjoy the same rain-shadow weather and offer wonderful boating and cycling opportunities. The best known and most populous islands, the Southern Group, stretch from Campbell River to Victoria: Gabriola, Valdes, Galiano, Mayne, Salt Spring, North and South Pender, and Saturna. North of Nanaimo are Lasqueti, Texada, Denman, Hornby, Quadra, Cortes, Sonora. Ferries from Tsawwassen on the mainland and various spots on Vancouver Island service the islands. For more information, call BC Ferries, (604) 669-1211. BC Ferries does not take checks or credit cards (and few islands have bank machines) so be sure to bring extra cash.

THE GULF ISLANDS: SONORA

LODGINGS

Sonora Lodge
*48 kilometers north of
Campbell River
(accessible by boat or
plane only),*
(604) 287-2869
*Mail: 625-B 11th Ave,
Campbell River,
BC V9W 4G9
Expensive; full bar; DC,
MC, V; checks OK*

We're sure it's not the *best* fishing lodge in British Columbia (that's got to be April Point), but it's certainly the most expensive. Even so, the $1595 you shell out for two nights and three days includes everything. *Everything*: airfare, guided fishing, meals, drinks, rain gear, fishing rods, six hot tubs and four steam rooms. The place is impeccable—especially considering this multi-million-dollar spot has been open for 10 years (and it's only open when the fishing is). There are 5 buildings with 54 very luxurious suites (some have their own Jacuzzis). Other amenities include a world-class billiards table, a small convention center, and five fully-stocked self-service bars open 24 hours. Special needs are catered to here (as they make a point of booking only up to about 40 rooms on any given night). The kitchen is competent and serves a well-selected variety of, of course, fresh fish. Occasionally a special chef is brought in for a fête around the Teppan cooker.

THE GULF ISLANDS: QUADRA

Quadra is the northernmost of the Gulf Islands, a 10-minute ferry ride away from the salmon-fishing mecca of Campbell River. A lot of artists and craftspeople live here, so it makes a fine place to sleuth around for pottery and other wares. You can pick up a detailed map of the island at the **Kwakiutl Museum**, an outstanding collection of Native American art. Their masks, blankets, and carvings rival Indian displays in ᵗhe finest international museums. Three kilometers south of the ferry dock on Green Road, (604) 285-3733.

The Cape Mudge Band of the Kwakiutl people recently opened the **Tsa-Kwa-Luten Lodge**, (800) 665-7745, which overlooks Discover Passage and Campbell River. The contemporary lodge, built in the spirit of a longhouse, has 26 rooms all with views and fireplaces and four fully equipped beach cabins. Thursday and Saturday buffet dinners feature local foods (salmon cooked over an open fire, clams, mussels, berries, fiddleheads). A tribal dance follows.

LODGINGS

April Point Lodge
*10 minutes north of the
ferry dock on April Point
Rd, Quadra Island
(604) 285-2222
Mail: PO Box 1,
Campbell River,
BC V9W 4Z9*

Between April and October this famous resort draws serious fishermen and celebrities from all over the world for the extraordinary salmon fishing: bluebacks in April and May, tyee July through September, coho throughout the summer. The staff, nurtured by generations of experience, expertly pair guides with guests. About 8 kilometers in either direction are exceptionally lovely beach walks: the lighthouse to the south, Rebecca Spit Provincial Park to the east. The cabins facing west are spacious, beautifully furnished, and graced with large fireplaces; they're also expensive.

Expensive; AE, DC, MC, V; checks OK
Open April-October

Facing north are thin-walled cabins overlooking the marina; you might be kept awake most of the night by late-drinking or early-rising fishermen in adjoining rooms. There's a seawater pool, but if you're not here to fish—really fish (the cost of which is *not* included in your already hefty fee)—you will probably feel like a tolerated outsider; there are no other amenities. Reserve at least three or four months in advance.

The main lodge is sunny and cheerful; the food is always good, and with new chef Gordon Cowan (Vancouver's Liaisons and Sooke Harbour House) it should be getting even better.

THE GULF ISLANDS: DENMAN AND HORNBY

Tranquil and bucolic, the sister islands of Denman and Hornby sit just off the coast of Vancouver Island. Denman, the larger (10 minutes by ferry from Buckley Bay, south of Courtenay) is known for its pastoral farmlands and its population of talented artisans. Its relatively flat landscape and untraveled roads make it a natural for cyclists. Hornby (10 minutes by ferry from Denman) boasts Helliwell Park, with dramatic seaside cliffs and forest trails, as well as a lovely long beach at Tribune Bay.

LODGINGS

Sea Breeze Lodge
Tralee Point,
(604) 335-2321
Hornby Island,
BC V0R 1Z0
Moderate; full bar; no credit cards; checks OK

Sea Breeze Lodge may have a reputation among islanders for being posh and exclusive, but off-islanders will find it quite unpretentious. Catch the ferry from Denman before 6pm (10pm Fridays) and find 13 warm and comfortable cottages on the beach, some equipped with fireplaces and kitchens. Gail and Brian Bishop are enlarging their dining room to accommodate nonguests (by reservation) for Gail's home cooking (from May to the end of October), which is fresh and inventive, and for the convivial atmosphere around the rustic oak tables. Alternatives to the beach here include tennis on a grass court or a soak in the new hot tub (enclosed in winter, open in summer).

THE GULF ISLANDS: GABRIOLA

Although this most accessible island has become a bedroom community for nearby Nanaimo (20 minutes by ferry), it manages to remain fairly rustic and beachy. Highlight of the fine beach walks along the west shore is the **Malaspina Gallery**, weird rock formations and caves carved by the sea.

LODGINGS

Surf Lodge
5 kilometers north of the

A striking rock-and-log resort on Gabriola's south shore, Surf Lodge features nine lodge rooms and eight

ferry on Berry Pt Rd,
(604) 247-9231
Mail: RR 1, Site 1,
Gabriola Island,
BC V0R 1X0
Moderate; MC, V;
checks OK

rustic cottages, along with lots of recreational options: swimming, tennis, badminton, horseshoes, and tide-pooling, to name just a few. The food in the dining room is surprisingly good, and hearty vegetarian meals are available. Views from the lodge are peerless. Dennis Deakin will meet you at the ferry on request; children over 4 are welcome.

THE GULF ISLANDS: GALIANO

Named after Dionysio Galiano, commander of the 1792 Spanish expedition that explored the North Pacific coast, Galiano is a secluded, narrow strip of lushly forested hills, 22 miles long. Watch eagles, ferries, and sweeping tides from **Bluffs Park** overlooking Active Pass, or bike the western coast untroubled by traffic. Canoe or kayak under high cliffs and rest in secluded coves. Breathtaking sunsets can be seen (weather permitting) at **Montague Harbour**, where camping and supplies are available; for moorings: (604) 539-5733. With fewer than 1,000 permanent residents, services on the island are not abundant and most are clustered at the southern end. There is one gas station, a couple of small grocery stores, but no bank. A ferry from Tsawwassen arrives in Sturdies Bay twice a day; ferries from Swartz Bay on Vancouver Island run to Montague Harbour four times daily Monday-Saturday, three times on Sunday.

RESTAURANTS

La Berengerie
On the corner of Clanton
and Montague Harbour
roads, (604) 539-5392
Montague Harbour Rd,
Galiano Island
Moderate; full bar; V;
checks OK
Dinner every day in
summer, Fri-Sun March-
June and Sept-Nov (closed
Dec-Feb)

★

The quaint 40-seat restaurant boasts devoted fans. Owner/chef/hotelier Huguette Benger, who learned the trade running a small hotel in Paris, offers a $20 set menu of soup, salad, main course, and dessert. Items change daily. On our last visit we were served a wonderfully textured but tasteless mushroom soup, romaine salad with vinaigrette, a gingered beef with saffron rice and crisp vegetables, and cheesecake. Service and atmosphere are casual. Huguette is often your server as well as chef. Many of the vegetables come from the restaurant's own garden. Reservations are a must. Upstairs are three modest guest rooms, one private (but not spotless) bath, and all with paper-thin walls. But the hot tub on the deck up at Huguette's house and the good breakfast make up for the flaws.

LODGINGS

Bodega Resort
Follow Porlier Pass Dr
22.4 kilometers north of
Sturdies Bay to Cook Rd,
(604) 539-2677
Mail: PO Box 115,
Galiano Island,
BC V0N 1P0

The six spacious chalets are furnished with care: you might find lace country curtains, custom cherrywood cabinets, or a cast-iron stove in the living room. Each unit has three bedrooms, two baths, a fully equipped kitchen, and two view decks. The ranch-style unit has three bedrooms, kitchen, living room, bath, and a large sun deck surrounded by a rose garden—perfect for

Moderate; MC, V;
checks OK

Sutil Lodge

*Follow signs for
Montague Harbour; after
long steep hill, turn left on
Southwind; last drive on
left, (604) 539-2930
637 Southwind Rd,
Galiano Island,
BC V0N 1P0*
Moderate; AE, MC, V;
checks OK

Woodstone Country Inn

*Turn left off Sturdies Bay
Rd to Georgeson Bay Rd,
follow signs,
(604) 539-2022.
Mail: RR1, Georgeson
Bay Rd, Galiano Island,
BC V0N 1P0*
Expensive; full bar; MC,
V; checks OK
*Dinner every day in spring
and summer (days vary
off-season)*

family getaways. A lodge with a conference room also has a few rooms available. For fun there's horseback riding, a trout pond, and hiking trails amidst the 25 acres of meadows and trees. Prices are remarkable for such generous accommodations.

Ann and Tom Hennessy have completed the period renovation of their rambling 1928 clapboard, situated on 20 secluded acres of beachfront on Montague Harbour. The Hennessys' labors are to be commended. Rooms have been restored with the original fir paneling and filled with authentic 1930s furnishings. Travel there with someone you like to be close to; the seven guest rooms are tiny (but not cramped). Front rooms have stunning water views; the others face (in season) lush cherry blossoms and an expansive lawn which was, in early days, a grass tennis court. The communal sitting room and dining area both have fireplaces. Among the Hennessys' seagoing vessels is a 46-foot catamaran, on which they take guests on tours of the islands followed by picnic suppers on the beach. Fabulous off-season rates.

Once the newness wears off (there are some charms money simply can't buy) and the landscaping is completed, this promising country inn will come into its own. Until then, the 12 rooms at this genteel inn, which straddles wood and field, are sweet and bright. All have private baths and most have fireplaces. The best rooms possess a dreamy view of green pastures. Guests with children are discouraged, even though the surroundings would be a wonderful spot for families. Our morning meal was the rich Eggs Pacifica—poached eggs with capers and smoked salmon topped with hollandaise sauce. The inn maintains a walking trail that takes guests out to a viewing platform overlooking a marsh which in the morning mist is filled with birds. In the afternoon, guests regroup for tea.

Dining here (available to non-guests as well) is even more of a delight and gives Galiano its first peek at elegant dinners. The windows of the restaurant open onto an expanse of green, visited by deer and birds and dotted with horses (we even spotted a bald eagle above). The lighting is low and the servers soft-spoken. For $21.50, you might encounter a deliciously hot spinach salad with curry vinaigrette, freshly baked soda bread laced with thyme, a small plate of pasta in a red pepper sauce, and an exquisite lightly braised salmon in béarnaise sauce accompanied by crisp vegetables and a rich almond butter. Dessert is extra.

THE GULF ISLANDS: SALT SPRING

Named for the unusually cold and briny springs on the north end of the island, Salt Spring is the largest and most populated of the Gulf chain, and its population is growing steadily. It's accessible by ferry from Tsawwassen (to Long Harbor, 2½ hours); Crofton, near Duncan on Vancouver Island (to Vesuvius, 20 minutes); or Swartz Bay (32 kilometers from Victoria) on the Saanich Peninsula (to Fulford Harbor, 30 minutes). All roads lead to Ganges, as the natives are fond of saying. Ganges, the largest town on the island, has a colorful Saturday morning farmers' market, several pleasant cafes, a condominium overlooking the harbor, and a flurry of retail development.

Good camping facilities are available at St. Mary Lake, Ruckle Park, and Mouat Provincial Park on the southeastern tip of the island, where you'll find a spectacular mixture of virgin forest, rock and clamshell beach, and rugged headlands. Or drive Cranberry Road up to the top of **Mount Maxwell** for a panorama of the archipelago from Salt Spring to the American mainland. For information call the tourist bureau, (604) 537-5252.

RESTAURANTS

Bay Window Restaurant (in the Booth Bay Resort)
3.2 kilometers north of Ganges on the main road; look for signs,
(604) 537-5651
375 Baker Rd,
Ganges
Moderate; MC, V; checks OK
Dinner Wed-Sun, brunch Sun

On a protected bluff overlooking pretty Booth Bay, the wood-paneled Bay Window dining room with deck gives the English-country-manor tradition a Pacific Coast accent. Former Hastings House chef (and the owner's brother) Steven Lynch presides in the kitchen now. He's consciously trying to present a more accessible menu than that in his former venue, and seems to do well with the seafood standards common to Gulf Island cuisine and with the local specialty, lamb. Steven's Sunday brunch is worth the drive if you're staying elsewhere on the island. The 11 rustic cabins (most with fireplaces) went through a serious decline awhile back, but they've been spruced up and have regained their cozy comfort.

Vesuvius Inn
At the northwest point of the island,
(604) 537-2312
Vesuvius Bay Rd, Ganges
Inexpensive; full bar; MC, V; local checks only
Lunch, dinner every day

The big draws at this rebuilt version of a turn-of-the-century loggers' and fishermen's inn are the variety of brews and the spectacular view from the waterside porch of the ferry dock with Crofton in the distance. Also good at Vesuvius is the food—Caesar salads (which are ubiquitous on Salt Spring), fish 'n' chips, burgers, Northwest Mex—and entertainment. A very casual place—order at the bar as you go in and find a good spot on the porch.

LODGINGS

Hastings House
Just north of Ganges at 160 Upper Ganges Rd,
(604) 537-2362

Nestled among fruit trees, gardens, and rolling lawns that overlook a peaceful cove, Hastings House resort goes a long way toward satisfying the hideaway fantasies of most people. It stands in all its gentrified splendor, imbued with an almost formidable air of

Mail: PO Box 1110,
Ganges, Salt Spring
Island, BC V0S 1E0
Expensive; AE, MC, V;
local checks only
Dinner every day,
brunch Sun

genteel hospitality. The accommodations consist of 12 suites in five revamped farm buildings, plus a recently renovated Cliff House. Each is individually furnished with down quilts, antiques, and thick carpets. Our favorites are the Hayloft, with its bay window seat, Franklin stove, and quaint folk art; and The Farmhouse, a charming stucco and half-timbered house with two suites—ideal for two couples. Although service here strikes some as just a little too *too* (new towels are supplied every time you leave your quarters; a personal note, thanking you for your stay, follows the visit), the guest gradually discovers that in spite of that, and the stiff tariffs ($255-$395 in high season, which included a morning wake-up coffee, breakfast, and afternoon tea), and the almost palpable air of formality, Hastings House is a remarkably warm place, thanks to a friendly staff.

In the morning, a hamper of coffee and muffins is delivered to your room; later you breakfast in the dining room on farm-fresh eggs and produce. Saturday night stays include an outstanding Sunday brunch. Chef Lars Jorgenson, formerly of Vancouver's William Tell, recently took over the kitchen. He will continue to offer a nightly $48 five-course table d'hote dinner, beginning promptly at 6:30pm with cocktails on the lawn or drinks in the parlor. A recent meal began with three prawns in an unexciting dressing followed by a luscious wild mushroom soup spiked with sage and decorated with sour cream; a tiny breast of squab on sherried lentils; cleansing melon and crème de menthe sorbet; tender veal stuffed with prosciutto; and finished with a pear poached in red wine and presented in a pool of Belgian chocolate. Both dinner and Sunday brunch are open to non-guests by reservation.

Weston Lake Inn B&B
3.6 kilometers east of
Fulford Harbour at 813
Beaver Point Rd,
(604) 653-4311
Mail: C34 Beaver Point
Rd, Fulford Harbour,
BC V0S 1C0
Moderate; MC, V;
checks OK

The owners of this contemporary farmhouse just above Weston Lake, Susan Evans, Ted Harrison and Wilson (their sheep dog), have become experts at fading into the background and letting their guests enjoy the comfortable space. Their touches are everywhere: in Ted's petit-point embroideries, framed and hanging in the three guest rooms (all with their own baths), in Susan's excellent, hearty breakfasts, in the blooming results of their gardening efforts. Susan knows and loves her island and is a fount of knowledge about activities, eating places, and quiet entertainments such as swimming, biking, and fishing. Guests have access to a comfortable lounge with fireplace, library, TV, VCR (including a decent collection of cassettes), and most recently a Jacuzzi out on the deck. Open all year.

THE GULF ISLANDS: MAYNE

Rolling orchards, sheep farms, and warm rock-strewn beaches abound on this rustic 8-square-mile island. It's small enough for a day trip but pretty enough for a lifetime. Sink your teeth into a burger at the comfortably dilapidated **Springwater Lodge**, 400 Fernhill Drive, (604) 539-5521, hike out to the grassy point of the Indian Reservation, drop by the lighthouse, or stroll up to the top of Mayne's mountain for a view of the Strait of Georgia, and you'll begin to discover what Mayne's all about. By ferry the island's usually the second stop from Tsawwassen (1½ hours), and the fourth or second from Swartz Bay (1½ hours).

LODGINGS

Oceanwood Country Inn
A 12-minute bike ride, 25-minute stroll, 3-minute drive or 25-cent phone call from the island's ferry dock at 630 Dinner Bay Rd,
(604) 539-5074
Mail: C2 Leighton Ln, Mayne Island, BC V0N 2J0
Expensive; full bar; AE, MC, V; checks OK
Dinner every day, brunch Sun

Jonathan and Marilyn Chilvers' relatively new inn is run with the kind of confidence (and exactitude) that should carry it through many more successful years. It is set on a wooded cove with a tree-webbed view of Navy Channel and North Pender Island. The best thing about Oceanwood, however, is that you feel comfortable here. It's big enough for all eight rooms to be booked without the sense that you'll be stumbling over your neighbors at breakfast, yet small enough that you're part of the family, especially at teatime. The best rooms are upstairs, especially the Rose Room with its marble-faced fireplace and a whirlpool bath with a view of the channel through French doors. The three rooms downstairs are slightly less private, as they open onto the terrace and the Jacuzzi. All the rooms have bathrooms. There's a meeting room attached to the garage, equipped with a screen, whiteboard, VCR, and flip chart, where conferences of up to 12 people can be held. Breakfast is simple and plentiful.

Equal efforts are spent on dinner. Chef Ranada McAlister, who apprenticed at West Vancouver's popular Chesa, changes the menu nightly: a soothing cream of cauliflower and cress soup, a tangy, earthy toss of warm wild mushrooms on a bed of silky baby lettuce sprinkled with a balsamic vinaigrette, an herbed Cornish game hen, fettuccine alfredo, and a whole bulb of fresh roasted garlic. The carefully chosen wine list is culled entirely from West Coast vineyards. A smooth lemon mousse topped with Whidbey Island loganberry liqueur–laced whipped cream is the perfect finale.

Fernhill Lodge
Left onto Village Bay Rd from the ferry terminal, go about 3.5 kilometers to Fernhill Rd,
(604) 539-2544
Mail: PO Box 140, Mayne Island, BC, VON 2J0

The Crumblehulmes' eccentric taste permeates every corner, from Mary's vast collection of English pewter to the eclectic selection of books in the library to the eight guest rooms, each decorated in a period theme— Jacobean, 18th-century French, Victorian, Oriental, Canadiana, Farmhouse. The newest rooms display Moroccan and East Indian themes. The rooms are dark and a bit stark, but guests are welcome to stroll through the herb garden, relax on the discreetly placed

Moderate; MC, V;
checks OK
Dinner every day,
brunch Sun

benches peppering the hillside, or enjoy the wood-fired sauna under the trees. Brian Crumblehulme's passion is historical cookery. An unusual evening feast is prepared on prior notice (the first party to reserve gets to select one of five menus). Guest breakfast consisted of a copious fruit platter, warm scones and orange muffins with fresh cream and jam, an herb-and-mushroom egg puff and a folded cheese omelet, fresh-squeezed juice, and good, dark coffee. The Crumblehulmes' hospitality is boundless—from loaning bikes to sharing a soothing cup of tea out on the patio.

THE GULF ISLANDS: NORTH AND SOUTH PENDER

Green, rural North and South Pender islands are separated by a canal and united by a bridge, from which you get lovely views of both Browning and Bedwell harbors. The ferry lands at the dock at Otter Bay on North Pender. South Pender is better for biking (fewer hills).

LODGINGS

Cliffside Inn-on-the-Sea
Follow signs to Hope Bay
government dock, turn on
Clam Bay Rd to
Armadale,
(604) 629-6691
Armadale Rd, North
Pender Island,
BC V0N 2M0
Expensive; MC, V;
no checks

You're perched at the edge of a bluff beside a staircase leading down to a mile-long beach, with a sweeping view of the channel, the islands, and Mount Baker beyond. It all may be a little too gingerbread-cute for some tastes, but the emphasis here is on privacy: each of the four Laura Ashley bedrooms has a private entrance, deck, and bath. Three face the ocean. The hot tub on the cliff-hanger deck with the 280-degree view can be reserved for private sessions well into the night. Hostess Penny Tomlin—a third-generation resident of this property—is eager to please (she'll even sit down and do a map reading with you). She will prepare gourmet dinners for guests, arrange boat excursions and island cookouts, and even transport you to and from the ferry (bike and all if you'd like). Breakfast, served in the solarium dining room, might be stewed rhubarb with yogurt and homemade muffins. For dinner, there's usually a choice of three entrées, (usually seafood, lamb, or Cornish game hens) with salad from her garden and soup (Brazilian black bean, outstanding gazpacho). Desserts almost always are something with raspberries. Adults only, and smoking outside only.

Corbett House B&B
Call ahead for directions,
(604) 629-6305
Mail: RR1 Corbett Rd,
Pender Island,
BC V0N 2M0

Owners John Eckfeldt and Linda Wolfe run a fine B&B in a beautiful pastoral setting. The Yellow, Red, and Blue rooms are all equally cozy. The first is the only one with a full bath (though water pressure is minimal) and a private balcony. The parlor is open to guests, who often gather round the fireplace for evening coffee or quiet reading. The hosts provide an ample breakfast

Moderate; MC, V;
checks OK

of fresh baked goods, fruit, coffee, and varying entrées, all generally from local sources. Long country walks fit in well here.

THE GULF ISLANDS: SATURNA

RESTAURANTS

Boot Cove Lodge and Restaurant
Follow the signs from the ferry, (604) 539-2254
Mail: Box 54, Saturna Island, BC V0N 2Y0
Moderate; beer and wine no credit cards;
checks OK
Dinner Fri-Sun (two seatings per night)

Proprietor Peter Jardine triples as the maître d', waiter, and sommelier. He doesn't let a detail slip by him. This lovely frame house high on a hill overlooking an inlet and an oyster farm serves a wonderful five-course meal. Entrées change with the seasons—you'll often find salmon, prawns, or lingcod in the summer and some lamb variations in the fall. The menu changes nightly. You might start with asparagus, snow pea, and sorrel soup. It could be followed by a papaya-prawn salad on a bed of spinach and wildflowers; a savory (though slightly overcooked) entrée of lemon garlic beef and spring vegetables; and a mango sorbet with strawberry sauce garnished with a sugared pansy. Reservations are a must.

There's a large fireplace (crackling warm when it's cold outside) in the oak-trimmed waiting room (which doubles as a living room for the inn's guests). A pretty banister carries the oak-and-peach theme upstairs to the three bed-and-breakfast rooms ($55).

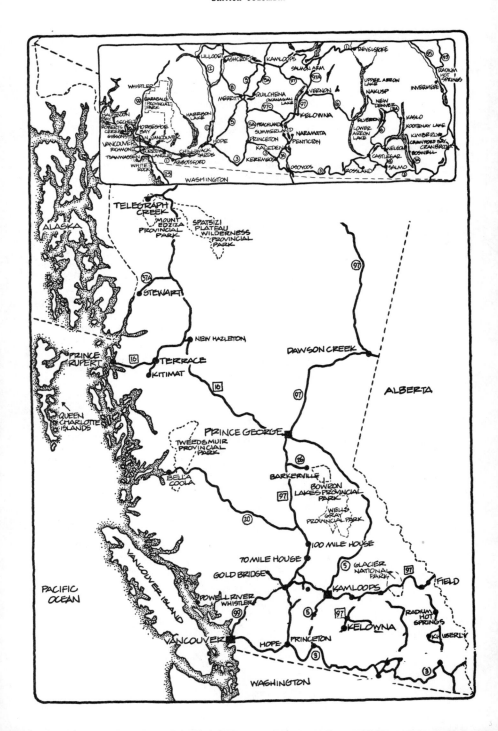

MAINLAND BRITISH COLUMBIA

First, north from Vancouver along the Sunshine Coast to Powell River, then inland to Whistler, Lillooet, and Gold Bridge. North to Prince George then west to Prince Rupert and the Queen Charlotte Islands. Then the eastward route out of Vancouver, through Harrison Hot Springs and Hope, turning northward at Manning Provincial Park, through Kamloops and Ashcroft. The Okanagan Valley at Osoyoos, then north along Lake Okanagan, east to the Rocky Mountains, turning south, then westward again along the southern rim of the province.

WHITE ROCK

RESTAURANTS

Cosmos
Corner of Elm and Marine, (604) 531-3511 14871 Marine Dr, White Rock Moderate; full bar; MC, V; no checks Dinner every day

Right near the border, Cosmos is pure Greek taverna, with an atmosphere that can be so electric it can make you forget the food (which is very Greek and very good). The taramasalata, moussaka, and tender quail are excellent choices. Desserts range from a rich baklava or bougatsa to a lighter orange sponge cake. Belly dancers are a likely sight on weekends.

THE SUNSHINE COAST

Inside the rain shadow of Vancouver Island, this aptly named area begins just west of Vancouver at Horseshoe Bay. The coast used to be—and still is—where Vancouverites vacation. But lately, as Vancouver expands in every direction, it is also where many of them are settling in an attempt to escape the madding crowds. There's even the possibility of a frequent foot ferry on the first of two ferry crossings on this coastal route. Call BC Ferries for schedule information, (604) 921-7414.

Prices in the British Columbia section are given in Canadian dollars; distances are quoted in kilometers whenever possible.

For the traveler, the crescent-shaped inlet of Howe Sound at Horseshoe Bay, flanked by green and snowy peaks, hints at the pleasures yet to come on the lower British Columbia coastline. Heading north, first on the ferry, then on Highway 101, you'll traverse lush wooded areas and rapidly growing small towns. Gibsons is home to a pioneer museum, but locals are eager to talk about more recent history: it was here that Canada's longest-running TV show, *The Beachcombers*, was filmed until 1990. Other highlights along Highway 101 include a local arts center in Sechelt and **Saltery Bay Provincial Park** near Lang Bay. Just north, the Earl's Cove-Saltery Bay ferry takes you to **Powell River**, the largest timber-and-fishing town on the coast. Highway 101 ends at the little fishing village of Lund.

HORSESHOE BAY
RESTAURANTS

Bay Moorings
Across from the ferry terminal, (604) 921-8184
6330 Bay St,
Horseshoe Bay
Moderate; full bar; AE, MC, V; no checks
Lunch, dinner every day

This pretty pastel-colored view restaurant is a rarity in its genre: its food is generally a match for the scenery. The handsome proprietor, Gus Tsogas, serves consistently fine seafood (aromatic calamari, rich chowder) and Mediterranean specialties such as lasagne, plus pizza with a light spicy sauce and lots of topping choices. The preparations are careful, and the service is topnotch. They also have take-out, but with such a dramatic ocean view, you won't want to leave.

Ya Ya's Oyster Bar
Take the Horseshoe Bay turnoff from the Trans-Canada Hwy,
(604) 921-8848
6418 Bay St,
Horseshoe Bay
Moderate; full bar; AE, MC, V; no checks
Lunch, dinner every day

The name came from a nasty joke and the idea came from the natural surroundings. Mahogany and copper decor and a pleasantly noisy ambience give the place a casual feel, and a special ale brewed on the premises provides a bit of authenticity. The oysters are excellent (and very fresh). Oddly enough, the nicely steamed mussels we sampled on a recent visit were from New Zealand. They're not shy with the garlic on the Caesar.

GIBSONS
RESTAURANTS

Ernie and Gwen's Drive-In
In the middle of town,
(604) 886-7813
Hwy 101, Gibsons
Inexpensive; no alcohol;
no credit cards; no checks
Lunch, dinner every day

This is a down-home picnic-table kind of place. If burgers and fries and "real milk" milk shakes are your thing, stop at Ernie and Gwen's after your trip on the Langdale ferry. You can adorn your burger with multitudinous condiments. It all tastes real. (Off-season, it's not a sure bet that you'll find this place open.)

LODGINGS

Bonniebrook Lodge
Outside Gibsons at Gower Point, (604) 886-2887
Mail: RR4, S10 C34, Gibsons, BC V0N 1V0
Moderate; full bar; MC, V; no checks
Breakfast, lunch, dinner every day

This simple yellow clapboard house on the water has been a guest house since it was built in 1922. Six homey rooms of varying sizes (all share three baths) may not be for everyone, but the views of the Strait of Georgia are lovely, and proprietors Barb and Ken Norton are friendly hosts. If you prefer, there are a few campsites behind the lodge and on the water. Breakfast is served in the restaurant (which is closed to non-guests off season). RV campsites available.

ROBERTS CREEK

RESTAURANTS

The Creek House
Roberts Creek Rd and Beach Ave,
(604) 885-9321
1041 Roberts Creek Rd, Roberts Creek
Moderate; full bar; MC, V; local checks only
Dinner Wed-Sun

Here's a restaurant with continental cooking—by which we mean the continent of today, not the one enshrined in hotel cooking of 50 years ago. This restaurant is owned and operated by Yvan Citernesch (former owner and chef at Le Bistro in Vancouver). Situated in a house with a view of a tree-filled garden, the restaurant is decorated simply inside with white walls, light wood floors, flowers on the tables, and original contemporary art on the walls. On a given night, you may choose from 10 entrées that change seasonally: roasted duck, rack of lamb Provençal, or sautéed prawns. Fresh local seafood is usually offered too. Desserts include mango mousse.

LODGINGS

Country Cottage Bed and Breakfast
9 miles from the ferry off Hwy 101 at 1183 Roberts Creek Rd,
(604) 885-7448
Mail: General Delivery, Roberts Creek, BC V0N 2W0
Moderate; no credit cards; no checks

Philip and Loragene Gaulin's charming butterscotch farmhouse is surrounded by a cherry orchard and over 100 rosebushes. You stay in a one-bedroom cottage with an antique iron bed, a pull-out couch for kids, and a wood-burning stove. Or you can stay in the sunny Rose Room with your own bath and solarium and a view of the grazing sheep that Loragene raises for wool. In the morning, your uncommon, genial hostess will prepare you a breakfast from what's in season: garden-fresh asparagus crêpes with cheese and fresh fruit on our visit. Later on, join the Gaulins for a full afternoon tea in the garden or the parlor. You're a pleasant five-minute stroll from a sandbar beach, and they have bikes to borrow. No smokers, no kids under 10.

The Willows Inn
Beach Ave and Marlene Rd, (604) 885-2452

Just behind John and Donna Gibson's lovely log house on a large wooded lot is this charming cedar cottage. Newly planted vines ensure privacy in the cottage; guests are invited onto the Gibsons' terrace for a late

3440 Beach Ave, Roberts Creek BC V0N 2W0 Moderate; no credit cards; local checks only

afternoon glass of wine or pot of tea. The cottage has an L-shaped living-room/bedroom area with cedar plank floors, skylights, a wood stove, and rustic furnishings. Donna provides a muffin-and-fruit breakfast. The beach (two blocks away) or the pretty country road make good places for a morning stroll. No children; no pets; no smoking inside.

HALFMOON BAY

LODGINGS

Jolly Roger Inn
Hwy 101, 5 minutes from Halfmoon Bay at Secret Cove, (604) 885-7184 Mail: Box 7 RR1, Halfmoon Bay, BC V0N 1Y0 Expensive; AE, MC, V; checks OK Open mid-March through mid-November

The Jolly Roger's main lodge and restaurant were in the throes of a major renovation at press time. Besides new carpet and paint, look for possible changes in the steak-and-seafood menu in the restaurant. This seasonal resort (although the new owners are considering staying open year-round; call to make sure) consists of a cluster of one- and two-bedroom dark-brown townhouses with fireplaces, kitchens, and decks; most have sweeping bay views. Boaters and fishermen find this spot enchanting: good fishing, a first-rate marina, pleasing accommodations.

POWELL RIVER

The last town of any size on the Sunshine Coast gives a sense of the industries that have predominated in this part of the Northwest for more than a century: timber, fishing, and limestone mining. The MacMillan Bloedel pulp-and-paper mill at Powell River employs 1,900 people in the area and is one of only two left on the coast (the other is at Port Mellon, near Gibsons). Powell River is separated into the original mill town which surrounds the plant, Westview, the newest residential area, downtown and the ferry terminal, and Cranberry surrounding Cranberry Lake.

The trail through **Willingdon Beach Park** is more of an open-air forestry "museum" (old lumber industry equipment placed throughout a wooded area above the beach). Across from Powell River is **Texada Island**, the largest island in the Strait of Georgia and the Pacific Northwest's richest source of limestone.

Powell River also is western Canada's preeminent **scuba diving** center, and offers superb trout and salmon **sport fishing** as well. For a while ferry service from Powell River to Vancouver Island was suspended, but it's scheduled to be back in service by late 1991; call (604) 485-2943 for schedule.

RESTAURANTS

The Seahouse
Duncan and Marine,
(604) 485-9151
4448 Marine Ave, Powell
River
Moderate; full bar; AE,
MC, V; no checks
Lunch Mon-Fri, dinner
every day, brunch Sun

unrated

One of your best bets for dining in Powell River has always been this spot, overlooking the arriving and departing Vancouver Island ferry (once it gets back into service). Start with a drink in the cozy bar on the lower level, then ascend to the comfortable dining room for a sunset dinner; as for the food, we can only vouch for the past owners, as new ones took over just as we were going to press. We just hope the recipe for that exceptional bouillabaisse came with the purchase.

LODGINGS

Beach Gardens Resort
Hotel
A half hour north of
Saltery Bay ferry,
(604) 485-6267
7074 Westminster Ave,
Powell River, BC
V8A 1C5
Moderate; AE, DC, MC,
V; checks OK

Sitting on a protected section of the Strait of Georgia, the Beach Gardens Resort is a mecca for scuba enthusiasts, who come for the near-tropical clarity of the water and the abundant marine life. Off-season, it's often filled with businesspeople who have come to see trade shows or attend training seminars and afterwards to relax on the tennis courts or in the indoor swimming pool or fitness center. There's a marina to accommodate boaters, a decent dining room with reliable seafood entrées (try the warm seafood salad at dinner), and a locally popular neighborhood pub. The rooms are comfortable—nothing sensational, except the views of all that clear water. Less expensive cabins without views are popular with divers. Book far in advance for summer months.

Rodmay Hotel
Right in town, in front of
the mill, (604) 483-3206
6251 Yew St, Powell
River
Moderate; MC, V;
checks OK

Over 50 years ago, Rod and May McIntyre turned the old Powell River Hotel (a 1911 building across the street from the Powell River Company, predecessor to the current MacMillan Bloedel mill) into the Rodmay. Under the current owners, the building has been renovated. Unfortunately, they've erased some of the hotel's older interior features, but the exterior retains its turn-of-the-century look. Many of the rooms have a spectacular view of the mill—quite striking, though not conventionally scenic. A popular pub and a coffee shop are attached.

WHISTLER

Highway 99, running north from Vancouver to Whistler, is an adventure in itself. The aptly-named Sea to Sky Highway hugs fir-covered mountains that tumble sharply into island-filled Howe Sound. The grandeur and the views are breathtaking, and the curves of the road often demanding. The drive to Whistler from Vancouver takes approximately two hours, depending on road conditions and photo opportunities. As an alternative to driving, you can take buses or train (BC Rail) from Vancouver or fly via shuttle from Vancouver International Airport. For details, call Whistler Activity and Information Centre, (604) 932-2394.

Whistler Village has gained a reputation as a world-class vacation resort—you'll hear plenty of Australian and European accents as well as Japanese and Cantonese spoken in the lift lines. The complex is now huge. The European-style resort is actually two "communities": Whistler Village, with 23 hotels, inns, lodges, or condos, and Blackcomb Resort, with 15 accommodations. The swankest of these allow such luxuries as an après-ski soak in a heated outdoor pool or a Jacuzzi situated under the chair lifts, or playing tennis in January in a covered year-round court, or (silly as it may sound in such a sportif place) working out in an exercise room that overlooks the slopes. Numerous shops tout everything from souvenir T-shirts to fur coats. One to check out is Gaauda Native Fine Art in Chateau Whistler, where knowledgeable gallery owner Gina Schubert, a native Haida, will explain the art and jewelry in detail.

The Whistler-Blackcomb ski area, at the edge of Whistler Village, comprises two mountains and boasts some of the finest skiing in the Northwest. The Seventh Heaven T-bar, which ran to the top of Blackcomb, has been replaced by a high-speed quad. Two additional T-bars have been added, providing access to glacier skiing (a truly lunar experience) and the opportunity to ski at both areas (or sightsee) throughout the summer. The two mountains now offer over 180 runs from 29 lifts; the resort's Ski Esprit ski school offers individual and group lessons for adults. Kids aged 2 and older can take a range of lessons or join Kids Kamp; those 13 and up can join racing teams; (604) 932-3141 (Blackcomb), (604) 932-3434 (Whistler). Heli-skiing is available from private concerns; 15 kilometers of cross-country ski trails begin just outside the Village and wind through the adjacent countryside (rentals available in the Village and Whistler Creek ski shops); 50 kilometers of groomed trails can be found 20 minutes to the south of Whistler; (604) 932-5128. Adventure activities include snowboarding (rentals and lessons are available) and paragliding (lessons are available done with or without skis), dogsledding, snowshoeing, snowmobiling, and sleigh rides. Call Whistler Activity and Information Centre, (604) 932-2394.

Reservations are recommended far in advance at most of the lodgings in Whistler Village or Blackcomb Resort. Call central reservations, (604) 932-4222; from Vancouver, dial 685-3650; from western Washington, (206) 628-0982; elsewhere, toll-free (800) 634-9622. For a simpler, less expensive stay, ask about the hotels, pensions, and "budget" (a different meaning in Whistler) accommodations outside the village. Many lodgings now require 30 days' cancellation notice, with a 3-day minimum stay.

The resort has done a lot in recent years to develop year-round recreation and is definitely worth checking out even when there's no snow on the ground. Besides summer skiing, hikers and bikers can take chair lifts to a network of alpine trails; mountain bikers can board their cycles onto Blackcomb's mountain express chairs to Seventh Heaven or take the gondola 3,800 feet above the Village for the ultimate mountain descent. Water sports abound at the five lakes in the valley surrounding the resort, all reachable from the resort by hiking, biking, or horseback riding along the Valley Trail. Summers are warm and ideal for fishing, swimming, boardsailing, canoeing, kayaking, sailing, or water-skiing. Golfers can try the scenic Arnold Palmer–designed Whistler Golf Club, recently rated as one of the best courses in the world by *Golf* magazine. A second course under construction on Blackcomb is scheduled to open in 1992. Concerts are performed daily on the Village stage from June to September, and the resort hosts Labour Day, Canada's Birthday (July 1), and Octoberfest celebrations as well as a country and blues festival (mid-June), a classical music fest (mid-August), and a jazz festival (mid-September).

RESTAURANTS

Rimrock Cafe and Oyster Bar
1 block north of the gondola in the Highland Lodge, (604) 932-5565 Hwy 99, Whistler Moderate; full bar; MC, V; no checks Dinner every day (winter and summer only), brunch Sun

This intimate cafe split into two rooms (smoking and non-, each with a stone fireplace) is housed in an unprepossessing hotel outside of the Village proper. Rolf Gunther's restaurant is remarkable proof that fresh seafood and haute cuisine are not anomalies in the mountains. It offers an exquisite menu of innovative entrées at surprisingly moderate prices. To order here, close the menu: the seafood's the thing and the daily catches are on the blackboard. A recent appetizer was a melting preparation of peppered ahi, lightly seared, with a soya-ginger vinaigrette. On a later visit, the mahi mahi came baked with a light hazelnut crust and the ahi (it was so good as an appetizer, we had to try it again) marinated in soya and sake and topped with wasabe butter. Great care is taken here, not only in the food's preparation and freshness, but with the vegetables (carrots, sweet peas, and asparagus) splayed on a vermilion pool of red pepper catsup and a golden pool of yellow pepper. Even if you prefer meat to seafood you'll be pleased here. Our meat sampling (beef tenderloin that has barely touched the grill, served with a mustard-caper sauce) was equally outstanding. Service was top-drawer—knowledgeable without the airs, upbeat without being hip. A white chocolate mousse pie with a dark chocolate crust and a raspberry sauce took us to seventh heaven. Reservations suggested. If you don't state a preference, you'll be seated in the smoking room, as the non-smoking room fills up fast.

Val d'Isère
Upstairs in St. Andrews House, (604) 932-4666 Whistler Village, BC Expensive; full bar; AE, DC, MC, V; no checks Dinner Wed-Sun

The younger sister to Vancouver's master of French cuisine, Le Crocodile in Vancouver, this restaurant escapes the usual twin banes of large-scale-resort dining—blandness and mediocrity—to maintain an intimate atmosphere and impeccably smooth, personable service. Best of all, the food is nearly as good as that at Le Crocodile—somewhat modified to accommodate the demands of its mountaintop location and its heavier flow of guests.

Still, we had no complaints about their rendition of Le Crocodile's signature Onion Pie, a dense, smokey specialty, or its conversation-stopping appetizer of crab-filled ravioli in a subtle cream sauce topped with slivers of smoked salmon. Reserve a window seat, where you can look past the huge evergreens and into Whistler Village from your second-story perch. Try the medallions of salmon in basil butter sauce or the seasonal venison with morels in red wine—as tender as filet mignon. If you're not sure what to order, leave yourself in the capable hands of maîtres d'hotel Michel Beranger or Hermel Rioux, or another waitperson. Desserts range from an extravagant chocolate orange torte capped with a white chocolate butterfly to a light, refreshing trio of blackcurrant, pineapple, and passionfruit sorbets in a raspberry coulis. At press time, plans for lunch on at outdoor patio were underway.

Il Caminetto di Umberto
Across from the Crystal Lodge, (604) 932-4442
Whistler Village
Moderate; full bar; AE, DC, MC, V; no checks
Dinner every day

The ubiquitous Umberto Menghi is at Whistler, too. Not surprisingly, it's *the* place to go in the Village; few things can top fresh pasta and a bottle of red wine after a day of climbing up or schussing down mountains. This perennial favorite is also busy, the tables are too tightly packed together, and noise from the bar and cabaret interferes with table talk. Aim for the specials, such as the New York strip with mushroom sauce or the poached salmon with passion-fruit cream sauce. Umberto's newest addition, the less expensive Trattoria di Umberto in the Mountainside Inn, appeals to the more informal crowd for pasta and items from the rotisserie.

Sushi Village
Second floor of the Westbrook Hotel,
(604) 932-3330
Whistler Village
Moderate; full bar; DC, AE, MC, V; no checks
Lunch, dinner Wed-Sun (weekends only off season)

Sushi Village is a welcome reprieve from the boundless activity that Whistler offers. A civilized hush hovers over this refreshingly modest Japanese eatery, where the staff is knowledgeable and gracious. Delicious sushi and sashimi plates are prepared by animated experts at the counter. It's straightforward and dependable, although the beer, as at most places in Whistler, is quite expensive. Reservations accepted only for parties of four or more. Tatami rooms available.

LODGINGS

Chateau Whistler
Whistler Village,
(604) 938-8000, or from the U.S. toll-free
(800) 828-7447
Mail: 4599 Chateau Blvd, Whistler Village, BC V0N 1B0
Expensive; full bar; AE, DC, MC, V; checks OK
Breakfast, lunch, dinner every day, brunch Sun

This is the place to see and be seen on Whistler—where else in Whistler will a valet put your ski gear away for you? This Paul Bunyan–sized country mansion (would Canadian Pacific construct anything that's small?) with 343 guest rooms designed by a world-class interior decorator opened with a splash in 1989. The lobby, appropriately termed the Great Hall, sets you amid a floor of giant slate slabs covered with oversized hooked rugs, walls decorated with huge hand-painted stencils of maple leaves, two mammoth limestone fireplaces, and a 40-foot-high beamed ceiling. The funky collection of folk art birdhouses and weathered antique furnishings make the place comfortable and even cozy. The health spa is especially swank: the heated pool flows both indoors and out, allowing swimmers to splash away under the chair lifts or soak in the Jacuzzi under the stars. Other services include a multilingual

(800)268-1133
PO Box 550, 4050
Whistler Way, Whistler,
BC V0N 1B0
Expensive; AE, DC, MC,
V; checks OK

staff, babysitting, room service, and a dozen or so shops. After the grand entrance, the rooms themselves are a bit disappointing (non-suite rooms are surprisingly small and the furnishings try too hard to look modern). Do it right and ask for a "ski-view" room, worth the token $5 per room per night surcharge.

The casual, spirited La Fiesta Hot Rock Cafe and the intimate Mallard Bar make for pleasant après-ski socializing, but the main dining event is the inventive Wildflower Cafe. Chef Bernard Casavant, formerly of the Four Seasons in Vancouver, uses local Northwest products—free-range chicken and lamb, wild salmon, and organic beef and produce—to create inspired dishes such as tartare of Pacific Salmon with won ton wafers, or game bird stew of pheasant, duck, and quail with mushroom and rosemary dumplings. The cheerful, airy dining room is popular for Sunday brunch (but it doesn't entirely escape the pitfalls of buffets—the meats were dried and the coffee overbrewed).

Le Chamois
At the base of Blackcomb
Mountain at Benchlands,
4557 Blackcomb Way,
(604) 932-8700
Mail: PO Box 1044,
Whistler, BC V0N 1B0
Expensive; AE, DC,
MC, V; checks OK

Le Chamois is as intimate, refined, sleek, and understated as Chateau Whistler is grand, loud, and splashy. This is the spot for a quiet, private retreat. The petite, six-story hotel (which opened in December 1990) makes a fresh, sophisticated addition to Whistler's growing collection of hotels. Rooms are larger and more aesthetically pleasing than those in most of the bigger hotels. Light, airy, and clean, they feature simple European-style furnishings and sleek, smart color schemes of maroon and navy against pinewood furnishings. Single bedrooms are built to accommodate four people; each includes a living area with either a fold-out sofa bed or a Murphy bed (and every room has a view, though that of the mountain will cost you an extra $20). Studio rooms and grand three-bedroom corner suites are also available. During high season the hotel requires a minimum stay of 5 days (3-day minimum during the off season). Unlike the other hotels we list, Le Chamois is a condo/hotel, meaning that all rooms are privately owned—so some have special touches. One of the three-bedroom corner suites is furnished with a piano, and others are equipped with mini-offices complete with fax machines. The compact kitchens stock all the utensils you need for quick meals: microwave, refrigerator, and all utensils, but no ovens.

Downstairs, McQueens specializes in seafood. There is also a small conference area, a fitness room with an outdoor pool, and a Jacuzzi. Children 12 and under stay free of charge.

Delta Mountain Inn
Whistler Village,
(604) 932-1982, toll-free

It may be not be as grand as Chateau Whistler nor as chic as Le Chamois, but the Delta Mountain Inn, one of the oldest and largest hotels in the resort, offers 300 rooms, restaurant and bar, exercise room, swimming pool, and dome-covered year-round tennis courts. It's a good spot for hosting business meetings with a conference area that holds 250. The rooms are plain; the better ones offer kitchen, fireplace, balcony, Jacuzzi, mini-bar, and view of the mountains. Delta sits just 50 yards from Whistler's base lift. Dogs allowed.

Haus Heidi
Whistler Way at 7115
Nesters Rd,
(604) 932-3113
Mail: Box 354, Whistler,
BC V0N 1B0
Moderate; MC, V;
checks OK

A short drive from Whistler Village, this eight-room owner-operated pension is a refreshing change from the resort scene at the base of the mountain. Hosts Trudy and Jim Gruetzke will make your stay comfortable--a personal touch often lacking at the large resorts. The rooms have private baths, and guests have access to a Jacuzzi overlooking the mountains. Two of the rooms are located a few minutes' walk away in a condo with a fully equipped kitchen and sauna. One awakes to a marvelous complimentary breakfast of fruit, croissants, and omelets.

Pension Edelweiss
1 mile north of Whistler
Village in White Gold
Estates at 7162 Nancy
Green Way,
(604) 932-3641
Mail: Box 850, Whistler,
BC V0N 1B0
Moderate; AE, MC, V;
checks OK

If you arrive late, hosts Ursula and Jacques Morel will probably leave directions to your room on the front door and chocolates on your pillow, and expect you late for breakfast. As accommodating as the hosts are, you'll probably be awakened by the *guests*, who clomp about in their ski boots come morning. This casual, nonsmoking guest house, built by Jacques himself, is run in European fashion. The eight rooms are simple and spotlessly clean (if a bit worn these days), with double beds, down comforters, and private baths. Extras include the shared sauna, new Jacuzzi, and massage on request. Jacques (a former competitive skier) and Ursula cook ample breakfasts.

Ask at least eight hours in advance, and your hosts will welcome you back from a day on the slopes or hiking trail with a raclette—a rich fondue-like treat made by wrapping melted cheese over ham, baby potatoes, bread, or vegetables—served with French or German wine and espresso drinks. If your legs are strong, Pension Edelweiss is within walking distance of the Village; elsewise, hop the free bus (it's easier than parking in the Village).

Timberline Lodge
Adjacent to Conference
Center in Whistler
Village, 4122 Village
Green, (604) 932-5211
or toll-free
(800) 663-5474

The enormous moose head that greets you in the lobby tells you this place has more of a sense of humor than the other big-name hotels. It's the kind of spot where you feel at home clomping into the lobby to warm your toes by the enormous fireplace. Timberline's 42 rooms are simple and rustic, with four-poster beds of rough-hewn wood. Some rooms have fireplaces and others have balconies. A heated pool and Jacuzzi are also available. For a taste of Whistler history, check out

Mail: PO Box 996,
Whistler, BC V0N 1B0
Expensive; AE, MC, V;
no checks

Myrtle's restaurant, named after Myrtle Phillips, the woman who reportedly discovered the area as a summer vacation spot around 1910. Timberline Lodge also boasts the hoppingest night spot in the resort: Buffalo Bill's draws big-name musical acts from BC and beyond. Be sure to request a room away from Bill's if you plan to turn in early; the dancing often lasts far into the night.

LILLOOET

Two hours north of Whistler on a gravel road, you'll happen upon Lillooet—mile zero of the Cariboo Gold Rush Trail. The best thing about Lillooet is getting there. The **BC Rail** line between Lillooet and Vancouver is a vital link to the outside world for the loggers, miners, and farmers who live in remote areas of the Coastal Range. It's also one of the most scenic stretches in British Columbia, along pretty Howe Sound and into the jagged mountains. The route links Vancouver with Whistler, Lillooet, and Prince George; any destination north of Lillooet requires reservations: (604) 984-5246.

GOLD BRIDGE
LODGINGS

Tyax Mountain Lake Resort
Towards Gold Bridge on
Tyaughton Lake Road,
watch for sign,
(604) 238-2221
Mail: General Delivery,
Gold Bridge,
BC V0K 1P0
Expensive; AE, MC, V;
checks OK

In the wilderness of the Chilcotin Range about a hundred miles north of Vancouver, floatplanes are seen dropping incoming guests off at the dock and taking fishermen up to Trophy Lakes; a helicopter out back lifts thrill-seekers to enjoy heli-*anything* (heli-skiing, heli-hiking, and even heli-fossilhunting). But it's not all a high-tech adventure: you can be just as happy canoeing, gold panning, ice skating, horseback riding.

There are 28 suites (with beamed ceilings, balconies, and down-filled quilts) in the freshly hewn spruce log lodge. We prefer one of the the three chalets (each with three to four bedrooms, kitchen, loft, and a balcony overlooking Tyaughton Lake and the mountains)—especially for longer stays. Other amenities include a sauna, a large Jacuzzi in the front lawn, a game room with a ping-pong table, aerobics classes, and workout rooms. They've got it all here; the only thing an active person might run out of in this paradise is energy (or money). The energy, at least, is easily replenished after a day of sunbathing at the lake's edge. Unless you're in a chalet, you take all your meals in the dining room. If you're without a floatplane, try the spectacular train from Vancouver to Lillooet; the resort will pick you up.

70 MILE HOUSE

LODGINGS

Flying U Guest Ranch
20 kilometers east of 70 Mile House on N Greenlake Rd,
(604) 456-7717
Mail: Box 69, 70 Mile House, BC V0K 2K0
Moderate; AE, V; checks OK

It's a working ranch, ideal for families who like to ride horses on their own. There are 25,000 acres to explore, and cattle to round up if you wish. Back at the lodge, you can stay in log cabins, canoe on the nearby lake, and you'll dine at the over-140-years-old main building. Movies, bonfires, hayrides, or square dancing often follow the meal. A new saloon features a full bar and snacks. Rates are $90 per day or $540 per week per adult, all-inclusive (3 meals a day, all you can chow).

100 MILE HOUSE

LODGINGS

108 Golf and Country Inn Resort
Hwy 97, 13 kilometers north of 100 Mile House,
(604) 791-5211
Box 2, RR1, 100 Mile House, BC V0K 2E0
Moderate; AE, MC, V; no checks

★

At what seems like the edge of civilization (8 miles north of 100 Mile House, hence its name), a full-scale resort covers thousands of acres of rangeland. The resort has been purchased by a Japanese family, but it's still managed by Red Coach Inn. The guest rooms have been remodeled, and doubles run between $77 and $112 depending on the season. There are horseback riding, a large pool, five tennis courts, and a topflight 18-hole golf course. In winter, the cross-country skiing is some of the best in the Northwest, with over 200 kilometers of well-maintained trails. The restaurant has a fine view of the golf course and two lakes, and a cheerful atmosphere, but the menu is limited to the expected steaks and seafood.

BARKERVILLE

Billy Barker found lots of gold here in 1862, whereupon the town became the largest city north of San Francisco; then it became a ghost town, and now it's a place revived for the tourist trade. It's not bad, really: restored old buildings, a melodrama, and a general store full of 5-cent jawbreakers and lots of retro '60s (that's 1860s) goods. The whole place shuts down after the summer season (May-September).

Canoe trips. Six lakes form an amazingly regular rectangle in **Bowron Lake Park**, a scenic and challenging setting for a 120-kilometer canoe trip (with a number of portages in between). Plan on spending a week to 10 days. For outfitting, a couple of lodges offer canoe, paddle, and lifebelt rentals. Becker's Lodge also has campsites, cabins, and a dining room; contact them at mobile phone N698 552, Wells YP (in winter (604) 492-2390); PO Box 129, Wells, BC V0K 2R0.

RESTAURANTS

Wake Up Jake's
In center of town,
(604) 994-3259
Barkerville
Inexpensive; beer and
wine; MC, V;
Breakfast, lunch,
dinner every day
(May-September)

There's nothing about this old-time saloon that isn't 1870s authentic: they don't serve French fries (which hadn't been invented yet); they don't use processed anything. Instead, it's all real: soups, caribou stew, sourdough-bread sandwiches, pot pies, steaks, flaky fruit pies, and even the specials—pheasant or perhaps cheese and onion pie—amid saloon decor.

PRINCE GEORGE

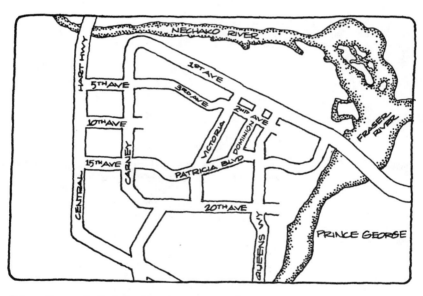

Prince George is the hub of north and central BC, and the jump-off point for brave souls heading up the Alaska Highway. The city sits between two mountain ranges on a dry plateau. Forestry is the main industry here, and loads of logging roads take hunters and fishermen back into remote and bountiful spots. The **Stellako River,** west of Prince George near Fraser Lake, is famous for its record trout. For recreational types, the **Cottonwood Island Nature Park,** along the Nechako River, has an extensive trail system suitable for hiking in the summer and cross-country skiing in the winter. Adjacent to the park is the **Prince George Railway Museum.** Two city galleries are of interest: **Prince George Art Gallery** features regional and national exhibits monthly; **Native Art Gallery** exhibits local native art and crafts.

Railroads. BC Rail will roll you through 462 miles of some of the most beautiful scenery in BC, from Vancouver to Prince George via Rail Canada in 13 hours; (604) 984-5246. Transfer to the passenger run to Prince Rupert, where ferries to the Queen Charlotte Islands, Vancouver Island, and Alaska depart regularly:

(604) 669-1211 for ferries within BC; toll-free (800) 642-0066 for Alaska Marine Highway information.

RESTAURANTS

Cafe New York
5th and Dominion,
(604) 564-1100
1215 5th Ave,
Prince George
Moderate; full bar; MC,
V; checks OK
Lunch Mon-Fri, dinner
Tues-Sat

A friendly spot, Cafe New York prides itself on an eclectic menu of entrées collected from a number of countries. The menu includes dishes such as a veal Marsala, chicken martina (prepared with garlic, capers, mushrooms, and vermouth), and pasta primavera (with hot Italian cappocolla, basil, garlic, and fresh veggies). Lunches are on the lighter side, which provides room for a slice of unbelievable cheesecake (they have over 100 different recipes).

The Achillion
4th and Dominion,
(604) 564-1166
422 Dominion St,
Prince George
Inexpensive; full bar;AE,
MC, V; no checks
Lunch, dinner Mon-Sat

Authentic Greek lunches and dinners can be found at Kostas Iliopulos' spot on Dominion Street. The combination plate is a good choice for two: you get pan-fried shrimp, beef shish kabobs, roast leg of lamb, potatoes, rice, and Greek salad or soup, all for $33.

LODGINGS

Esther's Inn
Off Hwy 97 at 10th Ave,
(604) 562-4131
1151 Commercial Dr,
Prince George,
BC V2M 6W6
Moderate; AE, DC, MC,
V; no checks

Bring your swimsuit to Prince George, even in the middle of winter, and pretend you're in the tropics. This Polynesian-style hotel comes complete with palm trees, swaying philodendrons, and waterfalls landscaped around a warm indoor swimming pool. For this dose of tropicana, rates are reasonable (about $55 a double); there are also three Jacuzzis, two indoor water slides spiraling into a separate pool, and a sauna. So they lay it on a little thick. The Tradewinds Dining Lounge and the Papaya Grove Coffee Garden are your dining alternatives.

PRINCE RUPERT

Prince Rupert began as a dream. Founder Charles Melville Hays saw this island as the perfect terminus for rail as well as sea travel and trade. Unfortunately, on a trip back from Europe, where he was rustling up money to help finance his vision, he met with an untimely death aboard the *Titanic*.

Seventy-five years later, a number of local folks rekindled Hays' dream. By the mid '80s Prince Rupert had two major export terminals and a booming economy. With this newfound prosperity have come culture and tourism.

The **Museum of Northern British Columbia** has one of the finest collections of Northwest Coast Indian art you're likely to find anywhere: 1st Avenue East and McBride, (604) 624-3207.

Ferries. Prince Rupert is called the gateway to the north, but it's also a place where ferries can take you west (to the remote Queen Charlotte Islands—see listing) or south (through the Inside Passage to Vancouver Island—see Port Hardy). The Alaska ferry winds north through the panhandle to Skagway.

RESTAURANTS

Smile's Seafood Cafe
*Follow 3rd Ave into
George Hills Way,
(604) 624-3072
131 George Hills Way,
Prince Rupert
Moderate; full bar; MC,
V; no checks
Breakfast, lunch, dinner
every day*

Since 1922, Smile's Cafe has been tucked unobtrusively among the fish-processing plants by the railroad. Favorites still include the fresh Dungeness crab, halibut, and black cod; the French fries are a perfect nongreasy, brown-skinned complement to the fish. The service is small-town friendly.

QUEEN CHARLOTTE ISLANDS

A microcosm of the British Columbia coast, the Galapagos of the Northwest, these sparsely populated, beautiful islands (150 in all) offer an escape to a rough-edged (and often rainy) paradise. There are countless beaches, streams, fishing holes, coves, and abandoned Indian villages to explore. Many unique subspecies of flora and fauna share these islands with the 6,000 residents.

The Haida Indians carve argillite—a rare black rock found only on the islands—into Northwest figurines.

Pacific Synergies offers sailing excursions in the area, (604) 932-3107. Or explore the island via kayak with the help of **Ecosummer**, (604) 669-7741.

Transportation. There are only 75 miles of paved roads in the Queen Charlotte Islands. Take the six-to-eight-hour ferry from Prince Rupert, fly in to the small airstrip on Moresby Island, or take a seaplane. Food and lodging are available, mainly on Graham Island, but most people who come camp. You can get tourist information through the local Chamber of Commerce, (604) 626-5211, or call Kallahin Travel Services (out of Queen Charlotte City) for island-related excursions from a bus-tour package to arranging a pick-up for you and your kayak, (604) 559-8455.

QUEEN CHARLOTTE ISLANDS: MASSET

LODGINGS

Copper Beech House
*Right by the fishing boat
docks at Delkatlah and
Collison, (604) 626-3225
1590 Delkatlah, Masset,
BC V0T 1M0*

The garden's a bit tangled, and so are all the memorabilia and collectibles inside this turn-of-the-century home, but come spring the garden smells wonderful and come morning so does breakfast. David Philips cans his summer fruits for year-round breakfasts and smokes his own seafood—which if you re-

Moderate; no credit cards; checks OK

quest dinner, will probably be one or more of the six appetizers. Upstairs there are two guest rooms decorated with Mission oak furniture: one has its own living room. Philips also caters dinner for groups.

QUEEN CHARLOTTE ISLANDS: QUEEN CHARLOTTE CITY

LODGINGS

Spruce Point Lodge
5.6 km west of ferry, left after Chevron station, then second left, at 609 6th Ave, (604) 559-8234 Mail: PO Box 735, Queen Charlotte City, BC V0T 1S0 Inexpensive; DC, MC, V; checks OK

What started as just a lawn and a shower offered to the occasional kayaker who needed a place to stay is now a cedar-clad building wrapped with a balcony on Skidegate Inlet that attracts families and couples alike—and still, most often, kayakers. There are seven clean rooms—each with a full bath, cable TV, and locally made pine furnishings. The price ($50 for a double) includes a continental breakfast and an occasional barbecue of whatever seafood the local fishermen drop off. Mary Kellie and Nancy Hett's lawn is not available anymore, but kayakers and adventurers on a budget will appreciate the hostel rooms (sheets and pillowcase provided) for $12.50 a night. There's use of the kitchen and laundry. Kayaks for rent. Pets and kids welcome.

FORT LANGLEY

RESTAURANTS

Bedford House
On the bank of the Fraser River in downtown Fort Langley, (604) 888-2333 9272 Glover Rd, Fort Langley Moderate; full bar; AE, MC, V; no checks Dinner every day, brunch Sun

A lovely place with a picturesque view of the Fraser River, this restored 1904 house is furnished with English antiques and has a pleasant, countrified elegance. The menu is rich with fancy continental cuisine: roast duckling with a fruit sauce, broiled fillet of salmon with hollandaise, or scallops and prawns served on puff pastry with a creamy champagne sauce.

CHILLIWACK

The name's not the only thing that's curious about this prosperous farming and dairy center: speakers set along the downtown portal blare easy-listening music, and antique cars seem plentiful. Local landmarks include an offbeat military museum at the **Canadian Forces Base** (open Sundays all year, midweek during the summer: (604) 858-1011), **Minter Gardens**, 10 large theme gardens (14 kilometers east at the Highway 9 junction: (604)794-7191), and **Bridal Falls Provincial Park**, 15 kilometers east on Highway 1.

RESTAURANTS

The New Yorker Steak House
Near Ontario at Yale,
(604) 795-7714
45948 Yale Rd W,
Chilliwack
Moderate; full bar; AE,
MC, V; no checks
Lunch, dinner Tues-Sun

This popular steak house in the center of town serves up enormous portions and consistently good quality. Charcoal-broiled Alberta grain-fed beefsteaks come in four different cuts and seven sizes, the most expensive being $13. You'll appreciate the whole sautéed mushrooms arranged on top. Chilliwack residents swear by the mushrooms Neptune (baked with cream cheese, shrimp, and crabmeat) and the hefty seafood platter. For a lighter lunch, order the Greek salad, prepared in true Greek fashion with tomatoes, cucumbers, lots of crumbled feta, and no lettuce. The decor is BC casual, with the usual fringed cloth lampshades.

La Mansione Ristorante
Near Williams St at Yale,
(604) 792-8910
46290 Yale Rd E,
Chilliwack
Moderate; full bar; AE,
DC, MC, V; no checks
Lunch Mon-Fri, dinner
every day

There's a menu of mixed delights in this handsome mock-Tudor mansion with leaded-glass windows and a warm fireplace for winter evenings. (Beware the air conditioner in summer; sitting near it can easily ruin the meal). We sampled a delicious seafood chowder, brimming with shrimp, crab, and clams. The veal pan-fried in butter, lemon juice, white wine, and capers was good and tangy. The dinner menu offers a wide variety of seafood dishes and pastas; other specialties include Chateaubriand, rack of lamb, and veal scalloppine Sergio (the legacy of the former owner). This is a good place to sample wines by the glass; new owner Peter Graham carries an extensive selection. Service is efficient. New banquet facilities for 45 are found on the second floor.

HARRISON HOT SPRINGS

Situated at the southern end of Harrison Lake, the town is a small, quiet row of low buildings facing the sandy beach and lagoon. The hot springs themselves are in a strangely enclosed temple with sulfur steam billowing out and an occasional Coke can strewn along the bottom of the pool. But don't be dismayed; the public soaking pool (which has cooled hot spring water pumped into it) is large and wonderfully warm (100 degrees average). In addition, there are sailboards and bikes to rent, hiking trails nearby, helicopters to ride, and a pub or two. In winter, skiers use Harrison as their spa after a day on the slopes at Hemlock Valley (a 40-minute drive).

RESTAURANTS

Black Forest

1 block west of Hwy 9 at Esplanade,
(604) 796-9343
180 Esplanade Ave,
Harrison Hot Springs
Moderate; full bar; AE,
MC, V; checks OK
Dinner every day (closed
Thurs off-season)

Bavarian food seems a staple in BC, and here's an authentic restaurant serving more than just schnitzels. Mr. and Mrs. Helpmueller run this family place, and the decor reflects their heritage; if you're a fan of goulash soup, schnitzel, and beef *rouladen*—sirloin stuffed with onions, pickles, mustard, and bacon, braised in red wine, and served with red cabbage and spaetzle—then you'll warm to the ambience too. The place is popular, so stop by on your evening stroll and make a reservation.

Conca d'Oro

Next to the public pool on Esplanade,
(604) 796-2695
234 Esplanade Ave,
Harrison Hot Springs
Moderate; full bar; AE,
MC, V; no checks
Lunch every day
(summer), Sat-Sun
(winter), dinner every day

This dark restaurant serves the familiar continental fare (schnitzel, seafood, veal), but you'll also find very good cannelloni and lasagne and great pizza. At dinner opt for the upper dining room with patio and lake view. Afterwards, if you have room, try the moist, homemade cassata, layered with creamy ricotta cheese, and then boogie it all off at the adjacent Lido cabaret. Avoid lunch: the midday menu is a small-scale offering of grilled cheese and fish 'n' chips.

LODGINGS

The Harrison Hotel

West end of Esplanade,
(604) 796-2244
100 Esplanade Ave,
Harrison Hot Springs,
BC V0M 1K0
Expensive; AE, DC, MC,
V; checks OK

Located at the southern shore of long and beautiful Harrison Lake, this legendary hotel is really a better place to view than to visit. The first hotel was built here in 1885 to take advantage of the hot springs; it burned down, and the present "old" building dates back to 1926. Since then the additions have changed the hotel into a sprawling mishmash of unrelated architecture. Grounds are quite lovely and spacious, with tennis courts and exercise circuit, but the best part about the place is definitely the hot spring water: two indoor pools (103 and 90 degrees) and one outdoor (90 degrees)—open only to hotel guests. A scenic golf course is 3 kilometers away.

Staying here is expensive (there are extra charges for almost everything), so you need to know what you're doing. Most of the rooms in the old wing still have 1950s decor. And since the hotel won't guarantee lake views, a safer bet is to book a room in the new tower (on the east side), where the more modern, spacious quarters are and where your chances of a view (lake or garden) are better. There's no air conditioning as yet, so you need to keep windows open or ask for a fan. The restaurants are nothing special. Our advice would be to use the place for a short stay, arriving in time to enjoy the excellent pools and a poolside drink and then promenading down the street to eat. The clientele will make you think you've retired to Florida.

MANNING PARK

LODGINGS

Manning Park Motel
Just off Hwy 3 in Manning Provincial Park, (604) 840-8822 Mail: Manning Park, BC V0X 1R0 Moderate; MC, V; checks OK

Situated within the boundaries of this pretty provincial park, the simple lodge gives you easy access to both gentle and arduous hiking trails. With a short drive, you can be paddling a rented canoe on Lightning Lake or riding a horse through the surrounding country. Besides the 41 motel rooms, the low-key resort includes a restaurant, a coffee shop, cabins, and triplexes—all in the same plain, functional style. If you have 39 friends, however, book the Last Resort a few yards down the highway, a real old-fashioned '40s charmer that sleeps 40. In winter (two-day minimum then) the park turns into cross-country and downhill ski heaven: Gibsons Ski Area is just out the back door.

PRINCETON

RESTAURANTS

The Apple Tree Restaurant
Vermilion at Dixie Lee, (604) 295-7745 255 Vermilion Ave, Princeton Moderate; full bar; MC, V; local checks only Lunch Tues-Fri (Tues-at July-Sept), dinner Tues-Sun

The big crabapple tree across from the Esso station marks the site of Douglas and Mary Rebagliati's excellent small restaurant, in a house filled with greenery and fussy wallpaper. Expect such appetizers as escargots cooked in mushroom caps (an Okanagan favorite) and good, hearty, homemade soups (such as Slovak sausage and sauerkraut); hope for the deceptively simple oregano chicken, marinated in olive oil and herbs and broiled. Desserts receive just as much attention (the reputation of the Louisiana mud pie has spread to Vancouver). The thoughtful wine list focuses on Okanagan Valley wines and BC ales and cider. The patio in the back is pleasant come summer. Have an early supper here and make Osoyoos by nightfall.

QUILCHENA

LODGINGS

Quilchena Hotel

Remote Quilchena Hotel captures the ambience of southwestern BC's cattle country, and it attracts a

Take the second Merritt
exit off the Coquihalla
Hwy, (604) 378-2611
Hwy 5A, Quilchena,
BC V0E 2R0
Moderate; MC, V;
no checks
Mid-April through mid-
October only

motley assortment: moneyed urbanites who fly over (the Quilchena has its own landing strip) in search of relaxation; cattle barons who come to buy livestock; gentlemanly senior citizens in search of the perfect golf course; and cowboys, Canada style (French accents belie their Texan appearance). It's a delightful stew, and meant to be that way: there are no phones or TVs in the 16 rooms; guests share bathrooms and dine together in the parlor. The rooms are decorated with the original iron bedposts and printed wallpaper. It's not elegant, but there's a worn comfort about the place, which was built in 1908 as a hotel for cattle ranchers traveling between Merritt and Kamloops. Guests often gather around the parlor's piano for an impromptu recital. Daytime finds you riding horses, playing tennis, golfing on the adjacent course, or searching the nearby fossil beds. For extended stays there's a three-bedroom ranch house on the grounds. There is lots of beef on the restaurant's menu; the old saloon is now open and features appetizers and local wines; the coffee shop is open all day.

MERRITT

LODGINGS

Corbett Lake Country Inn
16 kilometers south of
Merritt on Hwy 5A,
(604) 378-4334
Mail: Box 327, Merritt,
BC V0K 2B0
Breakfast, lunch, dinner
every day (closed
November, March-May)

French-trained owner and chef Peter McVey came from England to British Columbia on a fishing trip—and it must have been good. McVey's country inn caters to lovers of fly-fishing in the summer and cross-country skiers in the winter. There are three nondescript rooms in the lodge, but most choose to stay in one of the ten simple cabins, each with its own kitchen. The three new duplexes all have fireplaces and separate bedroom/living rooms. Aside from the outdoor activities, the food's the thing here. Dinner (by reservation only, guests and non-guests) is something different every night. McVey creates wonderful four-course evenings starting with soup (perhaps fresh mushroom), a salad (Caesar, hot German, or cucumber) and continuing to an entrée which could be anything from loin of pork with Dijon mustard to beef Wellington with Yorkshire pudding. Corbett Lake holds plenty of fish, but an extra fee gains you the privilege of angling in two private lakes stocked by McVey himself. You can catch as many trout as you'd like, but only two go home.

Did we lead you astray? Send us your gripe on the report form at the back of this book.

KAMLOOPS

RESTAURANTS

Minos

*1 kilometer north of
Overlander Bridge,*
(604) 376-2010
*262 Tranquille Rd,
Kamloops*
*Moderate; beer and wine;
AE, MC, V; no checks
Lunch Mon-Sat, dinner
every day*

Minos is a family-owned operation, with owner/chef Mike Frangiadakis' family living overhead. Wood furniture and lively-colored tablecloths help create a warm atmosphere. Service is exceptionally friendly and prompt; our waitress was well informerd and painstakingly patient. We enjoyed the chef's special, Mike's mezethes: bite-size pieces of chicken, pan-fried with mushrooms, onion, and wine, served with pita bread and tzatziki. Also good are the various souvlaki of lamb, chicken, and seafood. Minos' desserts are quite tasty; try a piece of honey-sweet baklava with a strong cup of Greek coffee.

LODGINGS

Lac Le Jeune Resort

*Off Coquihalla Hwy, Lac
Le Jeune exit 29
kilometers southwest of
Kamloops,*
(604) 372-2722
*Mail: PO Box 3215,
Kamloops, BC V2C 6B8*
*Moderate; full bar; AE,
MC, V; checks OK
Breakfast, lunch, dinner
every day*

Well-equipped and pleasant, this lodge puts you right on the lake for fishing and at the edge of the wilderness for hiking. You can stay in the lodge, in a self-sufficient cabin (perfect for families, and you can bring your pet), or in a chalet. The resort includes an indoor whirlpool and sauna, meeting rooms for up to 200, and a restaurant featuring breakfast, lunch, and an evening buffet. Adjacent is a downhill ski area; over 100 kilometers of cross-country skiing trails wind through the property. Boats and canoes are available for rent (the famous Kamloops trout are great to catch—and eat). Large tour groups tend to book the place en masse during the summer months, so reserve early, or take a chance on a last-minute cancellation.

ASHCROFT

RESTAURANTS

Ashcroft Manor Teahouse

*10 kilometers south of
Cache Creek,*
(604) 453-9983
*Trans-Canada Hwy,
Ashcroft*
*Inexpensive; full bar;
MC, V; local checks only
Breakfast, lunch, dinner
every day (open mid-
March through
November)*

A beautiful, airy roadside tearoom now sits just behind the original Ashcroft Manor, which was built in 1862 to accommodate travelers on their way to and from the gold fields. For breakfast, owners Tom and Susan Saunders offer a fresh fruit platter with hot scones, eggs any way you want, or huge, fresh cinnamon rolls (a meal in themselves). Lunch fare includes seafoods, salads, stir-fries, and fresh pasta dishes; dinners range from T-bone steaks to red snapper poached in orange sauce. The "changeable chicken" is most popular (a boneless breast prepared differently each night—120 recipes and growing). Outdoor seating in summer under the flowering trees.

LODGINGS

Sundance Ranch
8 kilometers south of Ashcroft off Highland Valley Rd,
(604) 453-2422
Mail: Box 489, Ashcroft, BC V0K 1A0
Moderate; MC, V; checks OK

Here's a dude ranch set in high plateau country, with the Thompson River cutting a deep gorge just to the west. Low-lying buildings of dark-stained wood contain handsome pine-paneled rooms and public rooms, all of which were renovated in 1989. Children can stay in their own wing or with their parents. For a real family retreat, stay in the nearby fully equipped lodge (holds up to 20), complete with wrangler to show you the saddle. The pool is quite grand, and the tennis court suffices, but the real attraction is the corral, where 100 good horses await you for the two daily rides, morning and late afternoon. It can get very hot here during the day, but if the sun is not too brutal, the rides will be simply wonderful. Over a dozen buffalo live in the adjacent fields. During the evening, the excellent meals are often served on the barbecue patio, and rustic rooms set the scene for drinks, parties, and games. You'll sleep well, breathing the cool, sage-scented air.

THE OKANAGAN VALLEY

The Canadian Okanagans, from Osoyoos at the border to Vernon to the north, are a summer playground. The valley is laden with orchards, making it especially appealing in spring when the fruit trees are in full bloom. The best time to pick up some of the valley's bounty is mid-August through early September; however, beginning as early as late June the fruit starts ripening: cherries (late June to mid-July), peaches (mid-July through September), pears (August through September), apricots (mid-July through mid-August), plums (September), apples (August through October), and grapes (September through mid-October).

Nevertheless, **wine-making** is the hot ticket in the Okanagan. British Columbians have long taken inordinate pride in their wines—even when those mostly came from a few largish factories like Kelowna's **Calona** (on Richter Street, (604) 762-9144) and Penticton's **Cartier** (on Main Street, (604) 492-0621). However, ever since British Columbia authorized estate and smaller farmgate wineries, many excellent small wineries have popped up. Some of the best estate offerings come out of **Gray Monk**, 8 kilometers west of Winfield off Highway 97, (604) 766-3168; **Cedar Creek**, 14 kilometers south of Kelowna in the Mission, (604) 764-8866; **Sumac Ridge**, off Highway 97, just north of Summerland, (604) 494-0451; and **Hainle Vineyards** in Peachland, (604) 767-2525. A couple of farmgate vineyards to keep an eye on are **Quail's Gate Vineyards** in Westbank, (604) 769-4451, and **Wild Goose Vineyards** just south of Okanagan Falls, (604) 497-8919. Other notable wineries to visit: **Mission Hill**, south of Kelowna in Westbank off Boucherie Road, (604) 768-5125; **Gehringer Brothers**, 4 kilometers south of Oliver off Highway 97 on Road 8, (604) 498-3537; **Brights Wines**, between Oliver and Vaseaux Lake on Highway 97, (604) 498-4981; **Divino**, (604) 498-2784 and **Okanagan Vineyards**, (604) 498-6663, both 5 kilometers south of Oliver off Highway 97. Most offer tastings and seasonal tours; call ahead for times and dates.

Skiing is still the biggest hook the Okanagan swings. The local climate is a powdery medium between the chill of the Rockies and the slush of the Coast Range, and the slopes are distributed along the valley. **Silver Star**, east of Vernon, has full resort facilities (information: (604) 542-0224). **Last Mountain** is the nearest stop from Kelowna for day schussing, (604) 768-5189, but **Big White**, (604) 765-3101, to the east has many more runs (44, up to 1,850 vertical feet), full facilities, and even cross-country trails, and claims the greatest altitude of all the ski areas in the province. **Apex Alpine**, Penticton's full-facility resort known for its challenging terrain, has added a number of "family" runs to complement its harder stuff; (604) 292-8222. Southwest of Penticton on Highway 3A, the **Twin Lakes Golf Club** doubles as a cross-country course in winter; (604) 497-5359. There's more downhill at **Mount Baldy** west of Osoyoos, (604) 498-2262—one of the first mountains in the area to have snow.

OSOYOOS

Osoyoos bills itself as "the Spanish capital of Canada," but not because of any pioneer ethnic roots. In 1975 the city fathers realized they needed a gimmick, saw that the Bavarian motif had been preempted elsewhere, so decided to slap up some fake red-tile roofs and goofy matador billboards and "go Spanish." The climate is Canada's driest, with 10 inches of rain a year and, Osoyoos Lake is reportedly Canada's warmest freshwater lake.

A good short hike is up Mount Kobau, just west of Osoyoos off Kobau Road. Take the Kobau Lookout trail (2 kilometers) to fire lookout or Testalinden Trail (5 kilometers) loop trail with views of the Similkameen Valley.

RESTAURANTS

Diamond Steak & Seafood House

Main St near 89th, Osoyoos, (604) 495-6223 Moderate; full bar; MC, V; no checks Dinner every day (closed February)

Just about everyone in Osoyoos likes this casual steak, seafood, and pizza house on the main street of town. The decor carries off the town's ersatz Spanish theme better than most, with brick window arches and black leatherette chairs with shiny silver buttons. The pizzas are quite good, if you like crust that's crisp enough to snap, and the Greek salad is the best in town. No wonder—the owner is Greek. The wine list shows a collection of labels (literally) from several valley wineries, and there are refreshing Okanagan apple and pear ciders too.

LODGINGS

Inkaneep

3 kilometers north of Osoyoos off Hwy 97, (604) 495-6353 Mail: RR 2, Osoyoos, BC V0H 1V0 Inexpensive; no credit cards; checks OK

Down a steep winding road to a little peninsula in Osoyoos Lake is this unassuming resort—one of the first on the lake. The best thing about it is location: all 10 beach-level rooms face directly south (maximum sun) and open only feet away from the water's edge (the two dark cabins are north-facing). Families (some in their third generation of vacationing here) don't mind the fact that the accommodations are a bit campish because they really come for the sun. Don and Esme

Hellyer book rooms by the week in the summer, love kids, and eschew loud boats and pets.

KEREMEOS

LODGINGS

Cathedral Lakes Resort
Call ahead for directions, (604) 499-5848 (or Kamloops radio phone off season N6-99700) Mail: RR1, Cawston, BC V0X 1C0 Moderate; no credit cards; checks OK

To say this resort is remote is more than an understatement. First you have to get to base camp, which is a 21-kilometer gravel-road journey off Highway 3 along the Ashnola River. Once you're there, a four-wheel-drive vehicle from the resort picks you up and takes you on a one-hour 14.4-kilometer journey to the lodge. The resort is heavy on recreation (hiking, canoeing, fishing), light on modern conveniences (such as phones and TVs). All rooms have hot water and views of the lakes and peaks that surround the resort. Choose a cabin (which can accommodate up to eight) or a room in the chalet or the lodge. Showers and toilets are shared. Two big meals are served (breakfast and dinner), so pack extra vittles if you get hungry midday (box lunches are available upon request). Make your reservations early, since the season is short and space is limited.

Located inside the Cathedral Lake Provincial Park, the entire area is a protected wildlife refuge and a unique geological region. At 6,000 to 8,000 feet, the air is cool and dry, the views of surrounding Cascade mountains spectacular. Mount Baker, Mount Rainier, the Coast Range, and the Kootenays are all visible from Lakeview Mountain, a day hike from the lodge.

KALEDEN

LODGINGS

Ponderosa Point Resort
319 Ponderosa Ave, (604) 497-5354 Mail: Box 106, Kaleden, BC V0H 1K0 Expensive; no credit cards; local checks only

Ponderosa Point's compound of 26 individually owned rental cabins on a peninsula extending out into Skaha Lake is an ideal spot to take a thick book for three days in the off season or a week in the summer (minimum stays respectively). The most attractive units are the one- and two-bedroom Pan Abodes set on a Ponderosa pine–covered bluff above the lake. There's a 600-foot sandy beach, boat rentals, tennis courts, a playground, and a big grassy central compound. The cabins, named after trees, are all individually furnished by the owners. They're not plush or contemporary, but they're universally comfortable and clean. Try Greasewood if there are two in your party—the furniture has a hand-hewn look that's perfect for the setting.

PENTICTON

Penticton takes full advantage of its dual lakefronts. The south end of town (with its go-cart tracks, amusement centers, miniature golf courses, water slides, and RV parks) touches the north shore of Skaha Lake. The north end of town sidles along the southern tip of the 70-mile long Lake Okanagan.

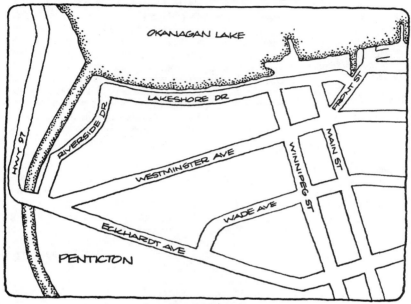

RESTAURANTS

Granny Bogner's
2 blocks south of Main,
(604) 493-2711
302 Eckhardt Ave W,
Penticton
Expensive; full bar; AE,
MC, V; checks OK
Dinner Tues-Sat

★★★

One of the province's best restaurants is also one of the most consistent. Regulars never tire of German-trained chef Hans Strobel's escargots and veal, and even when they think they'll venture farther down the menu, they end up ordering the same favored dishes again and again. Indeed, Strobel's capable of a lot more—meltingly tender sweetbreads; a fragrant goulash soup, and expertly herbed salmon. The menu remains admirable—poached halibut, duck in its own juices, beef filet with bèarnaise, excellent Russian eggs as a starter—and the preparations are consistently infused with creativity. Desserts remain outstanding, especially the fresh, lightly sweet strawberry tart.

Ambience is number one, with substantial old wooden chairs, cloth-covered tables well spaced throughout the rooms, and Oriental carpets and a brick fireplace to remind you that this was once a home. It's all just shy of precious, with fancy lace curtains and waitresses in floor-length paisley skirts. The bar with its comfy chintz chairs invites brandy and dessert. The wine list does a grand job of representing the best local estate wineries.

Theo's

Near the corner of Main and Eckhardt,
(604) 492-4019
687 Main St,
Penticton
Moderate; full bar; AE, DC, MC, V; no checks
Lunch Mon-Sat, dinner every day

The ever-popular Theo's sports a series of sun-dappled interior patios, roofed with heavy rough-sawn beams, floored with red tile, walled in white stucco. There's a two-sided fireplace to cozy up to in winter, healthy greenery, and lots of Greek memorabilia. The bar is hung with copper vessels and dried herbs. Patrons say Theo's cooks an excellent rabbit (from nearby Summerland) and swear by the octopus. We agree, but we wish the accompaniments (white rice, carrots, and over-cooked potatoes) were a little more inspired and the taramasalata more authentic. That said, by all means go in the late afternoon for an aperitif and a plate of excellent fried squid, or late at night to eat moussaka. The belly dancer's only there on special occasions these days, as the place is usually too busy to bother.

Tumbleweed Grill

Near Nanaimo and Main, (604) 493-6556
314 Main St, Penticton
Inexpensive; full bar; MC, V; no checks
Lunch Mon-Sat, dinner every day, brunch Sun

This bright, colorful, playful Sante Fe–style restaurant is a delightful addition to the Okanagan Valley restaurant scene. Peach stucco walls, Southwest-sky-blue trim, pink highlights, tall trees that stretch up toward the skylights, and a corner fireplace emit a good feeling well before the food arrives. Owners Rob and Donna Wylie and Andrew Brice (also of the summertime Salty Beach Cafe) have created a menu that perhaps originated in Sante Fe but doesn't hesitate to dip into California or the Far East. We like the way Tumbleweed plays with foods, placing chicken marinated in ginger and soy on top of udon noodles, presented on a corn husk, or tossing prawns in tequila and lime. Reports say this place is exactly the shot of sunshine Penticton needed to jolt its restaurant scene into the '90s.

LODGINGS

Coast Lakeside Resort

Main and Lakeshore,
(604) 493-8221
21 Lakeshore Dr W,
Penticton, BC V2A 7M5
Expensive; full bar; AE, DC, MC, V; checks OK
Breakfast, lunch, dinner every day

The Coast Lakeside (formerly the Delta Lakeside) is the flagship of the Lake Okanagan shore. This sprawling resort hotel is also the most expensive place in town, but since it's the only place with its own beach front it's hailed by locals, conventioneers, and tourists alike. There are 204 light, airy rooms with balconies: the north-facing rooms have lake views. There are outdoor tennis courts and an indoor pool that looks out to the lake beyond. The restaurants are better-than-average hotel restaurants. One of those, Peaches and Cream, makes a pleasant breakfast spot; the other, Ripples, features continental dishes plus a teppan table and such deliriously unusual (for the Okanagan) items as sake mushrooms and chicken yakitori. There's also the Lakeside Patio Grill and Lounge.

Penticton Inn

Martin St and Nanaimo,
(604) 492-3600
333 Martin St, Penticton,
BC V2A 5K7
Expensive; AE, DC, MC,
V; no checks

It's big, pink, and right in the middle of town. This once very smoky, seedy hotel has been completely remodeled under new ownership and reopened its doors in mid-1990. The 120 peach-colored rooms with deep green floral-patterned rugs are tasteful. It's not on the water, but there's a modest pool and sauna room. Conference rooms fit from 10 to 400. The elegant Prince Charles Dining Room does a good job of trying to use local ingredients whenever possible.

NARAMATA

RESTAURANTS

The Country Squire

Take Naramata Rd, left
on Robinson, right on 1st,
(604) 496-5416
3950 First St, Naramata
Moderate; full bar; MC,
V; local checks OK
Dinner Wed-Sun

Every meal becomes an event at this clubby old house. Dinner might take up to four hours; however long it is, the table's yours for the night—you can even take a walk in between courses if you'd like. Master of ceremonies is Ron Dyck, who owns and operates this shrine of Okanagan cookery with his wife Patt. Some think the flourishes are simply too much; others like all of Ron's personal touches. The opening act takes place when you call for reservations, at which time you are asked to choose from among several seasonal entrees: stuffed loin of lamb with mint, Béarnaise, and a touch of tarragon; pork filet with green peppercorn sauce; fresh Dungeness crab cakes with basil; or the ever-popular beef Wellington. Upon arrival you find a formal card detailing the courses to come: perhaps a coarse duck pâtè surrounded with Cumberland sauce to begin; a soup; your entrèe; a platter of well-selected cheeses and fruit; and dessert, such as the chocolate ginger pear, poached in sauvignon blanc. The food is good, if rococo, with only the occasional inexplicable lapse. The price is a flat $32—and Ron is at your side throughout the meal, decanting of one his 350 wines, flambéing the steak Diane, or carving the Wellington. He's also a splendid resource on local wines, many of which reside in his own deep cellar.

LODGINGS

Sandy Beach Lodge

Off Robson on Mill Rd,
(604) 496-5765
Mail: Box 8, Naramata,
BC V0H 1N0
Moderate; MC, V;
no checks
Open May through
September only

Here is the archetypal summer-lodge-on-the-lake, where the same families have signed up for the same two weeks in the same cabin for as long as anyone can remember. So long, however, that the place began to deteriorate without anyone really noticing. On our latest visit, we were pleased to see plans for the new cathedral-ceilinged lodgettes that are slotted to replace the squat brown bungalows over the next year. The spiffier new ones will be leased by the week on a 10-year basis. Non-regulars will have to settle for one of the five small rooms upstairs in the varnished pine-log lodge. Here the furnishings are old but good: heavy drapes and matching fitted bedspreads; wrought-iron-and-glass side tables and dressing tables. It's all too period to be tacky. The setting is just about perfect: a wide green lawn, breezy with stately pines and shady maples, sloping down to a quiet cove with a sandy beach perfect for horseshoes, croquet, or shuffleboard. Tennis courts, a small swimming pool, rental boats, and wooden lawn chairs provide ample diversions.

SUMMERLAND

A theme town done in the same spirit as Osoyoos, only this time they chose Tudor. Old Summerland is down on the water, but most of the town's business now thrives on up on the hill.

RESTAURANTS

Shaughnessy's Cove
Lakeshore Dr in Old Summerland,
(604) 494-1212
12817 Lake Shore Dr,
Summerland
Inexpensive; full bar;AE,
MC, V; no checks
Lunch, dinner every day

Shaughnessy's strong suits are its dramatic view of Okanagan Lake (it's built as close to the water as the law allows) and its airy atmosphere. The restaurant is tiered into four levels, with two outdoor decks, 20-foot ceilings, an old oak bar, skylights, three fireplaces, and pleasant decor. The seasonal menu features fare from fish 'n' chips to chimichangas to a filling stew served in a hollowed-out loaf of bread. The Caesars are so powerful, you'll also get a stick of Dentyne for later. Owner Mark Jones emphasizes service and atmosphere: both are excellent. Watch for the new outdoor margarita bar and firepit for summer evenings.

PEACHLAND

RESTAURANTS

Chinese Laundry
Follow signs from Hwy 97
to Peachland, then signs
to Chinese Laundry,
(604) 767-2722
5818 Beach Ave,
Peachland
Inexpensive; full bar;
MC, V; no checks
Lunch, dinner every day

On Front St in the Valley
Motor Inn,

True enough, the building once used to have a laundromat that doubled as a restaurant; however, the word is they did more laundry than dishes. But when Frank Jung opened his Cantonese and Sichuan restaurant in the same restaurant a few years ago, he latched onto the name and, so to speak, the concept. The place is filled with laundry-related antiques (washing machines, sewing machines, and interesting pictures documenting Chinese and their role in the laundry business). At first people came to the family-owned Laundry because of its strange name, now they return for its good food. During the middle of the day you can get a hamburger but after 4pm it's strictly Chinese. A popular place especially on summer eves. The new

(604) 492-2828
123 Front St,
Penticton

Penticton location is slightly bigger; but we prefer the Peachland original.

KELOWNA

On the east side of Lake Okanagan, Kelowna is the largest and liveliest of the Okanagan cities, with some noisy nightlife, some culture (an art museum and summer theater), a growing range of continental and ethnic restaurants, a big regatta in July, and an interesting historical preserve at **Father Pandosy's Mission**, (604) 860-8369. It even has its own version of the Loch Ness monster: **Ogopogo**. Keep a look out for him (or her) while supping on the gaily-decked-out paddlewheeler *Fintry Queen* or touring aboard the *Okanagan Princess*.

Houseboating on 70-mile-long Lake Okanagan a is good three- to seven-day vacation alternative for the entire family—most houseboats sleep up to six ($1200 per week). No previous boating experience is necessary—they'll give you a "Captain's lesson" when you arrive; Shelter Bay Houseboats, (604) 769-4411.

RESTAURANTS

Papillon
Near the corner of
Pandosy and Leon,
(604) 763-3833
375 Leon Ave, Kelowna
Moderate; full bar; AE,
MC, V; no checks
Lunch Mon-Fri (except
July-Aug), dinner
every day

With the departure of social chef Jean Peeters (who spent more time in the dining room than in the kitchen), Willi Franz and René Haudenschild (of the William's Inn) have expedited the service, stepped away from the strictly French menu, and added a number of pastas to keep up with the trend toward less-expensive dining. You'll still find the standard French offerings such as moules à la marinière, escargots en croute, steak au poivre, and wild duck a l'orange—all presented with flair—alongside more Italian infusions such as fettuccine alfredo, gnocchi with a meat sauce, and tortellini primavera. The wine list includes a smattering of everything, from European to local. Decor is contemporary but comfortable.

Vintage Room (Capri Hotel)
Gordon and Harvey,
(604) 860-6060, ext 229
1171 Harvey Ave,
Kelowna
Moderate; full bar; AE,
DC, MC, V; checks OK
Lunch Mon-Fri, dinner
every day, brunch Sun

Nobody really wants to like this elegant, pricey restaurant on the ground floor of the Capri Hotel. Maybe that's what makes the Vintage Room try so hard—and most often succeed. The service is impeccable, and the restaurant bends over backward to accommodate your whims. Only want a few appetizers, half-orders, or dessert? No problem—there's no pressure to order more. It's some of the most sophisticated food in the Okanagan with items such as a clear oxtail consommé, a watercress salad with a light Dijon-honey vinaigrette and tomato wedges with fresh basil. Vintage favorites include sweetbreads piccata or a spring salmon broiled with pesto and Pernod. Avoid the imported pastries and the runny chocolate mousse. The only other drawback is the tour groups that book here in summer.

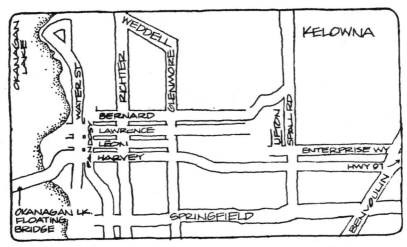

Talos Greek Restaurant
Bernard and Water,
(604) 763-1656
1570 Water St, Kelowna
Moderate; full bar; AE,
MC, V; no checks
Lunch Thurs-Fri, dinner
every day

For 14 years now Talos has been turning out superior Greek cuisine, and it just seems to be getting better. Favorites on the menu include horiatiki salad; very nice, creamy tzatziki with just enough garlic; and a dynamite souvlaki sandwich with thick slices of freshly grilled beef or lamb, stuffed into chewy pita bread. The last comes with a good Greek salad. All this takes place in a handsome, simple space, cool and pleasant, with checked tablecloths and lots of bare wood—like Greece, only better. Gallons of lemon juice go into the vegetables and grilled meats, and the prawns are reportedly excellent.

Guisachan House Restaurant
Cameron and Gordon,
(604) 862-9368
1060 Cameron Ave,
Kelowna
Moderate; full bar; MC,
V; no checks
Lunch, dinner every day

unrated

The original 1885 house was a summer lodge for the Aberdeens, who developed the big Coldstream Ranch east of Vernon. Careful restoration brought all the details back to the original design (fir floors, decorative mantels; even the vintage wallpaper was preserved and cleaned by a museum curator). Technically, it's owned by the City of Kelowna, but chef George Rieder recently leased the restaurant. At press time it was open only for lunch and afternoon tea. We suspect Rieder's waiting for the okay from the city to open for dinner before the efforts we know he's capable of make an appearance here.

LODGINGS

Hotel Eldorado
Follow Pandosy (which
becomes Lakeshore) for
6.4 kilometers south of the
Okanagan Floating
Bridge, (604) 763-7500

Hands down, this is the best place to stay on Lake Okanagan—that is, if a boardwalk will do instead of a sandy beach. Originally located a few miles uplake, Eldorado Arms was built for a countess of Scottish descent in 1926. After its move to its current location in 1989, it caught fire and burned almost to the ground.

*500 Cook Rd, Kelowna,
BC V1Y 9L5
Expensive; full bar; AE,
MC, V; no checks
Breakfast, lunch Mon-
Sat, dinner every day,
brunch Sun*

Consequently, the rebuilt manse feels very new yet has the grandeur of a bygone era. Each of the 19 rooms (even the least expensive) has an antique armoire and a couch, most have balconies, and some have Jacuzzis. Best are the lakeside or corner rooms. The boardroom with a large patio is an excellent meeting place for 10 to 60 people. The round house nearby can hold up to 85 for banquets.

There's not much of a lobby, as the restaurant and lounge take up most of the first floor. Fortunately, these are both places we don't mind spending a lot of time in. On one early spring visit we sampled an excellent roasted breast of duck with peach brandy and pink peppercorns which was accompanied by spaghetti squash, sweet peas, and roasted red potatoes and preceded by a chunky tomato and gin soup. There is a good selection of British Columbia wines. If you'd like to try some by the glass, just ask—there are often a few bottles open. Breakfast in the sun room is an extremely pleasant way to wake up. On summer afternoons you can have a hamburger on the Boardwalk. Rotary Beach is just a short walk away.

Lake Okanagan Resort

*2751 Westside Rd, 17
kilometers north of
Kelowna, (604) 769-3511
2751 Westside Rd,
Kelowna,
BC V1Y 8V2
Expensive; full bar; AE,
DC, MC, V; no checks
Breakfast, lunch, dinner
every day*

You reach the 300-acre resort via a beautiful, pine-clad winding road on the west side of Okanagan Lake. The place shows a little wear and tear, but the appointments were never first-cabin to begin with. Still, it's the best destination resort in the Okanagan. Now open year-round, it offers sailing, swimming, golf (18 holes), tennis (7 courts), and horseback riding to keep you busy. You can stay in a large condominium, or a smaller chalet (both with wood-burning fireplaces), or any of four different inns. All rooms have kitchens and rent by the night. Since the resort is located on a very steep hillside, many of the rooms are a good climb or a steep descent away from the activities, but a resort shuttle makes a quick job of it. The evening restaurant, Chateau, in the white Art Deco clubhouse serves fancy continental-resort fare such as wrapped and sauced veal and Chateaubriand. The informal Fresco Cafe is open all day. A poolside lounge makes for an interesting social setting.

Capri Hotel

*Gordon and Harvey,
(604) 860-6060
1171 Harvey Ave,
Kelowna, BC V1Y 6E8
Expensive; AE, DC, MC,
V; checks OK*

All of the 184 rooms have seen an upgrade. The best still look out to the courtyard (with its outdoor hot tub and pool), but privacy is lacking on the ground floor. There are two dining options here, the informal Garden Cafe and the outstanding Vintage Room (see review). For relaxation there's an outdoor hot tub and pool, men's and ladies' saunas, and for a taste of nightlife, there's Angie's Pub or Cuzco's Lounge.

The Gables Country Inn & Tea House
Off Highway 97 south of Kelowna, turn east at Old McDonald's Farm to 2405 Bering Rd, (604) 768-4468 Mail: PO Box 1153, Kelowna, BC V1Y 7P8 Moderate; no credit cards; no checks

The Gables sits on Indian land amid vineyards and open space yet is only 10 minutes from downtown Kelowna. The expanded late-1800s house, filled with antiques, was remodeled with salvageable lumber and appointments from other old homes bidding adieu in the area. The three rooms are large and ornately decorated. The largest has a balcony with view of the secluded sunken garden and pool. Breakfast includes fresh fruit and hot-out-of-the-oven scones.

VERNON

Vernon is the most commercialized tourist center in the Valley, the main jumping-off point for skiers and the main landing pad for conventioneers. Nightlife is lively, but the dining scene is generally uninspired.

O'Keefe Historic Ranch, 11 kilometers north of Vernon, is one of the original cattle ranches from the late 1800s. Now a museum, the compound contains most of the original buildings and equipment from the era. Tours run April-October; (604) 542-7868.

RESTAURANTS

Intermezzo
On 34th Ave near 32nd St, (604) 542-3853 3206 34th Ave, Vernon Moderate; full bar; AE, MC, V; checks OK Dinner every day

This musty green-colored restaurant looks like it has been around for 20 years, and in fact it has been here for nearly 15. Chef Jim Grady's been cooking here since its beginnings, so you can count on consistency and big servings. If you don't feel like eating in a windowless room, take your hefty order of cheesy lasagne, fettuccine pesto, or perhaps even some barbecued pork ribs to go.

LODGINGS

Best Western Villager Motor Inn
At the north end of town, directly across from Village Green Mall, (604) 549-2224 5121 26th St, Vernon, BC V1T 8G4 Moderate; AE, DC, MC, V; no checks

In terms of plush carpeting, contemporary accoutrements, and upkeep, this half-timbered-and-brick motel on the Highway 97 strip is the best in town. Of the 53 rooms, 24 open onto the inviting atrium pool and hot tub, but the regular rooms are quieter.

SALMON ARM

RESTAURANTS

Orchard House
22nd Street NE,
(604) 832-3434
720 22nd NE,
Salmon Arm
Moderate; full bar; MC,
V; no checks
Lunch Mon-Sat, dinner
every day

A retired British colonel built this lovely house in 1903, planting an orchard and tulips on its surrounding 20 acres. Now it's a restaurant, serving seafood almost any way—baked, fried, poached—but the rack of lamb shipped from Australia is the starring item. Four rooms have been converted into dining areas: try to get into the glassed-in verandah with a view of Shuswap Lake, or the living room with its glowing fire.

SICAMOUS

Houseboating. You and your family can explore the 1,000 miles or so of the Shuswap Lake shoreline at the northern end of the Okanagan Valley on a houseboat—complete with everything from microwave oven to a water slide. Seven-day trips run you between $1645 and $1745 during peak season, not including gas (plan on $25 a day extra); **Waterway Houseboats**, (604) 836-2505.

REVELSTOKE

Heli-skiing. For the serious skier, Revelstoke serves as a base camp to some amazing runs in and around the Albert Icefields. The catch: you need a helicopter to get there. Selkirk Tangiers Helicopter Skiing Ltd., (604)837-5378, boasts over 200 runs. For a few grand, Canadian Mountain Holidays will take you out, for a week at a time, to one of their fully staffed lodges in remote hideaways for some great skiing and hiking; (403) 762-4534.

RESTAURANTS

Black Forest Inn
5 kilometers west of
Revelstoke on the
Trans-Canada Hwy,
(604) 837-3495
Trans-Canada West #1,
Revelstoke
Moderate; full bar; AE,
MC, V; local checks only
Dinner Wed-Mon, lunch
in summer (closed
November)

Inside this A-frame you'll find a bit of Bavaria, with cute cuckoo clocks and German souvenirs cluttering every spare inch of space. Fondue Provençal, British Columbia salmon fillets, and a variety of beef tenderloins round out a rather extensive menu; we recommend one of the Bavarian dishes such as sauerbraten or schnitzel. Swiss-born chef Kurt Amsler's specialty is rainbow trout from a local hatchery; the servings grow larger as summer and trout progress. Try a glass of schnapps or a slice of Black Forest cake, made locally with cream and kirsch.

The 112
McKenzie and 1st,
(604) 837-2107
112 E 1st St,
Revelstoke
Moderate; full bar; AE,
MC; no checks
Lunch, dinner Mon-Sat

Located in the Regent Inn downtown, The 112 is a unanimous favorite among locals. The masculine decor of dark cedar paneling, historical photographs of the Revelstoke region in the 19th century, and soft lighting blends well with the continental cuisine. Chef Peter Mueller specializes in veal dishes, but the cioppino and lamb Provençal also come with high recommendations. Most of the seafood is frozen except for the BC salmon. The wine list has been expanded to include some French and Australian labels but still emphasizes British Columbia's own vintners. A variety of after-dinner flaming coffees are good for show but little else.

GOLDEN

RESTAURANTS

Mad Trapper
1½ blocks north of traffic
light, (604)344-6661
1105 9th St, Golden
Inexpensive; beer and
wine; MC, V; no checks
Lunch, dinner every day

The Mad Trapper is the après-ski hangout for helicopter skiers in the Purcell Mountain Range (who often include big ticket Hollywood types like Robert Redford and Lee Majors). The burgers and beer are strictly tavern—but great after a day in the white. The hook of the Trapper is that you sign a dollar bill and staple it to the wall. Autograph hunting is a favorite activity.

FIELD

LODGINGS

Emerald Lake Lodge
8 kilometers north of the
Trans-Canada Hwy in
Yoho National Park,
(604) 343-6321
Mail: PO Box 10, Field,
BC V0A 1G0
Expensive; AE, MC, V;
checks OK

In the middle of Yoho National Park, surrounded by the Kootenay Mountains and truly remarkable views, is the Emerald Lake Lodge. The geography is enough to lure you here, and the comfortably plush log lodge will keep you here. The owners (who gained their experience from running the Deer Lodge at Lake Louise) have brought in all the luxuries of a classy woodsy resort: numerous decks, three comfortable lounges with large stone fireplaces, a dining room, a billiards room (with a real English snooker table), a hot tub, sauna, and weight room. Stay in a suite (high season: superior $200, deluxe $240, executive $265); each has a deck, fireplace, and queen-size bed. The deluxe and executive rooms have "guaranteed" views (do you get your money back if you don't like it?) and mini-bars. Breakfast is well done and served buffet style. Dinners (a sort of mixture of California and Pacific Rim cuisines), are inventive.

The lake is too cold for swimming, so most people opt for horseback riding, fishing for trout, canoeing, or hiking (there's a nice trail around the lake). Come winter, there's access to nearby helicopter skiing, or make the pilgrimage to Banff to cross-country ski out to hot springs. Smoking and kids *are* allowed; but at least there aren't any TVs.

RADIUM HOT SPRINGS

Radium Hot Springs makes an ideal soaking stop at the base of the Kootenay mountain range. The hot springs, open to the public year-round, are equipped with two pools: one heated, the other cooler for more athletic swimming. If you didn't pack your bathing suit, don't worry; they'll rent you one for a buck. On Highway 93, 3 kilometers from Radium Junction, (604) 347-9485. Nearby you'll find golfing, camping, lodging, and tennis.

INVERMERE

RESTAURANTS

Strand's Old House

In the middle of town,
(604) 342-6344
818 12th St, Invermere
Moderate; full bar; AE,
MC, V; no checks
Dinner every day (closed
in November)

Built in 1912 by pioneer Alexander Ritchie, this house has been converted to an idyllic setting for some of the finest dining in eastern British Columbia. Beyond the beech tree–lined yard are gardens with views to the mountains. Chef Tony Wood makes everything from scratch, right down to the mayonnaise served with the steamed artichokes, and prepares a different special each evening (around $15). Don't shy away from the elaborate leather-bound menu, though, which features page after page of outstanding appetizers and entrées. A cold, spicy avocado soup started our meal, followed by a well-prepared veal steak with a morel mushroom sauce and an exceptional chicken Oscar, stuffed with crab and covered with a cream sauce. Regional wines and beers add gusto to occasional evenings of live music. A light menu (smaller portions of the regular fare) is offered after 9pm. Be sure to make reservations.

LODGINGS

Panorama Resort

18 kilometers west of
Invermere on Toby Creek
Rd, (604) 342-6941
Mail: PO Box 7000,
Invermere, BC V0A 1K0
Moderate; AE, MC, V;
no checks

More than a resort, Panorama is its own village—a sprawling establishment in the Purcell Mountains that contains a seven-lift ski area, condos and a hotel (even kennels for your dog), lots of restaurants and night-spots, and outdoor recreation aplenty. Eight well-maintained tennis courts, horses, hiking trails, and river rafting on Toby Creek relieve the resort from dependence on the winter ski trade. But ski season is still the time to go. The snow is deep, white powder (World Cup competitions have been held here), and if nature doesn't dispense the white stuff, machines will. We recommend the condos over the hotel units: they're more expensive, but they all have kitchens. Wherever you stay, you're never more than five minutes' walk to the chair lifts.

KIMBERLEY

Like many foundering mining towns in the early 1970s, Kimberley looked to tourism (and chose a Bavarian theme) as the panacea for a faltering economy. At 4,000 feet, Kimberley is (not surprisingly) the highest incorporated city in Canada. Views of the snow-capped Rocky Mountains are stunning, especially from the Kimberley Ski Resort, which has three chairlifts and a T-bar and over 30 downhill runs. There are 26 kilometers of Nordic runs, 3 kilometers of which are lit at night.

The town was named in 1896 by Col. William Ridpath and James Hogan of Spokane, after Kimberley, South Africa, because of a rich outcrop of minerals at the Sullivan Mine. Now owned by Cominco Ltd., Sullivan Mine is one of the largest lead, zinc, and silver mines in the world. It once employed 1,200; now half that many work there (the town's population is 6,700). The mountainside was initially mined as an open pit, and even though the pit was filled in, it remains as an ugly scar. Ore is now mined two miles deep into the mountain and carried by railcar to the Cominco smelter in Trail, BC. Gardeners shouldn't miss the teahouse, greenhouse, and immaculately kept gardens, once maintained by Cominco and now under the care of the city, on the grounds of the Kimberley District Hospital.

The Heritage Museum, 105 Spokane Street, (604) 427-7510, has an excellent display of the town's mining history and memorabilia, such as hockey equipment from the town team that won the World Senior Amateur Hockey Championships in 1937. For a good selection of regional books, try Mountain High Book Store, 232 Spokane Street, (604) 427-7014. Skiers and mountain bike enthusiasts (rollerbladers too) should check out Rocky Mountain Sports, 185 Deer Park Avenue, (604) 427-2838. Accordion music is played on loudspeakers on the bandstand at the center of the Bavarian Platz (the town's three-block walking street). For a quarter, a puppet pops out of the upper window of Canada's largest cuckoo clock and yodels. The Bauerhaus Restaurant on Gerry Sorenson Way (named for Kimberley's 1982 Olympic downhill-gold medal winner) has an outstanding view of the mountains; however, the well-reputed restaurant, dismantled from Austria and reconstructed here, is open only during ski season and for a few months in the summer; (604) 427-5133.

RESTAURANTS

Chef Bernard's Kitchen
On the Bavarian Platzl,
(604) 427-4820
170 Spokane St,
Kimberley
Moderate; full bar; AE,
DC, MC, V; checks OK
Breakfast, lunch, dinner
every day

Originally a fresh pasta eatery, Chef Bernard's has expanded its menu to include items such as pork tenderloins cooked in honey, walnuts, and cream; a variety of fondues; and a host of nightly specials which might include Florida alligator tail, Chilean trumpet fish, or British Columbia salmon. Nice tries; but the fresh pasta's the thing here. Try it with chicken filets, raisins, coconut, pineapple, and curry, or with Italian sausage, tomatoes, and basil. The restaurant boasts an impressive German and Austrian wine list, alongside some of the better BC offerings. There's the fresh cream torte every day.

The Snowdrift Cafe
On the Bavarian Platzl,
(604) 427-2001
110 Spokane St,
Kimberley
Inexpensive; beer, wine,
and liqueur; no credit
cards; checks OK
Lunch, dinner every day

The local hangout for the young sporting crowd, this small eatery located in a 100-year-old converted house boasts plenty of healthful foods—homemade whole-wheat bread and muffins, vegetarian chili and pizza, spinach and Caesar salads. There's also the lasagne special with garlic bread and salad for those who need to carbo-load for vigorous skiing or cycling, and a variety of cheesecakes. The Hungarian mushroom soup, flavored with dill and loaded with mushrooms, comes with thick slices of the whole-wheat bread. Locals claim this is the best coffee in the Kootenay Mountains.

LODGINGS

Kirkwood Inn/Inn West
At the top of the hill at the
Kimberley Ski Resort,
(604) 427-7616
Mail; PO Box 247,
Kimberley, BC V1A 2Y6
Expensive; AE, MC, V;
checks OK

Five kilometers from Kimberley, adjacent to the ski and summer resort, is the Kirkwood Inn. There are hotel rooms, but opt for a condo instead. The condos have kitchens, fireplaces, access to laundry facilities and sauna, hot tub, and swimming pool (seasonal), and the balconies have views of the Rockies (through the trees in front of some). The trailhead of the nordic ski trail system is across the parking lot, and the ski lift at the downhill area is a block away.

CRANBROOK

Cranbrook straddles the main highway north and hence has built several strip malls alongside the highway; however, the **Cranbrook Railway Museum**, Highway 3 and Baker Street, (604) 489-3918, takes visitors through a railroad yard of elegantly restored Canadian Pacific Railway TransCanada cars. Following the tour, tea and scones are available in the dining car.

LODGINGS

Glen Flora Castle House
Turn onto Baker St
from Hwy 3 and go
south on 10th,
(604) 426-7930
324 10th Ave S,
Cranbrook, BC V1C 2N6
Inexpensive; no credit
cards; checks OK

This really *is* a castle, complete with turret. Built in 1909, it was restored to the original design by owners Paul and Bernice Sargent. Located in a quiet neighborhood adjacent to an elementary school and five minutes from downtown Cranbrook, the castle's grounds are landscaped in the formal English tradition. The hosts prefer non-smokers for the two guest rooms, one with its own bath, one with a bath en suite. Continental breakfast is served.

BOSWELL

LODGINGS

Destiny Bay Resort
40 minutes from Creston on Hwy 3A,
(604) 223-8455
Destiny Bay, Boswell,
BC V0B 1A0
Moderate; beer and wine;
MC, V; local checks only
Breakfast, dinner every day (April-November)

German-born Rolf and Hanna Langerfeld brought a bit of Europe to the little town of Boswell on Kootenay Lake. You stay in one of the five grass-roofed cabins which easily sleep two or three (and possibly a close family of five), or in one of the three suites in the lodge. Tall pines obscure the view of the lake from the decks, and the road is a tad too close for such a remote place. We don't mind the absence of TVs or phones, but we might wish they had kitchens—if it weren't for the reasonably priced good food prepared by Hanna herself (some of the best food for miles). On sunny days, the wraparound deck on the second floor is the spot—for seafood to schnitzels to herring salads, for the view, and for smokers.

CRAWFORD BAY

The tiny community of Crawford Bay, accessible via an hour's ferry ride from Balfour (32 kilometers east of Nelson), happens to be the home of one of BC's finest golf courses, **Kokanee Springs Golf Course**, (604) 227-9226. Just up from the ferry dock is the **Last Chance Restaurant**, a local hangout with darn good sandwiches, (604) 227-9477.

LODGINGS

Wedgwood Manor
East of Nelson on Hwy 3A, take Balfour ferry to Kootenay Bay and head south, (604) 227-9233
Mail: Box 135, 16002 Crawford Creek Rd, Crawford Bay, BC V0B 1E0
Moderate; MC, V; local checks only
Open April through October only

On 50 acres that tilt westward toward the Purcell Mountains, this lovely 1910 board-and-batten house has recently become one of the finest lodgings in southeastern British Columbia. Downstairs there's a dining room and a semi formal parlor with a fireplace (where afternoon tea is served). There are five rooms (all with baths en suite). The newest (and smallest) room is just off the parlor, but its wainscoting, leather-trimmed bookshelf, and fireplace make up for its size and central location. The four spacious upstairs rooms open onto a quiet, comfortable reading room; the Charles Darwin and Commander's rooms get most of the afternoon sun. In summer, the large front porch is a very pleasant spot from which to gaze out over the big lawn and vegetable garden (where many of Joan Huibert's breakfast ingredients come from) to the Kokanee Glacier beyond. The owners have taken over the former servants' quarters next door, so the house is entirely yours, so to speak.

NAKUSP

RESTAURANTS

Lord Minto
*5th Ave between
Broadway and 1st,
(604) 265-4033
Box 889,
Nakusp
Inexpensive; full bar;AE,
DC, MC, V; no checks
Breakfast, lunch, dinner
every day*

At almost any time of day, the Lord Minto is the busiest place in town. It's named after the *SS Lord Minto*, a paddlewheeler which used to haul supplies and passengers up and down Arrow Lake before the road went through. Owners Lorraine Kellock and Karen Hamling work just as hard as they waitress, cashier, and cook. A great spot especially for lunch. The juicy Greek burger on our last visit was piled high with feta, onions, lettuce, and tomato with a side salad that was a meal in itself. Dinners extend to a vegetarian lasagna, salmon steak, and perhap some stroganoff. Especially good after an afternoon at the hot springs just 8 miles up the road.

ROSEBURY

RESTAURANTS

Wild Rose Cafe
*In Rosebury, 4 miles
north of New Denver,
(604) 358-7744
Hwy 6, Rosebury
Inexpensive; full bar;
MC, V; local checks only
Dinner Wed-Sun (Fri-
Sun winters)*

★

It's no problem finding the restaurant, just tough to find the town. Highway 6 used to run right through the middle of town, and now it's routed behind it. A small side loop takes you into the bustling town of almost 50 people. But its not just townfolk who line up out the door of this tiny Mexican cafe. It's a pretty drive from Nelson, and for the past 10 summers, people have been dropping in for some of Andrea Wright's great Mexican food. Everything's homemade, right down to the beans. Sit out on the porch and enjoy the evening.

SILVERTON

LODGINGS

Silverton Resort
*On the lakeshore in
Silverton, (604) 358-7157
Mail: Box 107, Lake Ave,
Silverton, BC V0G 2B0
Moderate; MC, V; local
checks only*

You'll be pleased with this little resort in the heart of the Hidden Valley. New owners Bill and Lorraine Landers took over these cabins on the shores of Slocan Lake in 1991. It's a great place if you like water play; bring your own or rent their canoes, windsurfer, or rowboat. There are a couple of mountian bikes available too. You stay in one of the five hemlock-log cabins—all spotlessly clean and simple and each named after a mythological hero. Some have sleeping lofts, all have kitchens and southfacing decks. They're all at the water's edge (though not far from the road either), but Thor 4 (situated just right) is our favorite. A lakefront resort backed by a glacier in the Valhalla Provincial Park: it's a fine spot to do absolutely nothing.

NELSON

Nestled in a valley on the shore of Kootenay Lake, Nelson sprang up with a silver-and-gold mining boom in the late 1890s and has retained its Victorian character. Its main street has changed little in its 90-year history. Over 350 heritage sites are listed in this small picturesque city. In recent years, Nelson has become known as the set for the two films, *Housekeeping* and *Roxanne*. Nelsonites are pleased with the attention these two movies brought them (though some still snicker at the fact that the bar Steve Martin walked out of was actually the courthouse) but wearily remind recent visitors that Nelson is a lot more than just a pretty stage set.

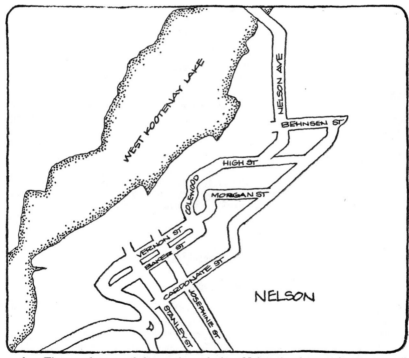

Art. The art shows and theater brought into Nelson by the town's arts council are well selected. From theatrical productions to wildlife lectures to classical guitars to nationally known folk-rock groups, there's almost always something going on at the operatic-style **Capitol Theatre**, (604) 352-6363. From June through August the entire town turns into an art gallery, with artists' work exhibited in almost 20 shops, restaurants, and galleries. Maps of **Artwalk Gallery Tours** can be picked up at the Tourist Information Bureau at 225 Hall Street, (604) 352-3433, or contact Artwalk, Box 422, Nelson, BC V1L 5R2; (604) 352-2402. For a calendar of weekly events, pick up a free copy of *The Kootenay Weekly Express*.

Skiing. The small local ski area, **Whitewater,** provides some of the best (and most) powder in the lower Kootenays. There are only 3 chairs, with about 11 expert runs out of 22 total, and the summit chair is especially challenging; call (604) 354-4944 or (604) 352-7669 (24-hour snow report). The closest accommodation to the mountain is the inexpensive, double-bunk-style **Whitewater Inn,** popular with ski hounds and bargain-hunters. Good **cross-country ski** trails begin at the Whitewater Inn, just at the base of Mount Ymir.

A scenic day trip through sleepy villages follows highways 31, 31A, and 6, then loops around to arrive back into Nelson. On the way, take the two-hour (round-trip) Balfour ferry across Kootenay Lake. It's a pretty trip and happens to be the world's longest free ferry ride. Don't miss **Ainsworth Hot Springs,** (604) 229-4212, where for a couple of bucks you can explore a cave of piping-hot waist-deep water or swim in the slightly cooled-down pool (open 365 days a year), and **Kaslo,** a town famed for its bakery—Rudolph's Pastries, 416 Front Street, (604) 353-2250.

RESTAURANTS

Fiddler's Green

On the north shore, 6 miles north of town,
(604) 825-4466
Lower 6 Mile Rd, Nelson
Moderate; full bar; MC, V; local checks only
Dinner every day and brunch Sun in summer, winter hours vary

It's really best in the summer when you can dine in the garden. But regardless of the season, this is Nelson's favorite spot for a special occasion. Locals quibble over whether the food is really the best in town, but they agree unanimously that this old estate house has the best atmosphere. There are three intimate dining rooms, one larger area (if the season calls for inside dining, ask to sit next to the fireplace), and the only garden dining in Nelson. At dinner, you may encounter decent Indonesian gado gado next to overfried lumpia, an undermarinated lamb topped with artichokes: or an uninspired chicken with mushrooms. Overcooked vegetables come draped with a cream sauce. The focus is definitely not on the food—but sometimes, when you're seated next to the fireplace (or at Sunday brunch in the summer garden) and conversation flows, the stale bread comes and goes without your even noticing.

Le Chatelet

Along Lakeside Park,
(604) 354-3911
903 Nelson Ave, Nelson
Moderate; full bar; MC, V; checks OK
Dinner Wed-Mon

Unlike Fiddler's, this little castle is very spare in atmosphere but, according to locals, more particular about the food. Chef/owner Eric Eriksen and his wife Essylt, originally from the French Alps, have created a country French menu. There have been disappointing reports on the veal stew and the lamb chops, though people who dine here often know to stay with the turnovers (which resemble calzones and are baked in their huge brick-lined, wood-burning oven). We sampled a delicate pheasant and liver mousse turnover. The salads are outstanding: impeccably fresh assorted greens dressed with chopped garlic were delicate and subtle in flavor. Desserts aren't too sweet. Essylt is attentive and always seems to know what you need.

Main Street Diner

Across from the Queen's Hotel at the north end of Baker, (604) 354-4848
616 Baker St, Nelson
Inexpensive; beer and wine; MC, V; local checks only
Lunch, dinner Mon-Sat

It used to be Millie's Fish & Chips, so owners Con Diamond and Linda Jamison decided to keep the famed—and still great—fish'n'chips on what's now a predominantly Greek menu (try the moist souvlaki or the warm pita bread with tzatziki) with a smattering of steak-and-chips entrées to appeal to the local appetites. We like their Athenian twist on the burger: a thick patty with tzatziki and feta. It's a bit noisy, and no wonder: it's the most popular eatery in town.

LODGINGS

Willow Point Lodge

4 kilometers north of Nelson on Hwy 3A over Nelson Bridge to Taylor, (604)825-9411
2211 Taylor Dr, Nelson, BC V1L 5P4
Moderate; MC, V; local checks only

Sue and Alan Dodsworth changed the name (it was formerly the Selkirk Lodge) but little else. You feel quite welcome in their large rambling 1922 Victorian perched on a hill in the middle of three and a half acres. The living room has a large stone fireplace. There are five guest rooms, all restored with period furnishings, and two on the third floor have been combined into a suite. Those on the second floor are best: three have window seats—looking east toward the mountains and lake—and one (our favorite) sports a private balcony. You'll need to remember your own soap and shampoo. With a little advance notice, Alan Dodsworth will organize mountain biking trips, exquisite alpine day hikes, sailing on Kootenay Lake, and even some spelunking. Breakfast is up whenever you are and always includes granola, homemade muffins, and perhaps some waffles with Okanagan raspberry syrup. No smoking is allowed, and reservations are requested.

Heritage Inn Bed and Breakfast

In the heart of town across from City Hall, (604) 352-5331
422 Vernon St, Nelson, BC V1L 4E5
Moderate; AE, DC, MC, V; no checks

In 1897, the Hume brothers decided Nelson (then a bustling town of 3,000) needed a first-class hotel—so they built one. Over the years the Hume Hotel, as it was known then, became quite run-down. In a recent remodel, the hardwood floors and fireplace in the bar (called the "Library") were rediscovered. Restoration is complete above the noisy rooms above the bar will stay unfinished and unrented, unless upon demand). Almost everything but the hallways seems polished. The spacious rooms are decorated with floral prints, lace curtains, and four-poster beds. The Library is the most comfortable meeting place in town with its big fireplace and high-backed floral print chairs. The Boiler Room (a disco) and Mike's Place, with a big-screen TV, can get rambunctious, especially on weekends. Breakfasts are ordinary fare, but the good Sunday brunch continues to attract locals.

ROSSLAND

This 1890s gold-rush town has been experiencing a second boom recently. This time the gold is not in Red Mountain but on it. **Red Mountain Ski Area**, 3½ miles southwest of town, is one of the more challenging ski areas in British Columbia with runs steep enough to keep even the most adventurous skiers alert; (604) 362-7700, toll-free (800) 663-0105, or (604) 362-5500 for snow conditions. There are over 40 kilometers of cross-country ski trails (about half are groomed); for information call **Black Jack Cross-Country Ski Club**, (604) 362-5811.

In the summer, the colorful turn-of-the-century main street of tiny Rossland bustles with hikers bound for alpine lakes, mountain bikers enroute to explore the numerous trails, or scenery-seeking visitors. A good place to get a good look at the town (and its surrounding scenery) is from the rooftop cafe of **Rockingham's** (2061 Columbia Street, (604) 362-7373), with over 30 appetizers. **After the Gold Rush Espresso Bar and Book Store** (2063 Washington Street, (604) 362-5333), with live Celtic music most Sunday nights, is a good place to linger over a latte and a good book.

Tour the fascinating **Le Roi Gold Mine**, Canada's only hard-rock gold mine open to the public. Not just another roadside attraction (open May through September; call (604) 362-7722).

RESTAURANTS

Roundhouse Restaurant and Only Well Pub (Flying Steamshovel Inn)
At the corner of Washington St and 2nd Ave, two blocks off Columbia Ave,
(604) 362-5323
2003 2nd Ave, Rossland
Moderate; full bar; MC, V; local checks only
Lunch, dinner every day

The inn named after the fellow who flew (and crashed) the first helicopter (dubbed the Flying Steamshovel by local miners) in North America, is currently just a restaurant. You can sit in the formal Roundhouse or the boisterous Only Well pub. The atmosphere is minimal in the dining room, so we prefer the pub, where the pool tables, pull tabs, and loud conversation make for a sociable evening, and the menu from the Roundhouse is available in addition to lighter pub fare. The appetizers are only okay, so go directly to one of the favorite entrées such as the chicken curry (with fruit, coconut, and a mango chutney) on coriander fettuccine or the boneless breast of chicken stuffed with raspberries and cream cheese in a tart raspberry brandy creme sauce. Future plans include suites above the restaurants and a banquet room and conference center below. We hope they'll both be well insulated from the raucous bar.

Sunshine Cafe
In the middle of town on the main street,
(604) 362-7630
2116 Columbia Ave, Rossland
Inexpensive; beer and wine; MC, V; local checks only
Breakfast, lunch, dinner every day

Virtually anybody will feel comfortable in Rossland's favorite little cafe. Sit in the front of the restaurant or walk past the kitchen to the back room. Food doesn't try to be fancy—just good, and there's lots of it. You'll do well to start with the Malaysian egg rolls (ground beef, coconut, and spices) dipped in a plum sauce and then go on to one of the Mexican dishes, the Budgie burger (boneless breast of chicken with ham and Swiss), or a simple entrée like the curried chicken. Huevos rancheros are a favorite of the breakfast crowd. The staff is friendly, and if you happen to sit in the back room you may catch the kitchen staff being silly. No smoking.

LODGINGS

Ram's Head Inn
Red Mountain Rd, 3.2 kilometers north of Rossland,
(604) 362-9577
Mail: Box 636, Rossland, BC V0G 1Y0
Moderate; AE, MC, V; checks OK

Dave and Doreen Butler's comfortable, nonsmoking inn is the choice place to stay in this mountainous part of the province; it's just a few hundred yards' walk to the Red Mountain ski area. The nine guest rooms are homey, but the comfortable public room is best, with a lofty ceiling, a stone fireplace, and big windows looking out to the wooded back yard. Package deals combine lift tickets with a bed and a full breakfast, making a ski weekend nicely affordable. Skiing here is surprisingly good—especially when the Butlers' hot tub and sauna are waiting. Young kids are quietly discouraged.

Heritage Hill House
On the corner of Spokane and Phoenix in lower Rossland,
(604) 362-9697
Mail: PO Box 381, Rossland, BC V0G 1Y0
Inexpensive; no credit cards; checks OK

It seems everyone in town has stayed here at one time or another, as it used to be a boardinghouse for local, seasonal employees. Upstairs in this sprawling house, there are four simple, clean rooms. The two bathrooms are down the hall; there is no fireplace for the winter months; and the rooms are missing a few obvious amenities (such as mirrors); but new owners Jill and Chris Perry cook a skier's breakfast and so far seem to be filling a need for an inexpensive good night's sleep.

CALENDAR

▲

JANUARY

Chinese New Year
International District,
Seattle, WA
(206) 623-8171

In January or February (depending on the lunar calendar) the International District greets the Chinese New Year with a fanfare of festivals and displays and a lively parade complete with lion dancers.

Great Northwest Chili Cookoff
Memorial Park
Coliseum, Portland, OR
(503) 226-1561

For 10 years now, the chili cookoff has benefited the zoo, providing fund-raising for expansion and for the care of the animals. About 30 different chilis are sampled by no fewer than 2,500 visitors.

FEBRUARY

Chilly Hilly Bike Ride
Bainbridge Island, WA
(206) 522-BIKE

Held the third Sunday in February, this 28-mile family ride sponsored by the Cascade Bicycle Club has come to be recognized as the opening day of bike season. Up to 4,000 cyclists fill the morning ferries to Winslow. Don't expect it to be warm or flat.

Fat Tuesday
Pioneer Square, Seattle,
WA (206) 622-2563

Seattle's own week-long Mardi Gras celebration brings a colorful parade and the beat of Cajun, jazz, and R&B music to the streets and clubs of Pioneer Square. Nightclubs levy a joint cover charge, and proceeds from several events benefit Northwest Harvest, a local food bank. Held the week before lent.

Northwest Flower and Garden Show
Washington State
Convention and Trade
Center, Seattle, WA
(206) 789-5333

This enormous horticultural happening occupies almost five acres at the Convention Center throughout Presidents' Day weekend. Landscapers, nurseries, florists, and noncommercial gardeners outdo themselves with over 300 demonstration gardens and booths. Shuttle bus service is available from Northgate and Longacres. General admission is $7, evenings $5.

Oregon Shakespeare Festival
Citywide, Ashland, OR
(503) 482-4331

An unassuming little college town, set in lovely ranch country, just happens to house one of the oldest and largest regional theater companies in the country. Almost 200,000 visitors a year (from February to October) attend the festival and crowd into the three theaters. Lectures, backstage tours, and Renaissance music and dance are other attractions theatergoers enjoy. Last-minute tickets are rare in the summer, but not impossible.

Rain or Shine Dixieland Jazz Festival
Citywide, Aberdeen, WA
(206) 533-2910

Every Presidents' Day weekend, rain or shine, Aberdeen hosts top Dixieland bands from up and down the West Coast. New bands take over every set. Multiple venues keep the town hoppin'.

24-Hour Ski Marathon
Grouse Mountain, BC
(604) 984-0661

Singles or teams of 6 to 12 skiers participate in this downhill ski marathon, with all proceeds going to help disabled children in the area.

Washington State Games
Call for location,
(206) 682-4263

What originated as the Washington Centennial Games is now the Washington State Games, a yearly event held in February (the summer games are in mid-August). The winter games feature downhill and cross-country skiing events; the summer games consist mostly of traditional Olympic sports.

MARCH

Kandahar Ski Race
Forbidden Plateau Resort, Courtenay, BC
(604) 334-4744

Now in its 42nd year, this is possibly the last amateur-status, freefall downhill race in existence. Anyone with the guts and a helmet can register. Generally held the first week in March.

NW Buddy Werner Ski Racing Championships
Call for location,
(206) 392-4220

An alpine ski event designed just for the younger members of your family. About 300 kids from 7 to 12 compete in the frosty event. Come out and watch Olympic hopefuls give it their all. Races are held in Washington, Oregon, or western Idaho.

Oregon State Special Olympics
Mount Bachelor, Bend, OR (503) 382-2442

Developmentally disabled athletes compete in ice skating and downhill and cross-country skiing just prior to the big international Special Olympics (usually held a few weeks later). Over 400 Olympians compete in the state meet.

Pacific Rim Whale Festival
Tofino, BC
(604) 725-3414

Migrating gray whales can be observed during March and April just off the shores of the Long Beach section of Pacific Rim National Park. Numerous charter boats and a seaplane company offer close-up looks at the pods. The actual festival, including dances and education programs, begins the last week in March.

Whale Migration

From March to May, the gray whales return to Alaska from Baja California, where they winter and calve.

For information, call the Westport, WA (206) 268-9422 or Newport, OR (503) 265-8801 chambers of commerce.

Along the Washington and Oregon coasts are a number of excellent whale-watching spots; some towns, such as Westport, Washington, and Newport, Oregon, offer charters especially for whale-seekers. The return migration happens from October to December, a less favorable time for whale watching due to the weather.

APRIL

Brant Festival
Parksville, BC
(604) 248-4347

The first annual Brant Festival, held in April 1991, celebrated the stopover of the brant (a species of geese) on their migration from Mexico to Canada. Staging areas provide fine opportunities to view the geese, once nearly extinct, as they feed. Wildlife art, photography exhibits, and carving competitions, too.

Cherry Festival
The Dalles, OR
(503) 296-2231

This event has parades, cherry orchard tours, dances, a carnival, and golf and tennis tournaments. Held the second Sunday after Easter.

Daffodil Festival Grand Floral Parade
Tacoma, WA
(206) 627-6176

The Daffodil Festival, a springtime tradition for over 55 years, celebrates the fields of gold in the Puyallup Valley. One of the largest floral parades in the nation visits downtown Tacoma, Puyallup, Sumner, and Orting, all in one day.

Hood River Blossom Festival
Hood River Valley, OR
(503) 386-2000

The coordinators of this event assure us that any similarities between it and the one in The Dalles are purely coincidental. Altogether, there are 30 to 40 different things happening throughout the valley. Tours of the blossoming fruit orchards and wineries along a 40-mile loop are available.

International Wine Festival
Vancouver Trade and Convention Center, Vancouver, BC
(604) 873-3311

The largest and most prestigious wine event in Canada, the five-day festival attracted over 6,700 visitors in 1990, when ten countries were represented by 103 different wineries and 370 wines. Events in this food and wine extravaganza include a Bacchanalia gala and complimentary palate cleansers; future festivals look equally promising.

Seattle Mariners Baseball
Kingdome, Seattle, WA
(206) 628-3555

The crowd is predictably loyal—even to a team whose performance is not so predictable. Although the playing can be truly inspired, the outlook for the next few seasons isn't particularly bright. The season lasts from early April through the first week of October (game time is 7:05pm weeknights, 1:35pm on Saturdays and occasional weekdays). Bring your own peanuts (Kingdome food is too expensive and not too good) and prepare to get lively if you're sitting in the left-field stands. Tickets are cheap ($4.50 to $10.50).

Skagit Valley Tulip Festival
60 miles north of Seattle via I-5, Mount Vernon, WA (206) 42-TULIP

When the 1,500 acres of tulips burst into brilliant color in early April, Mount Vernon seizes the moment and entertains visitors with a street fair and the Taste of Skagit. Makes a nice—and flat—bicycle trip.

TerrifVic Dixieland Jazz Festival
Victoria, BC (604) 381-5277

Twenty Dixieland jazz bands from all over the world shake up the town for five days in April. Sixty dollars gets you an event badge good for every concert in every location. Shuttle service is available between participating hotels and the eight concert locations.

Yakima Spring Barrel Tasting
Various wineries, Yakima, WA (call for map) (509) 829-6027

In late April, 20 wineries from Union Gap to Kiona hold special open houses to educate the public on the finer points of winemaking. Both owners and winemakers are on hand to explain the process, and wines from the barrel—some two or three years away from maturity—are available for tasting. Individual wineries add entertainment and food.

MAY

Bloomsday Run
Spokane, WA (509) 838-1579

Now the world's largest timed road race, Spokane's Bloomsday Run attracts thousands every year (over 65,000 runners) during the area's Lilac Festival, (509) 326-3339. Everyone who crosses the finish line gets an official Bloomsday T-shirt and his or her name in the city's major newspapers. Be sure to book hotel rooms well in advance (a year beforehand is advised).

International Children's Festival
Seattle Center, Seattle, WA (206) 684-7346

This popular event brings in children's performers from all over the world. Crafts, storytelling, puppet shows and musical and theater performances (some free) entertain kids and their parents for six days in early May.

National Western Art Show and Auction
Ellensburg, WA (509) 962-2934

For nearly 20 years the three-day event has brought artists from all over the country to this college town off I-90. A hundred display rooms turned into mini-studios offer paintings and sculptures for sale. Three auctions are held as well, including one benefiting Elmview Industries for the community's developmentally disabled.

Northwest Folklife Festival
Seattle Center, Seattle, WA (206) 684-7300

The largest folkfest in the nation runs throughout Memorial Day weekend and brings many ethnic groups and their folk-art traditions (dance, music, crafts, and food) to stages throughout the Seattle Center. A must.

Opening Day of Yachting Season
1807 E Hamlin St, Seattle, WA (206) 325-1000

Boat owners from all over the Northwest come to this festive ceremonial regatta, which officially kicks off the nautical summer. Arrive early to watch the world-class University of Washington rowing team race other nationally ranked teams through the Montlake Cut. Parade registration for watercraft is free.

Pole, Pedal, Paddle
Mount Bachelor, Bend,
OR (503) 388-0002

This grueling test of endurance is one of Central Oregon's most popular events. In '90, 3,500 people skied, biked, canoed, and ran in teams or by themselves (brave people) past 35,000 cheering spectators. Usually the weekend after Mother's Day, the original small-town run is now a full-fledged two-day event complete with street fair and food.

Poulsbo Viking Fest
Poulsbo, WA
(206) 779-4848

In mid-May, Puget Sound's "Little Norway" celebrates Scandinavian independence with a weekend of folk dancing and live music, a carnival and parade, and a lutefisk-eating contest (definitely an acquired taste).

Rhododendron Festival
Port Townsend, WA
(206) 385-2722

This is the oldest festival in town, and it improves every year. Highlights of this week-long event include a Rover Run (dog and owner), beard contest (scruffiest, longest), adult tricycle race, keg put, carnival, senior citizen coronation and dance, and more. The "Grand Finale" is a classic parade; the "Anti-Climax Grand Finale" is the 12K Rhody Run. See all of the Rhododendron Queens'cement handprints in downtown Port Townsend.

Sand Castle Day
Cannon Beach, OR
(503) 436-2623

Oregon's original and most prestigious sand castle contest is nearly 30 years old. Buckets, shovels, and squirt guns aid the 1,000-plus contestants in producing their transient creations. Upwards of 40,000 spectators show up to view the masterpieces.

Seattle International Film Festival
Citywide, Seattle, WA
(206) 324-9996

Founded in 1976 by Darryl Macdonald and Dan Ireland, the three-and-a-half-week Seattle International Film Festival brings films for every taste—high art to slapstick—to Seattle theaters every May. Fans of the obscure will appreciate the SIFF's archival treasures and independent films. Series tickets (full and partial) go on sale in January (Cinema Seattle, 801 E Pine Street, Seattle, WA 98122).

Ski-to-Sea Festival
From Mount Baker to
Marine Park,
Bellingham, WA
(206) 734-1330

A Bellingham civic festival over Memorial Day weekend that revolves around an 80-miles-plus, five-event relay race that includes skiing, running, cycling, canoeing, and sailing.

Slug Races
Old Town; Florence, OR
(503) 997-3128

In the Pacific Northwest spring and slugs seem to go hand in hand. During Florence's Rhododendron Festival the main attraction is the slug race. Watch the local gastropods slime their way toward victory.

Strawberry Festival
Lebanon, OR
(503) 258-7164

The main attraction at this festive event is the world's largest strawberry shortcake (see the *Guinness Book of World Records*). Standing several feet tall and weighing a couple of tons, it's big enough to give everybody a bite. Made with fresh strawberries, of course.

Swiftsure Race Weekend
Victoria, BC
(604) 592-2441

Held every Memorial Day weekend, this event attracts boats from North America and foreign ports (recently a boat from the USSR participated). Four races are held, the longest going west out the Strait of Juan de Fuca to the Pacific and back. Spectators can watch the vessels from Clover Point or Ogden Point.

Washington State Apple Blossom Festival
Citywide, Wenatchee, WA
(509) 662-3616

When the apple trees burst into bloom in early May, Wenatchee hosts an 11-day festival (the oldest in the state) featuring arts, crafts, and plenty of food.

JUNE

BC Lions Football
BC Place Stadium,
Vancouver, BC
(604) 280-4400

Some people feel that a wider field and one fewer down than in American ball make Canadian football more exciting. Well, action is the name of the game in this eight-team league. The season lasts from late June to late November and culminates in the Grey Cup Game, the Canadian version of the Super Bowl. Regular game tickets cost around $25.

Britt Festival
Jacksonville, OR
(503) 773-6077

This musical extravaganza runs from mid-June through September in the hillside field where Peter Britt, a famous local photographer and horticulturist, used to have his home. A handsome shell has been constructed, and listeners sit on benches or loll on blankets under the stars. Programs run the gamut from classical to folk, country to jazz, musical theater, and dance. Season passes are available as well as tickets to individual events.

Centrum Summer Arts Festival
Port Townsend, WA
(206) 385-3102

From June through September, one of the most successful cultural programs in Washington enlightens thousands with a multitude of workshops held by the nation's leading artists and musicians. For fiddlers, there's the Festival of American Fiddle Tunes. Jazz musicians can hone their skills at the Bud Shank Workshop or listen to the music at Jazz Port Townsend, one of the West Coast's foremost mainstream jazz festivals. Workshops are held at Fort Worden State Park; performances take place at the park grounds or various locations around town. There are also a writers' conference and theater performances.

Chamber Music Northwest
Portland, OR
(503) 223-3202

One of the finest summer festivals in the country, distinguished by the caliber of its performances, takes place in Portland at Reed College and Catlin Gabel School late June through late July.

du Maurier Ltd.
International Jazz Festival
Vancouver
Vancouver, BC
(604) 682-0706

Still relatively new to the international music scene, the du Maurier has not disappointed jazz enthusiasts. Last year over 500 musicians from Africa, Japan, Europe, and North and South America appeared during the two-week festival, which presents the full spectrum of traditional and contemporary jazz. Happens over Canada Day weekend at the end of June or in early July.

Everett Giants Baseball
Everett Memorial
Stadium, Everett, WA
(206) 258-3673

This Class A minor-league affiliate of the San Francisco Giants plays real baseball on real grass in real sunshine from mid-June through August. In 1990, the 1,800-seat Everett Memorial Stadium was enlarged to 3,000 seats to accommodate the ever-growing number of fans. Tickets are only $4.25 for adults, $2.75 for kids 12 and under; reserved tickets are a little more. Call for season schedule.

Northwest Garlic Festival
Ocean Park, WA
toll-free (800) 451-2542

This two-day affair attracts about 7,000 people each year. A street fair, live music, a garlic-peeling contest, and helicopter rides are just a few of the events that will keep you busy all day. A garlic-eating contest may keep your enemies at bay.

Rose Festival
Citywide, Portland, OR
(503) 227-2681

The Rose Festival is to auto racing what Seattle's Seafair is to boat racing. This 24-day celebration culminates in the running of the CART 200, a race featuring Indianapolis 500–style cars. Don't forget to catch the parade and stop in at the festival center.

Seattle to Portland Bicycle Ride
(206) 522-BIKE

There is a 10,000-rider limit for this 200-mile bike ride from Seattle to Portland sponsored by the Cascade Bicycle Club. Complete the course in one or two days (overnight facilities are provided at the halfway point). Registration is first come, first served, and in the past couple of years the limit has been reached.

Washington Special Olympics
Call for location,
(206) 362-4949

In 1968 an act of Congress created the organization known today as the Special Olympics. It has since grown to be the largest sports training and competition program in the world for the mentally retarded. The June event is the biggest competition in Washington.

Umpqua Valley Summer Arts Festival
Roseburg, OR
(503) 672-2532

Over 100 booths featuring every kind of art imaginable sprout up in the park around the Art Center in Roseburg the last weekend in June. You'll find pottery, silk scarves, jewelry, teddy bears, quilts, folk art, porcelain, woven baskets, and stained-glass items (just to name a few).

JULY

Albany Dixieland Jazz Fest
Albany, OR
(503) 928-0911

Bands from all over have participated in this music fest. A prepaid pass gets you in to all performances.

Bellevue Jazz Festival
Bellevue Downtown Park, WA
(206) 451-4106

Top Northwest jazz artists entertain outdoors for three days, the third weekend in July. Tickets are cheap (around $5) and one concert is free.

Bite of Seattle
Seattle Center, Seattle, WA (206) 232-2982

A big chompfest, which brings cheap nibbles from around 60 restaurants to Seattle Center on the third weekend in July.

Chinatown International District Summer Festival
Hing Hay Park, Seattle, WA (206) 623-8171

This mid-July extravaganza celebrates the richness and diversity of Asian culture with dancing, music and martial arts performances, Asian food booths, and arts and crafts. A children's corner features puppetry, storytelling, and magic shows; various craft demonstrations (classical ikebana, a Japanese tea ceremony, basketweaving, calligraphy, and Hawaiian lei-making) take place in the cultural corner.

Darrington Bluegrass Festival
Darrington, WA
(206) 436-1177

Every summer on the third weekend in July, bluegrass fans from all over the country turn their attention to the tiny town of Darrington, nestled in the Cascade foothills. Terrific foot-stomping, thigh-slapping bluegrass music is played outdoors by the country's best musicians. A convenient ticket package includes three nights of camping and three days of music: $60 for couples, $35 single.

Folk Music Festival
Jericho Park, Vancouver, BC (604) 879-2931

What better way to international peace and understanding than through the universal language of music? Last year over 200 performers from 12 countries came together for three days. There is a bewildering array of ticket options; the most economical is to form a group of 15 or more to qualify for a discount; a pass for the weekend is about $65. Buy early—admission is limited.

Fort Vancouver Fourth of July Fireworks
Vancouver, WA
(206) 694-2432

The best fireworks in Oregon are across the Columbia River... in Washington. Portlanders flock to the National Historic Site of Fort Vancouver for a day of activities and stage entertainment climaxing in the largest free aerial display west of the Mississippi. The bombardment lasts at least a full hour.

Fourth of July Fireworks
Seattle, WA
(206) 587-6500 (Ivar's), (206) 324-5939 (Fratelli's)

Seattle's dueling fireworks. Ivar's explode over Elliott Bay and are best viewed from Myrtle Edwards Park. Fratelli's rocket over Lake Union with good viewing from Gas Works Park. A lucky few who think to make reservations for a late dinner at the Space Needle can view them both. The pyrotechnics start just after dark.

Harrison Festival of the Arts
Harrison Hot Springs, BC (604) 796-3664

During this nine-day event, over 35,000 people visit Harrison Hot Springs to celebrate the musical, visual, and performing arts of a different set of countries each year. Theater, lectures, workshops, and live entertainment give visitors many activities to choose from.

King County Fair
King County Fairgrounds, Enumclaw, WA (206) 825-7777

The oldest county fair in the state is also its best, featuring five days of music by top country acts, a rodeo, 4-H and FFA exhibits, a loggers' show (remember ax-throwing contests?), crafts, and food. Begins the third Wednesday of July.

McChord Air Show
McChord Air Force Base, Tacoma, WA (206) 984-5637

Come see pilots in action as the F-16s do their thing. Afterwards, watch military demonstrations—from an all-services attack demo to antique aircraft—and get your picture taken in the cockpit of a jet. In July or August; call for dates.

Olympic Music Festival
Quilcene, WA (206) 527-8839

The Philadelphia String Quartet opens its season with one of Puget Sound's premier music festivals, held in a turn-of-the-century barn nestled on 40 acres of pastoral farmland on the Olympic Peninsula. Sit in the barn on hay bales ($15) or spread a picnic on the lawn ($6). The festival spans 10 weekends. Bring a blanket.

Pacific Northwest Scottish Highland Games
King County Fairgrounds, Enumclaw, WA (206) 522-2874

Kilts are not the only thing you'll find here. Scottish piping, drumming, dancing, Parade of the Clans, and games are the major attractions, not to mention a chance to sample authentic Scottish food and drink. Six dollars gets you in for the day.

Pend Oreille International Old-Time Fiddle Contest
Newport, WA (509) 447-4713

Competition is fierce as fiddlers from all over the country try to outdo one another with their renditions of "Soldier's Joy."

Renaissance Fair
Riverside Park, Grants Pass, OR (503) 479-1602

Local artists display their arts and crafts while the "jousters," knights in shining armor, rescue fair maidens during performances at various times during the day. Food and entertainment, too.

San Juan Island Dixieland Jazz Festival
Friday Harbor, San Juan Island, WA (206) 378-5509

A three-day festival, $35 for all three days, sponsored by the San Juan Island Goodtime Classic Jazz Association, brings Dixieland fans out to enjoy the jazz of yesteryear, mid- to late July.

Sand-Sations Sand Castle Contest
Long Beach, WA (206) 642-2400

Hundreds of children and children-at-heart flock to this annual event to build their sand-castle masterpieces. With judging in all sorts of categories (teamwork, effort, intricacy, suitability to sand) there are prizes totalling $3,000. At least 10,000 people show up to watch the artists at work.

Seafair
Citywide, Seattle, WA
(206) 728-0123

Seattle's frenzied summer fête has been around since 1950 and—to the chagrin of many locals—isn't likely to go away. The hoopla begins on the third weekend of July with the milk-carton boat races at Green Lake and ends the first Sunday in August, when the hydroplanes tear up the waters of Lake Washington. Bright spots include a couple of triathlons, the Blue Angels' air show, some excellent ethnic festivals (Bon Odori, late July; International District Festival, mid-July; Hispanic Seafair Festival, late July), and the Torchlight Parade (the Friday before the hydroplane races), which is a full-scale march in the downtown area and a kids' delight. Practically all Seafair events are free.

Sweet Onion Festival
Walla Walla, WA
(509) 525-0850

Fort Walla Walla Park celebrates the sweetest onion around with the onion-slicing contest, the two-headed onion shot put, the onion hunt, the onion dish recipe contest and cookoff, the onion ring toss, and a weekend full of fun.

Vancouver International Comedy Festival
Granville Island,
Vancouver, BC
(604) 683-0883

Watch out, *Improv*, Vancouver has a 10-day shindig with international comedians that'll knock your socks off. Roving street entertainers and scheduled shows give you the most diverse forms of comedy.

Vancouver Sea Festival
English Bay, BC
(604) 684-3378

This festival has everything from puppet shows and sand–castle building contests to a whole slew of sports demonstrations and competitions.

Victoria International Festival
Victoria, BC
(604) 736-2119

Artists from the Northwest gather at various Victoria venues to give classical music concerts, recitals, and ballet performances throughout the months of July and August. Ticket prices top out at $16 per performance.

Waterfront Blues Festival
McCall Waterfront Park,
Portland, OR,
(503) 282-0555

National blues artists (like Charlie Musselwhite) play at this three-day benefit for the Oregon Food Bank. The shows are free, although sponsors accept donations of food and money. A big event: in 1990, 40,000 fans turned out.

Winthrop Rhythm and Blues Fest
Winthrop, WA
(509) 996-2111

This late-July festival has attracted such national performers as Mick Taylor and John Mayall, as well as the best of the local bands. Now it's expanded to three days, and events include a New Orleans–style street dance in the Old-West streets of Winthrop, and a full day of steamy blues under the blazing sun at Twin Lakes. A popular event with the Harley crowd.

AUGUST

The Bite, A Taste of Portland
McCall Waterfront Park, Portland, OR
(503) 248-0600

Eat to your heart's content and help Special Olympics at the same time. Thirty restaurants and 20 wineries offer scores of delectables while performers at different venues entertain you.

Camlann Medieval Faire
Carnation, WA
(206) 788-1945

Held on Saturdays and Sundays in late August and early September, this "faire" attracts thousands of people. Dancing, medieval food, performances, and a tournament of knights highlight the event.

Coombs Country Bluegrass Festival
Coombs, BC
(604) 248-2990

A three-day weekend of gospel, country, and bluegrass. Performers such as Rural Delivery or the Rocky Mountain Boys have been major attractions in the past. Tickets are sold for each day. Rough camping is available on a first come, first served basis.

Evergreen Classic Benefit Horse Show
Redmond, WA
(206) 882-1554

Almost 500 horse-and-rider teams compete each year in this four-day A-system hunter/jumper show. Admission is charged during the weekend, but that's all right because proceeds go to Little Bit Special Riders, a program designed to teach disabled kids the joys of riding. And don't miss out on the $25,000 Cadillac Grand Prix of Seattle on Sunday—world-class riding at its best.

Evergreen State Fair
Monroe, WA
(206) 794-7832

For 11 days, late August through Labor Day, the Monroe Fair features country music headliners, roping and riding, stock-car races, a lumberjack show, a carnival, and a chili cookoff. Great fun.

Filburg Festival
Comox, BC
(604) 334-3234

A sophisticated arts and crafts show, this festival continues to grow in reputation as one of the region's finest juried shows. Woodwork, glass, pottery, and woven goods are just a few of the things on display.

Fine Arts Show
Sooke Region Museum, Sooke, BC
(604) 642-6351

Residents of southern Vancouver Island display their paintings and sculptures in the largest juried art show and sale in BC. A $2 admission is good for the entire 10-day event.

Gig Harbor Jazz Festival
Celebrations Meadow, Gig Harbor, WA
(206) 627-1504

The grassy natural amphitheater makes a great setting for a festival that draws national jazz artists. Boat owners can sail up to the site.

International Airshow/Airshow Canada
Abbotsford Airport, BC
(604) 852-8511

Want to see a Russian MIG up close or watch wing-walkers defy gravity? How about the flying acrobatics of the US Thunderbirds and the Canadian Snowbirds? Abbotsford Airshow has it all and more. Airshow Canada is a trade sale that happens in odd years.

Men's United States Tennis Association Challenger Series and Washington State Open Tennis Tournament
Seattle Tennis Club, Seattle, WA
(206) 324-3200

The top players in Washington and the men's western pro circuit compete side by side during the first week in August at the exclusive Seattle Tennis Club. Tickets range from $1 to $5, and it's worth the admission just to stroll the idyllic grounds. Order tickets in advance.

Mount Hood Festival of Jazz
Gresham, OR
(503) 666-3810

Definitely one of the premier festivals around, this weekend affair has featured such greats as Diane Schuur, Lou Rawls, and the Count Basie Band. Tickets are around $20 a day.

Omak Stampede and Suicide Run
Stampede Grounds, Omak, WA
(509) 826-1002

A hair-raising and controversial horse race: horses plunge down a 255-foot hill with a 120-foot vertical drop into (and across) the Okanogan River and into an arena (sometimes with broken legs). The stampede events last for three days; ticket prices range from $4 to $10.

Oregon State Fair
Salem, OR
(503) 378-3247

It's everything a fair should be: food, games, rides, horse shows, and live entertainment. For 12 days the people of Salem go hog-wild. Ends on Labor Day.

Santa Fe Chamber Music Festival
Meany Hall for the Performing Arts, University of Washington, Seattle, WA
(206) 622-1392

The cream of the chamber music festivals visits Seattle every August for one week of glorious music. The performers are fresh from Santa Fe's own festival, so this is relaxed, well-rehearsed music making. Regulars have included such distinguished musicians as Ani Kavafian and the Mendelssohn String Quartet.

Washington State Games (summer)
Call for location, (206) 682-4263

See February in this chapter.

Washington State International Kite Festival
Long Beach, (206) 642-2400

On the last day of this colorful, high-flying week, the Festival of Kites attempts to break its own record for number of kites in the air. Every day is a different event, from lighted kites to hand-crafted kites to stunt fun and games. The glorious spectacle is free to watch, but flying your own will cost you $17. The entire Long Beach peninsula is booked by January in anticipation, so plan (way) ahead.

SEPTEMBER

Artquake
Center for the Performing Arts and Park Blocks,

Over Labor Day weekend, Portlanders let loose a grand celebration of the performing and fine arts. The Center for the Performing Arts is the hub of the festi-

Portland, OR,
(503) 227-2787

val, although there are events throughout the downtown area, especially in Pioneer Courthouse Square. There is no admission charge for many Artquake events; others ask a nominal entrance fee.

Bumbershoot
Seattle Center, Seattle, WA (206) 441-FEST

The largest multi-arts festival north of San Francisco is a splendid and eclectic celebration of the arts. Select craftspeople, writers, and 500 performing artists on 15 stages throughout Seattle Center entertain the hordes over the long Labor Day weekend. A $7 daily pass ($6 if you buy in advance) is all you need to stay thoroughly entertained.

Classic Boat Fest
Victoria, BC
(604) 385-7766

Held every Labor Day weekend, this festival gives boaters a chance to show off their prize vessels. Discovery Reenactment, a society devoted to the re-sailing of Captain Vancouver's Northwest Passage itinerary, plans to stage the trip in 1992, with the culmination—the discovery of Vancouver Island—during the fest.

Ellensburg Rodeo
Ellensburg, WA
(509) 925-6144

The biggest rodeo in these parts brings riders in from far and wide for four days of Wild West events over Labor Day weekend. Admission to the big, colorful event is $9 to $13, depending on your seat.

Fall Kite Festival
Lincoln City, OR
(503) 994-3070

Lincolnites love to fly kites of all shapes and colors, and last year so did over 20,000 people who attended the festivities; these include a lighted show at night and a Japanese-style kite battle, which entails teams of 5-25 people trying to knock each other's kites out of the sky. Prizes are awarded in various categories.

Leavenworth Autumn Leaf Festival
Leavenworth, WA
(509) 548-5807

The last weekend of September is a grand time for a drive through the Cascade Mountains to Leavenworth, a mountain town gussied-up Tyrolean-style and home of this festival celebrating the glory of our deciduous trees. A parade, arts and crafts, and Bavarian music are all part of the festivities. Most events are free.

Pendleton Round-Up and Happy Canyon
Pendleton, OR toll-free
toll-free
(800) 45-RODEO

This four-day rodeo, complete with cowboys, bucking broncos, bulls, and clowns, is said to be one of the biggest in the country. Over 500 contestants and 50,000 spectators make it so. Admission ranges from $5 to $13. A carnival downtown keeps things hopping while the rodeo riders are recovering.

Seattle Seahawks Football
Kingdome, Seattle, WA
(206) 827-9766

Chuck Knox's Seahawks may play conservative ball (and may have seen better seasons than the next few promise to be), but the fans' loyalty is steadfast. Consequently, it's nearly impossible to get tickets ($19 to $35), and Kingdome-area parking is a crunch, so take a free bus from downtown. The season starts in September (pre-season games in August) and runs through December; games are Sundays at 1pm. Avoid scalpers.

Vancouver International Film Festival,
Vancouver, BC
(604) 685-0260

Similar to the one held in Seattle (see May), this event at the end of September/beginning of October features over 150 films from 35 countries. Prices are about $7 per movie. Pick up your tickets at the Ridge Theatre by mid-September.

Western Washington State Fair
Puyallup, WA
(206) 841-5045

This 17-day extravaganza begins in early September. It's the rural fair you remember from your childhood, only bigger. Rodeo, music, barnyard animals, carnival rides, exhibits, and vast amounts of food (including the legendary scones and onion burgers) make for kid—and grown-up—heaven.

OCTOBER

Children's Show
Pacific National Exhibit,
Showmart Building,
Vancouver, BC
(604) 684-4616

A plethora of activities, such as workshops, fashion shows, and entertainment, geared toward toddlers to pre-teens. A three-day kids' event ($6).

International Festival of Films by Women Directors
Seattle Art Museum and other locations,
(206) 623-8733

Despite its surge in popularity, this festival has retained its feel of intimacy. Films are shown in small theaters, and the directors usually make appearances for discussion afterwards. There's no political agenda to this internationally recognized series, but provocative and challenging films by rising stars and established artists are guaranteed to make you think.

Issaquah Salmon Days
Issaquah, WA
(206) 392-0661

Issaquah celebrates the return of the salmon the first weekend of October with a parade, food, crafts, music, dancing, and displays. At the State Fish Hatchery you can get excellent views of the Chinook and coho thrashing up the ladder.

Portland Winterhawks Ice Hockey
Memorial Coliseum,
Portland, OR
(503) 238-6366

See tomorrow's NHL players today in the WHL (Western Hockey League). This developmental league grooms young hockey players for the big time (34 former Winterhawks have already made it). The 72-game season runs from October through March, with prices topping out at about $9.50.

Salmon Festival
Oxbow Park, Gresham,
OR (503) 248-5050

When the salmon come home to spawn, the people of Gresham celebrate with an annual 8-kilometer run, a salmon bake, and arts and crafts. The name of the game here is environmental education. Old growth and salmon-viewing walks (where you can see the fish spawning in the Sandy River Gorge) are conducted to teach the importance of our natural resources.

Vancouver Canucks Hockey
Pacific Coliseum,
Vancouver, BC
(604) 280-4400

A promising NHL team that is still working on making a name for itself, the Canucks host such teams as the Edmonton Oilers and the Calgary Flames. Season runs from October through April and tickets are between $16.95 and $31.75.

NOVEMBER

Model Railroad Show
Pacific Science Center,
Seattle, WA
(206) 443-2001

A slew of different model train setups and clinics on how to make whistles, scenery, and train figures bring out the kid in all of us. Over Thanksgiving Day weekend; $6.

Portland Trailblazers Basketball
Memorial Coliseum,
Portland, OR
(503) 239-4422

The Portland Trailblazers are not the most winning NBA team, but their home games are among the most exciting (and earsplitting). They've sold out every home game for the last 10 years! Tickets range from $9.50 to $38.50.

Rainy Day Film Festival
Douglas County
Museum, Roseburg, OR
(503) 440-4507

For seven years now, the folks at the museum have been showing films on the second Sunday of the month from November through April. Themes in the past have been nature and history, and featured artists have included Buster Keaton and Alfred Hitchcock. $3.50 per family.

Seattle SuperSonics Basketball
Seattle Center Coliseum,
Seattle, WA
(206) 281-5850

From early November to late April, Seattle's home team tears up the court. In the past, the Sonics have played smart, competitive, and uneven basketball; they have a bright future, so grab tickets early ($5 to $25). Games are at 7pm.

DECEMBER

Christmas Lighting
Leavenworth, WA
(509) 548-5807

Crafts, music, and food are part of the ceremony kicking off the Christmas season. Around 4:45pm (usually on the first and second Saturdays of the month) the Bavarian village square is officially lit up for the season. Evening concerts and sleigh rides are the only things that require money.

Community Hanukkah Celebration
Stroum Jewish
Community Center, 3801
E Mercer Way, Mercer
Island, WA
(206) 232-7115

The arts and crafts, Hanukkah wares, games for children, and latke brunch are just the side attractions. The most significant thing about this event is the numbers—that is, the thousand or so people who come every year to the largest community Hanukkah celebration around. Everyone is welcome to take part in the *haimishe* (friendly) feeling the area's Jewish community creates when it gathers together for its festival of lights. You'll also find a vast selection of books on all aspects of Jewish life. The symbolic candle-lighting is quite moving.

Eagle Watching
Skagit River near Marblemount, WA, and Big and Little Qualicum Rivers near Nanaimo, BC; (206) 877-4590 (Washington) or (604) 752-9532 (Qualicum Beach)

Bald eagles converge on these rivers from December through February. These scavengers are best seen before noon, when they're hunting spawning salmon. Bring binoculars and wear rain gear.

First Night
Vancouver, BC (604) 669-9894

Downtown Vancouver (the first Canadian city to celebrate First Night) is the happening place to be New Year's Eve, when a full range of performance art (concerts, ballet, theater sports) entertains the masses in 35 different venues for the price of a $5 button. (If the Vancouver Symphony is performing, a separate $5 ticket is required; advance purchase is necessary.) The Grand Finale and Countdown begins at 11:30pm outside the Vancouver Art Gallery on the Plaza.

Whale Watch Week
Newport, OR (503) 867-0100

For one week after Christmas (and then again in March), volunteers from the Science Center in Newport teach interested folks how to watch for gray whales and report their sightings from various stations along the coast. Volunteers assist approximately 11,000 people from all over the world.

ACTIVITIES INDEX

Editor's note: This is an index to activities specifically mentioned in the book. See also the calendar of events.

INDEX

NORTHWEST BEST PLACES REPORT FORM

Based on my personal experience, I wish to nominate/confirm/disapprove for listing the following restaurant or place of lodging:

_____

_____

_____

_____

(Please include address and telephone number of establishment, if convenient.)

REPORT:
(Please describe food, service, style, comfort, value, date of visit, and other aspects of your visit; continue on overleaf if necessary.)

I am not concerned, directly or indirectly, with the management or ownership of this establishment.

Signed _____

Address _____

_____

Phone Number _____ Date _____

Send to: Stephanie Irving, editor
　　　　　Northwest Best Places
　　　　　1931 Second Avenue
　　　　　Seattle, WA 98101